F L/ 700

ary of Congress Cataloging in Publication Data

l, Allan L.
Modern applied salesmanship.

Bibliography: p. 453
Includes index.
1. Salesmen and salesmanship—Case studies. I. Title.
5438.R46   1975   658.85   74-16758
BN 0-87620-584-8

MODERN APPLIED SALESMANSHIP
SECOND EDITION

Copyright © 1975 by
GOODYEAR PUBLISHING COMPANY, INC.
Santa Monica, California 90401

Y-5848-0

Current printing (last digit)
10   9   8   7   6   5   4

Printed in the United States of America

Lib

Rev

HI
IS

SEC
MO
API
SALESMAN

ALLAN L. F

Vice President—
Special Publications Di
Prentice-Hall

Goodyear Publishing Company, Inc
Santa Monica, California

To my wife, Bessie

contents

preface

This can be one of the most personally helpful texts you have ever studied, or will study! Reason: A knowledge of how to sell yourself as a person, your ideas can help you attain success in sales or any other career, or in nonwork avocations involving close association with other people whom you hope to persuade or lead throughout your life.

This book is addressed to *you*—the individual student or reader, in a way that will unfold in the pages to follow. What you get out of it is strictly up to you. If you underline key passages and make notes on the pages to help study and restudy points presented, you will find this book useful to keep in your personal library and refer to time and again for years to come.

The text is divided into six parts, an overview of which will follow. A short list of *Learning Objectives*, sometimes called *Behavioral Objectives*, precedes each chapter. These are target guides to the key concepts to be learned in each chapter and they provide general checklists to use when you finish that chapter. Moreover, following each chapter is a list of key *Concepts to Remember* and a series of *Questions* on the material just covered. Two *Case Studies* follow each chapter; most are real-life examples from the business world, some are fictional, some are more detailed in concept than others. These case studies are not presented in order of increasing difficulty, but rather to illustrate points covered in the preceding chapter. However, most build on earlier chapters, so you will find that overall they offer progressive illustration of our unfolding study of principles, practices, and techniques of modern applied salesmanship. A *Sales Problem* follows these case studies (for each chapter except the last two); answers to most of these problems can be found in the chapter material which they follow.

Part I is an important one-chapter overview, both asking and answering the question: *What Do You Stand to Gain From Studying Salesmanship?* Hopefully, this approach will arouse your attention and interest and motivate you to *study* (not just skim-read) the balance of this text by answering promptly your legitimate question, "What's in it for me?"

Part II covers the theoretical concepts and historical development of sales/marketing to help you understand the *why* of certain principles, practices, and techniques that will be presented later in a very applied, "how-to" manner. The modern customer-society oriented marketing concept is stressed, market-forecast data for the late 1970s and the early 1980s is presented to help you prepare written assignments, and buyer behavior and the psychology of selling is explored. There is a chapter on social, legal, and ethical issues and *responsibilities* in selling; an important topic in view of the growing American consumer movement and the challenge it poses to sales/marketing professionals.

Part III deals with organizing, prospecting, and planning for personal selling; it works down from the top corporate or organizational level to personal outside or instore selling via a managerially-oriented approach.

Part IV presents the four basic parts of any logically organized sales presentation: *attention* (the approach), *interest* (how to create and hold interest), *desire* (arousing desire and securing conviction), and *action* (how to close the sale). Principles and techniques of handling challenges or objections are also covered.

Part V covers after-sale follow-up and follow-through, and special applications to retail, telephone, industrial, and group and trade show or exhibition selling.

Part VI offers a helpful chapter on how to sell yourself for the sales position of your choice; how-to-go-about-it information that also applies to helping you find and land the job of your choice in *any other career field*. The concluding three chapters outline how to achieve success most rapidly in personal selling or in working up to a managerial position, based on your own audit of yourself and your career objectives.

Please note that the terms *sales representative* (rather than the outdated term salesman) and *salesmanship* are used generally throughout this text, as they are in the sales/marketing profession, except in reference to retail selling, where *salesperson* is employed as the term in general use. The terms sales representative and salesperson include both women and men.

Good luck in your study; your author hopes you find this text interesting, informative, and challenging.

a note to the instructor
on the second edition

This second edition has been extensively reorganized, and new topics introduced based on recommendations of many lecturers in salesmanship, most of them from two-year colleges where the salesmanship course is most generally taught in the United States and Canada, others from four-year colleges and universities.

Briefly, these new features include a new approach and more theoretical concepts in Parts I and II; more real-life case studies from both small and large business firms (forty-two in this edition versus thirty-five in the first edition, twenty-one of which are new in this edition); more end-of-chapter problems (twenty in this edition versus eight in the first; twelve of which are new); and more dialogue illustrations in chapters, case studies, and sales problems suited to class-room role-playing.

Chapter 1, *What Do You Stand to Gain From Studying Salesmanship*, is a direct response to the many lecturers who urged that career opportunities be introduced at the beginning of the text, because today's students want to know *immediately* what can be derived from taking a course in salesmanship. Other new chapter and case study materials acknowledge their request for more material of specific interest to American minority groups—blacks, women, those of Hispanic origin, and those over sixty-five among others.

Chapter 3 includes statistical forecasts on what will be the two most important determinants of consumer demand in the late 1970s and 1980s: (1) the age mix of America's household population, and (2) the distribution of spending power. This has also been added at the request of several instructors, as has the new material on telephone, industrial, and group and trade show or exhibition selling. And there is more material throughout on retail selling.

Moreover, this second edition reflects far more American and Canadian examples and case studies. The important globally-oriented approach, so well-received in the first edition, has been retained, but because the basic market for the text lies in two- and four-year North American colleges, this edition reflects their more specific interests and needs.

Overall, this edition remains a reader-centered career guide, covering both the "why" (theoretical) and "how-to" (applied) principles, practices, and techniques of modern selling and salesmanship. The modern sales representative of the late 1970s and 1980s, outside and instore, will have to be better educated and more managerially oriented than in the past if he expects maximum financial rewards and the greatest opportunities for promotion to managerial ranks. At all levels, he is increasingly playing a more important role on the customer-society oriented marketing-management team that starts its planning with end-customers' needs and wants in mind. To help them prepare, this edition offers the following important features:

Managerial orientation is stressed throughout. The reader is taught that from the start he must learn to think like a manager by scientifically and practically learning to forecast, plan, establish procedures and programs, schedule work effi-ciently, and follow through in every way.

Principles with practical applications are carefully explained and illustrated through real-life examples and case studies. Although mainly presented from the point of view of those outside sales representatives of any field who are concerned mainly with closing sales, the material is equally valuable to sales promotion or instore retail salespersons.

The modern international sales/marketing approach of customer-society oriented problem solving is emphasized. This concept starts with the needs, wants, and problems of the end-customer and works backward, seeking to create products or services that will both offer value and benefit to the individual consumer and his society, and be sold profitably.

Concepts from the behavioral sciences are discussed. What causes people to buy what they do when they do? Can research really anticipate individual and group buying behavior? The behavioral sciences, though not yet exact, have given us many valid generalizations about individuals, groups, social processes, and interactions over the past eighty years. These are presented so that the reader may recognize and know how to apply, whenever possible, relevant, scientific principles of buyer behavior.

In summary, the second edition of *Modern Applied Salesmanship* is a reader-centered, goal-setting, managerially-oriented guide to selling with practical applications. It stresses the modern international sales/marketing approach to customer-society oriented problem solving, based on concepts from the behavioral sciences. Its forty-two case studies, twenty sales problems, and scores of examples, illustrate that the principles of modern salesmanship presented apply everywhere in the world when properly adapted to local conditions.

An instructor's manual containing answers to all end-of-chapter, case study, and sales problem questions, plus numerous true-false, completion, and multiple-choice tests and other useful material is available.

acknowledgments

A book such as this is the product of years of experience in working with others and in researching the writings of countless book-authors and contributors to journals and periodicals. I can only hope that I have contributed my own 10 percent plus to what has been learned from them and that others in turn will build on this endeavor.

My first specific acknowledgments go to a handful of men who in their own time, place, and way taught me so much of what is at the heart of this book. They include the late Paul W. Ivey, Ph.D., whose inspiring classes in salesmanship at the University of Southern California first opened my eyes to selling as a career; the late George L. McNelley, a grand railroad engineer turned direct salesman who taught me that cold-call selling is really "that adventure on the other side of the door"; and Richard P. Ettinger, Jr., the most conscientious and helpful field sales supervisor I have ever worked under.

The list continues with Kenneth C. Matheson, of Australia, the most capable professional salesman I have ever had the pleasure of working closely with; Hillard H. McMullen, of New Zealand, whose high ethical principles and goals in selling and business serve as constant personal inspiration; and Kenneth Thurston Hurst, from whom I have learned much about scientific management applications to selling and sales management.

My second special acknowledgments go to the following companies and organizations and their busy executives, who were kind enough to help provide practical and meaningful case-study materials: Shell Oil Company; the Singer Company; the Coca-Cola Company; Best Foods Division of C.P.C. International, Inc.; Volkswagen of America, Inc.; the Fuller Brush Company; Thomas J. Lipton, Inc.; R. T. Reid Associates, Inc., Goodyear International Corporation; Four Seasons Travel Agency, Inc.; the United Nations; the Royal Bank of Canada; IBM Corporation; the American Marketing Association; and CORO Inc. I also wish to acknowledge the permissions editors of the several book, magazine, and newspaper publishers cited as sources of quoted material.

Additional acknowledgements are also due:

To the following individuals, who assisted in providing or reviewing text or case study material: Arthur M. Rittenberg, George E. Frim, William H. T. Sie, Paul A. B. Poynton, Gordon D. Gram, Robert L. Young, Irving Krasner, and Donald T. Caldwell.

To the following individuals for their friendly and helpful professional assistance in allowing me use of their outstanding New York City reference facilities: Mrs. Marilyn Bochman, Head Librarian, Association of American Advertising Agencies; Mr. Tamsen R. Macwatt and other staff specialists, The Conference Board; and Mr. Bernard F. Kelley, Director, Marketing Information Center, Sales and Marketing Executives International.

To Leslie Kanuk, Ph.D. who kindly allowed me on occasion to meet with students of two of her salesmanship classes at Baruch College, City University of New York; and to the several academic reviewers who, through the good offices of Steven Lock, Editor, Goodyear Publishing Company, offered valuable critique of the first edition of this text.

To Colette Conboy, my production editor, Jan Deming, and Jane Hellesoe-Henon, of the Goodyear editorial staff, who worked so hard and ably on the production of this edition.

My last and most heartfelt acknowledgment belongs to my wife, Bessie, whose encouragement, inspiration, and long hours of critical reviewing, typing, and proofing helped make this book possible—and to whom it is lovingly dedicated.

PART I

WHAT DO YOU STAND TO GAIN FROM STUDYING SALESMANSHIP?

1
what do you stand to gain from studying salesmanship?

When you have mastered the content of this chapter, you should be able to:

Define the terms *selling, salesmanship, persuasion,* and *sales/marketing.*

Describe the importance of a knowledge of salesmanship in attaining success in both sales or nonsales careers, or in nonwork avocations involving close association with other people.

Summarize the advantages of a sales career and the monetary compensation such a career might offer you.

Describe meaning of the terms (1) *retail* (inside) *salesperson,* (2) *specialty* (outside) *sales representative* or *salesman,* and (3) *real sales representative.*

List the kinds of careers available in selling.

Outline the possible advantages of a sales career in terms of your own interests, educational background, and career aspirations.

Analyze whether or not you feel you would enjoy selling as a career and have what it takes to be successful in such a career.

Let us begin by talking about you, the reader—your hopes, your fears, your realistic ambitions in life. What kind of personal relationships with others do you hope for—to be liked, to influence others? What kind of career ambitions do you have—do you seek wealth, an interesting and challenging profession, status, career advancement, an opportunity through your work to make a contribution to society?

Have you ever been puzzled or confused by friends, fellow students, or fellow workers refusing to accept your ideas or opinions, or to behave or react the way you expect? Have you secretly envied the success of others in any of these areas noted so far and wondered why success came to them and not to you? Would you like to be as popular or successful as they are?

Why begin a book on salesmanship with questions like these? Simply because most of these things involve getting along with, working with, or leading other people; and salesmanship as a study basically is concerned with just that, especially with influencing and persuading others. In fact, a course in salesmanship, or your study of this book, could well be one of the most helpful, practical studies you will ever encounter, since it specifically relates to achieving personal, social, and career success.

We are going to talk in this book about how you can plan your future work so as to achieve your personal goals—whether they are wealth, status, career advancement, or leadership. Our framework will be salesmanship; you must be interested in the possibilities of selling as an avenue for achieving your ambitions or you would not have chosen to read this book. The principles we will be talking about relate to the achievement of success in business, industry, government, and in social work and other occupations or avocations involving close association with other people.

In this chapter we will discuss what you stand to gain from a study of salesmanship as applied to any type career or avocation you may follow, business or nonbusiness, and then consider the advantages of a possible professional sales career for achieving your goals.

But first, a word of warning! In spite of its very personal "you approach," this is a serious textbook on salesmanship. You will have to think and study, and start putting into practice immediately many of the principles, practices, and techniques we will be discussing, if they are to mean anything to you. A good way to start, if you are not in selling already, is to try to get a part-time sales job now, so you can start practicing and developing skills. Selling is like swimming: you can read all about it yet know little about it until you have jumped into the water, started kicking, and developed skill through practice.

If you are unable to get a part-time sales job, then at least get in the habit, starting today, of observing retail salespersons at work whenever you buy anything and evaluating their actions in terms of your current study of salesmanship. At the same time you can observe your friends and others "selling" their ideas, and practice the principles and techniques of salesmanship we will be studying in "selling" your own ideas to friends.

WHY STUDY SALESMANSHIP?

While we have already answered this question in part, let us consider the fact that literally everyone "sells" something; themselves, their ideas, services, or products. Actually, you started selling yourself immediately after birth, with your first lusty howl for attention. Throughout your life up to this point you have consciously and unconsciously sold yourself in many ways. And you must keep selling yourself—a marriage proposal, landing the career job of your choice, possibly even getting a loan at the bank, and in countless other ways—for the rest of your life.

Everyone sells—the politician trying to win an election has to sell his constituents on the idea that he is the best man to represent them; a minister or priest has to sell his religion (and sell his flock on the need for continued financial support).

The end result of any business venture, personal or corporate, is to profitably sell its products or services. Organizations have to sell their ideas if they want public acceptance.

This "selling" takes place in literally every aspect of life where people have to live or work together—with subordinates, peers, bosses, customers, or anyone else with whom you personally or the company, organization, or group you represent has to collaborate or work with.

If selling is that important, how does one go about it? Answering that question is what the study of salesmanship, and this book, is all about. You will learn how to sell—yourself, your ideas, and things—in the pages to follow, as we consider principles, practices, and some proven techniques of modern selling and salesmanship that apply not only to a sales career, but to any other career or noncareer associations involving other people with whom you might be associated in your lifetime.

WHAT DO WE MEAN BY SELLING AND SALESMANSHIP?

Traditionally, most definitions of *selling* have been in the strictly commercial sense. The American Marketing Association, for example, defines selling as "the personal or impersonal process of assisting and/or persuading a prospective customer to buy a commodity or service and to act favorably upon an idea that has commercial significance to the seller."[1] Another definition asserts that selling is persuading people to want what you have—in terms of products, services, or ideas. It is the dual instrument of discovering and persuading: discovering human needs and wants and persuading people to use your products or services to meet them.

Authors have defined *salesmanship* in various ways: one definition holds that salesmanship is the art of teaching or helping others to buy; another, that salesmanship is the persuasive leadership that influences people to buy goods and services. A third and broader definition asserts that salesmanship is learning the customer's viewpoint and making him see yours by getting him to think or act. Still another definition maintains that salesmanship basically is the art of persuading somebody either to accept or to follow our ideas, and thus lead them to the action we desire.

PERSUASION IS CENTRAL TO SALESMANSHIP

All the above definitions clearly indicate that *persuasion* is at the core of selling and salesmanship. In fact, persuasion is central to decision-making in most areas of life: professional, social, business, or political. A sale is made whenever two people disagree on a subject that is eventually resolved; one has persuaded, or sold, the other on his point of view. Persuasion means to move a person or persons to a belief, a position, a point of view, or a course of action.

Salesmanship is the practice of selling, and if mere persuasion is the end objective it could either be harmful or beneficial. But, as we shall discuss more fully in Chapter 2, modern selling and salesmanship goes far beyond merely persuading another to accept your ideas or buy your product or service. It is also concerned with offering something of value and benefit that will result in *buyer satisfaction* and *the welfare of society*—highly desirable, worthwhile objectives.

IMPORTANCE OF KNOWLEDGE
OF SALESMANSHIP FOR NONSALES CAREERS
It Can Help You Land a Job of Your Choice in Any Career Field

One of the most important problems facing many college students is whether to pursue a college course that will train them for a specific job-related career field, or one that will provide a general liberal arts education. Many feel it more impor-

1. From *Marketing Definitions: A Glossary of Marketing Terms,* (Chicago: American Marketing Association, 1960), p. 21. Reprinted by permission.

tant to gain a broad background, yet as they begin to recognize that graduates who majored in social sciences and the humanities have the most difficulty in finding desirable jobs in those fields, they wonder if they might not have been better off to major in a job-related field. Women especially haven't traditionally felt the kind of necessity that men have felt about studying for a field in which they know they will be able to support a family. Only recently have many women begun to think more in terms of careers.

United States Department of Labor reports and other services indicate that almost one out of five recent college graduates is working in jobs unrelated to their major fields of study. As examples, one might cite cases such as a 1973 sociology major who is now an office receptionist in Chicago, an art history major who is working as an aide in a New York City law office, and an American Studies major who is working as an assistant buyer in a Miami department store.

The 1950s and 1960s were golden years for American college graduates, most of whom received several job offers regardless of their majors. But so far in the 1970s, good starting jobs have become more scarce, college graduates have grown more numerous, and in many cases company recruiters have been seen less frequently on campuses. While the number of college graduates has increased, the total number of graduates being sought today on campus by company or government recruiters is not as great as it was during the 1960s. Many experts feel this trend is likely to continue for the next few years at least.

Many authorities blame the colleges and universities for inadequate guidance and counseling in helping students learn more about the working world. The Director of the Labor Department's Bureau of Labor Statistics in a major city was quoted as saying, "Regretfully, many college youngsters today learn about career opportunities in the same way they learn about sex, through a peer process which differs only, perhaps, in that the classroom is not the street but the campus."

What do *you* stand to gain from studying salesmanship? At the very least, a knowledge of how to *sell yourself* for a job of *your choice*; in Chapter 18 we will discuss specifically how to accomplish that highly desirable objective. The examples will relate to obtaining a sales position of choice, but the how-to principles are the same for obtaining a job of your choice in any career field, regardless of college major.

It Can Help You Achieve Success in Many Nonbusiness Activities

Just as knowledge of salesmanship can help you "sell yourself" for a job of your choice, so can it help you sell yourself or your ideas in many other ways throughout your life. The same basic principles of selling a product or service in a business sense also apply to the marketing or selling of other things, such as political, organizational (private or government), cultural, social, and cause ideas or programs. Let us consider a few such activities in which selling or salesmanship (the practice of selling) applies:

Political. A candidate has to sell himself to his constituents in order to get elected. He is the product, voters are the prospects (potential buyers), and the sales job is to persuade the voters that this particular candidate is the best one to provide leadership for putting into effect the type laws they desire. This concept is aptly described in the book *The Selling of a President 1968* by Joseph McGinniss (New York: Trident Press, 1969).

Organizational.   Churches, as an example of private organizations, spend a great deal of time and effort not only selling their faith, but also in persuading members to give financial support. The Billy Graham organization is well known for its highly successful sales methods in selling its brand of religion. Many government organizations also actively sell ideas; the United States Travel Service, for example, was set up to sell foreigners on the idea of visiting the United States, as one means of earning dollars to help offset the flow of dollars spent abroad by American tourists. Its success can be illustrated by the fact that the flow of 2.4 million overseas visitors to the United States during the first eight months of 1973 alone represented a 26 percent increase over the same period 1972, and it did not include arrivals from neighboring Canada or Mexico.

Cultural.   Organizations, such as local symphony orchestras, have to seek basic financial support from government, business, and the general public. Their "sales presentation" often stresses that donations from the latter two sources are tax-deductible. Private universities also constantly seek continued financial support by selling the value of the university to the local community, along with the idea that business and personal donations may be tax-deductible.

Social.   Programs that will benefit society in general often have to be sold to the general public in order to gain widespread acceptance and support. Well-known such campaigns include "Keep America Beautiful," "Smokey the Bear," and "Buy Bonds and Support America."

Cause.   The campaign spearheaded by the American Cancer Society to warn of the danger of cigarette smoking and the anti-pollution campaigns mounted by many governmental and private environmentalist organizations are but two examples.

It is quite likely that sometime during your lifetime you will be engaged, individually or as part of an organized group, in "selling" one or more such non-business ideas. This "selling" may embrace a "mix" (meaning the relative proportions of each type necessary to achieve success) of sales/marketing methods —advertising, publicity, sales promotion, and personal salesmanship. Success will depend on persuading others to your point of view. Your current study of modern applied salesmanship will help equip you to effectively participate in such activities and possibly even lead them to success.

It Can Help You Achieve Success
in All Nonsales/Marketing Areas of Business

The purpose of any business, from a Mom and Pop corner delicatessen to a major corporation such as General Motors, is to make a profit. *Profit*, to any individual business man or woman, is the difference between income received from *sales* and all costs and expenses.

If you eventually enter your own business, whether it be a shoe store or motel, or professional practice, such as accounting, brokerage, or management consulting, you will be vitally concerned with sales. If you work for a large firm or corporation, in whatever capacity, you should constantly be aware of, and help to attain, the overall profit-goal—the end result of the business enterprise.

So, whether you enter into a business career on a self-employed basis or work for a small firm or large corporation as a manager, accountant, computer technician, or in production, or in any other capacity, your current study of modern applied salesmanship will help give you more awareness and understanding of the vital sales/marketing end of the business.

THE PROBLEMS OF CAREER SELECTION IN TODAY'S WORLD

The average young college student of today encounters a bewildering number of choices in making a career decision. Job counselors advise and common sense dictates that one plans a career in a growth industry in order to gain financial and material rewards. In 1900 the leather and shipping industries were excellent growth industries. Today, however, the electronic, scientific, and precision-equipment industries, to name but a few, have surpassed leather and shipping in growth potential.

The normal problems of career selection are compounded because we live in an unprecedented age of technological explosion and distribution revolution, affected by rapidly increasing world population, changing age structure with emphasis on youth, increasing population mobility, and rising levels of income, education, and leisure. These things will be considered in greater detail throughout these pages, especially in Chapter 3, in terms of planning and organizing for selling in a changing marketing environment.

For now, the point is that the needs and wants of the exploding and changing world population will continue to increase, and private or nationalized companies or organizations will be fulfilling the marketing function of supplying those needs. Marketing, as we shall further define in Chapter 2, is concerned with the many things that fall between manufacturing or producing goods or services and the ultimate consumer, with personal selling as perhaps its most important function.

Sales/marketing, the term we shall use often throughout this book to integrate marketing and personal selling, is thus a growth area, providing unlimited career opportunities for you.

Provided that you select a growth industry or organization in whatever field that interests you, the sales road to marketing management offers one of the quickest paths to career success. Opportunities for higher earnings or promotion to top management through selling have reached, and will continue to reach, new highs in most countries of the world for most individuals regardless of age, sex, race, educational level, or social origin.

In order to take advantage of these opportunities, however, you will have to develop your knowledge and skills through study and practical application, and become managerially oriented. A major purpose of this book is to help you accomplish this. But first, let us see whether or not the possibilities of a sales/marketing career hold any real interest for you.

WHAT DOES SELLING AS A CAREER HAVE TO OFFER YOU?

Let us start relating some of the above mentioned trends to your specific desires and interests, to ascertain whether you should spend your remaining working years in the field of selling. If you are seriously interested in selling as your pathway to career success, you should seek answers to these questions:

1. What kind of careers are there in selling?
2. What is the expected compensation?
3. What education or training is needed to achieve success?
4. What economic trends may affect the sales career selected?
5. What are the chances through selling of reaching top management?
6. What are the advantages and disadvantages of a sales career?
7. What personal responsibilities will future successful sales representatives face?
8. Where can one find desirable sales positions?

We will discuss most of these questions in this chapter. We assume (1) that you are ambitious and desire increased compensation and promotion during your career, and (2) that you intend working as a real sales representative—one who will contact buyers, purchasing agents, or the public in order to sell a product or service; or in retail selling.

Selling can be classified into two broad categories: retail and specialty. U.S. census figures indicate that 5.3 million men and women were engaged in some form of sales work in 1974. Of these, 3.1 million were engaged in *retail* (inside) selling, and 2.2 million in *specialty* (outside) selling. The distinction between these two broad classifications is not always clear; some sales representatives, for example, work on the floor in retail establishments part of the time and call on prospects in their homes the rest of the time. But basically we can outline the following differences between these two broad categories as follows:

1. Retail (inside) sales representatives normally work inside stores, where customers come to them.
2. Specialty (outside) sales representatives go outside to call on prospects in their homes, offices, or places of business.

FIGURE 1.1   Job Opportunities for Sales Representatives in the United States*

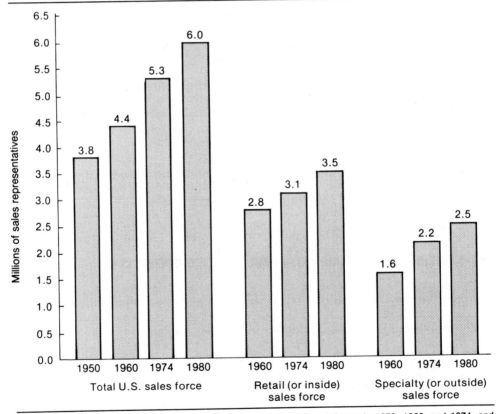

*Based on census estimates of employed salesmen in the United States in 1950, 1960, and 1974, and projections for the future based on 15 percent growth per decade.

Source: U.S. Department of Labor, Bureau of Labor Statistics.

We can make a further distinction between *real sales representatives*—who are vitally concerned with closing sales on most calls—and those missionary, route, or promotions sales representatives, or retail salespersons, whose company policy may not require them to try to close a sale during every call or interview. While most of the specific techniques and examples in this book are addressed to real sales representatives, much can be applied by the others to their own specific work.

Increased automation has taken its toll of some of the salesclerk (or order-taking) jobs, notably in the retail field. This development has led to a decline in the percentage of sales representatives engaged in business activity but has increased the importance of those so engaged. Nevertheless, as Figure 1.1 indicates, job opportunities are increasing and should continue to increase at the rate of approximately 15 percent each decade.

Selling offers excellent opportunities for rapid financial rewards and advancement to executive rank. By way of overview, to answer your first questions first and to point out some obvious advantages of a sales career, here are two positive thoughts regarding compensation and promotion. Selling is one of the best-paying vocations for both men and women, with many sales representatives earning more than their managers while having relative independence. Also, sales representatives with increasing frequency are climbing to the top of the corporate ladder.

Reflecting the increased sales/marketing orientation of top management is the fact that today one out of every three publicly owned U.S. corporations is headed by a person whose background is primarily in marketing and sales. Due to rapidly changing technological and social change, and a more affluent and demanding market marked by subjective choices, unpredictable consumer discretion, and impulse buying, top management must be highly sensitive to consumer demands. Thus the ratio of sales/marketing trained and oriented top managers will continue to grow.

WHAT KINDS OF CAREERS ARE THERE IN SELLING?

There are a few traditional area breakdowns for sales careers worth attention. Generally in each of them the sales representative's role is changing from that of being merely a seller of goods to that of being a market manager of his territory. Increasingly, job descriptions mention management activities such as advertising, finance, and understanding of automation. Changes in merchandising and inventory controls and increased reliance on the field representative are making many sales representatives more marketing- than product-oriented in the following areas.

Manufacturer's sales representatives. This category includes different types and specializations of representatives calling on industrial concerns; wholesalers, distributors, and dealers; and direct consumers. Some specialize in pioneering new products or brands, and, since good producers are always in demand, they can earn excellent compensation if they can overcome the challenge of stiff competition. The following sales groups are included in this category.

Dealer-servicing sales representatives call regularly on retail outlets in their territory, trying to write larger orders on each visit. For example, a representative for a hardware manufacturer brings new samples, checks stock, writes new orders, and even sets up window displays.

Sales-promotion representatives specialize more in sales promotion than in taking on-the-spot orders. Representatives of pharmaceutical houses, often referred to as detailmen, who call on doctors and publisher's representatives who present information about new or future books to university professors fall into this category.

Merchandising sales representatives include those who arrange newspaper and television publicity, hold product demonstrations for distributors' sales representatives, and even work with them in the field. Counselors for cosmetics companies are of this type.

Missionary sales representatives work through wholesalers, jobbers, or distributors, whose own sales representatives will sell to the ultimate customers. An example is a home economist for a dairy cooperative who sponsors demonstration classes for chain-store route or retail sales personnel.

Technical sales representatives are usually highly trained technical engineers who call on old or new customers to help solve their technical problems. The representative of a computer company, for example, has to be able to discuss entire systems and types of technical equipment that will best meet a customer's needs.

Wholesaler's sales representatives. These men and women represent the jobber or wholesaler, who carries stocks of many items from several different manufacturers. They serve the many retailers or other customers who find it more convenient to place one consolidated order for small quantities of many items rather than to send individual orders to all the manufacturers. Such a representative may represent a book jobber, who carries stocks of books from all publishers. He calls on libraries and perhaps displays a carefully indexed stock list or copies of publishers' catalogues; from these the librarian may order one copy each of 100 books from 30 different publishers.

Retail salespeople. The bulk of that portion of any national work force engaged in "sales occupations" is made up of retail salespeople. They are behind the counters in retail establishments all over the world. As automation and self-service have grown, their relative numbers have decreased. Often low paid and untrained, many can be classed as order takers rather than as sales representatives in the true sense. Others, however, are highly trained, earn excellent income, and enjoy favorable opportunities for advancement to store or corporate-chain management.

Specialty sales representatives. These men and women usually represent a single product or line which they sell by going directly to the consumers. The following are some of the more common classifications of specialty sales representatives.

Product or service sales representatives specialize in selling products or services used in the office or in the factory. They call on business or governmental purchasing officers or department heads, selling such things as computers, industrial or office machines, and training courses. They also sell accounting, insurance, and other services. Many such representatives in this area earn very high incomes, although in some cases they may have to work for years to make one large sale.

Inside-outside sales representatives is a broad category which includes both those working from a showroom or office and outside, such as automobile or insurance sales representatives, and those who operate a personalized route or direct-mail service from their home. Many retail stores have outside sales representatives, who call either on the store's existing customers to sell them more or on entirely new customer prospects at their homes. They usually try to sell expensive durable goods such as furniture, washing machines, and television sets, often bringing the interested customers back to the store to see the product. Most of the men and women in this sales category work on a straight commission or draw against commission, many of them earning very high incomes.

Door-to-door (or house-to-house) sales representatives are those direct sales-people who normally call on prospects in their homes. Such direct selling can bring high income to hard-working men and women of any age and with any degree of education. Encyclopedia sets and cemetery lots are sold this way, and some companies such as the Fuller Brush Company and Avon Products, Inc. (cosmetics) sell their products only through door-to-door sales representatives. This selling is perhaps the hardest of all since many doors have to be knocked upon and often several presentations made before a sale is closed. But with proper training and steady work habits, the law of averages works for these sales represen-tatives, and the commissions per sale are usually good. Direct selling of this type is often called walk-and-talk selling—the more you walk, the more you talk; the more you talk, the more sales you should make.

SELLING OFFERS MANY INTERESTING AND REWARDING CAREER POSSIBILITIES

Opportunities are there for you in any of the above traditional areas of selling, providing you are willing to put forth the effort and to follow the principles of salesmanship outlined in this book. Good sales representatives are constantly sought by every type of manufacturer, jobber, distributor, and retailer; but it pays to look carefully into the opportunities offered by each.

Perhaps the most important thing to consider is the growth potential of the sales area. Many fields will grow considerably in the years ahead. For example, within ten years sales of electrical distribution equipment may triple, a growth potential that applies to office machines as well. Sales of industrial instruments and controls may double over the same period. The chemical industry will also boom, needing improved machinery to produce new plastic materials and prod-ucts of all types for factory and home. The expanding population and rising income levels will create unheard-of demands for housing, furniture, appliances, carpets, and all the other goods necessary for home improvement. Longer life expectancy and stepped-up government medical programs should increase drug output threefold. The demand for good clothing for all age levels will increase, as will the demand for a wide variety of other goods and services. Since people will have more leisure along with more money, automobile sales will expand, and people will spend more on sports, hobbies, entertainment, and vacations.

Selling offers a wide variety of interesting, creative, worthwhile, and finan-cially rewarding careers; but it will pay to seek a professional sales career in a growth industry.

WHAT KIND OF COMPENSATION DOES A SALES CAREER OFFER?

In order to achieve personal happiness as well as financial security and growth in any career area, you should consider the intangible as well as tangible rewards. Let us relate both to a professional sales career.

Intangible Rewards

Many employers have wisely observed that for many people money is not the chief motivating factor in life or in work; they would rather be happy in their work with a reasonable income than to work for money alone. Perhaps you should seek to combine both—work you enjoy in a financially rewarding area.

Most sales representatives enjoy their work because they like the relative freedom of action, the fact that sales increases are a direct reflection of their own abilities, the quick recognition of such abilities, and the fact that opportunities for advancement in earnings or promotions are great. The salesminded person enjoys the opportunities such work offers to meet interesting people, to see what is going on in business and industry, and to be a participant rather than a desk-bound observer.

Opportunities to travel, the advantages of a probable expense account, and above all the challenge of matching wits with the prospective customer are all forms of compensation not readily found in nonselling vocations. Perhaps above all, the truly motivated sales representative engaged in worthwhile, creative work he enjoys has the feeling that his personal efforts can accomplish something now!

Monetary Rewards

The amount of money you can earn as a sales representative in the United States depends largely on what kind of selling area you enter, your educational background, the region or the area in which you work, and the compensation plan offered by your employer.

Certain industries pay sales representatives higher beginning wages than others do. For example, you can generally get a higher starting salary selling scientific and precision or electrical and electronic equipment, construction materials, or hardware than you can selling drugs, cosmetics, or glassware. The beginning income spread can be as much as $2,000 per year.

Average earnings per industry for experienced salesmen are generally higher in textiles and clothing, electrical and electronic equipment, and paper products than they are in printing and publishing, transportation, and retailing. The average spread of income between experienced men in these industries can be as great as $6,000 annually.

Industries offering the highest potential wages for qualified beginning sales representatives include furniture and home furnishings, primary metals, and various service trades.

Successful, experienced sales representatives earn higher income in such industries as paper and allied products, textiles and clothing, primary metals, chemicals, and petroleum. Income in these areas can run as high as $50,000 per year.

In view of this comparative income potential by industries in the United States, it is obvious that the highest beginning wages tend to be paid to those having technical education, knowledge, and skills. This observation is also generally true in the higher paid brackets. The textile and clothing industry is the exception—a thought that should encourage the nontechnical person.

The one industry, not yet discussed, that offers potentially high salaries at every stage is that collection of many vocations loosely called the service industry. Many sales representatives have made their fortunes in different ways within this area, real estate sales being one of the quickest avenues.

FIGURE 1.2 Annual Compensation Range for American Sales Representatives

Industry Range	Overall Earnings Range	Average Earnings Range
Advertising	$9,000 – $40,000	$16,000 – $18,000
Automotive	9,000 – 32,000	14,000 – 16,000
Apparel (wholesale)	9,000 – 50,000	24,000 – 26,000
Building and construction	7,000 – 30,000	14,000 – 16,000
Business services	7,500 – 27,000	16,000 – 18,000
Chemicals	8,000 – 32,000	14,000 – 16,000
Drugs	8,000 – 26,000	12,000 – 14,000
Electronics	9,000 – 25,000	15,500 – 17,500
Farm products	9,000 – 25,000	13,000 – 15,000
Foods, beverages	7,000 – 28,000	12,000 – 14,000
Hardwear	11,500 – 28,000	15,000 – 17,000
Housewear	5,000 – 30,000	9,000 – 11,000
Insurance	7,500 – 25,000	13,000 – 15,000
Metals	10,000 – 22,000	15,000 – 17,000
Office supplies	7,500 – 25,000	11,000 – 13,000
Publishing	7,500 – 23,000	11,000 – 13,000
Services (nonbusiness)	10,000 – 20,000	14,000 – 16,000

Figure 1.2, which has been compiled from several sources, indicates sales representative's annual salary ranges in a representative group of industries.

Compensation Plans

There are three general compensation plans in selling. The first is the *straight-salary* plan, in which an annual fixed salary is paid, plus perhaps an annual bonus or prizes or merchandise not directly related to individual sales efforts. Second is the *straight commission* plan, in which the sales representative is paid at a fixed or sliding rate in proportion to his sales or profit volume. This includes plans which offer a draw against commission.

The third and most widely used is the *combination salary-and-commission plan*, which can have many variations. Such a plan may offer a sales representative two-thirds of his total compensation in salary and one-third in commissions or bonus in direct relation to his sales or profit volume. Other combinations include a fixed salary plus a bonus for profitable sales above a fixed ceiling, or a salary plus profit-sharing.

Expense accounts and fringe benefits must be taken into consideration when comparing income from sales positions. Most companies pay travel expenses, many provide automobiles, and many reimburse sales representatives for entertainment and other expenses. Fringe benefits can include paid vacations; free hospitaliza- tion; life, accident, and medical insurance; stock options; pension plans; superan- nuation; and profit-sharing. In the face of the high national income taxes in most countries, fringe benefits can be worth more than a larger salary. For example, profit-sharing funds, which enjoy favorable capital-gains tax rates, may be more important to you on a career basis than more pay now.

The average sales trainee in the United States starts his career at an average annual income of around $8,000–$9,500, and soon is earning an average of $9,500–$12,000. From then on his income depends on several factors, notably his personal sales success. The average experienced specialty sales representative in the United States earns aroung $18,000 per year plus fringe benefits; the average experienced Canadian sales representative around $12,500–$14,500 per year plus fringe benefits. In both the United States and Canada, the man or woman on straight commission still earns the highest income, but since over half the American and Canadian companies are now paying on combination plans of salary and bonus or commission, income for their sales representatives is catching up with that of commission sales representatives.

Higher income can be earned in some parts of the country than it can in others. For example, salaries are generally higher in the United States on the eastern seaboard in the New York to Boston region than in North or South Dakota. Also many companies pay higher salaries at certain overseas posts than they do at home. The cost of living versus the take-home pay is an important consideration. A sales representative may enjoy a better standard of living in Sioux City than in crowded New York City, even though his income is considerably less.

Wherever he or she lives, whatever area of selling he or she is engaged in, the American sales representative earns better than average income; in fact, 50 percent better than the typical male worker, according to latest Census Bureau reports. It is not at all uncommon for a good sales representative to earn $30,000 per year or more, and the more he earns the better it is for his company. The average income, incidentally, is higher than that for engineers, accountants, and those in many other business categories. In many cases, crack sales representatives earn more than $100,000 per year—more than the presidents of their companies.

WHAT KIND OF EDUCATION IS NECESSARY FOR SUCCESS IN SELLING?

We have already observed that certain industries pay higher starting salaries than others do. Most of these are in technical fields, so they naturally try to employ university-educated engineering or science graduates, to whom they have to pay high wages. But it is not only the technical fields that seek well-educated sales representatives. Most industries seem willing to pay more for better education, and most companies within these industries are looking for applicants with at least some college or university background.

University graduates or college-educated sales representatives are in great demand. A relatively small percentage of firms now require a university degree for sales positions; but most of them require at least two years of college or university education. Trends indicate, however, that as more students earn university degrees, more employers will require them as a matter of policy. Within the next decade, a university degree may be a prerequisite for any important sales position, and advancement to key managerial positions will also require advanced training.

The 1974 Endicott Report[2] of company plans for on-campus recruiting, representing a detailed survey of 196 well-known business and industrial concerns about their campus recruiting plans, indicates that companies are looking for "outstanding achievers" with academic majors directly related to various specialized jobs for the better career positions being offered. Engineering, accounting, chemistry, math/statistics, sales/marketing, and economics/finance majors were reported in greatest demand. General business majors are acceptable and are being hired in large numbers as in previous years, but interest in liberal arts majors has diminished. Demand for M.B.A.'s continues high.

2. Frank S. Endicott, Northwestern University retired placement director and professor emeritus of education, *The Endicott Report, 1974, Trends in Employment of College and University Graduates in Business and Industry,* copyrighted by Northwestern University, 1973.

For sales positions, trends indicate a preference for applicants with a broad liberal education plus a good background in the behavioral sciences and business, marketing, and advertising. Study of quantitative methods, statistics, and applied mathematics may be necessary for future key managerial positions.

What is the future in selling for those who have not had or will not have a higher education? For those who do not have the time or money to spend on a university degree, there is also hope. Community colleges, technical schools, and universities are all offering adult night classes geared to the needs of local business, government, and industry. Executives of local institutions or firms teach many of these courses. Programmed instruction has speeded up the learning process in many areas, and many of these courses can be studied at home. Company training programs are increasing, and more companies than before are paying all or part of evening-course tuition for ambitious employees.

Sales opportunities that do not require a high level of education exist in the expanding areas of door-to-door selling, service agencies of all kinds, and franchise plans, in which management is provided for a self-owned and self-run business.

WHAT FUTURE ECONOMIC AND MARKETING TRENDS WILL AFFECT A SALES CAREER?

We have already noted some of the major changes that will affect sales work during the next quarter century at least. Overall major factors are the technological revolution, automation, the consolidation of business and industries, and the introduction of new marketing techniques brought about by changes in the marketing and distribution environment.

Most of these trends involve bigness in everything—larger and more complex marketing programs by fewer big companies and more complex and sophisticated roles for sales representatives. Markets have changed more radically than sales/marketing itself, however. The view from the marketing director's office is now often somewhat like the view of the world from a satellite orbiting 10,000 miles out in space. The problems of reaching the world market are greater than those involved in covering the neat little upstate sales territory, but the sales/marketing principles are basically the same.

Speakers before the Association of Canadian Manufacturers have painted a broad picture of what global marketing will be like in the future. They feel that the basic rules of pricing, producing, and promoting will still apply, but in unlimited new variations. Mass manufacturing and marketing will produce and distribute a broad line of simplified products. Because of the speed of modern, mass communication, rapidly changing products will instantly reflect consumer wants.

Business itself will be only one of the factors or institutions in our environment that will change or affect marketing. Government, for example, affects economic and marketing trends. High-level government officials are, in many countries, increasingly assigned the task of organizing groups of executives from business and industry to tour the world seeking new markets for national products, new areas for investment, and new ways to export national knowledge and skills. In effect, these teams are selling their national products to a world market, and their leaders have to be sales representatives in a very real sense.

In all these areas, personal salesmanship will continue to play a vital and important role. Some economists feel that personal salesmanship plays a key role in the entire economy. The spotty success of discount houses in the United States is but one proof that price alone is not the secret of successful selling. Offering real economic value helps, but just as important is the communication between sales representatives and customers. The need and opportunities for good sales representatives are greater than ever simply because people still do the buying, and people like to interact with other people. Vending machines and computers cannot do this, but you, as a sales representative, can.

OPPORTUNITIES FOR WOMEN, MINORITIES, AND OLDER PEOPLE IN SELLING ARE RAPIDLY INCREASING

The previously mentioned *Endicott Report* clearly points out the increased career opportunities opening up for women, blacks, and other minorities in the United States, especially in sales/marketing. Companies generally are implementing affirmative action plans to encourage women and minorities to pursue business or sales/marketing careers, to open up more good jobs for them, to observe equal opportunity hiring guidelines, and to offer more rapid opportunity for upgrading and promotion. But they are still hiring on the basis of qualifications, looking for a person capable of producing results, not hiring simply because the applicant is female, or a black or other minority. New careers for older men and women are also opening up in selling.

For Women

The traditional male fear that women would disrupt the sales force, antagonize buyers, or lower the company's selling standards is fast disappearing on the American scene. Women are rapidly being hired for sales positions ranging from field representative to sales vice-president, and results have been so encouraging that, according to a 1973 Sales Executive Club of New York survey, 71 percent of sales executives who employ female sales representatives would like to find and hire more good women. While the service and consumer product fields have hired most women sales representatives and executives to date, opportunities in the industrial products field (such as industrial chemicals) are increasing rapidly.

Direct, or door-to-door, selling remains one of the largest employers of women sales representatives. In the United States, as in Australia, where nearly all the 50,000 direct sales persons are women, women seem attracted to selling because of the recognition it gives them in their own community.

Sales positions are today opening rapidly for women in all sorts of formerly male-dominated areas. Leading magazines such as *Time, Newsweek* and *American Home* have added women to their advertising sales staffs. Many automobile dealers now employ women as salespersons, some of whom sell new cars at the rate of twelve or more a month to earn commission income of $12,000 to $15,000 per year. Some authorities predict that women may soon number 50 percent of the sales staff at every automobile dealership in the country. In 1973 Subaru of America, representing the Japanese auto manufacturer of the same name, launched a recruiting program that promised equal selling opportunities for saleswomen at its 520 U.S. dealerships.

Other types of companies now hiring women for responsible outside sales positions are IBM, Value Packaging (a sampling service), Cole National Stores, Dow Chemical, Alcoa, Xerox, Philip Morris, Best Foods, Central Gulf Railroad, Prentice-Hall, Inc., and scores of others. Arlene Dahl, the actress-tycoon, was recently elected director-at-large by the 25,000-member Sales and Marketing Executives International organization—her job is to recruit more women into sales and marketing. Says Ms. Dahl, "In sales/marketing, where the ability to communicate and persuade is a prime asset, an intelligent woman can build a career equal to any man's."

For Blacks and Other Minorities

Many American companies and organizations are today actively seeking qualified minority group members who can qualify for professional-level jobs that can lead to top managerial positions. Federal laws and regulations calling for positive action to assure equal employment opportunity are hastening this trend. Recent surveys indicate that desires for a business career, as executive or owner, are becoming more popular with minority groups.

Many blacks, Spanish-speaking Americans, and other minorities, however, still continue to view selling as a low-status career occupation. While equal and even exceptional opportunities are there, a sales career may present some psychological problems for some minority-group applicants, apart from status. To be successful in selling, one must have a positive mental attitude. Personal selling works on a percentage basis; a sales representative hears "no" far more often than "yes." If, due to past psychological blocks, an inexperienced minority-group sales representative reacts to a "no" by attributing it to white bias, then it may create a hostile potential buyer, or other problems, to the extent that initial failure can lead to more failures and even to rapid dissatisfaction with sales work. Success in selling for a minority-group person depends to a great extent on personal reaction to failure and a positive attitude toward life and work.

Studies indicate that minority-group members resent showcase hirings; they want to be hired, paid, and promoted on performance. Since higher earnings and promotion in selling are so dependent on results, selling offers you, if you are a minority-group American, unparalleled opportunities for rapid personal recognition and career success.

For "Golden Years" Men and Women

In 1972 there were about 39 million Americans aged fifty-five and older, and by 1980 their number will increase to 44.5 million. Prior to World War I about 10 percent of the population fell in this senior age group; today the proportion is almost twice that, and new developments in medical science are increasing longevity.

Many people in this age group face a drop in income, especially after age sixty-five, due to retirement. Many of these men and women wish to continue working, not only to increase their income, but also to keep mentally and physically active.

Career opportunities in selling abound for these "golden age" individuals. Some companies in fact are actively recruiting sales representatives from this age group. Texas Refinery, as one example, has over 500 sales representatives (out of 2,000) in this age group, many in their seventies, the oldest in their eighties. The company is primarily a roofing supplies manufacturer; its sales representatives usually sell complete roof repair jobs to homeowners, working without salary on a commission basis. The company feels its customers—mostly property owners, many of them older or even retired—relate better to older sales representatives. These Texas Refinery sales representatives average between $6,000 and $10,000 in annual earnings; some earn over $30,000. This company, and others, are actively seeking such sales representatives without restriction as to education, sex, race, color, social origin or experience.

ADVANTAGES AND DISADVANTAGES OF A SALES CAREER

The proper choice of a career is one of the most important steps you will ever make. The spirit and purpose of this book is to help you decide wisely whether salesmanship is the best vocation through which you can reach your own career goals. Different people have different needs and abilities, and if you enter a profession or vocation in which you will not find personal job satisfaction, then you probably will not be successful. You will waste your time, that of your employer, and that of prospective customers you may call upon. With this in mind, let us briefly examine some of the disadvantages as well as review the advantages offered by a sales career.

Disadvantages: Why Do Some Sales Representatives Fail?

Surveys indicate that in many American industries and companies about 20 percent of the sales representatives produce about 80 percent of the business. In addition, 10 to 30 percent of the sales force does not even pay its own way. Many of the sales representatives in this latter group either have to be dismissed or leave the selling field of their own volition—failures in either case.

Why do so many new sales representatives fail at such great cost to their employers and loss of time and self-confidence to themselves? Sales and Marketing Executives International, Inc. the most active sales/marketing organization in the world, offers the following breakdown in descending order of importance for our consideration:

Primary Factors

1. Lack of planning ability, time utilization, poor work habits.
2. Lack of industriousness, drive.
3. Lack of resourcefulness, aggressiveness.
4. Lack of observation, an eye for sales possibilities, vision.
5. Lack of self-evaluation and self-development.
6. Lack of self-confidence, enthusiasm, too easily discouraged.
7. Lack of ambition or desire to succeed.
8. Ineffective calls, could not develop interest-getting sales presentations.
9. Inability to answer objectives, slow, uncreative thinker.
10. Inability to develop successful closing techniques.

Secondary Reasons

1. He would not work.
2. He was unstable.
3. He could not assimilate training.
4. He was immature.
5. He needed more money now.
6. He lacked good human relations.
7. He felt that the new job offered more security.
8. He did not like to sell.
9. He had outside interests.
10. He felt the need for the security of a salary.[3]

---

3. "NSE Survey 'Why Salesmen Fail' Finds Weakness in Man, Manager," *National Sales Executives News*, No. 8 (May 1959): 1. Reprinted by permission of Sales & Marketing Executives International.

In view of the above facts, let us be honest, not negative, and review a few of the personal reasons why some people do not enjoy selling as a career and fail as sales representatives. Many men and women, for example, prefer a 9 A.M. to 5 P.M. job in which they can follow a set plan or procedure established by others. Many of them do not like to make constant decisions on their own, and many more want a job they can forget except during working hours. Many people dislike travel, even in a restricted territorial area, and even if the individual does like it, his or her spouse may not. Many do not like the constant pressure of meeting or even thinking about meeting sales budgets or planned objectives.

Perhaps the basic cause of most individual failure in selling, however, is a psychological inability to meet the challenge of constant face-to-face contact with people in a situation in which the sales representative is trying to persuade the other to make a decision. Selling is not visiting and talking about weather; it is hard physical and mental work. Most people basically do not want to make decisions, to change their attitudes or routines, or to buy anything. They constantly object to doing this or that. A sales presentation can basically end in only two ways: the sales representative sells the customer—persuades him that it is in his or her interests to buy—or the customer sells the sales representative on the idea that he or she is not buying. If you get discouraged easily and cannot keep up your positive, optimistic, cheerful, desire-to-be-helpful attitude after days of no's, then selling is not the career for you.

Advantages

The advantages of a sales career are just the opposite of the disadvantages cited above. If you enjoy being your own boss, like having relative freedom of action to do the job your own way, like the constant challenge of meeting people, thrive on personal challenge, enjoy travel, and appreciate the idea of your own abilities being recognized more rapidly through increased income and possible chances for promotion, then selling is the career for you. If you want to get to the top in business and industry, selling is perhaps the best vehicle because the decisions you make in managing your territory are very closely akin to those faced by top executives and decision makers in the professions, government, industry, and business.

The choice of whether or not to consider a sales career is up to you—the opportunities, advantages, and disadvantages have been fairly presented. From here on we will study the history and development of sales/marketing in some depth, plus the principles, practices, and techniques of modern applied salesmanship. Even if you do not elect to follow a sales career, this study will help you in many ways throughout your life and work, as we have indicated. If you are interested in selling as a career, you will learn how to become a truly professional sales representative—plus, if you have the ability, drive, and determination, how to get right to the top as a highly paid sales representative or executive.

SUMMARY

In this chapter we have defined *selling* and *salesmanship* and indicated the importance of a knowledge of salesmanship in attaining success in both sales or nonsales careers, or in nonwork avocations involving close association with other people whom you might hope to persuade or lead throughout your life. We considered the kinds of professional careers available in selling, the compensation (both intangible and monetary) to be expected, the opportunities in selling for women, minorities, and older people, and the advantages and disadvantages of a sales career.

CHAPTER REVIEW

CONCEPTS TO REMEMBER*

_____ sales/marketing	_____ persuasion	_____ everyone sells something
_____ growth industry	_____ salesmanship	_____ sell yourself
_____ selling	_____ profit	_____ cause selling

*For memory reinforcement, fill in the page number or numbers where the terms were described in this chapter.

QUESTIONS FOR ANALYSIS AND DISCUSSION

1. _____ is at the core of selling and salesmanship, just as it is central to decision-making in most areas of life: professional, social, business, or political. What is the meaning of the term?
2. At this point, what do you feel you personally stand to gain from your current study of salesmanship, as related to your past experience in life and work, and your future plans?
3. Describe selling activities of any two nonbusiness organizations in your local community with which you are personally familiar, or have read about or heard about from parents or friends. What additional selling activities do you feel each could do to enjoy greater success?
4. Assuming your father owns a retail business in your local community that you plan to enter and eventually take over and manage, what do you feel you can gain from your current study of salesmanship that might help you increase the profitability of the business?
5. Define, in your own words, the meaning of *selling, salesmanship,* and *sales/marketing.*
6. Job counselors advise that in order to achieve personal happiness and the best chances of financial security and professional growth in any specific career field, one should consider the intangible as well as tangible rewards that the career field offers. What is the meaning to you of the terms *intangible* and *tangible* rewards, in terms of your own objectives and expectations?
7. We have said that responsible sales positions in the United States are today opening rapidly for women, blacks, and other minority-group members. Have you observed this happening in your local community over the past two years? If so, explain. If not, why do you feel it has not happened in your area, since national trends clearly show the statement to be true?
8. Do you feel at this point that a sales career might interest you? What opportunities through selling do you now see for yourself? What type of selling appears of most interest to you now, and why?

COLLEGES SHIFT TO HARD SELL IN RECRUITING STUDENTS[4]

American colleges and universities, faced in the mid-1970s with declining enrollments and financial pressures they have not known since depression days of the early thirties, are increasingly resorting to the hard sell in recruiting students. While there has always been competition for the top athletes and the best scholars, many such institutions today face the major problem of keeping their classes filled in order to survive.

Across the country, the language of college officials is increasingly that of commerce and selling, the most common lament being that "it's buyers market." Their mood is one of longing for the heady days of the sixties, when even marginal institutions could pick and choose among big pools of applicants who were products of the post–World War II baby boom. That boom has passed, and increasing numbers of smaller colleges, those not so well known nationally or so richly endowed, who depend heavily on tuition fees to cover operating costs, are closing their doors in the face of declining enrollments.

This has led to recruiting and promotional techniques that colleges and universities never thought of, or rejected out of hand, a few short years ago—direct mail barrages, radio spot commercials, tuition rebates for students who recruit friends, and use of "recruiters" to sell "prospects" (potential students) in face-to-face interviews on the advantages of enrolling at this or that college or university.

Some of the recruiting aids the colleges are using are obvious enough. New York University, for instance, has only recently begun to include a return envelope when it responds to a prospective student's request for an application form. This of course is a technique long employed in direct-mail selling, to make it easy for the "prospect" to respond—now! Such direct-mail sales pitches, used for years by vocational schools but scorned by colleges, are scorned no longer. One Massachusetts high school senior had received 143 pieces of unsolicited college-recruiting mail by mid-March 1974, but had long since stopped reading it.

Other types of sales techniques being employed to find students (called "prospecting" in sales terminology) and sell them includes mass telephoning campaigns, usually by outside firms, participation in the growing number of "college fairs" for high school students, the radio spot commercials, and use of traveling recruiting vans.

This situation has led to a new type of sales-career opportunities for increasing numbers of men and women. Firms specializing in recruiting college students, some started by recent college graduates, have sprung up all over the country. They contract with colleges to handle their recruiting. Typically, such contracts set a "goal" for the number of students to be recruited; guaranteeing a number is considered unethical. The college, of course, retains control over admissions policy and final decisions about who is accepted. Use of such outside recruiting firms is controversial —some critics condemn it as verging on "bounty hunting."

Other institutions, like Grinnell College, a prestigious private college of 1,250 students in Grinnell, Iowa, employ their own full-time college admissions representatives (salesmen). Paul A. Lewis, a 1971 Grinnell graduate, for example, covers a region extending from Boston to Virginia from his New York home base, interviewing high school students from east coast states that normally provide Grinnell with about one-third of its enrollment.

Most often, his contact is with those students who have already written to Grinnell for information. As a new approach for the 1974 academic year, Grinnell purchased from the College Testing Service the names of 12,000 students east of the Mississippi who had attained a combined score of at least 1,150 on the college board examinations. Pamphlets about Grinnell, with business reply cards, were sent to all 12,000, and 600 of the recipients sent back the cards, seeking further information. Nearly one-third of the 600 interested students were contacted by Mr. Lewis by May 1974, by which time acceptances had been received and admissions deposits mailed to the college.

Enrollment results apparently justify employment of such full-time recruiters, and colleges using them claim that their activities are the best way to service prospective students. Employment of such full-time admissions representatives is by no means limited to smaller colleges; the Ivy League colleges are equally active, as colleges and universities throughout the nation energetically compete for new students to meet their enrollment objectives.

QUESTIONS FOR WRITTEN REPORTS OR CLASS DISCUSSION

1. Do you feel that starting a sales career as an admissions representative offers future growth potential? Explain.
2. Judging from the brief job description contained in this case study, would you classify Lewis' position as that of a promotions sales representative or a real salesman? Why?
3. Do you feel a woman would be as effective as Lewis in his admissions representative's position? Explain your viewpoint.
4. What human qualities do you feel would be most important in assuming greatest job success for a young admissions representative?

Case Study 1–2

IBM MARKETING REPRESENTATIVES DO MORE THAN SELL— THEY'RE SPECIALISTS IN PROBLEM SOLVING[5]

International Business Machines Corporation—IBM—ranked in 1974 as the *eighth* largest industrial corporation in the United States and the *tenth* largest in the world, with 1973 gross income of nearly $11 billion, is well known for its company slogan "THINK" coined by Thomas J. Watson, Sr., its famed chief executive from 1914 to 1956.

5. Material from IBM and other sources.

A more apt motto might be "SELL," for while IBM has certainly been an important innovator of new ideas and products their explosive growth since starting corporate life in 1911 under the name Computing-Tabulating-Recording Company (renamed in 1924 as International Business Machines Corporation in the United States), has been largely due to their belief and strength in sales/marketing. Mr. Watson, Sr., who joined IBM as President in 1914, had formerly worked for National Cash Register Company, where he was a branch manager at age 25 and later general sales manager. He had great confidence that good salesmen could do almost anything, and consistently promoted successful salesmen into jobs such as plant management, personnel, and other key nonsales positions.

As a result, a high percentage of today's IBM's top executives started out as salesmen, and the 10,000 strong worldwide IBM sales force continues to make IBM highly successful in the electronic data processing (EDP) and office products industry. During 1973, sales, services, and rentals of data processing machines and systems accounted for approximately 79% of IBM's worldwide gross income. And the future looks even brighter if EDP becomes, as forecast by many experts, the world's largest industry in the 1980s.

For many years, it has been IBM's corporate aim to anticipate the needs of the world's marketplaces; to innovate products and programs for special applications, to guide the installation of its products and insure their continuous reliability. IBM's 274,000 employees in 126 countries have produced and sold or leased, according to some experts, nearly 70 percent of the over 150 thousand computers in the world, and each year IBM's sales force sells over $500 million worth of typewriters, dictating machines, and other office equipment.

Among IBM's 12 domestic U.S.A. Divisions concerned heavily with sales/marketing are Data Processing Division, General Systems Division, Information Records Division, and Office Products Division. Successful college graduate applicants entering the sales/marketing end of these divisions, as "Marketing Representatives," enter a comprehensive training program, which can last in some cases a year or more, to equip them to contact and work successfully with management in all phases of business. Their sales duties include direct contact with IBM customers and prospects, with the opportunity to analyze business operations and recommend systems solutions, IBM machines and contract services to satisfy the requirements of business, industry, and government.

Marketing Representatives for the company's Data Processing Division, as a specific example, are trained to do more than sell—they become specialists in problem solving. They learn how to conduct detailed surveys to find out how businesses are structured, and how companies resemble or differ from others in an industry. They learn how to give presentations on their findings, and how to make recommendations to data processing management and executives. They learn to work as part of a team, working closely with other IBM technical professionals to provide customers with the best possible after-sale computer performance. The end-purpose of such training is to insure that the division's Marketing Representatives will serve their customers as valued problem solvers.

IBM makes a special company-wide effort to recruit and give more responsibility to women and minority group members. By early 1974, minority members represented 8.1 percent of the company's overall United States sales force, and women 4.5 percent; and the number of minority and women managers had increased sharply over previous years.

IBM, in recruiting applicants for Marketing Representative positions, seeks those men and women who look at new situations as opportunities, not problems; those who can work well with others, develop rapport, are self-starters, and who want to be winners.

Informed observers of the EDP industry indicate that customer loyalty plays a key role in IBM's continued success. Due perhaps to the huge cost involved of changing both hardware and software, this customer loyalty is at times phenomenal. The sales-minded executives who run IBM will undoubtedly insure that IBM Marketing Representatives of the future are trained and motivated to build on this existing customer satisfaction and loyalty.

QUESTIONS FOR WRITTEN REPORTS OR CLASS DISCUSSION

1. Into what category of selling, from among those presented in this chapter, do you feel IBM Marketing Representatives fall?
2. Do you feel that IBM might be a good company to join in order to pursue a sales career? Upon what factors is your opinion based?
3. Do you feel a woman would be as successful as a man in designing and selling expensive computer systems to government agencies, or business and industrial firms? Would a woman be equally effective in after-sale servicing? Upon what known or felt factors do you base your opinion?
4. Does IBM's sales success, as noted in the above case study, bear out the opinion of many experts that personal salesmanship plays a vital role in large-scale systems selling? Could IBM dispense with its Marketing Representatives and continue to maintain its huge sales lead in the future? Explain.

SALES PROBLEM 1–1

YOU MAY HAVE TO SELL YOURSELF TO OBTAIN A BANK LOAN SOMETIME—BUT BANKS HAVE TO SELL THEMSELVES TO YOU AND OTHERS ALL THE TIME

It was stated in this chapter that literally everyone, including you, "sells" something; themselves, their ideas, services, or products. It was suggested that you might have to "sell yourself" as worthy of being granted a bank loan at some time in your life. But banks also have to sell themselves to you and to other consumers. Here is some advice to bankers on that subject as published in *Banking* magazine.[6]

You are not going to attract new business to your bank from today's consumers by offering the same tired old product line. You are "people banks"—your life's blood is people. Your job is to meet their needs. What must you do to reach people?

---

6. The quoted material was extracted from an article by Gerald P. Feldman, "Clothing, Shelter—and Banks," *Banking, Journal of the American Bankers Association,* LXVI, No. 12 (June 1974), pp. 60–64. Copyright 1974 by the American Bankers Association.

If you haven't been in a big market lately, it may startle you to push a shopping cart through its quarter-mile of aisles. The shelves teem with products that did not exist a few years ago —breakfast cereals, cosmetics, cleaning agents, paper and plastic goods, pre-cooked and frozen ethnic delicacies, natural foods—often at prices the "old standard" products cannot hope to command. You'll see packaging ideas that are sheer genius—from putting pantyhose inside hollow plastic "eggs" to selling ordinary candied popcorn as Screaming Yellow Zonkers—and you'll more than likely see those packages in your own customers' shopping carts.

Surely all of this innovation would not exist if consumers were mere creatures of habit. Surely it would not succeed if it did not fill needs and desires that consumer marketers are well aware of. The fact is, companies that do not innovate, that do not learn the needs and desires of the market and develop their product line accordingly, get pushed off the shelves by those who do.

The fact is, scores of consumer product manufacturers now earn up to 80% of their profits from products that did not exist five years ago. And the most critical fact is, you in banking are competing for profits in the same markets that demand all these product and packaging innovations from food, drug, clothing, appliance and automobile manufacturers.

To reach, and get a positive response from people, you must sell what people want and need—not what you've gotten into the habit of offering. Customers do not owe you their patronage. You either earn it—by creating and selling the most advantageous, exciting and reasonably priced "product line"—or you watch the business go to the bank across the street.

Here are a few of the many new products or services suggested for banks later on in the article: money-dispensing machines, deposits and withdrawals by telephone, flat-rate checking accounts, photo IDs, family money-management counseling, and income-tax-return service.

QUESTIONS FOR WRITTEN REPORTS OR CLASS DISCUSSION

1. What examples can you present of the "selling" of products or services by banks in your local area? Have you personally been "sold" as a result of any of their sales messages? If so, explain what "sold" you on their offer.
2. Can you present examples of the "selling" of items in #1 above that both (1) do and (2) do not offer something of value and benefit, that will result in buyer satisfaction and increase the welfare of society?
3. Can you suggest any ideas of new products or services not listed above that banks in your local area could or should be selling; ones that might offer value and benefit and result in buyer satisfaction and the welfare of society?
4. Do you feel banking will be a growth industry over the next few years? Why? Do you feel that a sales career within banking is possible and might interest you? Explain.

2
selling:
the customer/society-oriented
marketing concept

When you have mastered the content of this chapter, you should be able to:
Define the terms *economics, business,marketing,*
market segment, customer-oriented marketing concept,
and *customer/society-oriented marketing concept.*
Describe the nature of business within the American free enterprise
economic system, marketing as a function of business, the functions of marketing,
and the four-part "promotional mix" employed in marketing.
List the three traditional forms of business organization and the newer fourth form.
List the two major market divisions and the three classifications
of companies who sell to these two markets.
Outline the historical development of marketing and of personal salesmanship.
List the eight functions of marketing presented.
Describe the role and employment of each of the four parts of the marketing
"promotional mix": advertising, publicity, sales promotion, and personal selling.
Summarize the changing role of modern salesmanship,
its future in an age of technology, and its impact
in terms of product presentation importance both on a national and global basis.
Analyze what is meant by the statement "a new supersalesman is needed
to meet the challenges of personal selling now and in the future."

In the preceding chapter we discussed some of the descriptive aspects of selling and salesmanship in relation to career opportunities. We will now trace the historical development of personal selling in relation to business and its environment in general and its important role as a marketing function in particular.

Your initial reaction as a reader may be to wonder why we start by considering some basic aspects of economics, business, and marketing, when this book is about personal selling. If you have taken basic college courses in these areas of study, some of the first part of the chapter may already be known to you. For readers who have not taken such courses, however, an overview of these areas is essential to thoroughly understanding the concepts of personal selling and the extensive how-to applications that will fill most of the pages to follow.

Special attention will be paid in this chapter to evolution of the marketing concept and how, in face of today's changing consumer values, it may evolve toward ever more social responsibility. And we will consider the rapidly changing role of the sales representative as a vital member of a modern customer/society-oriented company or organizational marketing-management team, in today's and tomorrow's global marketplace.

BUSINESS AND THE WORLD ECONOMIC SYSTEMS

In order to better understand the development, nature, and function of sales/marketing, it will help to briefly consider a few facts about the economic systems under which Americans and citizens of other countries live. Economics is concerned with how goods and services desired by a nation's people get produced and distributed. Once people organize to work together to accomplish this, an economic system evolves; the type of system selected governs the relative roles of private and governmental freedom and authority.

The United States is today one of a small group of nations having a basically private-enterprise capitalistic economic system, under which most productive resources are privately owned, and economic activity is largely determined by the flow or interaction of market supply and demand. This contrasts sharply with the communist economic system, involving one-third of the world's population, under which most productive resources are publicly owned and economic activity is largely carried out through centralized governmental planning.

Another major framework for solving economic problems is the democratic socialism of Sweden, Britain, India, and other nations. The underdeveloped nations of Africa and Asia seem generally to be heading toward economic systems involving more central control than free enterprise. The goal of every nation, regardless of its economic system is, on paper at least, to increase productivity so as to fulfill all the wants and needs of the citizens and thus to improve standards of living.

The American economic system is basically a private-enterprise one, based on the individual's rights to private ownership of property, opportunity to make a profit, freedom to compete, and freedom of choice and contract. These rights are basic not only to economic freedom, but also to the political and social freedom enjoyed by Americans.

The term *business* in the economic sense relates to the buying and selling of goods and services; in the commercial sense it relates more to a person, partnership, or corporation engaged in manufacturing, commerce, or service. In both senses the term *business* relates to profit-seeking activities. In practice, business is the whole system of interrelated activities acting together to make goods and services available in the marketplace. These activities are conducted both within the business enterprise, called a "firm," and between the firm and its environment.

The Growth of Business

In the beginning, business organizations started as *individual proprietorships* or small firms managed by a single owner who could oversee all aspects of the operation. As business grew more complex, requiring different managerial skills and greater financing, *partnerships* were formed between two or more individuals. As larger enterprises, such as barge canals, mining, shipping, and railroads, came into being, the modern *corporation* was created, combining the financial strength and diversity of many owners (stock or share holders) with the flexibility and efficiency of professional management.

As world population increased and economic problems increased in complexity, business changed in scope and function to meet consumer needs and wants as registered by purchases in the marketplace. In the United States especially, business has seldom been static—each generation has witnessed rapid growth and change. Today, Americans live in an era where some 1.5 million corporations have become the dominant force in business, employing as many people as the rest of the economy combined, including federal, state, and local governments, and paying out over 50 percent of the total national income.

The size and influence of larger corporations must be stressed, since the trend in the United States is toward fewer, larger, and more highly diversified companies run by well-trained professional managers. The biggest of the corporations are true giants, controlling great wealth and exerting great influence on society. Assets of American Telephone and Telegraph, the world's largest business, are over $63 billion; General Motors is over $24 billion. Annual sales of General Motors alone are greater than the entire gross national product of most nations.

In spite of the concentration of finance and industry especially in the hands of a relatively few large and powerful corporations, there are still far more small firms than large ones and approximately three out of four Americans work for smaller firms.

The 1960s saw the flowering of a new and independent force in the world called the *multinational corporation*, defined as a company with sales above $100 million, with operations in at least six countries, and having overseas subsidiaries that account for at least 20 percent of its assets. Over 4,000 companies qualify, accounting for over 15 percent of the world's gross national product. General Motors, Exxon, and Ford Motor Company, all American owned, are the largest in that order in terms of sales; Royal Dutch/Shell (British/Netherlands), British Petroleum (British), Philips (Netherlands), and Volkswagen (Germany) are the four largest non-American multinational corporations.

Operating easily within and across national boundaries, these fast-growing corporations saw sales increase from $200 billion in 1960 to over $450 billion a year in goods and services by 1973. Many critics feel this has led to far too much uncontrolled power in the hands of a few, and many international unions have begun exploring ways to neutralize their power and flexibility as a global employer. Within a few years we may see a clash of two giant forces—the economic power of the multinational corporations versus the political power of nation-states as to who shall control and regulate international trade and business.

Theoretically the consumer (all the buyers of the marketplace) registers his desires for what is to be produced through his purchases. But in practice, big national and multinational corporations and big unions often exert so much market power that they sometimes override the wishes of consumers. An example of this is the power that advertising has to shape consumer opinion or preferences.

Marketing As a Function of Business

We have noted that the marketplace is the central focus of all business activities. It is here, in competition with other sellers, that a seller presents his goods and services to consumers. It is here that consumers register their "votes" (through buying or not buying) and register changing wants and preferences. Over three-fourths of all the goods and services produced by American business are in response to consumer demands expressed by over 200 million Americans in the marketplace. These individual consumers, each allocating his income to fulfill his own needs and wants, provide basic signals to business producers telling what consumers want produced.

Business is carried on via several functional areas—production, marketing, finance, purchasing, planning, and administration. Of these, marketing activities are particularly vital since they are so directly concerned with sensing, stimulating, serving, and satisfying\specific consumer demands.

THE NATURE, DEVELOPMENT, AND FUNCTIONS OF MARKETING

Marketing can be defined in several ways. The American Marketing Association defines it as "the performance of business activities that direct the flow of goods and services from producer to consumer or user."[1] Another is "the set of human activities directed at facilitating and consummating exchanges."[2]

Authors of yet a third definition feel that the interrelatedness of product and market is an essential concept and should be included in a definition of marketing and also that there can be no marketing unless transfers of ownership occur. They thus define marketing as "the managerial process by which products are matched with markets and through which transfers of ownership are affected."[3]

Marketing and Market Segmentation

The terms *market* and *market segmentation*, as used by marketing people and sales representatives, should also be defined. A *market* can be described as the total or aggregate demand of the potential buyers for a product or service, aggregate being the composite demands of many consumers for a specific item. Within the total or aggregate demand are *market segments*, or groups of potential buyers who demand specific different requirements for the same item.

For example, the aggregate demand for automobiles is made up of several market segments—sports cars, small economy cars, large luxury sedans. Thus a market is not only an aggregate demand for a product or service, but the sum total of demands of several different market segments. In trying to fulfill customers wants, sales/marketing people carefully study changing market and market segment demands and trends in order to produce and effectively sell what will satisfy different groups of potential buyers.

This is done within the broad framework of two separate types or divisions of markets: the *consumer market*, made up of consumers who buy for personal or family consumption, and the *industrial market*, made up of those who buy to further production of other goods and services. For sales representatives, there are some differences in approach necessary in effective selling to each of these broad market divisions, which we shall be considering in the chapters to follow.

Companies who sell to these two markets can be classified into three types: *industrial products, consumer products,* and *services.* The classification of the types of products each sells will be discussed in Chapter 3.

Historical Development of Marketing

As a national economy develops, its functions also change. The first stage, in the face of scarcity, is to increase production; engineers are the chief innovators at this time. As production increases during the second stage, production is consolidated to maximize efficiency and profitability.

Then, as production increases to a high level and initial wants and needs are satisfied, a third stage—that of finding new and different market outlets or customers—is reached. The problem then is not so much a scarcity of goods but a scarcity of markets.

1. From *Marketing Definitions: A Glossary of Marketing Terms,* (Chicago: American Marketing Association, 1960), p. 21. Reprinted by permission.
2. Philip Kotler, *Marketing Management,* 2nd ed. (Englewood Cliffs, N.J.: Prentice-Hall, Inc., 1972), p. 27.
3. Edward W. Cundiff, Richard R. Still, and Norman A. P. Govoni, *Fundamentals of Modern Marketing* (Englewood Cliffs, N.J.: Prentice-Hall, Inc., 1973), p. 5.

In this third *sales-oriented stage*, faced with a shortage of customers, advertising budgets and sales forces are increased to stimulate demand for existing products, and all-out competition is waged for increased market share. In the United States, it was toward the end of this stage (in the 1930s and 1940s) that market research became highly developed, and sophisticated promotion and merchandising techniques were created. Since selling traditionally had been that specific function of marketing concerned with seeking out a new customer and persuading him to buy a firm's product or service, sales representatives played an increasingly important role, concerned as they were with face-to-face customer personal selling.

The Customer-Oriented Marketing Concept

By the mid-1950s business attitudes in the highly developed United States began to change. Prospective customers became more sophisticated, and marketing executives became aware that changing customers' wants to fit existing products and services was not good enough. They realized that they should adjust the goods before they were produced to fit the customers' wants or needs.

This resulted in articulation of a new marketing concept, which replaced the narrower sales-oriented concept which had been concerned only with increasing profits by ever more sales of existing products. This new marketing concept has perhaps been best defined by Professor Philip Kotler as follows:

The *marketing concept* is a *customer orientation* backed by *integrated marketing* aimed at generating *customer satisfaction* as the key to satisfying organizational goals.[4]

This truly creative American-originated concept rapidly caught the attention of companies, institutions, and nations where marketing as a definable, systematic discipline had seldom if ever been seriously considered. Under this concept literally all functions of business, from research and development to production, through advertising, selling, and customer service, became oriented not only toward the needs and wants of a customer but toward his after-purchase satisfaction as well. By putting the customer in the center, and by using market research efficiently to identify new market trends rapidly, firms were able to plan and compete more efficiently.

The new marketing concept was welcomed also by nonbusiness institutions and organizations such as educational institutions, hospitals, political parties, and government agencies. They realized that many of their problems of product or service development, information, persuasion, distribution, and customer service were similar to those that were being resolved so successfully be marketing management in business firms.

Marketing, as practiced in the United States under the modern marketing concept, is today widely studied and copied by managers of business and nonbusiness organizations around the world, in capitalist, socialist, and communist states alike.

HAS THE AMERICAN FREE-ENTERPRISE SYSTEM REALLY MET ITS PEOPLE'S NEEDS?

The United States is by far the richest nation in the world, with the Soviet Union (half as rich) in second place. All the other nations trail far behind, although the

4. Kotler, *Marketing Management*, 2nd ed., p. 17.

major developed countries, such as West Germany, Great Britain, France, and Japan, are far ahead of such underdeveloped countries as India, Bolivia, Kenya, and Syria.

The United States also has one of the best records in spreading its wealth among all citizens. The U.S. Department of Commerce estimates show the 1972 income of American families, based on the median family income of about $9,700, illustrated in Figure 2.1.

FIGURE 2.1 Percentage of National Income Received by American Households in 1972

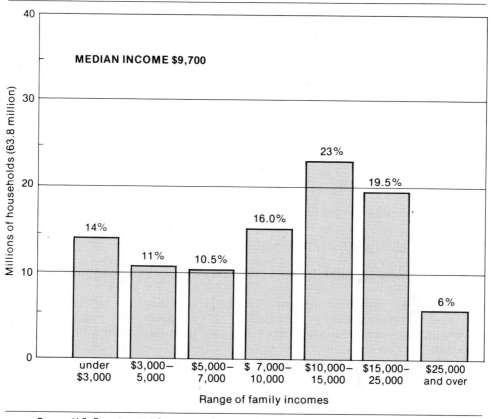

Source: U.S. Department of Commerce.

The bulk of the wealth in most nations is held by a very small percentage of the citizens, as little as 2 percent in some; the rise of the middle class in the United States has had profound implications for the American way of life and the material prosperity that the majority of Americans enjoy. This distribution of wealth to so many people over the past fifty years has been the real success story of American business and the free enterprise system in which it operates.

Bright as this picture appears on the surface, however, the bottom 20 percent of the American families in the 1972 figures just noted had incomes of less than $5,600. Several million of these families had money incomes of less than $3,000, and one million of these were raising four or more children on that income. Thus a large percentage of Americans have not received the material fruits of the national economic success. Too many Americans are still living in poverty, in slums, and in discontent.

In spite of its great success in many areas, several aspects of American business today, and especially sales/marketing, are being seriously questioned and challenged by critics, led in many cases by college students. These critics complain that too many new, unneeded wasteful products are being produced, that too many manufacturers and products pollute our water and the very air we breathe, and that the consumer faces so many choices he cannot make rational decisions and is often manipulated by deceptive advertising and selling practices. We shall consider these questions and challenges at greater length in Chapter 5.

EMERGENCE OF A NEW CUSTOMER/SOCIETY-ORIENTED MARKETING CONCEPT

Some of the critics of business and marketing have pointed out what they consider a serious flaw in the customer-oriented marketing concept. They have noted that while the customer is at the heart of all business and marketing planning activities, the end result is to "give the customer what he wants" with little consideration of whether "what he wants" is really beneficial either to him or to society. Are snowmobiles, that pollute clean country air and stampede wildlife even in the most remote areas, or throw-away aluminum beer and soft drinks cans that litter the countryside, beneficial to society?

Is it beneficial to society for business to cater solely to want-satisfaction of some individuals, when pursuit of such may be in conflict not only with their personal long-term best interest, but with society's as well? Is the customer-oriented marketing concept actually immoral in refusing to judge its activities in light of general welfare and long-term interests of both consumer and society?

Many sales/marketing leaders, recognizing that the public is increasingly holding them responsible for choices offered the consumer, are fast accepting a newer, still-developing marketing concept. Called the *customer/society-oriented marketing concept*, its aim is not only to fulfill consumer needs with something of value and benefit that will bring lasting satisfaction at a profit to the seller (the heart of the older customer-oriented marketing concept), but to *provide as well for a net improvement in the quality of life for all consumers and to the long-term benefit of society.*

Under the new concept, business plays a positive and vital role in helping solve society's problems. What greater a challenge for free-enterprise business than to satisfy the consumer at a profit and enhance the overall welfare of society at the same time!

Functions of Marketing

Nearly 50 percent of what a consumer pays for an item in a retail store goes to cover marketing costs. On the surface, this percentage cost seems high, yet when we consider all the marketing functions that take place as goods move from producer to consumer, it is easy to understand. These functions include market research, product planning, financing, buying, standardization and grading pricing, storing, transporting, risk bearing, promotion, and selling.

Merchandising is the overall term used to describe most of these marketing functions or activities. It can be defined as the planning and promotion of sales by presenting a product to the right market at the proper time, by carrying out organized, skillful advertising and sales promotion. It involves nearly every activity that influences consumers to buy the product except personal selling (but even here a sales representative often sells merchandising plans).

As we have already noted, and will continue to discuss throughout this book, the modern-day sales representative is fulfilling an increasingly important role on the integrated marketing-management team. He is becoming ever more involved in helping determine market needs and in finding production and marketing solutions to them. Thus, while engaging in his primary task of face-to-face selling, he must be informed on all the other marketing functions not only to provide feedback to his firm, but also to consult with his prospects or customers about these functions in a truly professional manner. While we can only deal briefly with them here, he needs to be well informed about these eight specific marketing functions in particular, for reasons given:

1. *Market research.* While most large firms have their own staff-level market research departments, they rely heavily on outside professional market research firms for market surveys and testing. The sales force can assist by providing ideas internally and field checking or testing research findings.

2. *Product planning.* Considerable planning is required to produce items that satisfy specific consumer demands. Product planning is concerned with decisions like the type of product or service to be offered, the number of items to produce, the design of the item, and periodic modifications or changes that may be necessary. Feedback from the sales force is highly important to such planning.

3. *Standardization and grading.* These operations improve marketing efficiency and benefit consumers. *Standardization* means establishment of constant physical characteristics that give unity to a group of products. Six- and eight-cylinder engines, for example, are common to different automobile manufacturers.

4. *Grading.* This is the sorting of products according to preset, generally accepted standards. A customer can thus select between high-test or regular gasoline, knowing that he can expect a difference in quality. A sales representative must understand these operations as applied to his products in order to describe them intelligently to buyers.

5. *Pricing.* Among the many factors that enter into the pricing of a product (such as markup above manufacturing cost to ensure a profit) is that of competition's prices for similar items. The sales representative can offer quick feedback concerning the competition's pricing. At the same time, the sales representative's knowledge of the greater value or quality that may have been built into his product versus a cheaper, similar-looking one helps him justify his higher price to a prospect or customer.

6. *Risk-taking.* For a high percentage of businesses, a major part of their working capital is tied up in inventory. If they are overstocked, and styles or models change or a new and better product comes out, they may have to return their stocks to the producer (if allowed to do so) or be unable to pay for them if credit has been extended. The sales representative, through observation or knowledge of the buyer's situation, can help his firm's credit department decide whether to extend credit in the first place and help his customer with returns or credit extension where necessary. And he can help both firm and customer by recommending proper buying and stock control so as to increase highest possible profitable turnover at least risk.

7.   *Transporting.*   Since most products have to be physically moved from producer to buyer, speed and cost of transportation are important. The sales representative keeps these elements in mind in advising his customer, and he follows through after the sale to see that items ordered were delivered safely and to ensure customer satisfaction.

8.   *Promotion and selling.*   This is the function of marketing entailing the most activity and requiring the greatest amount of personal and financial effort. From our point of view in studying selling and salesmanship, it is by far the most important of all the marketing functions, which we will next consider in greater detail.

Promotion and Selling–The "Promotional Mix" of Marketing

Promotion and selling is a major function of marketing. In the attempt to communicate with, inform, persuade, and sell goods, services, or ideas to consumers, the firm or organization employs a four-part "promotional mix" consisting of *advertising, publicity, sales promotion,* and *personal selling.* These four activities have separate yet overlapping capabilities and are carefully managed to produce optimum results as part of an overall sales/marketing program.

Historically, personal selling was the first of these separate activities, then came advertising, with publicity still later. It was not until the 1950s that sales promotion was considered, studied, or employed as a fourth distinctive activity of promotion and selling. We shall now consider these briefly and separately, listing personal selling last only because from that point on we will be discussing it in depth. Definitions of the four activities are those endorsed by the American Marketing Association.[5]

Advertising, defined as "any paid form of nonpersonal presentation and promotion of ideas, goods or services by an identified sponsor," is a varied activity. It employs many kinds of media, such as newspaper, magazines, radio, television, outdoor advertising (billboards, etc.), direct mail, directories and circulars, and novelties (book matches, calendars, etc.). It is used in different forms for different goals; national advertising, for example, asks consumers to buy a trademarked item (Kellogg's Corn Flakes), retail advertising asks the consumer to buy at a specific store, and mail order advertising asks a customer to mail in his order for the item or items advertised. Four broad classifications of advertising are: *institutional,* to build up a company image or name ("you are in good hands with Allstate;" "you have a friend at Chase Manhattan"); *brand,* to build up long-term brand image, *classified,* to tell about an event, a service or a sale; and *sales advertising* of various types.

Advantages of advertising are that it can be repeated publicly often in many different and dramatic ways; its chief disadvantage lies in its impersonal nature. Advertising can "talk to" people but not "talk with" them as can a sales representative.

Publicity can be defined as nonpersonal stimulation of demand for a product, service or business unit by planting commercially significant news about it in a published medium or obtaining favorable presentation of it upon radio, television and stage that is not paid for by the sponsor.

Many companies spend a lot of time and money creating "significant news" about which the press or television will give free coverage. United Airlines, for example, received excellent publicity by sending 2,500 executive secretaries a fresh rose, under a "Roses to a First Lady" program, each Friday for several weeks.

---

5.   From *Marketing Definitions; A Glossary of Marketing Terms,* (Chicago: American Marketing Association, 1960). Reprinted by permission.

The Bicycle Institute of America, a booster of safe cycling paths and cycling for health and fun, gained national publicity by persuading the U.S. Secretary of the Interior to lead a bike parade of congressmen from White House to Capitol.

Advantages of publicity are that many people are more inclined to accept or believe news stories about a product or company than paid advertisements, or than hearing about it from a sales representative. Disadvantages are that many potential buyers, suspicious of systematic efforts by public relations departments of firms to get "free publicity" through contrived "news," may react negatively.

Sales promotion can be defined as "those marketing activities, other than personal selling, advertising and publicity, that stimulate consumer purchasing and dealer effectiveness, such as displays, shows and exhibitions, demonstrations, and various nonrecurring selling activities not in the ordinary routine."

Sales promotions are usually short-term or temporary activities designed to support normal advertising and sales force activities. Those supporting advertising often involve the offer of "more for your money," like temporary price reductions. They fall into these three broad categories:

1. *Trade promotions* include such things as cooperative advertising, where retailer and manufacturer split costs of a retailer's newspaper ad featuring the manufacturer's product;
2. *free goods or special discount* for specified quantity purchase within a given period of time, such as a publisher offering booksellers one free copy for every ten books purchased by a certain date; and
3. *sales contests*, where prizes are offered the sales staff of the distributor or retailer in order to encourage them to promote the manufacturer's product.

Sales-force promotion—aimed by a firm at its own sales force, includes such things as cash bonus payments for sales above quota; contests in which prizes (normally durable goods such as luggage, or holiday trips) are given for extra sales during a given period; and enthusiasm-building sales meetings, often held at famous resort centers.

Consumer promotions—aimed at the end-consumer, include such things as the giving away of free samples; coupons which, whether mailed, on display at point-of-sale, or inside product packaging, are redeemable either from retailer or manufacturer for cash or other awards; premiums, which are special gift items given free or at low cost provided the consumer buys a particular product; trading stamps, which are given in proportion to size of purchase and are redeemable for merchandise; and public demonstrations, which either feature a product or how to use it, such as a fashion show during luncheon period at a large hotel, private club, or group meeting.

Personal selling—considered by many the most important element of the whole marketing process, as producer meets potential buyer face-to-face in the marketplace. It is the oldest of the marketing functions, expanding rapidly in importance in today's age of modern customer/society-oriented sales/marketing.

Let us now trace the historical development of the sales representative's role, explore in more detail his modern professional activities, and try to forecast in greater detail what his activities will be in the future.

HISTORICAL DEVELOPMENT OF SALESMANSHIP

If persuasion is at the core of selling, sales representatives have been at the heart of trading (buying and selling) since the first long-distance trade in sea shells occurred in what is now France over 10,000 years ago. Priests of Sumeria in 5000 B.C. were the first to keep written records of goods acquired through barter. As early as 4000 B.C. Arab traders traveled by caravans to market centers in the near and Middle East and Egypt. Early Greek and Roman traders traveled widely on land and sea. The ancient Egyptians in about 2000 B.C. were quite advanced in the fields of administration, diplomacy, and trade, and left us many written records of their activities. With a little imagination, we can conclude that these quotes from their scrolls contain advice on how to handle a persuasive sales representative of the time.

If thou art one to whom petition is made, be calm as thou listenest to what the petitioner has to say. Do not rebuff him before he has swept out his body or before he has said that for which he came. . . . It is not [necessary] that everything about which he has petitioned should come to pass, [but] a good hearing is soothing to the heart.
    Proclaim thy business without concealment. . . . One ought to say plainly what one knoweth and what one knoweth not.[6]

We certainly know that trader-sales representatives were active during the Bronze Age, about 1000 B.C., since archeologists have unearthed "sample cases" dating from that period.
    In the early days goods were sold on a barter basis after much haggling. By the Middle Ages, especially during the thirteenth and fourteenth centuries, trading became more refined and great Italian merchant princes especially ranged widely throughout Europe selling an increasingly sophisticated variety of products. Spices and other exotic goods from far-off lands were brought back by adventurous sea captains and eagerly purchased by royalty and the wealthy. With the advent of the Industrial Revolution, British sales representatives traveled the world selling manufactured items.
    Selling in North America was initially carried on inland by traders and peddlers and overseas by the captains of the great ships that traded throughout the world. These latter men were far more than master mariners. They were also international traders of a very high order. When a ship was dispatched, no advance arrangements had been made for sale of the cargo abroad; the captain had to negotiate the best price for his cargo and use the money to obtain goods that could be sold at the next port. Since voyages often lasted months, markets could disappear while the ship was at sea, and fortunes were made and lost on the voyage of a single successful trip.
    The earliest peddlers carried goods inland by backpack, by horse, or by boat. As trails were blazed, they employed carts or wagons to carry items essential to frontier life, such as cloth, tinware, flints, and bullets, other household necessities, and primitive luxuries. Many of them stayed at settlements along the way to open trading posts or general stores, carrying civilization with them wherever they went.
    In 1791, Alexander Hamilton, the first secretary of the treasury of the United States, called upon Congress to study the way Great Britain had spread "her factories and agents over the four quarters of the globe." By agents, he meant sales-representatives. Hamilton was thus one of the earliest American officials to pub-

6. Quoted in Adolf Erman, *The Literature of the Ancient Egyptians,* trans. Aylward M. Blackman (New York: E. P. Dutton & Co., Inc., 1927, pp. 55–60.

licly recognize the importance of sales representatives in increasing the prosperity of the nation.

Credit investigators were the earliest forerunners of modern sales representatives in the United States. During the early 1830s some eastern firms began sending credit investigators to frontier areas to collect past-due accounts and to report back credit data and other business information. They often sold goods along the way, and in time these sales functions became more important than the financial ones. Later on credit agencies or other financial institutions took over credit matters, but the investigators' sales efforts were so useful that they were kept on the road primarily for that purpose.

Drummers, or greeters, were next on the American scene, followed by "traveling salesmen." Prior to 1860 there were relatively few real salesmen as such in the United States and no real saleswomen to speak of. The custom was for retailers to visit manufacturers or wholesalers in the major trading cities once or twice a year. To make it easy for them to see goods fast, groups of firms or jobbers often jointly rented display rooms at one location and sent drummers, or greeters, to show the customers around, to entertain them, and of course to try to sell to them.

As new trading centers spread westward to Cincinnati, St. Louis, Toronto, and Chicago, many eastern jobbers and wholesalers began to send out traveling sales representatives to meet the competition. The growth of the railroads accelerated the use of this system; U.S. census figures record the growth in the number of traveling sales representatives: 1,000 in 1860; 7,762 by 1870; 28,158 by 1880; 58,691 by 1890; and 92,919 by 1900.

The two systems—retailers coming to visit the trading city and wholesalers and traveling sales representatives going out—existed side by side for several years. But the drummers and greeters were generally replaced in the early 1900s, and traveling sales representatives were busy everywhere. The railroads sped them and their samples about the United States and Canada; and the telegraph enabled them to keep in touch with their home offices to obtain rapid decisions regarding price quotations and delivery dates.

In time, selling and salesmanship became more customer-oriented. Slowly but surely, during this historical evolution, the manufacturers, the jobbers, and the wholesalers, and their drummers and traveling sales representatives began adding utility or value to their products in order to win customer acceptance and beat the competition. They improved product styling, added new lines for increased selection, made products readily available, and even commenced educating customers on the use of newly developed products. The selling process thus became a truly useful and productive area of marketing.

We in the modern age owe much to these early-day sales representatives, who played such a vital role in speeding world exploration and trade. They played an especially important role during the Industrial Revolution with their rugged individualism. They helped open the frontiers of the New World and break down the trade barriers of the Far East. Their sales tactics and strategies, crude as they often were, were accepted ones during the period.

Many of our modern merchandising and selling methods grew out of their collective experience. Sales representatives, not marketing professors originated such standard techniques as mail-order selling, installment-buying, market research, and sampling. Much of our modern sales sophistication is a direct result of the trial and error, ingenuity, and tenacity of the early sales representatives.

THE CHANGING ROLE OF MODERN SALESMANSHIP

Salesmanship fortunately has come a long way since the days of the drummers, whose job description could be summed up in one word: *sell*. These hard-sell sales representatives had little training or supervision, kept few records, and followed a lone-wolf life. This situation had to change if selling was to keep up with the times.

The half century between the end of the drummer era and the major American economic changes of the mid 1950s brought increased professionalism in selling. During this period, new developments in the areas of physical distribution, such as communication, transportation, and materials handling were made, changing the structure of retailing and wholesaling. The growth of information-processing following World War II led to the development of new mass-marketing techniques. These developments have not made the salesman obsolete; on the contrary, they have created a new breed of sales representatives, men and women, whose function can be described as follows: The modern sales representative helps his customers to understand already existing needs and to realize the value of his product as the best possible means of filling them.

The role of the sales representative in the modern American economy was aptly summed up by former president Lyndon B. Johnson in the following words, part of a message sent by him February 20, 1964 to Sales and Marketing Executives International, Inc., New York, in recognition of National Salesman's Week:

The salesman is a key figure in an economy which relies upon individual initiative and the competitive forces of the marketplace to stimulate full employment and achieve an orderly and efficient distribution of our goods and services. Our salesmen and women are the creative organizers of the free market so vital to the growth, prosperity, and well-being of our nation.

As the size and complexity of business and marketing have increased, the sheer magnitude and cost involved in making major marketing decisions have brought new responsibilities to sales representatives.

The Modern Sales Representative Is Being Integrated into the Marketing-Management Team

As noted earlier, the sales representative's role is rapidly changing from that of being a mere seller of products to that of being a proficient territorial business manager. He has thus become, in this modern viewpoint, a vital member of a customer-oriented, marketing-management team that starts its planning with customers' needs or wants in mind. Technical research, product design, manufacturing decisions, marketing and physical distribution are all based on consumer research. Striking changes constantly alter buying habits and patterns, and the sales representative, as the link between firm and customer, has acquired new importance in interpreting one to the other.

Each change presents a management problem, and the sales representative in effect has become a problem solver in approaching them. As part of the management team, he has to think analytically and systematically about the problems he encounters. He has to help plan, forecast, establish procedures and programs, fix schedules, and finally coordinate all these activities to achieve customer satisfaction.

Impact of Salesmanship on the International Marketplace

The first factor to consider when viewing the global marketplace from a sales point of view is that by 2000 there will be six billion people on this earth, 75 percent of whom will be living in Africa and Asia. The second factor to consider is that the tastes, attitudes, and desires of all these people are reaching a common international level. Nearly all these people will eventually have essentially the same basic desires and aspirations.

A third and important factor is that the world is becoming smaller and more closely knit than it has been before through rapidly developing and expanding communications. International television, for example, is rapidly breaking down national boundaries, and when 1,800 mph supersonic jets become operational, air-travel distances will shrink at a phenomenal rate.

The world is one big marketplace. All these factors point out that today there is only one market—the global market. Yet relatively few nations, companies, or sales/marketing executives today consider marketing and selling from a global point of view.

Nothing mysterious or different is involved in selling in other countries. Such selling is merely an extension of present local sales/marketing functions, not any basic change of function. All the principles and techniques of modern marketing and salesmanship apply to the global market if they are properly adapted to meet local conditions.

Corn flakes may be called "Flikk Flakk" in Norway, and "snap, crackle, pop," pronounced "knisper, knasper, knusper," in Germany, but they taste good everywhere. As Kellogg has proved, the techniques of selling corn flakes are basically the same the world over. Thirty percent of total Kellogg sales volume comes from the sale of corn flakes and other food products in over 100 foreign countries.

On the international level, American salesmanship has taken U.S. products to nearly every country in the world. Italian and Filipino businesspersons are likely to shave each morning with a Gillette razor blade and to brush their teeth with Colgate. In Singapore or Brazil businesspeople fill their car tanks with Exxon gasoline or petrol on the way to their offices. And once at their offices businesspeople the world over are likely to see Remington typewriters, IBM computers, and a host of American office machines and products at work. Their secretaries probably use Revlon or some other American cosmetic and wipe it off at the end of the day with a Kleenex. Most computers are American made; U.S.-owned or U.S.-controlled companies account for over a third of European auto production and a large percentage of the world tire and sewing-machine markets. In addition, most commercial jet airliners are made in the United States.

This American domination or control of so many key industries has given rise to concern in Europe especially. The communists call American domination "economic imperialism," and former French President Charles de Gaulle noted with concern the fact that American firms in France then controlled 40 percent of oil distribution, 45 percent of synthetic rubber production, and 80 percent of computer production.

Not all authorities view this situation with alarm, however. In his widely read book *The American Challenge*,[11] French author Jean-Jacques Servan-Schreiber, editor of the newsweekly *L'Express*, brims with admiration for the Yankee way of

11. Jean-Jacques Servan-Schreiber, *The American Challenge* (New York: Atheneum Publishers, 1969).

WHAT IS THE FUTURE OF SALESMANSHIP IN AN AGE OF TECHNOLOGY?

Because the concept of salesmanship and the role of those engaged in personal selling have indeed changed greatly, the sales representative of the future will need to be better educated and technically sufficient. He will be not only a sales representative but also a true consultant to his customers.

The sales force of the United States in 1950 numbered 3.8 million, had grown by 1960 to 4.4 million, and in 1974 reached 5.3 million. Projections[7] are that by 1980 it will reach 6.0 million, of which 3.5 million will be engaged in retail (inside) selling and 2.5 million in specialty (outside) selling. Some experts predict that the demand for sales representatives will grow at the rate of 250,000 jobs per year over the next few years, not including replacements.

This growth projection, while fairly consistent percentagewise with expected population growth, is considerably below the expected increase of 75 percent in national business activities. This decline in the percentage of sales representatives engaged in business activity is largely due to the consolidation of business brought about by changes in technology, automation, and distribution. Actually, the importance of sales representatives in the marketing process has increased, as we have discussed.

Trends indicate that the sales representative's job will continue to increase in importance, with each individual handling more of the business of the firm and playing a more important role in the overall plan of the firm than he does now. Along with his increasing management role will come higher compensation and more opportunities for promotion, in addition to increased responsibilities for which he will have to be better educated and trained. Here are some examples.

An understanding of customer needs and problems. The sales representative will have to know his customers thoroughly—what they want, how they buy, how they use the product, and how they react to it. He will also have to understand the buying process—why they buy. All this knowledge involves a sophisticated understanding of economics and psychological and sociological behavior.

An ability to speak the customers' language. The new technology will result in having products on the market that can be explained or sold only by sales engineers or technically trained sales representatives. And with the increasing use of EDP (Electronic Data Processing) at all levels, the sales representative will have to be capable of relating the firm to the customer and vice versa.

A thorough understanding of his customers' operations and facilities. Since he will literally be an account manager, he will have to be able to give advice on all aspects of his customers' business. For this role he will need an intelligent understanding of finance, credits and collections, inventory controls, purchasing, automation, advertising, government regulations, and tax and legal matters.

An ability to work at management level. Growth of the team concept in management has increased the trend toward executive and group buying decisions. The sales representative must be able to intelligently meet with and advise such groups. He must understand their methods of operation, marketing problems, and customer problems. Above all, he must understand the means whereby his customers make their profits.

7. The source of these projections is the U.S. Department of Labor, Bureau of Labor Statistics.

WHAT IS THE ULTIMATE CONTRIBUTION OF SALESMANSHIP TO THE WORLD MARKETING ENVIRONMENT?

It is impossible to separate the percentage of economic progress and marketing expansion due solely to salesmanship. But it is possible to point out significant examples of product, national, and international sales expansion that could not have easily occurred without salesmanship's playing a vital and perhaps decisive role.

Impact of Product Salesmanship

Let us think for a minute of four different products—Singer sewing machines, Coca-Cola, Encyclopedia Britannica, and Volkswagen automobiles. What would sales of those products be like today if sales representatives had not beaten paths to the far corners of the world to sell them?

Door-to-door sales representatives perhaps did more to spread a favorable impression of the United States by placing Singer sewing machines in homes around the world than did American diplomacy for half a century. Volkswagen sales representatives have done the same for West Germany since 1950. These two products are household words around the world, yet along the way they each faced competition that was as good mechanically. There are only two secrets to the marketing success of these two products: They offered real value and were sold.

What about Coca-Cola? No one really wants or needs Coca-Cola, yet the familiar sign is everywhere in the world, from the klongs of Bangkok to the dykes of Holland. And what about Encyclopaedia Britannica? Hundreds of direct sales representatives are knocking on doors of homes the world over each working day, selling hundreds of sets of this encyclopedia in over fifty non-English-speaking countries.

We may argue that these latter two products are not a necessity anywhere in the world. But their sales success does prove that good sales representatives can overcome objections and that the principles of salesmanship are valid anywhere in the world.

Impact of National Salesmanship

To view the impact and effect of a national effort in salesmanship, let us consider the economic competition of Japan and Great Britain since the end of World War II. Britain, who won that war, and Japan, who lost it, are small island countries with large populations. Both import food, neither has rich natural resources, and each has to import raw materials, turn them into manufactured articles, and export them in order to increase their wealth and continue desired economic growth.

Salesmanship has played a large part in Japan's economic growth. The rate of Japan's amazing economic growth (an average of almost 10 percent per year) has carried her to the point where she is today, in terms of total gross national product the world's third-ranking economic power, ranking behind only the United States and the Soviet Union in that order. In terms of per capita income, however, she still ranks about twentieth among free-enterprise economies. Some experts predicted, prior to the great increase in world oil prices of early 1974, that by 1978 Japan will be half as rich as the United States and twice as wealthy as West Germany, with per capita income the third highest in the world.[8]

8. According to 1974 United Nations projections.

Facing the fact that they had to export, the Japanese made a great effort to manufacture goods that would meet the needs and wants of the world market. They also sent teams of sales representatives all over the world to survey local market needs and to lay the groundwork for future sales. These efforts started paying off during the 1950s, when the Japanese, in spite of an unfavorable prewar reputation as imitators and producers of shoddy goods, launched world-wide export drives that captured quality markets for cameras, optical equipment, textiles, and transistor radios. Now they are competing with and most often outselling Britain in ships, steel products, and automobiles—areas in which Britain has long been a world leader.

A good part of Japan's gain has been in the traditional British markets of Australia, Southeast Asia, India, and Africa. The impact of this Japanese export-sales effort is highly visible today in such countries as Malaysia, where the streets of the cities are aglow with colorful neon signs advertising Japanese products. Malaysians ride to work in Japanese automobiles, buses and taxis and on Japanese motorcycles. They wear clothing made of Japanese textiles, wear Japanese watches, and relax by drinking Japanese beer before visiting department stores filled with Japanese goods.

Great Britain has not fared so well. Great Britain has lost ground in many of her former markets, and has also in many cases been unsuccessful in her home market in countering foreign sales efforts. A basic reason as noted during an April 1968 debate of the National Economic Development Council (NEDC), has been British marketing failures both at home and abroad. "There were not enough salesmen on the ground who knew what the foreign competition was offering or what they were fighting against and what the customer wanted,"[9] commented the director-general of NEDC in summing up the feeling of the council at that time: British companies were not selling hard enough or well enough on their own doorstep to counter the rising volume of imports. Following that meeting, the chief executive of British Leyland, a leading industrial export company, agreed that because of the absence of British marketing policy foreigners with a hard sell were outmatching home companies.[10] Another reason cited at the time for the failure of British sales representatives in general was lack of product information about their own products as well as about those of foreign competition.

Has better salesmanship made the difference in Japan's export-sales success? Why is Japan beating Britain in so many manufacturing areas in which the latter has enjoyed traditional leadership? And why is she getting such a big slice of business from traditional British markets? One answer is the presence of teams of alert Japanese businesspeople and sales representatives busily working in nearly every major city of the Commonwealth and the world. Perhaps the reason for their success is their progressive, modern attitude toward work, customers, and selling. Because they want export business, they work hard at giving a foreign customer what he wants. Better salesmanship is not the only explanation for the post–World War II sales differences between Japan and Britain, but it has played a vital role in Japan's success.

9. *London Daily Telegraph*, April 4, 1968, City Pages, p. 2. Reprinted by permission.
10. *Ibid.*

doing things, although he sounds the warning that within two decades the third greatest industrial power, just after the United States and Russia, will probably not be Europe but American industry in Europe; he suggests, in essence, that if Europeans want to avoid this situation they should imitate the Americans. His thesis is that American success is due to management imagination and talent for organization in marketing and selling its technology. He traces this ability back to lessons learned by Americans first in business schools and later in business itself.

Should the American success in international salesmanship lead to complacency? Why are so many American-made products sold abroad? Certainly not because of lack of inventiveness in other nations. After all, Europeans invented or discovered penicillin, jet engines, radar, and hundreds of other items. The big American achievement is in exploiting these and other products through organizing mass production and marketing products of value in order to fulfill the wants and needs of people everywhere. Could Americans have exploited these products to the extent that they have without aggressive, personal salesmanship? Probably not.

But Americans have little reason to feel complacent. As of mid-1974 only some 250 manufacturing firms accounted for 60 percent of all U.S. exports, and only 8 percent of all firms were in the export business, according to U.S. Department of Commerce estimates. The *International Traders Index*, a voluntary register of firms who have stated that they export, published by the U.S. Department of Commerce, listed up to 1974 only around 5,000 companies. It is surprising that so few American companies, in view of the huge global market potential, are internationally oriented today.

In face of increasing balance of trade deficits of recent years, many top government policymakers are voicing increasing concern over whether the United States can stay competitive in major world markets. They are concerned at the several areas (electronics and steel to name but two) in which foreigners are to some degree outproducing, outthinking, outworking, outtrading, underpricing, and *outselling* Americans.

Most foreigners consider American products to be of high quality—well worth the often high prices because of their dependability and superior performance. But Americans can no longer afford to sit back complacently in the belief that "Made in U.S.A." will find a ready market in foreign lands. In every country and city, European and Asian products and sales representatives are vying for attention. Because of this increasing competition, the need for aggressive American salesmanship abroad is vital and pressing.

International sales competition is becoming tougher, and keen sales representatives from other nations are fighting for business within the United States, as well as abroad. Who, for example, would have thought ten years ago that Japanese cars would have any appreciable sale in the U.S. market? Today, however, Datsun and Toyota cars are sold in increasing numbers, both in the United States and around the world. Canned Danish bacon, Thai silks for fashionable dress and home decoration, Hong Kong clothing, and beautiful Polish and Finnish glasswear are just a few of the products that have captured a top place in the American and world markets. The international marketplace is eagerly waiting for sales representatives with new and different products.

New Supersalesman Needed

Advocating the need for a "new supersalesman" to meet the challenges of personal selling now and in the future is Herbert E. Eagle, vice-president of marketing for giant, fast-growing Transamerica Corp. ($1.6 billion in sales in 1972), who coordinates the marketing and sales strategies for forty-two companies that field more than 6,000 internal sales representatives and handle everything from insurance and financial services to car rentals. Also serving as president of Sales and Marketing Executives International, Inc. a professional organization of over 25,000 members scattered through forty-nine countries, he is the closest thing to the world's top sales representative.

In articulating the enormous changes taking place in modern personal selling, he argues that today's sales representatives must do far more than fulfill the traditional role of merely being a seller of goods and services. In response to keener competition (both domestic and international), more systematic purchasing practices, and need to ensure customer satisfaction and benefit society, the modern sales representative must understand and relate to nearly all facets of his customer's business that bear on whatever he is selling.

Eagle's opinions, and those of other top American sales/marketing executives are aptly summed up in a special report entitled "The New Supersalesman,"[12] a magazine article that should be read by every student of salesmanship.

SUMMARY

We have reviewed in this chapter the economic and business foundations, with special attention paid to the nature, development, and functions, of modern sales/marketing. We discussed the customer-oriented marketing concept and newer emerging customer/society-oriented marketing concept. Knowledge of these foundations is essential in order to understand the evolving nature and role of modern personal salesmanship. We considered the four functions of marketing, of which personal selling is in our eyes the most important. Tracing the history of salesmanship, and its product, national and international implications, we concluded that the sales representatives of the future will be far more than a mere seller of goods and services. As a fully integrated member of the market/management team, their role will be that of a true consultant to their customers.

CHAPTER REVIEW

CONCEPTS TO REMEMBER*

____ marketing	____ promotional mix of marketing	____ market segmentation
____ customer-oriented		
____ sales promotion	____ business (in the economic sense)	____ customer/ society-oriented
____ global marketplace		
	____ multinational corporation	

*For memory reinforcement, fill in the page number or numbers where these terms were described in this chapter.

12. *Business Week Magazine* (January 6, 1973), pp. 44–49.

QUESTIONS FOR ANALYSIS AND DISCUSSION

1. What advantages are offered by the corporate business organization, as compared to proprietorship forms?
2. Can you name at least four functional areas through which business is carried on? Marketing is one such function; why is it such a vital business activity?
3. Name and describe the differences between the two broad types or divisions of markets.
4. Companies who sell to the two broad types of markets considered in question 3 above can be classified into three types. Name them and define what you feel are their differences.
5. Define and explain the new customer/society-oriented marketing concept. How does it differ from the customer-oriented marketing concept of the 1950s and 1960s?
6. Eight functions of marketing were listed and described in this chapter. Name and explain at least five out of the eight described.
7. What do we mean by the term "promotional mix" as used in sales/marketing terminology? What are its four parts?
8. What do we mean by the term "global marketplace"? Why is it important in today's world for sales/marketing people to "think globally—or internationally," as compared to simply domestically or locally?

Case Study 2–1

QUALITY PRODUCTS OFFERING USER SATISFACTION— THE KEY TO AVON'S HIGHLY SUCCESSFUL DIRECT SALES OF COSMETICS[13]

"Give others an opportunity to earn, in support of their happiness, betterment, and welfare ... "Quality products that will bring satisfaction to all users." These are among the basic guidelines quoted in "Great Oak", the little yellow booklet containing the highly successful formula for manufacturing and selling a line of goods direct from factory to consumer, expounded by David H. McConnell, a door-to-door book-salesman from Oswego, NY who founded in 1886 what in 1939, after several name changes, became Avon Products, Inc., today the world's largest cosmetic manufacturer.

Quality products, sold via a "value-and-variety" sales presentation direct by salespeople to prospects in their homes, have earned Avon an estimated 15 percent share of the US cosmetics and toiletries market. The cosmetic industry has a projected growth rate of 10 percent a year. International sales (16 countries), the fastest growing segment of the company's business, have flourished in the 16 countries Avon has entered since 1954. The successful American sales formula has worked equally well in Latin America, Europe and the Far East, with minor variations adapted to local cultures (in Japan, for example, the Japanese Avon Lady has to get her husband's permission before she joins).

13. Material from Avon Products, Inc., and other sources.

Selling entirely on a direct-to-consumer basis, over 680,000 active Avon Representatives, independent sales agents, call on households in USA, Canada and around the world. The USA Avon Representative—typically a mid-American housewife and mother in her mid-30's—calls on an assigned local-area territory of some 200 households. Earnings are in direct ratio to the amount of time a Representative devotes to her business.

Starting a new call-back selling cycle every two weeks, her basic selling aids are a 64 to 80 page Avon brochure, a new edition every two weeks, plus a few samples. At the end of this time she mails in her orders to her branch headquarters. In the US, the cost of merchandise to her is 60 percent of the recommended retail price and she earns 40 percent in sales that total $100 and more. Within a week, she receives her ordered merchandise, delivers it to her customers, is paid, and sends her check to Avon with her next cycle's orders. She can return unsold merchandise to Avon, which backs her with an unconditional guarantee.

The Avon product line is relatively simple compared to that of many heavily-advertised brand-name competitors. Uninterested in sensational product names, since it doesn't have to compete on the drugstore shelf or department store counters, Avon concentrates on wholesome, quality products geared to a mid-America, what everyone wants line that leads to user-satisfaction and continued repeat sales. Its thousands of Avon Representatives provide rapid market needs-and-wants-feedback to the company, enabling it to quickly anticipate changing tastes or trends. Looking ahead, based on continued consumer confidence and product diversification, the young (average 42) top Avon management, sees only continued growth as their Avon Representative salesforce continues to expand worldwide.

QUESTIONS FOR WRITTEN REPORTS OR CLASS DISCUSSION

1. How do Avon customers in their homes register their changing wants and preferences, via feedback conveyed by Avon Representatives to top Avon management, concerning the company's product line?

2. Would Avon in-the-home customers be considered part of the consumer market or industrial market? What is the difference in composition of these two types or divisions of markets?

3. Would you say that Avon's sales policies are customer-oriented? Why? Would you say they are customer/society-oriented? Why?

4. As the size and complexity of sales/marketing increases in face of fast-changing fads and trends, Avon, like all large corporations, faces new and costly marketing decisions. How do you feel Avon could make even better use of the Avon Representatives in your local area, as part of their integrated marketing-management team link between firm and customer, than was indicated in the above case study as it is currently being done?

THE REPS OF MEDIA SELLING GO MORE MARKETING ORIENTED[14]

The Reps. Their business cards may read sales executive, accounts supervisor, district sales manager or other variations on the theme of sales representative, but the busy band of men—and, rarely, women—who sell advertising time and space are known generically in the advertising world as The Reps.

Representing radio and television stations and networks, newspapers and newspaper chains, magazines and trade publications, transit and outdoor advertising companies, they call on ad agency media buyers and planners and directors, increasingly on account executives and supervisors, even creative departments, and on the ad managers with national advertisers.

Reps function in a world of "no," where "show me" is the warmest welcome to be hoped for. Advertisers don't really *want* to buy advertising; they do it because their competitors do it. Agencies *may* want to buy—long live the commission system, say the reps—but seldom, it seems, to buy just what, or as much as, the Rep hopes to sell them.

The Reps sell an intangible. They write orders in terms of thirty and sixty-seconds of time, and blank spaces of various dimensions, yet they're really selling the environment surrounding the time and space and, more specifically, the viewers and listeners and readers attracted to that environment, and the sales that can result from an advertiser filling the time and space with messages directed to those viewers and listeners and readers.

It's a highly competitive field. Each advertising medium fights the others for a share of the ad budget dollars. Within each medium, every market competes for attention. Within every market, each station or publication battles for a piece of the action. The ammunition is audience ratings, readership studies, market profiles, cost per thousand, things like that—and repmanship.

Winning ways, the infectious enthusiasm for the product, the instinctive exercise of applied psychology, is an important requisite for The Rep—but it's no longer the name of the game. Following the trend which has seen company ad managers, agency account, creative and media departments all become more marketing-oriented, today's Rep, the real pro, is also more marketing-oriented.

Hence today's Rep operates on two levels.

In the traditional role of the salesman, he makes the rounds of the media departments on his list, either as the pitchman making a presentation of new data on his station(s) or publication(s); or as the negotiator, presenting availabilities and recommendations; or as the order-taker, following up on previous calls. He has a ready smile and a new joke and the latest news, gossip and rumors about account-switching, who's looking for a job and why, where there are job openings and why. He's a valuable town crier. He may sit down with a newly-appointed media buyer and tell her more than she ever wanted to know about his medium and market and specific stations or publications. He takes someone out to lunch on the old expense account.

In his role as the marketing-oriented Rep, he calls not only on media departments, but on the account groups, and on the advertising managers, advertiser-side,

14. Material in this case study extracted from an article by Kit Morgan, *Stimulus,* November 1973, pp. 13–16. (Note: *Stimulus* is a Canadian magazine and may not be found in all U.S. libraries.)

even brand managers, to learn more about their products and their marketing strategies and problems, in order to plot the best use of his medium and markets and stations or publications to solve those problems. He makes tailored-to-measure, marketing-oriented presentations. He takes someone to lunch on the old expense account.

While the function of every Rep is to sell, the modus operandi, the income, the opportunities, vary according to whether he's employed by a radio and/or TV rep house, a newspaper, a magazine, a business publication, a newspaper chain.

Broadcast Reps: earn from $11,000 to $35,000 a year, with maybe a handful peaking at $40,000 to $45,000. Some work on straight commission. Others are paid a basic salary plus commission.

Newspaper Reps: earn from $11,000 to $22,000, straight salary, no commissions, with either a large metropolitan daily or the national ad sales operation of a newspaper chain.

Consumer magazines: earnings range from $7,000 to $8,000 (for trainees) or $12,000 to $25,000, with a handful at the top in the $30,000s, working on a salary plus commission or salary plus commission-over-quota basis.

Trade publications: earnings range from $8,000 (for trainees) to $17,500; from salary plus commission-over-quota to a straight $20,000 for the one-man national sales department for a small publication.

There's room at the top for the Rep with ambition and management skills. The qualities that make a good sales representative, however, do not necessarily make a good manager.

Many Reps choose to remain Reps. With experience as a memory bank from which to withdraw the most successful way to deal with any situation, ever-more-solid rapport with agency and advertiser contacts as juniors once befriended become media directors and marketing vice-presidents, the job becomes easier, the earnings better, and who needs the hassles and responsibilities of management!

Sales is a field in which promotion doesn't necessarily offer any financial incentive; top sales representatives can earn more than their superiors. Nor is the status of a management title any incentive to the average Rep; the status seeker would have crumpled early under the public image of the "seller" as a Fuller Brush man, door-to-door encyclopedia vender, or bait-and-switch vacuum cleaner sales representative.

QUESTIONS FOR WRITTEN REPORTS OR CLASS DISCUSSION

1. What are two major changing business trends that have led to increasing market orientation selling by media reps, as compared to their traditional level of selling?

2. Explain the meaning of this statement: "The modern media rep, in order to achieve greatest sales success, must learn to understand and relate to nearly all facets of his customer's business that bears on whatever he is selling."

3. In addition to learning more about his customer's products, marketing strategies, and problems noted in this article, what additional items discussed in the chapter material will a marketing-oriented media rep need to understand about his customer's operations and facilities in order to offer them better advice?

4. In order to help his customers more intelligently, the marketing-oriented rep should aim not only to be a good sales representative, but also (1) a problem solver, and (2) a true consultant to them as well. Explain the meaning of these two terms.

THINK CUSTOMERS—NOT JUST SALES

As noted in *Stores, The Retail Management Magazine* [15], under the above heading, statistics indicate that the average retail store loses 15 percent of its customers each year through death, moving, and age, among other reasons. This means, other things being equal, that you must get 15 new active customers for each 100 that you now have just to break even; 20 new ones to achieve a 5 percent increase.

Despite the lack of customer consciousness apparent in so many stores, customer loyalty is not dead—it's alive and well but needs constant nourishment in the form of service and recognition to keep those customers coming back.

Assuming you are a retail salesperson with some positive and practical ideas about how to solve the above problems, prepare a one-page written proposal outlining (1) the problems, and (2) your recommended solutions, to present to your store manager.

15. *Stores, The Heatil Management Magazine* (August 1973), p. 21.

3

forecasting, planning, and organizing for selling in a changing marketing environment

When you have mastered the content of this chapter, you should be able to:

Define the terms *objective* (or *goal*), *product, goods, management, top management, middle management, operating management, channels of distribution,* and *management by objectives* (MBO).

Describe the two most important determinants of consumer demand and explain why they are so important to sales/marketing.

Describe the four generally accepted management functions.

List the four elements of the "marketing mix" upon which any successful marketing strategy and program depends.

Describe the three classifications of any consumer or industrial product or goods that apply on the basis of their rate of consumption and tangibility.

Describe three types of goods or product classifications based on consumer shopping habits.

List the four major classifications of industrial goods.

Construct a chart illustrating the most commonly employed marketing channels of distribution.

Summarize the meaning and use of short-range objectives, long-range objectives, and sales and expense budgets for sales representatives.

Summarize broadly how companies organize for sales/marketing, how goods or products move through distribution channels from manufacturer to end consumer, how companies organize their sales force for selling, and some principles of training, supervising, and assigning sales representatives.

Having considered in Chapter 2 the nature and function of sales/marketing and the increasingly important role fulfilled by sales representatives, we will now turn our attention toward the planning and organization necessary for successful selling in the rapidly changing world marketing environment.

We will first consider some of the changes now taking place that will affect consumer demand and alter the composition of the marketplace in the decade ahead. Then we will note how companies or organizations plan their sales force objectives and training, within the framework of modern management theory, to cope with such changes.

Next we will study how companies organize for selling and relate principles of modern management theory to you, as sales representatives in your modern role of territory market manager. Finally, we will consider how companies determine their overall sales/marketing strategy and program and promotional strategy or mix, and how they organize their sales forces to accomplish their objective. Two end-of-chapter case studies will tie together much of what we have studied so far.

THE CHANGING MARKETPLACE

Sales/marketing has developed significantly since the end of World War II in 1945. We have seen the widespread development of suburban shopping centers and malls, credit cards, discount stores, super stores, rapid development of franchise operations, greatly intensified product differentiation, self-service selling, and improved packaging. The computer has played a significant role in the rapid development of several of these areas.

Some experts have predicted that the next several years will see even more changes in areas such as product planning and management, where product life cycles will be shorter and consumer/society benefits will be more carefully considered; in physical distribution, with increased automation and centralized warehousing; and in retailing, with increased around-the-clock and Sunday openings, more super stores, and more mixed business.

Personal selling, they predict, will become more complex, with fewer but better trained sales representatives in many areas, not merely selling goods or services, but acting as professional advisors to their customers in matters of market research, product planning, pricing, inventory control and analysis, and advertising. Research will determine how the sales representative influences the prospect, and vice versa. As prices and quality become more similar, the skill and ability of the sales representative will become a more decisive decision-making factor.

Factors that will largely determine consumer demands and sales/marketing trends in the future include such things as expected population growth, geographic shifts in population, population density in metropolitan areas, age composition and household formation, and income distribution.

Evidence from United Nations' sources and 1970 United States census figures gives us some indication of changes to be expected in these areas through the mid 1980s, as we shall note. Of greatest importance is the fact that there will be significant changes in the two most important determinants of consumer demand: (1) the age mix of America's household population, and (2) the distribution of spending power. The expected changes in these two critical variables will greatly alter the composition of the marketplace.

Population Growth

The world population explosion alone will bring with it tremendous new problems and challenges (see Figure 3.1). When the Christian church was established, the population of the world was only 250 million. It took 1,600 years for this figure to double to 500 million, less than the population of India alone today. By 1868 the world population had doubled again and stood at more than one billion; by 1968, a hundred years later, the figure had more than tripled to 3.5 billion. Currently the United Nations estimates a world population of around six billion by the year 2000.

In the United States alone, with a 1970 population of 204 million, projections are that by 1980 there may be 45 million more, for a total of nearly 250

FIGURE 3.1   The World Population Trend

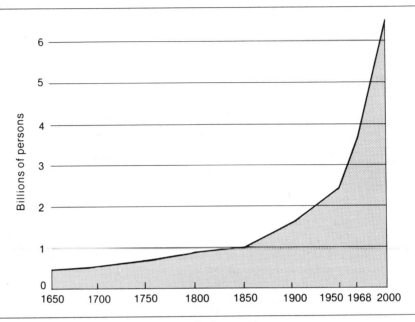

Source: United Nations World Population Studies.

million. In 1966 almost half were twenty-five or younger; by the mid-1970s there
were over 100 million under twenty-five. In 1960, Canada had a population of
17.9 million. Projections are that this will increase to about 25 million by 1980.
Mexico's 1970 population of 55 million, with an average age of fifteen, may equal
that of the United States before the year 2000.

Geographic Shifts in U.S. Population

In 1880, 70 percent of Americans lived on farms, but by 1967, 70 percent of these
had moved to urban areas, and by 1975 only 6 percent of the American labor
force worked on farms.
   Within the United States people continue moving, shifting into a few broad
regional areas of the country. In any average year, one American out of five
moves to different living quarters. Thus, in any given five-year period the equiva-
lent of the entire population moves to a new location.
   The most significant shifts in population which have occurred and are expected to take place are in the central cities and suburbs of metropolitan areas,
where two out of every three Americans live today.
   Nearly all of this shift, and continued growth of a few large metropolitan
areas, has not been in the inner or central city, but in the suburbs. Between 1960
and 1970 central cities grew only about one percent while their surrounding suburbs grew 28 percent, and Bureau of the Census projections indicate that by 1985
50 percent of all Americans will be living in the suburbs of these metropolitan
areas, one-fourth living in central cities, and the remaining one-fourth spread
about the rest of the nation. All that time, one-third of the central city residents
will be Blacks, compared to one-fifth in 1970.

Population Density in U.S. Metropolitan Areas

Eighteen new metropolitan areas were added to U.S. census rolls between 1960 and 1970, and the land area of some of the older ones was expanded during the same period. By way of definition, a metropolitan area consists of a central city of 50,000 or more population plus adjacent counties socially or economically integrated with that city.

Thus, even though Americans continue to move into metropolitan areas (estimates are 70 percent by the year 2000), due to the addition of new metropolitan areas and major growth in the suburbs, population density in metropolitan areas then will be considerably less than today.

Population Shifts and Density in Canadian Metropolitan Areas

Population shifts from rural to urban areas in Canada and population concentration in urban areas parallels that of the United States. Forecasts are that by 1980 over 80 percent of Canada's population will be urban (compared with 76 percent in 1971), with about 60 percent of the population concentrated in twenty-nine major urban centers, each having a population of at least 100,000. The problems of urban concentration are expected to be particularly acute along the Windsor-Montreal corridor.

Age, Composition, and Household Formation[1]

Consumer spending for goods and services in the United States is expected to increase 50 percent by 1980 over 1970, to around one trillion dollars (see Figure 3.4). Due to expected shifts in income distribution, the average American family may have a third more to spend than today. Since the age of a family has a lot to do with how it spends its money, the following trends are of special interest to sales/marketing people:

There will be a dramatic rise in the number of young adults between now and the mid-1980s. One-third the expected total population increase will be in the twenty-five to thirty-four age group, a result of the post–World War II baby boom.

Due to the sharp increase in this twenty to early thirties age group, the next decade will be the era of the young married. The current average million marriages per year will increase by the mid-1980s to around 2½ million, when we will need 2 million new homes or apartments per year to accommodate the newly formed households and expected large number of births.

Although there will be more births, the total number of children will remain unchanged, since children born during the post–World War II period will be reaching adulthood (over eighteen) at about the same rate.

Due to the rapid growth of young families, homes with children will increase nearly 20 percent.

There will be little growth in the middle-years, the thirty-five to fifty-four age group.

There will be slight decrease in the fifty-five to sixty-four age group.

There will be an increase in the sixty-five and over age group, from 13.5 million in 1972 to 17 million, or 20 percent of the population, by 1985.

---

1. Information here and under the heading "Income Distribution," extracted from Fabian Linden, "Reshuffling the Age-Income Mix," *Conference Board Record* XI, No. 3. (March 1974): pp. 58–60.

These age distribution changes, reflecting the rapid increase in young adults between ages twenty and thirty-four and a lack of growth in the forty-five to sixty-five age group, will especially affect school enrollments and career promotional opportunities for today's young people, especially in the growth area of sales/marketing.

More and better education for more people has already had a great impact on market trends and will continue to do so. The extremely high birth rates of the 1940s started an unprecedented increase in American school enrollments. The desire for more and better education has led to greatly increased college and university enrollments. One out of two Americans may soon be a college graduate. As the chart in Figure 3.2 shows, total American enrollments in all schools, colleges, and universities may surpass 70 million in the early 1980s.

While elementary school enrollments will rise only slightly by 1985 and high school enrollments will remain about the same as 1970, the number of college students may increase from 7½ million to nearly 11½ million.

FIGURE 3.2   United States Educational Enrollment Trends

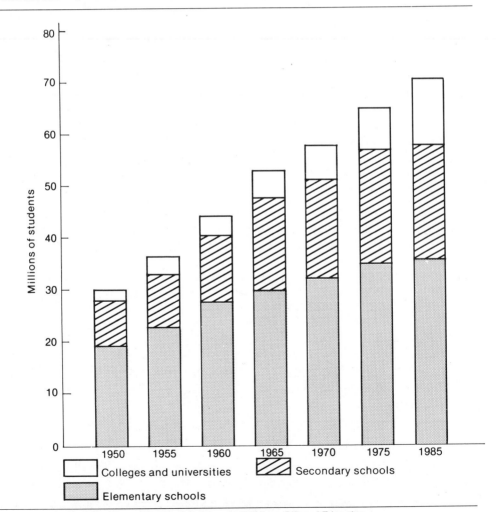

Source: U.S. Department of Health, Education, and Welfare, Office of Education.

More and better education leads to better income, especially in the United States, where the average lifetime earnings of university graduates are more than 65 per cent higher than those of nongraduates. Increased income means more money to spend on recreation and on cultural and leisure activities; this trend increases the demand for books, travel, art, and cultural activities of all kinds. See Figure 3.3.

FIGURE 3.3

Fast-Growing Leisure Markets	Fast-Growing Cultural Markets
Boating	Books
Skin diving	Theater
Travel	Drama festivals
Gardening	Educational records
Summer homes	Hi-fi and stereo
Private health gyms	Adult education
Adult camping	Art and sculpture

The trend toward higher education is noticeable in many countries of the world since the knowledge explosion and the demands of technology require that talent be continually improved through education. Because buyers of goods and services have more education, they demand greater choices and better quality; trained and capable sales representatives are necessary to intelligently present products or services to them.

Rapid promotional opportunities in growth career areas for today's youth in the twenty to thirty-four age group may result from the projected lack of growth in the forty-five to sixty-four age group. As population, business, and government expand and more of the latter group retire, we can expect to see more young leaders taking their place than ever before.

Income Distribution

Perhaps the single most important development which will affect the United States consumer market during the next decade is the expected continuous escalation of the income scale of American households (see Figure 3.4). The following trends are of special interest to sales/marketing people:

Families under thirty-five accounted in 1972 for approximately 25 percent of retail spending; by 1980 they will account for approximately 35 percent. Some 35 to 45 percent will earn $15,000 or more annually.

Not only will there be a sharp growth in young (under thirty-five) families, but spending power of families under thirty-five may double—a rate of increase nearly twice that expected of total spending.

By the mid-1980s, the thirty-five to forty-five age group will account for one out of every four dollars of household income. Between 50 and 60 percent will be earning $15,000 or more annually.

The forty-five to fifty-four age group, the one of greatest affluence, will shrink one million in size. Even though between 50 and 60 percent will earn $15,000 or more annually, due to the group percentage decrease it will control only 18 percent of all spending power, as compared to 33 percent in 1972.

Both the fifty-five to sixty-four and sixty-five and over age groups, while increasing slightly in size and income, will remain relatively stable in terms of spending power percentage.

FIGURE 3.4

Households by Age of Head and Income Class: Alternative Projections

(All figures in 1972 dollars)

	All Households	Annual Household Income (Before Taxes)						
		Under $3,000	$3,000-5,000	$5,000-7,000	$7,000-10,000	$10,000-15,000	$15,000-25,000	$25,000 and over
1972								
Households: Millions	68.3	9.4	7.7	7.2	10.9	15.7	13.1	4.2
Distribution	100.0%	14.0	11.0	10.5	16.0	23.0	19.5	6.0
Percent Spending Power	100.0%	2.0	4.0	5.5	12.0	25.0	32.0	19.5
Distribution by Age	100.0%	100.0%	100.0%	100.0%	100.0%	100.0%	100.0%	100.0%
Under 25	8.0	9.0	11.5	13.5	12.0	7.0	2.5	1.0
25-34	20.0	9.0	13.0	19.0	24.5	28.0	21.5	10.5
35-44	17.0	6.5	9.5	13.0	16.5	21.0	25.5	24.5
45-54	19.0	8.5	11.0	13.0	16.0	20.5	28.5	35.5
55-64	16.5	16.0	15.0	16.5	16.5	16.5	16.0	21.5
65 and over	19.5	51.0	40.0	25.0	14.5	7.0	6.0	7.0
1980 HIGH SERIES*								
Households: Millions	77.3	8.5	7.3	7.3	10.4	16.6	19.7	7.4
Distribution	100.0%	11.0	9.5	9.5	13.5	21.5	25.5	9.5
Percent Spending Power	100.0%	1.5	3.0	4.5	8.5	20.0	36.5	26.0
Distribution by Age	100.0%	100.0%	100.0%	100.0%	100.0%	100.0%	100.0%	100.0%
Under 25	8.0	8.5	10.5	12.5	13.0	8.5	4.0	1.0
25-34	23.5	9.5	14.5	19.5	25.5	32.0	30.0	16.0
35-44	17.0	6.0	8.5	10.0	14.5	18.0	24.0	27.5
45-54	15.5	7.5	7.5	10.0	12.0	14.5	20.5	30.0
55-64	16.0	17.0	13.0	16.0	16.0	16.0	16.0	19.0
65 and over	20.0	51.5	46.0	32.0	19.0	11.0	5.5	6.5
LOW SERIES*								
Households: Millions	77.3	9.3	8.1	7.7	11.2	17.8	17.0	6.2
Distribution	100.0%	12.0	10.5	10.0	14.5	23.0	22.0	8.0
Percent Spending Power	100.0%	1.5	3.5	5.0	10.0	23.0	33.5	23.5

Distribution by Age

	100.0%	100.0%	100.0%	100.0%	100.0%	100.0%	100.0%	100.0%
Under 25	8.0	8.5	11.0	13.5	12.5	7.5	3.0	1.0
25-34	23.5	10.5	14.5	20.0	27.5	33.0	27.0	16.0
35-44	17.0	6.0	9.0	11.5	15.5	19.0	25.0	27.5
45-54	15.5	7.5	8.5	10.0	12.5	15.0	22.5	29.5
55-64	16.0	16.0	13.5	16.0	15.5	16.5	16.5	19.5
65 and over	20.0	51.5	43.5	29.0	16.5	9.0	6.0	6.5

1985 HIGH SERIES*

Households:								
Millions	84.2	100.0%	7.6	6.7	10.1	16.9	23.2	11.7
Distribution	100.0%	8.0	9.0	8.0	12.0	20.0	27.5	14.0
Percent Spending Power	100.0%	1.0	2.5	3.5	7.0	17.0	35.0	34.0

Distribution by Age

	100.0%	100.0%	100.0%	100.0%	100.0%	100.0%	100.0%	100.0%
Under 25	7.0	8.0	9.0	10.5	11.5	9.0	4.5	1.0
25-34	24.5	10.5	12.5	18.5	26.0	31.0	33.0	16.0
35-44	19.5	7.5	9.0	10.0	15.5	19.5	25.5	31.5
45-54	14.0	6.5	7.0	9.0	10.0	12.0	17.0	27.0
55-64	15.0	16.0	12.5	14.0	14.5	15.0	14.5	17.5
65 and over	20.0	51.5	50.0	38.0	22.5	13.5	5.5	7.0

LOW SERIES*

Households:								
Millions	84.2	100.0%	8.5	7.6	11.8	18.5	21.1	7.6
Distribution	100.0%	11.0	10.0	9.0	14.0	22.0	25.0	9.0
Percent Spending Power	100.0%	1.5	3.0	4.0	9.5	21.0	36.0	25.0

Distribution by Age

	100.0%	100.0%	100.0%	100.0%	100.0%	100.0%	100.0%	100.0%
Under 25	7.0	8.0	9.5	11.5	11.5	7.5	3.5	1.0
25-34	24.5	11.0	13.5	21.5	27.0	33.0	30.0	16.5
35-44	19.5	7.0	10.0	12.5	16.5	21.0	27.5	30.0
45-54	14.0	6.5	7.5	9.0	10.5	13.5	18.5	27.5
55-64	15.0	15.0	13.0	14.5	15.0	15.0	14.5	18.5
65 and over	20.0	52.5	46.5	31.0	19.5	10.0	6.0	6.5

*The high series projection assumes an average annual real growth rate in total household income of 4%. The low series projection is based on a 3% growth rate.

Sources: U.S. Department of Commerce; The Conference Board

Source: From Fabian Linden, "Reshuffling the Age-Income Mix," Conference Board Record XI, No. 3 (March 1974): pp. 58–60.

FIGURE 3.5   The Projected Growth in the Consumer Market

(Personal consumption expenditures)

	1970 Billions of Dollars	Percent Increase 1970-1980
Disposable Income	$687.8	53.8%
Total Expenditures	615.8	53.1
Durables	88.6	82.5
Nondurables	264.7	39.7
Services	262.5	56.8
Durables	88.6	82.5
Cars	31.5	75.7
Tires, accessories	5.6	108.0
Furniture	8.0	39.7
Appliances	8.5	84.2
Television, radios, records etc.	8.3	152.4
Other household durables	12.4	69.2
Boats, sports goods	4.9	106.1
Other durables	9.4	69.2
Nondurables	264.7	39.7
Food at home	100.5	30.5
Restaurant food	28.4	24.3
Alcoholic beverages	17.7	39.7
Tobacco	11.2	21.9
Women's apparel	28.8	55.3
Men's apparel	15.5	48.0
Footwear	8.1	29.3
Housefurnishings	6.4	74.1
Household supplies	5.5	50.9
Drugs	6.7	89.5
Toilet goods	6.1	89.5
Gas and oil	22.9	56.8
Other nondurables	6.9	4.4
Services	262.5	56.8
Shelter	91.2	64.4
Household operations	36.1	58.3
Gas and electricity	15.1	72.4
Telephone, telegraph	9.8	106.1
Transportation	17.9	28.0
Automotive services	12.4	34.4
Intercity travel	3.0	74.1
Medical services	38.7	64.4
Physicians	12.4	52.3
Dentists	4.4	42.4
Personal care	4.0	39.7
Foreign travel	5.4	98.6
Higher education	5.2	93.1
Other services	64.0	43.4

Sources: U.S. Department of Commerce; *Conference Board Record* (June 1972); pp. 30–32.

FIGURE 3.6 Spending by Sector.   Chart 1.

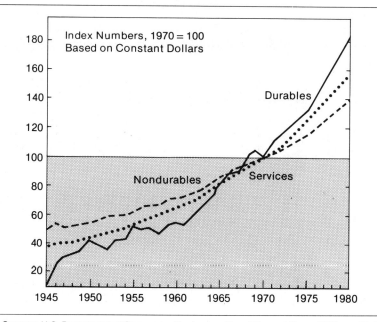

Sources: U.S. Department of Commerce; *Conference Board Record* (June 1972): pp. 30–32.

FIGURE 3.7 The Family's Shopping Basket.   Chart 2.

Total expenditures, 1980 = 100%

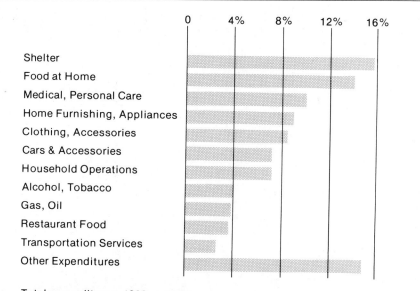

Total expenditures, 1980 = 100%

Sources: U.S. Department of Commerce; *Conference Board Record* (June 1972): pp. 30–32.

FIGURE 3.8 Where The Markets Are . . . And Will Be!

State and region	Total personal income (millions of 1967 dollars)			Population (thousands)			Per capita income (1967 dollars)		
	1969	1980	1990	1969	1980	1990	1969	1980	1990
UNITED STATES	**691,451**	**1,068,496**	**1,517,173**	**201,298**	**223,532**	**246,039**	**3,435**	**4,780**	**6,166**
New England	**43,110**	**66,580**	**93,422**	**11,735**	**12,954**	**14,130**	**3,674**	**5,140**	**6,611**
Maine	2,801	3,993	5,371	992	972	992	2,824	4,106	5,415
New Hampshire	2,287	3,778	5,388	724	843	919	3,159	4,483	5,863
Vermont	1,316	2,083	3,020	437	482	519	3,012	4,319	5,822
Massachusetts	21,136	33,024	46,443	5,650	6,267	6,876	3,741	5,269	6,755
Rhode Island	3,209	4,982	6,945	932	1,032	1,115	3,443	4,829	6,228
Connecticut	12,360	18,720	26,255	3,000	3,358	3,710	4,120	5,575	7,077
Mideast	**163,560**	**247,199**	**343,941**	**42,111**	**45,932**	**50,016**	**3,884**	**5,382**	**6,877**
New York	76,180	111,947	153,705	18,105	19,352	20,946	4,208	5,785	7,338
New Jersey	27,350	43,212	60,788	7,095	8,080	8,923	3,855	5,348	6,812
Pennsylvania	40,158	60,754	83,363	11,741	12,649	13,416	3,420	4,803	6,214
Delaware	2,163	3,415	4,914	540	627	707	4,006	5,450	6,946
Maryland	13,949	22,494	34,235	3,868	4,473	5,275	3,606	5,028	6,491
District of Columbia	3,759	5,378	6,937	762	750	750	4,933	7,170	9,249
Great Lakes	**146,289**	**220,315**	**307,441**	**39,904**	**44,005**	**47,688**	**3,666**	**5,007**	**6,447**
Michigan	33,252	49,562	69,602	8,781	9,743	10,645	3,787	5,087	6,538
Ohio	37,446	56,489	78,877	10,563	11,651	12,609	3,545	4,849	6,255
Indiana	17,537	26,577	38,027	5,143	5,784	6,364	3,410	4,595	5,975
Illinois	43,764	65,787	91,014	11,039	12,091	13,056	3,965	5,441	6,971
Wisconsin	14,289	21,899	29,921	4,378	4,737	5,013	3,264	4,623	5,969
Plains	**52,589**	**78,392**	**107,891**	**16,202**	**17,065**	**18,034**	**3,246**	**4,594**	**5,983**
Minnesota	12,478	19,731	28,279	3,758	4,119	4,553	3,320	4,790	6,211
Iowa	9,144	13,367	17,845	2,805	2,913	2,993	3,260	4,588	5,963
Missouri	15,141	23,224	32,467	4,640	5,071	5,439	3,263	4,580	5,970
North Dakota	1,730	2,281	2,917	621	579	563	2,785	3,941	5,177
South Dakota	1,852	2,609	3,384	668	655	648	2,772	3,986	5,227
Nebraska	4,914	7,000	9,450	1,474	1,499	1,557	3,334	4,670	6,069
Kansas	7,330	10,180	13,549	2,236	2,228	2,281	3,278	4,568	5,940

Southeast	**119,964**	**197,992**	**295,566**	**43,440**	**49,828**	**56,374**	**2,762**	**3,974**	**5,243**
Virginia	14,342	23,402	35,638	4,614	5,295	6,135	3,108	4,419	5,809
West Virginia	4,450	6,810	9,089	1,746	1,832	1,845	2,548	3,717	4,926
Kentucky	8,572	13,953	20,520	3,198	3,609	3,982	2,681	3,866	5,153
Tennessee	10,399	17,179	25,920	3,897	4,557	5,191	2,668	3,770	4,994
North Carolina	13,915	22,504	33,305	5,031	5,736	6,465	2,766	3,923	5,152
South Carolina	6,531	10,322	15,127	2,570	2,819	3,122	2,541	3,662	4,845
Georgia	13,181	21,182	31,940	4,551	5,147	5,907	2,896	4,115	5,407
Florida	20,871	39,988	63,320	6,641	8,926	10,978	3,143	4,480	5,768
Alabama	8,563	13,408	19,467	3,440	3,747	4,090	2,489	3,579	4,759
Mississippi	4,896	7,666	10,850	2,220	2,328	2,450	2,206	3,293	4,428
Louisiana	9,608	14,202	19,672	3,619	3,744	3,937	2,655	3,793	4,997
Arkansas	4,635	7,376	10,717	1,913	2,087	2,271	2,423	3,535	4,719
Southwest	**49,273**	**78,004**	**113,640**	**16,328**	**18,210**	**20,405**	**3,018**	**4,284**	**5,569**
Oklahoma	7,296	11,251	16,066	2,535	2,762	2,993	2,878	4,073	5,367
Texas	33,953	53,047	77,063	11,045	12,167	13,580	3,074	4,360	5,675
New Mexico	2,696	4,099	5,730	1,011	1,055	1,131	2,666	3,885	5,065
Arizona	5,328	9,607	14,782	1,737	2,226	2,701	3,068	4,316	5,473
Rocky Mountain	**15,007**	**23,976**	**33,864**	**4,943**	**5,455**	**5,936**	**3,036**	**4,395**	**5,705**
Montana	2,035	2,817	3,654	694	670	665	2,932	4,207	5,498
Idaho	1,996	2,899	3,954	707	708	738	2,823	4,095	5,360
Wyoming	1,041	1,490	1,947	329	331	334	3,165	4,503	5,828
Colorado	7,049	12,097	17,410	2,166	2,586	2,890	3,254	4,677	6,024
Utah	2,886	4,672	6,900	1,047	1,160	1,310	2,756	4,027	5,269
Far West	**97,635**	**149,609**	**211,967**	**25,596**	**28,904**	**32,086**	**3,814**	**5,176**	**6,606**
Washington	12,165	17,408	24,055	3,343	3,550	3,806	3,639	4,904	6,321
Oregon	6,686	10,466	14,754	2,062	2,335	2,537	3,242	4,483	5,815
Nevada	1,866	3,230	5,004	480	616	761	3,888	5,247	6,578
California	76,918	118,504	168,154	19,711	22,403	24,982	3,902	5,290	6,731
Alaska	1,193	1,875	2,795	296	333	391	4,029	5,625	7,145
Hawaii	2,832	4,555	6,646	743	848	979	3,811	5,374	6,790

The above figures, prepared by Bureau of Economic Analysis, U.S. Department of Commerce, indicate expected population shifts and income distribution in the United States for 1980 and 1990 compared to the situation in 1969. The figures illustrate where the markets will be.

Source: U.S. Department of Commerce, *Commerce Today*, May 27, 1974, p. 15.

Significance of These Market Changes to Sales/Marketing People

The significance of these projections to sales/marketing people is enormous. In 1967 about 55 percent of total household income accrued to families earning less than $15,000 per year, but by 1972, 53 percent of the total accrued to families earning $15,000 or more per year. This was an event of great importance—in those five short years the U.S. was transformed from a nation of predominantly middle income to one of predominantly upper income.

If the U.S. economy remains healthy, by 1985 nearly one out of every two families will control nearly 69 percent of the spending power (based on Figure 3.4, 1985 high series projections). Moreover, because of the combined impact of both income and population growth, the number of dollars in constant purchasing power at this upper-income level will probably be four to five times as great as it is today.

Figures 3.5, 3.6, and 3.7 offer some idea of how American families will be spending their income in 1980 as compared to 1970. Figure 3.8 indicates expected population shifts and income distribution by geographic regions in the United States for 1980 and 1990 compared to the situation in 1969; it illustrates where the markets will be.

By the mid-1980s, with an expected population of around 250 million, a sizable increase in young newlyweds, and a doubling of family money income, the United States will be the most affluent society the world has ever seen. Exciting times lie ahead, especially for those who pursue a sales career!

MANAGERIAL ORGANIZING FOR SELLING

Setting and meeting objectives are the key to success in every sales/marketing program, just as they are for any business or nonbusiness, group or individual action program of any type. An *objective* is something specific to be achieved.

In order to achieve success, any type of sales program—firm, organizational, or that of a sales representative in his own personal sales territory—has to be built around two essential elements: products and markets.

A *product* is what a seller has to sell; it can be goods, services, or ideas. *Goods* and *products* mean the same thing in sales/marketing; they will often be used interchangeably in this book. Each product is classified as either a *consumer* or an *industrial* product (or consumer or industrial goods). We will discuss and break these classifications down shortly. We defined *markets* and *market segmentation*, you will recall, on page 31 in Chapter 2.

Ensuring that goods and services desired by consumers are produced and supplied to consumers at the right time, in the desired amounts, and at an acceptable price, is the role and responsibility of business management. *Management* is defined as the process whereby resources are combined into an integrated system in order to accomplish the objectives of the system. Management, at its many levels, plans and sets objectives and strives to ensure that they are met.

In the preceding pages of this chapter we considered today's rapidly changing marketplace as it might appear to any firm with a product or service to sell. For our purposes we can consider it a business firm's market research findings, and thus we will now consider how the firm will plan and organize for selling in view of the data presented—especially the sales/marketing team, of which the sales representative is part.

How Do Companies Divide and Organize Managerial Activities?

From a managerial point of view, each individual in the organization plays a specific part in the over-all team effort. Direction in any group activity starts at the top, or policy-making, level. Thus the chairman of the board, or the chairman of directors as he is called in some countries, leads in establishing over-all company or organization policies and charges the president, or managing director, with their over-all implementation. He in turn delegates responsibility to various department heads in the functional areas such as research and development, personnel, finance, operations, production, and sales.

The degree of centralization of *decision-making* varies from company to company. Some companies organize their functional sales policies and planning in a highly centralized fashion. The head, or home, office does most of the planning for their sales activities. An executive committee decides which products are to be sold and their prices and also plans advertising, sales promotion, training aids, budgets, and specific territorial sales policies and procedures. If a company is highly centralized in this manner, the principal sales task of a sales representative in a territory may be to merely carry out the established sales program as effectively as possible rather than to generate new ideas.

Many modern companies favor more decentralized sales policies; that is, they allow the various branches or individual sales representatives as much freedom as possible to manage sales activities on a local level. The theory here is that the local sales representative on the spot is better able to plan for, to judge, and to solve local problems than anyone at the head office. Even in highly decentralized companies, however, the head office always makes these important decisions:

1. Products to be sold.
2. Prices for these products.

Actually, nothing is inherently wrong in either centralization or decentralization. Many companies use a varying combination of both to suit their needs. Even in highly centralized organization, the limitations can spur an individual sales representative to work creatively to succeed within the guidelines.

How Does Modern Management Theory Apply to You
As a Market Manager of Your Own Sales Territory?

Since we have stressed that a modern sales representative must learn to think and act like a manager right from the start, let us assume *you* are now, suddenly, a sales representative with our business firm, and start relating some management and sales/marketing theory to your specific needs and interests.

As we thus lead into specific techniques of planning your work and working your plan for your own sales territory, which will fill most of the chapters to follow, we should start thinking like and using the same vocabulary as some of the other key members of the overall management team: the president, or managing director; the vice-president, marketing, and the vice-president, sales; your sales manager; and you—the highly important local market manager.

Management at every level is concerned with seeing to it that the firm operates as efficiently and profitably as possible within the objective set. This is accomplished through four generally accepted *management functions*; planning, organizing, executing, and controlling. These are action processes essential to meeting objectives. They may occur simultaneously in different ways, at different managerial levels, at different times.

Planning is predetermining a course of action; it starts with the establishment of goals or objectives. It is essential to all activities, is performed by all levels of management and is a continuous, changing process. It involves, at all levels, the establishment of both long- and short-range objectives and includes formulation of policies, procedures, and programs through which the desired results are to be achieved. It involves all the functional areas of business, which we noted on page 30.

Organizing is the classifying and dividing of action work necessary to meet the objectives into manageable units. It involves grouping work activities into manageable units and delegating individual authority and responsibility, and like planning, is a continuous process.

Executing is the carrying out of the work necessary to success in meeting the objective. It is carried on simultaneously with the planning and organizing functions on a continuous basis.

Controlling is the constant checking of performance results against planned objectives. It involves control procedures, such as quarterly review of costs and sales versus budget; and control systems, such as manufacturing or shipping quality control checks.

The four functions are carried out simultaneously and with varying degrees of emphasis by the three broad levels of management found in any business firm or nonbusiness organization: top management, middle management, and operating management.

Top management consists of the board of directors, president, managing director and group vice-presidents, secretary, and treasurer, who are concerned with overall planning, policy-setting, organizing, staffing, directing, and controlling. *Middle management* consists of divisional departmental managers, such as production, research, traffic, marketing, and sales, who are responsible for executing, controlling, and supervising plans and policies of top management, and for control. *Operating management* consists of foremen, supervisors, district sales managers, and you, as a sales territory manager, who execute or carry out the activities essential to successful completion of the objectives (see Figure 3.9).

Later on, in Chapter 19, we shall relate these functions in greater detail to your specific role as manager of your own sales territory.

THE SALES/MARKETING STRATEGY AND PROGRAM

Now that we have an idea of the potential market or markets and the managerial organization necessary, we must consider our firm's product or service, in order to determine our overall sales/marketing strategy and the "marketing mix" to be employed in achieving our objectives.

Success of our strategy and program will depend on the proper *marketing mix* employed; the proper combination of four elements—the product, channels of distribution, pricing policies, and promotional methods. Since this is a book on salesmanship, not marketing, we will move quickly through this complicated subject. Our purpose is to give you, the sales representative, an overview understanding of these processes, in which you play such a vital role.

The Product—Its Nature and Classification

Product classification is based on the characteristics of our goods or products depending on their rate of consumption and tangibility and whether they are intended for either the consumer or industrial goods market (their nature).

FIGURE 3.9   Example of a Large Company Organization Chart. Showing levels of management authority and marketing and sales force organization. Smaller companies are organized in basically the same way.

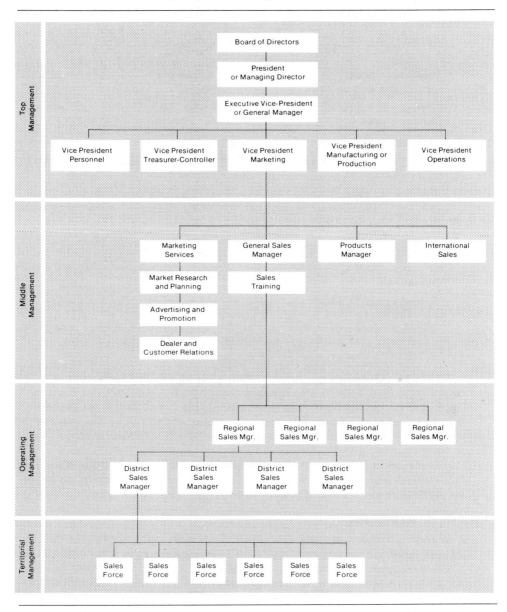

Consumer goods can include literally everything from A to Z (apples to zip-
pers). Professor Kotler[2] taking definitions from the American Marketing Association, has broken them down for ease of comprehension as follows:

2.   Philip Kotler, *Marketing Management,* 2nd ed. (Englewood Cliffs, N.J.: Prentice-Hall, Inc., 1972), pp.
95–96.

Durable Goods, Nondurable Goods, and Services

The first classification, which applies equally well to consumers' and industrial goods, distinguishes three categories of goods on the basis of their rate of consumption and tangibility:

Durable goods: tangible goods which normally survive many uses (examples: refrigerators, clothing).

Nondurable goods: tangible goods which normally are consumed in one or a few uses (examples: meat, soap).

Services: activities, benefits, or satisfactions which are offered for sale (examples: haircuts, repairs).

Convenience, Shopping, and Specialty Goods

A second goods classification, this one based not on the product's characteristics but on the consumer's shopping habits distinguishes three types of goods:

Convenience goods: Those consumers' goods which the customer usually purchases frequently, immediately, and with the minimum of effort in comparison and buying (examples: tobacco products, soap, newspapers).

Shopping goods: Those consumers' goods which the customer, in the process of selection and purchase, characteristically compares on such basis as suitability, quality, price, and style (examples: furniture, dress goods, used automobiles, and major appliances).

Specialty goods: Those consumers' goods with unique characteristics and/or brand identification for which a significant group of buyers are habitually willing to make a special purchasing effort (examples: specific brands and types of fancy goods, hi-fi components, photographic equipment, and men's suits).

Industrial goods can be classified, depending on the uses to which they are to be put, into these four major classifications: *production facilities and equipment* (such as major installations, minor equipment, plants and buildings); *production materials* (including raw materials and semimanufactured goods); *production supplies* (such as fuel oil and cleaning compounds); and *management materials* (such as office equipment and supplies).

Our purpose in presenting these classifications lies in the fact that knowledge of the degree and character of consumers buying needs and habits has an important bearing on the marketing strategy selected.

Channels of Distribution

A marketing channel, or channel of distribution, is the path traced in the direct or indirect transfer of ownership to a product, as it moves from a producer to the ultimate consumers or industrial users. The chart in Figure 3.10 clearly illustrates the most commonly employed marketing channels. Definition of distribution institutions in the left-hand column will be found in the Glossary of Terms in the back of this book.

Pricing Considerations

Pricing policies play an important part in the overall marketing strategy, especially in relation to promotional policies. For example, if a firm plans to sell a product at a higher retail price than competing products, and offers dealers a smaller discount than competition as well, it may have to spend more on advertising, sales

FIGURE 3.10   Marketing Channels Commonly Used in the Distribution of Industrial and Consumer Goods

	Industrial Market	Consumer Goods Market
Producers		
Agent Middlemen		
Wholesalers		
Retailers		
Industrial Users or Consumers		

Source: Edward W. Cundiff, Richard R. Still, and Norman A. P. Govoni, *Fundamentals of Modern Marketing* (Englewood Cliffs, N.J.: Prentice-Hall, Inc., 1973), p. 226.

promotion, and personal selling than the competition to offset these pricing disadvantages, in order to achieve planned sales objectives.

The Promotional Strategy or Mix

Having defined and briefly described the four-part "promotional mix" of promotion and selling in Chapter 2, we are aware that good promotional strategy employs all of them in combination. The proper combination or "mix" is that which will bring greatest results at least cost (see Figure 3.11).

Personal selling and advertising are the two most important of the four in terms of cost and market impact. Personal selling is nearly always supported by advertising, and often by publicity and sales promotion (especially point-of-purchase (POP) displays in retail stores or at merchandise marts). Personal selling is the most effective form of promotion, due to face-to-face contact and interpersonal communication between sales representative and prospective buyers, but it is also the most costly.

As an example of a highly successful sales/marketing strategy employing this four-part "promotional mix," let us consider Coca-Cola, one of the world's greatest sales to consumer success stories. It is a product whose quality never varies, yet continues to be sold ever more successfully year after year.

Keeping abreast of changing times and consumer tastes, Coca-Cola's sales/marketing strategy aims to make Coke drinkers out of each new generation of young people, as well as the young at heart (those 25 years of age, and even older), by getting them involved in a friendly and often emotional way with one of life's simple pleasures ("the real thing")—drinking a bottle of Coca-Cola.

Evidence of their advertising can be seen nearly everywhere; we will read in Case Studies 10-2 and 15-1 about Coca-Cola's dealer–sales-representatives in action.

SALES FORCE OBJECTIVES, SIZE, AND ORGANIZATION

For most companies, the sales force represents the most important ingredient in their entire sales/marketing strategy and promotional mix. The individual sales representative provides an irreplaceable link between the company and its customers. To many customers the sales representative *is* the company; to the company

FIGURE 3.11   The Overall Sales/Marketing Strategy:
"Marketing Mix and Promotional Mix"

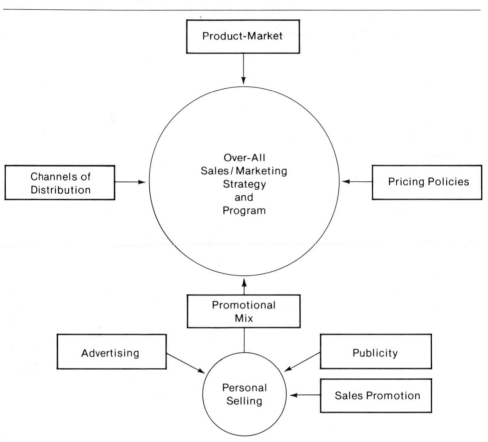

he represents not only the most effective source of sales, but the best source for rapid intelligence as to the needs, wants, and problems of the often rapid-changing marketplace. His monthly, weekly, and even daily sales successes and reports represent a barometer of the entire organizational success or failure in the competitive business world.

The objectives, size, organization, and responsibilities of individual company sales forces are as broad and varied as the thousands of different types of goods and services offered. The business a firm is in, the products it sells, and the level or type of customers it sells to determines its sales/marketing strategy and the educational level, specific skills, and abilities sought in hiring its sales representatives. It further determines the size and structure of the sales force, and the type sales training offered.

Role and Objectives

The role fulfilled by the sales force depends on such overall marketing objectives as the product markets sought, emphasis on both short- and long-range profits versus market share, and depth or degree of customer satisfaction desired. If rapid sales increases are sought, more sales call time may be needed to open new accounts. If a new product line is to be pushed, more personal sales time may have to be allocated to that line at the expense of current lines.

As well as planning how selling time will be utilized, companies plan their sales force objectives carefully in terms of overall *sales* and *budget* objectives. The overall sales-volume objective is broken down into specific goal-quotas by sales region, district, and individual sales representative. Expense budgets are broken down and assigned in the same manner. Profit objectives are made clear.

Let us assume, by way of example, that you are a sales representative working for a managerially-modern firm that thinks in terms of *management by objectives* (MBO). This entails joint participation by you and your sales manager in the establishment of clear and definite objectives for a given period. Normally done in advance of each sales year, the idea is to discuss objectives until an agreement on clear objectives is reached that is satisfactory both to you as sales territory manager and to your superiors.

Whether objectives are simply assigned, or worked out jointly MBO style, sales force objectives planning is normally concerned with *long-range objectives* and *short-term objectives*, or goals. For example, both your company and you may set as a long-range objective doubling sales and profits each five years. This breaks down to a 20 percent increase in sales and profits each year. Your immediate short-term objective is thus to increase sales and profits 20 percent in your specific territory next year. You can plan intermediate short-term goals within that framework simply as specific dollar and profit weekly, monthly, or quarterly objectives. You then plan a specific yearly *sales and expense budget* against which you can constantly check your progress. Figure 3.12 shows such a standard sales representative's annual sales and expense budget.

It is worth noting at this point that you as manager of your sales territory, in planning your territorial sales, expense, and profit objectives as illustrated above, are following the same procedure as your company president or managing director. You and he have a lot in common since you are both basically thinking and planning in the same way about your respective managerial assignments.

FIGURE 3.12 XYZ Company, Inc. Mid-Central Territory*
Annual Sales Representative's Budget† ($000 Omitted)

	1st quarter	1st 6 months	1st 9 months	Total year
SALES	20.0	40.0	60.0	80.0
Commission Income at 25 per cent	5.0	10.0	15.0	20.0
EXPENSES				
Salary	2.0	4.0	6.0	8.0
Travel & Entertainment	1.0	2.0	3.0	4.0
Promotion	.2	.4	.6	1.0
Total Expenses	3.2	6.4	9.6	13.0
Profit (before home office expenses)	1.8	3.6	5.4	7.0

*Includes states of Nebraska, Kansas, Oklahoma, Iowa, and Missouri.

†Example of a standard Sales Representative's Annual Sales and Expense Budget based on a territory with planned net sales of $80,000 by an $8,000 per year salaried sales representative.

Size and Organization

Most companies organize their sales force assignments along these three traditional lines:

Geographic territory.   Such territories, depending on actual or potential sales volume, may vary from one city block in New York City, to a single state, to a region such as six or more southeastern states. In establishing such territories, the number and clustering of current customers and prospects for efficient coverage (in both time and expense) is an important consideration, second only to profit-potential of the territory.

By Industry.   While assignment of a sales representative by industry may also fall within specific geographic areas, the idea is that he or she will sell only to a specified industry, such as to automobile repair shops, or to subdivisions of this or any other allied industry grouping. A major advantage of assigning sales representatives by industry lies in the fact that he or she gets to know the industry thoroughly.

By Product.   Such assignment by product line can also be made within a specific geographic area. Chief advantage of this form of assignment lies in the fact that the sales representative soon develops in-depth knowledge about his product. A disadvantage, if the company has several product lines, is that different sales representatives from the same company might call on the same prospect, and cause him to feel his time is being wasted through duplication of sales effort.

Other, more innovative types of specialized sales force organization used by some companies or organizations include such things as selling teams or special task forces. A selling team, assigned to a specified large account, might consist of a sales engineer, a marketing expert, and other experts as needed, to handle all customer requirements from selling through after sale servicing. Special task forces are often used to introduce a new product quickly to all accounts or prospects within a given area by telephone, special presentations, or sales calls. Sometimes the entire sales force is turned into a special task force, concentrating on nothing but one product, old or new, for one day, or an even longer specified period, at a time.

Whatever method is employed in sales force organization and assignment, the objective is that of earning profits in acceptable excess over the cost of getting the sales. The changing marketplace leads to constant re-evaluation, and often to sales-force changes of the type illustrated by the two case studies at the end of this chapter.

TRAINING, SUPERVISION, AND ASSIGNING OF SALES REPRESENTATIVES

The length of time a newly hired sales representative spends in training varies widely among companies. Certain industrial products and data processing sales representatives undergo perhaps the longest training programs. Due to the technical nature of their product or service, some of them are not on their own for many months. Most companies carry out their training programs in two or more locations: a typical case might be a formal training program at head office, then field training at one or more locations for a period of several weeks, then perhaps back to head office for a short review course that concludes formal training. Other companies concentrate on on-the-job training, with the new sales representative receiving his training from more experienced sales representatives or managers.

Some statistical figures concerning the average length of training for new sales representatives, compiled from a survey of over one hundred American companies, was published in 1974 by *Sales Management* magazine. Among its findings: "As expected, the industrial products companies have longer sales training periods. This is because their sales representatives sell more sophisticated products in a more complex environment. Service companies have the shortest training period—over 50 percent have programs of under six weeks. Note, however, that although 10 percent of the industrial products companies have training programs lasting more than one year, none of the consumer products firms do."[3]

FIGURE 3.13   Length Of Training Period For New Salesmen

	Type of Company		
Time Period	Industrial Products	Consumer Products	Services*
0 to 6 weeks	20%	34%	51%
Over 6 weeks to 3 months	24	38	9
Over 3 months to 6 months	13	14	15
Over 6 months to 12 months	33	14	21
Over 12 months	10	—	4
Total	**100%**	**100%**	**100%**
Median Training Period	**24 wks.**	**10 wks.**	**6 wks.**

*Includes insurance, financial, utilities, transportation, etc.

Source: *Sales Management, The Marketing Magazine,* January 7, 1974, p. 24.

Due to the high cost of recruiting and training sales representatives, companies pay careful attention to the content of training programs and training or teaching methods. Such programs normally feature knowledge of the company, its history, organization, and objectives; product knowledge, how and why it is produced and how consumers will use it; behavioral skills, or the knowledge of how and why different types customers buy different products; comparisons with competition; how to make effective presentations and close sales; and the mechanics of effective sales territory planning and follow-through, and managing (sales and expenses) for profitable results.

Training in, or teaching of, these things involves lecture-demonstrations, audio-visual methods of all sorts (slides, overhead projector, closed-circuit television, play-back cassettes), programmed learning and teaching machines. In-class role playing, field trips, practical work with experienced sales representatives, and constant testing are among other methods employed to increase the speed of learning, depth of knowledge, and degree of information-retention.

Once a sales representative is assigned to his sales territory or function, careful and formal supervision by sales management follows. This we shall consider more deeply in chapters to come.

SUMMARY

Having learned in Chapter 1 the meaning of salesmanship, the kinds of careers selling offers, and the degree of professional knowledge necessary for successful selling, we presented in Chapter 2 and Chapter 3 a broad but comprehensive overview of sales/marketing—what it is, how it is carried on in the business world, and how you as sales representative relate to it.

3. *Sales Management, The Marketing Magazine* (January 7, 1974), p. 24.

Since customer/society-oriented selling is based on satisfying consumer needs and wants (and to give lasting satisfaction and benefit society, don't forget), we first spent some time in this chapter analyzing what changes will occur in the marketplace over the next decade. We concluded that expected changes in (1) the age mix of household population and (2) the distribution of spending power are the two most important areas of change to sales/marketing people. Charts were presented to clearly illustrate projected changes in these two and other areas for the United States.

Considering this as completed market analysis forecast, we studied how a company organizes itself for profitable selling; first via overall managerial organization and function, then via the sales/marketing strategy and program. As part of the latter, we studied the necessity of product nature and classification, possible channels of distribution, pricing considerations, and the four-part promotional strategy or mix (advertising, publicity, sales promotion, and—most important of all—personal selling). These are all essential to getting the right product to the right place, at the right price, and at the right time.

Finally, we considered the sales force necessary to achieve the sales/marketing objective; its role, size, organization, and the training, supervision, and assigning of individual sales representatives.

Wherever possible, we tried to relate principles and some techniques to your own highly important role on the marketing/management team: that of individual market manager of your own sales territory or responsibility.

The two case studies that follow will help tie together in a practical way many of the things we have studied up to this point.

CHAPTER REVIEW

CONCEPTS TO REMEMBER*

_____ objective   _____ management by   _____ promotional strategy
    (or goal)   objectives (MBO)   or mix
_____ product/goods   _____ channels of   _____ industrial product
     distribution   (or goods)
_____ management   _____ consumer product   _____ determinants of
     functions   (or goods)   consumer demand

*For memory reinforcement, fill in the page number or numbers where these terms were described in this chapter.

QUESTIONS FOR ANALYSIS AND DISCUSSION

1. In terms of market forecasting and analysis, what are the two most important determinants of consumer demand? Of these two, which is more important, and why?
2. What is the difference, if any, in sales/marketing terms, between goods and products?
3. What do we mean by the statement "many companies favor decentralized sales policies," and what two decisions does top management always reserve for itself, even if it employs decentralized sales policies?
4. How would you define each of the four generally accepted functions of management? Are they carried out simultaneously or separately? Who carries them out?
5. Suppose you formed a company to manufacture hammers.
   a. How would you classify hammers as a product?
   b. Through what channels of distribution would you sell them?

    c. What considerations would affect the price you put on your hammer?

    d. What promotional strategy or mix would you employ to sell them?

    e. How would you train your sales representatives to sell hammers?

6. Would you prefer working as a sales representative with a company that plans in terms of management by objectives (MBO)? Why? What three objectives does annual MBO preplanning involve?

7. What do we mean by "product classification"? Why is it important, from a sales/marketing point of view, to classify products?

8. What overall factors determine the role to be fulfilled by the sales force of any company?

Case Study 3–1

MONARCH PROVES THAT FEWER SALES REPRESENTATIVES CAN SELL MORE— THROUGH SELECTIVE, TARGET SELLING[4]

Monarch Marketing Division, part of Pitney-Bowes Corp. retail systems group, sells tags, labels, and related equipment to retail and industrial accounts. It increased sales 19 percent to about $50 million in 1972, plus a further 12 percent increase in 1973, by *reducing* their sales force from 100 to 80.

As reported by *Sales Management* magazine, Monarch's sales representatives had been calling on thousands of customers. A market study showed that 76 percent of these accounts were unprofitable. A new marketing strategy and promotion mix was developed, which called for catalogue mailings only to this 76 percent, unless they specifically asked to see a sales representative for any reason.

The reduced sales force was reorganized; to the retail and industrial sales forces was added a third specialized sales force calling on major accounts only. Sales representatives in the retail and industrial sales forces now sell to just 75 to 100 customers apiece, and major accounts sales representatives call on as few as 2 and no more than 27 customers. This sales force realignment immediately resulted in increased efficiency and sales.

QUESTIONS FOR WRITTEN REPORTS OR CLASS DISCUSSION

1. Do you think Monarch would have achieved sales increases had it reduced its sales force without first making a careful market study? Why?

2. What do we mean by the statement "76 percent of these accounts were unprofitable"?

3. What do we mean by the term "major accounts"?

4. Into what product classification do you feel Monarch tags and labels fit? What is the basis for your determination?

4. Extracted from "Pitney-Bowes: Now For the Good News," *Sales Management*, December 10, 1973, p. 3. Reprinted by permission from *Sales Management, The Marketing Magazine.*

HOW A NEW SALES/MARKETING STRATEGY, REVAMPED SALES FORCE, AND SPECIALIZED SALES APPROACHES REGAINED LOST SALES LEAD FOR DYMO PRODUCTS[5]

Dymo Products is one of the ten domestic divisions and nine foreign operations of San Francisco-based Dymo Industries. Founded in 1958 as the original company (now a division) it soon had an instant success with its label-spewing vinyl-tape gun and other products sold through a distributor-oriented three-part sales force: (1) retail sales representatives, who dealt primarily with mass merchandisers and other high-volume consumer outlets; (2) commercial sales representatives, who sold to the stationery and office supply trade; and (3) a few industrial sales representatives, who called on industrial supply houses.

All of these sales representatives were calling on distributors, not on end-users. But by the mid-1960s when 3M, Avery Products, and Dennison invaded various segments of the label-making and tape-writing market, Dymo's market share, originally 100 percent, had dropped below 50 percent.

After careful market research, Dymo, in 1970 changed its sales/marketing strategy and reorganized and *enlarged* its sales force as part of a completely revamped promotional mix. Packaging was redesigned to develop a family appearance, the advertising budget was tripled, and the sales force, now end-user oriented, reorganized into two parts: (1) a consumer sales division, whose end users are the general public, especially housewives and hobbyists—and which sells to supermarket chains, discount houses, and other consumer retailers; and (2) a systems sales division, whose end users are office and industrial personnel and which sells through stationers and office and industrial supply houses.

Growth of the revamped consumer sales division was rapid; sales produced by the twenty-four-man sales force increased 25 percent in the first year, 1972, and 38 percent in 1973.

But it was through the newly created systems division that greatest success was scored. The word "systems" is important, because what this division's forty-five sales representatives stress in their sales presentations is that they are offering a system of communication to end users. By integrating a sign maker, a variety of tapes, and accessories like door plates and desk signs, a fundamental signs and labels system was created.

The systems sales division has two primary markets: (1) commercial users, such as offices, banks, and insurance companies, all of which need to label files, storage bins, equipment, and work areas; and (2) industrial users, such as assembly lines, parts depots, and maintenance shops, where the need for labeling is even greater. To reach these, three kinds of sales specialists were created: (1) the commercial sales representative, who spends 70 to 75 percent of his time at stationery stores and the balance calling on offices; (2) the industrial sales representative, who spends about 30 percent of his time calling on industrial supply houses, the balance calling on their customers; and (3) the end-user specialist, who calls on industrial end-users only.

5. Extracted from "Dymo's Deliverance," *Sales Management*, November 12, 1973, pp. 27–30. Reprinted by permission from *Sales Management, The Marketing Magazine*.

Although any one of these specialists can generate a major order, all sales go through the appropriate Dymo distributors. Dymo Products intends to continue building a force of specialized sales representatives for these different markets, because each requires different types of people and different kinds of skills and knowledge. The industrial sales representative, for example, has to go in and survey needs and make proposals. It is in this industrial market that Dymo sees greatest future growth potential.

These overall changes in marketing strategy—increased advertising through special interest (e.g., hobbyist) magazines, television, and company/dealer cooperative advertising; in-store demonstrations; and revamped sales force and sales approaches—have increased Dymo's overall market to perhaps 65 percent since 1971. The company estimates that what they and their competitors together sold over the past fifteen years represents only about 12 percent of the market. With virtually everyone a prospect for one or another of its products, Dymo sales representatives, geared to their end-user sales approach, will be trying hard in the years ahead to reach every potential prospect.

QUESTIONS FOR WRITTEN REPORTS OR CLASS DISCUSSION

1. What was the one major 1971 sales-approach change that has so greatly affected Dymo's sales increases since? Explain the differences in sales approach between the old and the new.
2. Would Dymo's products be classified as durable goods or nondurable goods —or would they represent services? What are the differences between these three types of product classifications?
3. Chart on blackboard or paper the channels of distribution employed from producer to end user employed by the post-1971 Dymo (a) consumer sales division and (b) systems sales division. Explain the distribution differences between the two divisions.
4. What sales advantages do you feel Dymo sales representatives enjoy by offering a "system of communication" in selling their variety of tapes and accessories, as compared to presenting each item individually?

SALES PROBLEM 3–1

HOW SHOULD ONE PLAN AND ORGANIZE FOR SELLING TO THE SPANISH-ORIGIN MARKET IN THE UNITED STATES?

Let us assume you have been appointed exclusive United States distributor for a Spanish-language edition of this textbook. You have just obtained an advance report of a nationwide study of the U.S. Spanish-origin population made in 1973 as part of the U.S. Department of Commerce, Bureau of Economic Analysis, Current Population Survey.[6] Your first task is to study the market, forecast sales potential for your product, and plan how to sell it—both in terms of sales/marketing strategy and sales force organization. The report shows these facts:

6. Factual material noted above was extracted from "Spanish-Origin Market in U.S. is Younger, City-Oriented Male," *Commerce Today*, May 27, 1973, p. 14.

The nation's Spanish-origin population totaled 10.6 million as of March 1973. This includes 6.3 million persons of Mexican origin; 1.5 million of Puerto Rican origin; 700,000 of Cuban origin; and 2 million of Central or South American or other Spanish origin.

Median income of families with a head of Spanish origin was $8,180 in 1972, about 8 percent more than the previous year.

The U.S. Spanish-origin population is about eight years younger than the rest of the population. The Spanish-origin median age was 20.1 years in March 1973, compared with 28.4 years for persons not of Spanish origin. Persons of Mexican and Puerto Rican origin were even younger, each group having a median age of 18.8 years.

Most families with head of Spanish origin live in metropolitan areas. In March 1973, over 1.9 million such families, or 83 percent of the total, lived in metropolitan centers.

There is a higher percentage of single men than single women among Spanish-origin persons fourteen years old and over. One-third of such men were single in 1973, but only about one-fourth of the women.

Families with a head of Spanish origin were likely to be large. In March 1973, these families averaged 4.0 persons; over 57 percent had four or more members per family.

Education attainment levels have been rising dramatically for persons of Spanish origin; one-half of young adults twenty-five to twenty-nine years old were at least high school graduates, compared with only one-fourth of those forty-five to sixty-four years old.

QUESTIONS FOR WRITTEN REPORTS OR CLASS DISCUSSION

1. How do these figures relate to the U.S. population in general as compared to United States changing marketplace information and figures presented in the chapter material?
2. What, briefly, would you set as your basic managerial long- and short-range sales planning objectives to sell your Spanish edition of the text?
3. Would you consider this product to be in the durable or nondurable goods category? Who would be your end customers? Depending on your answers, what marketing channel or channels of distribution would you employ in selling it?
4. What do you see as the role, size, and organization of your sales force? Where would you seek sales applicants; how would you train them for selling? Would you employ centralized or decentralized sales policies for your sales force? Why?
5. Prepare a simple model annual sales representative's budget for one of your sales representatives to illustrate how a similar one would be set up for all your sales staff individually.

buying behavior and the psychology of selling

When you have mastered the content of this chapter, you should be able to:

Define the terms *consumer, consumer* (or buying) *behavior, consumer research, behavioral science studies, needs, wants, buying process,* and the *self-concept theory of buying behavior.*

List the most prominent groups that are users, or potential users, of consumer research.

Describe the two basic motivations that cause people to buy anything, and some of the sub-motives affecting each.

List four basic common denominators of desire upon which individual needs and wants are based.

List the three major buyer groups within which each prospective buyer falls, to which different sales appeals may be addressed.

Summarize the meaning of the statements (1) "the selling process is a buying process," and (2) "the buying process is a decision-making process."

Summarize how a sales representative can influence buying decisions, and what he must always keep in mind in understanding what makes people buy.

Why do people buy what they do when they do? Sales representatives have been trying to figure this out from the earliest days. It was not until the 1960s, however, that consumer behavior research became highly developed in the United States. Since then much has been learned about the subject as a result of concepts, theories, and findings drawn from various social science disciplines; notably economics, psychology, sociology, and social anthropology.

While no final, perfect system for predicting buyer behavior has evolved, enough has been learned to greatly assist sales representatives in understanding what makes people buy. We will learn in this chapter, for example, that people do not buy without a reason or reasons. They are motivated to buy basically (1) by *internal*, rational, and emotional motivations, and (2) by *external forces*. As a sales representative, you should remember that whatever they finally do or decide is due to their reasons and not yours.

THE SELLING PROCESS IS ACTUALLY A BUYING PROCESS

The modern concept of salesmanship holds that the selling process is actually a buying process. Because the final buying decision is made in the mind of the buyer, the function of the sales representative is to help the buyer discover his needs, wants, and problems, and to help him to fulfill or solve them through buying that sales representative's product or service. In order to persuade the prospect that the product or service will fulfill his desires, the sales representative must present the advantages and benefits so that they meet the prospect's motivational needs. He must build his buying appeals around positive (desire for gain) or negative (fear of loss) selling points. The more he knows about the internal and external reasons the prospect thinks and acts the way he does, the easier it is for him to direct his appeals to the desires and self-interest of the buyer.

PERSUASION REQUIRES BOTH SYMPATHY AND EMPATHY

Persuasion lies at the heart of helping the prospect find fulfillment through the buying process. Once he is persuaded that he wants something, he will overcome all obstacles to get it. The great challenge to you as a sales representative is to convince him, through persuasion, to take buying action now.

If you want to persuade a person to do something, chances of agreement are greater if the two of you can understand one another. Understanding leads to acceptance and interaction, argument is averted, and you have a better chance of persuading the prospect to accept your point of view. The burden of trying to reach a sufficient level of understanding so that he will accept you with confidence and listen to your presentation falls upon you.

Both sympathy and empathy are important traits in creating this level of understanding and confidence with your prospect. You may feel sympathetic toward his point of view but still not be able to put yourself mentally in his shoes. Empathy, as used by modern behavioral scientists, is the ability to detect how the prospect feels and what his attitudes and opinions are. You not only understand how he feels but also can mentally and emotionally see the situation from his viewpoint.

Having empathy does not mean that you have to agree with all his opinions or conclusions, but it does mean that you must be able to appreciate, respect, and understand them. This feeling of empathy and an ability to project it to your prospect are two of the most necessary traits for you to have to succeed in selling. You can understand all the psychological and other scientific reasons why people buy and you can master all the techniques of persuasion, but you will not be a successful sales representative unless you can feel and project empathy. Fortunately, it is, for the most part, a learned quality.

CONSUMER BEHAVIOR:
ITS DEFINITION AND DEVELOPMENT AS A STUDY

Consumer behavior is the applied, multidisciplinary field of study concerned with the understanding, explaining, and predicting of human actions in the consumption role.

The most prominent users and potential users of consumer research are sales/marketing people. The other main user group includes government and social-action agencies interested in establishing or affecting public policy decisions relevant to consumer affairs. Examples of the latter are the Federal Trade Commission, and such privately based organizations as Action for Children's Television, which seeks changes in children's television programming and advertising policies.

Consumer behavior, utilizing findings from several areas of the social sciences, became a phenomenon of the 1960s, as a response, among others, to the widespread acceptance by sales/marketing people of the marketing concept which had evolved during the 1950s.

Along with *economics*, other social science disciplines involved in behavioral studies include *psychology*, as it concerns communication and attitude measurements; *sociology*, which deals with group behavior, social class, symbols and images, and group influences; and *social anthropology*, which investigates social systems and status, among other things.

WHY DO PEOPLE BUY:
FINDINGS FROM THE BEHAVIORAL SCIENCES

Perhaps the question, "Why do people buy?" should really be, "Why do people behave or act the way they do?" Sleeping, eating, working, and buying are but some of the dozens of human actions that scientists have studied over the years. Behavioral scientists study man as a social being—how he acts, how he reacts, the status he seeks, the role he assumes, the motivations and feelings that drive him. Scientists of different disciplines within this broad framework study various practical aspects of human behavior in areas such as communication, motivation, individual and group behavior, problem-solving, decision-making, and creativity.

The first formal explanations of buyer behavior were advanced by *economists*. They considered the subject from the point of view that man is a rational buyer with price as his strongest motivation; that all things being equal he will rationally and predictably buy maximum value at lowest price. The conclusion was that he ought to do this or that rationally if manipulated or guided toward selected sets of buying alternatives. While this theory might explain, for example, why a consumer might purchase a television set from one dealer instead of another (the one offering it at lowest price), it did not explain why he decided to purchase an RCA brand over a Sony, or a different size, model, or color.

Sales/marketing people—recognizing that there were many markets, not just one homogenous market for most products—soon concluded that consumer buying resulted not just from economic considerations, but from other reasons. Motivation research, led by its founder Ernest Dichter, seemed for awhile to indicate potential for real understanding of consumer buying and how to manipulate it. After a few years, however, its employment of depth interviews and projective tests were recognized as being a research tool of limited predictive ability. Concurrently, evidence had shown that motivational concepts play only a limited role in explaining consumer behavior.

Initially, most consumer research tended to be based around specific behavioral concepts, such as social class or reference groups. Since the late 1960s, however, emphasis has been on more process-oriented, or comprehensive-integrated research combining several different areas; for example, attitudes, perception, and social class. This view sees the buyer as a whole person feeling many emotions, such as love, joy, and boredom; and facing many problems, such as work and social environment; all of which ultimately involve his buying decisions and consumption. Thus a consumer is not just buying toothpaste, but rather solving the problem of oral hygiene; not merely buying a sports car for transportation, but rather fulfilling inner desires for status and recognition.

Behavioral scientists have concluded, through assumptions, insights, and empirical findings that still need considerable validation, that a buyer behaves both rationally and irrationally (or emotionally). These conclusions clash with the earlier ones of the economists; but behavioral scientists have yet to outline any one single theory explaining why people buy what they do when they do.

Since there is no single unified concept of buying theory, sales representatives find themselves caught in the middle of conflicting theories and sets of data about what people buy. Discovery of a perfect system for predicting consumer behavior is the goal of this aspect of behavioral science studies. Their findings to date, however, no matter how imperfect, can greatly assist sales representatives in understanding what might influence or motivate a person to buy, as we shall discuss.

Why Do People Act the Way They Do?

Certain basic differences among people cause them to think and act the way they do. National, cultural, and social backgrounds cause different individuals or groups to have different sets of values. Basic personality traits and habits, when combined with a given background and set of values, create fundamental differences among people. These differences influence behavior to such a basic degree that it may be impossible for a sales representative to overcome objections rooted in deep bias. He can influence attitudes and certain habits however.

People not only are different from each other, but also can, as individuals, act differently at different times. For example, a prospect whose office air conditioner has broken down on the hottest day of the year, who is tired from a sleepless night, who has missed lunch because of your visit, and who has a bad cold probably reacts to your visit differently from the way he would on a more normal day.

A sales representative tries, through questioning, listening, and observing to understand the personal, emotional, and social feelings of the prospect, and he adjusts his behavior and appeals to cope with them. Assuming a favorable physical environment and a certain degree of empathy, you as a sales representative face prospects who have certain basic motivations common to all men or women. With an understanding of these motivations, you can make well planned appeals and can present incentives for decision and action.

Buying Behavior Is Based on Needs and Wants

Human behavior, including buying behavior, involves a complicated series of stimulus-and-response reactions to many factors or motives. These motives may be expressed or unexpressed and are based upon deep-rooted needs or more openly felt wants. *Needs* operating just below the level of consciousness, are sometimes difficult to recognize since they were either inherited or learned. Needs may be deep, inwardly felt desires for love, affection, security, or safety—desires not even understood by the prospect himself.

Wants, on the other hand, are easier than needs to spot since they operate closer to the conscious level and reflect positive desires (pleasure, profit, approval) or negative desires (loss, disapproval, inconvenience). Wants are more broadly defined and psychological than needs and include, from a buying point of view, consumer desires, inward motivations, personal objectives, and mental satisfactions. When someone buys something, he psychologically satisfies both a need and a want. As products have changed, so has the consumer, or buyer. An average buyer today has more money than those of earlier years and normally has already fulfilled his basic needs for food, clothing, and shelter. He can now buy what he wants rather than what he simply needs. He no longer has to buy a particular product; a whole host of different products will satisfy his needs. He buys a specific product because it will provide him with certain mental or physical satisfactions.

As a result of this broadening of motivations, buying behavior has altered. Modern buyers want more than a mere listing of product features; they want to know how and why the product will benefit them. They are looking not only for what products can do but also for what they mean in personal, social, and cultural terms. They respond to buying appeals denoting the images and symbols that reflect their attitudes and satisfy their personal feelings and wants. Thus the professional sales representative today has to study and understand how his product or service can satisfy wants as well as basic needs. What are some of these basic needs and wants that motivate human buying behavior?

Four Basic Denominators of Desire

Motivational research by behavioral scientists has established four basic common denominators of desire upon which most needs and wants are based. Appeals to these can help you, as a sales representative, to strike a responsive chord in the prospect.

Physiological or biological needs. These are basic needs or desires such as for food, clothing, shelter, warmth, or money with which to buy these things. People often rationalize these desires to buy what they feel they must have to live comfortably. Given the slightest justification for considering a product necessary, they buy. Until they are reasonably well satisfied, these basic needs take precedence over all others. Once these needs are satisfied, however, other needs and wants become important motivators.

Social needs. Social needs are often called affiliation needs and include the needs to be accepted by other people and to belong to and to be accepted as part of the social group with which one desires to be identified. Psychologists have compiled long lists of social needs, among them needs of the individual to be with other people, to feel superior, to have recognition, and sometimes to dominate. If a product promises to raise our own or our neighbor's estimation of us, we are tempted to buy it.

Self-fulfillment needs. The desires to accomplish or achieve something, to do something worthwhile, and to enjoy the better things in life are all examples of self-fulfillment needs.

Psychological needs. Psychological needs include the needs for stability, or consistency, in ideas and beliefs; and the desires for personal, psychological integrity and individuality, and for an orderly environment. One such basic need is for safety; people tend to buy things, such as insurance, to ward off injury or misfortune.

HOW CAN YOU FIND OUT WHAT MOTIVATES A BUYER?

The big problem for you as a sales representative is to figure out what motivates your prospect. It is not enough to simply ask him because most people either do not know what really motivates them or give a rational answer when the real motive might be a deep-seated, highly irrational desire. Prospects generally have two reasons for buying or not buying—a stated reason and the real reason. Your very difficult task is to find out the real reason.

In most sales situations, several factors are influencing the buyer's decision. One basic factor may be that he does not like to spend his money; another, that he may resent the idea of a sales representative trying to sell him something, even if he really wants to make an affirmative decision. Relatively few prospects have a clearly expressed motive for buying; most have only a vaguely felt desire that they ought to buy or might be interested in considering buying.

It is your job to determine, through questioning, listening, and observing, what the prospect's real motivations or wants are and to build your sales presentation around them. Perhaps the most deeply rooted need of most people today is for personal welfare or a feeling of adequacy. If you have empathy enough to bring such deeply felt needs to the surface, you can possibly give prospects new perceptions about themselves and their environment. This may not only result in a sale but also actually aid them in their search for a feeling of adequacy.

Once you have determined the real reason your prospect wants to buy, you may have to consider your ethical and moral responsibilities as a sales representative. The power of persuasion, combined with psychological insight, sometimes is so great that experienced sales representatives can discover the real motivator or reason without the prospect realizing it himself. You may inwardly feel this need to be ridiculous, but your empathy should tell you that it is a real one for that individual, no matter how unimportant it may seem to you. You have the obligation to serve him out of genuine respect for his personality. And you have the serious professional responsibility of fulfilling this need by providing something of value.

WHAT MOTIVATES A BUYER TO ACT?

We noted in the beginning of this chapter that people are motivated to buy by external forces and internal forces, which include rational and emotional motivations. What do we mean by these concepts, and how can understanding them help make you an effective sales representative?

External Forces

External forces motivating buying behavior are those factors that make up an individual's social environment. These include nationality, geographical area of residence, race, religion, education, occupation, income, the products themselves, their price, and the effect of advertising. A consumer, or buyer, is a product of his cultural and social environment. His logic, value judgments, and thrift, as projected in his purchases, reflect what he believes to be culturally and socially acceptable. Findings of the behavioral sciences indicate that a man's attitudes and behavior are influenced by several layers of society. These include the culture and subculture in which he lives, his social class, his friends, his business associates, and his family.

The culture in which a man lives exerts a strong control over his attitudes and actions, and a subculture such as religion can further affect his attitudes. An Arabic-speaking, Egyptian Moslem for example, may have attitudes toward a given benefit or need entirely different from those of a Brooklyn-born, Irish Catholic.

Social classes within cultures also play an important part in determining attitudes. Upper-class people, for example, may place great value on expensive status symbols such as big homes in fashionable suburbs, even if they cannot afford them. Lower-class people may take great pride in personal maintenance of their own small, paid-for home in a less expensive neighborhood.

Individuals are strongly influenced by the groups with which they most often come in contact, such as close friends, fellow workers, neighbors, and family. This trend may be growing everywhere; it is certainly obvious in the wild teenage fashion and taste changes that sweep the world so fast and so frequently. The two most important external forces that may affect your prospect's buying behavior are his family and the organization for which he works. If you plan to influence his decision, you must ascertain their importance and plan your appeal accordingly.

The family probably plays the most important single role in an individual's early attitude formation and in determining his life-long buying behavior. Teenagers often rebel against their families' social values but often accept these again later. These family attitudes have a very important place in decisions on all family purchases.

It is important to discover who in the family is the decision maker for different products. In American families, the wife influences most of the buying and actually spends most of the family money. She usually makes the decision on buying a home, appliances, furniture, encyclopedia sets, and clothes, and on planning vacations. The husband usually makes the decisions on buying automobiles, sporting equipment, and insurance policies. The child is exerting an increasing influence on American family buying habits, because of sheer numbers and the fact that the family is often child-oriented. Giant food manufacturers, among others, vie on television and through packaging for the attention of the youngster in the house.

The organization to which a businessman or purchasing officer belongs plays a very important part in his buying decisions. The organization pays him to make purchases that affect the organization and often judges his effectiveness by the profits made through resale of the item or by the savings effected through the purchase. The organizational buyer usually is strongly rational in his decision-making. He is impressed by factors such as cost, quality, dependability, and follow-up service. But he also has his private thoughts and feelings, and if a persuasive sales representative can show him that it is in his own best personal interest as well as that of the company to buy a given product, he responds favorably.

Internal Forces

Internal forces motivating buying behavior include an almost endless list of physical and psychological variables generally classified into two groups: (1) rational motivations and (2) irrational, or emotional, motivations.

A prospect normally falls into one of three buyer groups, to whom you have to address appeals on different grounds. He can be an individual buyer, a family buyer, or an organizational buyer. But no matter which he is, you have to discover and appeal to his buying motives. He may make his decision alone or be influenced by or through consultation with others. Whichever is the case, rational motives, emotional motives, or a combination of both affect his buying behavior.

Rational buying motives. Rational buying motives include not only the immediate monetary cost but also all long-range costs affecting the buyer —durability, depreciation, length of usage, degree of labor necessary, and ultimate benefit. Businesspeople are usually more rational in their buying motives than are other buyers, but they too can be swayed by personal, emotional motives.

Emotional buying motives. Emotional buying motives cover a wide list of irrational motives including impulses, habits, and drives. These motives are varied in nature, and almost anyone could compile a long list of them. We discuss here some of the more generally recognized ones.

Ease and convenience. People like to be physically comfortable. They like a soft bed, an easy-riding car, good food, labor-saving devices, and innumerable conveniences at home, at work, and in recreation.

Profit and thrift.   Some people like to make money; others, to save money. The purchases they make enable them to gain monetary or personal benefits or to acquire better things at lower ultimate cost. A businessman may buy things he can resell at a profit. A housewife may purchase an item on sale now because it will cost more later.

Safety and protection.   People generally fear loss of life, health, friends, job, reputation, and comfort. They yearn for security, and as they grow older this fear becomes greater. They seek security through the purchase of homes, insurance policies, investments, locks for doors, and thousands of other items.

Play and relaxation.   Vacations, sports, and leisure-time activities are part of the good life desired by most people. Participant sports create desire for items such as new clothing, golf clubs, and boats. Spectator sports and recreational activities create desire for automobiles, books, television sets, and magazines.

Pride and prestige.   People like to feel important, to attain status among their peers, to keep up with the times, to achieve respectability, or to indulge in expensive status symbols. Once physical needs are filled, social wants become important. They create desire for education, theater and the arts, home improvements, and expensive home decorations, among other things.

Love and affection.   This category includes a sense of duty, a love of family and society, and a desire to see justice done to oneself and others. Many items purchased daily by millions fulfill desires motivated by love and affection.

Sex and romance.   This drive occurs in both young and old and involves pleasing the opposite sex. Cosmetics, wedding rings, dancing lessons, and wedding anniversary gifts are only some of the items purchased daily the world over to fulfill these emotional needs.

Adventure and excitement.   People are curious; they like new things, new experiences, and new places to go. They translate these feelings into purchases of the latest clothing fashions, new books, vacation cruises, and countless impulse-purchase items.

Other random emotional buying motives.   These include performance and durability, esthetic pleasure, and the urge to create. You, as an alert sales representative, must learn to identify the dominant emotional motives of the customer and how to appeal to them.

THE BUYING PROCESS IS
A DECISION-MAKING PROCESS

The Western, or Free World, marketing concept is based on the idea that human wants are endless in their variety and that the consumer himself selects the wants he will satisfy. Your product is often only one means among many for satisfying these wants. In addition people basically do not like to make decisions or to feel any need to make them now. Your job as sales representative is to translate these needs into the action of a purchase decision.

Many things may lead to a customer's actual purchase decision regarding your product. He may become aware of the product through advertising, may read about it in magazines or newspapers, or may hear about it through friends or business acquaintances. In effect he often moves through various stages—product awareness, knowledge, brand preference, and need conviction—before he reaches the point at which he considers gratifying his needs through purchase.

The purchase decision itself often involves a whole set of decisions. These decisions are based first on basic external or internal motives, which are orientations toward a basic product or service and, second, on the selective motivations, which are orientations toward a certain type or brand of product. Thus, the buying-decision process has two steps that narrow choice. The first leads to a choice of product or service in the broad sense as offering the fulfillment of or the solution to the felt need, want, or problem. The second step leads to acceptance of a specific brand item as offering the best fulfillment or solution in terms of benefit and value.

As a customer-oriented sales representative, your task is to explain convincingly, through demonstration and proof if possible, how your specific product or service best fills or solves the prospect's needs or problems. You should frame all your selling points around his interests and desires and direct your appeals toward what he stands to gain by having the product or what he may lose by not having it. To learn how to accomplish this goal, we shall examine briefly one key theory of buying behavior, the self-concept theory.

THE SELF-CONCEPT THEORY

This theory of buying behavior is one of the best-integrated attempts to relate consumer variables to an individual's self-concept: his perception of himself and his ego. It is based on the belief that a buyer perceives a product he would like to own in terms of its meaning to himself and others. For example, if a young male college student sees himself as aggressive and masculine he might buy a bright red, dual-exhaust sports car as an expression of how he sees himself and would like others to view him. In other words, he would see this particular car as somehow an extension of his own personality.

This theory hinges on the concept that an individual's real self and his ideal self are different, as seen in these four ways.

1. *Self-image*—how he sees himself.
2. *Ideal self*—how he would like to see himself.
3. *Looking-glass self*—the way he thinks others see him.
4. *Real self*—the way he really is.

A person's self-image or self-concept is a basic key to any form of behavior, buying or otherwise. His real self and ideal self are two different things, and throughout his life he strives to make his self-image and ideal self coincide with the way he would like others to see him. His ideal self is the goal toward which he strives, and he constantly changes his concepts throughout his life. This drive toward a steadily more satisfying self-concept is natural and proper from a mental health point of view.

This constant striving to match his real self with his ideal self influences his buying behavior, with motivation the driving force behind it.

The automobile sales representative, in our example, would try through questioning and observation to "size up" his young potential buyer. He would mentally ask himself: "How does this man see himself, how would he like to see himself, and have others see him?" Only by ascertaining this can he most effectively present that specific bright red, dual-exhaust sports car as a means of fulfilling this particular buyer's wants and desire.

The emotional buying motive of ego-gratification is based on this self-concept theory of human behavior. If you, as a sales representative, want to help your prospect fill his needs or solve his problems, you have to present the benefits of your product or service in terms of his attitudes and expressed or felt desires. With your knowledge, understanding, and empathy in interaction or communication, you should be able to build your appeals around his ego-gratification. In other words, find out what he wants, and present your product as a fulfillment in terms of his desires.

As we will discuss in detail in Chapter 12, you can employ several types of suggestive persuasion to help him see himself enjoying the benefits of your product in whatever way he would like to visualize it. But you should always keep on tap rational reasons to support your suggestions. A woman may desire a fur coat for prestige, status, or other inner needs but may feel guilty about spending so much money for it. If you can point out that the price is very low for the quality or that prices may go up next year, you can help provide rational reasons to justify the purchase.

HOW CAN YOU INFLUENCE BUYING DECISIONS?

In order to influence a buying decision you have to determine through empathy, questioning, listening, and observing on what the decision is to be based. Realizing that your prospective buyer is affected by both rational and emotional wants and motivations, you should strive to see things from his point of view and to help solve his problems and to fulfill his wants with valuable and beneficial products or services.

You can persuade him to accept your product through appeals to reason or emotion or through a combination of both. In most cases you make a sale by successful appeals to emotional wants or needs, reinforced by a careful outlining of benefits to be derived so that the buyer feels rationally justified in making the buying decisions. We shall be discussing, in far greater depth, how to put this theory into practice in the following chapters.

SUMMARY

We have tried to determine why people buy what they do when they do. We have concluded that they are motivated by internal wants and motivations, by other rational and emotional motives, and by external forces. These wants create problems, and the sales representative's task is to persuade and convince prospects that his product or service offers the best possible solution.

A successful sales representative develops the empathy to discover through questioning, listening, and observing what the customer feels. He then adjusts his behavior and addresses his appeals to take into consideration the prospect's needs, wants, and problems.

Concluding that the selling process is actually a buying process, we noted that consumer behavior has become, since the 1960s, an increasingly important area of research by behavioral scientists of social science disciplines such as economics, psychology, sociology, and social anthropology. Their findings are of special interest to both sales/marketing people and government and social action agencies.

While they have yet to develop a single, comprehensive theory explaining and predicting consumer behavior, behavioral scientists have discovered four major areas of basic needs or desires common to all people—physiological or biological needs, social needs, self-fulfillment needs, and psychological needs. The sales representative's problem is to translate these desires into a buying decision, which is made on both rational and emotional grounds, most often on the latter. We outlined in this chapter many such areas to which sales appeals can be addressed.

CHAPTER REVIEW

CONCEPTS TO REMEMBER*

_____ internal motivations	_____ inner wants	_____ physiological needs
_____ external forces	_____ positive desires	_____ self-fulfillment
_____ empathy	_____ consumer	needs
_____ real needs	behavior	

*For memory reinforcement, fill in the page number or numbers where these terms were described in this chapter.

QUESTIONS FOR ANALYSIS AND DISCUSSION

1. What does the term *empathy* mean to you?
2. Has a final, perfect system for predicting buying behavior been evolved? If not, why not?
3. What two desires are reflected through inner wants?
4. What motivates a person to buy anything?
5. Give some examples of how the self-image of a service-station operator and a college lecturer might lead them to act differently as a consumer, assuming equal income.
6. Select an item you would like to buy. List all the reasons possible why you want to buy it. Identify each reason as to the rational or emotional motives (or combination of both) affecting your buying motives.
7. Assume you are about to purchase a box of breakfast cereal at a supermarket. What basic need and what emotional buying motives are you about to fulfill? What is your basic reason for buying it, and your secondary considerations?
8. Explain how the purchase of an expensive bottle of perfume by a young secretary might really be based upon a deeply felt need, not even understood by the woman herself. What wants might also be involved in her buying decision?

WHY DO 82 OUT OF EVERY 100 RETAIL CUSTOMERS STOP BUYING AT YOUR STORE?

The above question was posed to retail store managers by Paul L. Pfeiffer, international marketing consultant and professor of marketing at Kent State University in a 1973 article published in *Stores*,[1] the well-known retail management magazine published by National Retail Merchants Association, Inc.

His answer to the question, based on surveys was: one was lost by death, three left when their favorite salesperson left the store, five left to buy from a friend or relative, nine left because they found they could buy at lower prices, fourteen stopped buying because of unadjusted complaints, and sixty-eight stopped buying because store salespersons were indifferent and showed no interest in the customer. Eighty-two out of every 100 customers were found to have been lost because of unadjusted complaints or salesperson indifference!

"Today, more than ever in American business history," warned Professor Pfeiffer, "there is a greater need for professionalism in the personal make-up of our [retail] salespeople. Today's customers are more mobile than ever before. If they are unhappy with the treatment they receive from your salespeople, they can easily shift their business to some other firm where their business will be appreciated. Any merchant who feels he 'owns his customers' and consequently takes them for granted is due for a rude awakening these days when he finds these customers have taken their business to a competitor who shows a sincere interest in their problems as well as the dollar volume. More competition in the marketplace means more professionalism in salespeople."

Concerning the problem of unadjusted complaints, he noted that many fine retail stores have a top management policy of "no sale final," meaning that no sale is final until the customer is completely satisfied with his purchase. "But in our work with many firms," he said, "we frequently find the 'no sale final' policy, decreed by top management, is interpreted by the salesperson according to his or her likes and dislikes. Salespeople often feel that they must protect their employer from what they believe to be unjust complaints, even though this is not in keeping with the company policy of 'complete customer satisfaction.' Such misinterpretation often causes dissatisfied customers, who become part of the fourteen who quit because of unadjusted complaints."

Turning to the problem of customers who stop buying because of indifferent, uninterested salespersons, he wrote, "when customers are unhappy with the service they receive from your store, they frequently stop buying from you without communicating their reasons. While they will frequently tell their friends and associates of their presumed shabby treatment, they will not, as a rule, tell those friends when they *are* satisfied with your effort. They assume that your salespeople should treat their business as valuable."

The professor added this telling statement: "There is an old business cliche that says, 'One satisfied customer may win you two; however, one dissatisfied customer may lose you fifty.' Even *one* dissatisfied customer is too much and should be avoided!"

1. Paul L. Pfeiffer, "Where Do Your Customers Go," *Stores, The Retail Management Magazine* (February 1973), p. 30.

Retail store managers and salespersons alike, faced with the facts presented in this article, should ask themselves this question posed by Professor Pfeiffer: "What are *you* doing today to stop this loss of your most important asset—your customers?"

QUESTIONS FOR WRITTEN REPORTS OR CLASS DISCUSSION

1. Do you feel that retail customers who stop buying at a given store due to salesperson indifference are turned off by the salesperson's failure to detect and appeal to any of the four basic denominators of desire (needs) discussed in the chapter? If so, which and why?
2. What rational or emotional motives, or a combination of both, might influence a customer to stop buying at a given retail store because of salesperson indifference, or failure to properly handle a complaint?
3. These lost customers must have felt a thwarting of their buying motive of ego-gratification due to indifferent salespersons. What feeling should the salesperson have tried to project instead of indifference, and how could they have found out how the customers really felt inwardly, had they tried?
4. What customer original buying motive, among those listed in the chapter, was probably frustrated most in face of an indifferent salesperson?

Case Study 4–2

THE EFFECT OF SALES REPRESENTATIVE SIMILARITY AND EXPERTISE ON CONSUMER PURCHASING BEHAVIOR (BRIEF OF AN ACTUAL CONSUMER RESEARCH STUDY)

From a managerial standpoint, the important question about sales representative–customer interaction is how the sales representative's behavior effects the outcome. What can the sales representative do to shape the course along which the interaction proceeds? Are certain selling strategies and techniques more effective than others in this regard?

Consumer behavior is studied by behavioral scientists and others concerned with consumer research. How do researchers go about such research studies? In order to get some idea, let us briefly consider some key points of an actual research study—how it was organized and implemented, and what conclusions were drawn—as presented in Journal of Marketing Research.[2] (Results and limitations of the study, too lengthy and statistically technical to include in this brief, can be read in the original source.)

BACKGROUND

Prior research studies by other researchers have postulated that power, attractiveness, and credibility characteristics of communicators produce three types of influences on

---

2. Arch G. Woodside and J. William Davenport, Jr., "The Effect of Salesman Similarity and Expertise on Consumer Purchasing Behavior," *Journal of Marketing Research* XI (May 1974), pp. 198–202. Reprinted from *Journal of Marketing Research* published by the American Marketing Association.

the customer: compliance, identification, and internalization. Also, it has been postulated that the greater the communicator's perceived credibility by the recipient, the
greater the likelihood that the recipient will accept the influencing message because it is
congruent with the recipient's value system, i.e., internalization has occurred. The
effects of perceived salesman similarity and expertise on customer purchasing behavior for a new product were investigated in this study.

HYPOTHESES

The following hypotheses were formulated to examine the effects of the selling
strategies discussed on customer purchasing behavior:

1. The greater the perceived expertise attached to the salesman, the greater the likelihood of
    purchase by the customer.
2. The greater the perceived similarity attached to the salesman, the greater the likelihood of
    purchase by the customer.
3. For the Extensive Problem Solving stage in consumer decision making, perceived expertise
    of the salesman produces a greater likelihood of purchase by the customer than perceived
    similarity of the salesman.

METHOD

The research design incorporated two levels of expertise and two levels of similarity to
enable comparisons to be made between treatment levels and across treatments (for a
total of four treatment conditions).

A salesman attempted to induce purchase of a new product innovation by consumers shopping for eight-track stereo music tapes in a small music store in Augusta,
Georgia. The salesperson was a woman in her late thirties who was the communicator
for all four treatment conditions. She was a part-time employee of the store, a high
school graduate untrained in marketing theory or sales psychology, and was not
informed of the predicted results of the study.

PRODUCT

A cleaning kit of materials to clean eight-track tape players, just put on the market, was
selected as test product. Such products are somewhat technically complex and its safe
use was assumed to be important to a user since the product had to be connected to the
tape player. The kit was mounted on cardboard, enclosed in a plastic container, and
had a retail price of $1.98. Operating instructions were printed on one side of the
cardboard.

PROCEDURE

The salesperson attempted to induce customers who had just purchased one or more
tapes to make an additional purchase of the cleaning kit. Selected customers were
randomly assigned to one of the four treatment conditions and to the control group.
Treatment conditions were typed and copies placed below the cash register in the store
after the copies were randomly mixed. Space was available on the copies to record
purchase information. Blank copies represented the control group assignment.

After the customer moved to the cash register area to pay for selected tapes, the
salesperson looked at the top treatment copy under the register and administered that
particular treatment. Purchase response was recorded immediately after the customer
left the store. The treatments consisted of the four combinations of two similar-
dissimilar and two expert-nonexpert levels. A total of thirty customers were assigned to
each combination and to the control group.

The following sales appeals were combined to form the four treatment conditions:

Similar. I hope you enjoy the tapes. They are of very good quality. I have these same ones in my collection and play them often.

Dissimilar. I hope you enjoy the tapes. They are of very good quality. I don't have any (. . . same type of music as buyer has selected) tapes. Mine are all (. . . most opposite type of music, e.g., rock-and-roll versus classical, soul versus country and western, religious versus party) tapes.

Expert. Here is a device we have on special that will clean the dirt and tape oxide from the guides, the head, and especially the drive wheels of your tape player. You just put a few drops of this cleaner on these two pads, stick it in just like a tape, let it run for about ten seconds while you wiggle this (point to head of cleaning bar). It will keep the music clear and keep the tapes from tearing up by winding up inside the player. It's only $1.98. Would you like one?

Nonexpert. Here is a thing we have on special that they tell me will keep your tape player clean. I don't really know how it works, but you can read the directions right here on the package as to how to use it and what it does. I never have used one, and really don't know anything about playing tapes except how to listen to them, but this thing is supposed to help the tape player a lot. It's only $1.98. Would you like one?

CONCLUSIONS

The findings fit into previously postulated theoretical research studies. Assuming that a product innovation, such as the one incorporated in this study, would cause the consumer to engage in Extensive Problem Solving, attempts to influence internalized values of the customer may be more effective than attempts to seek identification with him.

Further research would be useful for measuring the effects of compliance as well as identification and internalization. But conclusions of this research study point to the possible need for strong retail sales support to get customer trial and adoption of new products which may require Extensive Problem Solving. It may indeed be advantageous for a company not to introduce power and attractiveness attributes in its symbolic communication (mass media and personal selling) in all of those situations where the customer is primarily problem-solving-oriented.

QUESTIONS FOR WRITTEN REPORTS OR CLASS DISCUSSION

1. Define the meaning of the term consumer behavior. Who is interested in research findings in the field other than sales/marketing people?
2. As a salesperson of the eight-track tape cleaning kit used in this research study, do you feel its conclusion would have any bearing on your own sales presentation to retail store buyers? In what way or ways?
3. Based on conclusions of the research study, would you suggest to retail store buyers that they have their salespersons use any one of the four sales appeals (presentation) prepared for the study as is? If so, which one? Or, would you suggest an adapted one? If so, write your own suggested presentation, of approximately the same length.
4. Do you feel this research study does or does not develop a single unified concept of buying theory applicable to the selling by retail salespersons of any type product? Explain.

WHAT MOTIVATES PEOPLE TO BUY HOPE?

"Where vanity is—there shall be cosmetics" is a statement attributed to "the man who made Revlon" in a *Newsweek* feature article[3] on the multimillion-dollar American cosmetics and beauty industry. The article added, "The consumers don't have to buy a $10 or $15 face cream, but they buy it out of hope. That's what the industry sells —hope!"

The article quoted one authority as saying that the beauty industry fills no physical need for most people but does fill a psychological need. An executive of the Helena Rubenstein company agreed that cosmetics provide women with both psychological and tangible benefits. She felt that cosmetics "help women look better, therefore feel better, and as a result do things better."

Women have used cosmetics in one form or another since the beginning of time. The basic ingredients that go into the manufacture of cosmetics have not changed very much over the years, but the cost of buying hope has, in some cases reaching $50 for a day of treatments at New York Fifth Avenue beauty salons or $747.50 for a week at lush beauty spas (sometimes called "fat farms"). "And now to men," says the industry, which in recent years has seriously been promoting and selling cosmetics for men (colognes for example, with names like "Tiger Sweat" and "Studd") to the tune of hundreds of millions of dollars per year.

Hope is offered through the numerous cosmetics and toiletries lines sold in department stores, supermarkets, and drug stores, and by direct selling. Many of these items are also available at the more than 230,000 beauty shops and an even larger number of barber shops throughout the United States.

Here is one example, extracted from the article, as to how some salesmen and saleswomen sell hope in practice.

The hairdressers, themselves gorgeously coifed, dressed in London suits, often made up and occasionally decked in false eyelashes, are the aristocrats of the salon; then come the *visagistes,* with their trays of color and soothing chatter. "Oh, these lashes are just absolutely aching to go on those lids," coos a boy at the House of Revlon. "They'll be just divine. . . . Will they stay on in bed? Madame, it all depends on who you're with. . . ."

QUESTIONS FOR WRITTEN REPORTS OR CLASS DISCUSSION

1. Authorities quoted by the *Newsweek* article seemed to feel that cosmetics or beauty aids help fulfill certain psychological needs. It is also true that they fill certain social needs (or affiliation needs). What are social needs and how does purchase of cosmetics help fulfill them?

2. List two emotional buying motives that may be involved in a purchase of cosmetics or beauty aids. Describe how and why each may be involved.

3. Most of the material in this sales problem extracted from "A Beautiful $7 Billion of Moonbeams," *Newsweek* (June 3, 1968), pp. 80–84. Used with permission.

social, legal, and ethical issues in selling

When you have mastered the content of this chapter, you should be able to:

Define the terms *law, common law, statutory law, constitutional law, Uniform Commercial Code* (UCC), *business* (commercial) *law, ethics, business ethics, morals, consumerism,* and *consumerist movement.*

Summarize the types of basic business law with which a sales representative should have some familiarity, and give the reasons why.

Summarize some of the ways in which government regulates and affects sales/marketing, and give the forms of increased restraint employed in recent years that might be expanded in the future.

List some of the major laws of special interest to sales representatives that regulate business law and protect the American consumer.

List four "consumer rights" designed to protect the individual American buyer or consumer as advocated by Presidents Kennedy, Johnson, and Nixon.

Describe some of the social action views of the growing American consumerist movement and how this cause does and should affect business in general and sales representatives in particular.

Summarize some of the personal ethical standards toward which a sales representative should aim, and the personal responsibilities he should face in regard to his company, his customers, society, and himself.

Why consider social, legal, and ethical issues in selling immediately following a chapter on buyer behavior—before we discuss "how-to" personal selling? The key to the explanation lies in three sentences appearing on page 84 in the preceding chapter: "Once you have determined the real reason your prospect wants to buy, you may have to consider your ethical and moral responsibilities as a sales representative. The power of persuasion, combined with psychological insight sometimes is so great that experienced sales representatives can discover the real motivator or reason without the prospect realizing it himself. You have the serious professional responsibility of fulfilling his need by providing something of value."

What this means is that an experienced sales representative, in many types of selling, often encounters less intelligent or immature prospects who may be unable to resist his persuasion and want to buy something they should not buy. The sales representative is well aware, through his greater psychological insight, of this situation.

It is therefore important to understand just what social, legal, and ethical considerations are involved in such psychologically and emotionally difficult situations, so that when specific sales techniques are discussed in the pages to follow you will consider them as honest sales approaches, and not as "tricks of the trade." Good professional selling rests on solid ethical and moral foundations.

Having made this important point, let us enter the subject of this chapter by first considering some perplexing problems and questions that challenge all Americans.

ARE AMERICAN CONSUMERS BEING MANIPULATED?

A widely read and quoted author, Alvin Toffler, has written, "Pesticides and herbicides filter into our foods. Twisted automobile carcasses, aluminum cans, non-returnable bottles and synthetic plastic form immense kitchen middens in our midst as more and more of our detritus resists decay."[1]

Another, Hubert Marcuse, has said "false [needs] are those which are superimposed upon the individual by particular social interests. Most of the prevailing needs to relax, to have fun, to behave and costume in accordance with the advertisements, to love and hate what others love and hate, belong to this category of false needs."[2]

Are Americans being manipulated in some fashion to desire ever more gadgets that they do not really want and need, as these and other critics of business imply? Has American business, that social institution which employs most of our working population and provides our goods and services in such great abundance, overstepped its bounds by forcing upon society unneeded material goods and values? Since the economic organization of our country is based on private enterprise and competition in the marketplace, with planning and control of production determined largely by management teams of large corporations, do we know where they are leading us?

Young people especially have led in asking whether our great material affluence on one hand, and a deteriorating environment on the other, are not illogical. And the American public as a whole has followed their lead; witness the many private and governmental consumer protection movements. Their critical focus has been directed largely toward the marketing side of business, especially advertising and selling, as creating or abetting some if not most of society's ills.

The professional sales representative finds himself or herself on the firing line, and in the middle. The sales representative is paid to sell his company's products or services, yet he or she is also a consumer and a member of society. What can and should he or she do personally to further fulfillment of the modern customer/society-oriented sales/marketing concept? We will consider the problems, guidelines, and possible solutions in this chapter.

LEGAL FOUNDATIONS OF AMERICAN BUSINESS

William Pitt, First Earl of Chatham, the famous English statesman, once said, "where law ends, tyranny begins." All societies have devised laws to provide the rules and the methods of enforcing them to maintain order among their people,

---

1. Alvin Toffler, *Future Shock* (New York: Random House, Inc., © 1970), p. 380.
2. Hubert Marcuse, *One-Dimensional Man* (Boston: The Beacon Press, 1964), pp. 4–5.

provide individual and group protection, and serve as a final recourse in settling disputes.

Law itself may be defined as principles and regulations established by a government and applicable to a people, whether in the form of legislation or of custom and policies recognized and enforced by judicial decision. Western civilization has developed under two legal systems. Noncommunist European countries and most of the countries colonized by them live under Roman or Civil law, which was founded in the Roman Empire. Most English-speaking countries, including the United States, live under the English or Common Law system.

Legal Sources

The two main sources of law in the United States are common law and statutory law. *Common law* is based largely on custom and legal precedents which become established as successive similar cases are decided in the courts. When precedents become established under common law, they are often incorporated into written or statutory law.

Statutory law is written law resulting from legislation of federal, state, and local levels of government, or by government agencies. American federal and state constitutions, congressional and state legislative statutes, municipal ordinances, and rules and standards of federal regulatory agencies acting under the authority of statutes comprise statutory law.

Constitutional law is the highest source of law in the United States, followed by statutory law and common law in that order. Common law applies where there are no written laws applicable to the situation.

Only those specific powers delegated to the federal government by the Constitution are exercised at federal level; the rest remain with the individual states.

Uniform Commercial Code

Because state laws often lack uniformity, the National Commission of Uniform State Laws, working with the American Law Institute, drafted in 1957, a "Uniform Commercial Code" to standardize commercial transactions. Through 1974, it has been adopted by 49 of the 50 states, "The Code" or UCC, as it is commonly called, regulates, among other things, general sales, negotiable instruments, implied warranties, warehouse receipts, trust receipts, bills of lading, stock transfers, and certificates of deposit. Specific interpretations of the code are to be found in court decisions interpreting the code, rather than in the code itself.

Business or Commercial Law and the Sales Representative

Laws within common and statutory law applied to common business transactions fall into the classification of *business* or *commercial law*. Nearly every business decision or action has legal implications; disputes often arise between parties and have to be settled by due process of law.

Common law is the source of most laws pertaining to contracts, property, and agency; organizations such as corporations, partnerships and trusts, and many other activities of business, are subject to statutory laws.

A sales representative is often involved when differences or disputes arise, especially in matters of contracts, sales, and agent-principle relationships. While he or she is not expected to be an expert in legal interpretation and procedures, ignorance is no defense if he or she is implicated personally in a conflict. Every sales representative should have some familiarity with basic business law, especially concerning contracts, property, agency, negotiable instruments, and sales. Some recommended outside reading sources covering business law, and government and business, are listed in the bibliography at the end of this book.

GOVERNMENT AND BUSINESS

There are many ways in which government regulates and affects business. Ninety cents out of every dollar taken in by the federal government come from taxes, with sixteen cents of it directly from business profits. Types of taxes on business by all levels of government, particularly the federal government, include business income taxes, property taxes, excise taxes, and payroll taxes. As taxes keep increasing, prices of products and services keep increasing. But government spending also helps business in many ways, directly and indirectly, in areas such as national defense, transportation, research, and commerce.

Over the past fifty years in particular, as corporations have grown in size and power, the federal government has employed increasing restraints on business in the form of price and competition laws, consumer protection laws, anti-pollution laws, labor laws, and regulation of certain industries such as communications, public utilities, and transportation.

Some Basic Laws Regulating American Business

Some of the major laws that regulate business law and protect the consumer in the United States are of special interest to sales representatives, since many sales activities involve legal considerations. These include the *Sherman Antitrust Act of 1890*, which prohibited monopolies and certain types of restraint of trade; the *Clayton Act of 1914*, which supplemented the Sherman Antitrust Act by prohibiting certain specific practices and provided that corporate officials could be held individually responsible for abuses; the *Robinson-Patman Act of 1936*; which amended the Clayton Act; the *Miller-Tydings Act of 1937*, which further amended the Sherman Antitrust Act to exempt interstate fair trade (price-fixing) agreements from antitrust prosecution; and the *Antimerger Act of 1950*, which further amended the Clayton Act. *The Federal Trade Commission Act of 1914* set up a regulatory commission to investigate and act upon unfair competition in commerce, and was amended by the *Wheeler-Lea Act of 1938*, which extended the commission's mandate to include unfair or deceptive acts or practices. One of the first laws designed to protect the consumer was the *Federal Food and Drug Act of 1906*, which forbade the manufacture, sale, or transport of adulterated or fraudulently labeled foods and drugs in interstate commerce. This was supplemented by the *Food, Drug and Cosmetic Act of 1938*, which in turn was amended by the *Food Additives Act of 1958*. Other major laws include the *Meat Inspection Act of 1906* and the *Federal Alcohol Administration Act of 1935*.

Most recent laws include the *Automobile Information Disclosure Act of 1958*, the *Consumer Credit Protection Act of 1968*, and the *Federal Cigarette Labeling and Advertising Act of 1968*.

Buyers' Rights

Increasing attention is being paid to development of new legislation to protect the individual buyer or consumer and to more carefully regulate sales/marketing practices. Actions of Presidents Kennedy, Johnson, and Nixon led to presentation to Congress in 1969 of a "Consumer Bill of Rights," which guaranteed to the consumer:

The Right to make an intelligent choice among products and services.
The Right to expect that his health and safety have been taken into account by sellers.
The Right to accurate information on which to make his free choice.
The Right to have his complaints heard when his interests are badly served.

Will Government Regulation of Business Increase?

Laws and regulations affecting American business are constantly being interpreted by the courts and regulatory bodies, and many individuals and groups (private and governmental), are constantly involved in "selling" the public and legislators on the need to pass and enforce regulations to ensure product quality and safety and to protect the consumer from deceptive practices. As examples, consider the success of consumer advocate Ralph Nader in arousing public opinion and inspiring legislation that required the automobile industry to build more safety features into their vehicles, and the Surgeon General's Report and the American Cancer Society public-information program that led to government action in requiring warnings of the danger to health from cigarette smoking to be printed on each pack of cigarettes.

It seems certain that many new laws designed to regulate business and protect the consumer will undoubtedly be passed in the years ahead, especially in areas such as product safety, credit practices, packaging, and sales and advertising practices. The speed and degree with which this increased governmental regulation of business develops will depend largely on the speed with which business regulates itself by incorporating environmental and long-range public welfare concerns into its traditional profit-only concept in providing consumer needs and services.

BUSINESS ETHICS AND SOCIAL RESPONSIBILITY

More than any other of the world's peoples, Americans live in a business-oriented society. Business uses most of the natural resources, employs most of the workers, and provides goods and services for everyone. Business is the major force in American society; society is organized so that business values can be efficiently pursued. The success symbols of business-power—status, high income, and fringe benefits such as the expense account—are admired, envied, and sought after by a significant number of Americans who define and pursue their lives' goals in terms of business careers and values.

The right for a firm to make a profit by providing goods and services to others in a free and competitive marketplace has always been considered legitimate. The American capitalistic, free-enterprise system has given Americans in general the world's highest standard of living along with maximum individual freedom.

In the past, under the owner-entrepreneur business system, these rights were seldom questioned. But as large corporations have developed in size and power, their economic responsibility has in some cases come into conflict with their social responsibility. Americans are now questioning whether business has placed too much emphasis on the profit motive and too little on society-welfare values. Since there are often some business practices not in direct violation of specific laws, but not necessarily in harmony with them either, ethics becomes involved.

The term *ethics*, as derived from a Greek word meaning "custom," can be defined as the body of moral principles or values governing or distinctive of a particular culture or group.

Ethics within a given society pertains to commonly accepted standards of right and wrong behavior. *Business ethics* are the socially accepted rules of conduct that influence businessmen to be honest or fair in their dealings with others. Laws are specific, but ethics are based on consideration of individual or group conscience, the probability of receiving treatment in kind from others, and public opinion.

Society has the right to expect business and businessmen to be ethical. And to help ensure it, many trade associations, professional groups, and individual companies have drawn up codes of ethics to guide the behavior of their members.

Some codes of ethics of particular interest to sales representatives include those of The American Association of Advertising Agencies (see Figure 5.1), the Sales and Marketing Executives International (see Figure 5.2), and the Direct Selling Association.[3]

The American Management Association makes available over 400 examples of corporation codes of ethics. The Better Business Bureaus in scores of American cities receive financial support from member companies in their local communities, seek to promote codes of ethics for various business groups, and act as clearinghouses for complaints against local firms.

Today, due to the immense size of corporations and competitive pressures that can result in unethical practices harmful to society, more and more attention is being paid by the government, private consumer groups, and concerned individuals to the question of how business and society can exist in a way that benefits both at the cost of neither.

PERSONAL ETHICS AND MORALS

Since individuals have to make decisions, especially in business, that might affect others harmfully, personal standards of ethics and morals are important. *Morals*, defined as principles or habits with respect to right or wrong conduct, are usually identified with religion. The biblical Golden Rule, "do unto others as you would have them do unto you" is basic to the moral codes of many.

Personal standards of ethics and morals may vary between individuals or among different groups in a society. Some people believe that another's standards need not apply to them; some businessmen have one set of ethical standards for their personal lives and a less restricted set for use in business. In a free society, whose ethics should prevail? Legal rules governing conformity remain the major arbitrator, and they are constantly evolving as public opinion brings about changes in society's standards of ethical behavior.

Although every individual's behavior is influenced by law, personal morality, and group and social sanctions of right and wrong, ultimately it is the individual himself who chooses how he will behave. One's conscience will help guide his decisions and behavior. For a sales representative, the desire to sell something of value and benefit to his customers, something that will bring them lasting satisfaction and/or contribute toward the welfare of society, is at the heart of the ethical and professional standards toward which he aspires.

3. This latter association publishes a very specific, lengthy code plus regulations for enforcement copies of which can be obtained by writing Direct Selling Association, 1973 M Street Northeast, Washington, D.C., 20036.

CREATIVE CODE

American Association of Advertising Agencies

The members of the American Association of Advertising Agencies recognize:

1. That advertising bears a dual responsibility in the American economic system and way of life.

To the public it is a primary way of knowing about the goods and services which are the products of American free enterprise, goods and services which can be freely chosen to suit the desires and needs of the individual. The public is entitled to expect that advertising will be reliable in content and honest in presentation.

To the advertiser it is a primary way of persuading people to buy his goods or services, within the framework of a highly competitive economic system. He is entitled to regard advertising as a dynamic means of building his business and his profits.

2. That advertising enjoys a particularly intimate relationship to the American family. It enters the home as an integral part of television and radio programs, to speak to the individual and often to the entire family. It shares the pages of favorite newspapers and magazines. It presents itself to travelers and to readers of the daily mails. In all these forms, it bears a special responsibility to respect the tastes and self-interest of the public.

3. That advertising is directed to sizable groups or to the public at large, which is made up of many interests and many tastes. As is the case with all public enterprises, ranging from sports to education and even to religion, it is almost impossible to speak without finding someone in disagreement. Nonetheless, advertising people recognize their obligation to operate within the traditional American limitations: to serve the interests of the majority and to respect the rights of the minority.

Therefore we, the members of the American Association of Advertising Agencies, in addition to supporting and obeying the laws and legal regulations pertaining to advertising, undertake to extend and broaden the application of high ethical standards. Specifically, we will not knowingly produce advertising which contains:

a. False or misleading statements or exaggerations, visual or verbal.

b. Testimonials which do not reflect the real choice of a competent witness.

c. Price claims which are misleading.

d. Comparisons which unfairly disparage a competitive product or service.

e. Claims insufficiently supported, or which distort the true meaning or practicable application of statements made by professional or scientific authority.

f. Statements, suggestions or pictures offensive to public decency.

We recognize that there are areas which are subject to honestly different interpretations and judgment. Taste is subjective and may even vary from time to time as well as from individual to individual. Frequency of seeing or hearing advertising messages will necessarily vary greatly from person to person.

However, we agree not to recommend to an advertiser and to discourage the use of advertising which is in poor or questionable taste or which is deliberately irritating through content, presentation or excessive repetition.

Clear and willful violations of this Code shall be referred to the Board of Directors of the American Association of Advertising Agencies for appropriate action, including possible annulment of membership as provided in Article IV, Section 5, of the Constitution and By-Laws.

Conscientious adherence to the letter and the spirit of this Code will strengthen advertising and the free enterprise system of which it is part.   *Adopted April 26, 1962*

Endorsed by

Advertising Association of the West, Advertising Federation of America, Agricultural Publishers Association, Associated Business Publications, Association of Industrial Advertisers, Association of National Advertisers, Magazine Publishers Association, National Business Publications, Newspaper Advertising Executives Association, Radio Code Review Board (National Association of Broadcasters), Station Representatives Association, TV Code Review Board (NAB)

FIGURE 5.1

Sales and Marketing Executives International

Code of Ethics

SMEI shall support and preserve the highest standards of professional conduct in the field of sales and marketing management. Toward this end, its members should reflect this objective in their individual activities at all times under this code:

1. It is the responsibility of **SMEI** and its entire membership to maintain honesty and integrity in all relationships with customers, and to put first emphasis upon quality of product and service, with accurate representation to the public.

2. **SMEI** recognizes the basic marketing principle that there must be mutuality of benefit and profit to the buyer and seller in order to insure true economic progress, and thus to fulfill the inherent, responsibility of marketing to advance our country's standards of living.

3. **SMEI** is keenly alert to the need for constant advancement and protection of individual and corporate rights in the entire marketing concept. It is therefore inherent that **SMEI** shall always crusade to protect the freedoms of choice and competition which are a fundamental part of the free enterprise philosophy.

4. **SMEI** shall always strive for constructive and effective cooperation with governmental agencies in areas of appropriate interest, always with the objective of supporting and maintaining the free enterprise system.

5. **SMEI** shall ever be dedicated to the information and education of the public, in all its segments and age levels, to the true values and advantages of the free enterprise system.

Adopted May 19, 1963

FIGURE 5.2

CRITICISM OF SALES/MARKETING

Since business is such a major force in American society, critics associate many economic and social problems of our society with business. The marketing function of business, in all its aspects of advertising, publicity, promotion, and selling, has been singled out for the heaviest criticism, in spite of the fact it has been a major factor in bringing about such a high standard of living for Americans.

This criticism, by students, consumers, government, and even many sales/marketing professionals, has peaked during the mid-1970s, at a time when American sales/marketing methods are being widely studied and copied by both western and socialist countries elsewhere in the world and when nonbusiness organizations such as hospitals, educational institutions, political parties, and agencies of government are rapidly adapting sales/marketing principles and practices to their own nonbusiness activities. Politicians and social activists have been quicker than businessmen to recognize that a growing mass of American consumers are questioning strictly materialistic values and are becoming interested in the social aspects of consumption. This has led to increased social and political action and overall public concern via the rapidly growing consumer movements.

By way of definition, to *consume* means to destroy or expend by use—to use up. A *consumer* is one who consumes. *Consumerism* is the interaction of consumers, politicians, consumer advocates, business, and industry toward the achievement of consumer rights. Social action to achieve consumerism is called the *consumerist* movement.

Some of the major consumerist criticisms are listed below. They have been gleaned from many sources and are listed in no particular order of importance. They will serve to identify some of the specific issues of consumerism with which modern-day sales representatives should be aware:

1. The production and selling of many products and services often wastes resources, is built on trivial differences, and is often in conflict with overall social welfare.
2. Many forms of advertising and selling persuade people to buy products they do not need; many are actually deceptive.
3. Too many products damage the environment (disposable packaging) or blight the landscape (outdoor billboards).
4. Products are often unsafe, poorly built, not durable enough, and difficult and costly to repair.
5. American business has failed to raise living standards of the poor, the elderly, certain minorities, and other disadvantaged segments of American society; and often-deceptive sales/marketing practices hurt these groups most.

Consumerism is an attractive cause because the overall issues are real and of concern to all. The consumerist movement is here to stay. The professional sales representative must give careful consideration to its honest criticism and recognize his own ethical, moral, and social responsibility in his work.

WHAT SHOULD BUSINESS DO TO ENSURE ENLIGHTENED CUSTOMER/SOCIETY-ORIENTED SALES/MARKETING?

Business leaders, sales/marketing managers, and professional sales representatives should first recognize that consumer problems (and criticism) are problems of friction within a basically sound system. Like any good sales representative, they should welcome honest criticism or objections as a first step toward finding a solution to the problem, if a valid one exists. And then they should take positive steps to solve the problem by eliminating any abuses.

Two examples of widespread, often-justified post-sales complaints were cited by a high official of the Federal Trade Commission at a briefing on product liability and consumerism sponsored by the American Management Association.[4] The first is a failure to deliver merchandise a customer has ordered and paid for. The check is cashed but nothing is received. Letters of inquiry bring either no reply or a polite apology or promises, but no refund and no product. The chances are that the merchandise was never sent. The second complaint involves guarantees or warranties on anything from autos to record players. Purchased and taken to work or home, the item doesn't work. The customer takes it back to the sales-representative or dealer he bought it from, who either accepts it and fails to fix it, or tells the customer to mail it at the customer's own expense and inconvenience to the manufacturer.

The official warned the management group that companies must make certain these widespread abuses are rectified, since they fall with equal weight on "all groups of all citizens regardless of economic background, location, race, creed or color."[5]

Above and beyond correcting mere abuses however, business, and sales/marketing in particular, should strive in every way possible to produce and market goods and services that offer *real* value and benefit to both the individual consumer and society. Starting with end-consumer needs, wants, and problems, they should produce goods and services not for sake of change alone, but to provide something that makes a contribution to consumer welfare. This means thinking and acting beyond the traditional aim of profit-for-profit's-sake alone.

Some Companies (but Not All) Are Responding to Consumerism

Many companies have taken positive steps in this direction by forming consumer affairs departments staffed by experienced managers reporting directly to top management. Over 150 of these were formed between 1970 and 1974. Major functions of the departments include (1) resolving customer complaints and setting up more effective ways to cut down on the number of grievances; (2) influencing the design, safety, and servicing of company products; (3) screening and monitoring company advertising and promotional materials and sales policies; and (4) improving communications with outside consumer-interest groups.

While there is an encouraging development, not all companies have responded to the challenge of consumerism. Too many continue to see it as an "image problem" and have concentrated on face-lifting advertising and public relations campaigns. Others have chosen to simply ignore the problem and the movement, hoping they will eventually go away.

The problems, however, are real and consumer dissatisfaction is real—not a fad. There is a substantial gap in communication between consumers and business. Too large a percentage of the public feels that businessmen are not trustworthy and that more government regulation is needed to protect them. This feeling is widespread among America's 8 million college youth: one recent poll of 3,000

---

4. *Sales Managers Bulletin*, Bureau of Business Practice, Issue # 787 (October 30, 1971).
5. Ibid., p. 9.

students at 100 campuses showed many to be quite hostile to business; a survey of business administration and marketing majors showed only 37 percent felt they could believe advertising.[6] The conclusion seems to be that today's college kids don't want to be manipulated by hard sell, soft sell, or slick sell. This depth of feeling is important, since today's college youth will be the opinion-makers of the next four decades.

If business fails to act rapidly enough, if self-regulation does not work, then aroused public opinion will lead first to increased activities of social dissent such as picketing and boycotts, and then to increased governmental regulation. This could lead in turn to undesirable constraints on the consumer's freedom and range of choice.

If business does eliminate abuses and produces ever more socially desirable goods and services, it will please sales representatives, who can present them proudly, confident that they are helping fulfill real, not imagined or "created," wants and making a valuable contribution toward solving some of society's problems. To them, a satisfied customer and society will be their greatest reward for selling the right way.

WHAT ETHICAL STANDARDS SHOULD GUIDE A PROFESSIONAL SALES REPRESENTATIVE?

We have learned that the sales representative, as the face-to-face link between customer and producer, is fulfilling an increasingly important educational role by first determining and then helping solve real customer needs, wants, and problems by finding satisfying production and marketing solutions and servicing customers properly. Success depends in large part on the personal ethics and standards of the sales representative toward his company, his customers and society, and himself. Let us briefly examine some of the responsibilities you might face in these areas as a sales representative.

Toward Your Company

Upon joining a company or organization, we can assume in this day of enlightened business that it has extended to you many important rights, benefits, and privileges. But since any relationship is a two-way street, it is fair to examine the responsibilities toward your company you are expected to assume in return for your salary or commission.

To begin, if they have entrusted you with outside sales work, they are not going to know if you goof off or spend an afternoon a week at the movies. You are ambitious and naturally will not do that, but it is fair enough to state that your employer expects an honest day's work for wages paid.

Your company is something to be proud of. Some sales representatives think it is smart or clever to knock their company. This is an immature attitude, of course, and customers wonder what such a man may say about them to others. If you are willing to accept company pay, you owe it a certain loyalty or should get off the bandwagon.

Management expects you to get your paperwork in promptly, just as you expect them to get you a paycheck on time. They also expect you, as their ambas-

6. Edward P. Rearey, Jr., "Better Service: Society's Pressing Need," *Marketing Times* (May/June issue) p. 31.

sador in your territory, to keep them fully informed of all major developments there which have any bearing on your work or its potential. They should not have to constantly ask for it; you should train yourself to think as a manager does and to provide it beforehand.

A final personal responsibility is your attitude toward the spending of company money. You should always think of spending it wisely, as if it were your own, and make sure you get a good return on each dollar spent. When deciding whether to spend company money for something (such as entertainment), be practical; for a moment pretend you are in business for yourself. Then ask yourself, "If this were coming out of my own business pocket, would I spend it?" Remember, there are basically only two ways for your company to make profits: by keeping sales up and costs down. It judges you as a sales representative on both counts.

Toward Your Customers and Society

A sale should offer benefit to both buyer and seller. Before you can sell a product or service successfully, you as a sales representative have to first "sell yourself" as an individual whom the prospect can trust. This implies an obligation on your part to present features, advantages, and benefits truthfully—to avoid misrepresentation in any way. Personal integrity is an important factor here—full information should be given, not withheld; excuses should not be given, nor false information or data.

Confidences must be respected. If the customer discloses (or you yourself learn) trade or business secrets or plans, you should keep this information to yourself. You should never seek to bribe your way to a sale by offering under-the-table money, gifts, or any form of kickback; and should politely refuse any attempts on the customer's part to bribe you. If conflicts of interest arise, be guided by industry guidelines, company policy, and your own conscience in resolving them fairly.

Professional sales ethics require that you do not take advantage of prospect or customer ignorance, lack of experience, or inability to resist a psychologically persuasive sales approach; your guideline is to offer something of value that will bring real satisfaction. In presenting your proposal, treat competing products or services fairly if you have to make direct comparisons, and never knock competition. Once you've made the sale, follow up and through as time and circumstances permit to make certain the customer is satisfied with his purchase.

In all these matters, your goals and guidelines are those of creative, responsible selling; at the heart of this is service and mutual gain, with consumer and society welfare enhanced as a result of the exchange between buyer and seller.

To Yourself

In the final analysis, it is up to you as an individual to set and live by your own ethical and moral standards, both personally and in business. If you are honest with yourself, accept full responsibility for your thoughts and behavior, and treat prospects and customers as you would like to be treated in their place, then you will be known as an honest, respectable, trustworthy sales representative. The ethical way is the best way to success in selling or any other career.

SUMMARY

We have noted in this chapter that Americans live in a business-oriented society, the legal foundations for which we described. Business uses most of our natural resources, employs most of the workers, and has provided goods and services in such abundance that most Americans today enjoy the world's highest standard of living. But there is a growing segment of society that is questioning, if not rejecting outright, the materialistic aspects of business that aims to produce more of everything whether or not it is really wanted or needed, or beneficial to society.

This questioning of traditional business values, and many sales/marketing practices, has led to the consumerist movement which has effectively criticized and attacked many specific abuses such as demand manipulation, cultural and environmental pollution, and the sheer power of large corporations which increasingly control our lives. Their aim, as that of enlightened business, is to see goods and services produced that not only return a fair profit, but at the same time protect the consumer and contribute to long-range customer satisfaction and society's welfare.

We have concluded that consumer problems (and criticism) are problems of friction within a basically sound system. Although governmental regulation of business will grow, we discussed many things that both business in general and sales representatives in particular can do to help bring about improvements in the system. Fundamental to success are the ethical and moral standards to which our society aspires. The individual sales representative has both a professional and personal responsibility to set and follow responsible, highly ethical standards in his selling activities.

CHAPTER REVIEW

CONCEPTS TO REMEMBER*

_____ consumerism	_____ business self-regulation	_____ Consumer Bill of Rights
_____ Uniform Commercial Code (UCC)	_____ business ethics	_____ social responsibility
_____ professional sales ethics	_____ consumer affairs department	_____ consumerist movement

*For memory reinforcement, fill in the page number or numbers where these terms were described in this chapter.

QUESTIONS FOR ANALYSIS AND DISCUSSION

1. Explain the statement "a sale should benefit both buyer and seller."
2. What lies at the heart of creative, responsible selling?
3. Do you agree or disagree with the statement "consumer problems (and criticism) in the United States are problems of friction within a basically sound system"? Explain your position.
4. What is meant by the term "consumerist movement"? Describe two examples of consumerist movement activities you have observed or heard about recently in your local community. Do you agree with their aims and methods? Explain why you feel the way you do about them.
5. As a consumer yourself, can you describe any recent advertising seen or purchase made which you feel to be deceptive and not in the best interests of other consumers or society? To what extent do you feel the companies concerned who manufactured, advertised, and sold the item should be held accountable? To what extent should the sales representative of those companies be held accountable?

6. As a sales representative, you have a chance to close a big sale that will mean a lot to you and your company. As an "implied condition" of giving you the order, however, the buyer, who is purchasing agent for his company, has hinted he would not be opposed to accepting a free gift of a three-day all-expense-paid trip to Las Vegas for himself and his wife during the upcoming Fourth of July long weekend. What would you do?

7. Figure 5.2 outlined a code of ethics for sales/marketing people drawn up in 1966 by Sales and Marketing Executives International, a leading professional organization. Do you think it should be revised in view of growing consumerist activities since that date? If so, what changes do you think it should incorporate? Prepare your complete, recommended draft for an updated code.

8. In order to sell a product or service most successfully, you as a sales representative first have to "sell yourself" as an individual whom the prospect can trust. What obligations are implied by the term *sell yourself?*

Case Study 5–1

CPSC—A POWERFUL U.S. GOVERNMENT AGENCY WATCHES BUSINESS AND INDUSTRY (AND THEIR SALES REPRESENTATIVES)

The Consumer Product Safety Commission . . . perhaps the most powerful federal regulatory agency ever created—gears up.

—Industry Week

Washington is getting set to toughen up regulation of consumer products that cause a high proportion of injuries in and around the home.

—U.S. News and World Report

Its power is staggering.

—The National Observer

The Consumer Product Safety Act was signed into American law in October 1972. In May 1973, the Consumer Product Safety Commission, created by the Act, went into business. Not every manufacturer or businessman is yet aware of CPSC or its far reaching options to impose new and stringent legal actions against individuals for any consumer product their company has made, supplied parts for, distributed, or sold that is found by the commission to be unsafe.

While top executives of offending companies are in gravest jeopardy, any other individual bearing responsibility for any part of production, distribution, advertising, or sales connected with any consumer product found to be unsafe may also be affected, conclude editors of the nationally known Bureau of Business Practice.[7]

POWER

CPSC, explaining its own power, has defined it this way: "It is unlawful for businessmen to manufacture, import, distribute, or sell any consumer product that

---

7. Material extracted from "CPSC—A Government Agency Watching You," *Executive Action Series,* Bulletin No. 172, Bureau of Business Practice, (June 1974) pp. 17–32.

does not meet an applicable Consumer Product Safety standard or has been declared a banned hazardous product. A product declared an imminent hazard is liable for seizure, recall, repair, refund, or replacement under a court order, and manufacturers, importers, distributors, and retailers may be required by the court to notify known purchasers and the public of the product hazard."

CONSEQUENCES

The Consumer Product Safety Act calls for both civil and criminal penalties. The most usual procedure is to notify the company or companies involved that a product is not considered safe by Commission standards and ask that it be recalled, repaired, or refunded. Should that method not succeed in removing the offending product from the marketplace, then the Commission has a number of alternatives open to it. These include civil penalties of $2,000 for every violation, up to a maximum of $500,000; and criminal penalties, for knowing and willful violation of the act, which can be as much as $50,000 and one year in jail.

HOW CPSC PINPOINTS VIOLATORS

One of CPSC's most active pipelines of information is hospital emergency rooms. Here's how that works: Hospitals spread over all geographic sections of the country, 119 of them to date, monitor every injury that shows up in their emergency rooms. If a consumer product was in any way involved, that information is funneled into NEISS (the National Electronic Injury Surveillance System) and they feed the data to CPSC. The system is operational 365 days a year. Injure yourself with an electric shaver this morning, and by ten o'clock tonight Washington can know about it.

CPSC has two other sources of information that go into its compilations of products that may be posing a threat to consumers:

1. Consumers countrywide are being urged to make any complaints about product safety directly to the Commission. The call is toll free through 800-638-2666 (492-2937 in Maryland).
2. Consumers are being enlisted as local policemen to cover the retail marketplace. Volunteer Conşumer Deputies are trained by commission staff members to canvass stores, looking for products that are on the banned list and looking for products they feel merit investigation for safety hazards.

CPSC, after putting all this information together, makes up from time to time a list of products that have caused injuries and even deaths among consumers. This list is public information, available from CPSC. As each of the products on the list is investigated and its potential dangers are researched, the commission will decide what steps, if any, are necessary to protect the public.

WHAT HAPPENS TO VIOLATORS

At the top of most lists are bicycles and tricycles, followed by stairs, railings, and landings; nails, tacks, and screws; electrical appliances; glass doors, and so on. A list of the top fifty products associated with consumer injuries has been published and well circulated.

Much publicity has been given to the Commission's recalls of products from the marketplace and from consumers who had already purchased items before the hazards were apparent. When these recalls go out, there is a product named, a manufacturer named, and frequently labelers, retailers and advertisers named. The long list of products already recalled is growing daily, but here are a few of them:

1. Imported hand brakes on bicycles were recalled and repaired when it was found they might fail.
2. The users of 7,000 color television sets were found to be in danger of electrocution, and the sets were recalled.
3. A small TV antenna booster has been found to be a shock hazard. Its retailers have been publicly criticized for carrying the product, and its advertising has been turned over to the FTC for investigation as misleading and possibly fraudulent.
4. A novelty table lamp has sold more than 55,000 units. They have all been recalled since it was found that people using the lamp were in danger of receiving a fatal electric shock.

ACCOUNTABILITY AND A SALES REPRESENTATIVE'S RESPONSIBILITY

There are very few consumable products that do not come into the purview of the Consumer Product Safety Commission. Automobiles, cosmetics, and drugs are not included, everything else is. It is clear the commission intends to enforce the regulations.

Enforcement comes down to accountability, which the commission sees as extending down into every area of every company where there is a man or woman with any defined responsibility related to a consumer product or product line. This includes sales representatives!

Bureau of Business Practice editors advise individual employee acceptance of a personal responsibility to help make CPSC work effectively on behalf of all consumers. To sales representatives and others, they say:

A critical eye can save your company a fortune in time, effort, and most of all money, for recalls, bans, or court penalties. Whatever your bailiwick, if you see a possible hazard, have reason to question it, and, keeping CPSC in mind, you don't like it . . . *tell somebody!* You might be able to blow the whistle that stops the train before it runs into the CPSC. That's a move that would have to be appreciated in the long run.

QUESTIONS FOR WRITTEN REPORTS OR CLASS DISCUSSION

1. Under which of the two main sources of law in the United States (common law or statutory law) do you feel the Consumer Product Safety Act falls, and why?
2. Good personal ethics require a sales representative to sell his product honestly, avoiding any real or implied misrepresentation. But do you feel it is fair for him to face possible personal civil or criminal penalties in selling when he knows a product may be unsafe, if his company requires him to sell it? Explain.
3. If, as a sales representative, you discover that the product you are selling may be unsafe, what would you do about it first—call it to the attention of your sales manager or report it to the Consumer Product Safety Commission? Would you do this verbally or in writing? Why?
4. If an honest dispute arises between a customer and a company over the possible safety of a product sold to the customer, how should the dispute be resolved within the framework of the American free-enterprise system?

IS BUSINESS MORALLY ADEQUATE FOR THE U.S. SOCIETY OF TODAY AND TOMORROW?

"The answer (to the above question) is no, and the next question is how business morality might be improved," says author Max Ways in a May 1974 *Fortune* magazine article.[8]

He went on to explain that the Watergate scandals of 1973, with attendant exposure of many illegal campaign contributions by businessmen, followed upon a gradual rise in the level of moral anxiety that business had already engendered in the American public mind. He noted that, "among current movements contributing to antibusiness sentiment are consumerism, environmentalism, an aversion to big organizations, a tendency to confuse profit with exploitation, and a demand for more 'social justice.' "

He expressed the fear that sweeping generalized attacks on businessmen as a group, especially if expressed in the language of class conflict, might drive many businessmen toward a sullen disengagement from ethical problems that cannot be solved without their cooperation.

"What is needed is an approach that can be shared by business *and* many of its critics; a strategic theory explaining the present challenge in a way that can form the basis for an ethical advance," he claimed. He suggested that business management should develop a conscious, analytical, systematic interest in ethical questions and actively help build a two-way traffic of ethics-building between the business community and the larger society. The goal would be to help construct ethical norms for new moral questions being posed by our dynamic, changing modern society.

The author feels that for hundreds of years business has generated ethical norms valuable to society that influence the behavior of most businessmen most of the time—for example, modern accountancy, an information system upon which hundreds of ethical (and legal) norms have been constructed. But he feels businessmen have deluded themselves and much of the public into the notion that business has nothing to do with ethics. He feels that critics of business morals spend too much time attacking targets such as profits and corporate bigness. He feels that these questions are not central to today's ethical problems; that concentration by critics on them hardens resistance on the part of businessmen and is one reason why abuses are not being corrected as rapidly as they should be.

He fears that failure to establish a theory of modern ethics suitable to business and the public may lead to the creation of new regulations, codes, or rules that may deaden, rather than help protect, an individual's conscience.

The author concluded by saying, "A theory of business ethics adequate for the needs of a dynamic and liberating society would reflect both the selfish and the altruistic sides of reality. The same compound of self-service and other-service that produced life insurance and the system of promissory notes is surely capable of carrying its ethical evolution to a higher level."[9]

8. Material in this case study extracted from Ways, "Business Faces Growing Pressures to Behave Better," *Fortune* (May 1974), pp. 193–320.
9. Visit the library and read this entire excellent article, if possible. If it is not available, the above brief extract should in itself challenge your thinking in the face of the following questions.

QUESTIONS FOR WRITTEN REPORTS OR CLASS DISCUSSION

1. Life insurance, promissory notes, and modern accountancy are cited by Max Ways as examples of good business ethics. How would you define *business ethics?* In view of your definition, do you agree or disagree with his conclusions? Explain.

2. Do you share the author's feelings that American business should or could draw up a Code of Business Ethics for the seventies and eighties that might seem agreeable to both business people and most critics of business, or do you feel that Congress should or could draw up such a code? Explain.

3. Prepare your own ten point Code of Business Ethics for the seventies and eighties as a guideline to what you feel businesspeople and consumers would agree to be to the benefit of society.

4. Do you agree with the author's conclusion that business morality in general, as you currently observe it in your own local area, is inadequate for the American society of today and tomorrow? Explain.

SALES PROBLEM 5–1

AS A SALES REPRESENTATIVE, WHAT WOULD YOU DO IN THESE MORALLY AND ETHICALLY DIFFICULT SITUATIONS?

1. In order to quickly regain sales lost to a newly developed competing product, your company has made a couple of very minor changes in its own product and is widely advertising it as a newly developed product, which you know it is not. A good customer questions your firm's advertising and your sales kit material by asking, "is this really a newly developed product, or just a minor rehash of your old one?" What would you do?

2. You receive from your company advertising department a ditto sheet prepared by another sales representative in your division comparing one of your products with a competitor. The material unfairly disparages the competing product by name and by statements you personally know to be untruthful. A cover memo accompanying the sheet is from your manager. He urges you to show it to customers. What would you do?

PART III

ORGANIZING, PROSPECTING, AND PLANNING FOR PERSONAL SELLING

6

know your company – its products, policies, and promotional support – and know your competition

When you have mastered the content of this chapter, you should be able to:

Describe the importance to a sales representative of knowing as much as possible about his company—its products or services, the promotional support provided, the industry of which it is a part, and the competition.

Summarize the types of information a sales representative should know about several specific aspects of his company in order to intelligently answer questions buyers may ask.

Summarize the types of information a sales representative should know about several specific areas of knowledge concerning the product or service he is selling, including buyer questions he might face, answers to which he should be prepared to present in terms of user benefits.

List the four basic parts of a firm's overall marketing plan and some of the important topics that should be considered prior to formulating such a plan.

Describe basic factors influencing the effectiveness of advertising and the five presented forms of advertising, and describe how advertising and personal selling constantly supplement one another.

Describe the major difference between advertising and sales promotion from a retail merchandising point of view.

Summarize the types of information a sales representative should know about several specific areas of knowledge concerning competition, and give various sources for such information other than his own company sources.

"A few years back, it was usually the sales representative out there alone, pitting his wits against the resistance of a single corporate purchasing agent. Now more and more companies are selling on many different levels, interlocking their research, engineering, marketing, and upper management with those of their customers. This way, today's sales representative becomes a kind of committee chairman within his company. Some manufacturers call them 'account managers.' Either way, his job is to exploit the resources of his company in serving the customer.

As industries consolidate and larger corporations continue to swallow up the small fry, a growing number of companies are also 'preselling' their products through massive promotion, advertising, and improved communications between buyer and seller."[1]

The special 1973 report in *Business Week* magazine from which the above quotation was extracted went on to note, "At the consumer level, this shows up in the cutback of retail sales help and the huge expansion of self-service merchandising. At the industry level, it shows up in a whole new function for the industrial sales representative. No longer is he simply a pitchman or prescriber of his company's products. Now he must go beyond that and become a diagnostician."[2]

In this chapter we will consider the implication of the above statements as we study the knowledge and understanding needed by sales representatives at all levels of experience in all firms, whether they are consumer, industrial, or services oriented, and whether their sales work is retail (inside) or specialty (outside).

We will concentrate on the knowledge that is needed about one's own company, products, and promotional support for effective personal selling. We will also consider the importance of knowledge of these things in relation to your industry and your competition.

Our theme of presentation will continue to be built around you, as a newly hired sales representative now concerned with organizing your thinking, facts, and sales tools in preparation for prospecting (the process of checking out and looking up potential new buyers), planning your sales presentation, and contacting both potential buyers and established customers for sales interview appointments.

WHY IS KNOWLEDGE OF THE COMPANY AND ITS PRODUCTS IMPORTANT?

If you go to a doctor for medical advice concerning a suspected illness, you expect him to be well-trained, confident in manner, professional and helpful in his advice and possible treatment. As a modern "diagnostic" sales representative, it stands to reason that you also should appear knowledgeable, confident, and helpful to a prospective buyer considering your product or service as a possible solution to his needs, wants, or problems.

In a way, you face a more difficult problem than the medical doctor; his patients don't often know enough to question or challenge his statements or prescribed treatment, but in most cases yours will! Modern American buyers are, on the whole, far more sophisticated, better educated, and more demanding than those faced by sales representatives of past years. And as the economy becomes more consumer oriented, this trend will continue. Like the doctor, your role as sales representative is often that of identifying the problem and solving the problem, meanwhile prescribing your product as the best possible solution to the problem.

The first major reason that knowledge of your company and its products is important is that modern buyers, especially industrial buyers, demand and expect facts. If you want to succeed in selling you simply have to know your company and its products and policies thoroughly—from managerial policies to manufacturing to distribution—and be able to relate these to industry trends and compare them with competition. Second is the fact that only if you are armed with such knowledge can you face buyers with confidence and assurance to begin with, or hope to gain their confidence and trust. A third reason lies in the fact that much of modern personal selling is but the end of a sales/marketing strategy that sets

1. "The New Supersalesman," *Business Week* (January 6, 1973), p. 44.
2. Ibid.

many forces, especially the three other sales promotion forces, into operation long before your final sales-representative-to-buyer personal approach. You must know about the overall marketing and merchandising strategy and plan and understand how to build on it and use all aspects of it to your immediate personal sales advantage.

WHAT SHOULD YOU KNOW ABOUT YOUR COMPANY?

Some of the more obvious facts and knowledge you should have about your company are listed below. This is only a partial list. Much of such information is initially taught in company sales training courses, much else is gained from diligent and constant personal study, observation, and "question-asking." As in medicine, keeping up to date and thoroughly informed of all aspects of your firm's business is a never-ending task throughout your professional career. Many of the items listed below are in question form, representing types of questions buyers may ask. You should have ready, intelligent, informed answers for them.

Standing of your company within the industry and community. Before studying your company, you should research the beginning and development of the industry of which it is a part. What is the relation of the industry to other industries? What is the standing of your company within the industry, in terms of physical size, financial strength, credit standing, past and current standing in the stock market, product line, distribution methods, and future plans? What are current trends within the industry? What current or proposed government regulations or consumer demands may affect such trends (and your company)?

Of what industry or trade associations is it a member? What are your company's plans and policies within the industry as compared to those of its competition? What is the standing of your company globally, nationally, and within its local community? Are you proud of your company? Why?

History and current organization. Studying the history of your firm and learning about the men who devised its product and brought it sales success helps you to understand current policies better. Knowledge of the organization and its physical setup enables you to judge the quality of production, the standards of workmanship, and the efficiency and well-being of employees; this enables you to speak authoritatively about it to others. Why and how did your company originate? What new or unusual products has it developed? What contribution has it made to society? How did it get its name? Has it merged with or acquired other companies along the way? Has the buyer any reason to feel pride or unusual confidence through buying from your company?

Executives and key personnel. You should know something about the top executives of your company and about those to whom they are accountable. You can then judge their success for yourself by studying past annual reports issued by them. You can also learn from such reports something about the assets, liabilities, and overall financial setup of the firm. You have every right to learn everything possible about these matters and to judge the situation for yourself.

Were or are any of your company's founders or current executives well known internationally, nationally, or within their local community for any reason? Have any of them invented or developed any product or service of unusual interest? Have any of them served in a leadership capacity on government, state, or local advisory committees, or with social action, political, or community groups concerned with the welfare of society? Have any of them served as leaders in industry-related affairs?

Company policies in general.   Your knowledge concerning these is tied in with the reputation the company enjoys internationally, nationally, within the industry or trade, and with end-consumers. Is it generally considered a company of stability, integrity, and responsibility? Do its policies overall reflect a genuine interest in consumer satisfaction and the welfare of society? If so, how, in what ways? Can you give examples?

Its products.   Full knowledge is required concerning the type, quality, uses, and technical details of the product or product lines being offered, a topic that will be covered in greater detail shortly.

Sales/marketing policies and channels of distribution.   Both overall company policies and specific sales/marketing policies are decided by top management, not by you the sales representative. Prospects and established customers alike will often question certain policies, thus offering you an opportunity to turn them into selling points, where possible.

What channels of distribution does your company employ? What is your company's policy toward exclusives, marking products with jobbers' brands, or price maintenance? If your product is not marketed nationally, why is it available in some areas and not in others? What if your company sells both direct and through retailers; is this not hurting the retailer? What if your company sells to a large chain store and to independent retailers, and the former sells at lower prices—is this fair to the retailer? These are just some of the typical questions commonly asked by buyers; here are some others:

How are orders fulfilled, who receives them, how long does it take to fulfill them. When can I expect delivery and is the delivery date guaranteed? Who pays transportation costs? If an item ordered is out of stock and back ordered, will I be informed in advance of its date of shipment? A billing error was made, how can it be adjusted?

Selling is only part of a sales representative's duties—a great deal of his time is spent servicing his customers and answering questions about and solving sales/marketing problems such as these.

Price and discounts.   As any new sales representative soon learns, this is an item of deep interest to buyers. Price objections are constantly raised and have to be handled; we shall discuss how in Chapter 13. A high price often has to be justified in terms of superior quality (to end-consumer), or greater profit potential (to middlemen or retailers). If price seems low, it may have to be explained in terms of a better buy. Feedback from the sales force is an important factor in company pricing decisions.

Discounts are always of interest to customers who qualify and must be explained carefully. Knowledge of your firm's pricing and discount policies and procedures is essential to sales success, and you must learn to compute them quickly.

An understanding of the terminology of pricing and discounts used within your industry is important. These include such general terms as *list price, net price, FOB price, guaranteed price, quantity discounts, trade discounts, cash discounts,* and *price control;* definitions for these can be found in the glossary at the end of this book.

If given leeway to recommend special discounts in your sales territory, manage them carefully, keeping in mind that profitable sales are the objective of both you and your company. Greater profits often result from smaller sales and shorter discounts than from greater volume sales at excessive discounts. The sales representative who sells on cheapest price alone has nothing of real value to offer.

Credit and collection policies.   Many a sales representative has learned, to his or her regret, the truth of the old axiom that a sale is not complete until it has been paid for. If products are returned by a customer due to his inability to pay for them or the sale is written off as a bad debt because of inability to collect, the "sale" is deducted from the total, and the sales representative loses sales credit.

Most sales representatives are required to obtain and submit full credit information on a new account before the sale is approved by the company credit department and the order fulfilled (see Figure 6.1). In most companies the credit manager holds decision-making power over whether or not to approve credit. This is often frustrating to sales representatives, who are primarily interested in the sale alone. They do not realize that the credit manager is actually their friend; that the credit function and the brakes it employs along the way are designed to help, not hinder, sales representative and customer alike. In most companies, the sales and credit departments work closely together to overall customer and company advantage. Most companies need healthy middleman and retail accounts and often go to great length creditwise to help them stay in business.

One good way for you as a sales representative to avoid possible credit problems is to put all terms of sale down on paper, explain them carefully, and obtain the buyer's signature. In cases where you are asked to help effect collections personally, an often distasteful task to sales representatives, you should handle them along the lines suggested in Chapter 15 on page 321.

WHAT SHOULD YOU KNOW ABOUT YOUR PRODUCTS?

Product knowledge is essential to successful selling. As a "problem solver" you will have to thoroughly understand your product or products in order to show prospects how and why they stand to benefit by buying.

This task can be never-ending if your product line consists of hundreds or thousands of different items or variations of items. Your company training program, its manuals or sample range, and your own study will furnish you with the necessary initial background to start your calls. After that, it is up to you how fast you gain additional knowledge. Most people are not blessed with the power of total recall and have to absorb bits and pieces of information each day until the mind, like a computer, puts them together clearly in some flash of insight.

The best way to become an expert in product knowledge is to try to learn something new each day, building systematically on previous knowledge. Your customers will gladly help you learn; the best way to get this help is to become sincerely interested in trying to understand and solve their problems.

The following is a list of some of the more important areas of product knowledge about which you should be informed. But first, let us note once again that knowing a lot about your product is not enough; the main thing is that you be able to express this knowledge in terms of user benefits. If your prospect is more interested in quality than price or service, you must be able to illustrate, prove, or demonstrate convincingly the quality-features, advantages, and benefits offered by your product.

AS OF (DATE) _____

ACCOUNT NAME _____

ADDRESS _____

_____

OFFICERS (IF A CORP.) _____

OWNERS (IF A PROPRIETORSHIP OR PARTNERSHIP) _____

BALANCE SHEET

ASSETS		LIABILITIES & CAPITAL	
CASH		ACCOUNTS PAYABLE	
ACCOUNTS RECEIVABLE		NOTES PAYABLE	
INVENTORY		OTHER (LOANS, ETC.)	
OTHER	_____		_____
TOTAL CURRENT		TOTAL CURRENT	
PLANT & EQUIPMENT		LONG TERM DEBT	
OTHER		TOTAL LIABILITIES	
	_____	NET WORTH	_____
TOTAL ASSETS	_____	TOTAL LIABILITIES & CAPITAL	_____

OPERATING STATEMENT

FOR PERIOD _____ , THROUGH _____

SALARY			
RENT		SALES	
TAXES		COST OF GOODS SOLD	
OTHER	_____	GROSS PROFIT	
*TOTAL EXPENSES	_____	*LESS EXPENSES	_____
		NET PROFIT	_____

SIGNED _____

FIGURE 6.1 Example of Credit Information. This type of credit information is often obtained by sales representatives for their company's credit department.

Origin and history. Is your product a new invention? If so, what led up to the invention, and how was it developed into its present form? If your product is an improvement on earlier ones, what led up to the development? Try to develop an interesting (even dramatic) story about the origin and history of your product, a story that will illustrate one or more selling points.

Research and development. Can you build an interesting story about the initial technical research that went into the product? Was it created especially to meet specific consumer demands learned about through market research? Is it an offshoot of some exciting venture such as the space program? How long did it take to develop? Articles, charts, or tables that show depth and results of technical or market research can offer convincing proof that your product is indeed as good as you say it is.

Manufacturing/production. What is your product made of? You should know both the materials and their characteristics. How is it made? Can you describe the process in an interesting way and show pictures to illustrate various stages of production? What is the quality of the workmanship? Can you show samples or illustrate or demonstrate quality features in any way?

What about its design? The engineering that went into its manufacture? What improvements does it have compared to earlier models or to the competition? What new scientific developments does it incorporate? What safety features?

The physical product/operation, and performance data. You must be able to describe your product in every physical detail and relate key features as a means of solving needs or problems. What will the product do? How does it work? How long will it last? What will it cost to use or operate it; can you break these costs down into man-hours saved or other cost reductions? Knowledge of technical facts and performance is what buyers are normally seeking. Features should be translated into user benefits at every opportunity, in every sales presentation.

After-sale servicing. Will your company help teach the buyer or his staff how to use or utilize the product or service? Will you personally follow up to see that they are utilizing it properly and are satisfied with their purchase? Does your company have trained technical or service representatives that can be called upon for technical or professional help? What about a guarantee, if any? How will your firm back up its guarantee?

It may frustrate you as a reader to read obviously incomplete lists like the above and see so many questions without answers. We cannot, however, go much further here into specific company or product knowledge required, since we do not know what products or services you do or may represent. But we can stress once again the importance of knowledge. The more knowledge you have, product and otherwise, about your firm and its business, the more respect you will get from your customers. This respect leads to sales and profits because if you have knowledge and work in a professional way you will get results. Also, as you gain respect, knowledge flows back from the customers through you to your firm so that better products can be devised to fill their needs.

WHAT PROMOTIONAL SUPPORT
CAN A SALES REPRESENTATIVE EXPECT?

In our Chapter 2 overview of the development, nature, and functions of marketing, we defined and briefly discussed the four-part "promotional mix" of promotion and selling, probably the most important of the eight functions listed. Advertising, publicity, sales promotion, and personal selling are the four parts of that mix.

Since no two marketing situations are exactly the same, the proper mix depends on the objective. Of course, the overall objective of the sales/marketing effort is to maximize profits, but the day-by-day activities are planned in terms of intermediate goals which ultimately lead to accomplishment of the objective. In most companies this is outlined in a carefully prepared, written marketing plan. We will now consider this plan, with emphasis on its advertising and sales promotion aspects.

The Marketing Plan

This usually written plan, covering any agreed-upon time period, is normally drafted in four parts: (1) the situation, (2) problems and opportunities, (3) strategy, and (4) tactics. The last is the basic working section, outlining within the overall marketing plan the tactics (various goals) to be implemented by the advertising, sales promotion, and public relations departments, and the sales force. The company's marketing, sales, and advertising directors normally are all vitally involved in final formulation of the overall plan. During such formulation, the sales force is often called upon for marketing feedback or suggestions.

Once the overall marketing plan is approved by management it must be put into action. It is the step-by-step master action plan, periodically reviewed by management to check progress on implementation and effectiveness of its various parts, flexible enough to allow for any adaptations in tactical plans required by any along-the-way changes in the marketplace.

Once this plan goes into effect, a whole series of preplanned interdependent merchandising activities take place involving the advertising program, publicity, and sales promotional activities—all designed to pave the way through information and preselling for your personal selling efforts.

Advertising

Advertising and personal selling are by far the two most important parts of the promotional mix. They work as a team toward the same end—that of selling goods and services. The role each plays is determined by the product being sold and the overall marketing plan. In cases of companies like Avon Products (cosmetics) and Electrolux (vacuum cleaners), who concentrate on door-to-door or home selling, little is spent on advertising. Other companies, such as direct-mail houses, utilize advertising almost exclusively. For most companies, a closely coordinated program of pre-selling by advertising (to gain interest and acceptance of the product and build goodwill), lays the groundwork for the sales representative to present final selling points around the prospect's needs or wants and close the sale.

Factors Influencing Effectiveness of Advertising

Advertising is most effective in impersonal selling to a mass audience (such as in retail self-service stores) and encompasses all merchandising activities that take place *outside* the store. Shoppers in such retail stores make quick selections, spending little time in deliberation. Brand identification plays a vital role in their selection. The job of advertising here is to presell shoppers on the producer's brand beforehand through such means as TV commercials, radio announcements, magazine ads, billboards, and the store's own ads in newspapers.

Certain conditions help ensure maximum effectiveness of advertising in any situation. These include such things as having a good product (if it is not good, customers will seldom become repeat buyers), having a significant difference from existing similar products (like Lipton Flo-Thru tea bags), and having an easily identifiable trademark (like Chiquita bananas). The product should also have a consistent quality and be one that can be sold impersonally to a mass market.

Advertising is least effective for higher-priced items such as automobiles or industrial products where buyers need explanations and demonstrations of technical features. In such cases the sales representative plays the most important role in the promotional mix.

Advertising is highly important in the selling of products such as foods, beauty aids, and soft drinks; and for services such as car rentals, insurance, and packaged travel tours. It also plays an important role in institutional- and organizational-cause selling. Institutional advertising is concerned with telling about the company or industry (for example, "savings and loan associations are a good place to invest money"), rather than about a specific product. Advertising is used to sell causes like fighting drug addiction or supporting your local police, and to raise funds for various purposes.

Types of Advertising

Various forms of advertising are employed along the way from producer to buyer which normally are part of an advertising plan mix within the complete marketing plan. They include:

National advertising. This is advertising by the producer aimed at the end-consumer, asking them to buy the trademarked product through retail outlets. Examples include countless well-known brands such as Lipton tea, Volkswagen automobiles, Singer sewing machines, Crest toothpaste, and Kellogg's Corn Flakes.

Retail advertising. This is also aimed at the end-consumer, but is done by retail chains or independent stores like department stores and supermarkets. Some of this retail advertising is for nationally advertised products (often through co-op ads where manufacturer and retailer share cost of the advertising), but it can also be for non-nationally advertised manufacturers brands, or for the store's own brand (often featured by chain-store organizations).

Trade (and professional) advertising. Advertising by the producer aimed at middlemen or retailers who will buy large quantities of the product for resale to end-consumers is called *trade advertising*. Such advertising stresses why they should buy and resell the product offered. *Professional advertising* is directed by the producer to those who can either recommend its use to end-consumers or who buy it for their use (such as pharmaceutical houses advertising specific drugs or medications to doctors).

Industrial advertising. This advertising is addressed to manufacturers who use the offered product in the making of their own product (such as a tire manufacturer advertising to Ford or General Motors).

Direct-response advertising. This is advertising by the producer direct to the end-customer in which a direct response is sought, either in the form of an order or a request for additional information by mail, or through a sales representative. Such advertising can be done by direct mail, telephone, television, or radio. Direct-response advertising seeks an immediate reply in response to the ad.

Overall, advertising assists the total marketing effort of a firm in many ways. Apart from increasing sales directly, it benefits the middlemen and retailers by supplying product information that enables them to buy wisely and more economically, thus increasing their profitable turnover. In addition, it helps the retailer build store prestige and increase in-store traffic.

Advertising benefits you as sales representative by helping secure leads to potential new customers, preselling prospects and customers prior to a personal sales call, reinforcing selling points, and contacting prospects or small-volume customers you might not be able to reach or visit otherwise due to time limitations.

Above all, from your point of view, advertising is working for you twenty-four hours a day, seven days a week, throughout the year—between calls, while you sleep, when you are ill or on vacation. Advertising and personal selling constantly supplement one another; a good mix of the two produces greater results for most firms than either could do alone.

Sales Promotion

We covered this topic adequately for our overview purposes in Chapter 2, where we noted that sales promotions are usually short-term or temporary activities designed to support advertising or sales-force activities and often involving "more for your money" or temporary price reductions. The three major types of sales promotion and types of activities within each were explained.

A major difference between advertising and sales promotion from a retail merchandising point of view lies in the fact that whereas advertising applies outside the store, sales promotions normally take place *inside* the store. Within the retail store, in order to give maximum exposure of the product to shoppers, *shelf-arrangement* is a separate area of attention, along with special sales promotions. The best combination of display (sales promotion) and shelf arrangement is sought by sales-promotion sales representatives selling to retailers.

In line with our theme of considering you as market manager of your sales territory, it should be noted that a manager does not simply passively accept what is handed down to him. He *manages* events, within the limitations of his responsibilities and authority. Thus you should learn everything about and get to know personally all key people possible concerned with your firm's advertising, sales promotion, and publicity or public relations departments. Don't just wait for them to help you; actively seek their extra help to ensure your personal success. Far too few sales representatives make any attempt to do this; the others' loss could be your gain.

WHAT SHOULD YOU KNOW ABOUT YOUR COMPETITION?

We said early in this chapter that you should learn everything possible about your industry, your company (products and policies), *and your competition*, in order to measure up to the modern concept of a problem-solving, diagnostic sales representative prepared to discuss all aspects of his business with his prospect or customer. Information should be sought in these basic areas:

Basic information about the industry and its markets. You need to know overall market potential and sales histories of your major competitors and their current market and individual product share in terms of dollars and units. Major current market trends must be studied, as well as economic factors affecting them.

How are products within the industry sold and distributed? You should seek information about the sales, cost and profit, history and current picture of key competitors' major competitive products, and relate them to your own products. Distribution channels should be studied, and sales methods that affect sales through these channels.

Individual competing products should be studied in comparison with your own. Information needed for such comparisons includes design, quality, sizes or models, packaging, delivery and after-sale service, plus overall performance comparisons.

Who uses the product—your competitors' and yours—and why? The end-consumer or prospective buyer must be identified and classified by age, sex, education, income level, occupation, and geographical location. What are his attitudes toward your product and service, and your major competitor's? What are his purchase habits, how does he use the product, and what trends may affect his future buying attitudes, purchase, and use habits? What are your competitors doing to capitalize on these trends?

Such information gathering is open-ended. First, you can turn to published information available from various sources. Second, you can learn by asking questions of experts within both your own company and your customer's firm. Published information can generally be found under these three broad headings: statistical data, individual company information, and industry or market studies. The following United States sources are among those suggested by various government publications.

Statistical data: Aggregate statistical data for companies classified by industry; or for plants classified by industry groups and industries; and for product shipments (or sales) classified by product class groups, product classes, and products themselves are available in different degrees of depth for different parts of the economy. Such data can be used to trace trends and to derive estimates for the future.

Financial data are, for example, available by 2-digit (broad-gauge) industries for all types of businesses in the *Statistics of Income* series published annually by the Bureau of Internal Revenue of the U.S. Department of the Treasury. Similar financial data are available for manufacturing corporations in the *Quarterly Financial Report for Manufacturing Corporations* now published by the Federal Trade Commission.

Trade data for 2-digit, 3-digit, and 4-digit manufacturing industries, as well as for 4-digit product class groups, 5-digit product classes, and 7-digit products, are published every five years by the Bureau of the Census as part of the *Census of Manufactures*; related data for wholesaling, retailing, and service industries are published by the Bureau of the Census as part of the *Census of Business*. Similar but less detailed data are also published annually—and in some cases on a monthly or weekly basis—by the Bureau of the Census.

Industry data are also published by other U.S. Government agencies, such as the Department of Agriculture, the Bureau of Mines, the Maritime Commission, and the Interstate Commerce Commission. Industry data are also available from the Federal Reserve Board, which publishes production indexes by industries, and from the Bureau of Labor Statistics, which publishes industry data on payrolls and hours worked; it also publishes a wholesale and a consumer price index, broken down by industries and/or products. The *Survey of Current Business* published by the Department of Commerce carries industry data on the components of GNP (Gross National Product) as well as other industry series.

Many trade journals also carry specialized data series for the industries they cover and additional statistical data are available to trade association members in many industries; these series supplement government series. In addition, many brokerage firms and investment advisory services publish information by industries, as do such general financial services as *Moody's* and *Standard & Poor's*.

Much of this data can normally be found in any large public, business, or university library. The data can also be obtained from various government offices, trade associations, or other sources, provided you know where to go and what to request.

Company information. Information for registered corporations is available in financial statements and prospectuses. While the complete documents, by definition, contain more information than condensations, the abbreviated material that appears in the *Moody's* manuals and such publications as *Standard & Poor's* is more readily available for a check of financial or product data for companies that can be identified by name. The *Fortune Directory* identifies major corporations by rank in sales. It does not, however, include data on nonlisted corporations. Information on the relative sizes of a more extended set of companies, by industries, is available in the *Newsfront Directory*, which classifies companies by 4-digit SIC categories.

Industry or market studies. Special government reports and hearings on specific industries are sometimes available. For a few industries, there are pamphlets or books in hardcover. These are often available in libraries.

Articles in business publications, such as *Fortune, Baron's, Forbes,* and *Business Week,* carry industry information of current nature. Most major corporations carry on their own market research and many also buy research from specialized organizations. Such material normally contains valuable industry insights and can be found in company libraries. Investment advisory services also frequently carry information organized on an industry basis.

SUMMARY

We have, in this chapter, continued to develop the theme that you as a modern customer-oriented, problem-solving sales representative must know a great deal about your industry, your company (its products and policies), and your competition. This is essential if you are to truly become a diagnostician, able to discuss intelligently and professionally all aspects of your prospects' or customers' business, and advise solutions to their problems in the form of your product or service, presented in terms of user-benefits.

Without knowing what type of selling you are now in, or may enter, we discussed generally the type and degree of knowledge you need about your company and its products. We then considered the promotional support your company provides, or should provide, to assist you in your personal selling. This was presented first in light of the overall marketing plan, for which you might be called upon to provide suggestions, and then in terms of the advertising and sales promotion parts of the four-part promotional mix which constitutes the total, integrated sales/marketing program for any firm's product or service. All this build-up leads to your personal sales task of meeting individual buyer needs and closing the sale.

Finally, tying in both the company and product knowledge needed, and the marketing plan and promotional mix, with similar knowledge about your competition, we presented various sources of information from which you can obtain data about your industry and competition other than your own company sources.

CHAPTER REVIEW

CONCEPTS TO REMEMBER*

_____ advertising mix   _____ Census of   _____ Trade Advertising
                                  Manufacturers   _____ Fortune Directory
_____ shelf-arrangement   _____ national advertising   _____ direct-response
_____ market plan   _____ industry standing   advertising

*For memory reinforcement, fill in the page number or numbers where these terms were described in this chapter.

QUESTIONS FOR ANALYSIS AND DISCUSSION

1. What is the meaning of the statement "a sale is not complete until it has been paid for"?
2. Describe and explain one good system that you as a sales representative might employ at the time of making a sale to avoid future credit problems between your company and your customer?
3. Would you consider advertising to be more effective in selling lower-priced mass-market items such as canned fruit, or higher-priced items such as data-processing systems for a business firm? Why?
4. What two terms do sales representatives often use to describe sales promotion activities that take place inside a retail store? Describe at least three such activities you have read about or seen.
5. What is a marketing plan? What are its four parts? Which of the four most concerns the field sales representative?
6. In order to get maximum exposure of your product in a supermarket, what two-part promotional arrangement would you as a sales representative seek to promote or sell? Describe differences between the two, and why both together would be more effective than simply one or the other.
7. Describe the difference between retail advertising and trade advertising.
8. Assuming you are an experienced typewriter sales representative, in what ways do you think you could usefully advise management in the early stages of drafting a market plan as to what advertising mix and sales promotion should be employed in introducing a newly developed "talking typewriter" (you talk and it types what you say)?

Case Study 6–1

SALES/MARKETING WITH LIPTON: SOME EXCERPTS FROM THEIR NEW SALES REPRESENTATIVE TRAINING COURSE

In 1871, an enterprising twenty-one-year-old opened his first provision shop in Glasgow, Scotland. He had a real talent for selling, and he combined it with efforts to sell his customers nothing but the best. By the time he was thirty, he had a chain of twenty shops and was selling throughout the United Kingdom. Tea was among the items featured in his growing chain of stores, and to ensure consistent top quality he traveled to Ceylon and bought his own tea estate. By the time he was forty, he was known as "Mr. Tea" and had the commission to supply Queen Victoria with tea. He was, of course, Thomas J. Lipton.

He was the first to package tea and sell it under a name brand, so that his customers could be sure they were getting the same high quality each time they bought Lipton's tea. Lipton was also the first to advertise tea. His prices were reasonable, his quality was always the best. Sir Thomas began marketing tea in North America in the 1890s, as well as throughout other parts of the world. Today Lipton's tea is world famous.

The growth of Thomas J. Lipton, Inc. in the United States has been rapid and innovative. Since 1938 a part of Unilever, one of the world's largest international corporations, it is today a large and highly respected member of the American food industry, with annual sales of over $400 million. In addition to tea, the company's 450 person sales force offers a diversified range of brand products including soup mix (Lipton), salad dressing (Wishbone), canned meat products (Morton House), noodles and macaroni products (Pennsylvania Dutch), pet foods (Tabby), ice cream products (Good Humor), and Knox Gelatine.

Lipton's programmed sales training course is one of the best in the food industry. Here are some extracts (in text form) from their sales training manual[3] that illustrate how Lipton sales representatives first learn about many of the topics covered in the chapter material just presented.

WHO BUYS LIPTON PRODUCTS?

1. Lipton is a consumer goods company, which means that our products are bought and used by consumers such as yourself or your family.
2. We're not in a service business, because we sell products rather than services. We're not an industrial goods company, because our products are consumed.
3. Because our focus is on the consumer, marketing is the heart of our business. Marketing includes all the many things that fall between manufacturing and the ultimate consumer.

WHERE DO CONSUMERS BUY OUR PRODUCTS?

1. The final step in marketing is sale to the consumer. From your own experience, you know that this sale takes place in grocery stores.
2. More specifically, most sales take place in supermarkets. You're probably familiar with supermarkets from shopping in them, or perhaps from working in one. But, technically, a supermarket is a grocery store doing over $500,000 in business per year. In other words, the definition is based upon the size of the store's sales.
3. Most sales of our products take place in stores doing a minimum of one-half million dollars a year; namely, in stores defined as supermarkets.
4. Supermarkets are surprisingly big business; they do over $89 billion a year.
5. In fact, the food industry as a whole is America's largest retail industry. Most of the industry's sales are through supermarkets.
6. There are many things that characterize supermarkets—self service, a variety of departments, check-out stands, etc.—but the industry's definition is: a store with over $500,000 of sales per year.

HOW DO OUR PRODUCTS GET TO THE STORE?

1. The marketing steps between Lipton and the consumer are determined in part by the sheer numbers involved. Consider these statistics: in round numbers, they are:

200,000,000	consumers
200,000	grocery stores
450	Lipton sales representatives

   Obviously we don't sell directly to the consumers. Similarly, we don't sell directly to all those stores.
2. The customers to whom we sell directly are the wholesalers and some of the stores.

---

3. Material excerpted from *Marketing with Lipton, Course I,* Thomas J. Lipton (Englewood Cliffs, N. J.: Thomas J. Lipton, Inc.) pp. 1–3. Reprinted by permission.

WHAT INFLUENCES BUYING?

1. Merchandising is that part of buying that most directly influences the consumer. Merchandising includes nearly everything that influences people to buy our products. (Your own personal selling is an exception; but, even there, you'll often be selling merchandising plans.) One influence that applies outside the store is advertising; other merchandising activities take place in the store.
2. Two other influences that apply in the store, while a consumer is shopping, are sales promotion and shelf arrangement. As the terms imply, sales promotion is a means of promoting sales, and shelf arrangement is the way our products are arranged on the grocer's shelves.
3. Short-term, or temporary, activities designed to increase sales are called sales promotions. They very often, but not always, involve the offer of "more for your money," such as a temporary price reduction.
4. One example of sales promotions are displays. Displays are extra space for our products. They're temporary, and they're in addition to the regular space for our products on the shelves. They're part of sales promotion because they influence buying.
5. Shelf arrangement is the way our products are ordinarily made available for sale to the consumer—the way they're shelved, in other words. Unlike advertising, this kind of merchandising takes place inside the store. Unlike sales promotion, it's relatively permanent.
6. In some respects, shelf arrangement is the most critical merchandising activity, because it influences the vast majority of our sales. The amount of space allocated to a particular product and the condition of the product are very strong influences on the consumers. Thus, shelf arrangement is a very strong part of merchandising.
7. So, the three main parts of Lipton's merchandising are (1) advertising, (2) sales promotion, and (3) shelf arrangement.
8. Merchandising is one part of marketing; personal selling is another. Personal selling means the kind of face-to-face selling you'll be doing when you call on the trade. Since supermarkets are self-service, the trade sells to the consumer mainly through merchandising but not through personal selling. We sell to the trade through merchandising and through personal selling.
9. In personal selling, you have a kind of double role; the grocery trade is our customer, but it's also our partner in selling to the consumer. One way of putting this is that your job is to "aid and persuade the trade." Because we sell to them we depend upon you to persuade. Because we depend upon them to market our products effectively, we depend upon you to aid.

PLANNING FOR SELLING LIPTON PRODUCTS

1. The third major area of marketing is planning. The first two, which we have already discussed, are merchandising and personal selling.
2. Our planning is based on what is sometimes called the "marketing concept." This means that we plan all of our operations to produce a profit by meeting the needs of our customers and their customers. In other words, the single most important question to consider for each of our products is: "Will it sell?"
3. We plan all of our operations (1) to produce a profit and (2) to do so by meeting the needs of our customers and their customers. Thus, planning starts with the needs of our customers, the grocery trade, and the ultimate customers, the consumers.
4. Consumer needs are the basis for a product concept. On the basis of consumer needs, we develop a product that has certain features which will produce the benefits the consumers need or want.
5. A benefit is a need that has been met. The characteristic of the product that produces the benefit is a feature. Taken together, the characteristics and benefits form the product concept.
6. One feature of our Instant Tea is that we remove elements that would cause cloudiness when the tea is prepared by the housewife. The benefit that results is clear, non-cloudy tea.
7. "What's in it for me?" is something we all want to know before we buy. So, in selling it's more effective to stress benefits than to stress features.
8. New product planning starts with the product concept, then continues through the market research and test market phases. Then, if the product has proven itself to be a winner, it goes into the national introduction (launch) phase.

9. The first few weeks of a new product's life make it or break it. If the introduction isn't successful, the product very probably won't survive.
10. The merchandising of a new product in the store is the critical factor in the introduction. One of your most critical sales responsibilities is to ensure the successful introduction (merchandising) of new products.
11. Annual planning is the marketing planning that is done for established products. A plan is developed for each category—Soup Mix, Wishbone, Instant Tea, etc. The plan is developed each year.
12. An important part of annual planning is development of an attainable volume (sales) objective. We call this objective *proforma*. Proforma is developed for each product category for the coming year. Proforma is an attainable volume objective. Or, in other words, it's a reliable projection of sales for the year.
13. Besides estimating our sales figures, or proforma for the year, we also plan the profits and costs for the year. As a formula, it could be put this way: proforma = costs + profit.
14. One of the major factors in cost is the amount we invest in advertising and sales promotion. We develop these costs at the same time that we develop the figures for proforma and profit, and we actually make these investments well in advance of sales.
15. Achieving proforma requires skill in each area of marketing. Thus, your responsibility is to achieve proforma through planning, personal selling, and merchandising, the three main types of sales/marketing that concern us most.

QUESTIONS FOR WRITTEN REPORTS OR CLASS DISCUSSION

1. Do you feel the above information tells a new sales representative enough about Thomas J. Lipton, Inc., and the American food industry? If not, what other information should be presented, so that he will go into the field thoroughly informed of all aspects of Lipton's business?
2. Concerning tea as one of Lipton's products, what would you as a new Lipton sales representative want to learn about it?
3. Brand identification plays a vital role in quick-selection decisions by shoppers in supermarkets. What type outside-the-store advertising do you think Lipton should do for its Flo-Thru tea bags, to presell these shoppers most effectively?
4. From what sources could you, as a new Lipton sales representative, learn everything possible about the competition you can expect to face for each of your different product lines?

Case Study 6–2

SALES REPRESENTATIVE AND CREDITMAN— PARTNERS TO HELP THE CUSTOMER

Approving or rejecting credit is not a whimsical matter. Most companies' credit department policy is (a) "Know your customer," and (b) "When in doubt as to whether to approve or reject, resolve that doubt in favor of making the sale."

To the sales representative, an order is a piece of gold. It represents profit to the company, possible bonus for himself, and an ever expanding market for future sales. To the creditman, at the company home office or branch, it may represent just one more piece of paper. He may lose sight of the fact that behind that piece of paper is a flesh-and-blood, living human being whom the sales representative has cultivated as a *customer*.

Modern, customer-oriented credit theory recognizes the importance of close cooperation between the sales representative in the field and the home office, or branch; that there should be recognition and respect for each other's problems. Such cooperation results in teamwork that promotes profitable sales and harmonious customer relations.

Today, it is more necessary than ever before for companies to maintain tight control of their money. The experience of having to "write off" $150,000 due from one bankrupt account is traumatic. It is equally traumatic to write off 150 accounts owing $1,000 each. The close cooperation and continual two-way flow of information between credit and field, and field and credit is more essential than ever before in the history of American business.

Here are some practical guidelines for the sales representative concerning such cooperation that are typical of those formulated by many American business firms:

1. Complement the creditman's efforts by acting upon his communications. Copies of letters are supplied to inform the sales representative of the status of overdue accounts. Primarily these are for information only and most require no action. But if a direct memo is sent, specifically spelling out a particular problem, the sales representative should take immediate action—otherwise (in the absence of any response) the creditman will feel that the sales representative has no interest in the case.
2. Volunteer information about special circumstances affecting an established customer —good as well as bad. For instance, the customer may be planning an autograph party or a special sales campaign. Conversely, he may be having trouble with his landlord, or sickness in the family, or damage due to a flood or a fire. Keep the creditman informed ahead of time if possible.
3. Counsel a customer who has been receiving collection letters (sales representatives are normally sent copies). Advise him that the credit department is under constant pressure (especially in any period of difficult economic climate), but that the creditman will be sympathetic to any special problem. Remember, though, that the creditman is in a far-away office and won't know about any extenuating circumstances unless the customer or sales representative advises him.
4. It is particularly important to submit financial information promptly on new customers. A businessperson expects to be asked for references. It is best to report information you have gained in:
    (a) *New customer information*—this may be a memo, or company-supplied form for this particular reporting. It should include not only factual information (type of business, number of employees, etc.), but also your personal comments. These should include your general impressions such as age and health of the principal, general housekeeping, size of store, whether the principal is mayor of the town, president of the local library association, etc.
    (b) *Financial statement*—this is a standard business format form showing assets, liabilities, and other basic financial information (see Fig. 6.1). He may have such a form on hand, recently prepared. If he has one, ask him for it. If not, ask him if he has filed such a statement recently with Dun & Bradstreet. If neither, leave a form (most companies issue them routinely to sales representatives) and ask him to fill out the data and mail it promptly to your company credit department. Attach one or both the above reports to your initial order to speed processing.

QUESTIONS FOR WRITTEN REPORTS OR CLASS DISCUSSION

1. In addition to submitting the two reports noted above when submitting an initial order for a new customer, what additional things could you as sales representative do at the same time to help ensure prompt credit-department approval and order fulfillment?
2. Do you feel your customer might get offended by your asking him the detailed financial questions shown in Figure 6.1. Why?

3. Assuming you are a sales representative needing such financial information, how would you go about asking your new customer for it?
4. Why is it particularly important for a sales representative to submit complete as possible credit or financial information promptly to his company on new customers?

SALES PROBLEM 6-1

CAN POTTERBRIDGES' PAPER SACKS BE SOLD PROFITABLY TO WINTERBOTTOM IN PEAS POTTAGE?

This is not a tongue-twisting riddle but a serious problem in paper-sack selling to Paul P., who represents Potterbridges' Proved Paper Products, Ltd. (fondly known through the trade as PPPPL in southern England) out of his home town of Newton Poppleford, Devon.

Paul, his company, and his prospect may be mythical, but paper-sack (not bag) selling is a big and very competitive business in Cornwall, Devon, Hampshire, Dorset, Somerset, and Wiltshire counties. Heaps of potatoes, fruits, vegetables, chemicals, coal, seeds, wheat, corn, and refuse all go into paper sacks in this part of England.

Our friend Paul has just spotted a potential new sales prospect: Frisky Fido Food ships its product in big paper sacks. Thinking quickly, Paul decides that there could be one dog for every 10 people in southern England and if Frisky Fido reaches even one in 100, it could mean many extra paper-sack sales—in the hundreds of thousands over a period of time!

He notes that the manufacturer of Frisky Fido is A. Winterbottom & Sons Fertilizer Processing Co. Ltd., of Peas Pottage, Hants. Being a customer-oriented sales representative, Paul decides to scientifically study the needs of this potential customer and to prepare a sales presentation of PPPPL paper sacks that can offer Winterbottom better value for his money. Price means everything in the competitive paper-sack business, so his basic problem is to offer Winterbottom this better value at a lower price if possible and still to allow PPPPL to make its profit.

Here are some of the problems Paul has to solve in order to come up with an answer to Winterbottom's packaging needs.

CUSTOMER INFORMATION

(1) How big a supplier is Winterbottom? (2) How many sacks of Frisky Fido does he ship per week or month? (3) What other products does he manufacture and ship in paper sacks? (4) What other products does he ship in competitive packaging (i.e., cardboard cartons, wooden crates, or plastic containers) that could be shipped in paper sacks?

PACKAGING INFORMATION

(1) Who manufactures the currently used Frisky Fido sack? (2) How much does the presently used sack cost Winterbottom? (3) What is the quality of the competing

sack: how many layers does it have, what are the properties of each layer (i.e., waterproof or extra tough), and what are the reasons for extra layers if any?

PRODUCT INFORMATION

(1) What are the properties of Frisky Fido, the product being shipped? (2) What properties are necessary in the PPPPL sack to protect the product being shipped (i.e., waterproofing, oil base)? (3) What strength PPPPL sack is needed to ship Frisky Fido properly?

PAUL'S OVERALL PROBLEM

Through knowledge of his product, the competing product, and the customer's needs, he must work out what it would cost PPPPL to produce a better sack at a lower price if possible. If a lower price is impossible, then he will have to use extra value to justify the difference.

QUESTIONS FOR WRITTEN REPORTS OR CLASS DISCUSSION

Assuming you are Paul, how would you gather the above information prior to contacting Winterbottom? You should have the answers before making your sales presentation if at all possible.

7
prospecting and organizing your prospect list

When you have mastered the content of this chapter, you should be able to:

Define the terms *prospect, prospecting, qualified prospect, sales lead, referral leads,* and *cold-call canvassing.*

Describe two common steps employed in the prospecting process and the difference between prospecting and the preapproach.

List many specific sources of locating new prospects (leads) from within your company, from your present customers, from competitors, by canvassing your industry, through social contacts, and through other initiatives.

Construct a direct-mail prospecting letter that will also serve to qualify the prospect.

Summarize the importance of qualifying a prospect prior to a sales presentation, and give the three questions that must be answered in order to ensure proper qualification.

Describe certain advantages offered by the telephone in prospecting and selling.

Outline six progressive steps involved in pre-call planning prior to qualifying prospects and making appointments by telephone, and give key factors to be considered under each.

Summarize basic principles and techniques in properly using the telephone for (1) qualifying prospects and making the appointment, and (2) selling.

A major first step in analyzing your sales territory is to determine which firms or individuals are or could become customers for your product or service. Your company will provide you with a current customer list, but it is basically your job to increase sales by finding more customers. You want to find new ones not only from a personal point of view but also to replace the average 10 to 20 percent of customers normally lost by any firm during the year for one reason or another.

Why do regular customers drop away and need to be replaced? Transfers, deaths, retirements, liquidations, corporate takeovers, and real or fancied grievances are but a few such reasons. Another is your competition, whose eager and aggressive sales representatives like nothing better than increasing their business at your expense. You have to be competitive in spirit, and sales and service-minded enough to hang onto your current customers and to increase their business where possible. You also have to be prospect-minded, constantly alert to the fact that a steadily expanding list of qualified prospects is vitally important to the increased sales necessary for your success.

What do we mean by a qualified prospect? What is prospecting? How does one find and qualify new prospects? These are questions we will now consider.

WHAT DO WE MEAN BY QUALIFIED PROSPECTS?

There is a big difference between a mere list of possible customers, called leads (pronounced lēds), and a list of qualified prospects. A dictionary definition of lead is "that which acts as a guide or clue." In sales terminology, a lead becomes a prospect (person, firm, or institution) when it has been determined that it can benefit from the product or service. A qualified prospect not only needs and can benefit from it but also must be able to afford it and be able to make the decision to purchase it.

We can further illustrate the importance of finding qualified prospects. No matter what work you are engaged in as a real sales representative, you are interested in discovering potential customers who have a basic need for your product. Through persuasion you have to change that need, first into a want and then into the action of a purchase. You may easily find those who need your product and whom you can convince to want to buy it now. But if they do not have the money to buy or do not have the authority to make an official company decision to buy, you will be wasting your time.

WHAT IS PROSPECTING?

Different sales representatives encounter different problems in finding qualified prospects. In general however, the process involves two common steps: (1) checking all possible sources for leads that may become prospects and (2) qualifying these prospects as to their buying potential.

This process of looking up and checking leads is called *prospecting*. It involves collecting the names of people who on the surface appear to want or need your product and checking further to determine whether they can become prospects. These further checks are called *qualification*. In this chapter, we will examine first where you can find prospects and then methods of qualifying them. Finally, we will discuss the use of the telephone in carrying out both the above steps and also in making an appointment to see the prospect.

Before going on, however, we should understand the difference between prospecting, which we are now studying, and the preapproach, which will be covered in Chapter 9. The steps involved in prospecting are obtaining lists of names (leads) which are further qualified to turn up prospects who need and will benefit from your product and who have the money plus the decision-making ability to buy. Collection of or action on any further information or data is part of the preapproach.

We will illustrate some of the steps involved in finding prospects with examples from several specific types of selling. We cannot cover everything in these few pages however, so you are again urged to apply the principles discussed to your actual or hoped-for sales position. Apply what is useful to your situation, and ignore ideas which are not applicable. The list below is fairly comprehensive and practical and should be a useful reference in both your salesmanship studies and your sales position.

HOW YOU CAN LOCATE NEW PROSPECTS

The basic equation of selling is sales representative + prospect = sale. You as the sales representative represent one-half of this equation; but where do you find prospects, the missing part? The answer is almost anywhere and everywhere. The sources for finding prospects are all around you. You have to discover what these sources are and employ all the initiative and persistence necessary to put them to work for you.

What are some of the sources for finding prospects? Your company, your industry, business competitors, customers, and even prospects who do not buy from you—these are but a few. One secret of prospecting success is to utilize each to the greatest depth possible. Here are some hints.

Leads from your company.   These are the easiest to obtain, yet it is amazing how few sales representatives use initiative enough to get maximum benefit from all possible company sources. Sources for leads exist in many different divisions and departments of each company but are seldom available from one single source in easy-to-obtain form. You may find it worthwhile to meet various department heads and to ferret information out for yourself from among the following sources.

Current active customer lists are the easiest lists to obtain and are normally handed over to you as a matter of course. But what about customer lists from other divisions of your company? Another division may sell a different product with its own sales representatives, mailing lists, and records. If your company has such different divisions, check them to see if they have any additional names, apart from those on your own lists, who may be potential customers for you.

Credit departments are useful for inactive accounts or for credit bureau rating reports on noncustomer accounts. You can often turn people who bought from your company in the past once again into productive customers. Even if they cannot be resold, they can often tell you about others who may buy from you. Your credit department probably subscribes to a credit-rating service that gives information about newly formed companies, yet credit department personnel may not be sales-minded enough to even think of turning over such names to the sales department as potential leads. Can you get them for yourself?

Company service department records may indicate calls to service equipment for which a new replacement may mean savings for the customer. Service person-nel may or may not be trained to report such possibilities to the sales department. Perhaps such people can become bird dogs for you, reporting to you alone (per-sonal gifts or a commission cut would help win them over) on all sorts of sales possibilities inside firms or homes on which they make service calls.

Advertising plays an important part in every company promotion plan. It will pay to know what advertising will be going out and to what specific lists well in advance of publication and mailing. You may be able to personalize such ads to your advantage. Few sales representatives take the trouble to initiate meetings with key advertising people and thus miss good opportunities. Would it not be helpful if a higher than usual percentage of customer reply cards were handed over to you personally by your friends in the advertising department?

Exhibits, conventions, and trade fairs in which your company participates are excellent sources of leads. Attend all these you can, even if you are not a delegated representative, and exchange business cards with everyone you meet. Study these afterward, and ask yourself which ones may need your product or service. Then write or phone them, saying that, since meeting them, you have thought of an idea which may benefit them.

People who attend such exhibits or conventions are usually interested in the products on display. You thus have a chance to meet prospects from areas you may have overlooked on regular calls, and certainly have an excellent opportunity to talk easily with a larger than average number of potential prospects during the day or evening.

Direct mail, either on a systematic company basis or through your own initiative in utilizing company resources and lists, can work while you work, getting new leads for you. A well-written, direct-mail piece contains triple bait for prospects —news, benefits, and confidence—these help set the stage for your personal follow-up call.

Direct mail is a relatively inexpensive prospecting technique that helps qualify a prospect. Your company can send such letters out for you, or you can have it done at your own expense. Insurance companies often send out such direct-mail letters, in which, for example, a small free gift may be offered in exchange for either the prospect's birthday or that of a friend he suggests. (See Figure 7.1.) If the information is returned, the name and birth date become a lead to be followed up by a qualifying phone call or even by a personal visit from the sales representative.

Direct mail prospecting is also employed by many nonbusiness organizations, commonly to obtain members to support a cause of one kind or another. Figure 7.2 illustrates an example of such solicitation by Common Cause, an independent, "citizen's lobby" of concerned citizens dedicated to making government at all levels more responsive to needs of United States citizens.

Telephone prospecting will be discussed at length later on. But we mention here that some companies have special operators who do it on a large and systematic basis. They call home or business telephone subscribers, often offering special prices if the prospect agrees to see a sales representative in his home. The lead is thus qualified, and a sales representative calls on what is considered a prospect. Individual sales representatives can employ the same technique on a similar basis, either through company or personal arrangements.

Inquiries from interested firms or individuals may come into various departments of your company. These may be in response to advertising, referrals, or word-of-mouth information about one or more products or services. Does your company have a system for turning these over as sales leads? If not, try to find out who receives such calls and whether the potential leads from them could be turned over to you.

Canvassers are employed by some companies or by some individual commission sales representatives to take part of the burden of cold-call canvassing or prospecting away from the real sales representatives. Often called spotters or bird-dogs, they most often use the telephone in prospecting, but frequently call door to door to qualify prospects and to arrange appointments for evening or other call-back interviews. Firms selling such things as encyclopedias, oil burners, vacuum cleaners, and automobiles often employ canvassers.

Some commission sales representatives use a modification of this system. They employ such people as elevator boys, barbers, bartenders, or waitresses to be their bird dogs in spotting potential customers.

New clients are often excellent sources of leads. They are likely to refer you to other good prospects if you relate your request for their assistance to the same reason that caused them to buy from you.

Your own records can be a profitable source of leads if kept up to date and properly indexed. A prospect may say, "I'm not interested now but may be next summer." If you feel it to be a valid lead, you should put it in your follow-up file and call again in the summer. The same holds true if you learn of future industry or prospect developments that could mean one or more sales at a later date. A professional sales representative takes note of everything of potential interest learned on each call and turns his files into a rich source for future leads.

INTERGLOBAL INSURANCE COMPANY

New York — London — Beirut — Tokyo — Buenos Aires

Fred Roberts
Branch Manager

60081 Eastern Avenue
Dallas, Texas
_____

PHONE 312-0896

March 30, 1975

Mr. Ian Stevenson
General Manager
Fosters Products, Inc.
43 Tightrope Walk
Flintknoll, Arizona

Dear Sir:

Would you mind just giving me your date of birth below so that
I may furnish you data on a new executive protection plan,
which, due to its low cost, is probably the most discussed
policy in the insurance world today.

A self-addressed, postage-paid return envelope is enclosed for
your convenience.

Very truly yours,

Fred Roberts

Fred Roberts
Branch Manager

Name _____

Address _____ City _____

Telephone Number _____ Date of Birth _____

FIGURE 7.1 Example of a Direct-mail Attempt to Qualify a Prospect. The prospect's
name could have been obtained from any number of sources.

 **common cause**

2030 M STREET, N.W., WASHINGTON, D. C. 20036

John W. Gardner, Chairman   (202) 833-1200

Dear Friend:

One of our members has suggested that you, like thousands of other citizens, are concerned about what is happening in and to this country -- and want to do something about it. We have enclosed material which will answer any questions you may have about who we are and what we are doing.

Common Cause is a very uncommon organization -- a constructive, independent, non-partisan movement of concerned citizens -- over 250,000 strong and growing -- determined to help rebuild this nation. We invite you to join us. We are Americans who don't believe that mere complaining gets results. We intend to do something. Many things are wrong. Many things must be done to correct them. And wishing won't make it happen. Action will. Our institutions don't move unless we push them -- and push them hard.

We are building a true "citizens' lobby" -- concerned not with the advancement of special interests, but with the well-being of the nation. War, discrimination, poverty, pollution and legislative irresponsibility threaten our existence as a united, democratic country. And we dare not be so skeptical as to say there is nothing we can do about it. Common Cause is proving we can do something about it.

When you become a member you will be doing more than just lending your financial support -- you will become a part of a strong growing core of enlightened citizens who are doing something. And together with them, you will carry on the tough job of making government at all levels more responsive to the needs of its citizens.

You will find a Common Cause Membership Form in the enclosed material. We urge you to fill it out and mail it back today. Together, we can build a better America.

Sincerely,

John W. Gardner
Chairman

enc.
JWG:mm

FIGURE 7.2 Example of a direct-mail solicitation by an active cause organization.

Leads from your present customers. These are perhaps your best single source. A fundamental fact of selling is that it is usually easier to sell to a current satisfied customer than to a new one. If you have done a good sales job and your customer is pleased with your products, company, service, and you, he will be only too happy to pass the good word along. Few of them volunteer however; they have to be asked.

You can get leads from satisfied customers in several ways. The first is simply to ask for their assistance. You may say, for example, "Mr. Brady, do you know of any personal or business acquaintances who may benefit, as you have done, from my product?" You may then suggest, "Do you mind my using your name as an introduction when I contact him for an interview?" Quite often your customer will be unable to think of a specific person he feels may consider your product. It may therefore be useful to ask him a question in general terms such as, if you are selling insurance, "Do you know anyone who has gotten a good promotion or raise lately? If so, I wonder if you could help me meet him."

Called *referral leads*, these specific leads given you by a satisfied customer, are generally considered the most valuable for getting you in touch with truly qualified prospects. The best kind of referral lead is a formal letter of introduction, recommending both you personally and your product. Few customers are willing to take the time to write such a letter, but if a customer allows you to prepare a draft for his approval, it is very easy for him merely to turn it over to his secretary for typing.

FIGURE 7.3 Customer's referral to a business friend, written on the back of his business card.

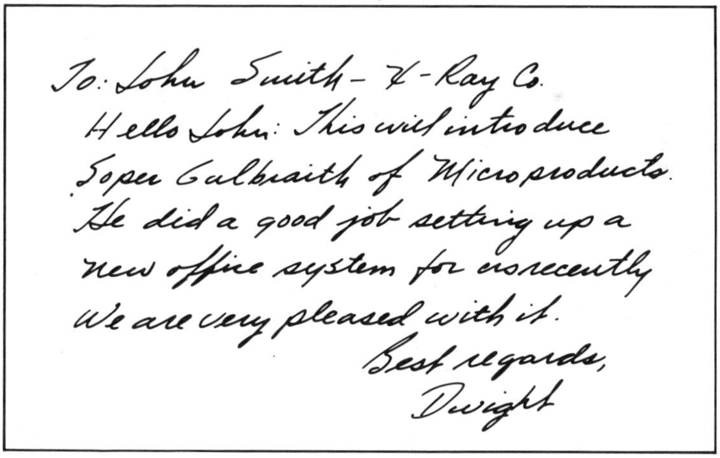

To: John Smith - X-Ray Co.
Hello John: This will introduce
Joseph Galbraith of Microproducts.
He did a good job setting up a
new office system for us recently
We are very pleased with it.
             Best regards,
                Dwight

Perhaps the easiest system of getting customer referral leads is to have the customer dash off a brief note of introduction on the back of his business card. Such a note need only be something like the one in Figure 7.3. You can also ask him to jot down such a brief introduction on the back of your calling card. In this case, you should ask for his full signature. Either way, this personalized card serves as a quick, valuable, attention-getting lead and should enable you to get in to see the new prospect without delay.

You can also obtain business-card referrals from a prospect you fail to sell! You can ask for his help in recommending new prospects, providing you did a good selling job and feel the climate is right for making such a request. He probably will feel a little bad about having turned you down and will therefore be glad to do you a small favor by suggesting one or more good potential prospects.

You can make the same request to a prospect to whom you have just made a sale, whether he be an old or new customer. You simply ask him if he has friends or business associates who may have problems similar to the one for which your products or services have just provided a solution. If you have sold him an encyclopedia set, for example, you may ask, "Mr. de Pinzon, can you give me the names of any friends or relatives with children around the age of your own who may find such a set useful for school-work reference?" Such customers may even write you a testimonial letter which you can show all future prospects.

If you are an industrial sales representative calling on company purchasing agents, the question is basically the same. In fact, you should talk up your own business in every way possible with each regular customer or new prospect you meet. Tell them what you are doing, what you hope to accomplish, and ask for their advice and guidance in reaching new prospects. If your listeners are not in the market themselves for what you sell, they may know someone else who is or who could become interested if he knew about it.

Leads from competitors and noncompetitors. Leads from competitors can be obtained by tracing the movement of competition products. You can learn of such activities from your own customers as well as from industry journals, the newspaper, or organizations such as your local chamber of commerce.

Sales representatives of noncompeting companies can be especially good sources for leads. They often have inside information on company buying policy, names of key decision makers, and dates purchases will be made. You may, for example, sell typewriters and learn from a friend in an employment agency that a given company plans to double its secretarial and clerical staff early next year. This can be a valuable lead to a quantity sale of your typewriters plus other office machines produced by your company. It pays to cultivate sales representatives of noncompetitive products and to reciprocate by providing them with information when possible.

Canvassing your industry. Another way to obtain excellent leads is to canvass your industry. You can get lists of potential customers from trade journals, chambers of commerce, credit bureau reports, and other sources. Many of these list names of purchasing officers or key department heads. These sources also often indicate the growth potential and latest developments of the industry and of companies within the industry. If conditions are changing, then you possibly can move in with new ideas that will help individual companies retain or improve their competitive positions.

Business and financial news within the industry or associated ones is especially important. A new contract, a merger, a building permit, a new bond issue, or a dramatic increase in profits spell opportunity for you. News of promotions or new appointments can mean sales of real estate, investments, insurance, or new automobiles. Management changes of any sort are especially important.

You can find worthwhile industry leads in the yellow pages of your telephone directory, and in city, trade, social, and professional directories. You can canvass leads obtained in this way by letter, by telephone, and through personal office calls.

Governmental departments, business libraries, and clipping services are all additional sources for leads. Many companies and many commission sales representatives or individuals subscribe to clipping services, whose staffs read all journals and newspapers, both national and local. For a fee, they cut out and mail all clippings that may be of interest to the subscribers.

Social contacts.   Social contacts are an excellent source of leads. Many sales representatives are not only members of but also active leaders in such organizations as Toastmasters' Clubs, Rotary, church, golf or other sports clubs, and all kinds of community and social organizations. The element of reciprocal selling is strong in many of these groups, but the wise sales representative keeps social contacts social. Such contacts often turn into good leads, but selling should be done during business hours. It may help a sharp young insurance sales representative to be thought of as "that terrific song leader at our club-sponsored picnic," but not as "that bore who tried to sell insurance at our club picnic."

Many aggressive and successful sales representatives respect their social responsibilities and treasure their personal lives, to the extent that they refuse to sell to relatives, close friends, or even neighbors. This gives them an ease in social relationships that is denied the hard-sell character always trying to use friendship as the means to an easy sale. Sales representatives who clearly separate their business and personal, social life are generally admired.

Finding leads on your own.   Called *cold-call canvassing* this is still the backbone of creative prospecting for most sales representatives. The trick here is to know all the potential markets for your product or service and then to classify all potential buyers who have a need for it and who can easily be contacted. Since there could be hundreds of such prospects, proper organization of your prospect list is highly important. You first have to list companies, agencies, or individuals who (1) have a basic need for the product and (2) have the money to pay for it. Once the listing is made in order of apparent potential, you should make persistent, systematic calls on all groups or individuals listed.

Some successful sales representatives organize their cold-canvassing prospect list along the lines of the yellow pages in the telephone directory. If, for example, you are selling air-conditioning equipment, you can parallel the listings in the yellow pages with a list of potential users for your product, arranged by industry with sublistings of companies or individuals.

No matter how you organize your list, the possibilities for finding leads are virtually unlimited, depending of course on the potential need for your product. Here are but a few sources for such leads.

Door-to-door canvassing. This can be done in residential areas house-to-house or on an office-to-office basis in a large building.

Your own creative ideas can provide leads. You may, for example, read about a new product being developed by a local company. Perhaps you can devise a way it can be combined with your product and thus open entirely new sales possibilities for that company—and yourself.

From other people with whom you do business. If you are a home owner and married man or woman, you deal with many people: banker, home builder, electrician, plumber, grocer, doctor, milkman, lawyer, and retailers of many types. Any of these can either become a prospect or refer you to others.

Special-need groups can provide leads for finding prospects. Does your product appeal to working adults, retired people, white-collar workers, teenagers, executives, lawyers, artists, people who sit while at work, or fishermen? If you list such special-need groups and find out how and where they can best be reached, you may be on your way to rapid sales success.

Newspapers provide new potential prospect names by the scores each day if you know where to look for them. Birth, promotion, business, financial, and real estate notices or stories can, when linked to your product, lead to new prospects.

Influentials, or people in your area who know many others and are known, can provide excellent leads. Newspaper editors, presidents of Chambers of Commerce, leading bankers, or well-known socialites can, if convinced of the merits of your product, express favorable opinions and give recommendations that make your selling job easier.

Your friends and acquaintances may know people who are good prospects. Even if you do not like to sell to your friends, you should ask them for leads. If your products offer real benefit, do not be afraid to tell your friends in a conversational manner what you sell, what it can do, and why it is good.

Join professional organizations, participate in their activities, and read their journals. Sales and Marketing Executives International is an important professional sales organization with national clubs in over forty-nine countries of the Free World and with local chapters in various cities. The American Management Association, with head offices in New York City, has affiliated chapters in most major American cities. Similar, internationally affiliated, national management groups exist in most countries. These are but two examples of professional organizations you may find worthwhile joining where possible.

Other ways of finding leads through personal initiative include examining where possible the files of trust companies and the deed recordings at municipal offices and reviewing newly issued business licenses.

HOW CAN YOU QUALIFY NEW PROSPECTS?

It costs you and your company time and money to locate new prospects. This time is wasted if you make a sales presentation only to find that your prospect is unable to consider your proposal for honest reasons—including lack of money in the budget or lack of authority to make a decision.

Your initial task therefore is to qualify your prospect before getting into the sales presentation. The depth of qualification depends in part on the product you are selling. If you are proposing employee accident insurance to a firm, you must find out who (which individual or group) makes the decision, when present coverage if any expires, and when the firm will be able to make a decision. If you are selling a diaper or baby napkin service, you must find out whether there are small babies in the home and whether the family already subscribes to such a service. If you are selling an automobile, you need to find out how the prospect will use it, so you can help him select the proper vehicle.

Proper qualification of a prospect involves obtaining satisfactory answers to these questions:

Does he have a need for the product or service?   If you determine that your product can help your prospect make money, save money, or do a better job, or otherwise honestly benefit him, then a need exists. You still have the task of persuading him to want the product now, but at least you have qualified him as to need.

Does he have the authority to buy?   Getting the answer to this question is just as important when calling on business firms as when calling on home owners. Qualification of the authority to buy involves determining whether the prospect can make the buying decision by himself. In selling to prospects in their homes, you should keep in mind that in most American homes the wife plays the key role. Husband and wife make most expensive purchases jointly however, although the woman may still make the final decision. Thus, in selling a children's encyclopedia for the home, you should make your presentation to the husband and wife together.

If you are selling a computer to a company, you may have to see several decision makers individually or make a presentation before a group of executives. Key questions to ask before making your presentation are: "If interested, Mr. Lombardo, will you be the one who makes the decision alone or will others be involved?" If others are involved, you can continue by asking, "How can I best present my product for the benefit of your entire purchasing committee?" It often saves time to ask his advice and help in such situations.

When two or more people are involved in a buying decision, determine who the key prospect is and plan your presentation accordingly. In the case of a husband and wife, the wife may be the key prospect. In a partnership business, you may first ask to see the "partner who usually does the buying." In companies, your key prospect may be the department head whose people will be most actively using your product. You can save time and money by trying to locate the key prospect or decision maker at time of qualification.

Can he pay for it? Qualification of a prospect's ability either to pay in cash or to qualify for credit terms often depends on your personal estimate of his surroundings, status, and occupation. He may appear willing to pay but really not be able to afford to do so. If a cash payment is required, it doesn't take long to find that out—he either has the cash or doesn't. But if credit is involved, caution is called for. There are certain types of prospects who have no scruples about signing an agreement to purchase something on a credit terms basis, with little intention to pay if they can possibly avoid it. Others readily sign up either knowing then, or discovering later they really can't afford to meet the payments as they fall due. Remember, no sale is complete until it has been paid for! If you are selling to home owners or individuals, you can tell a lot about a person's financial position by the way he dresses, the way he talks, the kind of car he drives, and his readiness to disclose the name of his bank or other companies with whom he does business.

When selling to firms, ask your company credit department for a credit check before spending time on a full-scale presentation. Commission sales representatives often find it worthwhile to subscribe to credit-rating services, such as Dun & Bradstreet. Trade commissioners or consuls of most nations gladly assist sales representatives selling in a foreign country to obtain credit information. Better Business Bureaus in many cities of the world help obtain credit information. The Chamber of Commerce is yet another organization that may be able to assist and advise you in such matters.

Newspaper reporters get all the facts on a potential news item by seeking answers to who, what, when, where, why, and how. A good sales representative asks himself the same questions in order to completely qualify his prospect.

USING THE TELEPHONE TO FIND, QUALIFY, AND SELL PROSPECTS

Up to 20 percent of your selling time is often wasted simply waiting to get in to see and talk to your prospects, even if an official appointment has been made. Someone else is often in the prospect's office first, and you have to wait your turn.

One secret for making more prospect calls in less time and for less money is the telephone. The law of averages normally applies here: the more prospects contacted, the more who are qualified; the more qualified, the more chances to make effective presentations; the more effective presentations made, the greater number of closes; the more closes, the greater your sales volume. Proper use of the telephone can often help sales representatives in certain fields to greatly increase their volume. Some companies sell entirely by telephone, and telephone companies in most major cities of the world are ready to advise sales representatives on proper telephone-selling techniques.

Certain advantages of telephone-prospecting are obvious. It enables you to identify yourself, your firm, and your business, and gives you a chance to quickly qualify your prospect and make a specific appointment. It helps you screen prospects in advance and avoid unnecessary travel time and expense. The prospect is prepared to see you when you appear for your appointment and usually waits to hear your story before making a buying decision.

There are also some disadvantages! A secretary may prevent you from talking to the prospect. If she does, she may remember you on personal callbacks and still not let you contact him. So, you have to face her as an inbetween person that has to be sold before you can contact the key prospect. And if you do get to talk to the prospect, he or she may also turn you down before ever hearing your full story. The telephone is a cold, impersonal instrument. It is psychologically easier for a secretary or a prospect to turn you down over the telephone than to do it in person.

Certain techniques, apart from those of normal face-to-face selling, apply to successful telephone-prospecting or telephone-selling. You may turn your prospecting call into a presentation and a sale closed on the spot. Thus you must be knowledgeable and alert enough to manage the situation, whatever it is, to your advantage.

We will discuss basic principles and techniques in two parts: (1) qualifying prospects and making appointments, to be considered now, and (2) the complete telephone sales presentation, which we will take up in Chapter 17. For a complete overview of telephone-selling, both sections should be studied together.

Qualifying Prospects and Making Appointments by Telephone

Careful planning and step-by-step following of the plan will assure greatest success in using the telephone to qualify prospects and make appointments. We will discuss this in two parts: (1) pre-call planning, and (2) the telephone call.

Pre-Call Planning

This planning involves thinking through and putting down on paper an outline of exactly what your objective is and the words you intend to say. This careful planning will save time and produce most successful results. Your planning should involve these six logical, progressive steps:

1. *Decide on what basis you will qualify prospects.* The basis selected will depend on the product you are selling. If you are selling power lawn mowers to homes you can phone homeowners, but you must find out if they have lawns. If selling a product to a business firm, you may need to know the type and size of the prospect's business, the facilities for handling, storing, or using your product, and how or if the prospect can pay for it. If you are selling heavy-duty trucks, large contracting firms would obviously be better prospects than bakeries who use light delivery vans only. If you aren't certain whether a

firm to be called is a potential customer for your heavy-duty truck, you will have to frame questions to find out quickly.

2. *Draw up a list of prospects.* Again, this list depends on the type of product or service you are selling. Once you identify the type of individual, business, or organization that seems to represent market potential, then you have to draw up a list of such prospects. If you are selling electric golf carts, your logical market might be sporting goods stores, country clubs, or large department stores. You could get lists of these from such sources as telephone directory classified pages, the chamber of commerce, or local trade associations.

3. *Outline your opening statement.* It is important to know exactly what you are going to say the first ten to fifteen seconds. The telephone is such an impersonal instrument that unless you quickly arouse the prospect's attention or interest, he may say no and hang up quickly. An effective opening statement should include these three essential steps:

   a. *Identify yourself, your firm or your organization:*
      "Good afternoon, Mr. Jones, my name is Tom Edwards of Anscon Products Corporation."

   b. *Quickly attempt to establish rapport,* to overcome any negative reaction to your call and warm the prospect up to listen to your sales message. This can be done in one of these ways:
      Make a friendly remark: "It is a pleasure to be speaking to such a well-known leader in community affairs."
      Mention something you and the prospect have in common: "I understand you are an alumnus of City College, as I am; that makes us fellow Bears (name of the school athletic team)."
      Tactfully acknowledge that he is probably busy: "I realize you are a very busy person, but . . ."
      Say something to stimulate his pride: "I've been reading in the newspaper about the grand opening of your new store, it must make you feel proud to have helped plan it."

   c. *Make an interest-arousing statement about your product:*
      "Did you see the picture in last week's newspaper of our Senator _____ and the president riding together on one of Anscon's new electric golf carts at the Pebble Beach Golf Course in California?"

4. *Outline fact-finding questions to be asked.* You need to ask fact-finding questions to help determine whether or not he is a qualified prospect. Open-ended who, what, when, where, and how questions are best:
   "What kind of sporting goods sell best in your store?"
   "Where do your golf customers buy their electric golf carts?"
   "How much of your business relates to golfers?"

5. *Outline your sales message.* In order to make an appointment, you must present enough sales points to arouse enough interest on the prospect's part that he will agree to see you at a specific date and time. This can be done by presenting no more than one or two *features* and *benefits* of your product. A feature is a description of the product; a benefit the satisfaction the prospect will receive from the feature. Each feature should be turned into a customer benefit (which represents value), since it is really benefits that customers buy. Both features and benefits should be described in interesting, sales-vocabulary words that help the prospect visualize it mentally over the phone.
   "Our new electric golf cart the senator and the president were riding on is an all-new, sturdy, dependable vehicle, with silent but thrusting power. It

represents a real breakthrough in electric golf cart development. They seemed to be enjoying their ride, probably because it operates so easily and is so much fun to drive."

6. *Outline your request for an appointment.* This has to be presented in two parts, the lead-in and the request itself. The lead-in should point out how the prospect will benefit from making an appointment.

"I would like to meet with you to explain exactly how you could gain sizable, extra sales volume by working with Anscon Corp. to promote sales of our electric golf cart through your stores."

The request, which follows, is the actual question you will use to get the appointment. The *wrong* way to do this is merely to ask if you can visit him sometime; this makes it easy for him to say he's too busy. The *right* (best) way to do this is to ask him to make a choice between two appointment times. If he doesn't like either, it is easy for him to suggest an alternative.

"Would 10:15 Thursday morning or Friday at 3:15 be better for you?"

The Call Itself

In order to further illustrate, in a slightly different way, some of the principles and techniques we have just considered in our planning, let us assume we are listening in (as sales trainees) to a telephone approach being made by our sales manager, Lyall Gleeson. Some new elements are introduced, so pay particular attention to how he handles the three people he will talk to and the qualifying techniques he will employ.

The Telephone Call

Lyall Gleeson sells a *Young Executives' Business Encyclopedia* and has just dialed XYZ Company.

Sales and Telephone Techniques Involved

He has observed the first rule of good prospecting by listing companies that should have a need for his encyclopedia. He now wants to find the decision maker, qualify him, and make an appointment to see him in person.

Company switchboard operator. "Good morning, XYZ Company."
Gleeson. "Can you help me please? Which of your corporate executives is most concerned with executive training or development? The key man? Can you give me his name please and put me through to him?"
Operator. "That will be Mr. Rodney Horwitz, our personnel manager, I'm putting you through to his secretary."
Secretary. "Mr. Horwitz' office."
Gleeson. "Mr. Horwitz please, Lyall Gleeson calling."

He does not know whom to ask for and has framed his question so that the operator will give him the name of the key decision maker. Note that he has gotten the name from the operator and not the secretary. The complete name and title!

Gleeson is trying to visualize Horwitz as a friend and to ask for him in a casual way, smiling into the phone. Note that he does not ask if he is in and thus risk being put off by the secretary. In a high percentage of cases, Gleeson finds that prospects personally take such calls.

Secretary. "From what company, please?"
Gleeson. "Executive Publishing Company; is he there?"

His answer to her question is rapid and straightforward. If Horwitz is in, and she is busy, the easy way out for her is to put Gleeson right through to him.

At this point many secretaries want to know what Gleeson is calling about. He usually tries to avoid that question by first asking, "May I have your name? Are you his secretary? I'm calling to make an appointment; may I speak to him directly?" If she still persists in knowing what the call is about, Gleeson tells her very briefly and again asks to speak directly to Mr. Horwitz. If she suggests calling someone else because Mr. Horwitz is busy, Gleeson replies, "Good, I'll be glad to talk to the other gentleman after speaking to Mr. Horwitz. When would you suggest I call Mr. Horwitz again?" Gleeson always tries to use the confident, direct approach first in his telephone calls, and, as in this case, usually gets through.

The Telephone Call	**Sales and Telephone Techniques Involved**
Horwitz. "Horwitz, speaking." *Gleeson.* "Hello Mr. Horwitz, this is Lyall Gleeson of Executive Publishing Company. We have a new junior executive training aid that could be of real value to your in-plant executive training program. Aren't you the one who supervises your company's executive training?" *Horwitz.* "Well, we have only an informal program with about six people in it, but I guess I am in charge. What type of training aid is it?"	Gleeson identifies himself and his company and starts his qualification. If XYZ Company does not have a program, Gleeson may then try to sell Horwitz personally. If they do have such a training program but Horwitz does not supervise it, the question is framed so that he should give the name of the individual in charge. The lead has been qualified; the company does have a small program and Horwitz is in charge. And by asking, "What do you have?" he has tossed out a buying signal. Gleeson now classifies him as a qualified, live prospect.
Gleeson. "Our material must be seen to be appreciated, and we tailor its use to your specific needs. May I have an appointment to show it to you at 3:15 P.M. tomorrow or would 10:30 A.M. Wednesday morning be more convenient?"	Gleeson uses a preplanned presentation involving visual aids. He wants to present his product in person. Beforehand, he will make up a card file with XYZ Company stamped on the cards, plus a sales story built around whatever else he learns about the company between now and the appointment. Note that Gleeson gives Horwitz a choice of appointment times, thus eliminating the possibility of a "next-year" answer.
Horwitz. "How about making it Thursday at 2 P.M.?" *Gleeson.* "Thank you, I'll be at your office Thursday at 2 P.M. sharp and look forward to meeting you personally. Goodbye."	Gleeson is careful to repeat the place, date, and time. This fixes it clearly in the minds of both men. Gleeson immediately writes the appointment information down after hanging up.

Good telephone prospecting and selling techniques involve careful preparation of opening statements and of questions that will rapidly qualify your prospect. The opening sentence is especially important at each stage, as was illustrated in this example.

SUMMARY

We have discussed in this chapter the need for you as a sales representative to constantly develop new lists of prospects. Even though your company provides a current customer list, a certain percentage are lost each year for various causes. You need to replace them and also to seek out new qualified prospects whose needs can be converted into wants and those in turn into the new sales necessary for volume increases.

Finding these prospects involves building up lists of firms or individuals who may have a need for your product and then checking them out in order to discover whether they have a need, the authority to buy, and the money with which to make the purchase. This procedure is called prospecting; and the result is a qualified prospect to whom you can make your sales presentation.

We discussed in some detail how to go about finding new prospects and concluded that for many products the possibilities for finding prospects are virtually unlimited. We then explained how to qualify these prospects.

Finally, we discussed the specific use of the telephone as one special means, among many, of finding and qualifying prospects. We treated this method separately from direct-mail or face-to-face prospecting methods because the special techniques employed can often lead right into a sales presentation.

Constant, systematic, persistent prospecting is an absolute necessity if you are to always have available what every top sales representative needs—an endless supply of potential customers.

CHAPTER REVIEW

CONCEPTS TO REMEMBER*

_____ leads (as used in selling)   _____ canvassers   _____ key prospect

_____ qualified prospects   _____ referral leads   _____ prospect-screening

_____ prospecting   _____ influentials   _____ cold-call canvassing

*For memory reinforcement, fill in the page number or numbers where these terms were described in this chapter.

QUESTIONS FOR ANALYSIS AND DISCUSSION

1. Explain the difference (in sales terminology) between a lead and a prospect.
2. What are the two main problems faced by most sales representatives in prospecting, and what steps are involved in solving them?
3. Proper qualification of a prospect involves obtaining satisfactory answers to what three important questions?
4. What are two major advantages in using the telephone for prospecting? What is the major psychological disadvantage of using the telephone?
5. What do we mean by the terms _junior sales representatives_, _spotters_, or _canvassers_? How are they used in prospecting, and by what types of sales organizations or individual sales representatives?
6. What is a referral lead? Why is it considered the most valuable type of lead for putting salesmen in touch with truly qualified prospects? What is the best single type of referral lead?
7. Assuming you are a real estate sales representative selling family homes and are planning to call numbers cold from the telephone book, describe two qualifying open-ended questions you expect to use.
8. Your company is a manufacturer of automatic coffee pots. Translate each of these two features into a benefit:
   Feature: Makes from one to four cups. Benefit:
   Feature: Takes one minute per cup to make. Benefit:

SINGER SALES REPRESENTATIVES' "MAGIC" WORDS FOR CHAIN-REACTION REFERENCE LEADS

In the United States alone, more than 50 million household sewing machines are in use, most of them Singer machines. Over 1½ million new household sewing machines are sold annually in the United States, almost half by Singer. These machines are sold through a network of over 2,000 company-owned or Singer approved independent dealers by (1) outside sales representatives and (2) shop demonstrator-salespersons. Traditionally, most of their leads for new prospects have come from satisfied Singer customers. Here is a summary of what one training leaflet had to say to new Singer sales representatives about where and how to get good leads through customer reference.

OBTAINING REFERENCE LEADS

A sure indication of a successful Singer sales representative is his ability to develop chain-reaction references sales. Most of our top-flight producers can point to four, five, or six sales that are direct results of proper cultivation of a single customer. Women interested in home sewing usually have close friends who share their interest. They usually know other women who need a modern sewing machine. Thus you can get reference leads on home calls as well as many other places during the course of your field work. Here are some examples.

    1. *In a home,* on almost any kind of call—repair, free service, new sewing machine, or rental delivery—you can obtain reference leads by using these seventeen "magic" words—memorize them: "Whom do you know who might be interested in a wonderful buy in a Singer sewing machine?"

    2. *In the field,* ask on every opportunity! Even after business hours, never forget that you are a sales representative of one of the finest lines of consumer products in the world. Be sure your friends and relatives know that you are working for Singer and that you are looking for leads. Some of them may be planning to buy a new sewing machine, and you can be sure that they would rather see you get the sale than give it to a stranger. The same thing applies to the merchants in your community. You buy from them, and they will be glad to buy from you if you let them know what you are selling. By being alert to opportunities after hours—in fact, any time, any place, anywhere—you will find many people who are in the market for a new Singer sewing machine or who know someone who is! Just ask them!

ONCE YOU HAVE ASKED THE "MAGIC" WORDS

1. Keep suggestions coming from neighbors, relatives, bridge-club members, church groups, etc., by asking questions.
2. Do not start qualifying until you have obtained all possible leads—then go back for details.
3. Review each lead to find out how to locate, special interests, age of children, etc.
4. On every reference sale go back immediately and personally thank your reference source—you will often find that in appreciation of your courtesy she will give you one or more additional leads.

149

QUESTIONS FOR WRITTEN REPORTS OR CLASS DISCUSSION

1. If you were a new Singer sales representative, would you be content with only the leads obtained from the suggestions noted above? Where else could you obtain leads that might be equally good?
2. Would you consider the name of a next-door neighbor, given by a satisfied housewife customer to whom you have just delivered a new Singer sewing machine, to be a good lead? Why? Explain fully all your reasons.
3. Assuming you feel the neighbor's name given by the customer noted above to be a good lead, how would you follow it up?
4. Assuming you follow up the lead above and make either telephone or personal contact, how would you qualify your new prospect? What would your opening remarks be?

CASE STUDY 7–2

PROSPECTING AND SELLING, LATIN AMERICAN AND PUERTO RICAN COMMISSION-MAN STYLE

The following case study, extracted from a Pan American World Airways publication[1] presents an interesting example of prospecting and selling Latin American and Puerto Rican style.

Appliance dealers in most Latin countries use outside sales representatives paid strictly on commission. They are called *piratas* in Venezuela and *coyotes* in Mexico and give the retailer the additional marketing tool of door-to-door coverage.

All the *pirata* does is to take dealer literature and canvass his own neighborhood. If he convinces a neighbor to go to the dealer in question, he will usually trail along to make sure the right store is visited—not a competitor. If the sale is made, commissions range from 3 to 5 percent on large appliances—refrigerators, washing machines, stoves, and up to 10 to 15 percent on small appliances—toasters, ironers, blenders. *Piratas* and *coyotes* can also play the field (hence the name), soliciting orders for competing dealers—and then steering the customer to the store with the best commission arrangement.

In Puerto Rico, a *piratas* variation is the *orejas* (ears), furniture-store salesmen who prick up their *orejas* when they hear about-to-be marrieds discuss kitchen appliances. Out will flash the salesman's card: "Go across the street to Juan Gomez. He has the best deal on refrigerators—and tell him I sent you."

QUESTIONS FOR WRITTEN REPORTS OR CLASS DISCUSSION

1. Do you feel that the Latin American *piratas* or Puerto Rican *orejas* help appliance dealers find qualified prospects? Why?
2. What principle of prospecting does use of *piratas* or *orejas* follow?
3. What is the closest United States' counterpart to *piratas*?
4. Do you think this system of prospecting would work in your local community? Explain your reasons.

1. Richard Lurie, "Trade Winds," *Clipper Magazine* (October–November 1967), p. 22. Reprinted by permission.

PROSPECTING FOR
FUTURE HONEYMOONERS

Honeymoon trips are one of the most lucrative and steady sources of business for travel agencies, and the airlines, railroads, shipping lines, hotels, and resorts they represent. Finding out in advance when weddings are to take place however provides some problems in prospecting.

4-Seasons Travel Agency, Inc., Englewood Cliffs, New Jersey, U.S.A., has devised one good idea for obtaining leads and qualifying prospects quickly. They combine with the bridal department of a leading New Jersey store to place newspaper advertisements at regular intervals announcing bridal fashion shows at which many splendid prizes will be awarded through drawings.

Prospective young brides and their grooms-to-be must write or telephone in advance for invitations. Names and addresses (leads) are obtained in this way, and the couple is sent both the formal invitation and a 4-Seasons form (Figure 7.4) which, when filled in completely, gives them a lottery-type chance to win a free one-day sightseeing trip.

ONE-DAY SIGHTSEEING TOUR FOR TWO
Anywhere You Go On Your 4-Seasons Honeymoon

Name _____

Address _____

City _____

Date of marriage _____

Telephone number _____

Drawing to be held on _____ (date) _____

Winner need not be present.

FIGURE 7.4

All forms are followed up by telephone, mail, and personal visit if necessary in order to qualify the couple as prospects. And each couple is offered the prize personally—providing, of course, that their honeymoon trip is booked through 4-Seasons Travel Agency!

QUESTIONS FOR WRITTEN REPORTS OR CLASS DISCUSSION

1. Can you think of three other effective ways 4-Seasons Travel Agency could prospect for prospective honeymooners? Describe how to plan and follow through on each.

2. Let us assume you have obtained the names of a young couple who are soon to be married and, as 4-Seasons sales representative, plan to telephone one or both to qualify them as prospects for one of your honeymoon trips. Outline on paper your planned ten-to-fifteen-second, three-step opening statement.

3. Assume you have qualified the young couple (in 2 above) as prospects in a telephone call now in progress with the young lady and are about to make an interest-creating comment to focus her attention on your 4-Seasons honeymoon trip service. Which of these two statements do you feel would appeal to her most, and why?

    We've just booked an entire small but very quiet and beautiful mountain resort hotel next month for the exclusive use of young honeymoon couples.
    We are having a honeymoon trip sales contest, and if I could sign you two up it would put me in first place.

4. Would a young about-to-be married couple you have just signed up for a 4-Seasons honeymoon trip be a likely source for referral leads? If so, what help would you ask of them?

8
planning your presentation

When you have mastered the content of this chapter, you should be able to:

Define the term *sales presentation.*

Summarize the importance of planning your sales presentation in advance in terms of knowing *why* you will say or do what you plan rather than just how or when to do it, so you can *react* to the prospect rather than simply *present* to him.

Describe the four basic, logical steps essential to any effective sales presentation.

Describe many of the key principles involved in effective two-way communication and understanding, such as how to be a good listener; correct word usage; proper use of words, eyes, and body; and proper use of demonstration, sales tools, and other techniques that aid communication.

Summarize through examples the importance and proper use of negative and positive facts or words in planning or making a sales presentation.

Summarize the objectives and importance of presentation planning which will tie together those principles, practices, and techniques essential to sales success.

Analyze the difference between a good properly-planned, organized, and effective sales presentation and a poor one.

You have qualified your prospect as to his need for your product and are confident that he has both the money and the authority to buy! You are now ready to plan your presentation, tailored to his needs. It would be nice if prospects were highly aware of their needs, wants, or problems, but most aren't. One of your first tasks will be to uncover any needs or wants, or suggest benefits that will suggest or create wants and desires in the prospect's mind, and to obtain his recognition and acceptance of them. But even when a prospect agrees he has a need or want, it always requires an effort or extra work to make changes. It is always easier for a prospect to maintain the status quo. You must exert some force to make him aware of his needs and to make him go to the trouble of doing something about fulfilling them. In short, you have to persuade him that a need exists and that you have the product or service to fill it. You have to motivate him to take action. Thus, you plan your sales presentation to inform, persuade, and initiate action, once the need is ascertained.

You can assume your prospect will have these questions in mind; careful planning of your sales presentation beforehand will help you answer them:

Do I have a need? Or a problem?

Would this product fill that need? Or solve my problem?

Is the price right?

Is this the right company for me to deal with?

Is this the sales representative I want to do business with?

Should I buy now? Is the time right?

The most important of these, the questions always at the back of his mind, are "Why change?" and "Why should I buy your product now?"

A good way to start planning how to answer these questions is from a problem-solving point of view. Here are the basic problems you face:

1. How to discover the prospect's basic need or want.
2. How to fit your presentation around the product or service that will best satisfy his need or want.
3. How to adapt your presentation to his interests through pointing out features, advantages, and benefits of your product.
4. How to shape his questions, complaints, or objections into reasons to buy.
5. How to close the sale.

We will discuss the above points in this chapter and in Chapters 11 and 12, where we will elaborate upon and extend our concepts of principles and techniques of a complete and effective presentation.

IMPORTANCE OF KNOWING WHY AS WELL AS HOW IN THE TOTAL SELLING PROCESS

We are now ready to consider the basic structure and steps involved in planning and making the sales presentation. But first we must stress that the presentation to come will be a dynamic process with constant action, reaction, and interaction between you and the prospect. The word *presentation* has an unfortunate connotation, since it denotes the act of presenting or delivering *to* someone; actually, the kind of sales presentation we will discuss involves a total communications interaction *between* prospect and sales representative.

The strategy and concepts—the why of what you are planning and will do during the physical presentation—are more important than the how-to tactics you will employ. In presenting the anatomy and structure of a planned, organized, logical-sequence sales presentation, we will provide a basic framework of principles, practices, and many specific techniques around which you can build any presentation of your own (business, cause, or personal). But you should constantly be aware that understanding *why* something is done is more important than just knowing *how* or *when* to do it. Knowing how and when to *react to* your prospect will close more sales for you than just knowing how to *present to* him step by step.

Your planning, therefore, is basically to set the strategy you will follow in the presentation: to plan, analyze, and set objectives around which you will adapt, react, and move your prospect to the close during the dynamic interplay of the face-to-face total selling process.

ANATOMY OF THE SALES PRESENTATION

Good customer-oriented planning first involves mentally putting yourself in your prospect's shoes and viewing your proposition as it will appear from his side. Now you are ready to carefully plan how you will accomplish the following four steps, basic to any sales presentation:

ATTENTION: Introduce yourself effectively in order to gain and hold his attention and interest so that he will willingly give you the information that will enable you to determine his needs, wants, or problems. It is around these that you will build the appeal of your product or service, in terms of benefits and value to *him*.

INTEREST: Hold his interest while you help him to discover and clarify those needs, wants, or problems, to admit them, and to indicate his willingness to consider your proposal as a solution.

DESIRE: Arouse his desire to enjoy the benefits that your product or service offers in fulfilling his needs or wants, secure his assurance that the benefits offered are of value to him, and handle any questions or objections that he might raise.

ACTION: Close the sale, which means the action of getting the order.

Do not underrate the simplicity of these four basic steps, since they can be expanded in countless and often highly sophisticated ways, depending on experience, type of product or service being sold, or company training or policy. This simplified "sales handle" is often a valuable aid to nervous sales trainees or new sales representatives who find it easy to remember the logical four major progressive steps of any sales presentation by recalling the key letters A.I.D.A., in connection with the famous opera "Aida" by Verdi. Such memory recall word associations are called mnemonic devices. A.I.D.A. thus represents the four basic elements or steps that have to be covered in every sales presentation. You have to explain, in the approaching presentation, why the prospect should do what you suggest. If your reason is satisfactory, then he need only question details of the what, when, and how of your proposal. Careful advance planning will greatly increase your chances for success.

We can best explain and illustrate the above steps by example. Let us see how one world-famous company taught and trained its sales representatives to plan and accomplish these steps.

HOW TO DEVELOP, OUTLINE, AND PUT INTO WORDS AN EFFECTIVE PRESENTATION

The Singer Company has long been known as the American firm that introduced the sewing machine to the world. Few Americans are aware, however, that among other consumer items Singer markets in the United States are vacuum cleaners, which it has manufactured since the 1920s. A few years ago Singer decided to try to triple its share of the upright-cleaner market and to double its share of the canister-cleaner market within a year in the following way.

1. Selling two cleaners to every prospect who did not have a good upright or canister cleaner.
2. Selling an upright cleaner to every prospect who already had a new canister but not an up-to-date upright.

Market Research Indicated Potential and Need

This program represented positive sales thinking at its best, but Singer also knew that the market was huge (over 5 million vacuum cleaners sold annually in the United States to an average of one in ten homes, at an average unit price of $88.36) and realized that the need or want for clean homes is always present. In addition, Singer market research indicated (1) that the average life of a vacuum cleaner is seven to ten years, (2) that a high percentage of women buyers want to take advantage of new and improved model changes, and (3) that vacuum cleaners are impulse sales items.

A Combination Product Offered Quality and Value

In order to reach its goals, Singer devised a unique plan for presenting and selling not one but two vacuum cleaners (an upright and a canister model) for $99.90—only about $11 more than the average, industry-wide price of $88.36 for one upright cleaner with attachments. The only way Singer could profit at those prices was through volume sales. In short, Singer had to sell and to keep selling if it was to reach its first annual sales and profit goals.

Called the "Two for $99.90 Combination" and offering the very best in famed Singer quality and value, the plan was instantly successful. Within a relatively short period, Singer had taken an important place in the vacuum-cleaner industry. This bold upright-plus-canister—combination concept was a major step forward in vacuum-cleaner merchandising in the United States.

We are mainly interested here in how Singer sales representatives sold their cleaners that first year, what their presentation was, and how and why it was developed.

Planning the Singer Presentation

In planning the presentation for this *impulse item*, Singer had the advantage of having hundreds of retail stores throughout most cities of the United States with well-trained in-store sales personnel. Trained outside sales representatives also operated out of most of the retail centers. In addition the Singer brand name was well established and highly respected.

The presentation had to cover the basic elements essential to any sales effort.

> Get prospect's attention (the approach)
> Arouse interest
> Create desire (and secure conviction)
> Close the sale (action)

It also had to be built around a demonstration of the vacuum cleaners themselves. Here then is the basic presentation (in brief) as developed around the above four sales steps and communicated successfully by hundreds of Singer salespeople. We will assume that the presentation is being made in a Singer retail shop with models on display for demonstration purposes.

Development of the Singer Presentation: Questions, Outline, Words

The approach (and qualification of prospect)

Q.: Should you demonstrate vacuum cleaners to everybody?
A.: No. When selling vacuum cleaners, find out who the really interested prospects are by asking three key questions. This questioning will lead you very quickly to those women who are prospects and who, because they are interested, can be closed quickly. This way you use your time most efficiently because you do not demonstrate vacs to cold prospects. After all, time is your most precious tool. When you use it efficiently, following a sales plan, you have a good chance of success.

Q.: Why do you ask everybody the three key questions?

A.: A woman may be in the market for a new cleaner but may not be thinking about it at the time. The questions make her think about it.

Q.: What is the first question?

A.: What kind of cleaner are you using now?

Q.: What is the second question and what does it tell us?

A.: How long have you had it? This question tells whether it is worth continuing with her; her cleaner may be too new to replace.

Q.: What is the third question? What does it tell us?

A.: Have you ever thought of making a change? This question tells whether she is a prospect.

Q.: What is the key sign she may give you in answer to the third question?

A.: If she hesitates and does not immediately say no, she is a prospect worthy of your very best effort, and you should demonstrate to her.

Q.: Is there an ideal location in the shop for asking the three questions?

A.: Not really. Ask wherever the customer is. If she happens to be near the vac area, that is fine. If she has expressed interest and has given the right answers, you can easily ask her to step over to the vac area.

Q.: Where else, besides the shop, can we ask the three questions?

A.: Wherever we are with people we know—in our own homes, or in friends' homes, on service calls, and in many other places.

Arouse interest

Q.: After you have received the right answers to these questions, you have to decide whether to demonstrate an upright or a canister to her. What can you say to her and what do you ask her that helps you decide?

A.: Won't you step over to the vacuum cleaners, please? As you can see, we have both upright and canister models. And, as you know, we generally recommend an upright when a home has extensive carpeting, and a canister when most of the cleaning is of bare floors and is above the floor. What kind of cleaning do you find most important in your home? That is, which type would best suit your needs?

Q.: The canister demonstration differs from the upright in one important way. Why do you demonstrate the powerful suction of the canister cleaner before going into the other features? How do you demonstrate the powerful suction?

A.: To get customers into the demonstration quickly and to get agreement that the canister is a powerful cleaner. You establish the fact by inviting the prospect to hold her hand up to the end of the hose and to feel the powerful suction.

Create desire (and secure conviction). This is the heart of the presentation and involves pointing out, describing, and demonstrating the various features of the cleaner being presented. Throughout, the prospect is invited to touch, to hold, or to try herself some of the operations of the cleaner. A key prop of the presentation is a demonstration rug, use of which is explained as follows.

To sell vacuum cleaners, you have to be prepared to sell them. The vacuum-cleaner display area must be in shape and ready for selling. For an effective demonstration, we need a quantity of each of the materials that, when spread on the demonstration rug, just before the demonstration, represents the three kinds of dirt commonly found in the home today. The materials are:

1. Baking soda, which represents light surface dust.
2. Kapoc, which represents stubborn, clinging surface lint and litter.
3. Sand, which represents embedded grit.

Features of the Singer vacuum cleaner as presented in planned order include positions the cleaner can work in, different power settings, tool storage, and use of furniture nozzle and dusting brush. The sales representative cleans the different types of simulated dirt on the rug through demonstrations of nozzle and brush and of the most efficient cleaning strokes.

> Q.: How many steps are there in the demonstration? What are they?
> A.: (1) Show the suction; (2) show the features; (3) show and explain nozzle construction; (4) make parallel stroke test.

The sales representative can forestall two possible major objections, or reasons for not buying, at this point by anticipating them as questions and by asking and answering them.

> Q.: Now you may ask, Mrs. Barnes, why should a person interested only in an upright with attachments buy our "Two for $99.90 Combination"?
> A.: Because it costs only about $11 more to have two separate cleaners instead of one upright with attachments.
> Q.: And, you may also wonder whether there are any advantages to owning two cleaners in your home. May I suggest at least five such reasons: (1) The upright cleans better on carpeting. (2) The canister cleans bare floors and everything above the floor better than an upright cleaner with attachments. (3) The motors last much longer because they share the load. (4) Two people can clean the house at the same time. (5) If one cleaner needs repair, the other can do the cleaning job.

The close. At this point, or even earlier in the demonstration if the prospect acts or looks interested, the Singer sales representative goes into a trial close. Here are some of the questions he or she asks in order to effect a rapid close.

> Mrs. Barnes, if your present six-year-old vacuum cleaner had all these modern features, you would make good use of them, wouldn't you?
> Wouldn't it be a pleasure for you to own two such easy-to-use vacuum cleaners at such a low combination price?

You've thought that some day you'd like to have both an upright
and a canister vacuum cleaner like these, haven't you?
How long have you been wanting a vacuum cleaner like this?
You can readily see that you have a need for these two vacuum
cleaners, and you will use them to full advantage, won't you?

Once a yes, a nod, or an affirmative gesture or look is noted to trial-close
questions such as these, the sales representative can start talking about delivery
date, credit arrangements, or other formal closes (which will be discussed in
Chapter 14.

Singer Presentation Summary

A Singer summary of planning and remembering the above steps in this successful
presentation may run something like this.

> Q.: What are the four logical steps to a sale that we should re-
>   member when planning a sales presentation?
> A.: (1) Attention; (2) interest; (3) desire; (4) action (close).
> Q.: What can we do to help us remember these four steps to a sale?
> A.: Remember the key letters A.I.D.A. by thinking of the famous
>   opera "Aida" by Verdi.
> Q.: Name five secrets of successful creative salesmanship employed
>   in selling our "Two for $99.90 Combination."
> A.: (1) Acquiring a thorough knowledge of the product being sold
>   and preparing a definite sales talk and demonstration. (2) Getting
>   our prospect to talk by asking questions and then listening to her!
>   (3) Building desire by giving a complete, dramatic, enthusiastic,
>   and convincing demonstration. (4) Stressing quality and cus-
>   tomer benefits that relate to the prospect's interest. (5) Using
>   trial-close questions that get yes answers and buying decisions.
> Q.: What is the practical formula for sales success in presenting this
>   combination offer?
> A.: (1) Ask everyone the three questions. (2) Sell the two-in-one
>   concept. (3) Give a short demonstration to many people. (4) Try
>   for a fast close. (5) Do not overdemonstrate to a difficult pros-
>   pect. Save your time for the next prospect—she may be much
>   easier. It is not how long but how often we demonstrate that
>   counts.

HOW TO COMMUNICATE EFFECTIVELY
WITH PROSPECTS

Important to both planning and making an effective presentation is communication, or two-way understanding. You have to understand what your prospect is
saying and thinking, and vice versa, or the time spent may be wasted.
      You are attempting to communicate to your prospect information and ideas
which he must clearly understand before he can ever take positive action toward
accepting them. Since you are the sales representative, you should establish the
rapport and understanding necessary to talk to him in his own language and at his

level of interest and comprehension. The opening of such lines of understandable communication requires that you think, write, or speak clearly enough for him to understand what you are communicating.

Clear Thinking Involves Mentally Outlining Your Presentation

In planning your actual presentation you must consider several specific things that will help your prospect to understand you, and you in turn to understand him. These are based on your desire to inform and persuade.

1. Decide on the length of your presentation.
2. Cover all the steps of the basic presentation.
3. Learn to be a good listener, to absorb feedback, so you will be able to interact with him.
4. Sharpen the emphasis of your key points through techniques that aid the prospect's understanding.

How long should your presentation last? The length of your presentation depends in large part on what you are selling. You can effectively present some products, both tangibles and intangibles, in two or three minutes. Such brief presentations consist of perhaps 200 to 300 carefully chosen words. The average sales presentations lasts from ten to fifteen minutes, but others, especially those of a more technical nature, last longer. Many sales representatives feel that under no circumstances should any interview last more than thirty to forty minutes.

The presentation itself then should be carefully prepared to be delivered with maximum effectiveness within the shortest time and to ensure full understanding by the prospect. The length of the remainder of the interview then depends on the interest of the prospect as evidenced by the questions he asks. Most experienced sales representatives try to close the interview as soon as possible so as not to waste any of the prospect's valuable time. Their advice is to give your presentation, to get the order, and then to leave—all in the shortest time possible.

Cover all the steps of the basic presentation. These steps were covered at the beginning of this chapter. Briefly, they include introducing yourself, getting and holding the prospect's attention, arousing his interest in your product or service and then his desire for it, convincing him with proof of its benefits to him, and then closing the sale by getting him to take action toward acquiring it.

Learn to be a good listener. Perhaps the best way to discover needs or problems is to ask intelligent questions; in the following chapters we will go into considerable detail about effective question techniques. And, when you ask questions, be a good listener. One of the parts of being a good conversationalist, or a good communicator, is to be a good listener. Show your prospect that you are sincerely interested in what he is saying, and your job of persuasion will usually be easy.

Why discuss intelligent questioning and the art of being a good listener before mentioning the details of your carefully planned verbal presentation? Your first task in the interview is to get the prospect interested in you, your product, and your company, in that order. The best way to accomplish this objective is to develop a carefully planned approach that will, as soon as possible, get him telling you about himself, his job, his problems.

True professional selling often involves as much or more careful listening as talking. Many sales representatives have talked themselves right out of a sale, simply by not knowing when to start listening. In some sales situations, especially where tangibles are concerned, the actual sales talk is most effective when it is used basically merely to explain what it is the prospect is hearing, seeing, feeling, smelling, or tasting.

Sharpen the emphasis of your key points through techniques that aid understanding. This involves the development of skill in oral communication and in the effective use of sales tools. The purpose of your sales interview is to find the prospect's real want or need, to prove that need, and to convince him through demonstration or proof that your proposition will satisfy it.

Unless you are an expert, your prospect is not particularly interested in your personal opinion or advice. The best sales presentation, especially with sophisticated buyers, is one that is simple, frank, direct, and factual. To be most effective it should be built around (1) demonstrations, (2) sales aids, and (3) your oral sales presentation including negative and positive facts.

Clear Writing Involves Putting Your Presentation into Words

In order to gain the attention of your prospect and to hold it throughout the interview, your presentation has to be well organized and smooth flowing from start to finish. You should tailor it to the prospect's needs and point of view, fill it with facts that can be proven or dramatized, and present it effectively through well-chosen thought patterns and vivid, persuasive language.

Some companies require their sales representatives to memorize and strictly follow a carefully tested and written *canned presentation*. These presentations are especially useful to those selling the same product all the time. They are so carefully worked out that a high percentage of closes results from methodically memorizing and presenting the *canned* wording. Such presentations are dead or listless unless the sales representative, like an actor, strives to make the words come alive on each interview.

Most sales representatives resist such canned presentations but give considerable attention to structuring their thought and word patterns to allow for a logical, factual, persuasive, natural delivery to the prospect. They thus develop a structured and personalized sales message called a *planned presentation*. In it, the company provides or the sales representative writes his or her own key sections, the main points of which, with their carefully chosen wording, are committed to memory. This presentation has the advantage of being more conversational and less stilted than the canned presentation, but the sales representative still follows his carefully prepared outline and script during the interview.

In putting your own thoughts on paper, aim to include one or all of the following items.

1. A simple or detailed outline in either chart or graph form
2. Specific written proposals, which can be submitted either prior to or during the interview
3. A planned presentation—detailed outline with selected key points carefully written out for later word-for-word presentation
4. A canned presentation, in which the entire presentation is carefully written out and memorized in its entirety for later word-for-word presentation

You have only a limited time in which to make a complete presentation in terms of your prospect's values (which may differ from your own) and level of understanding. Thus, your presentation must be clear, convincing, interesting, brief, factual, and to the point.

Words make images.   Basic to any effective written or oral communication is the fact that words make images. Advertising copywriters take great pains in constructing the product advertisements in magazines and other media. They test, polish, and revise each word until it glitters with meaning. A good sales representative does the same thing in committing thoughts to paper when developing a presentation. His words have impact and are persuasive upon delivery.

You can make your presentation effective by using image-packed key words that give your prospect a mental picture of your sales points and of how your product will benefit him. A good dictionary or thesaurus is a rich source for vital, descriptive selling words, or picture-building words. Here are some examples of vivid words which, when contrasted with weak ones, better describe the sales points of an ordinary fluorescent desk lamp.

Weak descriptive words	Strong, image-building descriptive words
200-watt light.	An easy-on-the-eyes, soft but bright, 200-watt fluorescent light.
Good shade on top.	The adjustable shade cuts glare and prevents eyestrain.
Two-button light control.	These two conveniently placed buttons assure fingertip, instantaneous light control.
Heavy base.	This sturdy, graceful-looking base will not scratch your desk.

Correct word usage.   Know the meaning of words and how to use and pronounce them correctly. This knowledge is essential for using ordinary words and also for using the technical words of the industries or businesses to which you sell. If, for example, you are selling insurance and introduce "statistical facts shown by these actuarial tables," you should know the correct pronunciation, usage, and meaning of the word *actuarial*. Many sales representatives like to have others go over their written presentation to check the clarity and effectiveness of the wording and to catch any grammatical or technical errors.

Why discuss clear writing in presentation preparation?   Because clear writing is a logical and vitally important extension of clear thinking about the approaching interview, putting your thoughts down on paper enables you to do the following things.

1.   Decide what you are going to say and how and when you will say it.
2.   Organize key selling points logically so they can be easily remembered and presented more effectively.
3.   Use vivid, picture-building words that will enable the prospect to understand your key points and to visualize how your product will benefit him.
4.   Speak convincingly, with good grammar, logical organization, and understanding and correct usage of technical language.

Clear Speaking Involves Words, Eyes, Face, and Body

No matter how carefully you prepare and deliver your presentation, your prospect may understand or absorb only part of what you tell him. Oral communication is only about 30 percent effective in conveying an idea accurately. The problem is that both you and the prospect are communicating with words, and words have meaning only in terms of how one or the other of you use or react to them. Meaning does not exist in a word as such; it exists in the significance each of you assign to it in terms of your own experiences, attitudes, and beliefs.

It takes two people to communicate an idea, one to send it and one to receive it. If either you or your prospect fails to understand one another, your message won't get across. Such understanding is a two-way street: He must understand what you are saying, and you must not only understand what he is saying but also try to understand what he is thinking.

The burden of establishing this important level of understanding falls upon you, the sales representative. You have to consider his motives, prejudices, and the other things he may have on his mind. If you aren't careful he may miss your point and either be embarrassed to admit he doesn't understand or too proud to admit that he didn't get your full meaning.

There are two basic ways you can make certain your prospect understands your message, not his own interpretation of it. The first is to communicate clearly and carefully yourself; the second is to have him give the message back in his own words, and to *listen* carefully to what he says. If he gives back the same picture you tried to send him, you can be fairly certain you have been broadcasting on the right wave length.

In broadcasting your message, use all these "languages" to help insure that your communication gets across—words, voice, eyes, face, and body. To illustrate:

Words.　　Words make images, as we have already said. Use action words to get response: "*what* do you feel about that?"; "*how* do you like the feature I have just demonstrated?" Spice up your verbal presentation with words and illustrations that are truly arresting and imaginative. Use short sentences; use selling objectives and action verbs.

Voice.　　Speak clearly and with enthusiasm at a steady, not-too-slow and not-too-fast pace that is understandable to your listener. Avoid mumbling, unnecessary expressions such as "like" or "you know" to bridge phrases, droning, stridency, or listlessness in your presentation. Try to vary the pitch, tone, and speed of your voice; project warmth, vigor, vitality. Talk with your prospect, not simply to or at him.

Eyes.　　Try to maintain eye contact with your prospect as much as possible. Use your eyes to transmit enthusiasm, alertness, and sincerity. Use them to indicate you are receiving his communication in return—interest, approval, alertness. When selling to two or more people, let your eyes sweep from person to person while transmitting and receiving communication.

Face.　　Let your face register happiness, confidence, warmth, and conviction.

Body.　　Sit or stand upright and alertly, don't slouch or hang your head listlessly. Gesture only if it comes naturally to you. Your body stance should convey your confidence and interest.

Although we will touch on some of these points again in pages to follow, they are mentioned now in the planning stage because once you have planned and organized your presentation you should rehearse it, aloud, on your feet, two or three times, before trying it on a live prospect. You should tape it on a recorder and play it back to edit and polish any irrelevant or rough spots. If friends, family, or fellow sales representatives can hear your rehearsal and offer you helpful tips on improvement, so much the better.

Demonstrations and Sales Tools and Techniques
That Aid Communication

Unless you are an expert, your prospect is not particularly interested in your personal opinion or advice. The best sales presentation, especially with sophisticated buyers, is one that is simple, frank, direct, and factual. To be most effective it should be built around (1) demonstrations, (2) sales aids, and (3) negative and positive facts built into your oral presentation.

Demonstrations. These should be made whenever possible. Your prospect does not believe what you say nearly so much as he believes what he can see. A physical demonstration of the point you are trying to make is always the most effective, interesting, and believable sales technique. Here are some suggestions for putting it into practice.

Your verbal lead-in	Demonstration	Appeals to his sense of:
"Notice how quietly the motor runs."	Let him listen.	Hearing
"You can drop this shockproof watch and it still keeps running."	Let him drop it.	Seeing
"Feel how soft this strong new carpeting is."	Let him feel it.	Feeling
"Doesn't this new food product taste good?"	Let him taste it.	Tasting
"Your wife will like the scent of this new after-shave lotion."	Let him smell it.	Smelling

A physical demonstration so effectively dramatizes a sales presentation that it should be used whenever and wherever possible. If you cannot demonstrate the actual project, then try to demonstrate a reasonable imitation of it, all or in part, tangible or intangible.

Sales Aids. These can also be used to effectively dramatize your verbal sales presentation. Good sales aids can offer illustrations that enable your prospect to see as well as to hear what you are saying. Keep in mind that selling aids merely illustrate your presentation. When the prospect starts giving a reason why he should buy, quickly put the aid aside, even though you may be only halfway through turning the pages. You are there to write an order, not to deliver a lecture.

Here are some examples of selling aids that can be used along with your oral presentation and some tips on how to use them most effectively.

Sales kits. These usually contain several items such as brochures, samples, booklets, and information sheets. You should practice using this material as part of your presentation before the interview so you do not fumble or lose or drop anything in the prospect's presence. Above all, you should keep the kit neat and presentable, replacing literature or samples as soon as they become tattered, torn, or smudged.

Sales manuals. You must control the use of the manual in your presentation. Use it to illustrate points in turn as you come to them. Do not let the prospect take it away from you; to do so means possible loss of control of the interview. And, as with the sales kit, keep it neat and tidy. Nothing is so unprofessional as a tattered messy sales manual.

Catalogues. You must know how to find things quickly and accurately in the catalogue yourself before trying to locate items in front of your prospect. As with the sales manual, control it yourself and do not let your prospect have it until you are ready to turn it over to him. Use only a new, fresh copy if possible.

Samples. These should be clean and in good condition. Whenever possible, you should attach information that will help the buyer order by number, size, cost, etc. Try to show only those samples suited to a prospect's needs, not necessarily the whole range.

Charts and graphs. Tell your prospect what these illustrations mean before you show them to him so he will understand them correctly. Use them in a dramatic way by holding them up so that he can easily see them, and control their use as with the sales manual.

Testimonials. These can include letters from satisfied customers, photographs of your product in use, lists of prominent firms or individuals who use the item, or case histories. For best results they should come from an individual or firm whose opinion the buyer respects and preferably from someone in the same business and industry.

Order form. You can use order forms as effective sales tools simply by having them in sight at all times during the presentation. Information or specifications can be written onto the order form as a matter of course during the presentation. You can use it effectively to close the sale in this way: "Mr. Vanderhoef, I've been listing on this form all the specifications we have discussed. Will you look them over, and if satisfied just OK it by signing here on the signature line?"

Get Your Prospect Involved

In order to keep his interest, involve the prospect in the presentation as much as possible by giving him a job to do and by making him look and feel good as he does it. For example, if selling an automobile, ask him to sit behind the wheel and test the automatic gearshift, lights, and windshield wiper for himself. You can make him feel good by a comment such as, "Your neighbors and business associates couldn't help but be impressed at seeing you drive up in a powerful, beautiful new automobile like this, could they?"

Use of Negative and Positive Facts or Words
in Planning and Making the Sales Presentation

Since many buyers are often reluctant to bring themselves to the point of saying yes in a buying situation, part of the art of selling is recognizing their hesitancy and helping them make the decision. You can help manage this situation by planning key negative and positive facts or words.

Negative. Emphasis on negative facts or words often comes first in the presentation. If your prospect is considering changing to something new, he is probably already basically dissatisfied with the old. In order to bring him up to the point of buying the new, however, you should be aware of and be prepared to employ negative facts and words to help him become even more dissatisfied.

Questions asked during the information-gathering part of your interview can bring out his problems with and likes and dislikes of the old. You will not offend him by employing negative facts such as these.

Doesn't your current cumbersome system waste a lot more employee time than would be the case if you were using our modern product?

Your operating costs are much higher now than they would be with our new product.

Here are some examples of negative words.

Inconvenient	Unsafe
Old-fashioned	Inadequate
Inefficient	Wasteful

Positive. When speaking of the new product or service, present only positive facts, illustrated and dramatized with positive words. The following examples show the use of positive facts.

Our brand-new, space-age system will save you over forty man-hours a day more than your existing less modern system does.

Our new product will cut your current operating costs 50 percent and should increase your profits by at least 10 percent.

Here are some examples of positive words.

Convenient	Completely safe
Up-to-date	Highly efficient

SUMMARIZING OBJECTIVES OF PRESENTATION PLANNING

Let us now tie together the several principles, practices, and techniques we have discussed through the following illustration of notes for a planned presentation made by a sales representative of a new electronic office machine. Coupled with the earlier Singer illustration, it should offer you good indication of the type of careful planning that is essential to greatest sales success.

1. Briefly outline the topic (proposition) to be covered and the conclusions to be reached. "Mr. Evans, I would like to demonstrate how this new machine works in order to show how it can cut your costs by allowing the operator to process twice as much information in the same amount of time the machine you are currently using takes."
2. Simplify the complex by a step-by-step demonstration and explanation. "Step one, Mr. Evans, involves a single key-setting like this [demonstration]. Your current machine requires three similar procedures. Step two involves one movement of this other key. Try it [which prospect does]. Isn't that easier than the two comparable steps on your current machine?"
3. Present new, important information in small doses. "Technically speaking, Mr. Evans, this machine is better than others in the market in three basic ways: X. [Brief description.] Any questions? Y. [Brief description.] Don't you

agree this is an important feature? Z. [Brief description.] Please feel free to ask any questions."

4. Relate explanations to his problems and needs. "Mr. Evans, now that I've shown you how this new machine works, what specific problems can you see it handling more efficiently for your office?"
5. Use any devices or techniques that illustrate the point.
   a. Use of interesting stories that illustrate benefits others have gained from using the new machine. Such stories can put the prospect's imagination to work and can help him see solutions to his own problems through visualizing how someone in a similar situation was helped.
   b. Appeals to any of the five senses.
      (1) *Hearing*. "Notice how little noise the machine makes when turned on."
      (2) *Seeing*. "The designers did a good job on this machine. Isn't it modern-looking?"
      (3) *Touching*. "If you rest your hand on top here, you will notice the complete lack of vibration."
      (4) *Tasting*. (Not applicable with this machine.)
      (5) *Smelling*. "Since this machine doesn't heat up as your current one does, the operators can't complain of any odor from the ink."
   c. Example and comparisons that may help clarify the statement. "Mr. Evans, I've just demonstrated how this machine can enable an operator to do twice as much work just as easily in the same amount of time. For example, it would enable you to get your monthly statements out several days earlier. Couldn't you use that time saved for other things?"
   d. Use of any appropriate, available visual aids such as brochures, catalogues, samples, testimonials, charts or graphs, filmstrips, presentation kits, or photographs.
6. Check and recheck constantly through the question technique to make sure each step is fully understood. "Do you have any questions, Mr. Evans, about the operational step I've just demonstrated?"

   "Mr. Evans, how could the process I've just outlined apply to your own monthly statement problem?"
7. Summarize the original topic (proposition), the key illustrative points (proof), and the conclusions (benefits). "Mr. Evans, I have tried to demonstrate how this new machine can cut your costs by allowing your operators to process twice as much information just as easily in the same amount of time as with the machine you are now using. We discussed three ways in which this could be done. Briefly, they were (1) Step X, (2) Step Y, and (3) Step Z. Do you agree with me that its chief benefit to you would be the considerable time and costs it would save by enabling your office to process monthly statements five working days sooner than they do with the machine you are currently using?"

SUMMARY

One of the most important keys to sales success is planning, especially of the presentation itself, which consists of four basic elements: (1) the approach (gaining attention), (2) creating interest, (3) arousing desire, securing conviction, and handling any questions or objections, and (4) closing the sale (getting the prospect to take action). You have to persuade most prospects that a need exists, that your product will fulfill that need, and that they should take action. The sales presentation thus informs, persuades, and initiates action once a need or want is ascertained.

Since two-way communication is so important to understanding during the presentation, prior planning of it involves thinking points through carefully and putting your thoughts into words that will persuade and motivate. The first step in planning an orderly presentation around benefits that will arouse interest, create conviction, and motivate action is preparing a structured outline of the presentation. You can then develop this outline into a more or less detailed planned presentation or into a highly detailed, word-for-word canned presentation.

In this chapter we have considered most of the aspects and techniques involved in planning a presentation. These will be elaborated upon, and other concepts considered in Chapters 11 and 12. These three chapters together should be reviewed before you sit down to plan your presentation. The concepts covered here were illustrated by way of overview through the example of how the Singer Company developed a highly successful presentation-demonstration of their vacuum cleaners, and in the detailed presentation planning notes of our electronic office-machine sales representative. The case studies to follow will further develop these concepts, as did those studied in Chapters 6 and 7.

CHAPTER REVIEW

CONCEPTS TO REMEMBER*

____ testimonials	____ positive facts	____ complete presentation
____ canned presentation	____ negative words	____ image-building words
____ planned presentation	____ detailed script	____ sales kit

*For memory reinforcement, fill in the page number or numbers where these terms were described in this chapter.

QUESTIONS FOR ANALYSIS AND DISCUSSION

1. What are the four basic steps of planning and making any sales presentation?
2. What key factor does communication involve in the sales process? What three points have to be considered in planning a presentation to assure good communication?
3. Of what value is the phrase *words make images* to a sales representative planning or making a sales presentation?
4. The four major steps of the Singer vacuum-cleaner presentation were built around a key, central factor. What is that factor, and why is it so important?
5. How long should a sales presentation last? What determines its time length?
6. What are the two basic ways described in this chapter that a sales representative can make certain his prospect understands his message, not the prospect's own interpretation of it?
7. What particular type of demonstration of a sales point is always the most believable, interesting, and effective? To what senses can it appeal?
8. Halfway through your page-by-page sales presentation, using a binder with illustrations, charts, and graphs, your prospect says he thinks he would like to own the product being shown. Do you continue leafing through to the complete end of your visual/oral presentation, or do you stop then and there? Explain the reasons for your decision.

HOW BOB COLLINS GOES ABOUT PROSPECTING, PLANNING, ORGANIZING, AND SELLING CASH REGISTERS

Bob Collins is a young cash register sales representative for XYZ Company in a southern U.S. metropolitan area. He decides to adapt some of the famed sales techniques developed by several big American office-machine companies to his specific product and local market needs. He feels that he should work out a planned sales presentation based on sound sales principles, but one that employs persuasion that prospects in his local area will respond to and works to a strong close that will motivate them to buy now.

Let us look over Bob's shoulder as he goes about his prospecting and planning his presentation by putting yes-building persuasive points and tentative words down on paper. Let us also watch as he carries out a successful sale, paying attention not only to how he goes about it, but why he does what he does at various stages.

PREAPPROACH

In his territory Bob has some 1,200 business concerns that use cash registers. They range from movie theatres to department stores to butcher shops. He decides to plan his routing to work four blocks at a time methodically, making a cold-call approach to anyone he feels may use a cash register.

His scheduling calls for making these approaches at the prime time, between 9 and 12 A.M. on Monday through Thursday. Friday is for callbacks. He decides not to make any calls between 12 and 2 P.M. since that is the busiest period of the day for retail businesses. He feels he can use that time to scout his territory, prepare for presentations, and write reports.

THE APPROACH

Bob's first problem is to determine whether the prospect is currently using an XYZ machine or a competitor's machine. In either case he plans to talk about business systems rather than about cash registers.

If an XYZ register is being used, he decides to make this approach:

Good morning Mr. Alexander, I see you are using an XYZ cash register. "I'm Bob Collins from XYZ Company, and I'd like to ask how it's working and if you are satisfied with the system and the service we are providing.

Bob expects to get a stock reply such as, "I'm satisfied and don't need a new one." He plans to smile and nod and to try to get immediately onto common conversational ground with his prospect. If the call is on a butcher, for example, he may say, "How's the price of meat these days? Is it so high you have to sell short?" (a common, stock gripe of butchers). He wants to get the prospect talking about his problems with himself (Bob) as a sympathetic listener, but at the same time he wants to continue guiding and controlling the interview.

He will then ask whether he can render a service through such a question as, "May I take a look at your machine and see if it needs any maintenance?" As he performs the maintenance, with the prospect looking on, he will keep guiding the conversation, listening all the time for clues as to needs, wants, or problems.

If a competitive machine is in use, he plans merely to introduce himself and to start talking about something of interest to the prospect (e.g., if calling on a fruit and vegetable market, "How are the prices of tomatoes today?") In order to do this intelligently, Bob has to be informed about general business conditions. He keeps up to date by reading various newspaper and market reports each evening after dinner at home.

AROUSE INTEREST

Bob then decides on a key question that should arouse interest in either case (XYZ machine or competitive one).

Mr. Alexander, I've been able to help several businesses like yours to get better control over stock and money than they had before. If there were a system which could give you this control and if it were a good buy, would you want to know about it?

Bob realizes that his prospect may (1) say no at this point, but he does not plan to take no for an answer, (2) offer positive objections (which will represent difficulties to be overcome), or (3) advance negative objections (which probably will not represent real objections).

A normal retort may be, "I suppose you want to sell me a new [or, one of those] expensive XYZ machines. What would it cost me—several thousand dollars?" Bob feels this retort is a trap, and he does not intend at this point to talk about either XYZ cash registers or price. His planned answer runs something like this.

Well, I don't know whether you do need a new one because I don't know anything about your business or the way you handle money. May we take half an hour now or later at your convenience to talk about how you handle your stock and your money [the two greatest problems of any retail business]?

Securing agreement to carry out this survey will, in Bob's mind, qualify the man as a live prospect. He needs half an hour to do the survey properly and so will be happy to make an appointment to call back and do it at the prospect's leisure if he is too busy to do it then. The unobtrusive survey questioning will begin with this lead-in: "Mr. Alexander, I'm going to ask confidential questions as a doctor does, but I assure you that whatever you say will go no further."

Bob then plans to ask a series of indirect questions in order to get facts which suggest weaknesses. Once the survey is completed, he will depart and later write the prospect a letter stressing possible losses that could be suffered now or later as a result of the system currently being used. The psychological theme here will be fear of loss. The weakness and probable-loss points in the letter will be based on facts or figures from the prospect's own business which he will tell or show Bob during the survey.

As a conclusion to this letter and to the arouse-interest phase of the presentation, Bob plans to write something like this:

XYZ would be pleased to demonstrate to you a system which will overcome the weaknesses in your present system as described in this letter. We feel this system will place you in the position of knowing whether you are getting all the money and records possible for the goods and services you sell.

CREATE DESIRE (PHASE I)

Bob's next step will be to take this letter personally to the prospect and read it aloud to him point by point to secure his agreement that these weaknesses exist in his present system. Bob plans to gain this agreement by asking, after reading each point, a question such as, "Do you agree that this is a real weakness that could cause loss?"

Bob realizes that the prospect will not agree to every point and is quite prepared to concede that some points are not real problems. He will be most interested—as he watches his prospect's facial expression and movements and listens to his words—in which point or points seem to the prospect to be his real or imagined weaknesses or fears. Bob knows that what he thinks is unimportant; what the prospect thinks or feels counts.

Bob's plan is to try to sell the highest priced system he feels will be best for the prospect; he will work down to a less expensive one only if he has to. Since both XYZ Company and Bob personally are highly ethical in their customer problem–solving sales approach, they do not believe in either overselling or underselling. Bob sincerely wants to demonstrate the best system for his prospect's needs. He knows that in some cases he may be able to oversell but that the truth —that the system was too much and too expensive for the prospect's needs—will sooner or later emerge. Even if the prospect never knows, Bob will. And since he is a sales representative of high personal integrity, doing the right thing for his customer is important to hlm.

CREATE DESIRE (PHASE II)

Having read the letter aloud, including the final paragraph noted earlier, Bob then plans to say, "I have a new XYZ cash register in my car. I'll bring it right in now and demonstrate its features to you."

After bringing the machine into the prospect's place of business, Bob then plans to go into a canned-presentation demonstration of the machine itself. For this demonstration, he has memorized word for word twenty-five pages of technical features of the machine and has keyed them to demonstrations on or with the machine. He will not cover every point—only those of interest to his prospect. Since he has learned this canned part of his demonstration verbatim, he will not have any trouble integrating just those features of interest to his prospect into a smooth-flowing presentation.

Throughout this phase of his demonstration Bob plans to stress the benefits of those features that appear to be of most interest to his prospect and to skip all the others. He will constantly present a system and not the machine as such.

CLOSING THE SALE

Bob plans to try to close on a $2,000 system offer, employing one or more of the standard closing techniques he has studied (they are covered in detail in Chapter 14).

Only after his prospect has agreed to buy will Bob present the XYZ Company formal, printed purchase agreement and guarantee for his prospect's signature. Bob feels that since he is basing his sale around a tailor-made system, his prospect may resent his bringing out a printed agreement form earlier in the presentation.

FOLLOW-UP AND FOLLOW-THROUGH

As part of his after-sale service and follow-through, Bob also plans to help install his customer's new system by training the staff in how to use it. He intends to spend half an hour an evening (after completion of his own work) for a whole week to ensure that such training is comprehensive and that use of the system is thoroughly understood by everyone concerned. He hopes to be able to do his customer's daily records during this period to make sure Mr. Alexander understands how to use the machine properly in his business.

Bob also plans to call back once a week for ten to fifteen minutes for a month just to see how the system is working and to let the customer know of his appreciation for and continued interest in the sale. There is an incentive for Bob to make these callbacks. The XYZ purchase agreement calls for a 10 percent deposit with the balance within ninety days of delivery. Since Bob is on a draw-against-commission compensation arrangement, any commission paid out against such a sale can be charged back if the customer becomes dissatisfied and refuses to pay within the ninety-day period. He will also lose quota points for additional commission if the customer pays after the ninety days. Thus he plans his follow-up calls to ensure customer satisfaction and prompt payment.

QUESTIONS FOR WRITTEN REPORTS OR CLASS DISCUSSION

1. Four points noted in the preceding chapter material covered all the steps that have to be taken in every sales presentation. Do you feel that Bob's cash-register presentation plan covered all those points? Did he leave any points or parts of any points out of his presentation? Explain.
2. Bob's planning was built around getting specific information about his prospect and his needs through asking a series of survey questions. Could he have gotten much of this information before his call? How could he obtain such information in advance? Do you feel his method is best for his special sales situation? Why?
3. How could Bob plan to check his prospect's understanding of features being demonstrated during the presentation?
4. Bob feels that he has planned a structured and personalized sales presentation. How would you define those terms? Do you feel his presentation is structured? Why?

Case Study 8–2

THE ART AND SKILL
OF WRITING GOOD SALES LETTERS

In the chapter material just concluded, we learned that development of a good sales presentation should start with a written outline. The aim is to carefully select thoughts and words that will inform, persuade, and motivate the prospect to buy now. Writing good sales letters requires, in many cases, an even sharper appreciation of objectives, since success or failure to communicate and persuade depends on the short written appeal alone.

The following extracts from a Royal Bank of Canada publication[1] not only offer sound advice about how to write letters that sell, but also reinforce the ideas contained in the chapter material on how to develop, outline, and put into words a good sales presentation.

1. Material in this case study extracted from "Letters That Sell," *The Royal Bank of Canada Monthly Letter* 55, No. 5 (May 1974), pp. 1–4.

Everyone writes letters that sell, and every letter has as its purpose the selling of something: goods, services, ideas or thoughts.

Salesmanship of any kind is basically a person moving goods by persuading another person that he needs them, or winning that person's support or approval of an idea or a plan.

Some non-commercial type sales letters are those that champion good causes, such as community welfare or health standards or national unity. They seek to influence the thinking of individuals or groups.

It is not a simple task to compose a letter designed to sell. Like any other product of value, it calls for craftsmanship. There are techniques to be learned, techniques of conveying ideas, propositions, conclusions or advice appealingly and purposefully.

Let your personality show: Make your letter sound friendly and human: put your personality on paper. *Your letter is you speaking.* Some of the features in your personality that you can display are: friendliness, knowledge, keen-mindedness, trustworthiness and interest in the prospect's welfare.

It is not enough to write something so that it can be read. The degree to which communication occurs depends upon the degree to which the words represent the same thing for the reader as they do for the writer.

In the beginning: In creating a letter to sell something we need to begin by thinking about the person to whom we are writing.

The writer must anticipate and answer in his letter questions that will occur to the reader: What is this about? How does it concern me? How can you prove it? What do you want me to do? Should I do it?

It is a good rule to spend more time thinking about the reader than about what you have to say. Otherwise you may become wrapped up in the virtues of your product so that you forget that the decision to buy rests with your prospect.

The self-interest of the person to whom you write is a major factor to consider in successful sales communication.

Show some style: Never "talk down" to a reader. Make him feel that he knows a great deal, but here is something he may have missed. There is a big difference, when trying to build business, between making a suggestion and preaching a sermon.

Letter writing invites us to use the same etiquette as we use in courteous conversation. We look at the person with whom we are talking, converse on his level of understanding, speak gently, and discuss matters he considers important or interesting.

What the reader of your letter will notice is not its normal courtesy, but the extra touch that demonstrates care and understanding, a genuine interest in the reader's wants, a wish to do what is best for him, and the knowledge you show of how it can be done.

Use suitable formulas: Here are three formulas for letters. The first may be called the sales formula, the second the logical formula, and the third the rhetorical formula.

(1) Get attention, provoke interest, arouse desire, obtain decision. Attention is curiosity fixed on something; interest is understanding of the nature and extent of what is new and its relationship to what is old; desire is the wish to take advantage of the proffered benefits; decision is based on confidence in what the writer says about his goods.

(2) This is summarized: general, specific, conclusion. You start with a statement so broad and authoritative that it will not be disputed; you show that the general idea includes a specific idea; the conclusion is that what has been said about the general idea is also true of the specific.

(3) This is very simple: picture, promise, prove, push. You write an attractive description of what you are selling; you promise that it will serve the reader well in such-and-such a way; you give examples of the commodity in use, proving that it has utility and worth; you urge the reader to take advantage of the promised values.

The soft sell: The tone of a letter designed to sell something should be persuasive rather than insistent. It should seek to create a feeling of wanting, or at least an urge to "let's see."

People do not want to be told how to run their affairs, but anyone who shows them how to do things more economically or faster or better will find keen listeners. Soft sell gives the prospect credit for knowing a good thing when it is shown him, and acknowledges his right to make up his own mind.

Writing a letter that pleases the recipient is not enough: it must be designed to lead to action. Do not fear to be explicit about what you want. Coyness in a letter is not attractive, and it exasperates the reader. Answer the reader's questions: "What has this to do with me?" and "Why should I do what this person is asking me to do?"

You may answer these questions and encourage a purchase by appealing to emotional motives like pride, innovation, emulation, or social practice or to rational motives.

To summarize, the backbone of the principles of writing letters that sell is made up of these vertebrae—know what you are writing and what about; believe in what you are writing; be tactful and friendly and truthful; base your appeal on the prospect's interests . . . and check your letter and revise it.

QUESTIONS FOR WRITTEN REPORTS OR CLASS DISCUSSION

Simply reading about, or talking about, how to write a good sales letter is not enough. One has to practice writing them. The gist of the above article is that the basis of a good sales letter is you (the writer) writing in your own words to a prospect you mentally visualize a persuasive letter that appeals to his own self interest in such a way that motivates him to take buying action now. Most libraries have many reference books showing examples of good sales letters to which you can refer for examples. The best sales letter, however, is that composed by you in terms of the principles and techniques noted above.

1. Write a sample one-page sales letter to a movie theater manager in your local area, asking him for an appointment in order for you to verbally present additional information on the cash register you are selling. Necessary factual ideas and details can be obtained from Case Study 8-1 material (pages 169–172).
2. Write a sample one-page sales letter to a young lady in your local area whose engagement announcement you have just seen in the local newspaper, asking for an appointment with her and her fiancee in order for you to present additional information for your travel agency's Honeymoon for Two offer. Necessary factual ideas and details can be obtained from Sales Problem 7-1 material (page 151).

SALES PROBLEM 8–1

WHAT KIND OF SALES PRESENTATION COULD SHISEIDO DEVELOP TO RAPIDLY INCREASE DEPARTMENT-STORE IMPULSE SALES OF ITS JAPANESE COSMETICS IN THE U.S. MARKET?

An interesting article in *Marketing/Communications*[2] magazine tells of initial attempts by the internationally known Shiseido Company of Japan to launch its cosmetics and allied ranges in the huge American market through department stores.

The company was originally founded in Japan by Mr. Y. Fukuhara, who also founded the first American-style drugstore in Japan in 1872 and introduced the soda fountain to the Japanese. The company diversified and grew to the point where today, as part of its $160 million annual business, it holds a 30 percent share of the Japanese cosmetics market.

2. Extracted from "Action People," *Marketing/Communications,* 295, No. 8 (December, 1967), p. 17. Reprinted by permission.

The article notes that the move into the U.S. market obviously requires sales/marketing adaptation since buying habits in America are different from those in Japan. It quotes the top Japanese executive of the company resident in the United States as saying that "the Japanese woman, sometimes called a 'shopping animal,' shops every day and usually buys one item at a time." He further notes that "the American woman goes on periodic shopping safaris and stocks up, buying three, four, even five lipsticks or jars of face cream at a shot." This American buying habit poses a problem when it comes to persuading and motivating American women to try an unfamiliar brand of cosmetics. However, if one can be so persuaded, she may scoop up a whole handful of items at once.

The Shiseido American Ltd. company at first sent Oriental demonstrators into the stores to help introduce their cosmetics but found they were not needed. The products told the story. The article concluded with the observation that Shiseido would further modify its advertising and sales techniques to the American market. This modification would include, the executive noted, "things beyond the Oriental style, but not necessarily American. It will be, perhaps, something quiet."

QUESTIONS FOR WRITTEN REPORTS OR CLASS DISCUSSION

Based on the above information and your general knowledge of cosmetics-selling in department stores (without getting involved in technical details), prepare a written, planned, three-minute sales presentation for Shiseido cosmetics that could be effectively used by cosmetics salesclerks.

As you prepare this, please follow all the guidelines in this chapter for planning a sales presentation. You are free to draw on the mystery and allure of the Orient if you feel they may persuade American women to "scoop up a whole handful" of Shiseido cosmetics in an impulse purchase.

the preapproach:
getting in to see the decision-maker

When you have mastered the content of this chapter, you should be able to:

Define the term *preapproach.*

Describe the need to get as much information as possible in advance about the prospect to be seen and how to go about getting it: this includes personal information, information about his industry, his company, and his specific job function.

Describe the three most common ways to get sales interview appointments, and identify the one which is used most often.

Outline many specific techniques for obtaining an interview through (1) trying for an appointment by telephone, letter, and other means, and (2) securing it without a prior appointment on a cold call.

Describe what is meant by the statement, "No matter what approach you use in securing the appointment or interview, your objectives are to (1) sell yourself and (2) sell the interview, in that order."

Summarize the importance of the first five seconds with a prospect in terms of how he views the sales representative and how his impression can so vitally affect the rest of the interview.

In preceding chapters we discussed prospecting, or the qualifying of a specific prospect as to his need for, ability to buy, and authority to buy your product or service; and we discussed planning for the specific presentation you will make, tailored to his needs, wants, or problems. In this chapter we will cover the steps in bringing you face to face with your prospect, fully prepared for a successful interview.

This preapproach involves (1) finding out all you can about your prospect prior to the interview, and (2) getting the specific interview, either through prior appointment or without an appointment.

WHAT ELEMENTS ARE INVOLVED IN THE PREAPPROACH?

Once you have located a qualified prospect, your first tendency may be to rush over to see him as soon as possible, ready to start selling. After all, you have studied your prospect list thoroughly and have carefully planned what you feel is a great sales presentation.

But stop for a minute and consider these points! (1) How are you going to get in to see him—by appointment or cold call? And when you do get in to see him

(2) do you know how to adapt your knowledge to his specific wants or needs? Finally, (3) are you fully prepared to adapt yourself to whatever personality he has?

You strive to be professional in your sales planning and selling, so why not consider what other professional men do at this stage of their work? Doctors carefully diagnose a patient before prescribing a cure; structural engineers thoroughly consider all factors before starting work on a costly suspension bridge; and trial lawyers carefully study the jury before presenting their closing arguments. You, as a professional sales representative, should use this preapproach period to find out everything you can about the specific prospect, both personally and as a businessperson, so that you can most effectively build your presentation around his needs or wants.

You may feel that all these points have already been considered as part of your prospecting process. Indeed, it is often difficult to determine when prospecting ends and the preapproach starts. That point comes, however, when, in your own mind, you have qualified a prospect. But overlap occurs since you continue to find out even more about him during the preapproach process.

The preapproach period gives you an opportunity to consider different elements of the impending interview that may affect it in special ways.

Are there are special local conditions to consider?   Climate and ethnic, cultural, and religious backgrounds should be considered prior to the interview. People living in warmer climates often have more relaxed personal and business lives than do those living in colder regions. The fast-moving sales presentation successful in New York City may not be so useful in Mobile, Alabama, or Rio de Janeiro. And a prominent Seventh-Day Adventist businessman may not look favorably on a sales representative's trying for a Saturday appointment.

What will the interview situation be like?   Selling situations differ according to the products sold, the customers called upon, and how, when, and where these customers permit interviews. If you sell an intangible specialty product you may have to be prepared for a reception at the prospect's home, where his wife may influence his buying decision, rather than at his office.

If you generally call on wholesalers, retailers, or purchasing agents, your interview situation will normally differ from that of house-to-house selling. The former groups are used to seeing sales representatives and are generally friendly, while home owners may be initially suspicious or even hostile.

Selling to industry presents other possibilities for consideration, such as the necessity for group interviews or for making presentations to several individuals before obtaining a decision.

What will your prospect's personality be?   Since people differ in personality, you should try to anticipate in advance the personality of your prospect. If you cannot do that, then you can at least anticipate certain personality responses and know how to handle them. Here are a few standard personality types and some general techniques for handling them. We will cover these and other types in greater detail in later chapters.

The price-conscious type.   Can you blame him for being a shrewd buyer? Be honest and factual with him about prices; sell your product on the basis of benefits to him.

The grouchy type.   He may be ill or be having family or business problems; or, perhaps, he has a grudge against your company or product. Try to solve any problems quickly and then concentrate on your presentation, cheerfully and help-fully, and try to take his mind off his troubles.

The too-clever type. Baiting sales representatives may be a game with him. Just keep your good humor and meet his clever remarks with facts and proof of the merits of your product.

The self-important type. He may like to drop names or employ a knowing smile or supercilious sneer. Sell him the way he likes to be sold—let him feel he outbluffed you; what difference does it make if you get the order!

No two selling situations are exactly alike. Part of the fun and challenge of selling is matching your wits in differing circumstances against different prospects. There are obstacles to be overcome in all selling situations, and the surmounting of them depends on your initiative, resourcefulness, and imagination. Your goal during the preapproach is to try to anticipate the situation as far as possible. By anticipating certain elements, you can prepare yourself to meet them and thus increase your chances of getting the interview and of closing the sale.

FINDING OUT ABOUT YOUR PROSPECT
PRIOR TO THE INTERVIEW

The first phase of the preapproach is finding out, prior to making the appointment or call, everything you can about the prospect. The extent of this information-gathering depends in part on what you are selling. If you are presenting something for his personal use, you may be chiefly concerned with gathering personal back-ground information. If your prospect is buying for a company or organization, you should seek, in addition to personal information, facts about his industry, his company, and his specific job.

With all possible information on hand, you can sift it for clues to the prospect's idiosyncrasies and personal or business problems. This preapproach in-vestigation applies not only to new prospects but also on a continuing basis to customers on whom you make regular callbacks.

Systematic collection of this background information means deciding (1) what kind of information will be useful, (2) how to go about collecting it, and (3) how to organize it efficiently for permanent referral and rapid use, as discussed in Chapters 6 and 7. Let us, then, consider what personal, industry, and specific company information may be useful and how you can go about collecting it.

Personal Information and Where to Get It

If you know something about the personal background of your prospect and let him know that you have gone to the trouble of seeking it out, he is normally flattered and thus interested in you. Since your first job in any interview is to sell yourself, such research efforts help you gain the immediate attention and respect of your prospect.

What personal information may be useful? Why? Here are some examples. Can you think of others?

Names. People love to see their names written and to hear them spoken correctly! You must learn to spell and pronounce names correctly since mistakes can be costly. Ask his secretary or anyone who knows your prospect to spell and pronounce his name for you before the interview. If you are unable to do this beforehand, ask him promptly for his name, write it down in his presence, and use it often throughout the interview. He will not be offended if you do this; he will be pleased and flattered at your interest. If the name is a difficult one, jot down your own phonetic interpretation of it to help you remember its correct pronunciation. A person's name is one of the most beautiful sounds in the world to him!

Age.   Neither older men nor older women like to be reminded of their age, but if you are younger than they, they will appreciate an appropriate air of respect for their seniority. If the prospect is younger than you, he will normally respond to your recognition that he has achieved certain things (i.e., number of children, nice home, important job, position, etc.) at this stage of his life.

Education.   Since many people spend years getting formal general or professional education, they like to have these achievements noticed. If a man has a Ph.D. degree or a professional title, call him "Doctor" or whatever title is appropriate. Self-made men, who have achieved something without formal education, are proud of their attainments and respond favorably to your notice of them.

Family.   The response of most people is normally favorable if you know about or ask about their families. For example, what man would not be impressed by your saying that you had just read in the newspaper of his son's being elected captain of his college swimming team!

Place of birth and current residence.   People are often quite proud of their country or area of birth and enjoy talking about it. Others are proud of their neighborhood or area of current residence since it may reflect their social or economic status. Having this information helps you to determine a line of questioning that may appeal to your prospect along social or status lines.

Nonbusiness associations.   It helps to know of any religious, civic, and fraternal groups to which your prospect belongs. It may develop that you are members of the same religion, are fraternity brothers, or were in the same branch of military service.

Hobbies.   Perhaps you are fellow weekend sailplane pilots, stamp collectors, or sports fans. If you share similar feelings toward the same hobbies or if you know of his pet hobby and appear interested in it, it may be easy to establish a personal rapport.

Idiosyncrasies.   Does your prospect like to see sales representatives only by written appointment? Does he have a strong dislike for cigarette smokers? Many individuals have personality quirks, and if you know of them in advance, you can turn them to advantage.

Where can you get the personal background information we have just mentioned? (1) Track it down from various sources, and (2) ask someone who knows either the prospect or something about him. You can obtain personal information from telephone books; street directories; city directories; school, college, or university yearbooks; professional organizations; your company files; newspapers; and many other sources. Business associates, personal friends, neighbors, fellow social or sports club members, and other sales representatives both in and outside your company are just some of the contacts you can ask for personal background information.

Industry Information and Where to Get It

If your prospect is a business or industrial prospect, you need not only personal background information such as we have just discussed, but also information about his industry and company. In Chapter 6 we covered the topic of what kind of industry and company information in general might be helpful and where and how to go about getting it, but we should consider in greater detail the obtaining of information about your prospect's specific company or organization.

The more you know about the business he is engaged in, the more you know or are able to find out through intelligent questioning about his business problems. Gathering such information in advance allows you to plan your presentation around benefits that will help your prospect solve those problems.

It also helps to know the language of the industry or trade in which your prospect is involved. This knowledge allows you to talk to him on his own level and gives him assurance that the product or service you present will help him solve his specific problems. You do not necessarily have to be a chemist to sell industrial chemical products to a chemical engineer, but you should know something of the chemical industry and the processes used so that you can present your product intelligently.

The best way to get background information on the business or industry is to read its trade journals or other special publications. Such reading gives you a familiarity with its history, state of development, current problems, and goals.

Other sources of information include trade advertising produced by your company and competing companies, text or reference books, trade association publications and directories, and governmental publications. Another good way to get information is to talk to people engaged in the industry. People at all levels like to talk about their work and will usually be happy to explain their field to you if you express a sincere, intelligent desire to learn.

Specific Company Information and Where to Get It

Whether your prospect owns his own company or is employed by one, the more you know of its operations and its standing within the industry the better prepared you will be to help solve his specific problems. Here are some questions which you should try to answer prior to the actual interview.

Overall company operations

What kind of company is it—public or private?

What does it produce or offer for sale?

Who owns it, and who manages it?

What is the quality of its products and services?

What is its history and current standing in the industry?

What are its annual net sales, assets, liabilities, worth?

Is its management considered conservative or progressive?

What is its size? How many employees does it have?

What is the extent of its operations—locally, nationally, and internationally?

Is it considered a growth company? Why?

How has its stock fared in recent years? What is the current market price of its stock?

Do you know of any pending mergers or acquisitions in which this company is or may be involved?

Is its credit good?

What is its plant capacity?

What manufacturing processes are employed, if any? What kind of materials and what kind of machines and equipment are used?

What seasonal factors, if any, are involved both in production and in maintenance schedules?

Company purchasing practices

What purchasing systems and procedures are followed?

Does the company buy from single or multiple sources?

What lead time is involved in purchasing decisions?

What seasonal factors, if any, are involved in buying decisions?

What are the credit factors involved in doing business with this company?

Company personnel factors

Is buying done by individuals or on a committee basis?

Who are the heads of individual purchasing departments?

What is the specific name, job title, and buying authority of the actual purchase decision maker(s)?

What people within the purchasing department(s) may influence the buying decision?

Answering completely or partially the above questions and others helps you to become informed about your prospect and his needs. The more you know about his problems and needs the easier it is to build your presentation around reasons why your product or service will be of benefit to him. And the better prepared you are, the greater your confidence and the better your chances of closing the sale.

You can find answers to these questions in many of the published sources we have mentioned earlier. You may obtain specific company information from annual reports, house organs (internal company publications), advertising, your own company sales and credit files, and by simply asking people, both inside and outside that company.

HOW TO GET THE INTERVIEW

We have been discussing the first step in the preapproach process—finding out all you can about the prospect prior to the interview. Let us now turn our attention to how you are going to get that interview, with or without an appointment. We will assume that the qualification has been complete and that your prospect is the decision-maker, with full buying authority.

Bear in mind that the prospect does not owe you an interview or anything else! You are asking for a portion of his valuable time, and if he is good enough to grant it to you, you should feel professionally obliged to make the time spent worthwhile.

If you present and he buys your product or service and if it will increase his profits, cut his costs, or offer tangible or intangible benefits, then his time was profitably spent. If he decides that your offering is not useful to him, then you should at least leave him with the feeling that he has gained information of value and interest from your call. This will leave the door ajar for callbacks.

With these thoughts in proper perspective, we can now discuss some specific techniques for getting the interview by appointment.

Techniques of Making Appointments

Why make an appointment? The chief reason is so you will not waste time on a cold call to your prospect's office only to find that he is out of town, is in conference, is too busy to see you now, or sees sales representatives only on certain other days or periods of the week.

Specific appointments not only save you hours of travel and waiting time but also make the approach phase of your interview easy since the prospect knows at least your name and that of your company. It also means that he has set aside some time, hopefully free from interruptions, to give you his undivided attention. Having a firm appointment also adds prestige to your call.

Appointments save you time and energy, and they can also increase your earning power. Your time is valuable, and since appointments increase your face-to-face selling time, they lead to increased sales and income.

The most common way to get appointments is by telephone or letter either directly or through a third person. You can follow up advance advertising by a telephone or letter request for an appointment, or you can simply send your card in advance, saying that you will be calling at a certain time.

You can use many other methods apart from telephone or letter to secure appointments. You can send a telegram or cablegram, contact the prospect's secretary or wife to arrange it for you, ask other associates in his company or organization to arrange it for you, or employ more dramatic approaches. No matter which method you use, you must cover these points, which we discussed in Chapter 7 under the topic of qualifying prospects and making appointments by telephone:

1. Introduce yourself and your company.
2. Capture his immediate attention and interest.
3. Present a brief sales message of no more than two features and benefits of your product—stressing benefits that will turn his interest into desire.
4. Let him know how he can fulfill those desires (by letting you explain the benefits more fully to him in person).
5. Ask for a specific appointment date and time.

Attention-Getting Approach Suggestions

The key to any type approach is to quickly capture the attention and interest of the prospect. Here are some specific suggestions, which, although written in the form of telephone approaches (the most common form), can easily be adapted to letters, telegrams, or other methods for obtaining appointments that will be discussed shortly.

Solution approach

Mr. Amerman, this is Frank J. Rittenburg of Arno Office Services, Inc. Our new Zeno system has been especially designed to speed up your record-keeping at less cost to you.

May I call on you Wednesday at 11:30 A.M. to show you how it can be done in your office or would 2:30 P.M. Thursday be more convenient?

Service approach

Mr. Lynch, this is Ric Campbell of Industrial Chemicals. Many companies have been surprised and pleased to learn that we now handle industrial service and repairs on your type of plant equipment on an annual, modest, fixed-cost basis. May I call on you to explain details Wednesday at . . . ?

After-mailing approach

Good morning, Mrs. Ramos. I mailed you a letter and brochure last week about our new Ajax Kitchen Helper. What did you think of it?

Follow up immediately. If she likes it, make an appointment for a demonstration; if she has any objections, try to turn them to advantages and to arouse enough interest for a demonstration appointment.

Thank-you approach

Mr. Chapple, this is David Blum of Columbian Coffee Exports Co. I want to thank you for your August 5 order, which we just received. At what level does this put your stock inventory? May I add a reorder to it now for delivery later, and save you some money?

Congratulations approach

Good morning, Mr. Slawney. This is Joe White of City Chevrolet Co. May I congratulate you on the approaching wedding of your daughter Christina as announced in the society pages today? We have a beautiful new red convertible sports car in stock that would make a perfect wedding gift for such a well-known couple. May I show it to you this evening at 6 P.M. or tomorrow at 12 noon?

Social approach

Good Morning, Mrs. Hubert. This is Mike Gladishev of Royal Piano Company. You visited our store last month looking at pianos for your daughter but decided to wait for after-Christmas discount sales. Well, for one day only, next Tuesday, we are offering $100 off on all Rolay models, and you won't beat that anytime. Can you come in at 10 A.M. Tuesday, pick your model, and let us deliver it for Christmas Day? Or would 11:30 be more convenient?

Seeking Appointments by Letter

A carefully written letter gives you a chance to cover all your points without fear of the interruption that could affect a telephone call. Control is lost once you mail it, however, and unless it captures your prospect's attention and interest, it will not evoke a response.

Your prospect is probably a busy person, and your letter is only one of many that arrive in his mail each day. It comes as an uninvited guest, and if it does not stress benefits to him, it is not a welcome guest. Unless you secure the appointment, all your preliminary investigation and planning are to no avail, so as much care and attention should go into preparation of the appointment-request letter as into planning the presentation itself.

A good appointment letter will have the following characteristics.

Personal.   The prospect is not basically interested in you, your company, or your product. He is thinking only, "What's in this for me?" Thus, your letter should be personalized, addressed to him!

Positive in approach.   Both your opening and follow-up points should be positive, not negative. The letter should be forceful, interesting, and logical, built entirely on one major appeal.

Concise.   A letter that is clear, concise, forceful, and well-organized will be easy to understand. Make your point near the beginning of the letter, ask for action at the end, and include all the facts. Also, use simple, specific words and short paragraphs; limit sentences to one idea each.

Interesting.   Since he may receive other appointment letters or advertising at the same time, yours must obtain his immediate interest. Thus it should have an original, fresh approach, with clear, picture-building words that catch his eye and attention. Use action words to get response; words that tell the prospect to do something, such as:

"Send back the enclosed card."
"Pick up your phone and . . ."
"Act now to take advantage of our special offer."

Proper tone.   In order to be effective, a letter must be easy to understand. It must also have the proper tone. This means it should sound friendly, natural, and courteous.

Ask for action in the last paragraph.   The reader should not have to go back to the beginning of the letter to find out if the next move is up to him. Make your request or give him instructions at the end of the letter. *His* responsibility will then be uppermost in his mind.

Other Techniques for Appointment-making

You are limited only by your own imagination in employing techniques other than telephone or letter to secure interview apiointments. If you use dramatic means, they should be in good taste and should appeal to your particular prospect. Timing is important; and you should be prepared to follow up promptly, no matter what method you employ. Here are some examples of other appointment-making techniques.

Send a telegram or cablegram.   They are instant attention getters and are always read immediately. Here is how you may put this technique to use.

Arriving Chicago Wednesday August 10 stop. May I see you 10:30 A.M. or 3:15 P.M. regarding new personalized estate-insurance plan stop. Cable desired appointment time collect. Jim O'Donovan, Equitable Insurance.

Use a third party to get the interview for you.   Many successful sales representatives ask mutual friends, business associates, wives, or secretaries to write, to telephone, or to introduce them personally in order to get appointments.

Advertise for the appointment.   This is especially effective when combined with prospecting on a blanket basis. An insurance sales representative, for example, may send out form letters with an enclosed calling card and prepaid postcard on which the prospect asks for an appointment and lists convenient times. In a similar manner, automobile sales representatives can leave such return cards under automobile windshield wipers in supermarket parking lots.

Use radiation methods.   For certain types of selling, one sale can be exploited to lead to other sales in the same area. If, for example, you are selling a home-landscaping and yard-maintenance service, one nicely landscaped yard you have just completed may stand out in the neighborhood. You can then write, telephone, or personally call on neighbors, asking whether they have noticed the "new landscaping of your neighbors Mr. and Mrs. Joaquin Po." This question can be a lead-in for asking them for an appointment to discuss similar landscaping for their property.

Send an announcement card.   Many sales representatives use postcards as a simple, positive, and surprisingly effective way of obtaining appointments. A sales representative uses such an announcement most often on regular calls, when he or his company is known to the prospect, but he can also use it as a cold-call appointment-getting technique. It is not so effective as an acknowledged, specific appointment, but it does alert the prospect to your impending arrival.

Contact him at home.   If your prospect is difficult to reach during normal business hours because of his own out-of-office calls, you might consider telephoning him at home to arrange the appointment. If you have something of interest for him, he probably will not object to having his privacy invaded. Normally, however, this technique is a last resort.

The methods we have described are practical examples of appointment-getting techniques used daily by sales representatives all over the world. Make appointments whenever and wherever possible; they assure more face-to-face selling time.

But, what can be done if you do not have an appointment? Can you go directly to the prospect and stand a reasonable chance of getting an interview? The answer is yes, but you must be prepared to cope with a new set of problems, as we shall discuss.

FIGURE 9.1

```
                                        Sept. 12, 1975

     Dear Mr. Harned,

          I will be visiting your city
     next Tuesday, Sept. 22 and will be
     calling on you around 10:30 a.m.

                    Sincerely,


                    Sam Hector
                    ABC Products Corp.
```

How to Get the Interview without an Appointment

In professional sales terminology, going to see your prospect without a prior appointment, in the expectation of getting either the interview on the spot or at least an appointment for one, is called a *cold call*. The name itself gives an inkling of the problems to be faced. Your prospect may be busy, or he may be impatient at or even suspicious of your unannounced approach.

In any such cold call you must be prepared to sell yourself and to sell the interview. And you may have to sell these two points to others, such as a receptionist, secretary, or assistant, before getting in to see your prospect face to face. Thus you have to be prepared to face several possible types of situations and plan systematically in advance how you will meet and overcome them.

The problems you meet depend in part on what you are selling and the prospect you are calling upon. Purchasing agents are normally easy to reach if they are not busy since it is their job to see sales representatives. Door-to-door selling is more difficult than calling on purchasing agents since outright suspicion and even fear may be encountered.

The more important your business prospects, the more valuable their time; and they often jealously guard against unexpected interruptions with a series of buffers designed to protect them from unannounced callers and sales representatives. Part of the function of a good executive secretary or of an assistant is to protect the boss from unnecessary demands on his time. Some of them may be initially neutral, negative, or even cold toward your unannounced visit. They will not necessarily be unfriendly, but they may sometimes be negative rather than positive.

It is part of the selling game, as in any other profession, to take the bad along with the good. Negative or indifferent responses on cold calls is to be expected. Success is based on mathematics; the more calls you make the more prospects you will be able to make callback appointments with. A realistic percentage figure for an average sales representative in many types of selling might be one out of three. Since negative responses are quite common, you simply have to recognize them as sales problems to be handled. We will discuss some techniques for handling them, but first let us consider how the prospect views you!

Selling yourself.   You have walked in unannounced, full of enthusiasm, ready to solve the prospect's problems or to bring him health, wealth, happiness or other benefits. You are ready to get on with the interview or at least to get a specific appointment.

But to his way of thinking, you are or could be an unwelcome intruder on his time. Some prospects may take one look and make up their minds negatively about you forever. Others are more open-minded but still remain influenced throughout your call by the first impression they formed of you.

Many professional sales representatives feel that the first five seconds with a prospect are perhaps the most important of the entire call. During this time receptionists, secretaries, and prospects, men and women alike decide whether you are a person they would like to do business with. The reception you get depends to a great extent on which way their decision goes.

What do they look for in these first five seconds that can so vitally affect your whole approach?

Your appearance.   Is your dress and grooming up to the standards they expect from a professional sales representative in their business or occupation?

Your manner.   Do you approach a prospect with confidence and a smile, secure in the knowledge that you are sincerely trying to help him? Or, do you appear hesitant, nervous, or worried about your reception as if you have something to apologize for? If your approach is confident and cheerful and if you smile and look directly at the other person, chances are that his decision will go your way.

Selling the interview.   Having first sold yourself as a person worth talking to, you now have to sell the interview—either to get in immediately or at least to set up a specific appointment. You may simply have to ask for an appointment, but it may be more difficult than that if the interview is not readily or freely granted.

Your best chance for sales success is in an interview situation in which you can sit down face to face with your prospect alone, if at all possible, and have his undivided attention. Your approach should be aimed at gaining such an interview. Here are some of the problems you may normally expect to encounter and some techniques for handling the situation.

Getting past the receptionist or secretary.   Usually an attractive young lady, the prospect's secretary or receptionist can pose real problems on business and industrial calls. Sometimes instructed to act as a buffer between you and the boss, other times merely liking to feel important, she is either a potential ally or a real barrier between you and your prospect.

If she likes you, she will help you get in to see him; or if he is busy or is away from his office, she will help you set up a mutually convenient appointment date. If she decides she does not like you, she can be most uncooperative and can cause real trouble if you try to go around her or over her head once she has turned you away.

It is best to tackle the receptionist-secretary problem head on by trying to make friends with her from the start. It helps to find out her name beforehand if possible; if not, ask it of her, and use it often but not too often in your conversation. Your very best approach is simply to ask, "Can you help me?" If you call back regularly on the prospect, you may best gain her long-term friendship by sending a friendly note of thanks for her help and assistance. A warm smile and cheerful greeting always help win her over.

During initial cold calls, a receptionist-secretary can thwart your reaching your prospect in the following ways.

1. *Trying to find out your business and then deciding herself whether to let you see the boss.* Your best course is the direct, positive approach, which tells her as little as possible and discourages her from asking questions. Your approach may run something like this. "Good morning, will you please tell Mr. Moore that Mr. Matheson, M-A-T-H-E-S-O-N, is here?" Then move away and try not to invite further questioning. In most cases she will assume you are expected since you act expected and will ring through to the prospect. The odds of his seeing you at that point are favorable.

If she persists in asking what your business is, without contacting her boss, you might say, "Mr. Matheson of Southern Cross International. Will you please tell Mr. Moore that I would like to ask him a question? Is he in?" If she still persists, you may have to tell her a little more and ask her help.

It's about a possible new nonassociation-sponsored publishing plan for your firm. I would like to see him now if possible, but if he is busy, I could see him at 2:15 this afternoon. Will you ask him which time would be more convenient?

The aim of these progressive steps is to create the impression in her mind that you will be received. You must be truthful, but by confident manners and actions, you can imply a lot. This throws the problem of uncertainty on her, and her path of least resistance is to ring through to her boss and let him make the decision.

2. *Telling you that her boss is too busy to see you.* This may be a valid excuse. You can test it by replying, "Would it be more convenient for me to call back in half an hour?" If she is sincere, she will probably help you by arranging a convenient appointment time. If, however, she is merely using it as an excuse to get rid of you, then you should quietly persist by asking her if you may speak to him on the phone for a second. If you can do this, you are at least discussing the call with the prospect.

3. *Telling you that her boss will not be interested in seeing you.* You may have to be persistent at this point, as the following example illustrates, but you must be careful in what you say and how you say it (smilingly yet confidently, so as not to personally offend her).

Well, Miss, what is your name please? You are making a big decision that could cost your firm quite a bit of money. Don't you really think you should put me through to Mr. Moore and let him decide?

Getting past an assistant or subordinate.   This problem is sometimes caused either by the receptionist-secretary's directing you to an official other than your decision-maker prospect or by having your prospect tell her over the phone to send you to that individual first.

If you determine that you have to clear the appointment interview with this subordinate, then you have to concentrate on selling the need for the interview. In order to accomplish this goal you may have to state the essence of your proposal but without going into the details, especially concerning prices, etc., on which the final decision must be made. Your chief objective in this encounter is to sell this subordinate on the need for the decision maker to hear the full proposal and to have him arrange a specific appointment time for you.

Your cold-call approach on the prospect himself.   This approach should be the straightforward one of stating your name, company, and purpose in calling. You can use any of the techniques previously discussed in this chapter to arouse his interest and to create a desire to hear your whole story.

Your main task is to rapidly convince him that it is worth his time to see you. He will do this only if he needs or wants the benefits you describe. So you should first arouse his interest and then present a benefit you feel has the most immediate appeal to him, stressing what it will do for him rather than explaining it in detail since your objective is to secure an appointment for a proper presentation.

Remember your aims are to sell yourself and to sell the interview. Since you want to control the presentation, you should try to avoid a too-hasty stand-up, or reception-room interview. You may handle the situation something like this.

Mr. Nowell, I am Tom Paul of Marko Products Corp. Our new records system has helped more than twenty industrial firms in this area to cut plant overhead costs from 15 to 20 percent. I have made a tentative study of your operation and would like the opportunity to go over my checklist with you in the hopes of offering you a similar saving. It will take half an hour to explain my proposal fully in connection with your specific plant problems. Your time is valuable, I realize. May we sit down together now or would 2:30 this afternoon be more convenient?

This strategy is effective in most appointment-seeking cold calls, whether they be business, industrial, retail, or door to door. Know what you are going to say and appear intelligent and sincere in talking about your prospect's needs, profits, convenience, or whatever benefits are likely to have the most immediate appeal. If you approach him in this straightforward manner, the odds are very much in your favor that he will willingly grant you the interview.

THE HONEST, STRAIGHTFORWARD PREAPPROACH IS ALWAYS BEST

The method employed to secure the appointment interview is merely a means to an end. You can have a lot of fun in selling by constantly seeking new, interesting, and creative methods to accomplish your objectives. People like dramatic approaches if in good taste; and they like to have their interest and curiosity aroused. They respond to, respect, and remember your originality.

But you should remember that, while it pays to be creative and to come up with honestly conceived, ingenious ideas for securing the interview, there is no substitute for the honest and sincere approach. The easiest way to get the interview is simply to ask for it; the best way to start is to sell yourself as someone worth the prospect's time.

SUMMARY

In this chapter we have discussed the preapproach, or getting in to see your prospect by appointment or without it. We considered the need to plan this preapproach phase just as carefully as you do the presentation itself. Unless you are able to sell the interview itself, you will not be given a chance to make the presentation.

We considered the need for getting and how to get as much information in advance as possible about the prospect personally and, where necessary, about his industry, his company, and his specific job function. We then discussed techniques of getting the interview: first, trying for an appointment by telephone, letter, or other means; and, second, securing it without a prior appointment on a cold call. We illustrated these several techniques with many specific, practical examples used successfully in the past, as well as now by thousands of sales representatives the world over.

Our conclusion was that techniques are only the means to an end, and while prospects respond to creative approaches and techniques if in good taste, there is no substitute for the sincere, honest approach of simply asking for the interview. No matter what approach you use in securing the appointment or interview, your professional objectives are to sell yourself and to sell the interview, in that order.

CHAPTER REVIEW

CONCEPTS TO REMEMBER*

_____ preapproach	_____ radiation methods	_____ first five seconds
_____ tricks of the trade	_____ cold call	_____ thank-you sales approach
_____ sell the interview	_____ negative response	_____ selling process

*For memory reinforcement, fill in the page number or numbers where these terms were described in this chapter.

QUESTIONS FOR ANALYSIS AND DISCUSSION

1. List three advantages of making appointments prior to a sales call.
2. What are the three most common ways to get sales appointments? Of these three, which one is used most often?
3. Describe or outline a service approach you, as a sales representative for a home heating fuel oil company, might use in writing heads of households in your community for an appointment to call on them to sell your product and your home heating unit inspection and repair service.
4. What is meant by the statement "in order to be effective, an appointment letter should have a proper tone"?
5. In an appointment letter, should your action request be in the first paragraph, in the middle, or in the last paragraph? Why?
6. What types of third parties in your community could you call upon to help get appointment interviews for you? What two major action requests would you make of them?
7. What two major objectives must a sales representative plan to accomplish in making a cold call for an appointment with any type of prospect?
8. What is the best single approach a sales representative can make to a secretary in order to secure her cooperation in helping him obtain an appointment interview with her boss?

Case Study 9–1

GETTING THE APPOINTMENT WITHOUT TELLING TOO MUCH IS IMPORTANT TO INSURANCE SALES REPRESENTATIVES

Getting the appointment, either by telephone or personal call, without telling the prospect exactly what is to be discussed is a serious matter to agent-sales representatives of all insurance companies. They have to sit down face to face with the prospect to determine real need and to tailor an insurance plan to that need. Thus they have to handle questions and objections at this stage with only one objective in mind—to get the interview appointment without telling any more than they have to in the process.

Here, in his own words, is how one veteran northwestern United States insurance sales representative, Angus Haltiwanger, handles his problem of getting the appointment by telephone.

I work through referral leads, so I call the prospect by phone directly and ask to speak to him. If a secretary answers, I handle it this way (using a pleasant and authoritative tone of voice): "Mr. Stay, please," or "Will you put me through to Mr. Stay, please," or "Please let Mr. Stay know that Mr. Haltiwanger is on the telephone." (I never ask, "Is Mr. Stay in please?") Then, when the prospect himself answers, I go right into my appointment presentation as follows:

Good morning, Mr. Stay, My name is Haltiwanger, Angus Haltiwanger, and I represent Inter-global Insurance Company. We have a mutual friend (acquaintance) in Mr. Ed Thomas. I'm phoning you because I would like the opportunity of meeting you to discuss a new concept for thousands of people like ourselves who are interested in saving money. I would like to call and tell you a little more about the idea, and you could very quickly tell me whether it would be of value to you. I'm wondering if Thursday morning at 11:15 would suit you, or would you prefer Friday afternoon at about 3:45?

It may seem easier to say, "I have an appointment near your office, may I drop in?" etc., but such a wrong statement could lose the interview. I'm trying to convey the impression that I'm going to make a special trip to see him. That makes him feel important and makes it easier for him to say yes.

HANDLING HIS OBJECTIONS

Once in a while I secure an appointment immediately. Most of the time, however, I encounter objections. Here are a few examples of the objections I get, with the more or less standard ways I have of handling them. Although I may vary my pattern, I never change one thing. My last sentence always is something to this effect: "Will Thursday morning at 11:15 suit you or would you prefer Friday afternoon at 3:45?"

Objection: What is your idea about? Tell me a little more about it.
Answer: Frankly, Mr. Stay, it's a little difficult to explain over the telephone. It would hardly be fair to you or myself to do so since it requires certain visual aids. That is why I'm suggesting I call to see you on Thursday at 11:15, or would you prefer Friday at 3:45?
Objection: Is this life insurance? This is insurance, isn't it?
Answer: Well, Mr. Stay, I did say I was with an insurance company, so naturally there is a connection; but as I told you, many men in positions similar to your own have found this particular idea of tremendous value. This is why I would like to come along and have you tell me whether you are interested. Would Thursday suit you or would you find Friday at 3:45 more convenient?
Objection: I have plenty of insurance.
Answer: Mr. Stay, that's fine. I would be most surprised to come across a person in your position who didn't own a lot of insurance. In fact, if you didn't, this idea wouldn't be of the slightest interest to you. It is designed for people with a lot of insurance, and that is why I'm suggesting that I come to tell you more about it. Would Thursday at 11:15 be all right or would you prefer Friday at 3:45?
Objection: I couldn't afford any more insurance even if I wanted it.
Answer: Mr. Stay, I couldn't possibly expect that at the precise moment that I speak to you on the telephone (or to anyone else for that matter), you would be about to take out more insurance. What I am suggesting is that I come along to show you this idea. It may well interest you and help you, if not now, then perhaps at some time in the future. Would Thursday at 11:15 be all right or would you prefer Friday at 3:45?
Objection: I'm very busy. I can't spare the time to see you.
Answer: I have perhaps suggested an inconvenient time, but I promise you that it will only take you a few minutes to tell me whether you are interested. Looking at my diary again, I could make it at 9:45 on Monday, or perhaps Tuesday at 1:00 would be better for you. Which time suits you, Mr. Stay?

Please note that I have been very careful up to this point not to divulge any information to the prospect. It is vitally important that I arouse his interest and attention strictly by the offer to explain to him a particular idea.

If the prospect keeps switching to different objections, he is probably stalling, and I have to determine quickly whether he is worth spending time on. It is better to get on to the next call than to waste time with him. Sometimes the prospect asks me to send him an illustration by mail. This is a brush-off, and I never agree to such requests.

Do not be impatient to put down the receiver after making the appointment. Rather, in closing the conversation, I say slowly, "That's 10:15 on Thursday, the fifth then, Mr. Stay; I'm just entering it in my diary." (This will encourage him to do likewise.) "Thank you very much; I look forward to meeting you at that time. Good-bye."

QUESTIONS FOR WRITTEN REPORTS OR CLASS DISCUSSION

1. What major advantages does Haltiwanger gain by confirming such appointments by telephone rather than visiting the prospect at his office or home?
2. We noted in this chapter five basic points that should be covered when making an appointment by telephone or by any other means. What are these five points? Does Haltiwanger's telephone technique cover all of them to your satisfaction? Why?
3. List two disadvantages faced by Haltiwanger in using the telephone to make his appointments.
4. Do you feel that Haltiwanger uses proper techniques in his telephone approach? Does he cover all the aims of a good telephone approach?

Case Study 9–2

HOW SALESMAN TOM SMITH HANDLES TWO COMMON RECEPTIONIST PUT-OFFS

Tom Smith sells office equipment in a large North American city, concentrating on a systems approach that involves selling a complete integrated line of dictating machines and desk calculators which, if purchased as a system, offers significant cost-reduction. He favors cold-calls to seek interview appointments.

He often faces put-offs, or stalls, from receptionists or secretaries who are overzealous in protecting their bosses from unannounced callers. In his own words, the two most common put-offs he faces, and how he handles them in a friendly but businesslike manner, are these:

Put-off #1: "I know Mr. Rogers wouldn't be interested in buying a lot of new office machines."

Tom usually handles this by pointing out that her put-off could be costly to her boss: "Mr. Rogers must have plenty of confidence in you. He is letting you make a decision that could save him at least $2,000 over the next two years. Why don't you just tell Mr. Rogers I am here and let him decide whether or not he will see me?"

Put-off #2: "Mr. Rogers is busy right now; he's not seeing anyone."

Tom knows that this could be true, but feels he should make certain it's a fact and not just a put-off. He tests by seemingly agreeing with her statement: "I see. I know how busy he must be. When would be a good time to call back—say about 3 P.M.?"

Tom realizes that if she accepts his callback time suggestion, or suggests an alternative time, her boss really is busy right at that moment. If, however, she replies that he shouldn't bother to call back at any time, he knows she is acting independently in putting him off. If he feels it is a put-off, he then uses the same technique for handling the situation as in number 1 above.

QUESTIONS FOR WRITTEN REPORTS OR CLASS DISCUSSION

1. What would you do in Tom's situation if, after making the statement and asking the question noted in number 1 above, the secretary still won't announce him to her boss?
2. Can you suggest two different ways that Tom could handle the put-off noted in number 1 above?
3. Could Tom, or any sales representative on a similar cold call, do anything before asking if he can see her boss to make the secretary more inclined to try and help get him in?
4. Whether Tom is successful in getting past the secretary or not in such cold-call cases, how should he handle his departure so that he might call back in the future, as far as the secretary is concerned?

SALES PROBLEM 9–1

HOW WOULD YOU HANDLE THIS RECEPTION-ROOM WAIT?

THE SITUATION

The charming young blonde secretary has just told you that her boss and your important prospect, Mr. Bartlett, is in an important conference and will be delayed half an hour in meeting you for the scheduled appointment in his office.

YOUR PROBLEM

What to do the next half hour! You have driven 50 miles to keep this appointment, your first at this very large and potentially good company account. The highway was thick with traffic, and you feel that a cup of coffee would hit the spot. The secretary is pretty, seemingly friendly, and you and she are alone in the waiting room. She is busy, but some current popular magazines and a daily newspaper are on a small table nearby, plus some industry trade catalogues, company reports, and employee bulletins. You have another important appointment scheduled in 2 hours 10 miles distant, and you still have not checked the arithmetic of one of your proposals for this interview.

QUESTION FOR WRITTEN REPORTS OR CLASS DISCUSSION

What is your decision? What will you do with your time these next 30 minutes?

PART IV

WORKING THE PLAN: STEPS IN THE SELLING PROCESS

10
the approach:
the important first few minutes
of the interview

When you have mastered the content of this chapter, you should be able to:

Describe the purpose of the approach phase of the sales presentation interview, and give its three component parts.

Describe meaning and use of two generally accepted methods of presentation to induce (motivate) a prospect to do something (take action) differently: (1) logical reasoning and (2) suggestion.

Describe how much time is normally devoted to the approach phase and tell what two sub-phases it is broken into with regard to objectives and time.

Describe the two basic structured approach methods presented.

List four basic points to be covered in any type of approach.

List sixteen basic approaches suitable for use in a wide range of sales situations.

Summarize some basic principles and practical techniques of overcoming any fear or tension new sales representatives might feel.

Describe six different personality types a sales representative might meet on any given day, and some practical psychologically sound methods for warming up and relaxing each type.

Describe use of the question technique as a practical method for rapidly uncovering a prospect's needs, wants, or problems.

It has taken about half the pages of this book to get to this point—our opening words with the prospect in the presentation interview. Hours (perhaps days or weeks) of careful research, organization, and planning have led up to this moment. Even if the presentation interview is a cold call that may be concluded within a few minutes, every action and spoken word is the result of cumulative planning, preparation, and experience.

You may spend the next fifteen minutes—the average interview time in many types of selling—or longer with your prospect, depending on the situation, what you are presenting, and his interest in what you are proposing. The amount of time you spend is relatively unimportant; what you accomplish counts.

For many sales representatives, especially those selling a single product or service house to house or office to office, the presentation is an all-or-nothing process. They close the sale or do not. They apparently don't believe in the value of, or feel they can afford the time for, a callback or second try.

Some products or services do not lend themselves to a close on the first presentation call. The product may be left for a trial period, or further study may be necessary before an intelligent purchasing decision can be made. In some cases you may not effect a final close or even expect it until the third or fourth callback. Some sales representatives do not even try for a close on the first call and tell the prospect in the beginning that they are not trying to sell him anything. They use this technique to disarm him, to gain his confidence, and to develop their sales story before making a final close.

Regardless of whether you try to close the sale at this interview or merely sell the first stage in a planned multi-interview sequence, a sale of some sort is made. Either the prospect sells you on the idea that he is not interested or will not buy now or later, or you sell him on buying now or allowing you a follow-up opportunity.

The way the interview goes depends largely on what you do and say during the first few seconds and minutes. This important first presentation is called in sales terminology the *approach phase*. But before we discuss it, let us consider these two points:

1.   What the ideal sales interview is like.
2.   How persuasion is the key to motivation and eventual action throughout the entire sales presentation.

THE IDEAL SALES INTERVIEW

In the ideal presentation interview you and your prospect sit down face to face for an uninterrupted, relaxed, informal, conversational discussion. You immediately like and respect each other; he is interested in your proposal and senses that you are trying to solve one or more of his problems or to offer him a benefit.

Through questioning, you find out what those problems or wants are and persuasively explain verbally and with demonstration and proof if possible how your product or service will accomplish what he wants or needs. You answer his questions, handle his objections, and ask for the order. The whole procedure is relaxed and easy, and you probably spend considerably more time listening than talking. Once the sale is made, you each have a warm feeling: he is pleased with the benefits you have brought him, and you are pleased not only with the sale, but also with being able to help him.

Many sales are made just that easily. Many professional sales representatives, in fact, say that their biggest sales are often their easiest. Most sales situations however, are more involved, uncertain, and difficult than is the ideal one we have described. Your professional aim should be to work toward this ideal in every sales interview, but you should realize that only careful study, planning, and practice will make it an easy process for you.

PERSUASION IS THE KEY TO MOTIVATING
THE PROSPECT TO TAKE ACTION

One key word in the above description of an ideal presentation belies the ease with which the sale is made. That word is *persuasively!* If the presentation is not persuasive, the prospect does not feel any compelling need to buy at the time.

Early in Chapter 1 we stated that persuasion is central to salesmanship. Every sales presentation, easy or difficult, involves persuasion from approach to close.

You must persuade each prospect, before he decides to buy, that a need exists and then motivate him to take action to fulfill that need (through buying).

Persuasion is aimed at inducing (motivating) another to believe or do something (take action) differently. Persuasion is thus at the core of the selling process. A sales representative's task is to persuade the prospect that his needs or wants can be realized through using the sales representative's product or service. Then the sales representative, with an understanding of why people buy and the specific needs and interests of the prospect, motivates the prospect to take action toward obtaining the product or service (buying). No one buys anything unless he has been persuaded that it is in his interests, however; so the sales representative's first task is to uncover any unexpressed needs or wants and to pinpoint expressed ones in terms of how they can be fulfilled through his product. Unless a need or want exists or is created, chances of closing a sale are small. The sales representative discovers or develops these needs and wants, if they are not expressed openly, as he presents his proposal in terms of benefits and value to the prospect.

As we noted in Chapter 4, the prospect's reasons for buying or not buying are based on rational motives or emotional motives or a combination of both. Persuasion involves proper appeals to the prospect's strongest instincts or motives, whatever they may be, in an effort to secure conviction that he should take action (by buying) to fulfill them. In order to appeal most effectively to these needs or wants, the sales representative has the option of presenting benefits from both a positive (desire for gain) and a negative (fear of loss) point of view or from a combination of both. For example:

	Basically desire	**Basically fear**
Business people	Profit.	Loss, competition.
Purchasing agents	The greatest value for money spent.	Cheap, inferior products that cost more in the end.
Wholesalers	Something that can be resold quickly at a profit.	Items that do not move or that may become obsolete.
Retailers	Quick resale at a profit; having satisfied repeat customers.	Items that do not live up to promises claimed or that do not sell quickly.
Housewives	Ease, convenience, or fulfillment of other specific buying motives.	Buying something that does not fulfill their desires.

HOW CAN A SALES REPRESENTATIVE MOTIVATE A PROSPECT TO TAKE ACTION?

Two generally accepted methods of persuasion induce (motivate) another to believe or do something (take action) differently. The first is by logical reasoning; the second, and of greater importance to selling, is by suggestion.

Motivation by Logic

Logic or logical reasoning appeals to rational buying motives by presenting sales points that lend themselves to comparison. Logical reasoning is more likely to appeal to technical or to professional buyers, who tend to buy on rational grounds, than to the average prospect.

It is most effectively used when selling complicated proposals involving detailed cost comparisons or when the price is so great that the prospect must weigh every fact carefully before reaching a decision. It is also effectively used when presenting a radically new item. The selling or leasing of an expensive, new computer installation requiring a different programing language from the one being used is an example of a sales situation in which logical, comparative sales points are highly effective.

Logical reasoning is built around syllogisms, arguments (or sales claims) based on major premises, minor premises, and conclusions. Here is an example.

Major premise: This computer will save more executive time than any other.
Minor premise: You are a busy executive.
Conclusion: Therefore you should have this computer to save your time.

This argument is logical enough, but people in general do not necessarily react positively to such reasoning. Instead, they tend to react for emotional reasons (their reasons), and they often resent being convinced against their will.

Thus, in most cases, it is best to employ abbreviated syllogisms, which allow the prospect to draw his own conclusions from the premise. Here are three common techniques for accomplishing this aim.

1. *Offering alternatives* allows the prospect to draw a rational conclusion from two or more alternatives. The computer sales representative may say, "If you agree that our computer is the best and will save you time, let us examine what you may gain and lose by waiting until next year to buy and examine what you will gain and lose by buying now."

2. *Suggesting a comparision of similarities* invites an examination of two possible situations and a noting of the similarities. Our computer sales representative may give a reason such as this one.

Addo Company down the road faced a dilemma similar to yours six months ago, when they were deciding whether to install this computer or to wait a year. They elected to wait and just last month lost a large account because they were unable to process its orders rapidly enough.

The present customer can picture himself in the same situation and can draw the logical conclusion—that he should buy now rather than run the risk of losing potential new accounts himself.

3. *Employing the if-then technique* involves stating an assumed (if) premise followed by reasons based on it. For example, a sales representative may say, "*If* you wait a year before deciding to buy this computer and prices keep going up the way they have the past three years, *then* it will cost you more."

Motivation by Suggestion

Suggestion is a far more widely used key to motivation in selling than is logical reasoning. Psychologists agree that people respond more often to suggestion, involving their emotional buying motives, than to logical reasoning, directed at rational buying motives. They tend to react favorably to or to accept suggestions, ideas, or conclusions unless they have a strong reason to object. They react to suggestion on the basis of habit, instinct, imitation, and personal bias, and because it is the easiest thing to do.

Suggestion is always at work in our lives. You greet a friend, and he extends his hand; automatically you extend yours for a handshake. Someone smiles at you, and you find yourself smiling back. The restaurant waitress cheerfully offers to refill your coffee cup, and you smilingly nod assent, to find later that 25 cents has probably been added to your bill.

Psychological suggestion to motivate people to take action falls into three major classifications:

1. *Ideomotor suggestions* are statements that suggest that the prospect do something, such as, "If you will just OK this agreement with your signature, I'll have the item delivered to your home tomorrow by 2 P.M."

2. *Autosuggestion* involves setting the stage so that the prospect's own thoughts suggest action. An example is showing a colored sales-kit brochure picturing a young man sitting in a new sports car surrounded by beautiful and admiring girls. Any young man considering a new car can easily identify with such a pictorial autosuggestion and decide that he may also gain feminine admiration by buying a similar car.

3. *Prestige suggestions* offer a prospect the same benefits as those enjoyed by movie stars or other such personalities.

Here are several other persuasive suggestions that motivate a person to take action.

Direct suggestion. "Since you like the article and it's on sale today—three for the price of two—why don't you take six and save money?"

Indirect suggestion. "I appreciate your reasons for delaying a decision, but neither of us knows what it may cost six months from now, with prices going up all the time."

Suggestion through action. "Here, try it for yourself! Isn't it light and easy to move around?"

Positive suggestion. "You do like this article, don't you?"

Negative suggestion. "You wouldn't like to be without such a convenience for long, would you?"

Rational reasons to support suggestions should always be on tap. While more buying decisions are based on emotional than on rational motives, a sales representative must always be prepared to help the buyer justify his emotional decision. Thus, if a couple has just decided to buy a more expensive home than the one they had planned on, the sales representative can reassure them that they will never regret the purchase because of the higher resale potential or their increased status in the eyes of their friends and acquaintances.

WHAT IS THE APPROACH PHASE
OF THE SALES INTERVIEW?

The complete sales presentation, as we outlined previously in Chapter 8, is a smooth-flowing, integrated, four-step process. More or less time may be spent on the individual steps, depending on how the interview goes, but all the steps are included.

The approach phase, aimed at gaining and holding attention, is the first of these steps. It has three parts:

1. Introduce yourself so that the prospect feels it will be worth his valuable time to talk to you.
2. Sell yourself, your product, and your company, in that order.
3. Get and hold the prospect's attention and interest so that he will willingly give you information. From it you can determine his needs or wants, and around them you can later present advantages of your product or service in terms of benefits to him.

Many sales representatives consider the approach phase the most important part of the interview. For new sales representatives this opening step is often as difficult as closing the sale. It involves making a sale within the sale—selling yourself and the interview! Unless you accomplish this presale successfully, your prospect may brush you off before he hears your full story.

How Long Does the Approach Phase Last?

The approach phase covers the first few (usually less than five) minutes of the presentation. You should know exactly what you are going to do and say during this period. Plan and rehearse your opening remarks so that you can deliver them positively and confidently without thinking.

Your aims are to get down to essentials quickly, but not abruptly, and to control the interview from the start. The approach divides into these two phases.

1. *The first five seconds of the interview.* During this time your prospect decides that he will see you and will hear your story.
2. *The balance of approach time necessary to obtain your objectives.* During this time you establish rapport; briefly introduce yourself, your company, your product or service; ask questions and get the prospect to tell you his problems or needs.

What Does the Prospect See?

What the prospect sees during this entire period, especially during the first five seconds, when he sizes you up, may be equally as important as what he hears. Most sales representatives take a minute to consider, just prior to the interview, how they will look to the prospect from his side of the desk as well as what they will say in their opening remarks.

Many individuals pride themselves on being able to size another person up within a few seconds of meeting him. Most experienced sales representatives realize you cannot intelligently judge another person that quickly, but your prospect may not realize it. You have to assume that he may make his mind up about you in the first five seconds.

We touched on this first five-second problem in the preceding chapter by discussing its importance in initial meetings with receptionists, secretaries, assistants, or subordinates, as well as with the prospect. We concluded that they chiefly observe your appearance and your manner (e.g., air of confidence and sincerity). Let us now add mannerisms to these other two characteristics and give some further consideration to what positive or negative impressions your prospect may have as he observes you throughout the interview and especially in the beginning. We can do this most easily by considering some dos and don'ts suggested by professional sales representatives. These comments come from many sources, and many, we suspect, were learned the hard way!

Dos	**Don'ts**
Appearance	
Take your cue from the type of prospects you call upon. Wear the kind of clothing they wear and you will look right to them.	Avoid colors or patterns that clash.
Manner	
Be enthusiastic; look your prospect in the eye.	Avoid appearing overfriendly or unbusinesslike.
Bear yourself with dignity and composure.	Avoid showing impatience, even if you feel impatient.
Appear relaxed, poised, at ease, and confident.	Do not interrupt, contradict, or argue with your prospect.
Be an attentive listener.	Do not speak disrespectfully of your employer or of friends or business acquaintances of the prospect.
Mannerisms	
Develop the habit of repeating the prospect's name often.	Avoid both bone-crushing and wishy-washy handshakes.
Show, by your words and actions, appreciation for his time.	Do not smoke without your prospect's permission, or nod continuously at him.
Show genuine warmth in your smile.	Do not rub your chin, tap your toes, or toy with watch, chin, fingers, etc.
Stand and sit up straight; be businesslike.	Do not slouch or give the appearance of timidity or uncertainty.

Many of these points are so self-evident that they hardly seem worth mentioning, yet sales representatives who fail to heed them lose sales daily. In order to command respect and attention, you have to deserve it. If you do not look the part of a successful business person, you will not be able to command the respect of successful business persons. Gear your grooming to the prospect being called upon; what he or she considers appropriate counts.

But careful grooming alone will not impress a prospect; you have to be mentally and physically fit as well if you expect him to react favorably to your approach. If you have a heavy cold or a hangover or if your entrance is a shuffling gait and your handshake limp, he is bound to form an unfavorable opinion that will spoil your chances of success.

Many sales are also lost because the prospect becomes annoyed at some irritating mannerism of the sales representative. Most of these, such as slouching when seated, failing to look the prospect in the eye, and ear-pulling or chin-rubbing, are due to nervousness. Because you cannot see yourself as other people do, you may be unaware that you have these mannerisms. The best way to check is to have a friend or fellow sales representative listen to a demonstration presentation and tell you of any such irritating mannerisms. Once you become aware of them, you can usually easily overcome them.

Your Approach Must Gain and Hold Attention

Some sales representatives feel that the first sentence uttered in the prospect's presence is the most important of the entire presentation. A good idea, expressed in these opening words, can capture his imagination, interest, and attention.

These opening words are vitally important because your first task is to sell the interview—to capture your prospect's immediate attention and to arouse his interest in both you and the benefits your product or service appears to offer him. If you accomplish this initial sale within a sale, that of selling the interview itself, then the prospect is ready to hear your full presentation.

Ways to create interest are to smile, because it eases tension, and to use your voice in a pleasant, conversational manner that sounds positive and impressive. An inexperienced sales representative often talks nervously and rapidly in initial approaches. This mistake creates a bad impression.

Introducing Yourself, Your Product, and Your Company

You should spend time devising a proper approach, carefully designed for the specific prospect and interview situation. It is an insult to open with such phrases as "I was just passing by" or "I apologize for taking your time." Each call must be a planned occasion.

Plan your approach to accomplish these objectives:

Be different.
Gain your prospect's undivided attention.
Avoid a "No thank you, not today."

To accomplish these goals, you can structure your approach in one of two basic ways: (1) a natural introduction, followed by one of several basic approaches fitted to the particular call; or (2) a lead-in, attention-getting opening sentence, followed by the introduction of yourself, your product, and your company. The following examples will help illustrate their differences; sixteen practical variations of these basic approaches will be outlined shortly.

Example 1:

Good morning Mr. Gaines. I am Jim Parker from Arco Products Corporation, here to inquire whether you have seen a demonstration of our new AK model office duplicator. X-Ray Products Corp., just down the road from you, has found it cuts their duplicating costs 25 percent. Would you be interested in effecting such savings?

Example 2:

Mr. Gaines, your friend Mr. Drucker, purchasing officer at X-Ray Products Corp., down the road, suggested I ask whether you would like to see a demonstration of our new AK model office duplicator. It cut their duplicating costs 25 percent. I am Jim Parker from Arco Products Corp. May I have the opportunity to demonstrate how our machine may effect similar savings for your company?

The introduction of yourself and your company normally comes first. You should stand erect, speak clearly and confidently, and smile with warmth while looking your prospect in the eye. Do not shake hands unless he extends his first. Do not be seated until he asks you to do so; although if he does not do so shortly, as a means of controlling the interview you may suggest, "Do you mind if we sit down so that I can answer any questions with visual material from my presentation kit?"

Normally, you also state the purpose of your visit, mentioning briefly your product or service. In some cases, especially in specialty selling, it is desirable to avoid mentioning the product as long as possible. This technique is not trickery; the purpose is to prove that a need exists, then to show how your proposal can satisfy that need. In most sales situations, however, the honest, sincere, straightforward approach—a complete introduction and a brief explanation of the purpose of your call—brings best results.

The introduction should be a cheerful, natural one, based on your positive mental assumption that you are glad to meet the prospect and have something of value to offer him. You are, in effect, a guest in his place of business or home and want to get down to matters of specific interest to him as soon as possible.

When to Present the Business Card

When to present the business card is a problem that may come up during the approach phase of the interview. Sales representatives are divided as to when it should be presented. Normally, unless it has been sent in ahead through a secretary during a business call, it is presented at the time of the introduction.

Some sales representatives prefer to present it only at the close of the interview. For many, the problem is solved prior to the interview since they have presented their business card when requesting the interview appointment, either by letter or in person. When to present the business card may depend to a large extent on the type of selling you do, the individual interview situation, your company policy, or personal choice.

SIXTEEN USEFUL, BASIC APPROACHES

Here are sixteen basic approaches that may be useful to you. Explained and illustrated by examples, they are attention-getting, interest-arousing techniques adaptable to a wide range of sales situations. They can easily be adapted to fit any of the common buying motives that account for most sales. We covered these in Chapter 4: briefly summarized, they include the following desires.

ease and convenience	play and relaxation
profit and thrift	pride and prestige
safety and protection	love and affection
adventure and excitement	sex and romance

Any good approach should contain (1) a positive opening, (2) a benefit for the prospect, (3) something to arouse curiosity, and (4) assurance that you are not wasting the prospect's time. For example:

Good morning. I've got an idea here that can double your profit on every item that you sell. However, I know you're a busy person, so if I'm here over ten minutes it will be because you insist.

Use of dramatic devices or showmanship to show as well as tell can be highly effective when used in combination with the verbal approach, as some of the following approach examples illustrate.

1. Benefit approach. You can open the interview with a statement or a question which focuses the prospect's thoughts directly on the benefits your proposal offers him. When using this approach, you must make sure that you are stating a real benefit and not just a smash opener that can easily be punctured. A benefit, when used as an approach, should meet the following requirements.

1. It should be one the prospect wants.
2. It should be thoroughly substantiated in the rest of the presentation.

3. It must be something that you can deliver in full.
4. It should be specific. A dollars-and-cents offer is more effective than a sweeping generality to get attention.

You may phrase the benefit as a question:

Mr. Conroy, would a 15 percent saving on your present shipping costs interest you?

or as a statement:

Mr. Conroy, I want to tell you about a new type of shipping service that will save you up to 15 percent on your present shipping costs.

2. Curiosity approach. An unexpected approach immediately arouses a prospect's interest and curiosity. Use of a question or a gadget, honestly and not as a trick, can often lead quickly to a warm reception.

Here is how one coffee vending-machine sales representative approaches his busy prospects—normally owners or managers of small offices or businesses: "Mr. Melendes, how would you like an extra branch office that could earn you $69 a week without any extra work on your part?" He then explains that his vending company completely services the machine once a week and that its representative turns over a percentage of the coins collected at the time of servicing.

3. Dramatic approach. Everyone loves a show, and an eye-opening, dramatic approach always arouses interest. It works best when you can get the prospect into the act, as this example shows!

Ms. Wilkenson, our new shatterproof water tumblers for hotels, restaurants, and hospitals won't break when dropped. Here, try it for yourself! Just hold it up over your head and drop it here on the hardest part of the floor! You see, it didn't break!

4. Factual approach. You can turn an interesting fact connected with the product or service you are offering into an opening appetizer sentence. The facts must be true and the sentence brief. Such an approach is usually followed by the introduction.

Mr. Steiner, did you know that over fifty companies in this state alone increased plant efficiency 20 percent within the past twelve months without adding new staff? They have done it, as this report shows, by instituting the new system of Rablaco Corp., which I represent.

5. I-am-here-to-help-you-approach. Few people can resist a confident, direct, enthusiastic offer to help. This approach can be quite effective if you follow the opening sentence with facts that prove your proposal can help them.

Mr. Steen, I am here to honestly see if I can help you cut your plant operating costs 30 percent with only a small initial investment on your part. In these days of mounting costs, that's an interesting offer, isn't it?

6. Introductory approach. This approach usually features a letter, card of introduction, or testimonial from a friend, customer, or business associate of the prospect. It can be used as a lead-in to the presentation, as follows:

Mr. Baker, I am here at the suggestion of your friend Mr. Clements of Maxwell Products, Inc. He felt you would be interested in our new Argo conveyor system, which cut his plant operating costs 20 percent the first month. Here is a note he sent you through me. He said it would serve as his introduction and endorsement.

7. News approach.   Newspaper stories or trade-journal articles often provide personalized information about your prospect or his situation. You can use this information to lead into a specific presentation. An insurance sales representative may use this approach.

Mrs. Mustelier, I've just heard some more bad news about Bigtown Department Store, which burned down yesterday. The insurance covered only three-fourths of the damage. It's a warning to us all. May I go over your firm's present coverage with you, just to make sure you are protected 100 percent?

8. Opinion approach.   This disarmingly effective yet simple approach immediately focuses attention on your product and makes the prospect a participant in your presentation. The idea is simply to show or hand him your product, give an example of what it can do, or just provide an illustration of it, and ask, "Mr. Hudson, what is your honest opinion of this?" or "Mrs. Calissi, I would like your honest opinion as to whether this would be of benefit to you." If the prospect hesitates, you may suggest moving over to see it under better light or may hold it up at another angle for better display.

9. Premium approach.   Because everyone likes to get something for nothing, few prospects turn down a free gift or sample. By accepting it, they usually feel obliged to hear your presentation. The more interesting or unusual the gift, the warmer the atmosphere for the interview. The gift itself should tie in with what you are selling. For example, "Mr. Szvetics, here is a little complementary present for you. It is intended merely as a goodwill gesture and a way of saying thank-you for the time and courtesy you are extending in seeing me today."

10. Problem-solving approach.   Most prospects are interested in ideas that help them solve their problems. The more you know about specific problems the better, but you can also aim the approach at solving common problems, as this example points out.

Mr. Ristoli, your company, like others in your industry, can cut carton-banding labor time 50 percent and costs 15 percent by using our new tape-binding process instead of your older wire-banding machine. Would you like to know how it can be done?

11. Praise or compliment approach.   Honest praise or compliments are usually well received. False praise or flattery is not. If you notice something on the prospect's office wall or desk or in his home that may be a source of pride to him, you can often use it as part of your approach.

Mr. Tarasenko, may I ask what kind of sailboat that is in the picture on the wall behind you? Are you a sailing enthusiast?

Ms. Rodgers, do you mind if I compliment you on the orderly appearance of your desk? I know how busy you are, so it must mean that you have an unusual ability to manage your time and paperwork.

12. Product approach.   Many small and eye-catching items sell themselves. People like to see, feel, hear, taste, and smell things for themselves. This approach simply involves handing the item to the prospect and asking such questions as these: "Did you ever see anything more beautifully designed than this?" "Did you ever see a wristwatch with a built-in alarm system like this?"

13. Question approach.   This approach normally consists of giving an interesting fact about what you are offering, framed as a question. The question should be simple and noncontroversial and should call for a reply to stimulate the prospect's participation in the sales presentation to follow.

Dr. Larsen, have you ever seen a small, lightweight dictating machine quite like this? Don't you think that such a lightweight unit would appeal to your office staff more than the bulky, heavier one they are now using?

14. Service approach.   What person can resist the appeal of having some-one else do some of his work for him or relieve him of responsibility or worry? Offers that promise these services, especially at lower or similar cost, have wide appeal, as the two following examples illustrate.

Mr. Edwards, wouldn't you and your wife like to be completely free of fuel or unit-breakdown heating worries this winter? My firm keeps your oil tank full and guarantees free emergency unit-breakdown repairs day or night. All we ask is that you buy your fuel from us at normal rates. Can you beat a service offer like that?

Mrs. Cancio, our laundry van will call at your door every Tuesday morning whether you have anything to send out or not. Anything picked up will be delivered the following afternoon. Our charges are reasonable, as this list shows. All we ask is that you agree to sign up as one of our regular customers.

15. Shock approach.   A mild form of shock can be effectively used in many types of selling. Insurance sales representatives and memorial park counselors often employ a form which runs like this:

Mr. and Mrs. Kuhnert, as we sit here together talking seriously about that one fact of life from which there is no escape, do you realize that in nine cases out of ten the American husband passes away before his wife? Are you prepared for such a tragic possibility in your family? Don't you agree that now is the time to think about it—to lay rational plans—while you are both here together in good health?

16. Survey approach.   This technique can be used to qualify prospects as well as to lead into the presentation. You can prepare your own questions of any degree and depth desired about your product or service. Simple ones are, "Have you heard of our product?" "Do you now own one?" "What is your impression of it?" Others are more technical and specific.

Some unscrupulous sales representatives, especially those in direct sales, have used surveys as pretexts to get in to see prospects. People naturally resent such trickery. The survey approach works best as a legitimate activity for qualifying prospects and as a basis for making an appointment to call back later to give the presentation.

A door-to-door encyclopedia sales representative may use a survey approach in this fashion when making cold calls in a neighborhood. "Good morning madam. I am making a friendly survey on behalf of XYZ Company to find out whether you have an up-to-date reference encyclopedia in your home for your children." The reply may be, "No, we don't have an encyclopedia since our children are not yet in school," or "Yes, we have a set, but it's not very up-to-date." Whatever the answer, the sales representative has qualified the prospect and can try for a callback appointment if he feels it worthwhile.

Survey approaches are commonly used in business and industrial selling when study of a complex internal system or operation is necessary before an intel-ligent sales proposal can be made. Executives know that solving their problems involves study, and they normally pay attention to the sales representative who takes the time to survey in advance and to plan a specific presentation tailored to their needs. This is problem-solving selling at its best.

OVERCOMING FEAR AND TENSION

It is easy to write about how to make a proper approach and what to say in your opening remarks. It is much more difficult to write about how to reduce the tension and even fear that new salesmen and saleswomen often experience when knocking on strange doors, meeting people in unaccustomed surroundings, confronting different personality types, and always facing the unexpected. Many experienced sales representatives, like actors and actresses, are still tense as they go into important interviews. This problem is a common one, worth more attention than most of the sales literature pays it.

A certain element of tension is normally present when sales representative and prospect meet each other for the first time. You as a sales representative are facing the unknown, the prospect may be on the defensive against sales people in general, and you are each sizing one another up.

The burden is on you to be confident in appearance, manner, speech, attitude, and bearing in order to reduce the tension and to sell yourself and the interview. This task is not easy if you feel apprehensive. Just remember that thousands of salespeople face this same fear daily and steel themselves to overcome it.

Are you afraid to make this call? One of the greatest single reasons for failure in selling is the sales representative thinking, "I just can't get up the nerve to make the next call." It is easy to make excuses—to feel sick, to decide to have a cup of coffee instead, to postpone the call if at all possible. Many potentially excellent sales representatives quit the selling game before they master this fear of the approach.

Do not be alarmed if you have this feeling of timidity, apprehension, or fear. Modern selling requires the perceptive, sensitive person. If you feel bashful and timid it may be a good sign because you can understand and sense that your prospect may have similar fears.

Once you face this problem, it is best to tackle it head on. Turn on your will power and tell yourself that you will do it! Then switch your thoughts to your prospect, imagining that he has your fears and that your tasks are to put him at ease, to relax him, and to let him know that you sincerely want to like and help him.

Practical ways to overcome fear include making practice calls in which you work only on the approach and do not even try to sell anything. You may give away a few samples or small gifts that tie in with what you are selling. Just make the call saying, "Good morning, here is a small complimentary gift. It is a good-will gesture from my company. My name is Tony Lara, the new sales representative for XYZ Company in your area." The point is not to sell anything. You can answer questions and even take orders, but do not try to sell. After a few such calls you should be able to meet future prospects without hesitation.

Another useful technique for overcoming fear is especially valuable, even for an experienced sales representative apprehensive about facing a tough buyer or a technical buyer whose questions he feels inadequate to answer. Pick the toughest, most difficult prospect in your territory and go after him. Lay siege to him if necessary; think up and try every sales technique or device imaginable to sell him. Ask the help of your sales manager or a fellow sales representative in winning him over. Keep after him until you succeed, remembering always that if he really needs or wants what you are offering, he has to buy it from someone. Why not you? You may fail in your initial attempts to sell such tough prospects, but once you succeed, your new feeling of confidence will enable you to enter all future interviews with assurance.

The way you look to yourself and to others can play an important part in reducing fear and tension. If you wear good, appropriate, successful-looking clothing, you tend to feel good and to be success-minded. If you look and feel good, you think positively and act with confidence. Your prospects see and feel this; their fear is eased; and they tend to accept you readily.

ESTABLISHING RAPPORT AND GETTING DOWN TO BUSINESS

Once you have made your opening remarks and the prospect has accepted you by indicating a desire to hear more, here is your next task:

1. Get the interview on as relaxed a basis as possible; establish rapport quickly.
2. Get the prospect to willingly give you information that will enable you to determine his needs or wants. You can then shape the benefits of your proposal around them.

We have noted previously that in the ideal interview you and the prospect talk a mutual problem over in a relaxed manner, much like two acquaintances. Your aims in this situation are to create a good impression, to control the conversation, and to get your points across in as relaxed an atmosphere as possible. A certain amount of small talk may be necessary to reduce the tension and to give you and your prospect a chance to relax, but neither of you is there to visit. Your job is to get down to business, to get him talking about his problems, and, as you listen carefully to what he is saying, to try to determine his personality type.

The best way to get him talking is to ask a question that will also elicit some valuable information for you. Most planned sales approaches include at least one question within the first two minutes of the interview. Your questions and comments should also secure his agreement with what you are saying because you are trying to get him, from the start, in a yes frame of mind. Your yes-building introductory comments and questions may run something like these.

You: Mr. Comerford, you certainly have a nice office; the view outside the window overlooking the pond is very relaxing.

Prospect: Yes, it is a nice view.

You: But I am sure that a busy person like you doesn't have much time to sit around enjoying it.

Prospect: Yes, you certainly are right there.

You: It would be nice if some magic machine could do all your paperwork in half the time, wouldn't it?

Prospect: Yes, but I'm afraid I'll be out of this world before they ever invent magic machines.

You: Well, Mr. Comerford, it may surprise you to know that a wonderful new recording and memory-storing device can help busy men like you cut their routine paperwork in half. Are you interested in a time-saver like that?

Prospect: Yes.

Continue in this manner throughout the interview, changing the pace, but yes-building all the time.

BUILDING AN ATMOSPHERE OF WARMTH AND CONFIDENCE

Along with your efforts to get your prospect to start talking about his problems and to give you information, you must also create an atmosphere of warmth and confidence. The faster you develop this ease in communication, the sooner your prospect will be receptive to your ideas.

We have considered at some length the importance of creating a favorable, confidence-building image of yourself in the eyes of your prospect. What he sees in you during the first part of your approach goes a long way toward his initial decision to receive you or not.

You now have to size him up, to find out what type of person he is, and to create an atmosphere of warmth that will make it easy for him to tell you about himself and his problems. How can you create this atmosphere quickly with a perfect stranger?

People study is a fascinating hobby and a never-ending source of enjoyment for a good sales representative. Unless you sincerely like people, you probably would not have considered selling as a career. But merely liking your fellow man does not necessarily lead to sales success. You have to study people constantly to develop the flexibility to meet each prospect differently, according to his personality. You also have to study various sales approaches since different approaches work with different prospects.

We will discuss different temperaments and how to handle them at greater length in subsequent chapters. For now let us consider briefly six personality types you may meet in any given day.

Warm, but will not be pinned down.   He sincerely enjoys your visit as a break in his routine. He would rather chat about fishing or the international situation than about his problems. Unless you are careful, his interview time will run out before you get around to your presentation.

Cold.   He listens to your story without warmth or emotion and gives you a cold, but polite, "No, thank you."

Indifferent.   His attention may wander; he may ask completely irrelevant questions; he may turn to work on his desk as he talks; or he may make phone calls in your presence.

Warm.   A friendly, warm reception that encourages your presentation and usually leads to a sale.

Hard.   He may want what you are offering but challenge or bait you all the way, often leaving you mentally and emotionally exhausted whether you make the sale or not.

Unpleasant.   Possibly even rude, he could not care less about you or your product. He just is not interested in hearing you out.

The first practical step you can take to face these different personality types is to realize that you and every other sales representative have to take the bitter with the sweet. Then you can relax and start planning how you can meet and win over whatever personality type is next thrown in your path.

If you accept warming prospects up and winning them over as a challenge, you can continue to face even a series of hard prospects cheerfully. Just do not take the hard encounters personally. Try to make a game out of winning over all the different personality types; relax and enjoy it!

Here are some laws of human nature—of getting along with or handling people—that will help you rise to the challenge. They are powerful psychological weapons for you if used sincerely!

The magic of a smile.   A genuine, sincere, warm smile is one of the most pleasant sights. Even grumpy people warm up when faced with a cheerful, sunny disposition and sincere smile. If you strongly feel that you like the other person and if you try to project your feelings with a warm look and smile, he will find it very difficult to resist.

Call him by name.   A person's name, to him, is one of the most beautiful sounds. Use it two or three times in your opening statement and often throughout the rest of the interview. The more difficult a prospect's name, the more wonderful it sounds to him when used often—if pronounced correctly.

Take a sincere interest in him.   When someone takes a sincere interest in you, it is a pleasant experience. You cannot help feeling friendly. Your prospect will react the same way toward you if you show a genuine interest in him as a person, not just as a potential customer.

Be a good listener.   The more talking you encourage and let him do, the more you learn about him, his company, his problems, and his wants and needs. You also earn his goodwill since everyone likes a good listener.

Sympathize with him.   Everyone has problems, and it makes people feel good to talk about them—to get them off their chests! A prospect likes to feel that you agree that he has legitimate gripes.

Show respect.   Everyone likes to be respected. Nobody likes to be ignored, slighted, or looked down on. You can show respect by asking the prospect's opinion and by thoughtfully considering it. You do not have to agree with him, but you can do and say things that will make him feel good. You will not gain respect by fawning flattery or by disagreeing with him.

Make him feel important.   He is important to you! Compliment him and his company when a genuine opportunity presents itself. Show appreciation for his valuable time, his consideration, and his attention.

Those magic words: thank you and please.   What more needs to be said about these two truly magic words? They ring as genuinely in the business world as in a social setting. They are hard to wear out.

You are controlling the interview at this point largely by asking a series of yes-building questions that invite attention, easy response, and noncontroversial agreement. You are striving to warm the prospect up, to show such genuine interest and attention that he feels confident in telling you about himself, his business, his company, and his problems.

Your aim now is to get enough specific information to enable you to determine his wants or needs. You can accomplish this goal by asking questions designed to get specific information.

GETTING INFORMATION THROUGH THE QUESTION TECHNIQUE

One secret for rapidly uncovering problems, wants, and needs is to forget yourself and what you want for the moment. Try to put yourself in the prospect's shoes and to think from his point of view. You are interested in finding out what he knows and feels about your company, product, or service. Thus, you should direct your questions toward what you are offering and toward securing his agreement on various points.

Attempt to determine his problems and needs to find out what product he is currently using, and to break items down into characteristic components to find out what he likes about your product or service, what he dislikes about it, and what it can do for him (benefits).

It is easier to illustrate this technique than to discuss it. Since many people use typewriters or are prospects for one, we can put ourselves in the place of a typewriter sales representative and see how he may approach a prospect to sell a new electric portable model.

Let us assume that this prospect has replied to a mailed questionnaire. He is a typewriter owner or user and a prospect. In this example, the sales message is relatively unimportant; we are interested basically in the sales representative's approach—how he arouses interest and employs the yes-building question technique to ferret out problems, objections, and wants or needs.

Uses question approach. Has friendly smile. Introduces company and product.	*Sales representative*	Mr. Lawson, do you realize that you are a 1-in-500 person? According to a mail survey recently made by my company, Regal Typewriter Corp., to which you responded, 1 out of 500 people in this city owns or uses a typewriter. Yet only 15 percent have heard of our new, low-cost, portable, electric Stylerite model.
Makes personal introduction. Proposes a free offer with no effort involved on part of prospect and no obligation to buy. Assures prospect he will not have to make a decision now. Makes trial close.		My name is Tony Sirgy and I am here to ask you personally whether you would like a free, ten-day trial of it in your office (or home). There is no obligation on your part, of course. Are you interested?
	Prospect	Not particularly, my present machine is adequate.
Ignores negative answer and asks specific factual question. Uses his name.	*Sales representative*	Is it a big, standard, manual machine, or a portable, Mr. Lawson?
	Prospect	Well, it's a standard manual, but I'm not interested in a new typewriter.
Gathers more valuable information.	*Sales representative*	How old is it?
	Prospect	Eight years or so, I suppose.
Asks for a noncontroversial yes-getting response, acknowledging reliability of firm and product.	*Sales representative*	May I ask you a question? Are you familiar with Regal Typewriter Corp., and its national reputation of standing behind its products?
	Prospect	Oh yes, everyone has heard of your company.

Still appears not to sell, just asks personal information in a friendly inquiring manner.	*Sales representative*	Just out of curiosity, may I ask what kind of work you do on your machine and whether anyone else in your office (or home) uses it?
Finds out other users besides prospect and determines objections.	*Prospect*	My secretary (or my daughter) and I both use it, mainly for correspondence and reports. But look here, I am busy and am not interested in a new typewriter.
Apparently agrees with prospect, but asks another personal, inoffensive question in an interested manner. Uses his name.	*Sales representative*	Good! But Mr. Lawson, may I ask, does your work require a lot of carbon copies? And does hers?
	Prospect	Yes.
Breaks objections into components. Finds out what he likes best!	*Sales representative*	For my own information, what do you like best about your older manual machine?
	Prospect	I am used to it, and it does the job for me.
Finds out what he likes least!	*Sales representative*	What do you like least about it, again for my personal information. And how does your secretary (or daughter) feel?
Gains valuable, specific information around which benefits of new machine can be built.	*Prospect*	Well, my secretary (or daughter) says that she gets tired after using it a while and that it is pretty slow compared to the new models.
Secures agreement.	*Sales representative*	Would you agree, Mr. Lawson, that she has a good point?
	Prospect	Yes, I guess so.
Offers proof.	*Sales representative*	If I can prove to you that our modern, lightweight, Stylerite electric portable could do your work and hers easier and in half the time, would you be interested in a trade-in arrangement?
A buying signal! The prospect is interested.	*Prospect*	What would it cost me?
Avoids price if possible (but will disclose it if customer persists). Stresses benefits of saving time and of reliability. Closes on minor point of trial demonstration. Makes it easy for prospect to agree since he is not being forced to make buying decision now.	*Sales representative*	The cost is very low compared to a 50 percent saving of your valuable time. My company is interested only in having you try it in your office (or home) for ten days without obligation. We feel our marvelous, new Stylerite has to sell itself. May I bring one in for you tomorrow at 10:30 A.M. or at 2:30 P.M.?
Knows sale after trial is almost assured if Stylerite accomplishes benefits claimed.	*Prospect*	Yes, I guess so. I've got nothing to lose by trying it out, and it sounds interesting. Make it 10:30.

SUMMARY

In this chapter we have concentrated on the proper approach to use in calling on a new prospect. In many types of selling the job is not complete until after the third or fourth call, but such follow-up calls are built on the results obtained in the initial call.

As a lead-in to the approach, we stressed that persuasion is the core of the entire selling process and is related to all the basic steps from approach to close. We discussed logical reasoning and suggestion as the two generally accepted persuasive methods that motivate a prospect to take action (to buy), with the latter being more often employed.

The purpose of the approach is to gain and hold attention. It should be carefully planned and executed because successful accomplishment of this sale within a sale is often as difficult for new sales representatives as is the final close. Lasting from the first two to five minutes of the interview, the approach breaks down into (1) the first five seconds and (2) the balance of approach time necessary to gain your objectives. These objectives are to sell yourself and the interview and to avoid being brushed off.

We discussed the importance of creating a good first impression and of encouraging the prospect to accept you with confidence so that he will tell you his problems, wants, or needs, and hear you out. We stressed that your appearance and manner are equally as important as what you say.

We covered many specific approaches and approach techniques. We discussed the fear and tension commonly felt by new and sometimes even by experienced sales representatives and how to overcome them. And we noted practical ways through which the prospect can also be relaxed and encouraged to talk and by which a warm interview situation can be quickly established.

Finally, we covered the question techniques most commonly used to arouse and hold attention while getting information about the prospect's problems, objections, wants, and needs; around these you can shape benefits during the remainder of the presentation.

CHAPTER REVIEW

CONCEPTS TO REMEMBER*

_____ logical reasoning   _____ benefit approach   _____ question approach
_____ suggestion   _____ planned approach   _____ curiosity approach
_____ ideal sales   _____ mannerisms   _____ factual approach
          interview

*For memory reinforcement, fill in the page number or numbers where these terms were described in this chapter.

QUESTIONS FOR ANALYSIS AND DISCUSSION

1. What are the basic differences between persuasion based on suggestion and that based on logical reasoning?
2. How long does the approach phase normally last, and into what two subdivisions is it broken?
3. What do prospects see and judge a sales representative on inwardly during the first five seconds of the interview?
4. What three purposes does one seek to achieve by using a planned, proper approach?

5. What two generally accepted methods of persuasion are commonly used in sell-ing? Which of the two is the most widely used? List and explain two examples of the most widely used one.
6. Why are the opening words of the approach so important? In what two ways should they be structured?
7. Name three of the four requirements of a benefit used in a benefit approach.
8. What single technique can a sales representative use to most effectively ferret out problems, objections, and needs or wants?

Case Study 10–1

THE VOLKSWAGEN LOW-PRESSURE APPROACH TO SELLING

A postwar British commission made the following report after visiting the bombed-out Volkswagen factory in Wolfsburg, Germany, in 1945.

The VW, or People's Car, does not meet the fundamental technical requirements of a motorcar. . . . As regards performance and design, it is quite unattractive to the average motorcar buyer. It is too ugly and too noisy. A type of car like this will remain popular for 2 or 3 years if that. To build the car commercially would be a completely uneconomic enterprise.

As Volkswagen production increased—from 8,987 vehicles in 1947 to more than 100,000 in 1951 and to 1,800,000 in 1970—sales were made in one country after another until today the VW is sold and serviced in more than 130 countries. Over 20 million Volkswagens have been sold since that commission made its report.

The biggest market outside Germany is the United States, which now buys 25 percent of total VW production each year. By the end of 1974, over 5 million VW's were registered in this country.

REASONS FOR SUCCESS

What miracle caused the worldwide sales increases of a relatively unknown automobile from a war-defeated nation within a few years? How could a small and different-looking foreign car rise from nowhere to challenge even the mighty American auto manufac-turers of Detroit?

Volkswagen of America, Inc., with over 1,100 authorized dealers and 50,000 employees, has some answers. They say success is due to a fine product; a unique marketing and service concept; responsible, enthusiastic, customer-oriented dealers and sales representatives, and their low-pressure philosophy of selling.

WHAT IS THE VW LOW-PRESSURE SELLING PHILOSOPHY?

The Volkswagen sales philosophy essentially is that customers buy cars not only to fulfill a need (transportation), but also to gain basic and highly personal satisfactions. The VW sales strategy is to fulfill needs and to provide satisfactions on an individual basis. The company feels that there are three types of selling: high pressure, no pressure, and VW low pressure, as outlined below.

High-pressure selling is based on the premise that people do not like to buy and must be sold. In such selling, anything goes to get the sale. By using emotional or rational statements, the fast-talking sales representative just keeps trying until the prospect gives in. VW feels that the buying public today resents such selling and distrusts sales representatives who use high-pressure methods.

No-pressure selling is based on the premise that if you are just nice to people and give them only information, they will buy. Such selling involves little or no persuasion, and sales representatives consider it distasteful to ask for an order. This is passive selling, and VW doesn't feel it is successful as a technique or helpful to prospective customers.

VW low-pressure selling is active selling—aggressive yet thoughtful and imaginative. Sales representatives are trained to listen for prospect reactions so that they will know when and how to translate features into benefits. They use a planned sales presentation geared to the particular needs and interests of the individual prospect. This presentation lulls resistance but tends to gain customer confidence and trust because the VW sales representative is, in effect, a problem-solver rather than a product-pusher. His success comes not from pushing the prospect but from leading or helping him, gently but firmly, to make a satisfactory buying decision. The emphasis in VW low-pressure selling is on fulfilling the needs of the customer by showing him how the VW can satisfy him.

QUESTIONS FOR WRITTEN REPORTS OR CLASS DISCUSSION

1. Do you feel that the VW low-pressure sales approach is in line with modern customer-oriented, problem-solving selling? Give three good reasons to justify your conclusion.
2. The VW has undoubtedly been a world-wide sales success. Give two major reasons for this success.
3. Offer and explain in detail three reasons why VW enjoys far greater sales success in the United States than does the French Renault—a competitive car in price and quality.

Case Study 10–2

THE COCA-COLA COMPANY'S "SOFTEN HIM UP WITH COLD COKE" APPROACH SCORES IN 133 COUNTRIES

The business of The Coca-Cola Company is one of the greatest sales/marketing operations the world has ever known. Developing Coke in 1886, the creator of the formula, Dr. John S. Pemberton, thought of it primarily as a sweet syrup mix for the bitter prescription compounds made to order for physicians to give their patients. However, it has never been advertised as a medicine and no medicinal claims have ever been made. On the contrary, it was first advertised as a delicious and refreshing soft drink in the *Atlanta Journal* for May 29, 1886. Eighty-eight years later, over 165 million drinks of Coke a day are being consumed in approximately 133 countries, more countries than are members of the United Nations.

Coca-Cola became a wholesome family drink for all occasions. This most American of American exports, in spite of vitriolic attacks by the Communist Press, has successfully stimulated taste buds (and cracked the market) in Yugoslavia, Hungary, Poland, and other Communist satellite countries. Today, its combined net worth in assets, including the total value of independent bottling franchises, possibly make it the largest privately-owned enterprise in the world.

Who wants or needs Coke? Probably even the top company executives cannot say for sure, but they continue selling it the world over in ever-increasing quantities. They claim there is no market saturation point. Enjoy a drink of Coke, and thirty minutes later, you are theoretically ready for another. According to the Company, no one in the world between the ages of 13 and 50 is too poor to buy himself a drink of Coke a week. On a national basis, the average consumption of Coca-Cola is about 160 drinks per person per year.

Much has been written about the successful advertising programs for Coca-Cola, but little about the day-to-day sales activities of thousands of route managers and the average of five driver-salesmen they each supervise in those 133 countries. The drivers of these largely decentralized sales operations generally follow a simple pattern in making an initial approach to a prospective dealer. Analysis pinpoints geographical market areas, and such areas are assigned to one or more route managers. The route manager's list may be one of current soft-drink outlets or he may seek his own. Any place where people gather—schools, food markets, factory canteens, or cafes—is a potential market-place for Coca-Cola. An advertising campaign usually precedes personal sales calls in a newly opened territory or country, and potential dealer prospects usually know that Coke is being introduced in their communities before being called upon.

The route managers, or their driver-salesmen, have a secret weapon in the back of their delivery trucks—some ice-cold bottles of Coke. They take one or more bottles of Coca-Cola with them on their calls on prospective dealers; they ask for glasses, pour a glass of cold Coke for everyone, and only then do they talk business—while the prospect is enjoying his glass of cold Coke!

The general lead question, depending on the outlet situation, runs something like this: "How many cases of soft-drink do you sell a week?" Taking a percentage of that, the salesman then suggests, "Perhaps you should start with X (number of) cases per week" (citing a conservative figure).

The aim of this first call is to get even a few cases of Coca-Cola into the outlet. In a subsequent case study (15-1), we shall see how the major and sustained efforts for Coca-Cola helped the dealer sell the product through a highly organized follow-up and follow-through sales plan.

QUESTION FOR WRITTEN REPORTS OR CLASS DISCUSSION

Based on the information above, outline four various receptions a sales representative for Coca-Cola may get to the above approach and your suggested plans for handling each.

SALES PROBLEM 10-1

GOODYEAR TIRE DEALERS ASKED:
"HOW OFTEN DOES YOUR CUSTOMER GET A FRIENDLY GREETING?"

Sales management challenges dealers for the internationally known Goodyear Tire
Company with this question: "How often does your customer get a friendly greeting?"
This friendly greeting is the first of five company-recommended steps in a tire sale. Here
they are in order of presentation.

1. Give a friendly greeting.
2. Look at old tires and analyze the customer's needs.
3. Show recommended new tires.
4. Sell features and benefits.
5. Ask for the order.

But why, you may ask, does Goodyear consider the first step so important? It
should be obvious, and company sales managers readily agree that it is, yet their
surveys show that 36 percent of all tire sales representatives do not greet customers
in a friendly way. Goodyear tells these dealers that it is very important to size the
customer up and to make him feel welcome because every prospect wants to know
that he has come to the right place and that the sales representative is willing and
able to help solve his tire problem.

The best way to make him feel welcome, Goodyear feels, is to smile and give a
cheerful greeting. This simple act, ignored 36 percent of the time, disarms him and
paves the way for the next four steps in the Goodyear five-step approach.

QUESTION FOR WRITTEN REPORTS OR CLASS DISCUSSION

Assuming you are a Goodyear tire dealer-sales representative, write a brief planned
approach, based on a smile and cheerful greeting, that will lead through Steps 1 and
2, up to the point at which you are ready to show your prospect a recommended
new tire.

11
the presentation, part I: creating and holding interest

When you have mastered the content of this chapter, you should be able to:

List five decisions a prospect has to make in his own mind before agreeing to buy.

List the six essential points to be covered in any effective sales presentation.

Describe meaning of these statements concerning a sales presentation: (1) it must be complete, (2) it should eliminate competition, and (3) questions should be anticipated and built into the presentation.

List two useful techniques a sales representative can employ in bringing up and eliminating competition himself during a sales presentation.

Summarize the importance of questioning and listening, and give some specific principles and techniques that sales representatives should be aware of.

List eleven prospect personality types a sales representative can expect to encounter; tell how to identify and handle each.

Describe how to handle various types of interruptions that might be encountered during a sales presentation.

Describe various principles and techniques involved in arousing and holding a prospect's attention and interest.

The preliminaries are over, your prospect is interested in you and what you are proposing, and you are now entering the heart of your presentation. This is your big opportunity—will you make the sale or lose it? What you say and what you do during the next several minutes goes a long way toward influencing the decision.

You have aroused the prospect's interest, but can you hold it? Because his attention span is not long, your immediate task is to create continued interest—to hold it long enough to tell your story. What can you say or do to hold his interest? Will your words and actions bring him to the point of saying "Yes, I'll buy" or will they leave him cold and unsold?

Our thoughts in this chapter will center on the principles and techniques of creating and holding interest. We will cover a lot of ground in considering this subject, as the following list of topics shows. We will discuss them in this sequence during the remainder of this chapter.

1. Presentation overview: the strategic aims in Parts I and II.
2. Five decisions your prospect makes before buying.
3. Helping your prospect recognize and admit his needs or wants and his readiness to seek a solution.
4. Six essentials of a good presentation.
5. Some principles and techniques of questioning and listening.

6. Holding the interest of different personality types.
7. Handling interruptions during your presentation.
8. Clearly understanding how to arouse and hold your prospect's interest.
9. Four factors of holding attention and interest.
10. Accomplishing your objectives.

PRESENTATION OVERVIEW:
THE STRATEGIC AIMS IN PARTS I AND II

With success in the approach phase of gaining and holding your prospect's attention, you are now ready to continue with the presentation. Although it is a smooth-flowing, integrated process throughout (from approach to close), we will consider the body of the presentation as follows: Part I (creating and holding interest) in this chapter and Part II (arousing desire and securing conviction) in the next chapter. Following that we will cover the handling of objections and the close.

Let us first consider for a moment the strategy to be followed throughout Parts I and II as you persuasively lead your prospect from interest to desire to conviction to action.

Your objectives during Part I (creating and holding interest) are to help your prospect to discover and to clarify his needs, wants, and problems, to admit and to discuss them, and to indicate willingness to seek a solution. At this point you have already aroused his interest by establishing rapport and have made a few tantalizing suggestions as to how your product or service may benefit him. Now you are in a position to start finding out his real wants or needs or his *major* problems.

Your objective during Part II (arousing desire and securing conviction) is first to help your prospect realize that your product or service will provide solutions or answers to his needs, wants, or problems. Then, through proof and demonstration where possible, you seek to convince him that your offering will be the best possible way of fulfilling his desires.

FIVE DECISIONS YOUR PROSPECT MAKES BEFORE BUYING

Your prospect has to make the five decisions listed below before agreeing to buy. He may express these as questions or objections, or he may not express them. You must realize what they are and must build them into your presentation at the proper time in order to forestall his presenting them as objections and to provide facts upon which he can base his decision.

1. Need. No prospect buys until he recognizes a need or want. His first step in this direction is to feel dissatisfied with his present situation. Desire is aroused by pointing out the advantages of having your product or service (desire for gain) and the disadvantages of not having it (fear of loss). Stressing the benefits he now misses and which he would gain and enjoy by owning or using your product or service intensifies desire.

2. Product. Your prospect, before he buys, has to be convinced that your product (1) will do for him what is claimed for it, (2) is the best available for his special needs or situation, and (3) will be the best for some time to come (in order to justify the cost).

3. Service. He has to agree that your firm offers guarantees or other backing of his purchase and that it can deliver as promised. He must have confidence in the reliability of the source and of after-sale service if necessary.

4. Price. The prospect has to decide first whether he can afford to buy and then whether the benefits will offset the cost. He also has to make a value decision: Does the product or service offer more value than that of the competition?

5. Time. Your prospect has to decide whether he wants to enjoy the benefits enough to buy now or whether time of purchase is of little importance. He also has to take into consideration any promised delivery date.

HELPING YOUR PROSPECT RECOGNIZE AND ADMIT HIS NEEDS OR WANTS AND HIS READINESS TO SEEK A SOLUTION

Helping your prospect recognize his needs is the objective and heart of Part I (creating and holding interest) of the presentation. His needs, wants, and problems may be openly acknowledged or subconscious; your task as a sales representative is to help him discover, clarify, and intensify them.

In Chapter 4, we noted four common denominators of desire: (1) physiological or biological, (2) social, (3) psychological, and (4) self-fulfillment. People are motivated to fulfill these basic desires by deep-rooted needs or more openly felt wants. Real needs, operating just below the consciousness, are sometimes difficult to recognize since they represent deep-rooted urges either inherited or learned. Fulfilling a need may involve satisfying deep, inwardly felt desires for love and affection or security and safety—desires not even understood by the prospect himself. Wants, on the other hand, are easier to spot since they are close to our conscious level and reflect positive desires (pleasure, profit, approval) or negative desires (loss, disapproval, inconvenience).

Your function, as a customer-oriented, problem-solving sales representative, is to try to help your prospect satisfy his unconscious needs and conscious wants. You can accomplish this task by asking questions about his likes, dislikes, hopes, fears, and problems and by listening carefully for answers that give you clues to his strongest desires or greatest fears.

As you question, guide him toward a favorable image of and positive response to your product or service as a means of fulfilling his desires or solving his problems. By narrowing the questions down to the most basic or important needs, wants, or problems, you help clarify in his mind as well as in yours his area of greatest concern. You can intensify this concern by continuing to frame questions that require yes-building answers to the desirability of his obtaining the benefits you are offering. We will discuss this yes-building question technique in detail later.

SIX ESSENTIALS OF A GOOD PRESENTATION

Although we have already discussed the over-all aims of your presentation, some further clarification may be helpful as we consider the essentials for overcoming as many objections as possible while building toward desire, conviction, and action. First, you have to explain clearly and carefully, in a convincing manner, what you are proposing as well as its benefits. Second, you have to establish the fact that what you are proposing will satisfy one or more buying motives and will overcome to your prospect's satisfaction any questions or objections he raises. Finally, you have to arouse such a desire in his mind for the benefits it offers that he wants to buy it. These points may sound like a mere restatement of items previously discussed, but success depends on how closely your presentation follows this outline. Success also depends on how well you relate these points to your prospect's personality and response.

Six essential points to be covered in any effective sales presentation are the following. They are grouped as they will be covered in Part I and Part II of our discussion.

Part I

1. Your presentation must be complete.
2. It should eliminate competition.
3. Questions should be anticipated and built into the presentation.

Part II

4. Your presentation must be clear.
5. The question of price must be handled.
6. Logical and emotional selling points should be developed around needs and key buying motives so that they arouse desire and secure conviction.

---

1. Your presentation must be complete.   You should tell the whole story so that your prospect knows exactly what it is you are proposing. Completeness does not necessarily mean giving details about everything, but it does involve covering all the elements of the presentation: attention, interest, desire, conviction, and the close. Within this framework, you have to cover in logical sequence all the important points of your sales story.

We discussed in Chapter 8 ("Planning Your Presentation") the elements necessary for a complete presentation. That review covered such topics as effective communication between you and your prospect regardless of qualifications on the part of either and the advantages of a canned versus a planned presentation in different circumstances. It is suggested that you restudy Chapter 8 to further clarify what is meant by completeness of your presentation.

2. It should eliminate competition.   From your point of view, it is best not only to anticipate competition as a factor in most sales situations but also to plan to meet it. Building it into your presentation from the start renders it as harmless as possible or eliminates it completely in advance as a possible objection.

Your prospect may be a satisfied customer of a competitor or be aware of competing products against which he can or may desire to compare claims made for your product or service. You can handle either situation by first studying the products, advertising claims, or performance claims of your competition and then being prepared to point out specific superior points of yours.

Prior planning enables you to acknowledge competition while stressing the advantages your own proposal offers. These advantages may be better technical performance, new and unusual features, or lower price. If you cannot offer these advantages, you may have to emphasize faster delivery, better personal service, or more efficient follow-through servicing. Careful questioning as to what your prospect both likes and dislikes about competition presents ideas around which you can frame positive sales points.

Avoid mentioning the competition, either a company or a specific product, by name. Avoid derogatory comments at all costs; they only demean you and often have a way of getting back to competitors. If you make any comparisons or statements concerning the competition, be sure you can back them up with facts.

Even in the face of unfair competition, always be fair yourself and say only good things about that company or its products. This course will gain respect and will give your prospect confidence in both you and your claims.

Although we will discuss techniques for handling specific objections involving competition in a subsequent chapter, here are two useful techniques you can employ in bringing up and eliminating competition yourself.

1. Acknowledge Competition, Praise It, and Pass On.

Mr. Deeks, you are as aware as I, of the several excellent competing products on the market. We think ours offers you greater value for your money. For example. . . .

2. Meet Competition Head On, Armed with Facts.

Mr. Pellacani, our low-priced, American automobile delivers only twenty miles per gallon compared to twenty-seven for its chief competition, the well-known Brand X foreign import. But ours offers 136 horsepower compared to its 65, can seat six adults comfortably compared to four in theirs, offers more luggage space, and you can get service and parts readily in every city and town of the United States. Wouldn't you prefer all these benefits since the price is the same?

3. Anticipate questions and build them into your presentation. Your prospect wants to know and has every right to ask what your proposal will do for him, how it works, what is its price, and perhaps even how its technical details compare with those of competing products. You are asking him to spend his money, so it is only natural that he want these questions answered. You too probably take all factors into account when you consider a major personal or home purchase.

It is at this point that empathy becomes important. You will recall that early in Chapter 4 we defined *empathy* as the ability to detect how the prospect feels and what his attitudes and opinions are. He is a consumer like you, and you can expect him to question some or all aspects of your proposal, just as you do yourself when considering major purchases. So, both in planning for and during the presentation, mentally put yourself in his shoes and try to anticipate and build into your presentation the questions you would ask in his position. It will add conviction to your points and instill confidence in his mind that you really are offering something of benefit and value to him. Your ability to project empathy will go a long way toward helping him say yes to your offer.

You can help avoid questions becoming possible objections by anticipating them in advance. In the planning stage of your presentation, list every possible question you feel the prospect may ask. You can then work out planned answers to these questions and include them automatically as part of your presentation.

Another way of approaching the problem is to list all the key features, positive facts, or other advantages of both your product and your company. You can then rephrase these advantages in terms of benefit statements when planning your presentation. During your presentation, you can include them in your logical development of points, thus in effect answering your prospect's questions before he has a chance to ask them.

Perhaps the most effective sales presentation is one that anticipates and answers as a matter of course and logical development every question which the prospect may want answered. Upon completion, the story is so thoroughly convincing that your basic job is merely asking, "When do you want it delivered?"

SOME PRINCIPLES AND TECHNIQUES OF QUESTIONING AND LISTENING

The Importance of Questioning

You want to help your prospect solve his problems, but how can you talk about his specific problems and interests if you are not familiar with them? Fortunately for sales representatives, most people like to talk—especially about themselves. Thus, the best way to discover your prospect's problems is to ask questions. Get him to tell you his opinions, experiences, needs, and difficulties before you start to sell. Chances are, if he talks enough, he will show you exactly what you have to do in order to convince him that what you are offering is just what he wants or needs.

By getting him to talk, you also make him think. Perhaps he does not even know he has a problem. If so, your first step is to make him aware of it. If he does not have a problem, you should try to help him discover one. Until he recognizes a problem and appreciates its importance, you will not be able to hold his attention or interest.

You gain other advantages by getting him to talk: It makes him feel important and flattered, and he warms up to you as someone sincerely interested in him. When you show that you respect his opinion, he is likely to respect yours. And continuing to ask questions throughout your presentation helps uncover the key issue around which you can close the sale.

What kind of questions should you ask? The best are those that challenge him to think and to answer as a matter of personal pride. At any stage of the interview, you should direct them toward yes-building and closing the sale. Here are some helpful principles and techniques of good questioning.

Who, what, when, where, why, and how questions open discussion, create interest, provoke thought, help develop a subject, discover buying motives, and uncover hidden objections.

Short, specific questions, especially ones requiring a simple yes or no answer, help define points readily.

Ask questions directed at the prospect's specific situation.   If selling in his or her home or office, relate questions to that environment and situation. For example, "Mrs. Bernstein, wouldn't this color rug [showing swatch] look nice here in this living room with all your beautiful antiques?"

Ask questions aimed at specific, major buying motives.   Through questioning you can determine what is most likely to motivate the prospect to buy and then can further direct your questions to that major motive (convenience, profit, prestige, etc.).

Ask questions to make sure he understands.   Stop after each point to ask the prospect whether he has any questions. For example, "Do you have any questions about what I've just demonstrated, Mr. Schulte?"

Ask questions that require him to observe what is happening.   For example, "Mr. Castro, how do you think the motor is going to sound when I push this button?"

Ask questions to get the prospect to answer his own objections.   The "why" question is commonly used, such as, "Why do you believe it costs too much?" "Why don't you like the push button instead of the older dial system?"

Ask thought-provoking questions to gain attention. For example, "Mr. Fernandez, can you really afford not to have this labor-saving device in your plant?"

Ask "why" questions—the hardest of all for a wavering prospect to answer. You can ask this simple question over and over again to pinpoint specific objections.

You can ask simple, direct questions in many ways and for many reasons: to open and control the interview, to draw out silent or hesitant prospects, to discover buying motives, to find hidden objections, and to help make the final close.

And now here is one great secret of effective question-asking! Once you ask your question, keep quiet, sit back, and listen attentively so you will learn something!

Learn to Be a Good Listener

It is one thing to be able to ask questions in such an interested, forthright manner that your prospect wants to tell you about his problems and needs. It is quite another thing to be an intelligent enough listener to turn what he is saying into sales points that help you guide him toward a favorable buying decision.

Being an intelligent listener may not be enough, however. You should not only give him a chance to talk and encourage him to do so from time to time by asking him questions, but also *try to understand his feelings*, as well as his words. Once again, your empathy becomes important—your ability to understand how he feels. You don't have to agree with all his opinions or conclusions, but you should let him know that you appreciate, respect, and understand them.

It is to your advantage to be a good listener for four major, basic reasons.

1. You can win the prospect's attention, interest, and confidence by being a good audience. People in general like to hear themselves talk and to be listened to. If you show sincere interest in his thoughts and opinions he will like you and will be strongly motivated to repay you with an order.

2. You can determine his real interests and needs only by paying careful attention to what he says. Your prospect must have a chance to talk, to ask questions, and to state his feelings and opinions. Through careful listening you can discover his interests and reasons for buying. Many prospects do not know what they want, and the only way you can find out is to listen carefully and to frame new questions to draw them out.

3. You can check the prospect's understanding or comprehension only through feedback. People as a rule do not like to admit that they do not know or understand something. You can test your prospect's comprehension step by step by asking him to restate in his own words what you have said. This is called feedback. His answers to your questions reveal whether he is still with you or whether he has failed to get your message. If he misses your point, you may lose the sale.

4. You can realize when he is ready to say yes. Far too many sales are lost daily by sales representatives so interested in talking themselves that they miss buying signals or verbal expressions of interest that may indicate that the prospect is ready to buy. Sales representatives have the reputation of being glib talkers, and many do, in fact, talk themselves out of sales. Many professional sales representatives feel that a good presentation involves only 25 percent talking on their part and 75 percent listening. If this is true, if listening is that important, do you know (1) when to stop talking and start listening and (2) how to be a good listener?

You should stop talking and start listening when you recognize certain signals from your prospect, such as these.

1. *If he interrupts you.* If he wants to get a word in, let him as long as you still maintain control of the interview. Listen attentively, for he may be trying to say yes.

2. *If he starts to agree with you.* This may indicate that he is ready to buy. You can encourage him to continue expressing why he agrees, and he may further convince himself with his own words.

3. *If he says you have given him an idea.* If he does this, let him talk; he may give you pointers around which you can frame your selling points.

4. *If he says he likes what your product or service will do for him.* This means he is ready to buy; it is time for you to stop bringing up new points and to go into a trial close.

You can develop the art of good listening by observing the following dos and don'ts.

Dos	**Don'ts**
Give your full attention to what is being said.	Do not pretend to listen when your thoughts are elsewhere.
Listen for key facts rather than for overall ideas.	Do not get annoyed by phrases or words you find objectionable.
Look and act interested in what he is saying.	Do not allow yourself to be distracted by outside sounds, sights, or activities.
Mentally attempt to anticipate what he is trying to get at, what his point will be.	Do not try to take notes of what he is saying.
Mentally, summarize what he has said to be sure you get the point.	Do not interrupt him at any time.
Try to learn something from his words, manner, actions, tone, and looks.	Do not mentally criticize his looks, manners, tone of voice, or ideas.
	Do not try to rebut every minor negative idea he expresses.

Listening is an art that requires concentration and energy. You may become mentally tired after listening attentively to several prospects during the day, but you still have to be prepared to give your fresh, complete attention to the next one. You cannot hope to win and hold his attention and interest unless you can first project the feeling that you are sincerely interested in him.

Two-way communication requires an interchange of ideas, and a sales representative has to give the prospect a chance to talk. Since, according to psychologists, you can think about four times faster than he can talk, you have time to plan your strategy around his comments. You can best do this by listening attentively for expressions that may indicate his needs, expressed or hidden objections, and reason for buying. If you are alert to buying signals, you can base your closing efforts around his favorable comments.

How can you make sure your prospect is listening? What can you do if you suspect that his mind is wandering and that you are not holding his undivided attention and interest? How can you tell whether he is paying attention to what you are saying? If he seems too relaxed, just sits back and listens without offering either objections or positive comments, you probably are not holding his interest.

You can check this situation and force him to fresh attention by getting him to participate in the discussion: ask a question, invite him to read something or to check figures, or show him something and ask him a question about it.

How can you let your prospect know you are listening to him? One of the best ways of being empathic is to be a good listener. If your prospect senses that you are sincerely interested in him and his opinions, he will open up and tell you more. How can you communicate to him that you are listening attentively to what he is saying?

The best way is to briefly summarize what he has been saying. For example, "If I understand you correctly, Mr. Lombardo, you are most interested in the problem of preventive maintenance for your machine tools. Is that true?" Frame such summary questions so that he will give you a yes answer, around which you can build the next point in your presentation. As you proceed, you continue to hold his interest since you have demonstrated that you are a good listener and truly interested in his feelings and opinions.

HOLDING THE INTEREST OF DIFFERENT PERSONALITY TYPES

Once you have passed the approach phase of the presentation interview and aroused the prospect's attention and interest, you face the problem of holding his interest, whatever his personality type. Just as he has been sizing you up, you have been sizing him up. What kind of a person is he? How do you meet the challenge of his personality, his likes and dislikes? How can you get through to him? The place to start is with an analysis of your own attitudes and manner.

Are you mentally prepared to meet any situation? You have to be mentally prepared to handle any one of a number of generally recognized personality types on their terms and on their home ground. The first step is to adjust your own manner, words, and actions to those of your prospect. The second step is to judge him as rationally as possible before typing him. It is risky to make snap judgments—the most unlikely prospect may be the biggest buyer.

You can read about handling various personality types, but only you can train yourself to be sincerely interested, flexible, adaptable, and even-tempered. Start by refusing to accept your prospect's initial behavior at face value. Perhaps he is not feeling well, or perhaps his attitude or response is merely a defense he employs against or to test all sales representatives. Whatever the case, you should try to find his real nature—what the inner person is like. Do not worry about whether he likes you or is impressed with you; just act as though you like him and find him a reasonable and intelligent person, and control your own actions.

Can you remain cheerful, even-tempered, and calm regardless of the situation? You have to face whatever personality type you encounter cheerfully and with equanimity. If he is rude and unpleasant, you cannot afford to take it as a personal affront and let it ruin your day. Just accept his reactions as part of your work and refuse to let his rebuff get under your skin.

People in different positions and jobs think and act differently. Busy executives may be brusque and intent only on getting to the practical point immediately. Some business and home buyers are swayed by emotion rather than by reason. Technical-minded people may be slow and analytical in considering your proposal. The personality of each may change throughout the day because of work pressure, worry, fatigue, or even indigestion.

In order to arouse and hold the interest of your prospect you should be constantly alert to signals that indicate his mood and be prepared to handle it successfully. Although it is difficult to type any person specifically, sales representatives and sales literature have made some general breakdowns of personality types and have offered suggestions for handling them that may be useful to you.

PERSONALITY TYPES AND SUGGESTIONS ON HOW TO HANDLE THEM

How to identify them	*How to handle them*
The Glad-Hander Prospect	
He is glad to see you and is happy to talk about anything, to listen to your proposal, and to hear your story; but he is not interested in buying. If you are not careful, he thanks you graciously and sends you away empty-handed.	He may not be the real decision-maker. Ask him questions he finds difficult to answer: How could he use your product or service? When would he consider buying it? Can he refer you to anyone who may be interested in buying now? If you cannot get him seriously interested, then do not waste your time.
The Talkative Prospect	
He is so cheerful and talkative that he wanders from the subject. If you are not careful, he sidetracks you, and time runs out without your getting down to the business of closing the sale.	Give him a reasonable amount of time to talk himself out but use every opportunity to steer him to your proposal. Agree with a comment he makes and tie it in with your next one. Keep your own points in mind and guide the discussion your way.
The Impulsive Prospect	
He appears impatient and interrupts you often. He may agree to buy, then change his mind. He may try to stall or delay you. He may get bored easily.	You have to try to deal quickly with him, stressing benefits and making trial closes. Offer him proof if he wants it but keep pressing him in a friendly and businesslike way for an affirmative decision. If he seems bored, forget details, outline major benefits, and try for a close.
The Vascillating Prospect	
He probably hates to make decisions; he appears nervous, uncertain, and undecided in words, manner, and actions.	You can best help him by focusing his attention on a single course of action. Offering him a choice only makes him think he has to make the decision. Offer him authoritative proof and logical reasons for taking a specific course of action. Be firm with him.
The Deliberate Prospect	
He appears calm, serious, and unhurried in speech, manner, or actions. He listens carefully, asks detailed questions, and considers every point of your proposal thoroughly.	Be sure you know your product or service carefully as compared to that of the competition. Offer him plenty of proof as you stress the value of the benefits he will gain. Try to give him all the proof he wants since he is seriously considering your proposal.

The Silent Prospect

He may just sit there listening, saying nothing, without offering any clue by manner or facial expression to his inner thoughts.

He will be impressed most by facts. Offer him proof of the benefits and value he will gain by accepting your proposal. Treat him with dignity and respect. You should ask him questions in an effort to get him to talk, remaining silent yourself after each one and outlasting him.

The Closed-Mind Prospect

He is firmly satisfied with the status quo and with current suppliers' products and service and sees no reason to change.

Question him in detail about why he likes the present situation, and watch for clues that may indicate any dissatisfaction. Then try to find out what could be improved in his present situation and build your points around how you can offer him greater value.

The Shopper Prospect

He listens to your story, gets all price quotes and literature, and puts you off with a "I'll let you know later." You suspect that he will go elsewhere and try for a better deal. This type often plays one sales representative off against another, trying for special discounts or prices.

Try to create a sense of urgency in his buying from you now. Stress the benefits, such as faster delivery or lower price, he will gain by taking action. You must try to prove that it is in his best interests to decide now.

The Procrastinating Prospect

He listens to you but just will not or cannot make up his mind. He asks for more time in which to reach a decision.

Check his reasons for delay by asking such "why" questions as, "Why can't you make your final decision now?" Get him to outline affirmative and negative reasons and build your close around the affirmatives. Show him testimonials from satisfied users. Show him that he will save time by deciding now.

The Grudge-Holding Prospect

He sees you but promptly attacks your company or product for real or imagined lapses in past performance, for poor service, for credit troubles, or for any other unsatisfactory experience. His complaint may not even be specifically against your company but against industry policies in general.

Your first job is to find out whether he has a real problem that you can help him with. If so, meet it head on and do everything possible to solve it promptly. Then switch to a personal basis by saying, "I can't help the mistakes made in the past, Mr. Drake, but I can avoid them in the future. Will you give me a chance to prove that by considering my proposal today?"

The Opinionated Prospect

He is forceful and positive, a real or imagined know-it-all decision-maker. He intends to make his own decisions, and he may be brusque or even rude in language and manner.

Compliment and flatter this type; praise whatever you can about him or his business. Appear to respect his success, his intelligence, and his opinion. And, once he warms up to you, ask his opinion about your proposal!

It is easy to get carried away with typing prospects and planning sales techniques to hold their attention and interest. Common sense is the best rule to follow in meeting different people; and keep in mind these very basic rules for getting along with others:

1. Do control yourself, relax, ask questions about what your prospect likes and dislikes, wants or does not want; agree with him whenever possible; and remain alert, cheerful, and interested in him.
2. Do not lose control, get angry at or argue with him, appear nervous or jittery, offend him in any way, or talk too much yourself.

HANDLING INTERRUPTIONS DURING YOUR PRESENTATION

Relatively few presentations have no interruptions. The phone may ring, a secretary may appear with an urgent question, or a visitor may intrude. Whatever the case, the communication bond between you and your prospect has been broken. How do you pick up the threads again?

If the interruption is a long one or requires urgent attention or action on your prospect's part, you may do better to make a new appointment to continue at a more favorable time. If you are not sure of the situation it is best to ask him.

Mr. Williams, it is to your advantage that we spend at least another quiet ten to fifteen minutes together discussing this proposal. May we take that time now, or would this same time tomorrow be more convenient?

Most interruptions are short, but unfortunately just long enough to break the attention bond. The telephone is the greatest cause of such interruptions on business or industrial sales calls. If your prospect is a key executive, you may even have to put up with a succession of such interruptions during the interview. Here are some techniques for quickly focusing his attention back to the subject.

1. Just sit quietly until he has a chance to switch his thoughts back to you and your proposal.
2. Repeat the last point under discussion before the interruption:

Mr. Esposo, you were saying just before the phone rang that you were interested in the cost-cutting features of our service. In what way does this most interest you?

3. Briefly restate points covered prior to the interruption.

Just prior to the phone call, Mr. Esposo, we had covered the key features of our service and were relating them to your specific interest in cost-cutting applications. In what way does this most interest you?

4. Hand him a brochure or catalogue to create interest as you verbally reengage his attention.

Mr. Esposo, here in one of our advertising brochures is a photograph that illustrates the point you were making about cost-cutting. Is this illustrated situation similar to yours? If not, in what way does our cost-cutting feature most interest you?

5. Jot down some figures or make a rough sketch and hand it to him while asking a question similar to that in 4 above.
6. Ease back into the presentation by first talking for a moment about a subject of mutual interest:

Mr. Esposo, it amazes me how busy men like you can accomplish so much with constant telephone interruptions. How can you keep track of things? For example, we were just discussing cost-cutting. In what way does it most interest you?

During telephone interruptions you may feel uncomfortable listening to what may be a confidential or personal discussion. The best way to handle this situation is to offer by voice, look, or gesture to leave the room. Your prospect will appreciate your consideration and will indicate his desires. Even if it is unnecessary to leave the room, you should keep busy reading sales material, taking notes, or doing some other quiet activity that avoids any impression that you are eavesdropping.

CLEARLY UNDERSTANDING HOW TO AROUSE AND HOLD YOUR PROSPECT'S INTEREST

Are you interested in sex? In Chapter 4 we noted that sex and romance were major buying motives. Did you wonder at the time how or whether you could put sex or romance into your sales presentations? Let us see what the late Elmer Wheeler, a colorful and well-known American sales consultant, had to say about sex in selling as he found it in Paris!

First, a bottle was held up. Sometimes the name was given—usually not, for unlike a Swiss seller, they weren't interested in who or how it was made, but its effect on a man when a woman wore it. "Ah, zis has such a fragrance," they say. "Don't you agree?" The bottle, the stem, or the hand dabbed with the scent is extended toward your nostrils.
"This lady's glove is so delicate, so light," says the seller. "Here, hold it and see." They will invite madam to try it on, then they will stand away and admire how it "does something for you." You do not know who made the glove. But you are soon sold on what it will do to heighten you as a man-getter.
Romance is important in selling. It can be used even in life insurance, a dollar and cents business. The seller says, "This will assure for you a pleasant old age. You can spend your time at the beach and not worry about where the next dollar is coming from."
Sex can be put into lawnmowers, garden tools, into bread, butter, into automobiles, into stocks and bonds even, by the seller alert to the great appeal of sex. Only Boston objects to a sales manager standing up at a Monday morning meeting and shouting, "Let's put sex into our sales."
Sex makes the world of sales go round. [1]

Now that we have reengaged and are holding your interest, let us restate in illustrative form in Figure 11.1 some of the points covered in this chapter, as well as some we will cover in the chapter to follow. Make certain that you clearly understand the basic principles and techniques of arousing and holding your prospect's attention.

1. Elmer Wheeler, *Tested Selling Tips from Around the World* (Englewood Cliffs, N.J.: Prentice-Hall, Inc., 1961), pp. 182–83.

FIGURE 11.1

IN ORDER TO
CREATE INTEREST

OBJECTIVES	CENTER ATTENTION	TECHNIQUES
Make your presentation complete by making certain your prospect knows exactly what it is you are proposing.	by Discussing his needs, wants or problems and	*Reduce Tension* by asking his opinion, leading off with a story or "news" or by praising him.
Eliminate competition where possible by acknowledging it while stressing the advantages your own proposal offers.	helping him discover, clarify and admit them, then	*Win Undivided Attention* by catching his eye and ear and promising a benefit of value.
Anticipate and build questions into your presentation, so as to answer as many as possible before they are raised as objections or challenges.	HOLD HIS ATTENTION AND INTEREST	*Discover Key buying motive* through use of question-technique leading into yes-building features of the benefit you are offering.
(Be prepared at any time to go into a trial-close.)	to the point where he indicates a willingness to consider your proposal as a solution to them	(Listen and watch for buying signals all the time.)

then go on to convince him that your product or service offers the best possible solution to fulfill his key buying motive by pointing out
        FEATURES
        ADVANTAGES
        BENEFITS
His interest will turn into desire once the advantages and benefits of having it so dominate his mind that he is ready to take action (through buying) to obtain it.

FOUR FACTORS OF HOLDING ATTENTION AND INTEREST

Discussed below is a method of holding interest often described in the literature of education, psychology, and selling. This method involves appreciating and learning how and when to use four basic factors of arousing attention: intensity, contrast, interest, and novelty. If you find that you are not holding your prospect's complete interest, you can apply these factors in this way.

Intensity. Change the tone of your voice or pace of your delivery; pause; or repeat yourself.

Contrast. Employ verbal or illustrative differences to sharpen understanding and awareness. For example, you can compare profit versus loss or cost versus savings.

Interest. Ask questions about personal or business subjects that interest your prospect; try to get him talking.

Novelty. Employ any novel or unusual attention-getting technique or device that keeps him interested in you and your presentation.

These four factors apply to Parts I and II of the presentation and provide you with other frames of reference for handling the interview situation as well as the discussion (talking), demonstration (showing), and participation (doing) points we will be covering in the following chapter. The principles underlying all these methods however are the same. You must maintain attention and interest throughout the entire presentation, from approach through close.

ACCOMPLISHING YOUR OBJECTIVES

Our objectives during the first part of the presentation are to help our prospect discover and clarify his wants, needs, and problems. We can accomplish these objectives by asking questions framed around how our product or service may help the prospect solve his problems and by listening carefully for any clues that may indicate buying motives around which we can build sales points.

If you do a good job, both you and your prospect have a better idea of his wants and problems than you did before and are ready to see how your proposal will help meet his needs or desires. At this point he should have admitted any wants or problems, discussed them, and indicated a willingness to hear more about how your product or service will benefit him.

SUMMARY

We have focused our attention in this chapter on creating and holding the continued interest of your prospect. Your objectives during this phase of the interview are to help him to discover and to clarify his needs, wants, or problems, to admit them, and to indicate a willingness to consider your proposal as a solution.

We considered five decisions your prospect has to make before deciding to buy: (1) need, (2) product, (3) service, (4) price, and (5) time. We also discussed six essentials of a good presentation, covering three in this chapter: (1) completeness, (2) elimination of competition, and (3) questions that should be anticipated and built into your presentation. We shall consider the remaining three in the following chapter.

We discussed many principles and techniques of good questioning and careful listening and reviewed how to arouse and hold the interest of different personality types. We also discussed how to handle interruptions that may occur during the interview.

CHAPTER REVIEW

CONCEPTS TO REMEMBER*

____ positive desires   ____ eliminate competition   ____ intensity
____ negative desires   ____ body of the presentation   ____ contrast
____ complete   ____ yes-building questions   ____ novelty
     presentation

*For memory reinforcement, fill in the page number or numbers where the terms were described in this chapter.

QUESTIONS FOR ANALYSIS AND DISCUSSION

1. What is the basic objective during Part I (creating and holding interest) of the integrated body of the sales presentation?
2. How can a sales representative make certain his prospect understands or is even listening to him?
3. What four factors of holding attention were introduced in this chapter?
4. What two methods of eliminating competition were presented in this chapter?
5. How can a sales representative help avoid in advance the situation where questions his prospect might ask become objections?
6. Describe what factors would make for a most highly effective sales presentation.
7. What is the hardest of all sales technique questions for a wavering prospect to answer?
8. How would you as sales representative handle a prospect that just sits there listening, saying nothing, not offering any clue by manner or facial expression to his inner thoughts? How should you treat him? What will impress him most?

Case Study 11–1

A FULLER BRUSH SALES REPRESENTATIVE TELLS OF HIS RAPID-FIRE APPROACH TO CREATING AND HOLDING INTEREST

George Frim was for many years a Fuller Brush dealer (sales representative to us) in a medium-sized New Jersey city. Recently retired from selling, he still speaks with pride of his former company and of the scores of former customers that continue to speak highly of the cheerful service he gave them over many years.

The Fuller Brush Company, with a 25,000-strong sales force today, was a pioneer in door-to-door selling in the United States. It is well known to nearly all American housewives for friendly, highly ethical, personalized direct selling and for over 200 quality household items, including toilet articles, disinfectants, and cosmetics, as well as a famous line of brushes.

Many of the sales techniques that made George such a successful sales representative over the years are of interest to students of salesmanship. One of the most interesting of these is what he likes to call his "rapid-fire approach" to creating and holding interest and closing all possible sales within a very short period of time. Let us recall with George a typical interview and see how to put the famed Fuller sales techniques into action, as he knocks at the door of a home in a typical middle-class suburban neighborhood.

Comments	*The Presentation*
The Approach	
He knocks; when housewife answers he takes one step backward (so as not to alarm her at the sight of a strange man) and says:	*George:* "Good morning, I'm George Frim, your local Fuller Brush man. Here is a free sample for you."
This famed Fuller approach technique involves giving a small but useful gift, such as a wash-and-dry towel or small brush, absolutely free, without obligation.	*Housewife:* "Well, thank you very much." (She accepts the gift with a surprised, pleased smile.)
Having accepted the gift, most housewives invite him in.	*George:* "I am pleased to offer you this free gift in order to introduce you to Fuller Brush Company. May I step inside and show you our items that are on sale?" (He is smiling, relaxed.)
	George: (once inside) "Your name is Mrs. _____?"
	Housewife: "Mrs. Williamson."
After obtaining her name during brief small talk, he gets them seated.	*George:* "Your home is certainly nice (looking around the living room)! May we sit down a moment so I can show you the illustrations in my catalogue?"
	Housewife: "Yes, certainly. Won't you sit here?"
The Presentation	
Then without delay he produces his sales catalogue and order pad and goes into his rapid-fire presentation.	*George:* "Do you need anything? Are you short of anything around the house, such as cleaning materials, toilet articles, or brushes?"
If the answer is yes, George first fulfills the need, although nine out of ten of his customers reply, "No, I don't need anything." If the answer is no, or after he has fulfilled the request, he then continues.	*Housewife:* "No, I think I have nearly everything I need right now."
	George: "Fine, Mrs. Williamson, but may I mention our Fuller special offers of today? For example (pointing to an item in the four-color catalogue), we are offering two cans of spray insecticide for use both indoors or out at only $3.98. The regular price is $4.78. Are you interested?"
	Housewife: "Oh, yes. I can use that!"
He writes the order in his order book (If the answer had been no, he would have said "fine") and continues to the next item (pointing it out in his sales catalogue).	*George:* "Thank you very much, I'll just make a note of it in my order book." "Here is a handsome club brush-and-comb set with stand mirror for only $11.89 as compared to our regular price of $13.74. It makes a perfect gift for a man or teenage boy. Can you use one?"

Comments	*The Presentation*
He notes this interest in his notebook for a future pre-Christmas callback.	*Housewife:* "No, thank you; I'll save that for a later date, perhaps before Christmas."
	George: (Next item) "Would you like this?"
The Close	*Housewife:* "No, thank you."
George continues in this way to point out his no more than five or six specials, trying for a close after each, jotting the order down immediately if the answer is yes. He never tries to rebut a no.	*George:* (Next item) "Does this interest you?"
	Housewife: "Yes, I'll take that, it's nice." (etc.)
He calls this close indirect or low-pressure selling, or soft-selling. He feels a hard-sell close such as, "I'll put you down for two sets," is a mistake because he hopes to make each housewife a repeat customer.	
The Departure	*George:* "Well, thank you very much for your order, Mrs. Williamson (puts away his catalogue and order form, arises, and slowly moves toward the door, smiling at her). I will personally deliver these items to you Saturday morning to make certain you are completely satisfied with your purchase."
	Housewife: "Thank you for coming, Mr. Frim."

George worked on the law of averages, knowing that if he knocked on enough doors he would hit his planned sales goal. He established his gross sales goals by week and day. For example, if his weekly sales goal was $300, he knew he must sell $60 daily.

In order to reach such a goal in a middle-class neighborhood he knew he must knock on approximately seventy-five doors. He averaged thirty to thirty-five presentations, closing fifteen to twenty of them for an average of $3 or $4. He kept a weekly call and sales record showing street and house address.

THE FOLLOW-UP AND FOLLOW-THROUGH

His follow-up was a personal delivery of the items a week after closing the sale. On such follow-up calls he did not try to sell but usually mentioned an item he knew would be on sale in the future. For example, "May I mention a new item, sun-tan lotion, which will be a future special! May I bring a bottle on my next visit?"

COVERAGE

George covered his city territory of 4,500 homes each four to eight weeks and started over again. If the housewife did not buy on one visit, he called on her four weeks later. If she bought on that visit, he called on her eight weeks later. He always tried to satisfy promptly any customer complaints and aimed overall to establish a list of repeat customers on whom he called at least four times each year.

Proof of the success of this sales approach to George is the fact that as a Fuller Brush dealer for many years in his area, he was always warmly welcomed by his hundreds of satisfied, steady, repeat customers. "Direct selling of this type has been a most satisfying experience to me, all these years," says George.

QUESTIONS FOR WRITTEN REPORTS OR CLASS DISCUSSION

1. Does George's rapid-fire presentation indicate his interest in the housewife's problems and not merely his own desire to make a sale? Explain.
2. How does George make certain that his prospect is paying attention during his presentation?
3. What are the two basic principles of arousing and holding the interest of a prospect? How does George specifically employ these principles in his Fuller presentation?

Case Study 11–2

THE SHELL OIL COMPANY DEALERS PUT INTO PRACTICE THEIR COMPANY MOTTO, "SERVICE IS OUR BUSINESS"

The familiar Shell emblem at service stations throughout the world is well known to motorists of many nations. Like most major oil companies, Shell has gone to great lengths to make sure its dealers maintain high standards of service and cleanliness. It has tried harder than most, however, to train its dealers to build a profitable business based on complete customer satisfaction. The aim is for customers to "think" Shell and to seek Shell service repeatedly. To Shell Oil Company, its best customers are repeat customers.

A Shell service station is like any other store in a neighborhood. It has things to sell and people to sell them to. To Shell, satisfied customers mean sales. Thus its dealers and service-station attendants are carefully trained to give the customer who drives into their pump station for gasoline or petrol the best possible service and attention.

Creating a favorable image or wanting to be friends in itself will not necessarily sell Shell products however. And this is where Shell salesmanship enters the picture. When a customer drives up to a Shell pump island for gasoline, a well-planned, customer-oriented, problem-solving sales presentation gets underway. Called the SHELL FIVE-STOP SERVICE it is basically a well coordinated, five-point sales plan, with lots of smiles and pleasant words for customers added for good measure. Figure 11.2 illustrates how attendants are taught to present it.

FIGURE 11.2
Courtesy Shell Oil Company, Retail Training, Houston, Texas.

Pump Island Service

SHELL

Shell five-stop service means
- **Satisfied Customers**
- **Greater Sales**
- **More Profit**

INTRODUCTION
(Time: 2 minutes)

Points to develop

It probably would be a safe bet to say that every man here has had a bad experience with a salesman...or clerk...or waiter...or somebody whose business is service...in the last month or so! No one likes to be neglected, ignored or not given service in the right way! Your impression of that place of business became negative because you thought nobody cared about you as a customer.

Well, the same is true in our business! Our customer also want service. They don't want to be ignored or given the "cold shoulder." It is up to you to give the customer a favorable impression of our station. We have to live up to that sign over the bay doors, "Service is Our Business." To every customer you service, you represent my station. So act like, look like and sound like you want to take care of that customer, and keep him coming back.

REMEMBER...for satisfied customers and greater sales all of us must follow the five stops in Shell's Pump Island Service. It's an organized plan for service and selling.

DISCUSSION
(Time: 8 minutes)

1—SERVICE AT THE ISLAND

The five-stops in Shell's Pump Island Procedure are:

1 Greet the Customer
Solicit a full tank
Suggest Super-Shell
Look and Listen for Extra sales
(Mufflers, Brakes, etc.)

2 Go to the Rear of the Car
Insert Nozzle in Tank and set on automatic
Wipe rear window (Drivers Side)
Check tail light lenses
Wipe other half of rear window
Check Tire Tread

3 Wipe Right Front Windshield
Check Wiper Blade and Arm
Observe Car Finish

Clean and Check Headlights
Check Tire Tread
Check Oil
Check Cooling System
Check Battery
Check Hoses, and Belts
Check Air and Fuel Filters
Check Windshield Washer Fluid
Look for other sales opportunities

Clean Drivers side of Windshield
Check Wiper Blade and Arm
Top off the Tank
Check Lube Sticker when possible
Collect the Money
Tell Customer about needs you have
    found— and, ask to fill them
Thank the Customer

2—SALES OPPORTUNITIES

Sell the customer.

If a customer drives into this station with a flat tire, what would you do? Right, fix the tire or sell him a new one! How about the customer that drives in with a leaking cooling system hose. Again, the answer is easy, you'd sell him a new one. But, in both of these situations, these service situations, the customer would have gone to the *nearest* station. The odds would have been against us in getting that business. Shell Five-Stop service, however, puts the odds in our favor. That's because if you properly give 5-stop service, you can spot trouble before it starts, and make the repair or replacement sales before somebody else

has had a chance. Now let's review the 9 most obvious sales opportunities on a car. (Note: Use Wall chart to impress the sales potential on each car...Ask how many more the men can name).

SUMMARY

(Time: 1 minute)

1. Follow procedure.

2. Lift every hood.

3. Look for sales opportunities.

4. Sell customer benefits.

5. Sell the customer.

Close with

a. Announcement of special promotions you may plan to run. Vacation, holiday or changeover specials.

b. Special awards or incentive plans you may want to begin to stimulate sales.

c. Set a definite period for these special events to take place.

Results from this excellent sales presentation are equally beneficial to the customer and to the Shell dealer. From the customer's point of view, worn-out parts can be an inconvenience, an expense, or even a danger. This preventive maintenance check thus locates trouble before it happens. If everything is in good condition, he is pleased that the attendant took the time to check and to reassure him that all is well. In either case, the customer is pleased with the attention and service. From the Shell dealer's point of view, the check may have uncovered one or more of the following nine replacement-part profit opportunities—the chance to sell.

oil change	tires	water pump or hose
air filter	battery	wiper blades
fan belt	sealed-beam headlights	muffler

QUESTIONS FOR WRITTEN REPORTS OR CLASS DISCUSSION

1. In addition to the above list, a Shell dealer-salesperson during his inspection may uncover the need for seven additional replacement parts or services. Can you guess what four of them may be?
2. Once the Shell dealer discovers a need for any of these items, what are two ways he can quickly bring up and eliminate competition?
3. If you see a need for any of the items, how can you as a dealer-sales representative quickly get the prospect interested in considering that he might have a need and best hold his interest?
4. What should the statement, "a sales presentation must be complete," mean to a Shell dealer-salesperson? Would there be any difference, considering your answer, in what it should mean to him versus a salesperson in any other business? Explain.

SALES PROBLEM 11–1

SELLING A BATTERY TO "TALKATIVE SAM"

You are a Shell service-station dealer, and one of your regular customers, whom you call "Talkative Sam," drives up to a pump island and stops short of the Super Shell pump. You ask him to drive forward so the hose will reach and notice that his battery seems to grind slowly and does not start the car promptly—a sign that it may be ready to give out.

During your Shell Five-Stop Service check (outlined in Case Study 11-2) you note that the battery connections are corroded. As you accept payment, Sam starts chattering about the latest scoring in the ball game being broadcast loudly over his car radio. You manage to ask him how long he has had his battery, and he simply says, "Three years, and don't you try to sell me a new one!" You realize that Sam's battery is ready to give out at any time and tell him so. He thinks you are joking and starts trying to make small bets with you and a customer at the next pump island on the outcome of the ball-game.

Since he needs a battery and Shell has an excellent one at competitive price, you want to make a presentation—if he would only stop talking long enough to listen! Your battery is very good, with extra-rugged container, extra plate area, and extra-strength grids. It has one of the best written guarantees in the industry behind it. You have a cutaway model by your battery test stand and want to get Sam over there. The ball game will be over in three minutes.

QUESTIONS FOR WRITTEN REPORTS OR CLASS DISCUSSION

1. How can you get Sam to listen to a sales presentation about a new battery when he is interested in the ball game and placing small bets?
2. How can you get him to recognize he has a need for a new battery?
3. What benefits would a new Shell battery offer him?
4. How can you demonstrate those benefits? How can you tell him about them so as to arouse and hold his interest?

12

the presentation, part II: arousing desire and securing conviction

When you have mastered the content of this chapter, you should be able to:

Describe the meaning of these statements concerning a sales presentation: (1) the presentation must be clear, (2) the question of price must be handled, and (3) selling points must be developed logically and emotionally around key buying motives to arouse desire and secure conviction.

Describe key factors involved in these three methods of getting and holding continued attention and interest: (1) discussion (talking), (2) demonstration (showing), and (3) participation (doing).

Analyze what is meant by the statement, "interest changes to desire when advantages and benefits so dominate the prospect's mind that he is ready to take action to gain them."

Describe two important factors necessary to secure conviction, and show how to incorporate them in a sales presentation.

Summarize key factors involved in three techniques of indirect suggestion: (1) narrative, (2) dramatic parallel, and (3) analogy.

Describe six techniques of handling challenges.

Analyze advantages of the "rifle" technique or concept of sales presentation versus the "shotgun" technique or concept.

Describe the "feature-advantage-benefit" technique of arousing and building desire and securing conviction, for each presented sales point of a sales presentation.

Summarize the importance of securing agreement after each point, so that the prospect recognizes and accepts the value of the benefits pointed out; explain how this is done.

As we discuss in detail the various aspects and techniques of the presentation, keep in mind our overall objectives and goals. Perhaps we can best sum them up and lead into this chapter, which covers Part II of our presentation, as follows: Your aim has been and continues to be that of holding the attention and interest of your prospect as you stress benefits that create desire and secure conviction. You are showing him how he can obtain these benefits and are motivating him, through persuasion, to take action now to obtain them.

We will focus our attention in this chapter on the principles and techniques of arousing the prospect's desire for benefits and of securing his conviction that your product or service does offer value. We will save the handling of specific objections for Chapter 13 but will discuss here as well how to handle certain possible challenges or negative responses during the development of your presentation.

Let us turn our thoughts back to the presentation overview portion of the preceding chapter. There we discussed the strategic aims in the presentation: Part I, to create and hold interest, which we covered in that chapter; and Part II, to arouse desire and to secure conviction which we will now consider.

As outlined there, your Part II objectives are (1) to help your prospect realize that your product or service will fulfill his needs or solve problems and (2) through questions, proof, demonstration, and other persuasive techniques, to convince him that your offering is the best possible solution now and for the future.

You will recall that the prospect has to make five minor decisions before deciding to buy: (1) need, (2) product, (3) service, (4) price, and (5) time. And, you will recall the six essential points that must be covered in every effective sales presentation. Three of them—(1) completeness, (2) elimination of competition, and (3) questions that should be anticipated and built into the presentation—were discussed in that chapter. The remaining three essential points of the effective presentation will be considered in this chapter in this order:

4. Your presentation must be clear.
5. The question of price must be handled.
6. Selling points must be developed logically and emotionally around key buying motives so as to arouse desire and to secure conviction.

Priority now centers on persuading your prospect that your proposal offers the best solution to his problems or needs. At this point you have succeeded in arousing your prospect's interest to the point where he has admitted his needs or wants, has discussed his desires or problems, and has indicated his willingness to consider a solution to them. Your task now is to convince him that your product or service offers the best possible solution. You can best do this in the following sequence.

1. Show him, to his complete understanding, exactly what your product or service is, how it works, and what it can do for him.
2. Help him recognize and accept that your product or service offers him the best possible solution to his problem or fulfillment of his desires.
3. Secure his conviction that by obtaining it he will find the satisfaction he is seeking.

We will now leave the above three important topics for a few pages as we conclude the final three essential points in a presentation. Following that review of principles and techniques, we shall again return to the above points and tie them together in a close-knit survey.

ESSENTIALS OF A GOOD PRESENTATION

Your Presentation Must Be Clear

Your prospect should understand exactly what your product or service is, how it works, and what it can do for him. We spent some time discussing the basic principles of clear thinking, writing, and talking in Chapter 8. There we noted the similarity of effective means of communication in both education and selling.

Educators and sales representatives each sell ideas and employ similar principles, tools, and techniques to impart knowledge, concepts, and ideas. From the field of educational psychology especially, sales representatives have learned that these are steps in the most effective method of presenting and developing ideas in terms of the prospect's interests or point of view.

1.   Briefly describe the topic to be covered and the conclusions to be reached.
2.   Break it into more readily understandable parts; present a step-by-step development of points reinforced by explanation and demonstration.
3.   Illustrate it as dramatically as possible with appeals to any or all of the five senses.
4.   Check and recheck constantly through the question technique to ensure full understanding.
5.   Invite participation by letting the prospect do something. This technique provides constant attention, interest, and involvement.
6.   Summarize the topic and points in terms of benefits and value to him.

Since your first task is to show your prospect, to his complete satisfaction and understanding, exactly what your product is and what it can do for him, you should know how to relate the above concepts to your presentation.

Your sales presentation is more than a mere dissemination of knowledge, however; its purposes are to convince the prospect that he wants or needs the benefits discussed and to motivate and persuade him to take immediate action to obtain them. Your prospect is motivated largely because the ideas presented seem to be consistent with ideas, values, and beliefs he already holds. He is interested in his problems, needs, and wants, not yours. It is your task to try to understand his self-image, or the way he sees himself or would like to see himself. You can role play, or act as necessary to make yourself understood, in order to establish good communication, rapport, and possibly complete empathy. This role-playing is one of the most important psychological techniques of a superior presentation. Through it you tell your story so completely in accord with what the prospect says, thinks, and believes that he feels it is directed to him alone.

As you size up the prospect and try to assume the role that will help him better understand you and accept your ideas, strive to get and hold his undivided attention and interest. Maintaining these throughout the entire presentation is vital to his perception, understanding, and motivation.

The six principles of presenting ideas we have just outlined are basically carried out through (1) discussion (talking), (2) demonstration (showing), and (3) participation (doing). Let us now relate some principles learned from the behavioral sciences to effective selling techniques in these areas.

Discussion (talking).   We have stressed consistently the need to get the prospect talking about himself and his problems as soon as possible in the interview situation. The chief purpose is to quickly set the stage for a two-way discussion so that a meaningful interchange of ideas can take place. The old-fashioned lecture method of education and the tell-it-to-them sales pitch of the drummer are far too ineffective for modern use. Neither invites the active participation modern sales techniques require.

Psychologists have shown that people remember only about 10 percent of what they hear. Since you will be engaged in talking and discussion throughout the interview, you want to maintain the prospect's level of attention and interest at the highest level possible. A high level of attention improves chances for under-standing and remembering. Here are some practical suggestions for making your speaking more interesting through the use of contrast.

Change the pitch or tone of your voice.   Nervous people often speak rapidly in a high-pitched voice; less nervous ones may speak more slowly in a deep, yet flat, monotone. Each can become monotonous and uninteresting if continued for any length of time. Your prospect is likely to remain interested in what you are saying if you change your pitch or tone of voice frequently. You may, for exam-ple, drop from a higher pitch to a lower, more deliberate tone when emphasizing an important fact or conclusion.

Change the pace of your delivery.   If, for example, you are speaking rapidly at a high pitch, you can not only lower the pitch when stressing an important fact or conclusion but also slow down your pace of delivery.

Add a pause for suspense.   A continuous flow of words, regardless of change of pitch, can become confusing. A brief pause, either before or after you say something important, helps make the point stand out in your prospect's mind.

Phrase or paragraph to make your points stand out.   By presenting one fact or conclusion at a time, you avoid an overlapping of ideas that may confuse your prospect. Your planning of the presentation should provide individual units of thought, and you should make them effective through your verbal emphasis.

Give a cheerful, positive, confident delivery to create interest.   A ready smile at the proper moment helps relax and reassure your prospect. A positive, flowing delivery helps create confidence, whereas a faltering one betrays anxiety and worry. If you believe in what you are selling and mentally picture the benefits you are proposing, you tend to speak with the confidence that enables your prospect to buy with confidence.

Speak clearly and distinctly.   If you talk too rapidly and mumble words, your prospect may have to ask you to stop and repeat yourself. Practice your presentation so that you speak clearly and distinctly enough to avoid any possibil-ity of misunderstanding.

Use precise words to emphasize specific thoughts and to maintain interest.   Exact, precise words not only prevent confusion and misunderstanding but also add power and contrast to your speech. Positive, vivid, picture-building words help emphasize important facts or conclusions. You should use short, sim-ple words that your prospect clearly understands.

Use proper body actions to add contrast to your speech.   Spoken words can be emphasized by certain bodily actions made at the proper moment. You can change position, stand up, walk over beside your prospect, sit down, raise an eyebrow, nod your head, or use gestures. Practice makes them appear natural and relaxed.

Repeat to enhance understanding.   Psychologists and educators tell us that we learn many things rapidly through repetition. Some prospects are more intel-ligent than others and can grasp even complex ideas quickly. Others may not understand until the point has been repeated a second or third time.

Your prospect may be reluctant to say he does not understand, but you can make sure by repeating the point two or three times during the presentation if you are in doubt. You can describe the point in a different way, such as through a story, and thus tell him again what you have already told him in an inoffensive way.

Use comparisons, such as similes, metaphors, and analogies, to add clarity and meaning. A *simile* is a comparison often made by using the words *as* or *like.* For example, "This new plastic tubing is as strong as iron." A *metaphor* is like a simile except the words *as* or *like* are omitted. For example, "He is a bear of a man." An *analogy* is a comparison between two situations, which though dissimilar have certain points in common. For example, "Having this fire extinguisher in your home is much like having a life jacket handy on overseas air flights. You don't expect to use it, but feel more comfortable knowing it's close at hand."

Demonstration (showing). Your prospect probably has a rather short attention span and has many thoughts and problems on his mind. Unless you arouse his interest and get his thoughts focused completely on your presentation, his mind is likely to wander. Mere words may soon bore him; thus you somehow have to add showmanship, drama, and sparkle to your presentation through demonstration. You have to bring your presentation to life and make it so intriguing and interesting that he cannot help but give you his undivided attention. Fortunately, many techniques and tools at your disposal help picture what your product or service will do for him. These tools illustrate far better than words alone the benefits and value to him.

"Seeing is believing," "a picture is worth a thousand words," and "everybody loves a show" are common expressions that illustrate what psychologists tell us about the importance of seeing as well as hearing. We noted previously that people remember about 10 percent of what they hear. Psychologists also tell us that what people see attracts their attention almost nine times more than what they experience through the other four senses combined. Furthermore, they remember approximately 35 percent of what they see. Thus, if you can demonstrate or show what you are proposing, as well as talk or tell about it, you stand a far greater chance of creating and holding interest and of assuring remembrance.

It is important to keep in mind two important principles concerning the use of visual demonstrations.

1. The objective of any visual demonstration is to show what the product can do rather than how it does it.
2. Demonstrating or showing is always accompanied by telling or explaining in terms of the prospect's needs.

An interesting demonstration is not an end in itself; it is a technique to enhance the point you are making by arousing and holding interest through appeals to basic instincts or motives.

Since sight plays such an important part in arousing attention and holding interest, you should use demonstrations and visual aids whenever and wherever possible. Here are but some of the sales tools and devices that can be employed. We described others in Chapter 8.

Pencil and paper. A moving pencil holds attention and enables you to sketch your own visual aids as you go along.

The product itself. If you sell an item too big to carry, perhaps you can use a smaller, working, demonstration model. If your product is small, get a bigger model for demonstration purposes. Tell the prospect what you intend to show him before demonstrating.

Photocopies of orders or repeat orders. These copies of orders and especially of reorders from satisfied customers offer convincing testimony to your claims.

Charts, graphs, tabulations. Such items reflect the experiences of individuals or groups of customers and make especially good demonstration aids. They can depict economies resulting from use, performance features, or increased production or sales.

A *telephone call.* This can be showmanship at its best. What better confidence can you display in your product than to call a current user from the prospect's own phone and to let a satisfied customer help you close the sale?

Demonstration aids or visual sales tools not only attract and hold attention but also help your prospect remember product or service facts and information. If used properly, they can offer dramatic proof of your claims and thus save time and discussion. They not only make your presentation more interesting but also reveal uses, features, and benefits better than verbal explanation alone does. They help focus your prospect's attention, often offer him an opportunity to participate in the demonstration, usually please him, and seldom irritate him. You can greatly increase your own selling power by using showmanship techniques in dramatizing benefits through the use of demonstrations.

Other Types of Demonstration Aids Include the Following:

Photographs	Flip charts
Sound filmstrips	Flash cards
Movies	Maps
Overhead projectors	Scrapbooks
Visuals	Exhibits or displays
Slides	Mock-ups
Presentation books	Blackboards
Sales portfolios	Flannel boards

Demonstrations are most effective when presented in the prospect's home, office, or plant—in the physical location where they will be used. You should avoid being overtechnical, tell him in advance what you are going to show, keep the demonstration short, and ask questions before starting and as you demonstrate to keep him thinking and to ensure complete understanding. Whenever possible, you should get him to take an active part in the proceedings.

Participation (doing). We can best indicate the importance of seeing, hearing, and doing by noting conclusions of psychologists that people remember up to 65 percent of what they see and hear and up to 90 percent of what they see, hear, and participate in. Thus, you can best arouse and sustain interest by showmanship sales techniques that bring your prospect into the act. As one veteran sales representative put it, "Stage a show with him as the star." You can accomplish this by letting him operate, clean, use, work, or experience your product or service. This participation should involve as many of the senses as possible.

If you are selling an automobile, let him drive it!
If you are selling a typewriter, let him type on it!
If you are selling textiles, let him feel them!

This participation is intrinsically interesting if you relate new information about your product or service to something your prospect is already familiar with.

All the areas we have just covered—discussion, demonstration, and participation—revolve around selling the prospect on the idea that your product or service meets his needs. You sought information about these needs from the start and continue to seek it through questioning and listening, as you develop your yes-building points. You can now extend these thoughts into the areas of logic and emotion, as you continue to frame yes-building points around the key buying motives that arouse desire and secure conviction.

First, however, let us consider how to handle that important question of price, should it arise at this early stage of the presentation.

Handling the Question of Price

The question of price comes up in nearly every sales presentation, so you should be prepared to handle it positively and with confidence at the proper time and place. You may want to introduce it early in the presentation and then justify it in terms of value, or you may elect to postpone it until you have stressed benefits and clearly demonstrated value. There is no rule as to when to introduce price; it depends in part on what you are selling and the prospect you face. You may even want to refer to it several times throughout the presentation.

Although we will discuss techniques for handling specific price objections in Chapter 13, here are some helpful suggestions for quoting and minimizing price and some techniques for postponing specific price quotes until you are ready to give them. They may prove useful if your prospect brings up the question at this stage of the presentation.

1. **Quoting price with confidence.**   Unless your price is without question the lowest, you should dwell on benefits and value and try to avoid a situation in which price becomes the point around which success or failure revolves. You may want to avoid it as long as possible without giving the impression of stalling.

When you do quote price, do so with confidence and in a straightforward manner. If your product or service does offer value, price may be of secondary importance. You should know the reasons why the price is as quoted and convey the feeling that you believe it to be fair for the quality offered.

If you are in a position to offer a range of prices it is normally best (except in retail selling, as we shall note on page 337, Chapter 16) to start with the highest ones first. You can always work down the scale from a higher price, but it is difficult to open with a lower price and try to work up.

Although price is nearly always an important factor in a sale, it more often than not is not the only or even the major factor. Your job is to offer proof of value, to stress the differences that make your product or service worth the price asked for it, in a positive, confident manner.

2. **Minimizing price.**   This can be accomplished by breaking it down into smaller units (such as operating costs per day instead of per month) or by using key words that tend to minimize price. For example, "Mr. Ohgaki, it will cost less than $2 a day for you to own this reasonably priced item."

You can also minimize price by suggesting higher prices for similar products or services or by emphasizing cost-cutting or other savings that could be effected. For example, "Mr. Joseph, wouldn't you expect a cost-cutting item like this to be worth $1,000 or at least $800? Well, I can offer it to you today for a mere $500."

3. Postponing price questions until you are ready to quote. Prospects often ask the price before you have had a chance to discuss benefits or value. In order to avoid a quick objection based on price alone, you may want to acknowledge but pass over a direct quote. Here are two practical suggestions for accomplishing this.

May I answer your price question in a moment, Mr. Poynton? I would like to show you this brochure first. What do you think of this specific illustration?

The final price depends on the style selected and the delivery date, Mr. Mulhall. May I first show you these illustrations of various models and styles? What do you think, for example, of this particular one?

Sometimes the prospect insists on knowing the price and refuses to let you pass it off. In such cases quote it promptly and then continue with your presentation.

Development of Logical and Emotional Selling Points
Around Key Buying Motives to Arouse Desire and Secure Conviction

Along with being complete and clear, your presentation should be developed logically and emotionally around those points that offer the greatest appeal from the prospect's point of view. While planning your presentation, you should list, review, and rank your selling points, stressing exclusive features first. As the presentation develops, determine which of these have the greatest appeal and attempt to pin down the key buying motive. You can then build your major appeals around this key buying motive or motives.

This point brings us once again to a consideration of the psychology of selling. What is going on in your prospect's mind now? What rational and emotional appeals will turn his interest into desire and conviction and motivate him to take action to obtain the benefits you are offering?

In a way, your situation at this point is somewhat like that of a fisherman whose bait has just been grabbed by a powerful, canny, fighting fish. You have him hooked, but if you are not very careful he may suddenly snap the line and get away from you. He may let you reel him in steadily and quietly without a fight, but he probably will do a lot of twisting, turning, and double tracking before you finally land him. Most prospects do not like to make a final buying decision any more than a game fish likes to get hooked! It is difficult to outguess either a hooked prospect or a game fish at this point. You have to play it by ear and feel, being prepared for anything, as you answer questions, try for a close, overcome objections, try for a close, and slowly play him until, with the swish of the net, you have him with a positive decision.

What motivates your prospect at this delicate stage of the presentation? In Chapter 4, when we discussed the psychology of selling, we pointed out that your prospect's buying decision is based on rational or emotional wants and motivations or on a combination of the two. A common fault of many modern sales presentations is that, while well organized from a logical point of view, they fail to arouse emotion. The importance of this emotional element can be illustrated by the fact that up to 75 to 95 percent of consumer goods sales and 50 to 60 percent of most industrial sales are based on emotional decisions.

Up to this point in your presentation you have aroused and held the interest of your prospect, but now you have to make him want or desire your product or service. Interest is largely a mental reaction, but want or desire involves the emotions. *Interest changes to desire when advantages and benefits so dominate his mind that he is ready to take action to gain them.*

While questioning and evaluating him, you have been seeking clues to the appeals that seem to arouse greatest interest. You have built your sales points around those buying motives that bring the most favorable responses. In essence, you have been judging the degree of logic or emotion to be used in your appeals both to his needs and to his emotional buying motives.

He may be a very shrewd buyer, one who buys strictly on the basis of logical reasoning. Many purchasing agents may make a decision based on 90 percent logic and 10 percent emotion. He may be a comparison shopper, looking for either the best value or the best deal for home or business. His decision probably will still be based on 50 percent emotion. Or, perhaps he is one of the majority of buyers who often make a decision based on 10 percent logic and 90 percent emotion. Whatever the case, his thinking is influenced by his background—cultural, social, psychological, and environmental. He tends to believe or accept what he has heard or read from authorities, advertising, business associates, or friends. And perhaps more importantly, he tends to believe, rationally or irrationally, what he wants to believe.

Bearing all this in mind, you should adjust your presentation to his beliefs or point of view so that he starts to accept your ideas as being his. Once he recognizes that a need exists and that what you are proposing is desirable, you should concentrate on that fact and personalize it in every way possible.

He will start desiring your product or service when convinced. Thus desire and conviction are intertwined, although we will, for clarity, now discuss them separately.

Arousing desire.   Interest changes into desire when these events take place:

1.   The prospect accepts the fact that a need or want exists.
2.   The benefits to be gained from fulfilling that need satisfy his emotional buying motives.
3.   The advantages of the benefits (value) dominate his mind.

It is easy to state the principles, but getting the prospect through these psychological steps requires all the art and skill of persuasive, convincing salesmanship that you can command.

Basically, most prospects prefer to put off the buying decision. They are afraid of being high pressured into something they do not want. Thus, if you bluntly ask them to buy your product or service, without leading them up to the buying decision properly, it is like taking them to the top of a tall diving tower at an unknown swimming pool and asking them to jump in. A better way to get a prospect into the deep end of the pool is to start at the shallow end and to let him wade in, to feel his way into the unknown deep end. And so it is in selling. Avoid a possibly frightening big decision by developing the yes-building little decisions, each leading on to the next.

Establishing a need or want is a major milestone along the road to sales success. You feel the prospect has a need, and he may even agree but not feel strongly about it. Thus you have to remind, show, and convince him that his need is important. Then you have to magnify the importance of that need to the point where he starts actively thinking that the benefits you are offering may be desirable.

Getting him to agree that your product or service would be useful and that he would like to have it is a little decision—he is not saying that he will buy it. Yet this decision is vitally important to you, for unless you can get him to decide that the product or service would be useful (would fulfill a need or want) and that he would like its benefits, you probably will not make the sale.

Showing how emotional buying motives can be fulfilled is your second goal. If he likes the product or service, you have to show him that your specific brand will do the best job of fulfilling his need and that its value justifies the cost. Then you have to prove that he can afford it and show how he can obtain it. You can create desire for your specific product or service by showing or demonstrating how it will do a better job for him than any other. By stressing, from his point of view, the exclusive or special features of your proposal, you can dramatize even minor points into desirable advantages.

Once he accepts the fact that he would like to have your specific item (a little decision that still does not require him to say whether he will buy it), you can start talking about color, style, and delivery dates. You thus assume that he will buy and switch him onto easy-to-answer secondary questions. This assumption technique frees him from the burden of facing directly the big decision of "Yes, I'll buy," or "No, I won't buy." Many prospects are relieved when the presentation develops this way and the decision is, in effect, made for them.

You can create desire further at this stage by helping the prospect justify his personal enthusiasm by pointing out that his feelings are a reflection of sound business or personal judgment.

Dramatizing the advantages of the benefits (value) to the point that they dominate his mind continues to involve devising little yes-building decisions that increase his desire. If he agrees that he would like to have what you are proposing, that its value is worth the cost, and that he can afford it (or, cannot afford not to have it), then you are well along the route to closing the sale.

You can now increase desire by personalizing or glamorizing your appeals and by showing how desirable the benefits are in terms of his needs and interests. Here are some illustrations of points around which such special appeals can be directed to various categories of prospects.

With retailers or wholesalers—talk profits, fast turnover, satisfied customers.
With individual consumers—talk economy, beauty, utility, prestige.
With industrial buyers—talk performance, savings, efficiency.

Once you have aroused desire to the point where the benefits (value) start dominating his mind, you promptly strive to secure conviction so that he can justify action to fulfill his strong desires.

Securing conviction. Your prospect may have developed a strong logical or emotional desire but may want to be further convinced that your proposal is sound or at least to have his inner conviction reinforced. Your entire presentation up to this point should have been planned and delivered around the idea of building up and securing conviction. This may be the time to reemphasize points made earlier, however, or to summarize evidence that your proposal is a sound one. Whatever the case, consider the two important factors that secure conviction in his mind.

1.   His acceptance of, and belief in, you.
2.   Proof that your product or service will furnish the benefits claimed.

Your attitude and manner go a long way toward securing conviction that your proposal is a sound one. If your attitude is that of the sincere, straightforward, customer/society-oriented, problem-solving, professional market-counselor sales representative we have depicted in the preceding pages, then your prospect will accept you with confidence. If you do not have that positive attitude and are merely out for a quick sale, your prospect will probably see through you and immediately lose confidence in your proposal.

If your attitude is sincere and professional, the positive, confident manner in which you conduct the presentation further reinforces conviction on his part. Here are some positive and negative mannerisms that decide the issue for him.

Conviction builders	*Conviction destroyers*
Being enthusiastic, yet realistic	Being excitable and unbusinesslike
Being calm, serious, deliberate	Being emotional
Speaking clearly and forcefully	Gushing or speaking falteringly
Explaining points carefully so that he clearly understands	Giving superficial explanations
	Appearing more anxious to close a sale than to render a service
Being cheerful and eager to please	
Showing loyalty to your company and product	Disparaging your or competing companies' products
Making only those promises you can keep	Making wildly extravagant promises or claims
Showing that you are thinking of customer satisfaction	Appearing self-centered

Proof or evidence to substantiate your claims is also necessary to secure conviction. Whether he is spending company money or hard-earned personal cash, he wants and expects facts that clearly show the value he will get for the expenditure. He also wants facts that will make him proud to recommend, use, or own the product or service—facts he can tell his superiors or business associates or his family, friends, or neighbors.

You can suggest believable facts or evidence, but the most effective proof is facts or evidence that the prospect can see as well as hear about. Psychologists estimate that a person receives over 85 percent of all impressions through his eyes and not his ears. Thus your actions, such as being confident in manner and willing to show visual evidence or proof of your claims, weigh far more heavily in securing conviction in his mind than do mere verbal statements.

Suggestion can be both direct and indirect. It involves the planting of an idea in the prospect's mind so that he accepts it uncritically without further proof or evidence. Suggestion works best when directed at the subconscious (emotional and instinctual) mind rather than at the conscious (reasoning) mind.

Suggestion as a psychological sales tool is valuable in preventing argument. For example, your argument may run, "This is the best industrial chemical on the market today." But a suggestion runs this way.

You want to get maximum efficiency at lowest cost. Ten out of twelve firms in this area have switched to our chemical because it offers just that. As a result, most of their buyers say that this is the best industrial chemical on the market today.

Sales representatives generally prefer indirect suggestion over direct suggestion; they employ indirect suggestion through techniques such as these.

Narrative involves telling a story about someone else (in a position similar to that of your prospect) who made the purchase and was very pleased afterward. Your prospect subconsciously puts himself in the position of the other person and deduces that he will also experience profit or pleasure from the purchase.

Dramatic parallel consists of asking a leading question that poses a challenge to your prospect.

Question: Is it company policy to keep equipment until it wears out even if it costs money?

Answer: No, our company doesn't have a policy like that.

Question: In that case, the facts I've presented as to how our new machine can cut costs should go over well with your divisional vice-president if you decide to take advantage of our offer.

Analogy (noted earlier) is a comparison between two situations which, though dissimilar, have certain points in common. You can apply it as a sales technique by describing a situation in another field and through inference suggesting that results would also be applicable in relation to your own proposal.

Visual proof is always best. You can present a forceful verbal sales story and even dramatically demonstrate it without securing conviction. Visual facts or evidence are the only effective, convincing way to back up, supplement, and explain statements and claims.

Today's prospect is a more sophisticated buyer than in the past. He may accept your claims at face value and appreciate your sincerity and desire to help him solve his problems but still not be convinced because he knows it is one thing to promise and quite another to deliver. One bad buying experience may have soured him on claims of any and all sales representatives.

This show-me attitude makes your sales job tougher than that of the old-fashioned drummer. It poses the challenge of preparing adequate visual, factual evidence to back up your promises and claims. Such facts and evidence should be truthful, specific, applicable, and understandable. Let us review some of the previously noted as well as new types of evidence that help you prove your point.

Demonstration. The most convincing proof is to show in your prospect's presence, in his surroundings, that your product does exactly what you claim for it.

Tests. If employed in conjunction with the demonstration noted above, tests offer extremely convincing proof.

Visual evidence. Photographs of machinery in operation elsewhere or photocopies of delivery orders or samples of equipment after use are impressive.

Testimonials. Written statements from satisfied users, stamps of approval from independent testing laboratories, or other forms of testimony from experts or customers offer persuasive evidence to back up your claims.

Statistics. Many technical or business buyers respond favorably to such visual evidence. They like, trust, and respect figures. You can often compile such statistics from government sources, from trade association publications, or from the records or research of your own company or organization.

Published articles.   People tend to respect outside magazine or newspaper articles more than they do advertisements or company-produced public-relations handouts.

Guarantees.   A written guarantee is one of the most convincing forms of proof. Since your company feels confident enough to prepare such a written warranty, your prospect also feels confident.

Case histories.   These are more detailed and specific than mere testimonial letters and as such are read with interest by your prospect.

Telephone testimonials.   A most convincing proof of the claims for your product is to call a satisfied user in the presence of your prospect and to let the two of them talk it over. People like to be asked their opinion, and your satisfied user will probably say only positive things about the item in question.

HANDLING CHALLENGES

We have already noted that most people prefer to put off a buying decision, even though they may want what you are offering. Thus they often attempt to stall, postpone, avoid, or otherwise delay the approaching decision. Your prospect, in his attempt to stall, may throw up many challenges or objections. These can range from requesting more information so he can avoid a decision now to challenging your statements as a means of putting you on the defensive.

Many people are afraid of sales representatives and basically resent the idea of being sold anything. Many of them feel quite helpless in the face of powerful, persuasive sales techniques or a sales representative who they feel can outtalk or outthink them. Thus many challenges such as those we have mentioned are not objections at all but merely defensive reactions made to avoid a buying decision. In many such cases, in spite of the words spoken, the prospect is really saying, "Why should I buy now? Give me a reason why I have to make a decision today." He may also secretly want you to make the decision for him.

We can briefly discuss these defensive reactions now in terms of challenges which can be sidestepped rather than as specific objections. We will cover the principles and techniques of handling specific objections in Chapter 13. Here are some techniques for handling challenges such as a statement like this from a prospect: "I question the statement you have just made. I read recently something quite different. Can you check again on your facts, so that we can talk about it some other time?"

Challenge his statement and ask for details.   "What were the specific facts? Where did you see them? Why do you think those facts are correct since my evidence indicates that ours are accurate?" The theory here is that his comment is a stall and that he will back down in the face of your challenging him for specifics.

Agree with his statement and continue.   "Yes, I think I may have seen something like that, but here are some more specific facts about my previous point that will interest you."

Agree, but counter with your view of the statement.   "Yes, you have a point there, but my figures are quite specific as this diagram shows, and I urge you to consider them as accurate in view of my sincere desire to help you solve the problem we have been discussing."

Act directly to confirm or disprove his statement. "You may have a point, but I don't believe they referred to the same problem. Shall we telephone that source right now to confirm it one way or the other, or isn't it that important to you?"

Agree he has a point and change the subject. "Yes, you may have a point there, but it may not affect your specific problem. Here is something else that may interest you."

Ignore it and continue with your presentation. If you sense it to be a mere excuse rather than a real challenge, you can sometimes continue with your presentation and ignore the challenge. Please read the full discussion about handling this delicate situation in Chapter 13, pages 267 and 268 before employing it as a technique.

APPLYING WHAT WE HAVE LEARNED TO YOUR SITUATION

Earlier in this chapter we noted that at a certain stage in the presentation interview you are ready to concentrate on priorities centered on persuading your prospect that your proposal offers the best solution to his problems or needs.

Since he will not buy until convinced of the merits of your proposal and its advantages to him, your first task is to help him understand exactly what your product or service is, how it works, and what it will do for him. Then you have to help him recognize that it offers the best fulfillment of his desires. When his interest turns into desire, build on it by securing his conviction that, by obtaining your product or service, he will find the satisfaction he is seeking.

We have considered many effective principles and techniques of leading a prospect through these steps. In order to tie all these together for simplified application, we will now try to target our thinking, words, and actions.

Rifle versus Shotgun Technique

This is not so much a technique as it is a concept. The idea is to "rifle" or concentrate your efforts on a few key specifics rather than "shotgunning" or talking so much you confuse your prospect. Having learned his problems or interests, you now concentrate on:

1. Presenting facts about your product that are specifically tailored to his problems, wants, or desires.
2. Show him exactly what your product will do for him.
3. Wrap up each point made with a commitment question.
4. If he voices any objections, acknowledge and handle them; turn them into reasons for buying, or otherwise to your advantage.
5. Close the sale as soon as possible; watch for buying signals, which can come at any time.

For each point you make, tell him what you are going to say, demonstrate or prove it to him, guard against overtalking or getting too technical, and involve him at each stage by asking questions that secure agreement which will add up to conviction in his mind.

Since he has admitted his needs or wants and discussed his desires and problems, he is now willing to consider your product or service as a fulfillment or solution. Basically he wants to be convinced that your offering (1) will do what is claimed for it and (2) is the best for his purposes now and in the future.

Features-Advantages-Benefits Technique

The most effective way to arouse and build desire, and secure conviction is to develop each sales point in this order.

Features—   Tell or show him exactly what your product or service is, how it works, and what it can do.

Advantages— Point out or demonstrate by examples how it will meet his needs or solve his problems.

Benefits—   Point out benefits he will obtain by having it (desire for gain) or may lose by not having it (fear of loss).

What's the difference between a feature and a benefit? We noted them in a preceding chapter, but to repeat:

A *feature* is a description of a product or service.
A *benefit* is the satisfaction your prospect will receive from the feature.

For example: If you tell your prospect "this coffee pot is automatically controlled," you are pointing out a feature. On the other hand, if you tell him "all you have to do is plug it in and forget it—it's automatic," you are explaining a benefit.

The benefits always have more sales impact; it is your sales job to interpret each feature of your product into a benefit, and describe it in vivid, picture-building sales vocabulary:

Expressive words—foolproof, luxurious, flawless, ultramodern.
Dynamic words—powerful, thrusting, energy-saving.
Personal words—you, me, I, we, our, us.

Features themselves have no impact. You as a sales representative have to give each feature a value (that is what benefits are), since *benefits are what he will really buy*. Benefits give him a reason for buying; your sales points should be based on benefits rather than features. We can define and illustrate in greater depth features, advantages, and benefits as follows:

A *feature* is a part of or a characteristic of your product or service. There may be many features to your specific product or service, each relating to a specific need, problem, or interest. Combined, they represent the total features. For example, (1) is portable, (2) can operate either on batteries or plugged into a light socket, and (3) is instantly convertible to either 110 or 220 voltage.

You normally present each feature separately so that you answer these two questions:

1. *What is it?* You can answer this by telling the prospect the name of the feature and pointing it out.
2. *What does it do?* You can explain and briefly demonstrate, adding further interest and conviction by letting him do it.

For example:

I gather from what you have told me, Mr. O'Carroll, that you travel both here and abroad and need a lightweight, portable tape recorder you can use easily anywhere in the world.

A key feature of our machine is its light weight. Here, won't you hold it for a second? Wouldn't you agree that it is almost as light as a camera? And it is easy to carry, too, don't you think?

A second feature of interest to you is that it can operate either on batteries (pointing them out) or plugged into any home, office, or hotel wall socket.

Advantages of the feature are how it helps solve problems or fulfill desires. Pointing out the advantages of the feature in terms of your prospect's interest and to his full understanding is highly important if you expect to arouse desire and secure conviction. Lead from the feature into the advantages through verbal phrases such as, "This is important to you because. . . ." "Others have found this useful because. . . ." "This will help solve your problem because. . . ." For example, "The light weight and portability of this tape recorder are important to you, Mr. O'Carroll, since you do so much traveling."

Benefits are the advantages your prospect obtains through ownership (desire for gain) or disadvantages he may suffer by not having it (fear of loss).

Here is an appeal to gain:

Based on what you've told me, Mr. O'Carroll, it appears that this lightweight, easy-to-carry, portable tape recorder will be convenient to use and will save you time on your frequent business trips. Such convenience includes the ability to plug it into either a 110 or 220 light socket anywhere in the world or to operate it on batteries at any other time, day or night.

Here is an appeal to loss.

Owning this machine will free you from the inconvenience and loss of time involved in not being able to record whenever or wherever you want, day or night, anywhere in the world.

Secure Agreement to Each Point

It is important that you secure agreement *after each point* that your prospect recognizes and accepts the value of the benefits pointed out. You do this by yes-building questions such as:

Don't you agree that this will help you?
It is indeed easy to operate isn't it?

If he doesn't agree, then ask why, in an effort to find out what real or imagined objection he might have, and handle it via the several techniques we will be describing in Chapter 13.

Remember, it is your responsibility to turn each feature of your product or service into something to be desired by your prospect. The key is to explain how he will benefit from the feature, through picture-building words or demonstration, and then secure his "yes" agreement that it is indeed desirable.

SUMMARY

We discussed in this chapter the principles and techniques of arousing desire and securing conviction. We started from the point at which the prospect had admitted needs or wants, had discussed his desires or problems, and was willing to consider a solution.

We continued by outlining progressive steps showing the prospect what the product or service is, how it works, and what it can do. We used a feature-advantage-benefit sequence for each point developed. The aim is to help him recognize that the specific proposal offers the best fulfillment of his desires. Once he recognizes this fact his interest starts changing into desire, and desire into conviction. We concluded that interest changes into desire when advantages and benefits so dominate your prospect's mind that he is ready to take action.

In order to make this psychological transformation as smooth as possible, we discussed how to plan for and build into your presentation certain factors that eliminate fears, questions, or objections before they are expressed. These factors include clarity of presentation, the handling of price, and that selling points be developed logically and emotionally around key buying motives.

Although arousing desire and securing conviction are intertwined as part of the developing presentation, we discussed them separately for clarity. We pointed out that conviction is secured chiefly through the prospect's acceptance of and belief in you and the proof or evidence that your product or service will furnish the benefits claimed. Your manner and attitude are chiefly responsible for his acceptance of you personally, and visual evidence is the best form of proof.

Along with the techniques of creating desire and securing conviction we briefly discussed how to handle certain challenges you may encounter.

CHAPTER REVIEW

CONCEPTS TO REMEMBER*

____ role-playing	____ feature	____ phrasing
____ pace of delivery	____ advantage	____ conviction builders
____ emotional selling point	____ benefit	____ indirect suggestion

*For memory reinforcement, fill in the page number or numbers where the terms were described in this chapter.

QUESTIONS FOR ANALYSIS AND DISCUSSION

1. What is your first sales task now that your prospect has admitted his needs or wants, has discussed his desires and problems, and has indicated a willingness to consider your solution to them? How do you accomplish this task?
2. What is your second sales task, following completion of the above task, recognizing that the two are actually intertwined?
3. At what stage does interest change to desire in the above process?
4. What are the two important factors that secure conviction in your prospect's mind?
5. Why is it important to change the pitch or tone of your voice or change the pace of your delivery during a sales presentation?
6. What two important principles concerning the use of visual demonstrations during a presentation should a sales representative always keep in mind?
7. List and explain four types of demonstration aids that might be effectively used during a sales presentation.
8. What two anticipated questions should be incorporated into a sales presentation for each product feature to be pointed out?

CONVINCING PROOF THROUGH DEMONSTRATION WINS THE SALE OF ELECTRONIC JET-ENGINE COMPONENT

Bob Reid is the energetic owner-president of R. T. Reid Associates, Inc., a small but highly regarded manufacturers' representative in Fort Lee, New Jersey, USA. He and his sales team successfully compete against some of the largest electronic manufacturers in the world in supplying vital components to the engineering, aviation, and space-technology industries in the eastern United States.

His engineer prospects are glad to see any sales representative who can offer them new and easy solutions to their difficult problems. They are very objective however, and since Bob and the group of small manufacturers he represents are often relatively unknown, he has to sell hard to prove the value of his components. Product knowledge is essential to his sales presentations, for unless his prospects feel that he knows exactly what he is talking about, he probably will not get their business.

Bob feels that proof through demonstration is the most effective way to arouse and hold their interest and to secure their conviction that his product provides the best solution to their problems. Thus he goes to great lengths, in time and effort, to demonstrate the claims for his products. Here, in his own words, is how he put his product knowledge and sales techniques into action recently to successfully close a very large and important sale.

"The company I was calling on is a large manufacturer of electronic jet-engine ignitions. In this ignition they use a high-voltage rectifier, which I was trying to sell them. My competitor had the business, so I had to prove beyond doubt that it would be to this company's advantage to modify its specifications to require my rectifier.

"I knew that jet-engine parts are subjected to high levels of vibration and that my rectifier, although higher in price, would withstand a higher level of vibration than would my competitor's. To demonstrate this I had one of my rectifiers, which is of solid encapsulated construction, ground down so that it was effectively sectioned in half and the internal construction could be seen. My competitor's rectifier was a glass tube with the parts inside held in contact with each other by a spring. I purchased a competitor's rectifier from a distributor, broke it open, and placed all the pieces in a lucite box.

"I called on key individuals in the engineering department, demonstrated the superior construction of my rectifier, and showed that the occasional intermittent contact they were experiencing was caused by the spring in the competitor's part which would flex, with sufficient vibration in the right plane. I demonstrated how this flexing could not happen with our part.

"I also emphasized that this problem with intermittent contacts was costing them a lot more than the small extra cost of my rectifier. I persuaded them to issue an amendment to their purchase-part drawing, specifying that rectifiers with springs could not be supplied. When the requirements went to the purchasing department, the amended drawing put me in a sole-source position, and I was able to obtain the business at a higher price."

QUESTIONS FOR WRITTEN REPORTS OR CLASS DISCUSSION

1. Bob knew from the start that he faced both a specific competitor and a lower price. How did he plan correctly in advance to handle competition and price during his presentation?

2. This sale was won by demonstrated technical superiority. Suppose the rectifier had been just as good as but not superior to the competition. What three reasons could Bob have advanced as to why the company should have let him supply the rectifiers anyway?
3. We do not know exactly when Bob introduced price into his presentation. Had you been in his place, at what point in the presentation would you have introduced it? What is the general rule for introducing price if there is such a rule?
4. What are the two most important factors that secure conviction in the mind of any prospect? How did Bob work these factors into his presentation?

Case Study 12–2

COMPONENT-COST COMPARISONS AROUSE DESIRE AND SECURE CONVICTION FOR REFERENCE-ENCYCLOPEDIA SALE

Mr. Alfiero Palestroni, a leading East Coast building contractor in the United States, tells this story of how he was convinced by a sales representative of the value of an expensive reference-encyclopedia set for his office.

"The sales representative phoned to make an appointment, saying I was one of a few selected executives whose opinion he would like to ask regarding the value of a new reference encyclopedia for firms in the building and contracting business.

"When he came, he seemed to know a lot about my industry and its problems and soon had me talking about my problems and plans for building thirty-six expensive new homes. It did not take me long to realize he was there to try to sell me a reference-encyclopedia set for my office rather than just to get my opinion of it. But as he showed me a sample book and colored brochures and pointed out all the easy-to-use features, illustrations, and special reference services for specific questions, I realized it was a good and useful set.

"It also looked expensive! I told him the set looked OK but that it probably cost too much to interest me. Then he really went to work on me, using the kind of arguments that make sense to me as a builder. He used a component-cost-comparison technique to handle the price issue.

Mr. Palestroni, you have several reference books in your office already, and you know how much they cost you individually. But you bought them not because they were books, but for information, didn't you?

"I had to say yes to that one!

Well then, let me just hold up this sample book, one of thirty in the set. It has 400 pages, is full of color illustrations and technical charts, is beautifully bound, and has an index designed for a busy executive like you. How much do you think it will cost you by itself outside?

"Technical books are expensive, so I told him $10 to $12 at least. 'Well then, Mr. Palestroni,' he said, 'if you bought thirty books at $12 each, how much would you be up for?' I told him $360, and he gave me a piece of paper and asked me to write it down. Out of curiosity as to what he would do next, I wrote it down as requested. 'I can tell, Mr. Palestroni, that as a successful executive in the highly competitive building industry you appreciate value. Am I right?' I could not disagree with that, so said yes. 'If you could obtain this $360 value today for only $199, would you be interested?'

"I was interested, and soon found myself signing an order form. I did feel that I had gotten a good buy on a very useful encyclopedia-reference set. More than that however, I was impressed with how he had come up with the best possible way to break down my price resistance. He had broken his proposal up into thirty components and had me assign my estimate of value to each. He then got me to mentally add it up and physically write the price down. When he finally did present his price, it looked very reasonable indeed compared to mine. Since the set did offer advantages to me and the value looked excellent, I felt I could not afford to pass the opportunity up."

QUESTIONS FOR WRITTEN REPORTS OR CLASS DISCUSSION

1. What was the real interest factor in this sales approach to Palestroni?
2. What other methods did the sales representative use to back up the image of value in the eyes of his prospect?
3. What excellent method did the sales representative use in relating value to something specific in the prospect's mind?

SALES PROBLEM 12–1

CAN "VALUE ANALYSIS" SECURE CONVICTION THAT WILL LEAD TO A SALE?

How do professional sales representatives get their prospects really interested during a sales presentation—interested enough to want the specific product or service they are selling? The answer is to offer benefits! And something called "value analysis" is the way a large percentage of them get their message across and secure the conviction necessary to close the sale.

What is value analysis? It can be summed up in one phrase: it's not what it costs—it's what it will save!

How do sales representatives use value analysis as an interest-arousing, convincing sales technique? They find out what job the prospect wants done or what problem he wants solved (e.g., better or less expensive ways); then they suggest cost-saving, alternative ways that involve the use of the product or service they are selling. A value-conscious company or government agency will nearly always be interested in making cost-saving purchases to fit all phases of its operations.

QUESTION FOR WRITTEN REPORTS OR CLASS DISCUSSION

How could you employ "value analysis" in selling in these functional areas:
1. Office
2. Manufacturing
3. Inventory control
4. Shipping

13
principles and techniques of handling objections

When you have mastered the content of this chapter, you should be able to:

Summarize what is meant by the statement, "The two greatest problems faced by both new and experienced sales representatives are (1) how to handle objections, and (2) how to close the sale."

Summarize why objections are raised and are to be expected, and what the attitude of a sales representative should be toward objections.

List two common honest objections of a business nature and three sincere objections of a personal nature that might be encountered in any sales presentation.

Describe these five classifications of standard or common objections, and some techniques for handling them: (1) price, (2) no interest or need, (3) product, (4) company or source of supply, and (5) stalling or procrastinations.

Summarize six principles involved in how a sales representative should react to any type of objection.

Summarize five strategic principles that can help turn objections of any nature into sales.

Describe six basic techniques for handling objections.

Analyze the importance of the statement, "With only rare exceptions, you cannot close a sale as long as the prospect has any major objection or objections. Thus you have to understand the principles and techniques of handling objections before attempting to master closing techniques."

The two greatest problems faced by both new and experienced sales representatives are (1) how to handle objections, and (2) how to close the sale. In the case of a new or inexperienced sales representative, fear is often part of the problem—fear that he will be unable to handle objections and will thus lose the sale. This fear is justified because, with only rare exceptions, you cannot close a sale as long as the prospect has any major objection or objections. Thus you have to understand the principles and techniques of handling objections before attempting to master closing techniques.

Objections or doubts are present in nearly every sales interview. They may be real or valid ones, hidden ones, or mere excuses to put you off. Once you learn how to anticipate, recognize, and handle them, your fear will vanish and the problem of facing them will diminish. True professional sales representatives not only welcome but also seek out objections so they can answer them to the prospect's satisfaction at the earliest strategic moment.

Once he has answered an objection, a sales representative can often turn it immediately into an excuse for a trial close (trying to get a quick decision). In some cases, even the first objection is a signal that the prospect is ready to buy. In those cases, rare though they may be, the sales representative can close within a few minutes. With such possibilities always present, the sales representative who knows how to handle the objection quickly thus becomes a better closer.

WHY ARE OBJECTIONS RAISED?

Since you have to deal with objections day after day, interview after interview, it may help to give some thought to why they are raised. Some objections are honest ones, others are mere stalls for time, and others are intended as bids for information. Many people object to the idea of being sold, others just do not like to part with their momney and thus try to avoid a decision as long as possible.

Honest objections of a business nature may involve the following points.

1. A desire to know all facts of your proposal as they affect the buyer's firm or organization. Since he is paid to handle the money of his organization carefully, he has every right to voice objections or doubts until he is fully satisfied.
2. A search for proof that your product or service will fulfill a need, will increase profits or cut costs, and will perform exactly as you claim.

Sincere objections of a personal nature may involve the following points.

1. A desire to feel that he (the buyer) is making the decision and is not being sold anything.
2. A desire to know all the facts so as to be reassured in his own mind that the purchase will be of value.
3. A need to be a participant or partner in the sale—to have his opinion listened to with respect.

A sales representative may encounter objections of both a business and a personal nature when selling to the buyer of a firm or organization. The buyer has to represent his organization effectively, yet is also influenced by his personal feelings and emotions.

Many objections, especially some of the standard ones such as "It costs too much," "I can't make a decision at this time," or "I'll have to think about it," are mere smoke screens and do not represent the real objection at all. Thus you cannot afford to take all such objections at their face value; you have to find the real objection and answer it. But this real objection may be so deeply rooted in preconceived ideas or prejudice that the prospect himself is not specifically aware of the inner reasons for his negative response. We will discuss methods for discovering the real or hidden reasons later. First, however, we will consider your personal attitudes toward objections in general.

WHAT SHOULD YOUR ATTITUDE TOWARD OBJECTIONS BE?

Your attitude should basically be that of welcoming objections and answering them positively rather than evading, ignoring, or resenting them. As we shall discuss later, timing and controlling the handling of them may vary, but you must finally acknowledge all objections to the prospect's satisfaction in order to close the sale.

However, you should frame closing questions or techniques to uncover objections, most of which can usually be handled, and to avoid a flat no. Once a prospect has said no, he has a position to defend, and your job of persuading him to say yes becomes much more difficult. Thus, yes-building questions are desirable, and it is best not to try to force a decision until you are fairly confident that it will be a favorable one.

Your major closing problems come more often from procrastinators, who cannot make up their minds, than from prospects who have a solid reason for not buying. But in either case, you should not consider a "no" or "not interested now" as final but merely as an invitation to continue selling harder.

Most objections are standard ones, common to all fields of selling, and sales representatives have devised many persuasive techniques to cope with them. Other objections require special handling and considerable knowledge, empathy, and flexibility on your part. Your attitude in all cases should be one of securing agreement rather than securing mere submission from your prospect.

You should welcome an objection because it offers a clue to what your prospect thinks or feels. It pinpoints an area on which you should concentrate and offers insight into his wants and buying motives.

PRIOR PLANNING CAN ANTICIPATE
OR FORESTALL MANY OBJECTIONS

What kind of objections may be encountered, and how can they be forestalled within the presentation? Here is a brief list of some common objections plus a few less common ones. We will cover in depth techniques of handling these and others later.

Standard objections	Less common objections
Your price is too high.	Your product is too new.
I cannot afford it.	I have heard that some other company had trouble with your product.
I am not interested at this time.	Your credit terms are not favorable
I am satisfied with what I am currently using.	enough. We have a better offer from your competitor.

Such objections can be forestalled by incorporating into the presentation certain arguments that counter the objection before it is voiced. This forestalling can be accomplished without your having to ever state the objection yourself. For example, if your product or service is higher priced than that of a competitor, you can openly acknowledge the fact, then proceed quickly to stress value, benefits, quality, performance, satisfaction, or any key features other than price.

Mr. Carruthers, ours is a quality product priced not to be the cheapest item available but to give you the high standards and long-lasting dependability you require. Its high quality will save you a great deal in the long run.

You can anticipate some of the less common objections, and, as in the case of the "your-product-is-too-new" objection, you can forestall them during the presentation in much the same manner as you can the price objection. Knowledge of what is going on in your industry and of what your competition is offering prepares you to handle promptly other less common objections.

A carefully planned interview, presented in a logical, clear, understandable, convincing manner, can effectively eliminate all or most basic objections. Nevertheless, prospects raise some objections in nearly every interview, so you have to understand the strategy, psychology, and techniques of dealing with them.

BASIC STRATEGY AND PSYCHOLOGY FOR HANDLING OBJECTIONS

During an average sales interview you may have to handle from two to five objections. Your first problem is to determine whether they are real objections or mere excuses or stalls. Your second problem is to decide on the strategy and tactics of handling them in order to retain control of the interview.

Your standard reaction to all objections should involve these principles:

Welcome the objection. Do not resent it or attempt to argue. The prospect may be offering you a point around which the sale can be rapidly closed.

Listen carefully to it. Keep quiet, smile, and concentrate on what he is saying. You may think the matter is trivial, but to him it may be very important. Because what he thinks or feels is important, give him the courtesy of treating his objections or doubts seriously and with respect. Careful listening involves not only hearing his words but also searching his eyes or bodily movements for clues that may reveal his real feelings. Give him time to express himself fully; let him finish what he is saying. Do not make the mistake of cutting him off in mid-thought even if you do recognize his objection and are eager to acknowledge it.

Rephrase and repeat the objections. By taking the time to rephrase and repeat his objection, you accomplish three major goals:

1. You assure him that you have understood and respect his objection and thus please him with your interest.
2. You gain time to think for a moment how best to handle it.
3. You can soften his objection by rephrasing it into a question, which is easier to handle than an objection, and you put yourself in the position of helping him answer it.

For example, if he complains that your product is too expensive, he may really be wondering if a cheaper one would not be just as practical. You can test this objection by rephrasing it into a question, such as, "Mr. Kobayashi, aren't you really wondering whether the expense for this item can be justified?"

Do not guess at the reasons behind his objections. Your aim is to try rapidly to pin down the real issue. Sometimes the problem bothering the prospect is not clear even in his own mind. You have to find the right question if you expect to handle his objection. You then have to give him facts that will influence him to answer the question favorably rather than unfavorably. Rephrasing and repeating his objection help clarify the issue for both of you.

Agree at least in part with him. By agreeing with his right to object and by agreeing that he has raised an important point, you avoid contradiction and take him off the defensive. You lose nothing by agreeing that his complaint is reasonable, logical, and worth thinking about. You can then supply additional facts that may help him to picture the situation differently and may turn his objection to your own advantage by making it a positive sales point.

Uncover hidden objections.   The process of rephrasing and restating objections into questions helps determine whether the objectives are valid ones or mere excuses or stalls. If your prospect offers more than five objections during the interview you can assume that he is probably stalling. Most likely he is hiding his real objection, and your problem is to bring it out into the open.

How can you uncover hidden doubts or objections? The best technique is to ask questions that bring them into the open. You have to watch as well as listen for clues since some prospects mask their real emotions or feelings. Keep searching for the real reason. Here are some question techniques that may be of practical value to you in uncovering hidden objections.

Mr. Smythe-Jones, I feel that there may be some reason that's bothering you other than the ones discussed. What is your real objection?

I feel that you may be holding something back. Would you mind telling me what it is?

You can be frank with me. What is your real objection to this proposal? Does it have to do with payments?

Let's forget that I am a sales representative and assume that we are two businessmen discussing a problem that offers a great deal to each of us. What is your real feeling about this proposal?

Ask what and why questions.   Asking questions prefixed by what or why helps uncover primary buying motives, clues to real or imagined objections, and countless other vital bits of information. *What* and *why* are perhaps the two most valuable tools in your sales word kit and you can use them as effective aids in your sales strategy and tactics as well as techniques. Here are but a few examples of how what and why questions can help you control and manage the interview.

What is your real purpose in considering purchasing what I am offering?

If you decide to purchase it, what do you hope it will do for you?

Why do you feel that way about it?

Why don't you purchase it now and start realizing its benefits immediately?

Make tact part of your over-all strategy.   Because you are interested in asking opinions and encouraging questions, you have to avoid being delayed by irrelevant objections. You are interested only in valid objections concerning your specific proposal. Many sales representatives make the mistake of getting involved in irrelevant discussions concerning politics, religion, local issues, or personalities. The danger here is that the prospect may sense your basic disagreement no matter how carefully you try to hide it. Thus you can lose a sale because of a totally minor and irrelevant point not at all connected with the proposal.

Good sales strategy and common sense dictate against allowing yourself to get trapped into such a situation. If caught, try to remove the "objection" from the prospect's mind without offending him. Here are a few statements that may help you get out of such a situation quickly without giving offense.

I respect your thinking on that matter, but may I ask you something specifically concerned with my proposal?

Your point is well taken, but perhaps you feel that way because I did not state the facts clearly. For example. . . .

Others have expressed the same thoughts to me, but perhaps this new factor could have some bearing on the situation. For example. . . .

HOW TO TURN OBJECTIONS INTO SALES

Underlying the strategy of handling objections, which we have just discussed, and the specific techniques, which we will cover in subsequent pages, are a few general principles that help turn objections into sales.

1. Place Yourself, from the Start, in the Role of a Question Answerer Rather Than of an Objection Handler

Invite the prospect to raise questions freely at any time since it is your duty to answer them. The psychological theory behind this technique is that a prospect does not feel he has to defend a question as he may feel he has to defend an objection. By placing yourself in the position of a question answerer rather than of an objection handler you probably will be in rapport rather than at odds with him. Here is an example of how you may initiate such rapport.

Mr. Engstrom, as we discuss this proposal, please feel free to ask questions at any time. It's my pleasure and my obligation to assist you by answering any question at any time. You are entitled to expect this of me; don't you agree?

2. Employ the Buffer Technique as a Further Means of Putting Your Prospect at Ease

Best articulated by real estate sales authority Chester H. McCall, Sr., this device is the starting point for handling all objections. This buffer technique is a refinement of the rephrase-and-repeat-the-objection and agree-at-least-in-part techniques discussed earlier; here is what this authority has to say about it.

The "buffer" is a statement made by the salesman before he starts to answer the prospect's objection. This shows that the salesman has respect for the objection and that it deserves proper consideration. It is an indirect agreement with the prospect, without necessarily agreeing that the objection is true, valid, or proper.[1]

Here is an example of how the buffer works in practice.

Prospect: I think the price of your item is way out of line.

Your Buffer: I'm sure you have some very definite reasons for feeling the way you do, Mr. Kuruvila, and I think we should discuss them thoroughly."

---

3. Deal with the Objection Initially as a Mere Excuse and Evade It Where Possible

As a follow-up to the rephrasing, restating, partial-agreement buffer, many sales authorities suggest the perfectly ethical tactic of evading the objection if at all possible. There is no use wasting time handling an objection unless it is a real or valid one. If the objection is not an important one, you may be able to pass over it and continue with your presentation. But always keep one fundamental rule in mind: *If the objection is truly important to your prospect, in most cases you should deal with it promptly and fully.*

1. Chester H. McCall, Sr., *Complete Guide to Turning Objections into Real Estate Sales* (Englewood Cliffs, N.J.: Prentice-Hall, Inc., 1968), p. 1.

Making exceptions to this rule is necessary (1) when a price objection is voiced before you have had a chance to explain fully all the features and thus to establish value and (2) when the objection can be answered more fully later on in the orderly development of your presentation. In such cases, you can recognize it as a valid objection and request permission to come back to it, in this way: "Mrs. Gobel, you have raised a very important question, which I will answer to your complete satisfaction in a moment. May I first point out these features by way of leading up to it?"

Nothing is lost by evading the objection until you are certain that it is a truly important one. If it is a mere excuse, this tactic may avoid your devoting time to acknowledging it. If it is a valid objection, one that your prospect raises again, then you must handle it promptly.

4. Ferret Out Any Hidden Objections

We have already discussed how to accomplish this, but we reemphasize its importance here as a means of turning objections into sales. Unless you bring all important objections into the open, the sale can be lost. Thus, a good sales representative constantly probes for any such hidden objections.

5. Close Immediately on Any Buying Signals

Although we will discuss closing techniques in detail in Chapter 14, throughout the interview the possibility always exists to turn an objection into an immediate close. Your prospect may make a statement in the form of an objection that is actually a buying signal. For example, "Your proposal sounds good, but I suppose I should think it over before finally deciding." "I suppose" indicates that he has decided to buy. If he has not yet decided he probably will say, "I will think it over." Facial expressions and general attitude as well as "maybe I will" or "perhaps I should" all represent buying signals. When you detect such signals, you should immediately stop selling and go into a trial close.

SIX TECHNIQUES FOR HANDLING OBJECTIONS

Once an honest objection has been raised, you can handle the situation in several ways. Sales authorities and trainers have refined rather standardized techniques, of which these are the six most basic.

1. Yes—but (indirect-denial) technique
2. Question (interrogation) technique
3. Boomerang (capitalization) technique
4. Offset (compensation or superior-point/fact) technique
5. Direct-denial (contradiction) technique
6. Pass-over (pass-by) technique

Yes–But (Indirect-Denial) Technique

This technique is perhaps the most widely used of the six. It is a tactful way of denying the validity of the objection without offending the prospect. No one likes to be flatly contradicted—to be told that his beliefs are wrong or his facts inaccurate. This technique enables you to dull the force of the objection, to flank it, and often to turn it to your advantage.

Suppose your prospect makes a flat statement such as, "I don't think your product is so good as you claim it to be." How can you use this technique to handle the objection? An incorrect way would be to say, "You are dead wrong, Mr. Gosling; you don't understand what I've been telling you." Such a statement would be in poor taste, would cost you the sale, and would probably cause the prospect to throw you out of his office. You do not have to agree with his statement, but the yes-but technique can help you handle the situation correctly: "Yes, Mr. Gosling, but aren't you impressed with this feature? May I show you how it works? See this red button. . . ." Or you can use words of indirect denial other than yes-but, such as: "I can understand, Mr. Gosling, that you may feel that way and for that reason would like to stress the superiority of our special feature. See this red button. . . ."

Question (Interrogation) Technique

If used sincerely, this technique not only can get the prospect to talk but also, if pursued, can help him clarify his own thinking. In many cases the use of a question to counter an objection causes the prospect to answer his own objection.

We noted earlier the importance of initially getting the prospect thinking in terms of questions rather than of objections. The same point applies to you; if you start thinking of every objection as a question, it will train you to quickly frame questions in employing this technique.

Basically, this technique involves agreeing that the prospect has raised a good question and inviting him to agree that his objection is a question. We can use the previous objection for illustration.

Prospect:	I don't think your product is so good as you claim it to be.
Sales Representative:	(using question technique): You have raised a good question, but aren't you really asking whether it will do a superior job for you, in your special situation?

The prospect may agree that it is a question but still persist in his claim. Your task is to break his general statement down to find out what his real (hidden) objection is. In a continuation of the above interview situation, you may find the word *why* of great assistance.

Prospect:	Well, yes, I guess that's the situation, but I just don't think your product is so good as you say it is.
Sales Representative:	Why do you feel that way?
Prospect:	It does not seem sturdy enough.
Sales Representative:	Aren't you really saying that it may not stand up to your specifications? If so, that's a fair question, and here are some facts to help you decide."

Boomerang (Capitalization) Technique

This strong technique involves turning objections back on your prospect as reasons why he should buy. Normally you should employ it only once during the interview and ideally should reserve it for handling the final objection that seems to be blocking the sale because proper use of this technique involves going immediately into a close. The combination of boomerang and proper closing techniques is commonly referred to in sales terminology as closing on resistance.

This technique is most effective when used by skilled sales representatives, and since it is a strong technique, it should be softened by a smile and friendly look. It is especially effective in meeting objections not strongly backed by facts or reasons.

Here are some examples of how you may employ the boomerang technique. In effect, and through different wording, you are telling the prospect that the objection he raised is the reason he should buy.

Prospect: I can't afford it now.

Sales   (using boomerang responses): Mr. Grabrovaz, it is only natural
Representative: that you should feel that way. But in this period of rising prices, can you really afford not to consider buying now? Mrs. Logan, you say you can't afford it now but that may be the very reason why you should consider buying now.

(She will probably ask why; the sales representative can briefly restate reasons for buying now and go into a trial close.)

Offset (Compensation or Superior-Point/Fact) Technique

This technique gives some validity to the objection but detracts attention from it by pointing out features that offset or compensate for the deficiency.

Very few products are perfect in all characteristics. Many of them embody, for a reason, design limitations to which a prospect may honestly object. Your job as a sales representative in such a situation is, through use of this technique, to persuade the prospect that the advantages outweigh the disadvantages.

Prospect: I was looking for a new home with a fireplace in the living room, but this doesn't have one.

Sales   (using offset technique): A fireplace would be nice, Mrs. Arm-
Representative: strong, but have you really ever seen a home within this price range with more extra features, such as. . . .
               Our architect thought of including a fireplace, Mrs. Armstrong, but since they cost so much to install, he decided to put that money into other features that would give you more house for your money. As an example. . . .

Direct-Denial (Contradiction) Technique

This technique must be carefully used because it flatly contradicts the prospect's objection and tells him that he is wrong. Use it only in those rare cases when he voices incorrect objections or attacks your company or product or service with a derogatory comment.

In such unusual cases, a direct denial may be the only way to meet the situation. However, use the yes-but technique first if at all possible. If offered with a smile and in a sincere manner however, the direct denial may impress your prospect with your sincerity and belief in the quality of your company or proposal.

The danger of employing this technique, especially for new or inexperienced sales representatives, is that unless very carefully handled it can offend the prospect. It should never be employed against egocentric individuals and is better suited to answering those objections voiced as questions rather than as statements of fact.

Here is an example of how it can be used in practice, assuming that it is the only effective way to handle the situation at the moment.

Prospect: Why can't your firm ever do anything right? Your shipping department must be the worst managed in the entire industry.

Sales Representative: (employing with sincerity the direct-denial technique): Mr. Smith, you and I both know that your statement can't be true. All my other customers tell me our shipping department offers generally the best service in the industry. Can you give me a specific example of recent poor service to you so I can take care of it now if possible?

(Some buyers are chronic complainers. They complain to every sales representative in exactly the same manner. By putting them immediately on the spot with a request for specifics, you can often put a stop to this kind of illogical objection at once. If they do have a specific complaint, try to settle it to their satisfaction immediately.)

The Pass-Over (Pass-By) Technique

This technique is generally used only in the face of trivial or flimsy objections. If the objection is too unimportant to waste time on, you can simply gloss over or ignore it if at all possible. In practice, the technique can be employed in this way.

Prospect: Your last statement sounds pretty farfetched to me.

Sales Representative: (using the pass-over technique): Well, Ms. Conboy, we try to point out everything of possible interest. You did seem interested in our other feature. If you will note this red button again. . . .

SOME TECHNIQUES FOR HANDLING SPECIFIC TYPES OF OBJECTIONS

As we enter a discussion of how to handle certain specific objections common to most types of selling, keep in mind the law of averages. You will not handle every objection successfully and you will not close every sale. But if you work hard, consistently, and intelligently the law of averages will be in your favor. Ten failures in a row are discouraging if you make only ten sales presentations and then give up in disgust. But if you make thirty presentations, ten failures, even in a row, are just part of the game. The average for many types of selling is one close for every three presentations.

The more professional you become at handling objections, the greater your number of closes. Many sales representatives become so adept at handling objections raised by even the most difficult prospects that they regularly close one out of every two presentations. This sales-close ratio depends, of course, on the type selling in which you are engaged.

Our discussion will now center on how to handle standard or common objections, along with some less common ones you will encounter.

WHAT ARE STANDARD OR COMMON OBJECTIONS?

No matter what type selling you are engaged in, you encounter certain standard or common objections. Classifying them as follows, we will discuss them in detail in subsequent pages.

1.   Price objections
2.   No-interest-or-need objections
3.   Product objections
4.   Company or source-of-supply objections
5.   Stalling or procrastination objections

We must consider these objections (as well as less common ones, which we will discuss later) in light of the following criteria.

Is it a valid objection?   If your prospect voices an objection relating to design, performance, construction, or other factual details, you have to consider whether it is a valid or genuine objection. A valid objection to one prospect may not be a real or important one to another.

Is it a stall, or put-off, objection?   Whatever the objection, you have to determine whether it is genuine or merely an alibi, stall, or procrastination. Since some prospects are simply afraid to make a decision on the spot, they try to stall or otherwise avoid making it. The common objection "I have to discuss it with other associates" (or my husband, my wife, my partner, etc.) may be genuine in some cases and may be a common stall or delaying tactic in others.

Is it a prejudiced or trivial objection?   Many objections may seem trivial or unimportant on the surface yet reflect prejudices which can spoil chances of a sale unless handled carefully. These objections may be based on deeply felt personal, social, religious, or business attitudes or prejudices. They may or may not be valid and may be based only on something the prospect has heard or feels instinctively.

Is it an impossible objection?   Valid reasons for an objection by one prospect may not apply to the next. If he does not have enough money in his current budget to buy this year or if he has already spent all allocated funds, then the objection may be valid and impossible to overcome. On the other hand, such an excuse may not be the impasse he pictures it to be. Creative thinking on your part may help him find ways of overcoming such a problem.

In dealing with the standard or common objection then, you first have to determine its depth and validity. Second, you have to determine whether it is the only or the real objection in his mind. We have already discussed how to do this.

WHAT ARE SOME LESS COMMON OBJECTIONS YOU MAY ENCOUNTER?

Some typical less common objections involve credit terms or other policy questions, legal questions, trade-in considerations, or technical performance questions. Your prospect may want to stock items on consignment to test resale rather than on outright initial purchase or may object even to your trying to close the sale or to other tactics.

Proper handling of some of these questions may require assistance from the head office of your company, assistance from outside sources, or rapid creative thinking on your part. Your initial job is to define them as to validity as outlined above.

PRICE OBJECTIONS

Price objections are generally the most common and the most difficult questions to handle. Countering such objections is and will continue to be perhaps the most frustrating part of the job for a very high percentage of both new and experienced sales representatives as they face statements such as these.

Your price is out of line.
Your price is too high.
I can't afford to buy it at that price.
The cost is far over our budget allowance.

No matter how carefully sales representatives plan their presentations or frame their answers, more sales are lost because of their inability to handle questions of price like these than for any other single reason.

What can you do to handle these serious and frustrating price objections, which you are bound to face so often? Successful sales representatives who have found their own answers to this problem have written thousands of words and have advanced hundreds of solutions. Basically however, these three general rules for handling most price objections sum up their findings.

1. *Since price is bound to come up in almost every presentation, anticipate and control its introduction to the greatest extent possible.* In some cases this means deliberately introducing price early in your planned presentation. If the prospect brings it up early, you may elect to ignore, evade, or pass over it, for the time being. If so, you should secure his agreement to do so, come back to it when you are ready, and answer it to his full satisfaction. Or, you may elect to meet it head-on immediately and deal with it at once, turning it into an immediate trial close.

2. *Do not attempt to answer or defend a price objection until learning why it has been raised and for what reason.* Use the question, or why, technique to find out whether it is a real excuse or a relatively unimportant question. Perhaps the prospect is really asking for more facts or is basing his objection on misconceptions.

3. *Handle the objection by making other considerations so overwhelmingly important in the prospect's judgment that the value and benefits of the product or service outweigh the cost.* Price is relative; people buy what they want even ahead of what they need. If you talk only price you probably will lose the sale because

someone can nearly always beat you on price alone. Your aim is to convince the prospect that he can afford what you are offering by showing him why he needs or wants it. Thus you stress value, quality, efficiency, ease of use, satisfaction, turnover, profit, economy, prestige, or whatever else appears to have the greatest appeal.

Successful handling of price objections must start in your own mind. You cannot dodge the issue; the prospect will raise it, and you must handle it. In many types of selling a sales representative seldom makes a call without being told his price is too high. In many cases the prospect simply hates the idea of parting with a sizable amount of money. In others, especially in industrial selling, the best price for value offered is the key issue for the professional buyer.

If you believe in your product and feel that it does offer value and benefits to your prospect, then you have no reason to fear the question. By eliminating fear of the question from your mind, you can concentrate completely on answering price questions in a positive, confident manner, keeping these thoughts always in mind.

1. If you have to sell on price alone, you basically are offering nothing of real value.
2. Any price must be justified only in terms of the ability of the product or service to fulfill a real or imagined need or want.
3. Your prospect decides to buy mainly because of (a) the desire to gain the benefits or (b) the fear of losing them.

The prospect determines whether value outweighs price. Just as you like to feel you are getting value for your money in any purchase, so do home, store, office, and industrial buyers. Proper and continued use of the question technique should bring out the buyer's feelings on the subject. Your detailed knowledge of your industry, your product or service, and what your competition has to offer helps reassure him of your claims.

Benefits that Help Justify Price

Profit (savings).   Business buyers are always interested in ideas that increase their profits or save them money. Industrial buyers are generally interested in such items as savings in operating costs, reduction of upkeep or maintenance costs, or labor or time-saving features. Home, business, and industrial buyers are usually interested in proof that your offering may in time pay for itself through lower operating costs or other economic advantages.

Quality.   The long-range value of quality often outweighs price in the mind of your prospect. Price objections can often be handled easily by proving or demonstrating that the quality of your product or service offers more and costs less in the long run than does the inferior quality of a cheaper product or service.

Satisfaction.   Higher price means quality, and quality adds up to fewer complaints and greater satisfaction with the purchase. Satisfaction can also come from the pride of owning a prestige product in quality or design.

Prestige.   Higher-priced items offer prestige to individuals and businessmen alike. To the latter, they also offer higher profits. Higher price is often due to national advertising, which helps build the image of prestige, quality, and desirability.

Performance. People often happily pay more for superior performance. They normally respond to claims that your product reduces maintenance costs; saves time; has a long, trouble-free life; and performs with efficiency and precision.

Service. Talk service instead of price whenever possible. Tell your prospect about each service or extra offered by your company, and stress any personal follow-up service you are prepared to offer.

Long-term value. Many industrial buyers in particular consider price as only one factor. They seldom buy costly plant machinery, for example, on price alone. The long-term value offered by your product or service interests most purchasing agents and other rational buyers.

Techniques that Help Prove Value and Justify Price

Break price down into small units. A high-priced item, especially if it is to be used over a long period of time, can be attractive if the cost is broken down into small units. A $1,200 machine sounds expensive compared to an $800 one, but when the cost is broken down a different picture emerges, as this comparison indicates.

The extra cost per week, Mr. Juselius, is only about $7.50; per day, during a five-day work week, only $1.50 extra; and for each hour of the eight-hour day it is less than 19 cents. Wouldn't it be worth 19 cents extra per hour to have all the extra features that add up to faster production and thus greater profit?

Use price-is-relative claims. You can often prove that your higher-priced item will be less expensive in the long run than an initially cheaper competitor's product by comparing the economy of better quality, trouble-free service, and longer life.

Stress exclusive features or differences. Since very few products are built exactly alike, it is usually easy to find, stress, prove, or demonstrate exclusive or different features of your product or service. By talking about differences you avoid making comparisons from which your prospect may conclude that he can get a product just like yours at less cost somewhere else. The more differences you can stress or prove, the less important relative price comparisons are.

Mr. Cousins, our storage tank is of standard size and looks on the surface like any one of its four competitors. But it costs one-third more. It costs more because we've made it rust free and guarantee it to last ten years. The others can't claim that, and not one offers a guarantee beyond five years. Don't you agree then that in the end ours will cost less and offer you longer guaranteed satisfaction than the others will?

Offer proof that the prospect will receive more than he gives. Your higher-priced item may look something like a less expensive one but may offer far greater value. Facts, figures, testimonial letters, written guarantees, or service contracts offer proof of that value. You can often demonstrate such proof with creative showmanship.

Here, Mrs. Jones, is proof of what I've been saying about confidence in our product. Will you look at the specific guarantees in this warranty? Have you ever seen such a comprehensive guarantee covering a two-year period?

Dramatize possible loss from not having your product or service. Price often becomes secondary when your prospect is dramatically shown how much he could lose by not having what you have proposed.

The superior quality and craftsmanship of our machine tool will free you from worrying about the costly breakdowns you may face by continuing to use your old machine.

Your neighbor, Mr. Gore, didn't think he could afford extra life insurance this year either, and now that he has just been operated on for cancer, he is uninsurable for the next ten years, even if he recovers completely.

Turn high price into an asset rather than a liability. You can often turn high price into the good news that, for slightly extra cost, many extra benefits can be acquired. High quality is a major benefit that often outweighs price because it brings satisfaction, prestige, profit, economy, or long, trouble-free service.

Admit high price and sell anyway. If your product is high priced, you can openly admit it and immediately start proving or demonstrating the special qualities that justify the difference. Rolls Royce or Tiffany jewelry sales representatives do not worry about price; they talk instead about the craftsmanship, quality, long-term value, and prestige that accompany the purchase.

Standard Replies to Common Specific Price Objections

"Your price is too high." Do not even try to compete on price alone. Talk to the prospect only about value, quality, satisfaction, profit, prestige, or service.

Yes, Mr. Takeuchi, our product is high priced, but since we sell thousands each year around the world, it must offer value to offset the difference. Here are some reasons why it will be worth the difference to you.

Your point is well taken, Mrs. Mazula. I make no claim to offering a cheap product. What I do offer is value for your money, and here are some reasons why.

"I can't afford to buy it at that price." If you qualified the prospect properly as to his ability to buy, this objection simply means you have not made him want or desire your product or service. Your tasks are to show him why he wants it and how he can obtain it most easily.

Is that the only problem standing in the way of an affirmative decision, Mrs. Adams? I appreciate your feelings, but perhaps you can't afford not to buy it now. By installing it now you will save money in the long run and enjoy the pride of immediate ownership for the following reasons.

I am glad you said that, Dr. Ottander, because it gives me a chance to explain how our exclusive features enable the service to pay its own way and, in the end, to save you money.

"Your price is out of line"; "I can buy something like it for less money." Very few products are exactly the same. Your tasks are to avoid argument and to concentrate on differences that avoid direct comparisons.

I don't doubt your statement, Mr. Perrot, but let me ask you a question. Would you rather have a major operation performed by the best surgeon possible or shop around for the cheapest doctor? You will be happy and satisfied with our product because of the superior craftsmanship and quality materials that go into its manufacture. Here are some specific reasons why it will offer you satisfaction.

Probably you can, Mr. Winsaki, but I know the craftsmanship and the quality of the materials that go into our product. That knowledge gives me the confidence to say to you that our product offers you greater value for your money than does anything else on the market. It is a better buy because. . . .

"The cost is far over our budget allowance."   Show the buyer through facts and figures how your product will increase profits or cut costs and how much it could cost him not to have it.

Budgets are a problem, Mr. Zamil, but let me show you with facts and figures how a modest expenditure for our product now can increase profits for you within this budget year. Will you check these comparison figures with me to make sure I've estimated your costs accurately?

Two of your three local competitors have installed our service within the past year, Mr. Zamil. I have some comparison facts and figures here that may convince you that even a month's delay may put your firm at a competitive disadvantage because of that fact. Will you go over them with me now?

NO-INTEREST-OR-NEED OBJECTIONS

Second to price in order of difficulty for many new or inexperienced sales representatives is a series of objections that can be brought together in the "not-interested" or "I-don't-really-need-it-now" categories. Inability to handle these objections successfully over a period of time can become most frustrating because such inability signals failure on the part of the sales representative to create interest or to present convincing reasons why the prospect should buy now.

Here are some examples of such standard or common objections.

No interest	*No need*
"I'm not interested."	"I'm all stocked up at present."
"I want to look around some more before making a final decision."	"The equipment I have is still good."
"I'm just shopping or looking around."	"I'm satisfied with my present product and don't see any need to change."
"Your product doesn't appeal to me."	"I don't have any need [or room] for your line at this time."

Why Is the Prospect Not Interested?

If your prospect admits to a need, takes the time to listen to your proposal, and then voices some of the not-interested objections noted above, you have probably failed to arouse his interest. Some prospects do shop before buying however and do not like the idea of rushing into a buying situation, even though they may not admit it. Others merely use the objection as a defense mechanism against sales representatives, viewing them in general as high-pressure types out for a quick sale and nothing else.

The important thing for you is not to get discouraged at hearing such objections. Such prospects do not always mean what they say, and you can turn so many such objections into sales that it pays to keep trying as long as any chance for success exists.

You can often avoid this objection by asking during the qualifying part of the interview such questions as "Are you considering this for yourself or someone else?" "Are you considering this item for immediate purchase?" or "If we can offer you exactly what you want at the lowest possible price, are you prepared to make an immediate decision?"

Your first step in the face of such objections is to try to find out the reason for the prospect's lack of interest and to determine whether that reason is a valid one or a mere excuse. One technique is to appear to give up, to ask him purely as a matter of interest why your proposal really failed to arouse him. Then be prepared to keep selling if his objection turns out to be a mere excuse.

Well, Mr. Khayat, I just want you to know how much I have appreciated the opportunity to tell you about my product. Since you aren't interested in buying now, would you mind telling me as a matter of personal interest the real reason why you aren't interested [or why you want to look around some more or what you really object to about our proposal]?

If after this question or succeeding why questions you decide he is just a shopper and probably had no intention to buy in the first place, close the interview as quickly as possible and depart. If his objection really means that he is not interested now but will be later on, try to arrange for a future delivery (thus a sale) or at least a future appointment for another try. If a genuine objection is uncovered that can be handled on the spot, go back into a presentation of the benefits he will obtain by making an immediate, affirmative buying decision.

Why Does He Not Need the Product or Service?

We have stressed that objections are useful sales tools and should be welcomed as such. If a prospect says he does not need or have room for your product, you can cheerfully use that objection to point out why he does need it or should make room for it.

"I'm satisfied with what I have; why change?" is a commonly held attitude and standard objection. Too many sales representatives give up in the face of such statements, unaware that there are many valid and convincing answers. Why is he so satisfied with what he has? Maybe it is because he does not know enough about the differences in similar products or services to even be able to compare them intelligently.

Your approach to this objection, no matter what product or service is involved, may be (1) to point out constructive reasons why his current situation may not be completely satisfactory to him and (2) to show him something new or different so that he is able to visualize contrasts, make comparisons, and have the basis for making an intelligent choice.

A simplified example is this approach by an oil-heater sales representative to a prospect who says he is happy with his twenty-year-old coal-burning home heating unit.

Apart from the possible problem of dirty smoke, Mr. Bona, do you know how much money you could save by using a cleaner-burning, modern oil heater over a year? May I show you these cost comparisons between older coal-burning units such as yours and our modern oil heater? They will help you visualize how our heater can pay for itself in only five years.

If a store owner objects that he does not have room to carry your product, you can point out that your line moves better than other lines and could thus mean faster turnover and greater profits for him. You can dramatize by selecting a specific window, shelf, or counter and comparing the turnover and profit advantages if your product or line were on display there. When making this comparison, forget the competition and concentrate on the benefits offered by your proposal.

PRODUCT OBJECTIONS

Prospects can voice objections to your product or service in many different forms, as these examples illustrate.

Your product is too new [or untried].
Your product does not fit into our normal range of stock.
Your product has been on the market too long.
Your product is not well known.
There is no demand [or call] for your product.
I have heard reports of customers' having trouble with your product [or of dealers having trouble selling it].
Your product would cause too many servicing problems.
It's too complicated for my people to operate.
I doubt that it will do the job for me [or what is claimed for it].

In general, if this objection is voiced early in the interview, it very likely is nothing more than an excuse and can be handled by the pass-over (or pass-by) technique.

If voiced again during or after your presentation, it is a serious objection that may indicate a directly competitive situation. What the prospect may be asking for is proof or justification of the benefits you are offering him. In other words, he may want to be reassured that he will be making the right decision. Testimonials from satisfied users, orders from other companies, and other visual evidence offer more convincing proof than words alone do.

Here are some practical suggestions for handling certain categories of objections relating to products.

Too new or not well known. Every product was too new when it was first placed on the market. You can tell about and show proof of the market surveys and pretesting that went into preparing your product. Why would your company spend money developing and marketing it unless it expected it to gain customer acceptance? Show the advertising that will help make it well known, demonstrate it if possible, and stress benefits, value, quality, and performance.

Has been on the market too long; no demand for it. Knowledge of your own and of competing products is essential in handling this objection. If your product sells well elsewhere, then back this fact up with evidence from your sales kit and proof in the form of statistics or testimonials. Perhaps the prospect needs advice or help in marketing it properly. If so, you should be creative and resourceful in offering practical suggestions as to how to increase profitable turnover. Your own enthusiasm can rebuild his.

Not in our line. Diversification of merchandise in a few large outlets has been one of the most striking changes in modern retailing history. This trend has been especially strong in the United States and is rapidly extending all over the world. Major retail buyers have to keep abreast of new product lines or lose out to competition. Small-store owners in particular face great competitive problems. A new line can help attract new customers and enable old customers to buy more than they did before when visiting the store.

Rumors of trouble or dissatisfaction with it. Your first step is to find out whether the dissatisfaction is a fact or merely a rumor. If a fact, try to solve the problem or let the prospect know that the trouble was handled promptly and that all is well now. You can then secure agreement that misunderstandings can always occur but do not necessarily affect the validity of the proposal. Once he becomes open-minded, continue stressing benefits to him, especially the guarantees or follow-up servicing offered by both your company and you.

Doubts that it will offer what is claimed for it.   Make every effort to pin down specific objections and to discover whether they are valid doubts or mere excuses. Find out specifically why the prospect has such doubts; do not accept generalities. Once you uncover his specific reasons, convince him with proof that your product performs exactly as you claim. Compare it with competing products, show testimonial letters or other visual proof; offer to telephone satisfied users and let the prospect talk to them.

Too complicated.   Show him once again how easy your product is to operate once the procedure is mastered. Let him and also those who may be working with it in the future operate it themselves. Offer to help train operators as time permits, and stress the benefits it offers. Product knowledge, confidence, enthusiasm, and showmanship should easily dispel this objection.

COMPANY OR SOURCE-OF-SUPPLY OBJECTIONS

Many specific objections belong in this category. Some have to do with past problems in dealing with your company or former sales representatives in the area. Others concern convenient competitive warehouse facilities, which may offer fast delivery or follow-up servicing, or the size of your company. Other objections center around the fact that the prospect is currently buying somewhere else and for a variety of reasons is reluctant to change.

Perhaps the best way to illustrate these objections and to consider how to handle them is to break them down as is done below. In general, they are best handled during the interview with attentive consideration. If expressed initially they may be excuses; if voiced once more or later on they deserve serious attention.

"ABC Company can give me better and faster service because its warehouse is close by."   Close proximity of central warehousing does not necessarily lead to fast or good service. But you have to present both solid reasons and factual evidence to justify claims that your company can offer comparable or better service. Testimonials from customers in the same or equally distant areas, written guarantees, or dated invoices and delivery dockets offer convincing proof that your service can and will meet requirements.

"We have bought from ABC Company for years and are satisfied with its service."   Your prospect will never know whether he can get better service until he gives you a chance to prove it. One excellent appeal is to suggest that two satisfactory sources of supply are better than one and that he can only benefit from having two firms in friendly competition for his business. You can also point out that it is good business for him to make the wisest buying decision and to get the best products and prices from any source possible. Ask him outright for an initial order to give you a chance to prove your claims.

"I buy from ABC Company because I have a close friend [or relative] who works for them."   His first duty to himself or to his company is to get the best value and benefits money will buy. Apart from the value of the product itself, guarantees or assurances of efficient follow-up service should outweigh personal friendship. Loyalty to one's friends or relatives is an admirable trait, but surely his friends do not expect the prospect to continue buying from them if it is to his personal disadvantage or to that of his company. Your task is to show him how it is to his advantage to give you at least part of his business and thus a chance to prove your claims of superiority.

"We have more or less promised to buy from some other sales representative." No order is firm until it has been officially placed by the buyer and accepted by the seller. The buyer's first duty to his company or to himself is to make the best buy possible. If your product is new, is inexpensive, is suited to his needs, or offers other immediate benefits, it is only to his own advantage to act now.

"I prefer to buy from a big [or small] company." You should treat the size of your company as an asset. Smaller companies can often render better personal service than larger companies can, and they may be more specialized. Larger companies offer other advantages. In general, however, the size of the company does not count so much as the quality and reliability of the product and the reputation and service behind it.

"Your company [or former sales representative in the area] caused me a lot of problems in the past, and I don't want to deal with you." Your immediate task is to find out exactly what the past problems were and to correct them immediately if still pending. Beyond that, your best rebuttal is to ask the buyer to forgive and forget and to let you try to make up for past problems by superior future service and special personal attention to his needs.

STALLING OR PROCRASTINATION OBJECTIONS

Few things are more frustrating in selling than to make an enthusiastic presentation to an apparently interested prospect who, when asked for the order, makes one of the following replies.

> I'll have to think it over.
> I'm too busy to make a decision now.
> I must discuss it first with my wife [or husband or business associates].
> Leave your card and I'll get in touch with you.

This situation is frustrating because you apparently have not lost the sale, but you have not landed it either. The prospect usually does not need the extra time to make his decision. The objection may signify that he has not been completely convinced or still has some hidden objection or some personal misgivings which have not been brought to light.

Since he has not said, "No, I won't buy," you should not accept his statement at face value but should try for an immediate decision. In most cases, the prospect is just trying to postpone a decision he ought to make. If you let him postpone it, he probably will never get around to it and will finally forget it.

Such objections are usually mere stalls or procrastinations. You should view them as buying signals requiring a prompt, strong close. Here are some specific suggestions for handling such stalling objections.

"I'll have to think it over." Your task is to find out the reason for delaying the decision; your most effective word tool is a simple why: "Why do you have to think it over?" If it is a mere excuse, he may not be able to think of a good answer and may agree that there is no valid reason for delay. In such a case, ask him again for the order. A valid reason is an objection that has to be handled. If it appears to be the only objection blocking the sale, then use of the powerful boomerang technique may be most effective.

Prospect: I'll have to think it over because of the cost involved.

Sales Representative: It is only natural that you should feel that way, but in this period of rising prices, can you really afford not to consider buying now?

Another effective retort is this one.

Prospect: I'll have to think it over because of the cost involved.

Sales Representative: Aren't there really two things to think over: (1) Do you need and want it and (2) can you afford it?

Prospect: Yes, I guess so.

Sales Representative: You know just as well today as you would next month that you need and can use it, don't you?

Prospect: Yes.

Sales Representative: And don't you know today as well as you will a month from now whether you can afford to enjoy its benefits?

Prospect: Yes.

Unless a valid objection is advanced, the prospect's problem is probably the psychological one of hating to make the decision. Thus you may have either to make the decision for him or to help him over the psychological barrier. Here are some suggestions.

1. Appreciate his caution.   Agree with him that it is never wise to rush into things but reemphasize the benefits that can be his immediately if he decides now.

2. Offer special inducements for an immediate decision.   Perhaps you can throw in a bonus for an immediate decision in the form of merchandise, extended credit terms, or use of the buyer's name or name of his organization in a forth-coming advertising or promotional campaign.

3. Offer protection against risk.   Since he may have to justify his purchase decision to others, you can stress again the guarantees offered by your company plus your personal involvement in protecting his interests and making sure that follow-up matters are handled in a manner satisfactory to him.

4. Make him feel obligated to you.   This involves doing something for him or getting something of value into his possession so that he may feel obligated to you, even in a very small way. You may act very eager to help or agree to send things anyway until he can make his decision. In effect, you are acting as though he has already inwardly made an affirmative decision.

5. *Stress the satisfaction that comes from having made a sound decision.* People who dislike making decisions usually feel quite relieved and happy once they have done so. By pointing out the pleasure and satisfaction that follow a sound purchasing decision, you help the prospect to think positively beyond the immediate decision, which then becomes a minor or secondary consideration.

"I'm too busy to make a decision now." If he had time to listen to your presentation, this objection is usually a mere excuse or stall. Again use the word *why*—"Why can't you take the time to decide now?" Use the technique noted in the "I'll-think-it-over" section above and press for an immediate decision.

If it is a valid objection, do not waste his time, but fix a definite later appointment: "May I call back tomorrow at 10:20 A.M. to settle details, or would 2:30 P.M. be more convenient?" If he agrees, he has probably decided in your favor, and you should talk and act from then on under that assumption.

"I must discuss it with someone else." If you qualified the prospect properly and know he has the authority to buy, this objection may be a stall. It usually means that your prospect is basically sold; he is just avoiding an immediate decision. You must immediately seek to find out why he has to talk to someone else and exactly who this person (or group) is. Suggest that the other person be brought in immediately so that you can talk to him or that you be allowed to go to see him at once.

If another discussion has to take place—between husband and wife or buyer and other business associates—make every effort to be present yourself. If this is not allowed, then go over the key points of your proposal once again with your prospect to make sure he understands them well enough to present them convincingly to someone else. Then try to set a specific time limit: "May I call back at 10:30 A.M. tomorrow for your final decision, or would 2:45 in the afternoon be more convenient?"

"Leave your card, and I'll get in touch with you." This is a polite way of brushing you off. You have failed to sell him. It does not help to ask "When will you call?" or to try to pressure him with "our-special-offer-won't-last" tactics. Just accept the fact that you have failed to hold his interest or pinpoint his needs, and make a fresh start.

One technique for handling this situation is that useful one of apparently giving up, engaging him in conversation only, and then going back into your presentation.

Fine, Mr. Hang, but before I go, for my own information, what point in my proposal appealed to you most? And what did you find most objectionable? Your comments may enable me to help someone else with problems similar to yours. Will you help me out by giving me the benefit of your honest opinion?

CONSIDERATION OF SOME LESS COMMON OBJECTIONS

Many less common objections can spoil a sale. Some are mere excuses, some reflect prejudice or misunderstanding, others result from previous, unfavorable experiences with your or some other company. Here are a few such objections that may confront you. In general, you should strive to get your prospect to answer them himself before you do. Ask him why he considers it a problem. His talking about it will uncover any hidden objections, and as he talks he may provide an easy solution for you.

Credit problems.   Such objections, which are usually mere excuses, may have to do with past credit or payment problems or with the fact that your credit terms are too difficult to meet. Usually, they are the standard gripes your prospect voices to competitive sales representatives as well. He is merely trying to get the best bargain or the best terms. From his point of view, he has a lot to gain and nothing to lose by objecting to terms that you may be able to improve to his advantage if you want his business badly enough.

If he has a current credit problem with your company, try to resolve it immediately. If he has been refused credit before, assure him that the judgment was impersonal and that your company has to adhere to good business policies just as he does if in business or would do if he were a businessperson. Try to get the facts, absolve yourself of personal blame, and let him know exactly what the credit conditions and terms of your company are.

You can point out justifications for such policies and help him see the reasonableness of them from your point of view. If you are honest and constructive in your approach, he will respect your loyalty to your company. In such cases, successful selling of your company leads to a sale of its specific product or service as well.

Legal department review.   If the prospect objects that his legal department or his attorney must review the agreement first, (1) be sure no other objections are involved, and (2) write up the agreement and get his signature, based on a brief written-in contingency clause that the agreement is not to take effect until it has been approved by his legal advisors. In many cases this procedure will satisfy him, and he will tell you to go ahead and fill the order as it stands, confident that you will stand behind the claims made.

Consignment.   Selling on consignment is generally a bad practice simply because a customer does not have any incentive to push your product. Normally, if a businessman stocks two items, one on consignment and one which he is committed to pay for, he is inclined to push the one he is obligated to pay for. This reason for not selling on consignment may make good business sense to him and cause him to drop the objection. You may be able to offer extended credit or returns concessions that reduce the element of risk from his point of view just as well as outright consignment does. Stand firm on your policy, and sell benefits; his objection is just an excuse.

Second-hand one is cheaper.   A buyer gets what he pays for. New products usually offer guaranteed performance and a known, high trade-in. Second-hand items usually cost more in the long run; in most cases they are turned in or offered for resale because they proved unsatisfactory. You can best prove cost differences by using facts and figures based on your prospect's cost or operating figures.

Trade-ins.   Trade-ins are often an important factor in many sales, especially those of durable goods such as automobiles, machine tools, or household appliances. Many suggested list prices, such as those in the automobile field, have built-in, sliding trade-in allowances.

Most sales authorities concerned with this problem suggest the following techniques for handling trade-ins, recognizing that the prospect normally places a higher value on the older article than what it is worth.

1. Sell the new item first; avoid handling the trade-in until the prospect has been completely sold on the desirability and benefits of the new item.
2. Have the prospect place a value on the item before it is sent out for appraisal (hoping that it will be low).
3. Have the appraising done by a third or outside party when possible and outside the presence of the prospect (to avoid argument).
4. Try to make the final close on value and benefits of the new item, with the trade-in handled as a secondary, or minor, consideration.

If the prospect then strongly objects to the trade-in valuation, you simply have to persuade him through facts, figures, and comparisons that the valuation is realistic.

SUMMARY

In this chapter, we first discussed the strategies, tactics, psychology, and techniques involved in handling objections. Handling objections and closing the sale are the two greatest problems in selling for both new and experienced sales representatives. Thus, you must understand the principles and techniques of handling objections before attempting to master closing techniques.

Our discussion covered why objections are raised, what your attitude should be toward them, and how prior planning can help anticipate or forestall them. We covered both the broad strategy of and the six basic techniques for handling objections, concluding with a number of observations that should enable you, with practice, to handle them successfully.

We then extended the discussion to consider in detail techniques for handling specific objections, standard as well as less common ones. We elected to call objections questions wherever possible and pointed out five major classifications of standard or common objections: (1) price, (2) no interest or need, (3) product, (4) company or source of supply, and (5) stalling or procrastination.

The point was made that an objection often provides an opportunity to go into a trial close. Thus we have touched upon closing a sale already; we will cover that subject in depth in the following chapter. Before moving into that chapter, however, we should recall part of our opening statement in this chapter, since it relates so importantly to what we have been covering and what we will cover regarding objections and closing.

With only rare exceptions, you cannot close a sale as long as the prospect has any major objection or objections. Thus you have to understand the principles and techniques of handling objections before attempting to master closing techniques.

CHAPTER REVIEW

CONCEPTS TO REMEMBER*

_____ real objection	_____ hidden objections	_____ boomerang
_____ pass-over technique	_____ standard objections	technique
_____ yes-but technique	_____ forestalling	_____ buffer technique
	objections	_____ buying signals

*For memory reinforcement, fill in the page number or numbers where the terms were described in this chapter.

QUESTIONS FOR ANALYSIS AND DISCUSSION

1. What should your attitude be toward objections raised by your prospect?
2. Why are objections so important to sales representatives?
3. What should be the standard reaction of any sales representative to an objection?
4. If an objection appears truly important to your prospect, how should it be handled?
5. What objections, commonly raised, are for most sales representatives the most difficult to handle?
6. Why is it so vitally important for a sales representative to understand the principles and techniques of handling objections?
7. What is role-playing, and why is it especially useful in connection with handling objections?
8. Since price is bound to come up in almost every presentation, what is the first thing you should do about handling it?

Case Study 13–1

HOW ROLLS ROYCE WON THE MOST AGGRESSIVE POKER GAME IN AIRLINE HISTORY (PART I: HANDLING THE OBJECTIONS)

Spring 1968 was the time, Washington, D.C., the center of action; Friday, March 29, the day of decision. For a few insiders high in the British government and for executives of Rolls Royce, manufacturers of the famed Rolls aerojet engines, waiting in tense excitement, this was the end of one of the biggest sales gambles in British history.

On that Friday, the final buying decision was made, with the announcement that Lockheed Aircraft Corporation would purchase Rolls Royce jet engines for its TriStar airbus, that Rolls Royce already had orders worth $360 million in hand, and that the value of the deal with Lockheed would probably reach $2 billion within a decade. It was the biggest export sale in British history. As startled American industrialists began asking how they were outsold, the Rolls executives sank back in exhausted relief. For them it was the exciting end to an incredibly unorthodox sales presentation that had begun in 1966.

By that time, Rolls Royce had spent millions of dollars in research in an effort to reach their 1954 sales goal—a major engine order in a major American airframe for a major American airline. By 1966, even though 60 percent of U.S. commercial air carriers already used Rolls aerojet engines, the die was cast for the British. Failure to sell British engines for the future airbus might mean the end of Britain as a leader in the aerojet-engine field. From 1966 until the day before the decision, Rolls executives had made over 230 journeys to the United States, just to sell the RB211.

Rolls had only three major U.S. airframe manufacturers—Lockheed, McDonnell Douglas, and Boeing—to deal with on the airbus order. The first break for Rolls Royce came in September 1967, when Lockheed decided to choose among three contenders: Rolls Royce and two giant American firms—Pratt and Whitney, and

General Electric. With full support of the British government, Rolls Royce went about proving to Lockheed that the RB211 offered benefits and value.

Rolls Royce faced the problem of handling and overcoming three major objections:

1. Price
2. Performance and reliability
3. Strong American industrial and political pressure to buy American

The British set up headquarters in New York for an intensive sales campaign. As described in newspaper accounts, their sales representatives saturated the American market with a tidal wave of propaganda. The gold lettering on one black-bound folder stated, for example, "Reasons Why Eastern Airlines Should Choose the Rolls Royce RB211 Engine for the Advanced U.S. Tri-Jet" and went on to explain with text and graphs. The folders sent to each airline and airframe company could be piled two feet high. Rolls even went so far as to compile a full social and economic history of Britain since World War II. They circulated this information, too, among American aircraft executives. Nothing was spared to present the benefits and value of the RB211.

Price was in their favor from the start. The advantages of thrust operating economy and weight were fairly evenly distributed among the three engines, but the Rolls engine scored heavily on capital cost—$100,000 cheaper than that of General Electric and about two-thirds the price of that of Pratt and Whitney. At the end of November 1967 devaluation brought Rolls another bonus. Within ten days of devaluation they announced a considerable price cut. The price dropped to $2.5 million per TriStar aircraft set of three engines and associated equipment.

This comfortable price advantage coincided with increasing appreciation by U.S. airline executives that the Rolls engine was technically superior—lighter and more powerful—to the two American engines. This fact plus the price differential caused Pratt and Whitney to drop out of the picture. The contest was now between Rolls Royce and General Electric.

Lockheed was now in the driver's seat, and Rolls Royce had aroused its interest. A trial close was agreed to—a straight offset deal: Lockheed would guarantee purchase of 144 engines; Air Holdings Limited, a British company, would purchase 50 aircraft. This "off-set" deal offer was a vital element at this stage, countering competitors' arguments about the threat to the U.S. balance of payments.

What happened next in this exciting sequence of events? The rest of the story, from this crucial trial close through breathtaking, give-and-take political, financial, and economic decisions, is told in Case Study 14-2.

QUESTIONS FOR WRITTEN REPORTS OR CLASS DISCUSSION

1. What do you feel would have been the key issue to Lockheed as far as the three competing aerojet engines were concerned?
2. Was the Lockheed feeling of "I won't buy from you unless you buy from me" a valid objection or mere excuse? Could Rolls Royce have avoided giving anything away at this point?
3. What were some less common objections that could have marred this sale at any time?
4. How would you classify each of the three major objections handled by Rolls Royce?

SALES LITERATURE OFFERS CONVINCING REBUTTAL TO CUSTOMER QUESTIONS AND OBJECTIONS

Why are there so many different forms of sales literature? Are they all necessary? Are they useful in handling customer questions and objections?

Answers to the above questions are contained in an article in *Advertising and Sales Promotion* magazine,[2] which illustrates how effectively such materials can be used. The article asks us to picture an industrial sales representative making a call on a multidivisional industrial manufacturer. In abbreviated form, the interview goes like this.

Our sales representative sells industrial controls which can be used to make equipment and machinery operate automatically, thus more safely and efficiently. He has secured an appointment with Mr. Blunt, plant engineer, whom he has qualified as a prospect with both the authority to buy and a new maintenance appropriation.

He soon discovers that Blunt has a problem and asks for a complete run down on it. The problem is basically simple: A tank full of valuable chemicals in one corner of the plant either overflows or runs dry intermittently.

"What I need," says Blunt to the sales representative, as they both walk out into the plant to look at the tank, "is a control system to regulate the tank level."

After looking over the tank and asking Blunt some technical questions, our sales representative tells the engineer he will need a level controller and shows him a *specification sheet* describing the device. He then points out the features that make the controller especially applicable to Blunt's situation.

"Have you got something that shows it all hooked up?" asks Blunt.

The sales representative then produces an *application bulletin,* which diagrams a tank level-control system similar to the one Blunt needs.

After satisfying himself on several other points answered by the literature, Blunt asks about cost. The sales representative takes out a *price sheet* and quickly writes up a quotation with a complete price for the level-control system. Blunt takes the work sheet and literature copies and studies them for a moment, then scratches his head in thought.

"You know," he remarks, "now that I recall it, your competitor from the ABC Company sent me something in the mail the other day that looked just like this. How do I know yours is any better? I'll show it to you."

Back in the plant-engineering office, after rummaging around his paper-strewn desk top, Blunt produces an ABC *direct-mail piece* describing a new tank level-control system and hands it to our sales representative. After looking the piece over carefully to make sure what the devices in the system are like, the sales representative reaches into his briefcase and extracts a *product brochure* describing his level controller. Because the brochure had been a key item in the promotional campaign for the new product, it places *graphic emphasis* on the features of the device and the benefits of its use, with *copious illustrations* of typical applications, a *point-by-point comparison* with leading competitive level controllers, and a *condensed list of specifications.*

The sales representative now talks through the brochure with Blunt, patiently comparing his own product with the competitive ABC product and silently thanking

2. Theodore K. Thomas, "Sales Literature Does Many Jobs," *Advertising and Sales Promotion* (February 1968), pp. 39–40. Reprinted by permission.

his lucky stars that the competitor's message is only briefly outlined in the direct-mail piece, while he now has the advantage of a complete, well-organized *sales brochure* to sell from.

The brochure does the job; Blunt takes the sales representative's quotation, tosses the competitor's folder into the wastebasket, and phones his purchasing department for an order number. As he does so, our sales representative is thankful that he had planned the presentation carefully enough to bring along all sales literature necessary to visually answer questions and handle objections. He is also aware, once again, that the printed word, pictures, and charts are still among the most powerful and versatile of all sales tools.

QUESTIONS FOR WRITTEN REPORTS OR CLASS DISCUSSION

1. Did Blunt's questions pose objections of a business or personal nature? Explain your reasoning.
2. Could the sales representative have done anything to forestall the question of competition after he had written up his price quotation? If so, what?
3. What good, basic, overall strategy and psychology did the sales representative employ in facing and handling questions?
4. What three major questions or objections did Blunt raise during the presentation interview?

SALES PROBLEM 13–1

HOW TO HANDLE STALLING OBJECTIONS WITH A "SALES ANCHOR"

Professional sales representatives know the value of a "sales anchor" that is stored in their mind, ready for use at any time during a presentation, from the first few minutes on. The "anchor" sets up something they can later fall back on if they have trouble closing the sale. It is especially useful in handling stalling objections.

For example, a sales representative can anchor his prospect time after time with a simple question.

Prospect (voicing a stalling objection): "I'm sorry, but we've been doing business with XYZ Company for five years. I couldn't consider buying from your company right now."

Sales representative (replying with his "anchor" question): "Mr. Prospect, I would never expect an executive like yourself to change something good for the sake of change alone. But a good businessman welcomes a change for the better, isn't that right?"

Since the prospect nearly always answers with a "yes," the sales representative can at any time from then on remind the prospect in his own words that he "welcomes a change for the better." He can pick up his presentation at any point from that anchor and can secure—more often than not—at least a trial order.

QUESTION FOR WRITTEN REPORTS OR CLASS DISCUSSION

Prepare three additional "anchor" questions, suitable for any sales situation, similar to the one illustrated above.

---

how to close the sale

When you have mastered the content of this chapter, you should be able to:

Describe, from a business point of view, the chief justification
for the existence of a sales representative.
Analyze what is meant by the statement,
"a successful close starts in the sales representative's mind and manner."
Summarize three actions or "buying signals" on the part of the prospect that
indicate it is time to try for a close.
Summarize three points of the theory of multiple-close, or trial-close, technique.
Summarize what is meant by the statement,
"selling starts when the prospect says no."
Describe how and when to use the thirteen closing techniques.

We are now ready to tackle our moment of truth—the close! To *close* is to end or terminate something one has set out to do. From a sales point of view, closing means getting the prospect's verbal or signed agreement to buy the product or service offered.

All your planning and hard work and your careful presentation have had one purpose—to secure your prospect's agreement or "Yes, I'll buy." Your build-up to this single objective involves the use of logic, reason, emotion, and impulse. During one or several moments during the interview the prospect may be ready to buy. Even the most experienced sales representatives feel a thrill of excitement at the approach of these moments.

What can you do at such times to help your prospect over the hump—to change his possible wavering indecision into either a direct or an indirect "Yes, I'll buy"? Answering this question is the objective of this chapter.

CLOSING THE SALE IS THE CHIEF OBJECTIVE FOR A SALES REPRESENTATIVE

Closing the sale or getting the order is the justification for your existence as a sales representative. Getting the signed order is your job; it is what you are or will be paid to do!

Strange as it may seem, many so-called sales representatives never understand or accept this hard fact of business life and wander along getting by but costing their employer and the public who holds shares in the company untold dollars in wasted expenses and lost sales. Even sadder to contemplate is the valuable time that has been and will be wasted by busy industrial and business buyer's seeing sales representatives who fail to close properly. If you seriously aspire to sales success or aspire to reach management ranks through selling, you have to accept and act upon the assumption that, unless you close sales, you will not be successful.

Very few prospects volunteer orders; they have to be asked for their business! Mere asking is not enough however; you, as a sales representative, have to ask in such a way that you get a "Yes, I'll buy now," instead of a no, a stall, or a put-off. This problem poses one of the greatest challenges to both new and experienced sales representatives. It involves knowing when to close and how to close.

A SUCCESSFUL CLOSE STARTS IN YOUR MIND AND MANNER

When considering the mental attitude of your prospect in a closing situation, put yourself in his shoes for a moment; try to see things as he sees them. He is comparing the advantages of buying now with the disadvantages. Unless the advantages offer great appeal, his initial reaction is generally that of caution—to either refuse or postpone the decision.

From your point of view, you are there (1) to help the prospect make up his mind, (2) to convince him that he does need or want your product or service, and (3) to persuade him to take action now to acquire it. If you feel confident that your product offers value to him and are enthusiastic in your presentation of the benefits, you tend to act with confidence and enthusiasm. He senses your confident attitude, which has a positive effect on him. Conversely, any negative attitudes, any wavering, hesitation, or lack of force in your verbal expression, attitude, or manner have a negative effect. Thus you have a good chance of closing if you can create the proper psychological climate by being positive in attitude and speech and confident in manner.

This positive attitude on your part together with knowledge of the proper strategy, tactics, and techniques of closing will help overcome any fear of asking for the order—a fear quite common among new sales representatives especially.

WHEN DO YOU TRY TO CLOSE (BUYING SIGNALS)?

In the early days of sales analysis and training, much was made of the so-called single psychological moment during a presentation when the sale would either be made or be irrevocably lost. This older single-moment theory has long been discredited.

The modern concept of salesmanship holds that there are many situations or psychological moments during a sales interview when the prospect may be prepared to buy. The yes may come following any plausible, believable, compelling reason to buy now. Such a compelling reason may come after the approach or after any one of the selling points in your presentation or after you have successfully handled an objection. Your prospect may also feel compelled to buy after your complete presentation.

Many sales representatives make the mistake of not trying to close until they have completed their entire presentation and thus miss earlier opportunities. How do you know when to try for a close? Here are some guidelines.

Spoken words.   The prospect may ask the price or ask that you repeat details or ask about delivery time or give other verbal indications of interest to you or to a third party who may be present.

Facial expressions. A raised eyebrow, a nod, an interested look in your prospect's eyes may indicate a positive interest and readiness to say yes.

Physical actions. He may examine details of your demonstration model closely, or he may pick up your agreement form and start reading it carefully.

All these actions are buying signals that indicate or express interest on his part. Whenever you notice them, you should stop talking and go into a trial close. You should try to close any time and every time from the start of your presentation that the opportunity presents itself or can be created. Here are some clues as to when to go into a trial close.

1. After any major presentation point that appears to interest the prospect.
2. After handling any objection he has raised.
3. Any time he indicates interest by words, facial expressions, or physical actions.
4. At the conclusion of your presentation.

THEORY OF MULTIPLE-CLOSE, OR TRIAL-CLOSE, TECHNIQUE

The modern approach involves trying to close at every possible opportunity or at least testing the prospect's readiness through multiple, or trial, closes, sometimes called experimental or test closes. You thus make several attempts to close throughout the interview. You may not succeed on any one try, but you have lost nothing and can continue with the next point in your presentation.

Key points of this dynamic theory are (1) it is never too early to try for a close, (2) try for a close after each strong point, and (3) a negative reply to a trial close is never to be regarded as final but just as an invitation to continue selling.

PRACTICAL SUGGESTIONS FOR CLOSING

Avoiding Atmosphere of Pressure or Tension

Some prospects have an illogical, emotional fear of making a buying decision. This can cause trouble in closing situations unless possible problems are anticipated and avoided. Some prospects are so nervous about being sold something that they resent any attitudes, words, or actions that to them might indicate high-pressure tactics.

In such cases you may have to help your prospect make his decision. You try to help him by giving reasons why he should buy. This should be done carefully, so as not to increase the emotional tension he feels or ruffle him. Do this by stating specific facts or benefits as reasons for buying, and base your closing attempt on them rather than on any emotional pressure. Thus we can reemphasize that before closing you should know what the prospect wants to accomplish or what his desires are and should direct your presentation and closing remarks to satisfying his needs or desires.

For example, in selling a Volkswagen to a woman who seemingly has agreed to all the points but who now just can't emotionally make up her mind to buy, using price as a reason for hesitation, you can ask quietly, "Is price your only reason for not buying?" If she agrees, then show savings she can expect in maintenance and fuel costs. Such a review of benefits will show the price to be reasonable. Then try to close again by saying, "Wouldn't you like to own this truly economical Volkswagen?" Make it easy for her to say "yes."

Another way to handle this emotional situation is to say, "Take your time in thinking it over. I don't want you to buy this car if you are not really convinced that it is both reasonably priced and the type you want. Suppose you think it over tonight, and I'll hold it for you until noon tomorrow. May I telephone you at 10:00 A.M., or would 11:30 tomorrow morning be better?" Not only have you relieved her anxiety, but if she agrees to your hold and call, it means the sale is in effect closed.

Handling the Order Form or Agreement

The order form or agreement frightens some prospects and should ideally be brought out at the start of the presentation so they can get used to it. Possibly you can write on it during the interview without offending him. If you take it out early and find that it does offend him, you can put it in with other sales material so that it is readily available at the proper time.

Positioning Seating for Control

A practical suggestion is to try to seat yourself to the left of your prospect so that visual materials, calculations, or the order form or agreement is in his line of vision. This position also enables you to control both the presentation steps and the closing situation.

SELLING STARTS WHEN YOUR PROSPECT SAYS NO

Very few prospects are ready to buy when called upon—they have to be persuaded to do so. Their initial reluctance to buy is therefore natural and to be expected, and their negative replies to trial closings are nothing to become unduly alarmed about. It is easier for a prospect to say no than to say yes because it is a safer position.

Selling really begins when the prospect says no. People find it easier to say no than yes because it is safer. What they often mean however is "maybe," "tell me more," or "I'm not exactly sure I know what you mean." General Dwight Eisenhower said no many times before agreeing to run for president of the United States in 1952, and most big American automobile manufacturers initially said no to the idea of producing compact cars to compete against the Volkswagen and other small European and Japanese automobiles. In other words, a "no" does not necessarily mean what it says; your prospect can always change his mind. You as a sales representative come in here; it is your job to be a mind changer, to turn negative doubts into positive desires.

HOW TO CLOSE THE SALE: THIRTEEN TESTED TECHNIQUES

The literature of salesmanship contains more discussion about closing sales than about any other single topic. Many complete books have been written on the subject, especially on specific closing techniques.

Perhaps the best known author of such books is Charles B. Roth, an American sales consultant. Here are his four basic closing secrets.

1. Start your presentation on a closing action, continue it on a closing action, and end it on a closing action. In other words, close, close, close, all the time.
2. Make it easier for the buyer to say yes than no.
3. Have at least one closing action in reserve to use when everything else has failed.
4. Try once more. Even when it seems impossible to make a sale, go back for one more try.[1]

Most of the books and articles on closing name and describe from six to fifteen specific techniques. These have been researched, redefined, and, with new material added, regrouped into the following thirteen tested closing techniques. As you study these various techniques and put them into practice, you will find that some are easier to use and bring better results than others. You can never hope to close every sale, but mastery of these techniques is esseential to continued sales success.

1. Ask-for-the-Order (Direct-Question) Close

This is the simplest and often the most effective closing technique—a logical conclusion to the rational presentation in which no unusual objections are encountered. This technique is based on the assumption that your prospect will buy. After the facts have been presented, what could be more natural than to ask for the order in a straightforward manner: "How would you like me to handle your order?" or "Can you give me your purchase-order number now?"

Many sales representatives, amazingly enough, do not frankly ask for the order because of a hidden fear that, after the presentation has gone so well, the prospect will suddenly say no. However, you will never know until you ask for the order. Simply asking for it under favorable circumstances can often settle the question quickly and easily.

Although this direct-question technique is normally employed only in the simple and easy situation just described, you can also use it in some unusual situations. For example, if competitive products and prices are about the same and you feel that the prospect likes you as a person, you can simply ask: "Since all things are equal, Mr. Ungerer, will you give me the chance to handle this order for you?"

2. Assumptive (Presumption or Assumption or Possessive) Close

This simple yet effective technique is based on your assumption that the prospect is going to buy and that only the details need to be worked out. You make a statement that presupposes his buying, and if he agrees with it the sale is closed.

You can accomplish this close by word, as this example shows.

Sales Representative:	Don't you really feel, Mr. Horlick, that this offer is a good buy?
Prospect:	Yes, I do think it's worth the money.
Sales Representative:	(Using assumptive close): I am certain you will be satisfied with it. I'll mark you down for immediate delivery if that is all right?

1. Charles B. Roth, *My Lifetime Treasury of Selling Secrets* (Englewood Cliffs, N.J.: Prentice-Hall, Inc., 1957), p. 110.

Or you can accomplish it by a physical action.

Prospect:	Yes, I do think it's worth the money.
Sales Representative:	(Simply hands him a pen and points to the X beside the signature line on the agreement form, indicating, without saying a word, that he is to sign.)

Or you can use a combination of words and physical action.

Prospect:	Yes, I do think it's worth the money.
Sales Representative:	(Handling the pen and pointing to the order form): If you will just OK this agreement with your signature by the X here, I'll mark you down for immediate delivery.

The psychology behind this close is that it is easier to get tacit approval than to get a specific yes. With this technique a nod, a grunt, or even silence signifies agreement. In effect, you are asking the prospect to stop or to deny your positive, confident action—a smooth-flowing, logical development of your yes-building steps of the presentation. If he does not stop you, then you have his approval, and the sale is made.

You do not offend your prospect if you go smoothly into this close following a positive statement. Do not use it after a strong objection or not-interested comment until that has been properly handled and positive agreement reached. He knows you are there to try to close a sale, and if you smoothly conclude it in this way he is in agreement with your words or actions.

If he objects he will tell you so and you can back off and start on another selling point for which you seek agreement. Then try this closing technique again or one similar to it, such as the minor-point technique, or a totally different one.

When the order form is introduced from the start and the sales representative writes upon it throughout the interview as a record, this assumption technique is of course being used powerfully.

You can soften this closing technique by using a few cushion words that further reduce chances of your prospect's getting the feeling that he is being nudged into a close. For example, the sales representative in our illustration might have said, "Assuming that you want me to mark you down for immediate delivery, may I have your OK by the X here on the agreement?"

This assumptive close is one of the easiest and most effective of all closing techniques if used at the proper time—following agreement to a positive statement or even following an affirmative silence after such a statement. It suits all types of selling and all sales personalities.

3. Minor-Point (Alternative or Choice-Technique or Minor-Issue or Double-Question) Close

This technique is especially suited to the vacillating prospect or to the one who honestly fears making a final decision. It involves passing over the big decision and asking him to make a choice between two minor issues. Making that easier decision implies an affirmative decision. For example, "I assume you like this item, Mr. Benincasa; would you prefer to save 2 percent by paying cash or would convenient, extended payment terms suit you better?" The attention of the prospect is thus drawn to a decision between cash or charge—a much easier decision to make than one on the object itself. The cushion "I assume" helps soften the effect. A hard but acceptable lead-in may also be "Do you want to pay cash and save 2 percent or charge it?"

The minor-point close is a modification of the assumptive close discussed previously in that it too involves an assumption on your part that the prospect is going to buy. Your aims are to secure his agreement to a positive sales point or statement, to assume he is going to buy, and then to offer him a choice between two minor alternatives, such as guarantees, dates of delivery, models, or color.

Would you prefer one-year payment terms or twenty-four months?
Would you like the agreement shown in your name or jointly with your wife?
Would you like shipment made here or to your overseas branch office?

Whichever choice the prospect makes, the sale is closed. If he refuses to make the choice, then you merely continue with the presentation.

4. Continued-Affirmative (Yes-Building or Continuous-Yes) Close

Some prospects apparently agree with all the major points of your presentation yet do not give final approval. They can often be closed with a rapid, enthusiastic, logical, yes-building summary of major issues from their point of view. The psychology of this approach is that a series of yes answers leads to a final, easy yes answer that brings the sale to a close.

Sales Representative:	If I am correct, you are most impressed with the quality and durability it offers in view of the reasonable price. Is that true?
Prospect:	Yes, those are the features that appeal to me.
Sales Representative:	In considering this proposal then, Mr. Cole, don't you feel that it offers real value?
Prospect:	Yes, I believe it does.
Sales Representative:	And don't you agree our payment terms are reasonable?
Prospect:	Yes, they seem to be.
Sales Representative:	Would you like to have delivery next Tuesday if it can be arranged?
Prospect:	Yes, that will be satisfactory.

5. Narrowing-the-Choice (Choice) Close

In many types of selling the prospect faces such a bewildering array of choices that he finds it difficult to make a decision. Consider this problem in a retail situation: a bewildered man trying to select a necktie from a wide assortment of colors and fabrics; or a perplexed woman seated before the store mirror, trying on one new spring hat after another from the nearby large collection of bright colors and styles. The situation in many American automobile showrooms is somewhat the same: selecting the brand (Ford, Chevrolet, Plymouth) is only a start; then come the various styles, models, price ranges, accessories, and color choices.

The sales representative can often bring a rapid close in such cases by helping narrow the choices, putting the items rejected, insofar as possible, out of sight and out of mind as decisions are made.

Do you prefer bright or dark colors?
Would your wife like this color best or that?
Any of these three would suit you. Am I right?
Don't you really like this one best?

This same situation can often occur as well with intangibles, such as life insurance or mutual-investment funds, when a wide variety of programs or plans is offered. The sales representative can help narrow the choice in such situations by offering a specific plan for the protection or investments desired or by determining the size of yearly or monthly premiums or payments. Proper use of this technique, especially in such technical areas as insurance or securities, not only helps close the sale but also offers guidance and service to the prospect. And, when the prospect has made his final choice, he has, in effect, given approval to your proposal.

6. Narrative (Report-Technique) Close

You can often restate closing points most convincingly in the form of a narrative or story that points to a situation similar to that of your prospect. Since we all like to profit or learn from the mistakes of others, this seemingly neutral approach can often be more effective than your personal sales summation.

The purpose of the story is to tactfully drive home the point that your prospect would be unwise to delay his decision. By pointing out the benefit gained by another who bought in similar circumstances or the loss suffered by one who failed to act, you help your prospect get the message.

Such narratives should sound plausible and not made up, yet it is not necessary to give names. Not using names often makes it easy for your prospect to picture himself in the described situation.

Here is how an insurance sales representative may employ the narrative closing technique.

Prospect: Your protection plan sounds good; but I'll have to think it over.

Sales Representative: I respect your thoughtful attitude, Mr. Wilkens, but sometimes it pays to act now. Just last month, for example, a gentleman in nearby Oakdale considered a $20,000 life insurance plan similar to this. He didn't have a lot of ready cash, but I helped him work out a convenient payment plan. One week later, just seven days exactly, he was killed in an automobile accident. He had paid only $100 into the plan.

The $20,000 from the policy he had just taken out one week, seven days to the day, earlier will enable his wife and two children to get along without her having to work. Don't you owe it to your wife and family to act now and to give them the same immediate protection?

---

7. Follow-the-Leader (Testimonial or Bandwagon) Close

Nothing succeeds like success, and this simple yet effective closing technique basically follows that line of reasoning. By looking over the biggest list possible of recent (and, through proof or implication, satisfied) buyers, your prospect, not wanting to miss out on a good thing, also gains the confidence or conviction to go along with the others.

When using this technique, cite by name those buyers who by sheer size or importance rate highly in your prospect's opinion. Apart from a list of these important trend-setting buyers, a lengthy list of recent buyers can often impress him. Showing copies of orders from your own book is convincing proof of your claims. Testimonial letters from recent buyers, citing impressive resales or performance results, offer further persuasive proof.

8. Summary (Balance-Sheet or Tip-the-Scale or T-Account or Build-up) Close

This technique can either be the simple one of holding up a finger for each major point or reason for buying, along with a verbal summary, or writing them briefly down in front of the prospect. Like a lawyer summing up the logical points of proof in a courtroom case, yet much more informally, you strive to build up a convincing list of reasons why the prospect should act now to obtain the benefits offered. This rapid summary or resume of points in which he seems most interested, when presented in a logical and enthusiastic manner, should build up in importance to the point that has the greatest appeal. You can tie in this build-up summary with any one of the other closing techniques to secure final assent.

The simple T-account of the sort shown in Figure 14.1 appeals especially to the rational business or industrial buyer accustomed to balance-sheet, asset-and-liability, profit-and-loss thinking. Needless to say, your list of reasons to act should be far longer and more impressive than the list of reasons not to act! A suggested close is "In view of these impressive facts, Mr. Parr, is there any reason not to act now?"

FIGURE 14.1   Example of a Simple T-Account Summary Often Written in Front of a Prospect in Closing Situation

Reasons not to act	Reasons to act
1. Budget problems 2. Must consult with others	1. Will save $1,000-per-year operating costs 2. Will do the job better and faster 3. Is easier for unskilled employee to operate 4. Can get immediate delivery if ordered now 5. Can save $300 by buying at special introductory price until the end of this month

9. Question (Why-Not or Doubt-Eliminating) Close

The purpose of this technique is to uncover any doubt that may be holding up a final affirmative decision. Acting as if and assuming that the prospect is going to buy you ask him in a straightforward manner what reasons, if any, he has for not acting now. Your question may be, "What have I failed to make clear that keeps you from acting now?" or "You seem to be hesitating, Mr. Easter; what is the reason?" His reply determines your course of action. You may elect to use his objection as the reason for buying now through employment of the trap, or boomerang technique, or you may use any one of the other closing techniques.

10. Surprise (New-Angle or Hat-Trick or Conquer-by-Yielding) Close

We noted earlier the importance of keeping at least one strong sales point up your sleeve for emergency use. The necessity of having that reserve ammunition becomes apparent as we consider this last-resort closing technique, to be employed only after all others have failed.

Some tough or sophisticated prospects refuse to be swayed by logical or emotional arguments. They do not offer any objections but just try to put you off with an "I'll have to think it over." They may really want to buy but for some reason do not want to give in to you.

In order to avoid a personal or emotional situation in which they may say no because of your insistence on bringing the issue to a close, you can appear to quit trying. By apparently giving up, or quitting, you relax their guard; they have the emotional satisfaction of thinking they have won a minor victory over you. This satisfaction switches their thoughts from resistance to the true picture of your proposal and its benefits to them.

Words such as, "Well, thank you for your time and attention, Mr. Lambert" or actions such as picking up your papers or even standing up indicate that you have given up trying to close the sale and are ready to depart, the prospect, sensing that you have quit trying to sell him, relaxes.

Sales Representative:	(Speaking casually): By the way, Mr. Lambert, before I leave, I wonder whether I could ask you one more question.
Prospect:	(Relaxed and happy to oblige): "Why, certainly, go right ahead.
Sales Representative:	(Bringing up an entirely new sales point): I almost overlooked a very important point in our guarantee. It provides free inspection and minor repair service for a whole year. Here is how it saves you up to $50 per year." (Goes back into this new sales point, around which he attempts another closing.)

The defenses of your prospect are down because he thought you were departing; his poise and self-assurance are shaken as you go after him with a new sales point. If it is a strong and convincing one, it can swing his put-off into a reason for acting now.

11. Emotional (Appeal-to-Pride, etc., or Fear) Close

As we have noted previously, the two most important factors in buying are the desire for gain and the fear of loss. Thus the final decision to buy now is based largely on impulse or emotion rather than on logic or reason. This closing technique appeals specifically to the emotions, such as pride, thrift, or prestige. It is normally used in a positive manner ("Wouldn't it feel good to be seen driving this powerful new car?") but can also be used in a negative sense in some types of selling. An insurance salesman, for example, may appeal to fear ("Have you considered your wife's situation if you pass away without any insurance protection?"). It is normally employed after a careful build-up to help certain slow-moving prospects make their final decisions.

The emotional close works most effectively with certain prospects—women home buyers, for example—and in certain types of selling, such as insurance. It is not an effective technique for selling machine tools to industrial buyers. Our previously mentioned man looking at new ties or woman looking at new spring hats may not need or even want one. But they can be moved to an impulse buying decision by a sales representative's emotional appeals, such as "It will make you feel good to wear it," "You will be in step with fashion," or "The color suits you."

A dramatic, emotional story to illustrate a closing point can be a powerful psychological weapon for an experienced sales representative facing certain susceptible prospects. As such, it should be used with care and with the highest ethical considerations. Especially when built around fear, these closes are last-resort techniques. They should ethically be used only when the prospect needs the benefits, can afford them, and has no real or valid objections.

12. Boomerang (Trap or Closing-on-the-Objection or Closing-on-Resistance) Close

As discussed earlier this technique involves turning the prospect's major objection for not buying into the reason why he should buy now. It is normally reserved as the most powerful last-resort technique for handling the final objection that seems to be blocking the sale. It is especially effective in meeting objections not strongly backed by facts or reasons. Ideally you should soften it by smiling and looking friendly.

Prospect:	I can't afford it now.
Sales Representative:	You really can't afford not to buy it now at this special, low introductory price. If I can offer acceptable payment terms, is there any reason not to act now?

13. Inducement (Standing-Room-Only or Inciter or Concession or Last-Chance) Close

In some cases an extra push is necessary to secure final agreement. You may be able to offer a special concession as inducement for an immediate affirmative decision. This closing technique is effective in final appeals to the two major factors that move prospects to action: (1) the desire for gain—"If you'll take it now, as a favor I'll phone our shipping department to deliver it tomorrow. Would you like that?"—or (2) the fear of loss—"Unless you decide now, I can't guarantee delivery for ninety days at least."

Many inducements urge the prospect to buy now: special extended credit terms, advertising allowances, seasonal packaging, an extra bonus, cash discounts (ethical, legal, and industry codes permitting), or other offers.

Usually you should hold this easy-to-use technique in reserve. A danger in using it is that a sharp trader may sense eagerness on your part and hold out for additional concessions.

SUMMARY

We have covered in this chapter the basic strategy, tactics, and techniques of closing the sale. Closing, or getting a verbal or signed agreement to buy, is the basic objective of every sales representative and the chief justification for his existence from a business viewpoint. We noted that the psychological climate for a successful close starts in the mind (having a positive attitude) and manner (being confident) of the sales representative.

We posed the question of when to try to close. The answer was basically close early, close often, close late. We discussed buying signals as clues to when to close; they involve spoken words, facial expressions, and physical action. Trial closes are part of the multiple-close theory of trying to close often throughout the interview. We offered some practical suggestions for making the physical and emotional setting conducive to successful closing.

We agreed that selling starts when the prospect says no or "not interested now"; such negative expressions not only should be expected but also should be considered as invitations to continue selling. In conclusion, we presented thirteen tested closing methods or techniques.

This now concludes our Part IV section on Working the Plan: Steps in the Selling Process. In Part V to follow we shall consider after-sale follow through and some applications of the principles we have been discussing in Part IV to some specialized areas of selling.

CHAPTER REVIEW

CONCEPTS TO REMEMBER*

_____ buying signals   _____ closing action   _____ bandwagon close
_____ trial close   _____ assumptive close   _____ technique of last
_____ high pressure   _____ physical action   resort
_____ agreement form

*For memory reinforcement, fill in the page number or numbers where the terms were described in this chapter.

QUESTIONS FOR ANALYSIS AND DISCUSSION

1. From a business point of view, what is the chief justification for the existence of a sales representative?
2. What does modern sales theory have to say about the so-called single psychological moment for the close during a sales presentation?
3. At what point during a presentation should a sales representative try to close?
4. Why was the statement made in this chapter that closing techniques should be built around yes-building questions?
5. In cases where a prospect apparently wants to buy but emotionally cannot bring himself to say "yes," what can an empathic sales representative do to help him decide?
6. What do we mean by the statement "selling starts when your prospect says no?"
7. What is the simplest and most-often effective closing technique any sales representative can use?
8. The minor-point closing technique is especially suited to the vacillating prospect or to the one who honestly fears making a final decision. What does it involve?

VOLKSWAGEN STRESSES THE GENTLE-BUT-FIRM APPROACH TO A SATISFACTORY BUYING DECISION

The point in our chapter 10 case study, "The Volkswagen Low-Pressure Approach to Selling," was that success comes not from pushing the prospect to buy but from leading or helping him, gently but firmly, to a satisfactory buying decision based on his best needs.

Two steps advanced by VW to use in leading up to this closing situation are (1) gauging the prospect's readiness to buy and (2) properly timing the closing. Let us examine in detail what VW means by these statements.

Gauging the prospect's readiness to buy means that you continue to qualify his interest by questions or statements that help measure it: (1) Ask open-end questions, such as "How do you like the car, so far?" or "Why do you want to wait until June to buy?" Such questions do not allow a yes or no answer. Instead, they encourage the prospect to reveal his true feelings. (2) Paraphrase or summarize his remarks, carrying them a little beyond what he intended.

Prospect:	Since there are only three of us in my family, I guess the sedan is big enough.
Sales Representative:	I see, then you feel that space is really no problem for your family?
Prospect:	(Explaining further): Well, I didn't exactly mean it was no problem. We plan on having another child someday, and then, too, we usually take my mother-in-law for a ride on Sundays.

By paraphrasing the prospect's statement and stretching it a little you have gained valid information and uncovered a true objection hidden from you in the first statement. (3) Ask "if" questions instead of direct ones, such as "If you buy a VW, you will save money, won't you?" The prospect feels comfortable answering since he can respond without committing himself. His response is thus usually free and candid.

Properly timing the closing involves both careful listening and skill in employment. You want to lead the prospect gently but firmly into a close but do not want him to feel you are interested only in making the sale and not in helping him. Careful listening involves catching key phrases that represent green lights or go-ahead signals for the close. These include: (1) Questions, such as "What color interior is available with a blue car?" "How much would payments be?" "If I buy, when could I get delivery?" "How much could I get in trade-in on my old car?" and (2) Statements of agreement, such as "It's a nice car!" "The VW is more economical than a big car!" "It's easier to drive than I thought!" "It probably would be a good second car!" "Yes, I can see the quality!"

Skill in employing closing techniques concerns the close used, which depends on the circumstances. One such technique (among many) is to use a question similar to an "if" question. For example: (1) "Mr. Lyon, you seem to like the blue and the beige sedans; which would you want?" (2) "We've looked at the sedan and the sun-roof models; which one would you want?" The conditional "would you want" is less direct than "do you want" and allows the prospect more freedom to answer. A trial close using this phrase may not always evoke a positive response, but it is often successful and does not make the prospect feel pinned down.

QUESTIONS FOR WRITTEN REPORTS OR CLASS DISCUSSION

1. What is the major purpose behind the VW gentle-but-firm lead-up to the closing situation?
2. From a sales point of view, what three major aims are behind all the VW sales representative's words and actions as he leads into the closing situation?
3. In the above VW statements, attention was given to listening for and acting upon certain words that are go-ahead or buying signals. What two other types of buying signals should the VW sales representative be alert to?
4. The last paragraph of the VW suggestions mentioned a trial close. What is a trial close, and when can or should it be employed during a sales presentation?

Case Study 14–2

HOW ROLLS ROYCE WON THE MOST AGGRESSIVE POKER GAME IN AIRLINE HISTORY (PART II: A SUPER CLOSE WINS THE SUPER ORDER)

An initial $360 million engine order is undoubtedly a super order, and Rolls Royce, after successfully handling the Lockheed objections regarding price and performance, seemed close to selling their RB211 aerojet engine by early February 1968. After all, a trial close had been agreed to, and seemingly all that remained was to secure the approval of the U.S. government.

As a last-ditch measure General Electric threw in a heavy price cut, but Rolls Royce matched it, bringing the price down to $2.5 million per engine set at the end of February. This cut seemed to increase chances of success, except for one seldom-talked-about but very real inwardly felt American objection. That objection—always hovering in the background—was "Why buy a foreign-made jet engine when American-made ones are virtually the same?"

The buy-American objection soon came to the surface. With hints of British-government subsidy and threats of U.S. unemployment, Republican Congressman Robert Taft played the last General Electric card. Taft claimed that buying Rolls would, by 1980, produce an additional $6,000 million deficit—half for engines and half for parts—and that award of the contract to foreigners would leave thousands of Americans unemployed. Taft's outburst of patriotism on the floor of Congress won a good deal of sympathy but failed.

An economy call by President Lyndon Johnson brought more doubts. These doubts were shrugged off however because of an understanding reached in 1967 by the British ambassador, Sir Patrick Dean, and the State Department that no political strings were attached to the purchase at all. The U.S. government treated the sale as a purely commercial matter.

There were doubts and jitters until the very end, but the high-level British lobbying in Washington, D.C., paid off and the sale was closed.

Was this sale of value to both sides? Certainly it was to Rolls Royce and to Lockheed, but what about the two governments concerned and their citizens? Was the sale of value to both the British and the American people?

Lockheed, with many firm advance-orders in hand, believes the potential market for all airbus-type aircraft will be at least 1,000 by 1980. Rolls Royce believes that its share of the engine market for these could earn it total orders of around $2,500 million, save the British aero-engine industry, and greatly contribute toward stabilizing the pound sterling. Thus the sale was of utmost economic importance to the entire British nation.

Although Britain obtained $360 million initially from the Lockheed purchase of Rolls engines, the U.S. balance-of-payments deficit would be more than offset by the British purchase of fifty aircraft through a company called Air Holdings. This purchase would in turn leave Britain with a deficit of $390 million, which would be more than offset after Air Holdings resold the planes to foreign airlines. These sales would be possible because of an agreement that Lockheed would sell to foreign airlines in lots of only five or ten units, thus protecting Air Holdings for small orders of one, two, or three units.

This super sale of a super-sized order was of mutual benefit to both the British and the American people as well as to Lockheed and Rolls Royce.

QUESTIONS FOR WRITTEN REPORTS OR CLASS DISCUSSION

1. Was there a psychological moment prior to the final decision in April when Lockheed seemed ready to buy? If so, at what stage of the presentation did it occur, and why was the sale not closed then?
2. Which of the closing techniques studied in this chapter seems to be the closing Rolls Royce was trying to make? Why?
3. Did Rolls Royce at any point attempt an inducement close? If so, at what point or points in their long presentation did they do so?
4. Congressman Taft's emotional appeal before Congress represented a third-party situation. How did Rolls Royce handle it?

HOW TO LOSE A SALE—HOW TO CLOSE A SALE: SELLING A MAN STOCKINGS FOR HIS WIFE[2]

Scene Number 1

Clerk (yawning): "Are you being waited on?"

Customer: "My wife needs some stockings. Can I look at some?"

Clerk: "Sure, what size does she take?"

Customer: "I really don't know."

Clerk: "Is her foot as large as yours?"

Customer: "No, only about two-thirds."

Clerk: "Then she will take size 10. Here's a swell pair for $2.00."

Customer: "Haven't you anything cheaper?"

Clerk: "Sure, here's some for $1.50."

Customer: "What's the difference?"

Clerk: "Fifty cents difference; but all we girls wear the $1.50 ones and we like them."

Customer: "Well, give me the $1.50 pair."

Clerk: "Why not be generous and buy her two pairs?"

Customer: "Nope, just one, hurry."

Clerk: "But my sales book is low today and I need some sales!"

Customer (walking away in disgust): "I'll come back some other time."

Scene Number 2

Clerk: (Smiling and alert) "Good Morning."

Customer: "Good morning." (Looks at stockings on counter.)

Clerk: "They are lovely stockings, aren't they?"

Customer: "Yes, my wife asked me to buy her a pair."

Clerk: "What size stocking does your wife wear, sir?"

Customer: "Oh! She forgot to tell me."

Clerk: "Then I'll give you 9½; that's the average size. Here is a very fine pair."

Customer: "How much are they?"

Clerk: "They are $2.00."

Customer: "Hm, do you have anything cheaper?"

Clerk: "Yes, sir, these are $1.50."

Customer: "What is the *difference* between the $1.50 and $2.00 stockings?"

Clerk: "The $2.00 pair will give your wife *more miles* of service!"

Customer: *"More miles of service!* Well, that's what she needs; she's always walking them out. I'll take a pair."

Clerk: "Does one of your wife's stockings wear out *before* the other?"

Customer: "Indeed it does. She's always tearing one and throwing the other away."

Clerk: "Wouldn't it be *good business* to buy two pair of the same color, so she can *alternate* if one stocking tears or runs?"

Customer: "Say, that *is* good business! I'll take two pair."

Clerk: "We have a special on this week for the $2.00 stockings — three pairs for $5.45. You can have the third pair for only $1.45. You save 55¢, the price of two good cigars with tax."

Customer: "I'll take three pairs — anything to save money." (Departs thinking — "Nice salespeople in this store. They are really helpful.")

QUESTION FOR WRITTEN REPORTS OR CLASS DISCUSSION

What is your opinion of the salesmanship involved on the part of the two sales-clerks? What principles and techniques of selling and closing are illustrated that apply to any sales presentation situation?

2. These scenes adapted from Elmer Wheeler, *Tested Sentences That Sell,* (Englewood Cliffs, N.J.: Prentice-Hall, Inc., 1962), pp. 158–159.

PART V

AFTER-SALE FOLLOW-THROUGH AND SPECIAL APPLICATIONS

15
the follow-up
and follow-through

When you have mastered the content of this chapter, you should be able to:

Describe how to properly depart from the customer after closing the sale, or from the prospect after failing to close.

Describe proper follow-up or follow-through steps to take to obtain the following: (1) a closed sale, and (2) one you failed to close.

List self-analysis questions to ask yourself after trying hard but failing to close a sale, in order to uncover clues that might help you succeed on future calls.

Summarize three major reasons why it is normally to a sales representative's advantage to ensure a customer's continued satisfaction with his purchase by proper after-sale follow-through.

The final close has been made; the sale has been either won or lost. What do you do now? How do you manage a proper departure, whatever the decision? Can you take any action now that will increase the effectiveness of a successful close? If the sale was lost, can you take any steps now to set the stage for a callback during which you can make a sale?

A professional sales representative never quits selling, so this is no time to relax. Whatever the decision, you now have to face these questions and to take whatever action is necessary to turn the situation to your present or future advantage if at all possible.

IS THIS JUST-CONCLUDED PRESENTATION ALL THERE IS?

In some types of selling, especially in the direct or specialty fields, you will never see the customer or prospect again. If the one-shot sale is made, your only task is to get on as quickly as possible to the next prospect once you have seen that delivery is made and payment is collected. If you failed to make the sale in such areas of selling, you merely make a quick and friendly exit and do not attempt a follow-up. Statistics show that the percentage of sales that may be closed on call-backs is very small compared to the much higher sales-close possibilities from calling on new, or first-time, prospects. If you are engaged in such selling areas, the experience, training, and policies of your company dictate your decisions at this time.

In most types of selling however, you can often turn even a lost sale to future advantage or repeat business. And, if you have closed the sale, you can use these final moments to set the stage for referral leads and possible reorders. We will address our thinking during the remainder of this chapter to this common sales situation, as we consider the following points.

1. How to depart after the close—win or lose.
2. Proper follow-up after landing the order.
3. Proper follow-up after losing the sale.
4. Follow-through for repeat business following a successful close.
5. Follow-through that may turn lost sales into future business.
6. Practical steps for efficient follow-through.
7. Special problems with follow-up and follow-through.

HOW TO DEPART AFTER THE CLOSE—WIN OR LOSE

Proper Departure after a Successful Close

For many inexperienced sales representatives, the period immediately following the signing of the order can be awkward. Some feel the inward exhilaration of victory. Others fear that their new customer may suddenly change his mind, and they want only to get away from the scene as quickly as possible so he cannot. Still others feel merely a sense of relief and are eager to go on to their next call without delay.

Professional sales representatives, however, use this opportunity to sincerely and naturally thank the customer for his time and business. Their words and attitudes, as expressed in actions and manner, can do much to assure that the sale stays closed and to set the stage for reorders.

Since time is valuable to both you and your customer, (1) thank him for the order, (2) settle any last-minute questions regarding delivery and follow-up service, and (3) assure him of your availability for answering questions and following up if necessary. By so doing you reassure him that he has made a wise decision.

You should do this naturally in a relaxed manner and then depart as quickly as possible. Do not make the mistake of staying for a chat and thus prolonging the interview unless your customer indicates that he would like you to do so. It is up to you to rise or to make other moves toward prompt yet relaxed and friendly departure.

Proper Departure after Failing to Close

The same procedure holds if you fail to get the order. Your aim is to thank the prospect for his time, to lay the groundwork for callbacks if you feel they would be worthwhile, and to depart promptly without appearing to rush.

Certainly, loss of a sale should not lead to any feeling of defeat or to sour grapes on your part. On the contrary, failure to get the order imposes some professional obligations. You should leave the prospect with the impression that his time has not been wasted by giving him one or more good ideas that will be valuable to him or at least by leaving him better informed.

You should also use this opportunity to leave him with a favorable image of you, your company, and sales representatives in general. And you should ask him for names of any friends or business acquaintances who he feels may be interested in your proposal. Perhaps he will write an introduction for you or even call them on the spot.

In effect, your words and actions at the point of departure, whether you close the sale or not, are the first steps of the follow-up and follow-through process.

PROPER FOLLOW-UP AFTER LANDING THE ORDER

Follow-up or follow-through is pursuing an initial effort through supplementary action. Proper follow-up is especially important after making the sale since it is your obligation to ensure prompt delivery, to see that any initial installation and operation is satisfactory, and to ascertain that the customer is completely satisfied in every possible way.

To a true sales representative, a sale does not end when the order is signed; the ultimate aim is to have a satisfied customer or user. Achieving this goal involves giving follow-up service to make certain he is satisfied and is secure in the knowledge that the sales representative is trying to take care of him and has his best interests at heart.

What kind of follow-up steps can you take after the order is signed to provide proper service and customer satisfaction? What will you each gain as a result of the time and effort spent in ensuring complete satisfaction? Here are a few concrete suggestions.

Give a warm and sincere thank-you.   This involves not only the immediate thank-you after the successful closing of the sale but also follow-up expressions of appreciation. A handwritten postcard or letter, a phone call, or a formal thank-you letter from your office a day or so after the sale makes your appreciation stand out.

Check delivery.   The best way to do this is through a phone call; the best time to do it, the day of delivery. Such follow-up action not only assures you that delivery was made in a satisfactory manner but also shows the customer that you care. If any damage occurred in shipment or if other problems have arisen, your phone call assures him that you will take prompt, personal action to correct the situation.

Check installation.   A personal visit immediately following delivery to supervise or check installation allows you to take action toward solving any problems. If there are no problems, your words and presence show the customer that this is the kind of service your company and you always give your customers.

Check operation and training of operators.   You can forestall many potential complaints about a newly installed product or service by helping employees of the buying firm learn to operate or use it properly. Your presence at such introductory training sessions not only proves your interest to the customer but also impresses the trainees. You also have a chance to get feedback from them as to performance and possibly even ideas as to how your product rates against competition.

Order adjustment.   Prompt follow-up after delivery can often lead to additional on-the-spot orders if the customer decides he wants more features or tie-in items, larger quantities, or additional supplies.

Ask for referrals.   Both the customer and his operator or user-employees, if any, often feel even more pleased with the new purchase at the time of delivery or installation than they did before. If you are there to check delivery and to solve any problems, you can often get them to express their satisfaction in the form of referral leads.

Set the stage for a long-term relationship. This initial follow-up, by telephone, letter, or personal call, can cement relations between you and your customer for the future. Your continued post-sale interest offers proof of the reliability of your firm and may lead to future business. You may find this period the best time to get on a friendly basis with him, and the relationship will be enhanced by the pleasant, mutually profitable sale just concluded.

PROPER FOLLOW-UP AFTER FAILING TO CLOSE THE SALE

Use This Defeat to Set the Stage for Future Sales

To a professional sales representative, a lost sale often spells opportunity to set the stage for callbacks that could lead to sales. A warm thank-you for the time and courtesy extended during the just-concluded presentation proves your sincere interest. People like to deal with sales representatives and firms with an interest in their business or personal affairs, and they remember how well you took defeat.

If you feel that your prospect should be using your product or service, then you have to try again later. Persistence does pay off in many areas of selling. Even if he is satisfied with his present situation, he may become dissatisfied later; and if you get in touch with him again at one of those moments, his business may be yours.

Proper follow-up after losing a sale to such a prospect is a sincere thank-you by telephone or letter a day or so later. This thank-you leads to sustained, long-term follow-through, which we shall discuss shortly. Proper, initial follow-up steps taken now can lead to success later.

Find Out Why You Lost the Sale–the Real Reason!

Use this follow-up period to find out the reasons you failed. If you take defeat well and honestly ask your prospect his real reasons for not buying now, he may give you interesting and helpful insights. As well as asking him, you should immediately analyze your failure by reviewing each stage of the interview and asking yourself, "What went wrong with my presentation?"

Ask your prospect his real reason for not buying. Did you lose out because of price, delivery date, credit terms? What other advantages may have outweighed these factors in the prospect's mind had you suggested them or been authorized to offer them? His feedback may help both you and your company to devise ways of overcoming such stumbling blocks in the future. Ask him these or any other questions about your specific proposal; you may find he is very glad to help you.

Mr. Blaisdell, you have been most generous in listening to my proposal. I appreciate your reasons for not buying now. But may I ask you, are there any factors regarding price, delivery, or anything else about my proposal that should be improved to make it attractive to other possible customers? May I have your honest opinion?

Perhaps your proposal was good enough but you simply failed personally to sell him. Was your preparation adequate, your presentation convincing, your manner in tune, your words or actions not offensive? If you ask, the prospect may answer you honestly, and you will profit greatly from his viewpoints.

Mr. Poulshock, I sincerely appreciate the time and courtesy you have extended in listening to my proposal. I appreciate your reasons for not buying now but somehow feel I may have failed in making my proposal sound convincing. I am sincere in wanting to improve my sales approach and wonder if you could help me.

Since you have seen many other sales representatives, can you offer any concrete suggestions as to how I could have improved my presentation just now? Could I have been better prepared? How could my actual verbal description or demonstration be improved? Is there anything I can do to improve my appearance, actions, or manner that would help me become a more professional sales representative?

Honest, sincere questions like these are very likely to bring honest answers. You may learn something, and the prospect will remember you for a long time. It is an easy way to set the stage for a callback.

Make a personal review and analysis of what went wrong with the presentation. You tried hard but failed to close the sale. What went wrong? Careful critical analysis of your just-concluded interview may uncover clues that will help you get the order on your next call. The best way to analyze your handling of the presentation is to ask yourself any or all of the following questions, or any others that seem applicable; answer them honestly for yourself on paper.

SELF-EVALUATION CHECKLIST

Yes No	Questions	How could I improve on my next call?
My Approach		
___ ___	Was I awkward in approaching and greeting the prospect?	___
___ ___	Did I greet him pleasantly and go right into my planned approach?	___
___ ___	Was I inwardly proud of being a sales representative and of my company and product?	___
___ ___	Was I businesslike in my approach?	___
___ ___	Did I feel nervous and timid?	___
___ ___	Did my opening remarks arouse his interest and make him want to give me some of his time?	___
___ ___	Did I find that the elements of a sale were really there: the need, the ability, and the authority to buy—the I of INP (Information, Need, Product)?	___
___ ___	Was my approach good? Could I have done better?	___
Creating and Holding Interest		
___ ___	Did I arouse and hold the prospect's attention and interest?	___
___ ___	Did I discover his problems, needs, or wants—the N of INP?	___
___ ___	Did I encourage him to talk and then listen attentively?	___
___ ___	Did I get him to ask questions and take the time to answer them to his satisfaction?	___
___ ___	Did I arouse his interest and then fail to follow through?	___
___ ___	Did I keep repeating myself until he lost interest?	___
___ ___	Could I tell when he was interested and when he was not?	___
___ ___	Did I create the impression that I was sincerely trying to help him solve his problems?	___

Yes   No

Arousing Desire and Securing Conviction

—— ——   Would my product or service have met the prospect's needs—the P of INP?   ——————

—— ——   Did I cover all the benefits of my product?   ——————

—— ——   Did I establish the need for at least two of those benefits?   ——————

—— ——   Were the benefits I stressed the ones of greatest interest to him?   ——————

—— ——   Did I bring out the strong points of my proposal?   ——————

—— ——   Was I enthusiastic enough about the benefits?   ——————

—— ——   Was I convinced that he would benefit from my proposal?   ——————

—— ——   Did I get point-by-point agreement on the value of the benefits?   ——————

—— ——   Did I prove the value of my proposal?   ——————

—— ——   Were my statements consistently positive and not negative?   ——————

—— ——   Did I win his confidence?   ——————

—— ——   Did I secure his conviction that my product could fill his needs?   ——————

—— ——   Did I recognize buying signals and try to turn them into trial closes?   ——————

My Demonstration

—— ——   Did I use all my sales aids effectively?   ——————

—— ——   Did I fumble or have trouble finding and using my sales-kit aids?   ——————

—— ——   Did I show all my samples or demonstrate my product to show its value?   ——————

—— ——   Did I show too many samples or sales aids and thus confuse the prospect in any way?   ——————

—— ——   Was my demonstration disjointed and thus unclear to him?   ——————

—— ——   Was I able to get him to participate in my demonstration?   ——————

—— ——   Did he fully understand all the points of my demonstration?   ——————

Handling His Objections

—— ——   Was I successful in getting the prospect to voice all his objections?   ——————

—— ——   Was I able to restate his objections in the form of questions and to handle them as questions which I was happy to answer?   ——————

—— ——   Was I able to get him to explain the basis of his objections?   ——————

—— ——   Did I show any irritation at any of his objections, questions, or negative responses?   ——————

—— ——   Did any of his objections or questions rattle me and throw me off track?   ——————

—— ——   Was I able to turn his objections into yes-building questions?   ——————

—— ——   Was I able to answer all his questions effectively?   ——————

—— ——   Did I attempt to turn any objections into a trial close?   ——————

Yes   No

_____ _____ Did I misrepresent my product or service in any way?   _____

_____ _____ Did he raise any questions which I disregarded?   _____

_____ _____ Was I well enough informed about my product and company policies to answer all his questions?   _____

_____ _____ Did I avoid or fail to answer any valid objections?   _____

_____ _____ Did I lack conviction, pep, or enthusiasm in answering his objections or questions?   _____

_____ _____ Did I listen carefully to his answers, after restating his objections or questions, and then handle them?   _____

_____ _____ Was I able to uncover all his hidden objections?   _____

_____ _____ Did I uncover his real objection?   _____

_____ _____ Was I able to handle his complaint or objection promptly, properly, and to his satisfaction?   _____

My Close

_____ _____ Did I use the trial closes I had prepared?   _____

_____ _____ Did I fail to recognize any buying signals or critical times to close during my presentation, prior to the summary?   _____

_____ _____ Did I secure the prospect's agreement to each point of my summary?   _____

_____ _____ Did I ever have him ready to say yes and then lose him by overselling or simply talking too much?   _____

_____ _____ Did I inwardly give up the first time he said, "I'm not interested"?   _____

_____ _____ Could he have sensed my discouragement at any time?   _____

_____ _____ Did I uncover all the reasons he would not buy?   _____

_____ _____ Did I ask for the order?   _____

_____ _____ Did I fail to suggest action now?   _____

_____ _____ Did I have only one closing argument?   _____

_____ _____ Did I keep a final, new, and strong reason to buy in reserve as a last resort?   _____

_____ _____ Did I know when and how to close?   _____

_____ _____ Did I let him sell me on the fact that he was not interested or ready to buy now?   _____

_____ _____ Could I sell him on a callback?   _____

_____ _____ Do I have some ideas as to what I can do to close the sale on a callback?   _____

My Personal Attitude, Appearance, and Manner

_____ _____ Did I have a proper, positive, will-to-win attitude throughout?   _____

_____ _____ Was I confident and cheerful?   _____

_____ _____ Was my personal appearance satisfactory—was I dressed appropriately and well groomed?   _____

_____ _____ In general, did I feel, look, and act in a professional and businesslike manner?   _____

_____ _____ Was I proud and enthusiastic about my company and product or service?   _____

_____ _____ Did the prospect seem annoyed at some mannerism of mine?   _____

_____ _____ Did I knock a competitor?   _____

_____ _____ Did we get into an argument?   _____

_____ _____ Did I talk too rapidly or too much?   _____

Yes	No		
___	___	Was I awkward and unsure of myself at any stage of the interview?	_____
___	___	Did I willingly discuss every important point he mentioned?	_____
___	___	Did I talk to him at his level in terms he understood?	_____
___	___	Did I avoid looking him in the eye or fail to smile often?	_____
___	___	Did I use too many I's and not enough we's or you's?	_____
___	___	Did I leave the interview pleasantly?	_____
___	___	Will I be welcome there again on a callback?	_____

The preceding series of self-evaluation questions covers fairly completely all the stages of the sales presentation. Answers to most of the problems such a review poses are in the preceding chapters of this book. All sales representatives would profit from seriously and honestly asking themselves the above questions upon failing to close after a full presentation.

The art/science/skill of salesmanship is a never-ending process of self-evaluation, study, and practice. You cannot hope to close every sale; but you can, through intelligent application of basic principles and techniques, increase your percentage of closes. And, as we have said, closing, or getting a verbal or signed agreement to buy, is your basic objective and the chief justification for your existence as a sales representative.

FOLLOW-THROUGH FOR REPEAT BUSINESS AFTER A SUCCESSFUL CLOSE

As stated earlier in this chapter, the ultimate aim of a professional sales representative is to have a satisfied customer (or user). You can make sure he is and remains satisfied with you, the product or service you have sold him, and your company, by providing follow-up service.

For many good reasons, in perhaps most types of selling, you should spend all the time and effort necessary to ensure the customer's continued satisfaction. Here are three major reasons:

1. It is easier in most cases to sell satisfied users more or something new than to find and sell entirely new prospects.
2. Satisfied users are the best source, through referral leads, for locating and gaining access to potential new customers.
3. Callbacks or user calls on satisfied customers give you an opportunity to see your product or service in operation. Through discussions with staff supervisors and line users or operators you can often discover new advantages or ideas for its use that can be applied elsewhere.

There are no hard and fast rules for when or how often you should make such follow-through callbacks or user calls. Because time represents money to both you and your company, the time thus spent has to ultimately result in profitable sales. Thus you have to ask yourself first, will callbacks on this customer pay for themselves, and second, how can they be made to pay for themselves? Deciding factors are the nature of your selling, the nature and situation of your customer, and your own experience, based on your records.

What can you gain from time spent on callbacks? And what can your customer gain? These are the two major questions you should keep in mind as we delve into the three major reasons, noted above, that justify sustained, follow-through callbacks.

It Is Easier to Sell Satisfied Customers More or Something New Than to Find and Sell Entirely New Prospects

Let us first consider this point from your view as a customer of all sorts of goods and services yourself. Do you not prefer to buy gasoline or petrol from the service station where the attendants greet you cheerfully by name, know your automobile through constant, repeat servicing, and give advice and have experience you trust? And do you not like to patronize the banks or department stores whose owners or employees recognize you and help you on a personal basis with your needs and problems?

Just as you like to deal with people, companies, and institutions you can trust to give efficient, personal, cheerful attention, so do your customers. In fact, a major problem for company and industrial buyers is to find sales representatives willing to give them such service since they are now buying increasingly on the basis of overall service rather than on price alone. And customers in general are not only expecting but also demanding more efficient follow-through service from sales representatives. In spite of new marketing approaches that tend to bypass the sales representative, your personal touch, your personal interaction with your customer on a face-to-face basis, continues to make the difference between volume sales and mere distribution or initial sales.

If your customer likes and trusts you, based most often on the follow-through service you render, he tends to give you his repeat business. Such business is easier to get than entirely new business since you eliminate all the time-consuming steps—prospecting, making the appointment, making the approach, and making that hardest sale of all—the initial one.

Keep in mind the useful advice passed along by veteran sales representatives through the years: "Never forget a customer; never let a customer forget you." We will discuss how to put this motto into practice in the next few pages.

Satisfied Customers Are the Best Source for Referral Leads or for Locating Potential New Customers

We have noted several times the importance of constantly asking everyone —friends, people from whom you buy, business associates, prospects, user customers, and prospects whom you fail to close—for referral leads—for names of potential personal, company, or institutional prospects who may have a need or desire for your product or service. Satisfied users are the best source for such referral leads. If they respect your follow-up interest and service, the easiest way for them to repay you is to give you names of others who may also be interested in the product benefits and superior follow-through service offered by you and your company.

Callbacks on satisfied users give you the relaxed opportunity and time to get to know the decision maker or other executives on a personal basis as well as the line supervisors and operators or clerks who may be able to give you specific referral leads. These can often be turned into immediate and profitable telephone or letter introductions or written testimonial letters. Because they are the best, you should follow up such referral leads promptly—immediately if at all possible. No better proof of the claims of your proposal can be offered than the testimony or recommendation of a satisfied, current user.

Callbacks on Satisfied Users Can Give You
New Ideas for Profitable Sales

For continued sales success, your product or service must serve the purpose for which it was sold. It is one thing to offer a product designed to produce specific results. What happens after it has been sold and put into use however may be quite another thing. The only way you or your company can actually know how well your product performs is to see for yourself! And because problems often multiply faster than profits, good follow-through service can pinpoint new ways your product can cut costs, increase sales, or boost efficiency.

Peter F. Drucker, leading American management consultant and author, pointed out this problem most tellingly in his book *The Effective Executive* when he said, "Failure to go out and look is the typical reason for persisting in a course of action long after it has ceased to be appropriate or even rational."[1]

Times change, markets change, and customer needs change constantly. If you as a sales representative and market manager are to keep up with these changes and are to provide necessary feedback and recommendations to your company, you have to get out and see the situation for yourself. User calls are the easiest, fastest, and most reliable way to keep up to date; they provide new ideas for future profitable sales.

Such calls are especially useful in uncovering creative new sales ideas when competing products all seem alike to the customer. For example, selling products such as matches and cooking oil depends largely on new sales ideas or packaging or better follow-through servicing in areas such as shipping and in-store promotions.

FOLLOW-THROUGH THAT MAY TURN
LOST SALES INTO FUTURE BUSINESS

Should you spend time calling back on your prospect after failing to close the sale? The answer depends largely on your careful evaluation of why you lost the sale and on whether you have enough interest or potential to make it worth your time to try once more.

You must decide whether your prospect had a need that your proposal could fill. If so and if he had the money and authority to buy, then he still remains a prospect. If that is the case, why did you fail to sell him? Did he have a valid reason for not buying now, such as no money for new expenditures during the remaining budget period? If it was a valid reason and if he appeared interested, then a callback or several callbacks may be in order. If his excuses for not buying were mere stalls or put-offs, you failed to sell him. Since you have already fired most of your sales ammunition on the initial presentation, will you be more successful next time?

How Much Time Should Be Allocated to Such Callbacks?

The amount of time to spend on callbacks to customers you failed to sell depends to a great extent on what you are selling and on the sales-call ratio in your industry. In many types of selling sales are seldom made until the third or fourth callback. And sales of some sophisticated equipment or systems may not be made until after many callbacks and perhaps after detailed bids or proposals. Your own sales records or those of other sales representatives in your company or industry may offer helpful guidelines.

1. *The Effective Executive* (New York: Harper & Row, Publishers, 1967), p. 142.

Some business or industrial buyers follow a policy of refusing to buy on any sales representative's first visit because too many sales representatives in the past promised but did not deliver on after-purchase service and follow-through. These buyers are often more interested in service than in price and want to see how regular and persistent you are in your follow-through efforts to get their business.

Keeping all these factors in mind, you have to consider whether you have a chance of making a sale if you do call back. If the prospect understands your proposal, if you are making progress with him, and if he either requested or is not opposed to a callback, then it may be worth your time.

What New Sales Approaches Are Necessary in Such Callbacks?

If you do plan a callback, you should present new and additional information and reasons for buying. You should find out the best time to call again by appointment and confirm that appointment by telephone shortly before the call. When you do see the prospect, your best approach is to briefly review major points covered during your initial presentation and to offer the new information or ideas you have developed since then.

If the business is worth having, many persistent callbacks following failure to close initially may be well worth the time and effort. Offer new facts about your proposal, new ideas or industry information, and let the prospect know that you are sincerely interested in helping him solve his problems. Seek even an initial small order that will enable you to get your foot in the door and thus give you a chance to show him how you can give superior service. It is hard for any buyer with a need to keep from saying yes to a friendly, sincerely interested, helpful, persistent sales representative.

PRACTICAL STEPS FOR EFFICIENT FOLLOW-THROUGH

To a large extent modern marketing and selling means discovering customer wants and needs and providing the products and services to fulfill them. The personalized, customer-oriented, problem-solving approach of the market-manager sales representative in this situation requires careful planning and efficient follow-through. Such follow-through is necessary especially to maintain customer satisfaction since increased sales volume is so closely tied to selling more and newer products or services. Because sales in many industries are made only after several calls, this efficient follow-through is also often necessary to ultimately sell those prospects who fail to buy initially.

Here are some practical suggestions you may employ in your own sales area to provide the efficient, systematic follow-through or servicing required by your increasingly sophisticated buyers. They are based on your sincere, continued interest in your customer's needs, problems, and general welfare and in maintaining his satisfaction with your products and service.

Practical Steps for Your Follow-Through

1. Develop a systematic schedule for checking on the performance of products sold through regular telephone or letter contact. And use this opportunity to present any new ideas on how customers may get even more use or benefit from them.
2. Meet and maintain regular personal contact with key management and purchasing agents who can influence the buying decisions of their firms or organizations.

3. Provide time for periodic calls on users or potential prospects not sold initially to maintain regular contact.
4. Make every effort to immediately handle personally or to follow up on company handling of any customer problems.
5. Try to make yourself always available to your customer. You can telephone him yourself at regular intervals or send postcards to let him know you are thinking of him. You can even leave your evening or weekend home or emergency telephone number. Customers seldom use the latter but are impressed that you are always available if they need you.
6. Relay promptly to all customers any new ideas developed elsewhere for your product or service that may increase their sales and profits, cut their costs, or increase their efficiency.
7. Put all your contacts to work for your customers. You may know of a capable executive who desires a change and of a position available in another company or you may learn of a company planning to purchase something sold by your customer. You lose nothing by putting them in touch with one another. If they get together for mutual profit, each will thank you. If they make contact but fail to reach agreement, they will thank you anyway. In either case they appreciate your thinking enough about their problems to try to help find a solution.

Practical Follow-Through Steps through Your Company

1. Make sure any complaints, problems, or requests for information from your customer to your company are handled promptly and efficiently. Your company office should handle these by phone or wire if necessary and keep you informed at all times so that you can take whatever action is necessary.
2. Keep your customer, his purchasing department, and key line supervisors on your company mailing list for new announcements, brochures, or other helpful information. Such advertising works for you in between your personal calls.
3. See to it that any promotional or advertising material developed by your company is promptly called to the attention of your customers and is made available to them. You save time by arranging for your company to do this directly.
4. Call to your customers' attention any national or local advertising by your company, especially that featuring specific products or service, so that they are able to benefit from it in every way possible.

These are but a few of the many practical ideas you and your company can employ as systematic follow-through steps to let your customers know you are constantly thinking of them. Your customers want and need all the ideas and assistance you can furnish them and will usually reward your efforts with increased sales volume.

SPECIAL PROBLEMS WITH FOLLOW-UP AND FOLLOW-THROUGH

Some problems with follow-up or follow-through require special attention and handling. We will touch on four of these in a general way: promises broken for reasons beyond your control, cancellations, specific complaints, and the dissatisfied customer.

Handling Broken Promises

At times circumstances beyond the control of you and your company lead to failure in providing the rapid delivery or prompt follow-up service you promised at the time you closed the sale. If your customer schedules costly operations based on delivery of your product at a certain time, he is bound to be unhappy if it does not arrive as promised.

Your proper follow-up in such cases is to notify him at once of the situation and to state the reasons openly and honestly. Break the news in terms of your keen personal sympathy for him and your understanding of the problems the delay is causing. You can then let him know that both you and your company are going to do everything possible immediately to help him solve those problems. Tell him specifically what you can do to help and what you cannot do.

Finally, suggest the best solution possible for his predicament, even if that means asking a competitor to give him immediate delivery. You may lose the order by such drastic action but may gain goodwill that can set the stage for future orders. Your first task is to help him solve his problems.

Handling Cancellations

There are many reasons for cancellations of orders placed, and you may experience many of them in your sales career. If cancellations are made for any legitimate reason beyond your control, they should be handled as outlined in the illustration above. Such cancellations may result from sudden financial reverses, illness, or loss of key personnel or staff.

Most cancellations however, result from your failure to sell your customer completely enough on the benefits he will derive from the purchase. You may make the sale more because of your strong personality than because of benefits and value. Then, after your departure, the customer becomes worried, talks it over with someone else, and suddenly phones in a cancellation to your company. In such cases, it is often difficult or impossible to resell him.

The best way to handle such cancellations is to avoid them in the first place. If you make certain that the prospect fully understands what he is buying, take the time to answer any last-minute questions, and reinforce his confidence in having made a wise buying decision, cancellations should not become a real problem.

Handling Specific Complaints

Customers often make specific complaints that your product simply is not doing the job they thought it would at the time of purchase. This and other specific complaints are, for purposes of our discussion here, beyond the control of you or your company. Your product may be good but their unique requirements may make it unsuited to their needs.

The temptation arises, in such a case, to hold the customer to his signed agreement and to let the problem remain his alone. But if you accept the proper viewpoint of serving your customer rather than exploiting him, you should make every effort to adjust the situation to his satisfaction. Sometimes technical or other experts from your company can solve the problem for him through adjustments or new techniques. You should make every effort to handle such specific legitimate requests in this way.

If all efforts fail, you should advise your company to take the long-range view and to help the customer out of his predicament in any way possible. This may entail cancellation of the order, payment adjustments, or other solutions. By making the situation right for him, you gain his goodwill and future business. The proper approach in such matters is to help him if you can and to turn the situation to your future advantage in every way possible.

Handling the Dissatisfied Customer

Sometimes the customer makes no specific complaint but is just generally dissatisfied with the product or your personal or company follow-through service. Often such a dissatisfied customer may be emotionally upset and may require special understanding and handling on your part.

Your first task is to approach him in a friendly manner that indicates your sincere desire to get to the bottom of his dissatisfaction and to help him if you can. A good way to start is to talk it over after taking him to lunch or even over a cup of coffee. Your second task is to hear him out and to try to find the real reasons for his dissatisfaction. Just giving him the chance to let off steam may go a long way toward placating him.

Once you get to the root of the problem, you have to decide what, if anything, can be done about it. Courteous, straightforward discussion can often lead to understanding if not complete agreement. Even when company policy decisions are involved, convey the impression that you consider it a personal responsibility to handle it yourself as best you can.

You may have to tell him in a straightforward manner that, although sorry, you are unable to help him in any concrete way. Then you have to sell him on the fact that the decision is the only realistic one you can make on behalf of your company. If you can make any adjustment by way of minor concessions, it may help overcome the harshness, in his opinion, of your big no. In any case, your prompt, honest, and undivided attention to his expression of dissatisfaction may mollify him to some extent and still allow you to retain his goodwill and a possible chance at his future business.

SUMMARY

We have considered in this chapter the proper follow-up and follow-through steps for both a closed sale and one you failed to close. Your ultimate professional aim as a sales representative is to have a satisfied customer or user. Planned, sustained, efficient follow-up and follow-through service is the best way to assure utmost satisfaction. Since many sales are not effected until after repeated callbacks, you should also extend such follow-through service to initial nonbuyers, providing you feel that possibilities exist to make a sale commensurate with the time expended.

We considered proper departure methods following both a successful and an unsuccessful sales presentation and offered a comprehensive self-evaluation checklist, against which you should check reasons for failing to close your sale.

We then presented reasons for after-presentation follow-through, win or lose, as well as specific practical procedures. In conclusion, we considered how you can handle specific complaints or after-sale problems such as cancellations, other complaints, and the dissatisfied customer.

CHAPTER REVIEW

CONCEPTS TO REMEMBER*

_____ one-shot sale   _____ callback   _____ follow-through
_____ follow-up service   _____ repeat business   _____ cancellations
_____ self-evaluation   _____ user calls   _____ user (customer)
      questions   satisfaction

*For memory reinforcement, fill in the page number or numbers where the terms were described in this chapter.

QUESTIONS FOR ANALYSIS AND DISCUSSION

1. What do we mean by the statement "to a true sales representative the sale does not end when the order is signed"?
2. What is the proper attitude for a sales representative to take after failing to close a sale?
3. When does a professional sales representative quit selling?
4. Why is proper follow-up after closing a sale important?
5. If a sales representative fails to close a sale and doesn't really understand why, what can he do to find out before leaving the prospect?
6. Name and explain two reasons why it is so important for a sales representative to have a satisfied customer (or user)?
7. Are new sales approaches necessary on sales callbacks? Explain.
8. If your company cannot deliver an item sold on the date promised by the sales representative at the time of the sale, what should the sales representative do about it—in terms of his customer?

Case Study 15–1

AFTER-SALE FOLLOW-THROUGH SECRET FOR SUCCESS OF COCA-COLA: HELPING DEALERS SELL THE COKE THEY HAVE PURCHASED

Our case study of Coca-Cola in Chapter 10 pointed out that the aim of the Coke route manager or his driver-sales representatives on their first call is to get even a few cases of Coke into a dealer outlet. From then on, helping the dealer sell the Coke he has purchased through all possible marketing means is the goal. Executives of Coca-Cola bottlers claim this after-sale follow-through to be the key to the phenomenal success of the Coca-Cola business.

How do they do it? After the first sale, the route manager and his driver-salesmen have three major objectives: to create demand, to create new consumers, and to create situations in which customers can consume Coke. Their aim is to get increasingly more customers to ask for Coke so that the dealer gets interested enough to promote and stock it actively.

Aiming for a bandwagon effect, they employ all sorts of sales and promotional techniques to push Coke as the drink suitable for all ages in any family or social gathering. They give free samples at picnics, supermarket openings, or sports or group meetings. They sponsor essay-writing and other contests through schools and clubs, show educational films, and erect Coca-Cola signs and billboards, which are often so numerous they appear to be part of the local scenery. All these activities stress the wholesome approach with Coke—the "happy" drink, always where the action is.

Selling Coke merely as a "Pause That Refreshes" is not enough for these energetic sales representatives. They picture Coke being consumed at meals in place of coffee, water, or milk, reasoning that if a consumer drinks anything with his lunch, why not 365 bottles of Coke per year! And to carry this vision even farther, why not drink it at dinner as well, making the number 730 bottles per year per person! As far as social groups are concerned, the aim is to create the impression that wherever there is a gathering of people Coke is or should be there.

This sales follow-through for Coca-Cola, through sheer ubiquity and untiring repetition, has made Coke a familiar trademark around the world. Thus, selling to dealers who want to get on the bandwagon is easier today than in the past. But a major sales problem for the route manager is to keep dealers interested and sales-minded.

Thus a major after-sale follow-up and follow-through effort is directed toward the dealers as well as the consumers. The route manager and his driver-sales representatives sell the dealer on the need (1) to provide advertising both inside and outside so customers know Coke is there and (2) to keep cold Coke at all times. This latter point is important because if the first bottle sold is not a cold one, all chance for a second sale is lost. Dealers are warned that if they serve warm bottles of Coke their customers will go elsewhere next time. Each route manager tries to call on each dealer covered by all his five driver-sales representatives at least once every two months. This sustained follow-up and follow-through sales effort puts into daily practice the feeling that good merchandising and salesmanship are "helping the dealer sell what we sell him."

QUESTIONS FOR WRITTEN REPORTS OR CLASS DISCUSSION

1. Early in this chapter, we stated that a professional sales representative never quits selling. In what ways does the follow-up and follow-through sales effort for Coca-Cola prove this statement true?

2. List three follow-up and follow-through after-sale steps, other than those mentioned above, that sales representatives for Coca-Cola may find effective. How would they work in practice?

SPLITTING PAPER SACKS PROVIDE AFTER-SALE OPPORTUNITY FOR INCREASED LONG-TERM SALES

In the Chapter 6 sales problem, we left Paul P., our British PPPPL sales representative, wrestling with the problem of devising a paper sack in which prospect Winterbottom could package his Frisky Fido dog food. He made the sale, for an initial 100,000 sacks a month, with prospects of larger reorders. But, two weeks after delivery, on a followup call, he found Winterbottom and his sons furious at both PPPPL and him. They had good reason to be angry; up to 30 percent of the PPPPL bags were splitting open before they could even be trucked out of the shipping yard to customers. Winterbottom threatened both to sue PPPPL for damages and to have his sons physically toss Paul out of their factory office.

Paul kept his head, however, agreed that the Winterbottoms had every reason to be angry, but asked if he could investigate their packaging and handling operation to see the situation firsthand in order to make prompt recommendations for adjustment. They had nothing to lose and told him to go ahead.

Knowing his product was good, better in fact than the previously used paper sacks, Paul felt there must be some unusual reason for the problem. He knew the sacks were tearing but had to find out why. He went through each step of the entire packaging and handling process, from machine-loading to transport out, and soon found the reason. The handling equipment that moved the filled sacks from the storeroom to the lorries (trucks) was a chain-and-fork affair, a loose section of which was making a very small tear in roughly one out of two sacks. When thrown by workmen into the lorry for stacking, many of the sacks split open.

Paul's recommended solution was immediate and inexpensive: switch to a leather-covered chain. Winterbottom was delighted because he had had this same trouble with the previously used competing sacks and had hoped the PPPPL sacks themselves would solve his problem. He, his sons, and his staff had never noticed the tiny cuts caused by their faulty conveyor system.

Two weeks later, on another follow-up service call, Winterbottom and his sons were so pleased with PPPPL sacks and Paul's service and help in solving their costly problem that they offered to give PPPPL first chance to quote on all the packaging for their entire mixed-product line.

QUESTIONS FOR WRITTEN REPORTS OR CLASS DISCUSSION

1. Paul proved the point made earlier in this chapter that a lost sale can often be turned to future advantage or repeat business. But there is one final thing he apparently failed to do to turn this situation to even greater advantage. What else should he have done at the time?
2. List and discuss three additional after-service steps Paul should now plan to take.
3. List two advantages Paul gains by callbacks on satisfied customer Winterbottom.

HOW CAN YOU AS A SALES REPRESENTATIVE GET YOUR OLD CUSTOMERS TO THINK OF *YOU* WHEN THEY HAVE A PROBLEM?

Far too many sales representatives settle for a comfortable order size or volume of business from old customers when they could be getting more. Without becoming overly aggressive, it is possible in a high percentage of such cases to sell these old customers on the idea that it may be to their advantage to buy more, or to buy a better (higher-priced) line than the one they have been using, from you.

Let us assume you are one of these sales representatives, and you want old customers to think of *you* when they have a question or problem concerning any phase of their operation with which you or your company might be able to offer advice or assistance.

QUESTION FOR WRITTEN REPORTS OR CLASS DISCUSSION

List and explain three ways you could systematically employ to get your old customers to think of *you* when they have a question or problem.

16

some special applications to retail selling

When you have mastered the content of this chapter, you should be able to:

Describe major trends and developments in retailing, and show how these may affect both consumers and retail selling and salespersons in the years ahead.

Describe the proper approach a retail salesperson should cover in a complete sales presentation.

Summarize sales techniques involved in handling two common retail objections: (1) excuses or stalls, and (2) indecision.

Summarize techniques that will help a retail salesperson solve four special retail sales problems: (1) the shopper, (2) two customers at once, (3) a group of shoppers, and (4) the complaining or irate customer.

Describe ideas for developing knowledge of merchandise and techniques for handling four common merchandise sales problems: (1) selling specials, (2) making second sales, (3) trading up for bigger sales, and (4) selling substitute items.

Describe proper follow-up or follow-through steps to take concerning special problem areas of (1) promises broken for reasons beyond your control, (2) cancellations, (3) specific complaints, and (4) the dissatisfied customer.

We noted early in Chapter 1 that approximately three-fifths of the total American sales force is and will continue to be engaged in retail selling. For clarity, we called them *retail* (or inside) salespersons as contrasted to *specialty* (or outside) sales representatives.

The major difference between these two broad classifications is that retail salespeople work inside stores, where customers come to them, whereas specialty sales representatives go outside to call on prospects and customers.

In the past, the term *salesman* was the most commonly used descriptive word for those (chiefly men) engaged in outside selling. In recent years, however, due to the ever-increasing number of women entering the field, the descriptive term *sales representative* has become the term of common business usage. We have stressed the modern term sales representative, above that of salesman, in these pages.

In retail selling, however, where the percentage of women has generally been high, the term *salesperson* has traditionally been, and continues to be, the descriptive term of common usage. In this chapter, we shall use the term *salesperson* to include both women and men.

The same principles and techniques of salesmanship apply generally to both categories of selling, especially as far as steps of the presentation are concerned.

Although the specific examples and case studies in this book have applied most often to outside sales representatives, we have illustrated many specific techniques by in-store examples. Certain case studies, especially those of the Singer Company and Shell Oil Company, have been retail-oriented to a large extent.

Nevertheless, the distinction between these two broad categories of selling is not always clear cut; thus we will soon take a close look at some special applications to the specific field of retail selling. First, however, let us focus our attention on some more detailed aspects of the rapidly changing retail scene that we briefly touched upon in earlier chapters.

THE CHANGING RETAIL SCENE

Retailing as we know it today evolved from the fifteenth-century trading post and the nineteenth-century general store. The general store has become the department and chain stores; its evolution continues today.

In Chapter 3 we noted how the changing marketplace since World War II has been marked in the retail area by the widespread development of suburban shopping centers and malls, and use of credit cards.

New mutations of retailing have included self-service warehouse showrooms and catalogue showrooms of various types. One newly developing variation on this theme is Cities Service Oil Company's catalogue showrooms at many of its gas stations, for members of a club who pay an annual membership fee. Warehouse outlets catering to special groups, such as union members or government employees only, have increased in number during the early 1970s.

"Super Stores," those of 100,000 square feet or more, which started in Europe, are increasing rapidly throughout the United States and Canada. At the same time the countertrend toward ever more of the popular ministores and specialty boutiques has developed.

Department stores have countered by setting up specialty shops or centers, both within larger stores and in separate locations. Discount stores have kept adjusting to hold the middle ground between the traditional department stores and the newer forms of mass outlets. Even newer forms of retailing have emerged, ones that bypass the traditional store methods by going to the customer directly via door-to-door salespersons or "party plan" selling.

Since we have indicated that these trends will not only continue, but accelerate, what will retailing be like in the 1980s? Definitely less wear and tear on the consumer, say retail industry leaders, who foresee these changes and innovations:

Electronic devices for filling prescriptions.

Completely automated food shopping in nearly unattended food stores. Shoppers will use computer cards and no carts. (This system is already in successful operation in western Europe today.)

Shopping centers in the sky. Chicago's John Hancock Building, for example, plans high floors devoted to shopping facilities.

Drive-in food stores and vending machines that accept credit cards. Shopping by closed circuit television and the telephone.

New methods of presenting merchandise and ideas. Changes in grouping merchandise. Show-business techniques.

New in-store operations. Instant information. Electronic intelligence. The modern electronic register.

Fads and fashions will change overnight. Shoes will become clogs, then shoes again. Dress lengths will ride up and down like an elevator. Hats, out now, will suddenly be in—then out again. Lifestyles and the things that accompany them will change rapidly.

Electronic point-of-sale registers, introduced in the 1970s, will be commonplace.

Technology, today keyed to general retail outlets, will rapidly expand to supermarkets, drug chains, and service centers.

Today's credit card, not yet an economic success, is a marketing success (consumers like it). Over the next decade credit card and transfer systems will be wedded to electronic point-of-sale terminals.

International point-of-sale transactions, now in the planning stage, will permit retailers to derive the full benefit of electronic transactions from across national borders.

How Will These Changes Affect Consumers?

While these changes may save the consumer wear and tear, certain of these trends indicate a serious imbalance against the customer. Automatic payments benefit the banker, credit union, savings and loan company, and mutual savings bank more than the consumer.

Bankers or retailers who assume that "what's good for the product is also good for the consumer" may find themselves in trouble. Systems that reduce paper burdens and man-hours, or improve bank accuracy, may *not* offer comparable consumer values.

If retail selling is to keep in favor with the changing consumer market we studied in Chapter 3, it must pay careful attention to consumer advantages and benefits—for the next decade will be increasingly consumer controlled.

How Will These Changes Affect Retail Selling and Salespersons?

The basics of retailing and retail selling will remain the same; they will be concerned, as they are today, with:

Merchandising: How goods are offered for sale as influenced by competition, characteristics of products, risk, overhead.

Retail selling: Conversion of shoppers into buyers through image, advertising, and face-to-face selling.

Some experts foresee that one of the greatest challenges in retail sales/marketing strategy will be to help the average consumer cut through the mass of sales/advertising messages he is exposed to daily—over 2,000, of which he remembers only about 75 the next day. One answer lies in the strategy now in effect at well-known Abercrombie & Fitch specialty department store in New York City; sell ideas, not items. For example, Abercrombie promotes not "French knives," but the "knives used by the chefs at the Paris Ritz." And its raincoat which comes with two linings is sold not as a "zip-in raincoat," but as a "365-day-a-year coat."

The trends toward bigness in the retail field will continue, with fewer large chains controlling more outlets. Career opportunities abound today and will continue with such organizations for sales-oriented young men and women, but these chains and large retailers are looking for ambitious, better-educated applicants, capable of fulfilling managerial roles. While smaller individually owned retail outlets will decrease in number in many areas, there will still be many thousands of them seeking sales-oriented salespersons.

Opportunities for good salespersons are excellent today and will be even better in the future because people still do the buying and like to interact with salespersons, not vending machines. Retailers are increasingly realizing how important well-trained salespersons can be as the role of the retail salesperson, like other sales areas, rapidly changes from that of a mere order-taker to that of a real problem-solver for customers.

Training of salespersons by larger retailers is increasingly concerned with understanding customer attitudes and motivations and developing communication skills (especially listening), as well as the steps involved in making a sale. Sales service is stressed in such programs as well, since modern retailing is increasingly concerned with providing complete sales service, with emphasis on this aspect of the inside salesperson's job.

Having considered these trends, we will now turn our thoughts to you in terms of your possible current full- or part-time work as a retail salesperson, or your career interest in this challenging field of selling.

ALL FUNDAMENTALS OF SALESMANSHIP APPLY TO RETAIL SELLING

The fundamentals of salesmanship apply to all fields of selling. In each, there must be advance preparation and planning, a proper approach, and a customer-oriented, problem-solving sales presentation based on offering benefits and value that will satisfy the customer's needs or wants. Proper handling of questions or objections and the all-important close, without which there is no sale, are also essential.

The fundamentals of human relations—knowledge of self and knowledge of other people—also apply to all fields of selling. If you are to be successful in retail selling, you should have a proper attitude toward life and work and toward your employer and customers. You should be sincere, courteous, tactful, and willing to work hard. In addition you must have or strive to develop a pleasing manner, appearance, and voice.

YOUR BASIC PURPOSE IS TO SELL!

In spite of self-service developments in chain stores and discount houses, if you hope to earn more income and promotions, you must always keep in mind that your basic purpose is to sell. The degree of sales persuasion you may be allowed to employ varies from store to store and depends upon the type of customer. The basic purpose of any retail business is to sell its goods at a profit however, and it employs you as a salesperson to help do just that.

If you are ambitious, you may have already taken heart from the Chapter 1 comparisons of average beginning earnings in various industries for both inexperienced and qualified salespeople. Retail areas such as clothing, furniture, and home furnishings generally offer better than average opportunities. For successful, experienced salespeople, the clothing and textile industries offer top earnings potential. A rapid route to success in these fields is to begin at retail salesperson level and to advance to store buyer or to specialty commission selling. Manufacturers tend to hire their often highly paid specialty sales representatives from among men and women with such a successful retail sales background.

Encouraging the concept that your basic purpose is to sell are the incentive programs of many large retail organizations. These include bonus or profit-sharing plans and excellent commission arrangements.

A RETAIL SALESPERSON IS A HOST

We have already noted that the basic difference between retail (inside) selling and specialty (outside) selling is that the prospect or customer comes to you in retail selling. A further difference is that the prospect approaching you very likely has some idea of what he is looking for. The specialty sales representative, on the other hand, often has to devote time to selling interest or to bringing the prospect to this point of awareness.

Since the customer has come to you, you are freed from problems of prospecting or the preapproach and are now ready to move into these two phases:

1. The approach (and qualification)
2. The sales presentation, consisting of creating and holding interest, arousing desire and securing conviction, handling questions and objections, and closing the sale

As we move into a brief review of some specific problems, approaches, and sales techniques involved in the retail situation, keep in mind that you as a retail salesperson are somewhat in the position of a host receiving a guest; your first aim is to make your approaching customer feel welcome and at ease.

GREETING THE CUSTOMER (OR THE APPROACH)

In greeting the customer what counts is not so much what you say but how you say it. He may be looking for a specific item, may have only a vague idea of what he is looking for, or may only be browsing or looking around. Whatever the case, your task is to recognize that he has or may have a problem that you can help him solve, but that he may be afraid to express it because of a hidden fear of being sold something he does not want—the fear of making a mistake.

Your first job is to sell yourself—to create the impression that you are a friendly, nice, sincere person who would like to help him. The warmth of your smile, the friendly, relaxed, personal look in your eyes, and your attentive manner all help get over any initial psychological barrier as you open the conversation with words like "good morning" or "good afternoon."

This cheerful greeting can be said warmly, yet with a question in your eyes. The idea is to show that you welcome and understand him. This gives the customer greater confidence to ask you for something.

Do *not* greet a customer with negative phrases such as "May I help you," "What can I do for you," or "Something for you?" To each of these, it is easy for him to say "No, thank you," which not only places a barrier between you, but may actually induce him not to buy anything.

If he doesn't ask for anything, but you sense through empathy that an approach may be in order, go right into any one of the sixteen useful basic approaches listed in Chapter 10. A good one might be a *benefit approach* such as this:

Have you seen our advertised specials feature for today? They are on that counter (pointing).

Your empathy plays an important role here. Some shoppers appreciate being noticed and helped promptly, others resent being bothered in store after store. So, while you should judge whether or not he will be receptive to an approach, don't hesitate to say something that might tempt a customer to consider buying something. After all, everyone who enters is a potential buyer and all the store's advertising, window and instore point-of-purchase displays, attractive merchandise displays, and you the salesperson are there to tempt them into buying.

Your next task is to establish a rapport that further convinces him of your sincere interest. You are trying to win his acceptance of you as a friend and to show him that you want to like and understand him. This rapport is called empathy; the best way to communicate empathy is by asking questions and listening.

Ask Relaxing Questions

To overcome the customer's possible inner fear of being sold something he does not want, reassure him that you do want to be of assistance and do not just want to try to sell him something. Since many shoppers do not know what they are looking for and do not like to be bothered by persistent salespeople, you can normally overcome initial resistance or even hostility by a statement such as, "Please feel free to browse; I am Mrs. Fowski and will be glad to answer any questions. Is there anything I can help you with now at this counter?"

If the customer indicates a desire to browse further on his own, do not bother him again unless he stops at and appears interested in a specific item. Then you can casually walk over and ask a trial-close question that may reveal buying signals. For example, "Would you care to see the same item in other colors? I have some I can show you." If the customer does not have an immediate interest and seems willing to continue the conversation rather than browse, you may try to arouse interest in a specific item. For example, "Have you had a chance to notice our special at the end of the counter? They offer splendid value at only $3.99, don't you think?"

The purpose of this kind of approach statement or question is to get the customer to relax by talking about himself or by giving an opinion which to him is apparently not related to a buying decision.

THE SALES PRESENTATION

Once your customer has asked to see or has expressed interest in a certain item, you are ready to enter a sales presentation. Since this presentation can involve showing many unnecessary items, it is best to ask a few more questions, particularly opinion questions, that help both you and your customer discover and clarify his problems and wants.

Many retail customers do not know what they are looking for, and you obviously cannot help them solve a problem or fulfill a need or want until you know what it is. Thus you have to get a prospect to reveal his problems or wants and what is important to him before you can help persuade him to solve his problem now. You can get him to reveal his problems through questions such as these.

Are you looking for yourself or another?
What do you think of this grade or quality?
Do you like this style?
Would this be comfortable?

Creating and Holding Interest

Once you have uncovered what you feel is the customer's problem or want, your aim is to move quickly to find the solution or fulfillment to it by a process of elimination, as the above questions illustrate. Here are two techniques that can help you find rapidly the price, item, style, and quality that seem to offer most appeal.

1. **Use interest-building sentences and words.**   The more carefully thought out the words and phrases you have at your command, the quicker you create and hold interest. Vivid, picture-building words ("season's newest fabric," "the very latest fashion"), well-known brand names, and manufacturer's claims ("won't rub off," "will cut your shaving time in half") are useful selling aids which can make your job easier.

2. **Demonstrate whenever possible.**   Seeing is believing, so when a customer expresses interest in or asks for an item, present it quickly if at all possible. As you show it, briefly outline the major features and through well-chosen words help him visualize the benefits he will enjoy after purchasing it.

Your aim at this stage of the presentation is to find the product solution or fulfillment to your customer's problem or wants. If you have asked the right questions and have narrowed the choice, your task now is to help him desire your product—a desire based on the conviction that it is the best possible answer to his needs.

Arousing Desire and Securing Conviction

The next stage of the presentation, based on securing desire and conviction, is aimed at accomplishing three goals.

1.   Help the customer understand exactly what the product is, how it works, and what it does.
2.   Convince him that it is the best solution to his problem or fulfillment of his wants.
3.   Reassure him that the product will bring him the satisfaction he desires.

Let us suppose that your customer is a young secretary highly interested in a newly introduced knit dress suitable for cool weather. In order to arouse desire and secure conviction you need to explain and demonstrate these points.

1.   Features (special characteristics of the product)
2.   Advantages (of those features)
3.   Benefits (she will gain by having it or lose by not having it)

Your presentation may run like this one.

You as Salesperson:	Based upon what you have told me, one of these [laying out two styles, one red and one blue] new Dacron-wool knits appears most suitable for you during the autumn months to come.
Feature:	Both these dresses, just coming into fashion, offer color and style and are suitable for smart work-day attire or for evenings in town.
Advantage:	This is important because you would be stylishly yet comforta-

	bly and warmly dressed for almost any occasion; don't you agree?
Customer:	Yes, that's true.
You	Wouldn't it also feel good to know you are dressed properly for
Benefit	an evening out right after work?
Gain	Knowing you were dressed suitably for any occasion would also
Avoid	help you avoid the worry of possibly not being properly dressed
(use one or	for an after-work event, wouldn't it?
the other)	
Customer:	Yes, it's certainly something to consider.

You can do many other things to point out and demonstrate other features, advantages, and benefits (such as quality, price, and value) to be gained by owning one of the knit dresses. Many suggestions were covered in previous chapters. Your yes-building questions bring out the customer's needs or wants, which indicate the points you should stress.

Basically, you have been selling the satisfaction the dress will give, so after briefly pointing out each major feature, illustrate or demonstrate it by using the garment itself. Hold it up for her to see or let her feel it or try it on. While demonstrating you can help her visualize the nice appearance she will have after making the purchase. Whenever you use the garment (or other item) in a demonstration, handle it with care and pride.

By using the words *when* and *your* during this part of the presentation, you help give the customer a feeling of ownership. For example, you could continue the presentation by saying, "When you wear one of these warm, colored knits, you will always have the feeling of being appropriately dressed."

Handling Questions, Objections, Excuses, and Indecision

In Chapter 13 on handling objections, the point was made that a good salesperson should always frame objections into questions which he is then only too happy to answer. We covered in that chapter various techniques for handling standard objections such as "It costs too much," or "I can't afford it now," plus some unusual types. Since those techniques apply to retail selling as well as to specialty selling, there is no need to repeat them here. We can, however, devote attention to handling excuses and indecision.

Excuses or stalls. These, rather than real objections, are often more of a problem for retail salespeople than for specialty sales representatives. Many store shoppers may want to buy but can think of any number of excuses to put off the decision. The table at the top of page 334 lists some standard excuses for not buying now and some suggestions for handling them.

Indecision. Another problem more commonly faced by retail salespeople than by specialty sales representatives is indecision. An example is a woman shopper who simply and illogically cannot make up her mind whether to buy. You do not want to force her decision and run the risk of losing her as a future customer, but you should try to help her decide to buy if you feel she wants the item.

Here are some suggestions extracted from *Retail Selling*[1] on helping a shopper who cannot make up her mind to buy.

---

1. *Retail Selling,* Brochure No. 106 (Waterford, Conn.: National Sales Development Institute, 1966), pp. 3–12.

Excuse	*One way of handling it*
"I'll have to think it over."	"Why do you have to think it over?"
"I'll come back and buy it later on."	"I appreciate your feelings, but it may be sold before you return. May I put it aside for you now?"
"I think I'll look around before deciding."	"Fine, but before you go, may I ask what feature appealed to you most?" Appear to give up, get the customer relaxed and chatting, and then go back into a close based on the feature with greatest appeal to the customer.
"I would like my husband to see it first."	This may be a valid reason or a mere excuse. If the former, try to set a specific time for them to call back together, saying you will hold the item until then. If you feel it is just an excuse, try to close immediately.

Present favorable alternatives. Ask which of two presented items she prefers rather than whether she likes either. Then she has a choice between two things rather than between something and nothing.

Mention testimonials. Whenever they are available, mention testimonials. For example, you may say, "It's featured in the leading fashion magazines," or "Margret Bidlingmaier, the television star, has one." You can also mention favorable comments of your own satisfied customers and can stress store or manufacturer's guarantees. The customer may like the item but be uncertain of its quality. Your explanation of the guarantee may provide a lead-in to a trial close.

Stress the timeliness of the item. Since women want fashionable items while they are still exclusive, you may say, "This style will be the height of fashion this season. If you get it now you'll be one of the first to wear it."

Suggest she take advantage of the price. If the item is specially priced remind her that it will not be on sale much longer. Or you may point out that the price is increasing and that she will save money if she buys now.

Stress limited quantity. If the item is in short supply, explain that she probably will not be able to get it later. You must be honest in your use of such a statement, however, since customers are wary of such warnings. Be sure the supply is limited!

Once you have handled a question or objection or turned the excuse or indecision into positive interest, you can briefly restate the features, advantages, and benefits the customer appears most interested in.

Closing the Sale

When you sense that your customer is interested at any stage in the above process, you should stop showing the merchandise and go immediately into a trial close. We outlined in previous chapters the buying signals that may indicate her interest and the several specific techniques you may employ in closing the sale.

HANDLING SPECIAL PROBLEMS IN RETAIL SELLING

As we lead into a review of how you as a salesperson may handle certain special problems often encountered in retail selling, we should note once again the difference between improper high-pressure selling and good customer/society-oriented, problem-solving selling. The basic difference is the customer's acceptance in the latter case of the fact that you are sincerely trying to help him buy wisely and are not just selling him anything for the sake of a sale.

If you are trying to help, then your suggestion of higher priced items, substitute items, or specials should not normally offend the customer. Thus your attitude and manner are basically more important than the specific words or techniques you employ in handling some of the special retail problems involving customer situations and merchandise (or product), which we shall now consider.

Special Customer Situations

The shopper.   A common problem faced by retail salespersons is how to get the shopper or browser interested in something you could turn into a sale. Far too many salespersons do nothing when, in response to an unwise and poor "Good morning, may I help you?" greeting, the customer replies, "No thank you, I am just looking [or shopping]."

We considered a few pages back how, once you have greeted him properly and gained his attention and interest, you may try to call his attention to certain items. Our suggestion in general was that you try to guide him at least to the proper section for the merchandise he may be interested in and to let him know of any specials. A second suggestion was to encourage him to continue looking around, not to bother him while he is looking, but to give your name and let him know you are available to answer questions. If you keep him in mind and are alert to move over to help if he does appear to find something of interest, you at least stand some chance of turning his "just looking" into a sale.

Our chief reason for bringing this common problem up again is to encourage you to think and to try to do something about the situation. Your degree of success in turning shoppers into buyers can spell the difference between being a mere ordertaker and being a professional salesperson.

Two customers at once.   Suppose you are waiting on one customer and another obviously interested one comes along. How do you as a salesperson handle the situation? Here are three suggestions.

1.   If another salesperson is available, call him over to help the second customer.
2.   Continue to assist your first customer but give a nod of recognition to the second to let him know that you are aware of his presence. If he is nearby you may even say, "Good morning, someone will help you shortly."
3.   If the first customer is just looking, excuse yourself for a moment to at least welcome the second and to get him started looking at a specific item. Before doing this, you should let the first know that you will be back to continue helping him.

Because most stores require that you assist the first customer before spending any time with the second, the issue presents problems. If the first just looks and the second appears highly interested, you may have to use your judgment, excuse yourself by telling the first you will be back with him shortly, and complete the sale with the second.

Group of shoppers.   A group of shoppers can pose problems to you as a retail salesperson. A common example is that of a friend's trying to dominate the buying decision of the customer. You may have to sell the friend in this case, but should pay primary attention to the wants and desires of the customer. If the friend is an annoyance, you may even signal another salesperson to engage him in conversation and allow you to concentrate on helping the customer. Some further suggestions for handling group selling situations are in Chapter 17.

Complaining or irate customer. Exchanges of merchandise, normal complaints (such as, "The toaster won't work," or "It won't do what was claimed for it"), and angry or irate customers often pose problems for retail salespersons. Even though the store may have an adjustment department, the customer usually first goes back to the original salesperson or department where the purchase was made with his complaint.

Although the fault may be that of some other department such as advertising, delivery, or accounting, such complaints are basically sales problems. Because the success of both you and your store lies in having satisfied, repeat customers, your basic sales tasks are (1) sincerely trying to help solve the problem to the customer's satisfaction if possible and (2) trying to turn his complaints into new current or future sales. Never argue with a complaining or irate customer. Here are some of the steps you should promptly take to handle the situation.

1. Acknowledge both his right to complain and his specific complaint at once.
2. Ask him for full details, listening carefully without interruption until he finishes.
3. Repeat the complaint to him to clarify both the problem and all details to your full understanding.
4. If the customer is right, admit the error and take steps to correct it. If he is wrong, do not try to prove him wrong, but instead ask him for his help and suggestions in trying to find an answer to the problem.
5. Call your manager or other store experts or executives for assistance if you are not able to resolve the problem to the customer's satisfaction.

Know Your Merchandise
and How to Handle Special Problems in Selling It

Having information about the merchandise you sell is vital to your success as a retail salesperson. You must be able to intelligently point out features, advantages, and benefits of an item to a customer constantly asking himself, "What benefits will I gain by buying it? What benefits may I lose by not buying it?"

The best way to become aware of the benefits of a specific item of merchandise is to understand what general types of benefits it may offer. As you study each item you sell in order to increase your product knowledge, look for these three types of benefits.

1. *Obvious benefits* are ones anyone can see, such as beauty, durability, or the purpose for which the item is made.
2. *Exclusive benefits* are advantages or features of an item which its competitors do not possess.
3. *Hidden benefits* are ones not readily seen or understood without explanation. For example, in the knit-dress sales situation discussed earlier, you as a salesperson were selling appearance and attractiveness for any work day or evening social occasion.

How do you find out about merchandise benefits?   Constant interest in and study of the items you sell bring product or merchandise knowledge. Here are some questions you may ask yourself about any item in order to discover what benefits it offers customers.

1. *What is the item to be used for?* How can it be used? Is it easy and convenient to use? Is it durable?
2. *What does it look like?* Is it attractive, unusual, colorful, novel? Does it have good style?
3. *How does it compare in price?* What is its price? How does that price compare with that of similar items? If less expensive does it offer real value? If more expensive does it offer compensating value?
4. *How do you care for the product?* Is there any feature such as ease of maintenance that you can point out to your customers?
5. *Can it be serviced easily?* Are replacement parts readily available? Does it have a guarantee?
6. *Are any testimonials available to back up claims?* What do the various independent consumer reports have to say about it? Does the manufacturer supply any performance data measuring it against competition?

The more you know about each item of merchandise you sell, the easier it will be for you to meet and handle the following special problems.

Presenting merchandise specials.   Most retail stores advertise specials to attract customers to their place of business. Nothing is more discouraging to a shopper than to enter a store in response to such an advertisement only to find that the salespeople know little or nothing of either the ad or the item.

You should read your store ads daily not only to know what specials are being offered but also to know the price and other features so that you can make an effective sales presentation. Even if your customer does not know about or ask for such specials, your telling him about them presents an excellent chance to make new or second sales.

Making second sales.   The above-mentioned specials offer just one way to turn a just-completed sale into a new or second sale. If a customer, for example, has just purchased some new shirts, you can call his attention to a range of new ties and suggest that the styles and colors go well with the shirts. If you have just sold a new steam iron, you can suggest a new ironing-board cover. In such cases show the second item if at all possible.

When a customer buys anything he is in a buying mood, and if you know your merchandise and features that tie in with the initial purchase, second sales are often easy to make.

Trading up for bigger sales.   When a customer asks to see certain merchandise, start by asking qualifying questions regarding size, style, color, or the use to which it may be put. You should not ask what price he wants to pay.

After asking a few but not too many such questions begin your presentation by showing him your medium-price range. This gives you a chance to discuss quality and a chance, if he does not indicate price resistance, to introduce a higher-priced item by way of comparison. You can then demonstrate that far greater value can be realized at only slightly higher price. You can also talk quantity at this point, especially where specials are concerned.

If a customer wants a low-cost item, he will tell you. If he does not mention price, a fundamental rule of good retail selling is to start in the middle price range and trade up, i.e., show higher quality or priced items.

Selling substitute items.   When a customer asks for a certain item by brand name or price range and you have it in stock, you may have the opportunity through substitution to trade up. If you do not have it, you either have to present an acceptable substitute or lose the sale.

Since many customers object to your mentioning substitutes if the item asked for is in stock, you must handle your introduction of a possible substitute carefully. Show the item asked for, then introduce the second item casually.

Here is the item you mentioned, and it is indeed good. But may I, by way of comparison, also show you a newer and slightly more expensive item should you desire to compare difference in quality?

The words *should you* provide a reason for the suggestion and eliminate the overt impression that you are trying to sell something other than what was asked for. If your customer is interested in a comparison, you may be doing him a favor by presenting greater quality at only slightly higher price. Your product knowledge and skill of presentation can thus often lead to a substitute trade-up sale that helps both you and the customer.

If the item asked for is not in stock, you can explain that you do not have that specific item and politely inquire about the customer's needs and wants. You can then show him a comparable or even better item from your stock. Your product knowledge comes in handy as you compare the features of your item point by point with those of the item originally asked for. The best way to arouse and sustain interest is to get your substitute item into his hands as quickly as possible after admitting that you do not have the one asked for and to explain its features positively and with confidence.

TO YOUR CUSTOMERS YOU ARE THE STORE

To most customers, and this includes you as a customer in your outside-of-work life, a store, business, or company is the people who sell and provide service in it. Thus to your customers you, the salesperson, are the store.

Just as you expect prompt, cheerful, willing service from the salespeople from whom you buy, so do your customers expect, appreciate, and remember the same kind of reception from you. No matter how good the merchandise or how beautiful the displays, your store will not enjoy a good reputation or attract satisfied, repeat customers unless you play your part in making it a pleasant place in which to shop and buy.

You as a retail salesperson have a heavy responsibility—as an official host—to ensure that your customers are always met and treated in the courteous, pleasant way in which you would expect to be received at their places of business or in their homes.

As customers depart, take a moment to smile at them and say, "Thank you for shopping with us."

SUMMARY

Since approximately three-fifths of the total American sales force is engaged in retail (inside) selling as contrasted to specialty (outside) selling, we devoted our attention in this chapter to some special applications of salesmanship to the field of retail selling. We concluded that all the fundamentals of salesmanship studied so far apply to retail selling. Some differences in techniques and applications are, however, of special interest to retail salespeople. Since customers come to the retail salesperson, he or she is in effect acting as a host in meeting them. The degree of persuasion salespersons are authorized to employ is determined by the store, which has to keep in mind its customers and trade.

After reviewing the steps of the sales presentation within the retail setting, we discussed the problems of handling excuses and indecision, noting that detailed procedures for handling objections and closing the sale had been covered in earlier chapters. We then went into the handling of special sales problems (e.g., the shopper, two customers at once, a group of shoppers, and the complaining or irate customer). We then emphasized the importance of knowing one's merchandise and gave suggestions for developing such knowledge and for handling merchandise sales problems (e.g., selling specials, making second sales, trading up for bigger sales, and selling substitute items). We concluded with the thought that, to the customer, you as a salesperson represent the store and thus have a heavy responsibility as an official store host.

CHAPTER REVIEW

CONCEPTS TO REMEMBER*

____ retail salesperson	____ merchandise special	____ the shopper
____ incentive programs	____ selling satisfaction	____ exclusive benefits
____ relaxing questions	____ favorable alternatives	____ hidden benefits
____ trading up	____ second sales	____ substitute items

*For memory reinforcement, fill in the page number or numbers where the terms were described in this chapter.

QUESTIONS FOR ANALYSIS AND DISCUSSION

1. As a salesperson, how could you help a customer overcome a possible inner fear of being sold something he does not want?
2. What are three things you as a retail salesperson may do to help a woman shopper who for no apparent reason cannot seem to make up her mind to buy?
3. What is the first selling job a retail person has when greeting a customer?
4. What is the basic difference between retail (inside) selling and specialty (outside) selling?
5. What are the best kind of questions a salesperson can ask a customer or shopper? Why are they the best kind?
6. What is it, basically, that a retail salesperson is selling when showing new fashions in clothing to customers?
7. What is the best single way to handle objections or questions?
8. If a customer comes to you with a complaint about an item, and you are the retail salesperson who sold it to him or her, what two sales tasks should you immediately try to accomplish?

EFFECTIVE POINT OF SALE RETAIL MERCHANDISING AND PERSONALIZED SELLING KEEPS CORO, INC. THE WORLD'S LARGEST MANUFACTURER OF COSTUME-JEWELRY[2]

Based on the belief that the world's women will continue to individualize their appearance with costume jewelry, as they have done through the ages, Coro, Inc. a subsidiary of Richton International Corporation, with sales of over $30 million per year, is today the world's largest manufacturer of costume-jewelry, in what is a big and growing $500 million industry.

From assembly lines in its Providence, Rhode Island factory, some 600 workers turn out a wide range of merchandise in various price lines ranging from its mass merchandising line of costume-jewelry under $2 to its "Coro" line, retailing from $2 to $5, through its "Vendome" line, retailing from $5 and up—Coro's own large designing department, operating at an annual cost of more than $500,000 per year creates new styles at such a prodigious rate that domestic and foreign competitors alike find it difficult to compete.

Even good designs and new styles have to be sold however, and Coro's innovative and highly successful point of sale merchandising and personalized sales technique glitter as brightly as do many of their products.

Most of Coro's over 6,000 customers are costume-jewelry departments located in department or chain stores. On initial calls, Coro Sales Representatives concentrate on selling free-standing, attractive display cases, each holding as many as sixty dozen items in earrings, necklaces, rings, and bracelets. These space-saving cases offer the advantage of displaying a large selection, attractively presented, to allow customers to get a close look and physically pick up merchandise for a closer look if they so desire.

Once the initial sale is made and the display cases set up, the sales representatives visit their customer regularly every four weeks to take inventory, write up replacement orders, and present new products. Their sales records and personalized feedback to headquarters keep Coro fully alert to new fads or trends that the company's design, manufacturing, advertising and sales departments can swiftly capitalize upon. Good design, new styles, a wide choice, attractive point of sale display and methodical follow up by the sales representative is still not enough for Coro, however. Realizing that customers still have to be lured to the Coro display, the company, at considerable expense, put in skilled personnel at scores of costume-jewelry departments all over the United States to pierce the ears of prospective earring customers. Over 500,000 pairs of ears were pierced during 1972 and 1973 alone according to some estimates.

Another innovative Coro activity, was the installing of engraving machines in these costume-jewelry departments so that customers could have personal or gift purchases personalized with engravings on the spot. These ear-piercing and engraving sales promotion activities naturally aroused customers' attention and interest, and helped sell a lot of costume-jewelry that would not have been sold

---

2. Material from CORO, Inc. and other sources.

otherwise. It is through these, and more innovative retail merchandising and personalized selling ideas to come that Coro, Inc. intends to maintain its sales lead in the industry.

QUESTIONS FOR WRITTEN REPORTS OR CLASS DISCUSSION

1. Would you consider the basic idea behind Coro's ear-piercing and engraving sales promotion ideas to be that of selling ideas or selling goods? Explain.
2. Do you think Coro's sales would increase or decrease if they changed their display cases to a vending-machine style, so a customer could put money in and receive merchandise on the spot without having to bother with a retail salesperson writing up the sale? Explain?
3. Do you feel a Coro program to train retail-salespersons in customer-oriented techniques of presenting and selling costume-jewelry would result in increased sales for Coro? If so, please outline what you feel such a training program should cover, and over what period of time.
4. Name two "hidden benefits" you as a Coro sales representative could point out to a prospective retail store buyer considering whether or not to stock Coro jewelry?

Case Study 16–2

HOW ONE RETAIL SPECIALTY STORE IMPLEMENTS THE SOFT-SELL

A customer entering the well-appointed clock and jewelry store in a large midwestern American city is greeted immediately by an attractive and smiling saleswoman who urges him to a seat in front of a blank display table in a long and narrow room. The saleswoman brings articles to him for personalized display once he makes his interests known. She serves coffee, engages in pleasant conversation with him, and makes sure the atmosphere is relaxed. She puts on jewelry for display, calls others over for opinions, and makes every effort to satisfy the customer's every wish. She puts as much care and attention into the display of inexpensive articles as into the display of very expensive ones.

Once the sale is made she sends it out for wrapping and offers the customer a small gift, such as an attractive miniature souvenir spoon—compliments of the house. The customer feels comfortable, relaxed, and flattered at all the attention.

The saleswoman then smilingly invites him, while the item is being wrapped, to see a special upstairs "exhibit." The exhibit is a display room filled with every article the store sells! The still-smiling saleswoman keeps urging him to "look at this next unusual item—it's so reasonable and would make such a cute gift." They are normally alone in the room; the tour is a personalized one.

As the customer leaves the store with his purchase (or purchases), all the smiling salesstaff free for the moment are at the door waving him off and urging him to come again. He leaves with the feeling of having gone through one of the most pleasant and thorough soft-sell experiences of his life.

QUESTIONS FOR WRITTEN REPORTS OR CLASS DISCUSSION

1. What successful techniques did the saleswoman employ to rapidly reach a bond of understanding between the customer and herself?
2. What three basic customer denominators of desire did the saleswoman play on in handling her sales presentation the way she did?
3. Did the saleswoman try for a second sale? If so, how did she go about it, and what buying motives did she appeal to in the process?
4. The above noted soft-sell sequence plays throughout on one important and deeply rooted need common to most people today. What is that need, and how did the saleswoman play on it?

SALES PROBLEM 16–1

INDECISION DURING A CHINAWARE SALE

A husband and wife approach the department-store chinaware area where you are a salesperson on duty. You greet them properly and show them several sets of fine china that arouse their interest. They both ask questions and then tell you they will talk it over and come back in a few minutes.

QUESTIONS FOR WRITTEN REPORTS OR CLASS DISCUSSION

1. You answer questions raised by both but direct your appeals to one of them. To whom, husband or wife, do you direct your appeals, and why?
2. Should you let them depart to talk it over privately or try to close without giving them such a chance? Why?

SALES PROBLEM 16–2

HELPING A MAN SELECT A PRESENT FOR HIS WIFE

A male customer approaches a lingerie counter in a fashionable women's apparel shop. He appears slightly ill at ease because two or three women shoppers are just browsing there. You as a salesperson ask whether you may help him. He explains that he is looking for a nice birthday gift for his wife—something very feminine. He does not appear to know exactly what he wants and keeps looking at his watch.

QUESTIONS FOR WRITTEN REPORTS OR CLASS DISCUSSION

1. What psychological facts should you as a salesperson recognize in this situation?
2. What sales approach should you use?
3. How can you best close the sale?

---

some special applications to telephone, industrial, group, and exhibition selling

When you have mastered the content of this chapter, you should be able to:

Define the terms *purchasing agent, value analysis, cost analysis,* and *group selling.*

Describe what is meant by the term *telephone itinerary* and how to properly prepare beforehand for selling by telephone.

Outline ten steps involved in a complete telephone sales presentation.

Describe the special importance of voice and word usage in telephone selling, and give some techniques for proper use of each.

List the two basic groups of buyers that constitute the industrial market, and some features that distinguish industrial buyers.

Describe the special importance in industrial selling of understanding the buyer's values.

Describe how to plan for and conduct a formal sales presentation before a group.

Describe how to plan and organize for trade show or exhibition selling, and how to personally sell at such shows.

As in the preceding chapter on retailing, we will review in this chapter some of the special considerations and attention needed to sell successfully in a few other special categories. These categories include selling by telephone, selling to industrial and government accounts, and selling to groups and organizations. We will also consider how to plan for, organize, and handle prospecting and selling at trade shows or exhibitions.

The same basic principles of selling we have studied up to this point apply to each. Our theme in presenting these principles, however, has been centered largely around the specialty (outside) sales representative selling a product or service direct to a single prospect or buyer in a face-to-face interview situation. Now we will consider application of these principles to the special situations indicated in greater detail.

SELLING BY TELEPHONE

Selling by telephone is a far bigger business in the United States than most people realize. Products sold directly over the phone range from housewares to industrial chemicals. We can dramatize this statement by noting that boats, lumber, banking services, heavy construction equipment, magazine subscriptions, home food plans, women's wear, office supplies, jewelry, catering supplies and servicing, home and office decorating supplies and services, electronics equipment, and children's toys are but a few of the hundreds of items being sold today by telephone throughout the country.

Every major city now has anywhere from ten to fifty or more highly organized phone rooms worked by full-time or part-time professional telephone selling staffs. Telephone companies work closely with these professional groups and with individual companies, organizations, or individuals in helping them get set up for telephone selling and training telephone sales representatives.

Direct telephone selling is employed by growing numbers of manufacturers, wholesalers, retailers, and fund raisers. Ever-increasing postal rates have speeded use of the telephone as an advertising, merchandising, and sales-promotion medium. Low-cost, flat-rate telephone service is now available in most metropolitan areas. Development of W.A.T.S. (Wide Area Telephone Service) lines offered by telephone companies has opened up whole states—and the entire nation—to low-cost, toll-free blanket service for subscribers. This has led to a situation where telephone calls in volume are often less expensive than mailing pieces—and can be up to five times as effective. It offers firms and individual sales representatives new opportunities to increase sales volume at less cost. It is most cost-effective when used to sell high-priced items or sets or groups of lower-priced items.

The Telephone Is a Useful Sales Tool for Many Reasons

Not only is the telephone useful for prospecting and making appointments, as we discussed in Chapter 7; and for direct selling, advertising, merchandising sales promotions, and fund-raising in general, as noted above; it is also used in countless specific ways. You might find the telephone useful for your own selling purposes, such as:

The price increase. Your product or service is scheduled for a price increase. Phone your present customers—giving them a chance to buy while the lower price is still in effect.

Introduction of a new line. Your company will soon introduce an entirely new line of goods. Who deserves the first crack at them? Good customers, of course—and the telephone offers you a chance to reach them all, cheaply and quickly.

Inventory clean-out. Here is a situation where the cost of your products is being reduced. These are the same products that your customers have been buying all along. Now, who will buy them at the reduced price, and who will appreciate the chance to buy them cheaply? The same steady customers who have been buying all along, naturally. So, here you have a chance to sell, and again, the telephone is a useful tool.

The pending event. From time to time, a pending event will increase the demand for a product. For example, when a new law is about to be passed that affects the operation of a business, it often opens opportunities to get in under a deadline. This is a key selling time, and the telephone increases many times over the amount of people you can reach in a short time.

Encourage customers to phone in regular orders. Inbound W.A.T.S. toll-free services designed to encourage phone-in orders are used by many companies, such as American Hospital Supply and Inland Steel, with successful results. Many of these companies have enlarged their customer service departments with inside sales representatives especially trained to handle inquiries and write sales orders.

For follow-up and follow-through. Your use of the telephone rather than trips or personal calls can save time, cut costs, and is often equally or even more effective.

More important than "handling" current accounts is generating new orders by telephone. A good example is Bell and Howell's highly effective "telesell" campaigns where the company pulls its entire consumer product sales force off the road two or three times a year so that the sales representatives can "telesell" key dealers from their homes. This is done on the last day before a price increase, to help the dealers get their order in under the wire. Similarly, the sales representatives get on the telephone at the end of a promotion period, to help the dealers take advantage of the promotion's benefits by anticipating future needs.

Organizing for Effective Telephone Selling

Telephone selling is a special form of selling requiring careful preplanning, organizing, and special sales techniques in order to achieve desired results. Here are some of the most important guidelines to consider.

Develop a "telephone itinerary." You should plan in advance exactly which accounts will be called, and with what frequency. Most professional full-time telephone selling in the United States is aimed at the residential or home market. Where there are plenty of prospects, calls can profitably be made from 9:00 A.M. to 9:00 P.M. Best-results periods are normally in the morning, and in the evening from 7:30 to 9:00 P.M.

Calls being made in the best interests of commercial or industrial accounts can normally be made at any time during the business day. The best times to call retailers are the half-hour before the store opens, the hour from 11:00 to 12:00 A.M., and during the afternoon from 2:00 to 3:30 P.M. During the rest of the day, retailers are generally too busy with customers of their own to be receptive to telephone sales calls.

As in any form of selling, the more people called, the better the results. Telephone selling can be productive at almost any time; timing of calls at certain times on specific types of prospects or customers simply produces better results. In general, Friday afternoon or evening is the poorest time to call; Saturday is often the most productive day. Telephone selling should never be attempted on Sundays or holidays.

Set telephone sales objectives. Each call, as well as the entire telephone effort, should have a specific sales objective. Since time is so limited, these objectives and your opening statements should be carefully set down on paper beforehand. It is best to stress no more than one or two major features, advantages, and benefits.

Prepare sales tools beforehand. Sales aids or tools should be specifically designed for telephone tools; do not try to make field-sales tools do double duty. Aids should consist of factual and statistical information—laid out for immediate reference, ready for use in conversation with prospects.

Study, develop, and rehearse beforehand proper telephone techniques. These techniques will be discussed shortly.

Plan to save call time.   The more calls made, the better your results will be. These practical guidelines to save time should be followed:

Know exactly why you are calling—and what you want to say—before lifting the phone. This makes calls as brief and efficient as possible.

Make as many calls as you can at one time—say, between 9:00 A.M. and 10:00 A.M. You "get in the groove" and don't have to interrupt yourself later in the day.

Don't hang on the line while a long-distance operator tries to reach your party. Tell her to call you back when she gets your man.

Say what you want to say—clearly, concisely, and quickly. Beating around the bush and discussing unimportant details will cost you time. But be sure you include all essential facts relating to the discussion, or you may end up making another call later.

Hang up when purpose of call is completed. Don't get involved in any unnecessary, extra conversation.

Use a three-minute egg-timer, if necessary, to help force yourself to complete calls within the time limit. Set the timer at the beginning of the call.

Evaluate results and redirect efforts and techniques as needed.   It is necessary to evaluate results in terms of orders written, or in any other type of specific, pre-set objectives; do not evaluate in terms of goodwill achieved.

Plan direct mail follow-up.   A systematic program of mailings—even if it is only handwritten postcards—should follow telephone calls to confirm what was agreed to. It is desirable to develop special after-call mailing pamphlets and folders summarizing the sales presentation for (1) repeat customers and (2) hard-to-sell prospects.

ANATOMY OF A TELEPHONE SALES PRESENTATION

In Chapter 7 we presented in detail the basic steps to follow in using the telephone for prospecting and making appointments. We will not repeat all the basics presented there; study that section again in connection with this information. Our purpose now will be to outline, illustrate, and explain use of the telephone in making a complete sales presentation. It is done in this sequence:

1. Identify yourself and your firm.
2. Establish rapport with the prospect.
3. Make an interest-creating comment.
4. Ask fact-finding questions.
5. Deliver your sales message.
6. Ask for the order.
7. Handle objections.
8. Close the sale.
9. Confirm details of the order.
10. Express your thanks.

To illustrate these steps, let us assume you are selling subscriptions to a ficticious well-known national magazine called *Business and Industry Weekly* to businesspersons connected in any way with nationally known advertisers in the magazine. Let us further assume that Ford Motor Company is one of those advertisers, and that you are now working your way through the list of Ford dealers in your area as listed in telephone book yellow (classified) pages, and that you have previously obtained the name of this particular dealer whom you are now calling, who has just picked up the phone.

The presentation on page 348 was adapted in large part from a highly successful midwestern United States telephone promotion used a few years ago to promote *Life* magazine subscription offers to businessmen. Published analysis[1] of its effectiveness shows that one out of every two prospects (those who were not already getting *Life*) said "yes" after the initial thirty-second presentation (lines 1 to 10 in our presentation), and three out of every four prospects said "yes" after the second thirty-second part (lines 11 to 19 in our presentation), where it was used.

Very little time was spent handling objections in the *Life* promotion; due to the effectiveness of the presentation, it was easier to sell the next prospect than to try to convert a turn-down. The wrapping-up part (with a repeat of the price and terms) of the *Life* presentation took another thirty seconds (illustrated by lines 20 to 28 in our presentation). Total presentation time, depending on questions or objections, averaged only one and one-half to three minutes.

Three out of four closes on short but effective sales presentation such as this is, of course, very good. This high close rate was the result of a thoroughly planned, professional telephone sales promotion. The above example clearly illustrates how an effective similar promotion can easily be devised by any manufacturer, wholesaler, retailer—or by you as a sales representative on an individual basis.

Analysis of the Presentation

Let us now analyze some of the reasons why this presentation was so effective by relating it to our ten-step sequence given at the beginning of this section. We will recognize why certain key words or phrases were used:

Step 1. This was accomplished in lines 1 to 4. Sales representative puts himself on a first-name basis while maintaining a respectful "Mr." address of the prospect. The call is treated as a business call by prospect because sales representative mentioned business. Sales representative gives prospect a reason for the call before prospect can decide for himself what the reason is.

Step 2. Lines 4 to 6 establish a rapid, subtle rapport suggesting both sales representative and prospect share overall Ford interest. Line 5 flatters prospect ("as you know") by giving him credit for knowing more than he does.

Steps 3 to 6. Lines 7 to 10 are the key presentation-offer words. Specific figures and dates are given to reinforce credibility. The word "if" on line 10 leads prospect to feel this is really a soft-sell offer rather than a sales pitch (which it is). Repetition of word "mail" successfully plants the idea that the entire transaction is handled without any signing of contracts or personal follow-up calls. These three steps are combined in this presentation; the only question being asked is whether prospect wants it mailed to his showroom or home. This is actually a combination assumptive/minor-point close; sales representative assumes prospect will approve, passes over the big decision, and asks prospect merely to choose between showroom or home. Making that decision implies an affirmative decision.

1. Alfred Griffin, *How to Get the Most out of Promotional Telephoning* (Englewood Cliffs, N.J.: Prentice-Hall, Inc., 1966), pp. 15–22.

The Sales Presentation (Time Length, Approximately 1½ Minutes)

Sales Representative:	1. "Good morning, Mr. Smith, my name is Jones, . . . 2. Bob Jones. I'm with the business office of *Business* 3. *and Industry Weekly*, and the reason I'm calling 4. is because of the money we are getting out of your organization. 5. As you probably know, Ford Motor Company pays us 6. $47,000 a *page* to advertise in *Business and Industry Weekly*. 7. To go along with that, starting May 15 we are mailing *Business* 8. *and Industry Weekly* to every Ford dealer we can reach at a 9. special rate of 38¢ a copy and I'm simply calling to ask 10. if you want yours mailed to the showroom or to your home.

Sales representative waits for an answer. If answer is affirmative, he will complete the sale using steps 9 and 10. If "no," he *continues as if no reply was heard.*

Mr. Smith:	"That may not be a bad offer! How does it work?"
Sales Representative:	11. "There's only one catch to it Mr. Smith, and that's the 12. fact that you can't get it indefinitely at that rate. 13. With over 7,000 Ford dealers in the country, we can't send 14. it free, so the 38¢ covers the cost of postage and 15. bookkeeping. We can send it to you at that guaranteed low cost for as long 16. as you want up to, but not exceeding, 150 weeks. 17. That's almost three years, and that's sticking our necks 18. out plenty if postage rates go up again. Are you 19. willing to go along on that?

Sales representative waits for answer. If "yes," he will complete the sale using steps 9 and 10. If "no," he has the choice of either closing the call with a thank-you or asking, "Do you have any questions?" in an attempt to draw out questions or objections, which he can then handle before trying once again to close.

Mr. Smith:	"OK—sign me up."
Sales Representative:	20. "Thank you Mr. Smith, I shall enter your subscription 21. to *Business and Industry Weekly* for 150 weeks at 22. a cost of 38¢ per copy including postage. I'll mail you 23. a brochure outlining this special offer this evening; 24. my business office will bill you within a few 25. days. Thank you for joining so many other 26. Ford dealers in taking advantage of this special 27. offer. *Business and Industry Weekly* appreciates 28. working with Ford.
Mr. Smith:	"OK—thanks for calling."

Step 6. The basic purpose of lines 7 to 10 (heart of the presentation) is to get prospect to agree, through acceptance of one of the two offered places, to mail the magazine to one of them.

Step 7. Anticipating a possible objection, and sensing that prospect is probably thinking "What's the catch," sales representative quickly puts the prospect off balance by saying (line 11) "There's only one catch to it." Prospect's reaction is to think subconsciously that if this limitation is the worst news, the good news is that he could get this special offer indefinitely.

Use of "over 7,000 Ford dealers" (line 13) infers, but does not say, that these dealers are going to get the magazine and appeals to prospect's desire for conformity. The word "free" (line 14) is one of the most powerful words in selling; by using it sales representative plants the idea even while denying it. Use of "38¢ covers the cost of postage and bookkeeping" after "free" further implies in prospect's mind that it is a very good offer.

Lines 15 to 18, especially the words "for as long as you want" and "that's sticking our necks out if postage costs go up" again infers a soft-sell offer and adds conviction that it is a good, safe offer to accept.

Step 8. "Are you willing to go along with that" (lines 18 and 19) represent the second closing attempt—by asking easily for a "yes" answer.

Steps 9 and 10. Since there are no visual means to hold attention in telephone selling, it is necessary to restate what has been offered or agreed to, repeating price, terms, and other necessary details. This and the concluding expression of thanks for the order are combined in lines 20 to 28.

Some Observations
on Proper Telephone Sales Techniques

There are certain psychological factors to consider and plan for before making a telephone sales call. Since the telephone is a very impersonal instrument, unless you have your questions and presentation framed carefully it is very easy for the person on the other end to tell you he is not interested and cut you off. It is always wise to write an outline beforehand of what you plan to cover in the conversation. In face-to-face conversations, expressions, gestures, and posture help add meaning to words, but words alone have to communicate by telephone, so you should frame them carefully beforehand so as to be certain your message gets across as desired. Even though you have outlined your presentation beforehand, you should say it in such a way that it does not appear to be merely a "canned" outline you are reading to the other person.

Your *voice* is the major thing you have going for you over the telephone. The warmth of your voice, the inflections you use, and the specific words used are all very significant. It is important to try to project yourself over the phone, especially your warmth and interest. One way to do this is to smile when you are talking; to imagine you are face to face with your prospect and trying to project your personality to him.

When talking, it is important to try and involve the prospect as much as possible, avoiding a monologue. One good way to do this is to ask involving questions from time to time. If he voices questions or objections, you can establish better rapport by indicating that you are listening carefully to what he is saying. This can be done by using words like "yes," "that's right," and "I agree with what you are saying." When he says something of obvious importance to him, use the technique of repeating the substance of his remark, so he knows you heard it.

The telephone can be a valuable, time-conserving, money-making sales aid in prospecting, selling, and after-sales follow-up if used properly. This is the age of the tape-recorder; use it to practice your telephone calls before you make them, so you will know in advance how your voice and words will sound to others.

INDUSTRIAL SELLING

Early in Chapter 2 we discussed the two broad types of markets—consumer and industrial. In defining both, we noted that the industrial market is made up of those who buy to further the production of other goods and services (rather than for personal or family consumption). At that time we also noted that some differences in approach are necessary to effectively sell to the industrial market.

Both products and services are sold to the industrial market, which is comprised of two basic groups of buyers: (1) business enterprises and (2) nonprofit institutions (such as government agencies, schools, and hospitals) or organizations. Some features that distinguish industrial buyers include:

They usually buy in much larger quantities and over a longer period than individual consumers.

They normally employ full-time professional purchasing agents, trained to buy rationally (where they can think the selling proposal over carefully and analyze, measure, evaluate, and discuss it rationally over a long period of time). Others in the company or organization besides the purchasing agent may have to be involved in the purchase-decision.

They often buy on a basis of specifications which are put out for bid. Performance, quality, or other special features may outweigh price as a key factor in their buying decision.

They may seek, or even be required to seek, alternate sources of suppliers for various needs.

Due to the size of most industrial purchases, special specifications that often must be met, and other reasons, much industrial selling is direct between producer and user, although various types of middlemen also sell to industrial buyers. Industrial sales divisions of companies are normally smaller in numbers than consumer sales divisions, and these fewer sales representatives, many of them engineering or science university graduates, often undergo training programs that can last up to two years.

The Changing Nature of Industrial Selling

Traditionally, highly trained industrial sales representatives were more product-oriented than customer-oriented in their selling. Product knowledge, in great depth, was considered more important than any other sales or knowledge attributes. Today, however, as industries consolidate and larger companies take over smaller ones, economic factors are creating a new trend. As costs of plant and equipment have skyrocketed and product technology becomes more complex, companies have responded by taking a longer-range look at their objectives, considering all aspects of their product planning, pricing, quality control, inventory, and marketing. This has led to decrease in item-by-item, or current requirement-by-requirement buying; and to an increase in the systems or overall approach to buying.

Purchasing agents, who are the officially appointed buyers for large companies or organizations, are far better trained today than in the past. Most are skillful, technically oriented men, often with an engineering or production background. Most large companies, such as General Electric and IBM, conduct lengthy training programs to teach purchasing agents how to buy. These men are thoroughly familiar with such things as costs, manufacturing schedules, technical and logistical support.

Due to growing cost-consciousness, upper management is increasingly getting involved in major buying decisions, as are top technical people. Thus the purchasing agent may be but the first level of decision-making. Often many top executive or technical people have to be contacted. In some cases it takes an industrial sales representative or team up to a year just to get to know all the key people, study the operation, and identify any problems of just one large account; and the stakes may be enormous.

To illustrate this last point, consider the problems faced by sales representatives of Boeing's Commercial Airplane Group Sales Division when they set out to sell the new 747 jet—at $20 million per plane! The sales representatives saw everyone of importance in their prospect-airline companies and employed every conceivable visual aid—but they weren't having much luck. Then Boeing found the answer: to sell jets effectively, you have to demonstrate! They did this by getting all the people involved in one airline's buying decisions into a real-life, full-length, 200-foot mock-up of the 747—where they could see, feel, and move about. Disbelief suddenly changed to enthusiasm, and within a short time Boeing sales representatives sold 192 of the Jumbos to twenty-eight airlines.

In order to sell creatively in such a situation, a sales representative must be proficient not only in product knowledge and the psychology of selling, but also in understanding the buyer's values. The sales representative's values are unimportant; what counts is how well he understands the buyer's time value, performance values, ease-of-handling values, assurance-of-supply values, and cost reduction values. To compete successfully, today's industrial sales representatives must have a wide knowledge and understanding of business; and they must be able to understand and discuss such things as value analysis and cost analysis.

Example of a Modern Industrial Sales Representative in Action

Let us assume that a young man we know, Joe Marks, is an industrial sales representative for a plastics container company calling on two manufacturing companies in his territory. He elects to approach Company A with a sales presentation built around *value analysis*. His presentation to Company B will be built around *cost analysis*. Let us see how he goes about each, and with what success.

Company A

The plan.   Joe knows that *value analysis* is a modern, cost-cutting technique built around three simple questions: (1) What does it do? (2) What does it cost? (3) What would do the job cheaper? He decides that if he can come up with the right answers, he's got a sale.

Results.   Joe asked permission to study their manufacturing and shipping operation in which items were packaged in plastic containers. He got all specifications and cost figures for their operation and found his firm could provide equally acceptable containers of a slightly different type for half the price of the competitor's container they were currently using. Since they spent $20,000 a year on containers, and Joe proved he could save them $10,000 a year by answering the three *value analysis* questions, he got the order.

Company B

The plan.   Joe knows that the most important processes for his account are manufacturing and marketing; they are the principal areas of major costs. He decides that they are also the most attractive targets for cost reduction and builds his approach around proving how his products can (1) reduce the company's manufacturing cost, and (2) increase salability of their products. Company B is a manufacturer of household products.

Results.   Joe's approach was to ask, "May I make a two-day study of your operations to see if I can help you cut costs?" The company had nothing to lose, so they gave him permission. After studying their manufacturing, shipping, and sales/marketing, Joe came up with the following:

Manufacturing—he found a way to repackage two of Company B's products in equally acceptable but slightly lower-cost containers; he suggested an idea that eliminated one stage in the manufacture of one of their products; and by suggesting round-edged square containers rather than the round ones they had been using, he reduced their shipping costs 10 percent. Overall cost savings per year resulting from all this was estimated at $10,000.

Sales/Marketing—Joe came up with new design ideas for his containers that so improved packaging appearance of the two repackaged products that Company B's sales manager estimated it would not only be worth an extra 10 percent increase in market share at retail-store point-of-sale, but should gain that even by increasing the retail price 5 percent. Overall extra profit at no extra cost was estimated at $5,000 over the next year.

Joe's twin-pronged *cost analysis* sales strategy and final presentation were gratefully received. He closed by offering to imprint the new design at no extra cost provided Company B gave him a two-year rather than the normal one-year contract. They said yes—and Joe thus in effect doubled the size of the order.

Industrial Selling Summarized

While the basic principles and step-by-step process of approach through close are those common to other types of selling, there are two special aspects to industrial selling worth emphasis. These are (1) the primary concern for buying and (2) the dominant buying urge that influences the final decision. The primary concern is nearly always rational; the dominant buying urge is nearly always emotional.

While a prospect's primary concern may be to buy a better machine tool in order to increase production at less cost, he is human and subject to all the emotional considerations that move anyone to buy anything. Possibly he is in competition with another buyer, perhaps he hopes for a promotion if he buys wisely or fears not being promoted if he buys unwisely. In order to close the sale, an industrial sales representative has to find the key to both.

Once the need, want, or problem is determined, in order to find the acceptable solution it is necessary for the sales representative to establish a real dialogue with his prospect. This is done by asking questions, offering him choices, and asking his opinion. The purpose is not only to hold interest or obtain agreement to rational points, but also to allow the sales representative to observe the prospect's behavior and personal characteristics. A carefully planned presentation that involves the prospect, proves selling points logically, and allows interpretation of inner personal feelings that may influence his buying decision stands the best chance for success in industrial selling.

This is basically the way industrial sales representatives sell products and services to large business firms, government agencies, school systems, hospitals, and nonprofit organizations of various types.

SELLING TO A GROUP

Since industrial selling often involves selling to a group (two or more individuals as contrasted to a single person), attention has to be paid to some specific techniques involved in group selling. We briefly considered this subject on pages 335 and 336 in connection with a retail closing situation but will now discuss it further.

Often a large company or government or private organization publically announces that bids will be accepted for certain items for certain purposes at a stated place and time. Usually certain specifications are announced at the time. In such cases, the buyer brings together a group of purchasing officers, technicians, and executives to hear a formal sales presentation by a sales representative or a sales team from different producers. In some cases the groups will tour factory locations, observe special showings (such as the 747 mock-up in our Boeing example), or see the item in operation at some location.

Planning for Group Selling

Prior to such formal gatherings, you as sales representative or sales team leader should try to meet, or at least find out all you can about each individual member of the group. Your purpose is to try and discover each one's rational and emotional likes and dislikes, both about your product and competing products. Armed with this information, you can then carefully prepare your formal presentation and assemble all necessary samples, charts, statistics, testimonials, and the visual aids necessary to demonstrate and dramatize them most effectively. Whether you are given a specified length of time for the presentation or the time-limit is self-established, you should practice and polish your delivery and demonstrations step by step beforehand.

The Presentation before a Group

Once a formal presentation gets underway, you will normally present your case point-by-point, asking for and accepting limited questions from time to time to keep the group involved, but always maintaining control of the situation. While progressing, you try to determine from attention, facial expressions, or body motions or positions, the degree of acceptance, indifference, or opposition to your points. While deferring to the formal leader of the group, you must try to include each member—by looking at each one individually from time to time, or through question and discussion breaks.

Interestingly enough, in most such situations one or more of the group will probably take your side. Once this becomes evident you can often work through this person, especially if differences of opinion break out among various group members. Also, in such groups one or two people (often not the leader himself) turn out to be the real "influentials," selling others of the group on their point of view. A major purpose in trying to meet each member privately prior to the formal meeting is to try to anticipate who such influentials might be. If one is very much in favor of your proposal, you can play off him by asking his opinion concerning a point you have just made. Conversely, a prior knowledge of possible opposition and the reasons for it may enable you to build any negative points into your presentation and handle them before they are vocally raised as objections before the group.

Most questions are reserved for a question and discussion period following your presentation; lengthy or off-the-point queries should be discouraged during the presentation. This can be done merely by acknowledging the question and asking consent of the questioner to return to it later.

A close, as practiced in face-to-face selling to one person, is seldom applied in such formal group presentations; although in some situations it can be done. Circumstances will dictate your closing action or end-of-presentation statement. Sometimes the group will hear presentations by several sales representatives, one after the other, at an all-day sitting. Normally they advise you beforehand in such formal-presentation situations when the decisions will be announced.

While the above discussion centered on a situation where you as sales representative had been called upon for a presentation at a stated time and place (such as a bid-situation), the same principles apply when you on your own initiative organize a group of two or more people for a formal presentation. In this case, you can more easily attempt to close on the spot.

TRADE SHOW AND EXHIBITION SELLING

Nearly 8,000 trade shows and countless large and small special exhibitions at which sales representatives represent their firm or organization are held each year in the United States. Costs of participation are often very high; for some companies such exhibitions are worthless in terms of specific sales, yet necessary from a sales promotion point of view. Other companies write almost a third of their annual business at such events.

Whatever form of selling you engage in, chances are you will be involved in planning, organizing, attending, and later following-up sales leads obtained at one or more such shows a year. Your participation may range from being part of a company sales team to that of organizing your own one-person show. Your efforts may be highly productive or a waste of time and effort, determined in large part by how well you and your firm or organization plan, organize, execute, and follow-up before, during, and after the event.

Careful Planning Is Essential to Success

In order to obtain maximum results, pre-show planning from a managerial point of view should include (1) establishing clear-cut exhibit goals; (2) discussing these goals thoroughly with your firm's advertising, sales, sales promotion, and public relations staff; (3) planning and coordinating strategy with all these people and with your exhibit designer if you are using one; and (4) communicating the goals and working plan to all sales representatives who will attend. Successful exhibition or trade show selling is, in most cases, the result of a carefully planned, integrated team effort.

Organizing the Show

A trade show or exhibition is one of the few places where the prospect comes to the sales representative. It offers opportunity to write orders on the spot without having to waste time in a waiting room or fighting for a busy buyer's time. But such shows often attract large numbers of visitors—up to 10,000 over a three-day period in some cases. Some are just lookers, some are real prospects, others are valuable established customers. With so little time and so many people crowding around, asking questions and interested in possible detailed explanations or demonstrations, how can you as sales representative-on-the-spot sort, qualify, handle, and sell selectively? The answer lies in careful planning, preparation, and organization; here are some of the major factors to consider:

The physical exhibit. What is it about the exhibition that is likely to attract prospects of interest to you? What will attract and hold prospects to your particular exhibit (which may be only one of many)? Answers to those two questions are essential in planning the physical layout of your exhibit, the effectiveness of which in turn depends on what emphasis you desire to place on selected products or product features. Past experience of your company or fellow sales representatives at such exhibits, good reference books such as *Trade Show Director* (Budd Publications), exhibit organizers, and outside exhibit designers are all good sources of information for effective physical exhibit-booth layout.

Proper booth location in large exhibition halls often plays an important role in attracting and holding visitors. If possible, you should study the floor plan and overall exhibit-booth layout, and select the specific space location best suited to your activity and desired traffic flow. Your firm's sales promotions staff, or other sources previously noted, can offer you guidance concerning product display, demonstration space, catalogue displays, and proper use of lighting, audio-visual equipment, and other matters.

Ample catalogues or other give-away literature must be made available, and plans must be made for its effective distribution. If products are to be demonstrated or audio-visual equipment used, you should know exactly how it works and practice beforehand to make certain you do.

Pre-show buildup. This takes two forms: (1) to obtain maximum publicity so as to attract potential new buyers, and (2) to make certain key prospects and important established customers are individually invited in advance to visit your exhibit.

Proper coordination with your firm's advertising department will help insure effective pre- and post-show advertising in journals and magazines to promote your exhibit. A special "invitation to attend" might be included in any regular advertising mailing scheduled before the exhibition date. Similar coordination with the public relations and sales promotion departments might suggest prior coverage or other attention-getting ideas to attract prospects to your exhibit, both in advance and during the exhibition.

Your sales department should know beforehand which customer companies or organizations are likely to send representatives. Pre-show promotion, through advertising and the field sales force, can alert them and invite them to attend your exhibit booth.

Above all, you should make a special effort to personally invite *your customers* to attend and meet with you. Some you will want to write or telephone, in order to arrange specific appointment times. Others you will merely want to invite to contact you upon their arrival, so you can then arrange a mutually convenient specific meeting time at the booth or elsewhere. One highly effective way to do this is to mail two postcards in an envelope to each of the key people you want to see (potential prospects or regular customers) two weeks before the show. One is a

FIGURE 17.1 Example of a pre–trade show or exhibit invitation written two weeks in advance by a sales representative to a key prospect or customer he specifically wants to meet at the show.

```
Hello, Mr. Jones,
     Hope to see you at our X-Company exhibit booth at the
National Y Exposition to be held May 18-20 at the Plaza Hotel,
San Francisco.
     Won't you let me know where you will be staying, or can be
contacted, on the enclosed post-paid card?
     We have something interesting to show you—it could save
you quite a bit of money!
     I'll be staying at the nearby Oceanside Hotel myself, but
will normally be at our booth from 9A.M. to 9P.M. daily.

                         Sincerely,
```

postpaid, self-addressed reply card addressed to you. An example of the other card is shown in Figure 17.1.

Selling at the show. A carefully designed exhibit and good pre-show promotion may draw initial attention to your exhibit, but they don't sell your products. You, and your fellow sales representatives (if any), do that. Your overall sales problem is somewhat like managing your sales territory. Your aim is profitable sales; to make enough sales to pay all costs of the show (salaries, promotion, etc.) and show a profit. As in your territory, the more qualified prospects or customers you contact at the exhibit, the greater your chance of success. As a guideline, you should aim to make as many effective sales contacts in one day of exhibit selling as one week of field selling.

This may sound like a lot, but exhibitions normally run day and evening and sales representatives manning booths normally put in twelve-hour days, with good prospects possibly visiting at the rate of up to six or eight an hour. Your problem, especially during peak visitor hours, is to separate prospects and buyers from other visitors and handle all properly. Overall, you are in effect your company's host at the show, acting both as sales representative and public relations specialist. Buyers won't waste time standing around waiting for long; so you have to acknowledge and meet with them as soon as possible. Yet you also have to greet and be considerate to all visitors. And you have to be prepared to employ far more rapid-fire selling techniques, due to the short time available, than the normal more relaxed kind of selling done in a prospect's office or home. Here are a few basic guidelines for working effectively in such an often-crowded exhibit-booth situation:

Greet everyone individually if possible, saying something like:

Hello, I'm Tom Jones. As you can see, I'm going to be tied up for a few minutes. Won't you please look around, and I'll join you in a moment.

Qualify each quickly as to their degree of interest—if they appear to be real prospects but you don't have time to handle them then and there, either make an appointment for another meeting at the booth or away from it later during the show, or for after-show follow-up.

Since you won't be able to remember every visitor, ask those showing any degree of interest to either fill in a card with their name, title, business address, telephone, and area of interest, or log it quickly yourself in your own exhibit-log book. Such exhibition prospecting is an excellent way to develop new sales leads.

As visitors depart, try and thank each one for visiting your booth and give them all available literature concerning their area of interest to take with them.

Rapid sales-presentation techniques common to exhibition selling where time may be very short are similar to those we covered in selling by telephone. For example, it is best to stress no more than one or two major features, advantages, and benefits of your product; arrange a later appointment or after-show call if longer time is necessary to explain or answer questions.

After-show follow-up. Your initial pre-show planning should have provided for a system of post-show follow-up and evaluation of results in terms of pre-set goals versus actual or potential sales. All sales contacts, specific leads, or later appointments made during the show should be followed up as soon as possible by telephone, mail, or personal calls.

SUMMARY

Building on previous chapters where our theme generally stressed a sales representative selling face-to-face to a single buyer, we considered in this chapter some special applications essential to successful selling by telephone, industrial and group selling, and prospecting and selling at trade shows or exhibitions.

Noting that telephone selling is a far bigger business in the United States than most people realize, we followed up our Chapter 7 discussion of prospecting and getting the appointment by telephone with an analysis of how to make the complete telephone sales presentation. Illustrations and specific techniques presented should enable any company, organization, retailer, or individual sales representative to use the telephone as an effective sales tool immediately.

Industrial selling, we concluded, covers two basic groups of buyers: (1) business enterprises, and (2) nonprofit institutions (such as government agencies, schools, and hospitals) and organizations. We went into some detail as to the changing nature of industrial selling and how industrial sales representatives sell. A summary of how to handle group selling (two or more people) followed, since much group selling is involved with industrial selling.

Our chapter concluded with an overview of important trade show or exhibition selling; including principles, practices, and several useful how-to-do-it techniques, applicable to any such business or nonbusiness event.

CHAPTER REVIEW

CONCEPTS TO REMEMBER*

____ telephone itinerary	____ purchasing agent	____ trade show
____ W.A.T.S.	____ telephone sales objectives	____ value analysis
____ industrial market	____ group selling	____ telephone voice

*For memory reinforcement, fill in the page number or numbers where these terms were described in this chapter.

QUESTIONS FOR ANALYSIS AND DISCUSSION

1. Name and explain three of the four features described in this chapter that distinguish industrial buyers.
2. What information does a sales representative seek in trying to meet individually with members prior to a formal group sales presentation? How would the sales representative use information so gathered?
3. If you were making a formal sales presentation to a group of government officials, and one asked a question having nothing to do with the immediate topic, how would you handle the situation?
4. Assuming you are sales representative for a firm whose $500 product X is scheduled for a 10 percent price increase in one week, outline a forty-five second telephone sales presentation you would like to make concerning the increase to your regular list of 100 customers. Be prepared to present it in a classroom role-playing situation.
5. What is it about a trade show or exhibition that makes a selling situation for a sales representative so different from his normal field selling activities? Describe and explain your answer or answers.
6. Pre-trade show buildup was described in this chapter as taking two forms. What are they? Why are they important?
7. An industrial sales representative has to know his product, have a knowledge of buyer psychology, and understand the buyer's values. What do we mean by "the buyer's values?" Please enumerate three such values and explain their meaning and importance in terms of both sales representative and buyer.
8. You are a retailer, planning to have your sales staff make a reduced-price color TV set offer by telephone this week during slack business hours. What prospects would you have them call? Where would you get their phone numbers? What time periods during the day would you ask your staff to place calls? What times would be best for the majority of your pre-selected prospects to favorably respond to such telephone sales calls?

A NEW KIND OF CHALLENGE FOR INDUSTRIAL SALES REPRESENTATIVES

In the face of mid-1970s worldwide shortages of many basic commodities such as steel, aluminum, plastics, and synthetic fibers, one might suppose that industrial sales representatives could take life a little easier, letting customers come to them for badly needed goods and materials.

In fact, though, as noted in an interesting *Fortune* magazine article,[2] they are in effect required to administer complex rationing programs for many vital materials. At the same time, fully aware that their markets could again become highly competitive, they have to look to the future and deal carefully with their purchasing-agent customers.

Four such sales representatives were profiled in this article, including Charles E. Wright, a thirty-four-year-old graduate of Colorado State University who is an industrial sales representative for Armco Steel based in Houston, Texas. Armco customers in his territory include companies that manufacture such things as tankers, drilling rigs, and electric utility poles. When the steel shortage first hit in late summer 1973, Wright, for the first time in his sales career, found himself in the position of having to ration steel to his customers.

Prior to that shortage, his job was in most respects like that of any other industrial sales representatives. His primary objectives, he says, were to "get orders from anybody who could put a carload together," and to "do a lot of survey work—find out who was buying what kind of tons from whom." Wright was vying for steel-tonnage orders with seven domestic competitors, as well as foreign producers like the Mexicans and Japanese, not to mention makers of such substitute materials as aluminum. Steel prices and demand were flat, and he customarily spent a lot of time prospecting for sales leads, spouting a quick jargon in a midwestern accent about such commodities as "alloy plates, SSS 100, A 514, Grade E, quenched and tempered."

In those days he would visit regularly with both established and prospective customers, looking for chances to beat competitors. To find new customers, he would get leads from Armco's market-development group or ask his customers who their competitors were.

Wright says that "cold calls" on new sales prospects were the most interesting. "I'd try to find out as much as I could about a prospect's company, the products he made, what problems he had in selling them. Suppose he made oil pipes. I'd bring in our market-development people to help him find new markets for them. Or maybe he had a manufacturing problem requiring technical help. I'd bring in our welding engineer—he's second to none." Wright would describe Armco's mill facilities and available services. "And then I'd say, 'Let me have a chance to quote on your steel requirements. Let me have a trial order.' "

Calls to regular, "buying accounts," on the other hand, were full of "a lot of B.S. about football scores and the weather," he says. "You establish good personal relationships, you really are interested in how his wife and kids are, how his new house is coming." But between pleasantries, Wright would always be asking about the

2. Material in this case study extracted from an article by Michael B. Rothfield, "A New Kind of Challenge for Salesmen," *Fortune*, April 1974, pp. 156–166.

product, how it was being used, and if there were any problems. He concerned himself even with shipping tags that fell off bundles of steel, resulting in transportation delays and resentment toward Armco.

The steel shortage has practically put an end to Wright's calls on new customers, and his relations with old ones have become strained. Nowadays, he can sell steel only to those customers who have a buying "history" with his company. Armco has established a strict allocation program, based upon a customer's record of past purchases.

The allocation program leaves little room for new accounts, which is especially frustrating for Wright and other Armco sales representatives, who would like to keep their sales growing. But they realize that a rationing plan based on previous buying experience is easier to explain to querulous purchasing agents. And they know that allocations, which may deny steel to customers now, can also be a valuable tool for building future sales. Wright tells those customers who bought a lot of foreign steel when it was cheap that they don't have enough "history" with Armco to get all the steel they need. And he leaves them with the thought that when steel again becomes more plentiful, it would be wise for them to establish a more stable relationship with a U.S. supplier—for instance, Armco.

While good-naturedly warning loyal customers against falling into bad habits in the future, Wright does everything he can to keep them supplied now. If he hears that one of his competitors has stock that he lacks, he'll pass the good news along to his customers. He'll also help his customers by telling one of them when another has usable leftovers from its manufacturing process.

In short, he is making the best of a bad situation (temporary shortages), trying to be as honest and as fair as he can with all customers, and is busily laying the groundwork and goodwill for greater sales when steel is once again abundant.

QUESTIONS FOR WRITTEN REPORTS OR CLASS DISCUSSION

1. Would you say that prior to the steel shortage Wright's sales approach was more product-oriented or customer-oriented? Why? Is his post-shortage sales approach any different? In what way?

2. What sort of customer values do you feel Wright must fully understand in order to sell steel to them effectively?

3. With steel in such short supply, if you were in Wright's shoes would you spend time prospecting for new customers? Why?

4. What steps, other than those mentioned in the profile, do you feel Wright could take to impress his old customers with his genuine interest in their problems and his desire to help them in every way possible?

BLACK TRADE FAIRS BOOST
FLEDGLING MINORITY-OWNED BUSINESSES

Trade shows, traditional corporate marketplaces, are increasingly being used to give a boost to fledgling minority businesses. In a unique turnabout of exhibit roles, major American corporations are buying and manning booths, and minority vendors with goods to sell to corporations are the attendees. In this way the corporations demonstrate both their commitment to social change and their willingness to give minority businessmen "a piece of the action." Such shows have been staged successfully in cities like Chicago, Cleveland, and Philadelphia. As described by *Sales Meetings* magazine[3], a Philadelphia venture called the *Minority Business Opportunity Fair* was organized and run as follows:

The fair was a venture of the Philadelphia Regional Minorities Purchasing Council—assisted by the Business Resource Center. The council is a group of fourteen major Philadelphia corporations that actively seek minority suppliers. A BRC consultant supervised most of the fair promotion and planning.

The primary problem was promoting a climate of trust. BRC enlisted the aid of local black civic groups, including the Urban League and National Business League, and the influential black newspaper, the *Tribune*. These supplied BRC with a list of several hundred potential show visitors (prospects) from their contacts in the community. Only wholesalers, people who were manufacturers, or suppliers of materials and services to industry were considered. Pre-registration forms were sent to each, on which they had to indicate the goods or services they offered. Meanwhile, the purchasing council was rounding up exhibitors. Letters and brochures went out to 400 members of the Philadelphia Purchasing Management Association, inviting their participation. (Fee for a booth at the fair was $100.)

Ten days later, the BRC organization began a telephone follow-up, calling every company that had not returned a reservation form. Company forms had space on which to indicate which goods or services the company was interested in purchasing. An index of this information was published in a booklet so each vendor knew immediately which companies he might see.

Three months after the start, the fair opened at the Sheraton Hotel, with seventy-six exhibitors. Booth setups were simple and each one was the same—a curtain backdrop with the name of the company on it and a table with chairs. Free coffee was provided at one end of the hall.

Show sponsors insisted that each exhibitor have a "decision" man in the booth, one who could say yes or no and could award contracts. The idea behind this was for each vendor to be able to shake hands with the man who counted. Some 250 suppliers attended the three-day fair, which started daily in the afternoon and lasted through early evening.

Special forms were supplied to exhibitors. On them the interviewer filled in his name, the exhibitor company, and the name of the booth visitor. The name of the interviewer, details on what the visitor could supply, and specific information on who the visitor would contact for a follow-up interview were all recorded in triplicate; one copy each went to the company and the visitor, the third to BRC for later follow-up.

3. Material in this case study extracted from "Black Fair Scores," *Sales Meetings*, March 1974, pp. 58–96.

A few weeks after the fair, a BRC executive began a personal follow-up of the leads and contracts recorded on triplicate forms. Final results directly attributed to the successful fair were over $650,000 worth of new business generated by twenty-four locally-owned minority companies who signed a total of fifty-eight different contracts.

QUESTIONS FOR WRITTEN REPORTS OR CLASS DISCUSSION

1. In what ways did careful advance planning and organization contribute to the success of this fair?
2. A major problem faced by sales representatives manning trade fairs in general is to separate prospective buyers from "lookers." The "decision maker" manning each booth at this Philadelphia fair did not face such a problem. Why?
3. In addition to the BRC advance contacts, what steps could individual suppliers have taken in advance to ensure that they would have adequate interview time with desired exhibitors during the Philadelphia fair?
4. Assuming you are a sales representative for one of the suppliers attending the Philadelphia fair, what after-fair follow-up action would you take separately from the BRC follow-up to capitalize on this successful fair?

SALES PROBLEM 17–1

HOW WILL NEW INFORMATION AND COMMUNICATIONS RESOURCES AFFECT TELEPHONE, INDUSTRIAL, GROUP, AND EXHIBITION SELLING IN COMING YEARS?[4]

Over the last decade, technological advances in basic electronics have had a significant impact in both computer and communications industries. As a result, sales/marketing people have available today a wide variety of information and communication resources. They are going to find it essential to their survival, and that of their firms, to maximize use of these resources.

There are many reasons for this: utilization of these advances will provide better overall knowledge of the marketplace; make data available faster, for more timely decisions; improve customer services; and enable a corporation to field a more effective sales force—to name a few. New technological advances will bring cost reductions that will also lead to increased utilization. For example, consider these services that are rapidly being made available by the telecommunications industry alone.

Picturephone service and the higher quality TV-type services are going to be feasible, and they are going to have major impacts on marketing activities. Customer contacts conducted via visual communications can practically eliminate the need to travel to customer locations. All the benefits of a face-to-face contact can be achieved by use of the appropriate visual communications service. Products and presentations can easily be shown to prospective customers. This

4. The above material was extracted from a contribution by Robert R. Tupper, in *Tomorrow's Marketing: A Symposium* (New York, N.Y.: The Conference Board, 1974), pp. 40–45.

will undoubtedly require a new type of sales personality—and a production staff of make-up men, hair pieces to reduce reflections, color coordinators, studios rather than sales cubicles, and working demonstrations rather than brochures.

Along the same lines, visual display terminals for accessing electronic data sources will be widely used. There are already a wide variety of these terminals available today.

Bid specifications, technical descriptions, wiring diagrams, copies of contractual arrangements, catalogs of products or parts, and price lists are just a few items that consumers will soon expect you to provide to them via the visual display terminal. You can expect customers to call your system and have your technical descriptions displayed on their terminals. They may well have your competitor's technical specifications on their adjacent terminal. There will be a great deal of pressure for you to market your products in this manner in the near future, particularly at the wholesale level and from volume customers.

QUESTIONS FOR WRITTEN REPORTS OR CLASS DISCUSSION

1. The author of the above article is vice-president, marketing, Chesapeake and Potomac Telephone Companies, a leading firm in the American telecommunications industry. Do you feel he might be making a bit of a "sales pitch" in his article? Explain.

2. Do you agree or disagree with his statement, "all the benefits of a face-to-face contact can be achieved by use of the appropriate visual communications service"? Why? Please relate your answer, in turn, to: (1) telephone, (2) industrial, (3) group, and (4) exhibition selling.

3. What do you feel might be the advantages and disadvantages offered by picturephone and TV-type services to each of the four kinds of selling noted in 1 above?

4. What "new type of sales personality" do you feel may be required for picturephone and TV selling, as contrasted to personality of successful face-to-face sales representatives?

PART VI

HOW TO REACH YOUR PERSONAL SALES OR MANAGEMENT OBJECTIVES

18
how to sell yourself
for the sales position
of your choice

When you have mastered the content of this chapter, you should be able to:

Describe how to go about getting a desirable sales position: where to look for such positions, and how to contact firms or organizations that may offer positions of interest.

Summarize how to contact companies or organizations you might be interested in joining, either through an employment agency or on your own.

Construct a proper, attention-getting sales job application letter and experience resumé.

Describe three common steps in the employment process, and tell what to expect and how to handle each.

List several basic personal traits and characteristics a prospective employer looks for when considering an applicant for a sales position.

Throughout these pages, we have told you about selling—what it involves, the excellent career opportunities it offers, and how to sell. While concentrating on the "you approach," as though you were a newly-hired or experienced sales representative reviewing fundamental theory, principles, practices, and techniques, we also involved those readers who, though they might not follow a sales career, may find the information presented helpful in any career or non-career association involving close work with other people throughout their lives.

In this final section of the text, we will assume that you wish to enter upon a sales career, and you want to know how to:

Sell yourself for the sales position of your choice (this chapter).

Manage your work so as to achieve success in the shortest possible time (Chapter 19).

Program your career toward higher earnings and possibly top management (Chapter 20).

After doing this, we will conclude with a final review, in Chapter 21, of what it takes to be successful in selling (or any other career field) and ask you to judge if you have the will and determination to succeed. From then on, words alone cannot help—only what you *do* will!

Let us begin by suggesting how you can best select and obtain a suitable sales position of your choice.

HOW DOES ONE GO ABOUT
GETTING A DESIRABLE SALES POSITION?

One of the first hard facts you must face as a job applicant is that, stripped of all the fancy words, you are selling your services, and the potential employer is buying your services. Many companies and government agencies spend much time and money recruiting, especially from among university and college seniors, but they are searching for good people, not just bodies, and for potential executive talent.

In India, where good jobs are scarce, university graduates know they must plan carefully for and fight hard to get through job interviews leading to a desirable position. Young American graduates, on the other hand, often seem quite unprepared by education or outlook for the penetrating depth interviews and psychological testing used by many companies and organizations to screen applicants. All too often they approach such interviews without any preparation and when rejected are angry or demoralized, not knowing what hit them or why.

To put it bluntly, a company buys your services at the going market price for people of your age, education, intelligence, and skills. The more desirable and sought-after the position, the tougher the competition and the more selective the employer can afford to be.

The employer is buying your services in the expectation that you will eventually become a productive asset to the over-all team effort. Business firms exist to make a profit for their stockholders or owners, and the executive who decides on your application is in turn judged by his overall success in hiring people who become successful producers for the firm. The decision is an important one for the firm because it probably will spend several thousand dollars on your training and development before you ever start earning your own way or earning a return on its investment.

The world does not owe you a living; you are going to have to earn your keep, and if you want to fight your way to the top of the executive pyramid, you are going to have to produce more than your competitors all along the way. This situation exists in every social system and in every country of the world today; the sooner you accept it, the sooner you can get along with the job. The way to start "managing" this situation to your own advantage is to first sell yourself for a sales position of your own choice.

Where does one look for a good sales position? In order to get the position best suited to your career goals, you must start planning long before the job interview. You should select not only the growth industry or area in which you want to work but also the best company or agency within that area. You have to study the industry and companies or agencies carefully, decide which offers you the best vehicle for meeting your own career goals, and then go after a position with them!

In order to determine whether you would like a sales career and to get some idea of sales work you would most enjoy, you may first try to get a part-time job in selling. Many companies offer such part-time work to students and housewives. Even though you are presently engaged in other work during the day, you may get a part-time sales job in the evening or on weekends. Door-to-door selling is one such area, and if you are successful at it, your experiences will certainly help you land a permanent sales position.

How does one go about contacting firms or organizations that may have desirable sales openings? Once you have decided on the area of selling which you think you would like and on the product or service you feel you would enjoy selling, your problem is how to contact companies or organizations you feel you might consider joining. This is done in two basic ways: (1) through an employment agency, or (2) on your own.

The Employment Agency

While state employment agencies often list sales positions, generally speaking they list mainly jobs in unskilled or semi-skilled categories. Private employment agencies specializing in sales or executive positions offer greater selection. These can be found listed in telephone book classified pages or in newspaper advertisements. The National Employment Association (2000 K Street, N.W., Washington, D.C.) offers at modest cost a *Private Employment Agencies Directory* which lists such agencies throughout the United States and gives their specialties.

The problem here is to find one that will really try to help you match your interests to the most suitable openings. Some are interested only in their fee, which the employer normally pays (but not always, so ask), and not in really helping you. Check them out with friends and local businesspeople, and judge them for yourself on personal calls. You can often sense their attitude in the attention, time, and respect they pay you, and through questions you can soon determine how well they know and handle their business.

How to Get Job Interviews on Your Own

One good source for locating sales openings is in the classified section of your local newspaper. Also, many trade associations act as clearing houses for sales jobs in their fields. Your local library may have an *Encyclopedia of Associations* to help you locate them, or your local Chamber of Commerce may be able to help. In many cities throughout the world, local sales executives clubs offer advice. College or university placement services serve their students or graduates, and their placement officers can often prove very helpful.

Direct mail may be your best source. Simply write the president or sales manager of any and all firms within industries that interest you; their names and addresses can be easily found through the several sources noted above. Answering newspaper or trade or professional journal or magazine ads is another good way to establish contact.

The best way to contact these sources or advertisers is to either write a letter requesting an appointment, contact them by telephone for an appointment, or simply cold-call on them in person. Whichever way you elect, prepare carefully beforehand, with a single job objective in mind and a structured sales approach to fit that objective. Prepare to "sell yourself" as a person, as you would a product, by convincing the "buyer" that your experience and talents will help him.

PERSONAL LETTER AND EXPERIENCE RESUMÉ

A personal letter, requesting an interview, is the most effective way to contact companies or nonbusiness organizations or agencies of interest to you. We mention nonbusiness organizations as well as companies since many employ sales representatives (under another guise) to sell their cause or service. You should

4632 South Bandicoot Lane
Los Angeles, California 09342
March 20, 1975

Mr. Colin Utterson
Vice-President, Sales
Latin American Export Corporation
178 Fifth Avenue
New York, New York

Dear Mr. Utterson:

I have long been aware of the international operations of
your company and would like the opportunity to join your
organization in a sales capacity. I have been preparing
myself for such a career in international sales/marketing
at Thunderbird Graduate School of International Management,
Phoenix, Arizona.

At Thunderbird, under professors experienced in foreign
trade, I have become familiar with the techniques of
international trade and how to apply them. I read, write,
and speak Spanish. I have an understanding of the social,
political, and economic situations in Latin America, both
through study and personal travel in that area of the world.

This specialized training, travel abroad, and graduation
from the University of Virginia, where I studied business
administration and marketing, are among the qualifications
I have to offer for your consideration. They are explained
in greater detail in the enclosed resume.

If you have any sort of a position in international sales
for which I might be considered, I would be happy to supply
further details. If you so desire, I would also be prepared to visit you for a personal interview at my expense,
anytime at your convenience between September 1 and September 20.

Will you please write or telephone me your decision? My
home telephone number is OR2-4168.

Sincerely, yours,

Rodney A. Molitor

Rodney A. Molitor

FIGURE 18.1

PERSONAL AND EXPERIENCE RESUME

RODNEY ANTONIO MOLITOR

4632 South Bandicoot Lane
Los Angeles, CA 09342
Phone: OR2-4168

Photo

Attached

CAREER OBJECTIVE

The opportunity to participate in the growth and expansion of
an international business in the field of selling and ultimately
sales management.

QUALIFICATIONS

Through association with businessmen friends, prominent in
foreign trade, I long ago developed an intense interest in
international sales management. As a result I have oriented my
academic program toward such a career and hope to be given the
opportunity to prove my worth to your company in this field.

EDUCATION

THUNDERBIRD GRADUATE SCHOOL OF INTERNATIONAL MANAGEMENT,
Phoenix, Arizona (1974-1975) Bachelor of Foreign Trade degree,
June 1975.

> A specialized postgraduate school emphasizing the practical
> aspects of international trade. Courses of instruction
> included: international commerce and finance; international
> marketing, where I acquired first-hand experience in the
> various means of international marketing, including foreign-
> market surveys, distributions, and sale of products abroad;
> and area studies, where I became familiar with the political,
> social, and economic problems of Latin America. Through study
> under a native-born instructor, I became fluent in written
> and conversational Spanish.

Extracurricular Activities:

> Marketing Club, Spanish Club, intramural athletics,
> Phi Delta Epsilon

THE UNIVERSITY OF VIRGINIA, Charlottesville, Virginia (1969-1973)
Bachelor of Arts degree with Honors, 1973.

> Majored in business administration with a minor in marketing.
> Courses of study included: Spanish, marketing, finance,
> economics, accounting, and political and economic geography.

Extracurricular Activities and Elected Offices:

> Omicron Delta Kappa (national honorary leadership fraternity),
> Dean's List every semester. Captain of varsity golf team,
> varsity soccer, advertising manager of University of Virginia
> yearbook, and second lieutenant in Army R.O.T.C.

FIGURE 18.2

```
EXPERIENCE

The Anniston Star, daily newspaper, circulation 37,000
Anniston, Alabama, 1969 to 1973 (Summers only).

        Position:  Classified and display advertising salesman.
                   I was personally responsible for a 20 percent
                   increase in classified space through intro-
                   duction of a new technique.

I earned 25 percent of my college expenses through various
types of summer employment and through positions in college.
As advertising manager of the school yearbook I increased
advertising revenue 62 percent, working on a commission
basis.

MILITARY SERVICE

I was commissioned second lieutenant, U.S. Army Reserve,
June, 1973.  I was honorably discharged, May, 1974.

PERSONAL DATA

        Single                      Born July 12, 1952
        United States citizen       in Gulfstream, Alabama
        6'½", 170 lb.               Excellent health

REFERENCES FURNISHED ON REQUEST
```

FIGURE 18.2 (Continued)

contact all possible by personal letter. It pays to write to several if possible, since you will want to be in the position of choosing among several positions rather than just taking the first job available.

While some authorities do not recommend attaching a resume to your personal letter, probably most recipients appreciate it since it will help them evaluate you better in connection with any openings they might have available now or in the near future.

Whether sending personal letter alone, or a letter and resumé, treat and carefully prepare each as if it were the most important document you will ever write. Consider it as a sales-promotion piece. Since the prospective employer is basically interested only in one thing, what you can do for him, concentrate on your accomplishments and not on your biography or academic or other qualifications. The more specific accomplishments you can relate to the sales position sought, the better. Use a command close in your letter. Just as in selling, if you want your prospect to buy, you have to ask for the order.

Figure 18.1 illustrates a good personal letter of application, but there is no set form to follow. Many such applications include a brief cover letter with a detailed resumé, or a listing of educational background or experience, attached on a separate sheet (as in Figure 18.2). This procedure is recommended when an applicant has a lengthy academic or job record.

If you do not have such extensive qualifications, your application can be a one-page letter.

Since this letter represents the first step in selling yourself as a desirable employee, you should do it in this way:

1. Type it neatly, being careful to avoid misspelled words or grammatical errors.
2. Present briefly and factually all important personal, educational, and work or other experience data that will enable the company to consider your potential qualifications.
3. State briefly, without being bombastic, why you feel you would like to join the company, and what you feel you have to offer.
4. Request an appointment for a personal interview at their earliest convenience.

STEPS IN THE EMPLOYMENT PROCESS

Upon receipt of your letter of application most companies or organizations will respond by (1) informing you that no openings are available, (2) enclosing a detailed application form for you to fill in and return for their further consideration, or (3) inviting you for a personal interview. In the event of either of the latter two responses, you should follow up by telephone either to make an interview appointment or to confirm your acceptance (or to request rescheduling) of the time, date, and place they may have suggested.

Filling out a detailed application form is the first step.   They may ask you to do this in advance of their confirming a personal interview appointment and prior to any depth interviews. Far too many applicants fill out these application forms hastily, not realizing that misspelled words, sloppy handwriting, or errors in or omission of facts are quickly noted. Care must be taken in listing personal or business references because the latter especially will probably be checked out in detail.

The second step is the personal interview.   This is generally a brief screening interview, followed by several depth interviews by different people. You have selected this company or organization yourself and intend to join it if at all possible. Thus, prior to the interview, you should learn all you can about the company. One way to get such information in advance is to write the public relations department for a copy of the company history, latest annual report, or any other helpful information they may have. Another suggestion is to find out how the stock has fared over the past year or its price on the market the day of the interview. By discussing the company positively, as you can do if you prepare beforehand, you immediately get the interviewers interested in you because you are selling—you are telling them how you can help them accomplish their goals. Most applicants ask only what the company can do for them; you are telling the company what you hope to be allowed to do for it.

It is not wise to be brash or "smart" in such interviews, but do not be afraid to say what you think. Interviewers do not care what you say so much as how you say it. They are basically looking for a confident, energetic team worker who can accept training and instruction and effectively carry out policies and procedures. They are more interested in evaluating your attitude and personality than in hearing how much you know about marketing or selling.

The key thing to remember in such interviews is that you must keep their interests in mind as you sell yourself; answer with confidence and enthusiasm the questions they ask and ask them questions in turn. The best kinds of questions for you to ask are intelligent ones as to what opportunities exist and what you will be expected to do in order to attain success in any specific positions under discussion.

The third step is for you to take a series of job-aptitude tests. These are most often given after you have filled out the application form and gone through a preliminary interview. Companies usually give the important depth interviews only after you have taken and they have evaluated such tests. Many of the questions raised in these depth interviews relate to your test answers and scores.

Such tests help the interviewers evaluate your mentality, drive, persistence, poise, sociability, and aptitudes for the particular position under consideration. Some people resent such tests and either refuse to take them or quit in anger halfway through. This justifies the whole testing process to the employer because if an applicant cannot take *that* little irritation, he certainly cannot cope with a rough business situation in which the penalties to the company for his blowing up could be severe.

Many of these tests are designed merely to ask you to tell the employer more about yourself. Since you provide the answers, it is not the employer's fault if negative traits show up. Actually, you should welcome the opportunity to take such tests because they often shed a great deal of light on your suitability for the position. If they help point out that you do not have the necessary traits or aptitudes for success in selling, it is better to find it out now rather than later.

Companies justify such tests on the grounds that mistakes in selection are costly and can often be avoided if careful selection procedures are applied. It costs American companies an average of over $10,000 to pick and train a new sales representative. Whatever the exact monetary value, errors in selection are expensive to a company in many ways, as pointed out by this quote from a news article:

The overall costs (when we make a mistake) in hiring a sales representative, including the cost of recruitment, cost of time spent in interviewing, cost of training, supervision, fringe benefits, and sales costs in excess of those for trained sales representatives as well as the less intangible loss of goodwill resulting from careless handling of customers by inexperienced sales representatives, can add up rapidly.

In companies with a high staff turnover, when we multiply these costs per man by the number of sales representatives who leave or are dismissed, the effect selection mistakes play on company profits is dramatic. Poor selection results in a direct loss of profits.

Thus there is nothing personal involved in a prospective employer's asking you to take such tests. The company is not trying to be big brother; it is only trying to help you and itself to avoid a mistake. It may cheer you up to know that very few employers base their final decisions on such aptitude tests.

One purpose of giving such tests prior to depth interviews, as noted earlier, is to point out a possible lack of interest in selling or basic traits or attitudes that may lead to failure as a sales representative. An interviewer normally frames questions around such areas of potential weakness so as to further explore real interests or aptitudes. He may throw out unusual questions during this exploration process to get some idea of your reaction to the unexpected. Do not be surprised at anything, just meet the situation normally and cheerfully and observe how well the interviewer does his job.

Factors influencing sales position hiring decisions. Many sales executives feel that the worst mistake they can make is to rush into a hiring decision. Basically they are looking for the following traits and characteristics:

Initiative and perseverence. These are the two most important personality traits needed. The reason is that sales representatives have to be self-starters. Close supervision is often difficult, and salary or incentive plans can only complement and support the innate drive and determination that motivates a sales representative.

Realistic viewpoint. They look for applicants who are interested in career opportunity rather than in getting rich quick. Training costs are high, and salaries the first two years are often low to compensate for that. If an applicant seems to want to get rich overnight, chances are he won't be hired.

Team player. Questions asked include not only how customers will accept the applicant, but how well he will fit on the company team.

Final steps in the hiring procedure involve reference checks, a physical examination, and, in some cases, the signing of a bond or employment agreement. Since key personal and employment references are nearly always checked carefully, you should, as mentioned earlier, list them carefully and accurately. Physical examinations are a normal requirement for hiring in most companies or organizations, either at their expense or yours.

As a final step to formal hiring, some companies ask the applicant whether he is prepared to sign a bond which will protect the company against certain actions on his part. This procedure is usually followed only when the company plans to entrust the representative with valuable and expensive samples or demonstration equipment or when the representative will be handling cash. Many companies require such bonds as a matter of practice, so there is nothing unusual in their asking you for one.

Other companies may ask that you sign an agreement to remain with them a minimum period of time. They make this request most often when expensive, technical training is involved. Such agreements represent an attempt to ensure that an applicant will not accept a position merely for the valuable training and then promptly resign to look for a better position elsewhere.

These are only three of the several factors considered in selecting and hiring of sales representatives, of course, but they serve to give you an idea of what your prospective employer will be carefully evaluating while considering you as an applicant. If you were in their position you would want to make a careful selection too. So be patient if the hiring process drags out awhile and you are called in for interviews by several people. It means they are interested in you—in terms of what you can do for them!

Once hired, you enter the company or organization training program and are officially on your way. A major step toward your ultimate career goal has thus been taken; you have obtained the position you sought. Now you have to produce in order to justify your employer's faith in you.

SUMMARY

Assuming you wish to enter a sales career, we noted in this chapter how to do so: where to look for a suitable position of your choice and how to apply for it.

We suggested employment agencies or getting job interviews on your own as being the two most generally used methods of contacting prospective employers. How to prepare a personal application letter and personal resumé was explained and illustrated.

Steps in the employment process were described, and suggestions were made as to how you can "give them what they want" by selling yourself in terms of what you can do for them—their real buying reason.

CHAPTER REVIEW

CONCEPTS TO REMEMBER*

_____ buys your services	_____ factors in hiring decisions	_____ personal resumé
_____ experience resumé	_____ employment process	_____ personal application letter
_____ depth interviews	_____ aptitude tests	_____ command close

*For memory reinforcement fill in the page number or numbers where the terms were described in this chapter.

QUESTIONS FOR ANALYSIS AND DISCUSSION

1. What major thread of thought ran through our discussion of how you can best seek and land the sales position you desire? What must you always keep in mind throughout the entire application-interview process?
2. What is a hard fact of life that a job applicant should keep in mind when applying for a desirable sales position?
3. A prospective employer is basically looking for only one thing when considering sales applications. What is that one thing?
4. How should an applicant for a sales job end his or her initial personal application letter?
5. Why is it so important to prepare a personal and experience resumé so carefully?
6. What is the first step in the employment process?
7. What key point should a sales applicant keep in mind throughout all personal interviews, no matter what the questions?
8. What is your personal opinion concerning aptitude tests for sales applicants? If you were an employer, would you use them? Why?

Case Study 18–1

A TOP PERSONNEL EXECUTIVE TELLS WHAT HE LOOKS FOR IN APPLICANTS SEEKING SALES POSITIONS

[**Author's Note:** *This case study outlines candid, off-the-record comments by the top personnel officer of a major American company who, along with his staff, interviews hundreds of sales-job applicants each year. His name must remain anonymous because he tells frankly why some applicants impress interviewers and why others fail to do so.*]

In our large company, the screening process consists of the appointment, a brief preliminary interview, filling out of the application blank, testing, the main interview, and, if the applicant seems promising, careful reference checks. If those prove satisfactory, he goes through a final selection by the responsible sales manager, and if hired, a physical examination.

We require that applicants write for an appointment and attach a resumé of their educational and employment background. We do not look for any set form of letter and resumé, but we do expect them to be neat and orderly. We are especially leery of statements that tend to oversell or statements that when challenged later in the interview turn out to have skirted the truth. We immediately notice any poor spelling, time unaccounted for, or past earnings not shown on both the resumé and the later employment application.

Our initial reception-room impression of the applicant means a lot. His appearance and general manner and attitude toward our secretaries or other people in the reception area give us clues on how he may fit into our company or act toward our customers. We expect him to be neat, well-dressed, courteous, and patient.

Above all, we expect him to be on time for his appointment. If he cannot make it on the set date, he should call and reschedule it. We do not mind his rescheduling the interview time to suit his convenience, but since we are also busy, we expect him to be courteous enough to notify us of any such change.

Since we do observe our applicant while he is in the reception room, we notice favorably such things as his picking up our company literature from the tables and thus gaining knowledge of our company as he awaits his interview.

OUR SELECTION CRITERIA REVOLVES AROUND FIVE BASIC AREAS

What is he like personally?   During the interview, we again note his appearance, manner, and decorum. We realize that his inner attitude is "What can the company do for me," but we on our side are thinking, "We are going to spend money on you, so what can you do that merits our investment in you?" The responses he gives to our questions are most important—we like positive, enthusiastic responses best. We try to judge him as a customer would, and for sales representatives, such judgments can be vitally important.

What has he done?   We like enthusiastic yet objective responses to questions about his education, training, and past work experience. For first-job applicants we like such statements as "I was editor of our school paper in high school" or "I worked my way through college but still got good grades." Our company does not view high scholastic grades as being overly important, but good grades do indicate native ability, intelligence, and willingness to apply oneself. We also like to see evidence of extracurricular activities. For those with past work histories, we look for evidence of job-hopping, amount of past earnings, and what his employers thought of him and he of them.

What does he know about our company?   We expect him to know something about our company, its past and present operations, and our standing in the industry. We also ask and expect him to have given serious thought to where he expects to go with our company. We are looking here for evidence of clear thinking rather than for specific answers.

What does he want to do?   He is applying for a sales position, but we look for any signs of misguided interest. We know that he will not stay with us unless he is basically interested in selling, so we try to draw out his real interests during the interviews.

We like questions from him such as "Where can I expect to be in two years?" or "Will I get recognition for hard work?" We dislike too many questions about money, coffee breaks, time off, etc. We feel our kind of sales representative wants to learn about the job and where it can lead him first. We normally raise the question of money ourselves halfway through the interview.

What are his potentialities? We use tests to help determine his intelligence, aptitudes, and skills in reference to our particular sales requirements. We consider test results as only part of the interview process but expect him to take them willingly as one means of discovering to our mutual satisfaction whether he stands a good chance of being happy and successful in our sales work.

My personal peeve is the know-it-all or bombastic applicant. The ones I respect most are the very few who write follow-up notes thanking me for the interview; it can often tip the scales.

QUESTIONS FOR WRITTEN REPORTS OR CLASS DISCUSSION

1. Why would this or any company want to hire you? Explain.
2. When should you start planning in order to get the position you would like with this company?
3. What key thoughts should you always keep in mind during employment interviews, as brought out in this case study?
4. Do you consider it reasonable or fair for a prospective employer to ask you to take written tests? Why?

Case Study 18–2

MEET THE MODEL MEDIA SALES REP

What makes an ideal media sales representative—as seen by a major advertiser? The following eleven-point view of the Model Media Rep evolved during a seminar sponsored by *Media Decisions* magazine at the Harvard Club in New York City in late 1973. They are hereby presented as published by the magazine in its June 1974 issue.[1]

1. *He's honest*—not simply concerned with selling us just because it's part of his job.
2. *He understands us.* Something about our company, our people and the way we're structured, our products, our customers, our goals/our strategies.
3. *He understands the value of time . . .* and uses ours *and* his wisely.
4. *He's an idea man* (not just full of facts that are on the rate sheet which, by the way, he knows well). He's constantly thinking about how his product can best be adapted to fill our needs.
5. *He's an account marketing service manager . . .* not a "peddler." Which means—
6. *He's prepared when he comes to call on us.* He has a strategy and objective in mind.
7. *He covers all the bases . . .* and sells "top down" and "bottom up" including product managers, group marketing directors—and the agency . . . everyone involved in the planning and decision making process.
8. *He's a positive individual . . .* a forward thinking individual. He doesn't carp about why he might not have gotten the business last year . . . but how/what he can do about next year's plans.
9. *He's totally involved in his product . . .* and doesn't need a "canned" pitch to sell it (oh, he may use one occasionally but it's always tailored to our needs).
10. *He likes what he's doing* and you can tell it immediately. His enthusiasm for his product is infectious on all his contacts.
11. *He's a good arbitrator,* representing his company's policies and point of view when he should and our interests when he should.

1. "The Model Advertiser Meets the Model Rep," *Media Decisions* (June 1974), p. 64.

In Summary: He's interested in what we're trying to do rather than in what he's trying to sell. He makes our life easier because he's there to help us solve *our* problems. If he's only trying to solve his problem, it doesn't work. If he can help us solve our problems, we're going to do business with him.

QUESTIONS FOR WRITTEN REPORTS OR CLASS DISCUSSION

1. What ideas could you adapt in preparing your own job application resumé, or during the application interview process for any sales position, from the eleven points listed above?
2. What two key personality traits discussed in the chapter material support the inner drive and determination that would motivate the Model Media Rep?
3. What are the best kinds of questions to ask (1) by our Model Media Rep during each of his calls, and (2) by applicants being interviewed for a sales position?
4. Media sales reps sell a service; a job applicant seeking a sales position also has to sell. What does the latter sell, and what does he have to convince the "buyer" (the job interviewer) of?

SALES PROBLEM 18–1

WHICH OF THESE TWO SALES JOB APPLICANTS WOULD YOU HIRE?

Let us assume you are an employer who has advertised for a sales representative. Introductions have been completed, the position described, and you are observing how these two applicants handle themselves during a morning's interviews.

First Applicant	*Second Applicant*
Applicant: "Well, I need a job and I'd like to take a shot at yours."	*Applicant:* "From your description, it sounds like you have some problems that a good sales representative could help you with."
Interviewer: "What is it about the position that most interests you?"	*Interviewer:* "Yes, you are right; we really are anxious to line up some new accounts."
Applicant: "The hours are good and having a company car as part of the deal sounds good, since mine has just about bombed out."	*Applicant:* "May I visit a couple of your type of accounts this afternoon, think overnight about how I might be able to approach new ones as your sales representative, and bring in a brief written proposal sometime tomorrow at your convenience?"
Interviewer: "What makes you feel you will be successful?"	*Interviewer:* "Splendid, make it 3 P.M. What is it about this position that most interests you?"
Applicant: "I've got a good personality and I like getting around and seeing people."	*Applicant:* "You have problems that would be interesting to try to solve. I like challenges, and your position seems to offer a great deal of opportunity for me to prove myself by getting good sales results for you."

QUESTION FOR WRITTEN REPORTS OR CLASS DISCUSSION

At this point, which applicant are you most likely to hire? Why?

19

plan your work, work your plan: the self-management of selling

---

When you have mastered the content of this chapter, you should be able to:

Define the terms *planning, forecasting, composite inventory, territory value analysis, territory screening, programming, production requirements, production plans, scheduling, sales call patterns, follow-through* (from a managerial point of view), *controls, quantitative reports,* and *qualitative reports.*

Outline a simple four-part grouping of desirable customers or prospects for a sales territory, which will enable a sales representative to make a value analysis of that territory.

Describe why proper scheduling is so important to a sales representative, and give the two most important factors involved.

Describe two types of account card systems that a sales representative can set up to quickly enable him to make an efficient territory analysis.

Summarize how a sales representative can set up an easy, efficient account classification system and put it to use for bigger sales.

Describe how to set up sales call patterns for both a fixed and irregular routing, and how to set up the most efficient route coverage for (1) a large territory or area, and (2) a smaller local area territory.

List six factors in a planned territory sales program that involves constant analysis and checks on progress and results, both by a sales representative and by management.

List seven good habits to develop that will make planning, organizing, and implementing work second nature to a sales representative.

We will now assume you have successfully landed the sales position of your choice, have completed the initial training program, and have been assigned as outside sales representative to a newly created sales territory. We are not concerned with what you are selling or to what specific type of customers; our aim is to discuss the principles, practices, and techniques that apply to any such assignment regardless of product or service, or specific types or combinations of industrial, retail, or end-user prospects or established customers.

Starting with the concepts of modern management theory surveyed in Chapter 3, we will relate more specifically the four basic management functions considered there (planning, organizing, executing, and controlling) to your immediate problems. We will assume you have been given an annual sales and expense

379

budget which outlines your objectives in those areas, plus an estimate of desired profit goals. Your task now is to plan and organize your work to accomplish those objectives, just as the more experienced sales representatives in your company do each year.

Your assignment is the vital, responsible one of *local market* (your sales territory) *manager*. As such, you are expected to think, plan, and work from the start as a manager does.

YOU, YOUR COMPANY'S PRESIDENT, AND YOUR COMPETITION HAVE MUCH IN COMMON

Selling is a competitive profession, and competition provides half the fun of being a sales representative. The company has said you are good and has asked you to think as a manager does; why not start by reflecting on the similarity of the problems faced by you in your sales territory and by the highly paid president (or Managing Director) of your company? And, think at the same time of the five (statistically average) competitors who are hard after your customers in the field every day.

As individuals you each start with native intelligence; varying degrees of education, knowledge, and experience; and the same 24 hours a day, 52 weeks and 365 days a year. You are each positive-minded, enthusiastic, healthy, and a hard worker. With so much in common basically, what secrets must you learn in order to become more successful than your competitors and even aim if you so desire toward the ultimate company position of president (or Managing Director)? The basic secrets are (1) proper planning and (2) an efficient management of time and work.

PLANNING YOUR WORK

Planning, as we learned in Chapter 3, is predetermining a course of action; it starts with the establishing of goals and objectives. Based on company policy, your planning involves the identification of problems you logically expect to solve to accomplish goals as efficiently as possible, and the practical actions necessary to accomplish them. We will now consider this in terms of forecasting, programming, and scheduling your work. Once your work is planned, you will follow your plan, reviewing it constantly, adapting it when necessary to meet changing conditions.

Forecasting

Forecasting involves collecting facts or data upon which you try to calculate or estimate in advance what will happen within a specific time. For example, you collect all the data available from your company about past accounts in your territory and thus get a picture of past yearly sales and profits. You then assemble all available facts about new prospects, market trends, and competition sales, and any other information to get some idea of how well past yearly sales compared to actual market potential. This collection of facts should include everything you can relate to the five W's and the H of basic reporting or fact-finding: who, what, when, where, why, and how.

Once you have collected the information, you can then make a composite inventory of your territory, which includes a value analysis.

A *composite inventory* involves territory-screening, or listing all accounts, both current and potential. Only when you have done this can you determine intelligently when and where you are going to start working, what you are going to do in what order of priority, and how you are going to go about developing your territory to its full potential.

Part of this decision-making involves making a *value analysis* of your territory. This analysis sorts out and classifies your desirable customers or prospects into simplified groups, so that you have an order of priority for calls and time to be allocated. You may set up such a simple grouping in the following four parts.

Prime potential
Better-than-average potential
Average potential
Poor potential

Normally, such a forecast indicates that you should call on customers or prospects in order of their business potential to attain greatest results. Other factors such as scheduling and time-call patterns may affect the picture however, so forecasting up to this point is only a part of your overall planning picture.

Programming

Programming is planning the specific activities or procedures necessary to successfully accomplish the planned goals. This step involves setting *production requirements*—how many calls per day are necessary to accomplish your objectives—and making *production plans*—the breakdown of those calls (e.g., 75 percent active accounts and 25 percent new ones). It is fairly easy to establish the overall objective, such as a 20 percent increase in sales and profits within the next year. It is more difficult, however, to plan how to reach the objective.

Your action, therefore, is (1) to determine a series of attainable intermediate goals that will enable you to systematically work your way to successful accomplishment of your overall objective, and (2) to plan the step-by-step procedures to be followed in meeting them within specified, planned time limits. These procedures are thus the step-by-step details of your overall sales plan.

By way of illustration, let us suppose that you have a sales objective of $100,000 net volume in your territory next year. Taking off two weeks vacation time leaves you fifty working weeks and a weekly sales goal of $2,000. These smaller weekly goals seem easier to attain than the $100,000, but your problem still remains—how to go about hitting that target figure each week.

It is easy to say, "I'll just go out and visit as many good prospects as possible, and if the law of averages is with me I'll make my sales." Unfortunately, it is not that easy. Here are just some of the factors and activities you have to consider in advance of actual interview calls.

Which prospects are you going to call on? In what order? How often?

How are you going to arrange your call schedules to visit key prospects at the best time for them?

How can you best handle your travel and routing problems?

What is involved in planning good, effective interviews for different prospects in different geographical areas?

When will you be able to do all the necessary reports and paperwork?

What delays will be caused by customers who are not in or by problems they need your help in solving?

How much nonproductive selling time will you have to devote to servicing or follow-up calls?

These are some of the problems faced daily by sales representatives. If you want to achieve sales success, you should plan your sales program well in advance, carefully anticipating as many such problems as possible and establishing procedures that will allow you to overcome all problems and still meet your sales goals on time.

Scheduling

Scheduling is arranging and managing the time necessary to carry out your sales program, and involves *planning routes* and *scheduling time* in order to cover your territory most effectively. Schedules should always be flexible enough to allow you to do unexpected things; but every successful sales representative not only schedules his work carefully but also tries as consistently as possible to follow his schedule.

By way of illustration, let us assume you are planning scheduling to enable you to achieve a $2,000-a-week, $100,000-a-year sales goal. You may decide to plan a six-month travel itinerary that will enable you to proceed from one geographical area to another at least cost of time and money, spending enough time in each place to see all key prospects plus a certain percentage of new ones. Within this schedule, you should plan to visit the key prospects at the time when past records indicate they are most likely to buy.

Your daily objectives call for you to visit your prime prospects first, then your next-best potential customers, planning each day (by appointment wherever possible) to make ten calls. Perhaps you have already worked out that if you can make eight such calls a day, you will be able to average four good presentations and one or two actual sales. By doing this consistently each day, you can expect $1,800 sales that week. But where will the additional $200 come from? Your scheduling allows you time to visit each day perhaps two new potential prospects that you have not called upon before. In other words, you are following an 8-2 daily call formula: eight regular customers and two potential customers. The extra business should come from these new customers. Such a schedule also allows you time to do your paperwork, such as sending in orders and reports, at the end of each working day.

What if the unexpected happens? You may be asked to attend a conference or meeting or be called to help a customer in a nearby city with an emergency problem. You can solve this by dropping the two end-of-the-day new-potential-customer calls. If the problem requires a longer period of time, you will most likely resume your itinerary, simply skipping those calls in between.

Scheduling should be flexible, but the most certain road to sales success lies in carefully planning your work and, through proper scheduling, in working that plan as consistently as possible.

SOME PRINCIPLES OF SUCCESSFUL WORK-PLANNING AND FOLLOW-THROUGH

At this point, you may wonder how you can relate some of the managerial concepts and techniques we have been discussing to your specific sales territory and situation. There are many different sales activities, each with varying successful techniques, employment of which should bring sales success. Your own employer can provide you with training in these specific techniques. Thus it may be helpful to you if we delve into some of the principles applicable to any form of selling. We can relate these to what we have already touched upon in the following areas.

Management of time

Efficient territory analysis

Account classification for bigger sales

Most effective territory coverage

Some basic routing plans that save time

Management of paperwork and reports

Management of Time

Let us assume that there are approximately 240 working days or 1,920 working hours in a year. Divide your salary by 1,920, and you can readily see what your time is worth. If your salary is $6,000 per year, each hour of your working time is worth $3.13. If you double your earnings to make $12,000 a year, each hour of your working time is worth $6.25. If you earn $24,000 a year, your time is worth $12.50 per hour. If you are paid on a commission basis at the rate of 20 percent of net sales volume, you have to sell $62.50 worth of goods or services each working hour!

That is not the whole story, however. Because of all the other factors involved, such as travel time, waiting time, paperwork, and nonproductive activities, even top professional sales representatives find that only about one-third of their time is spent in productive, face-to-face interviews with prospects. That means you have only about 640 hours in which to make your sales. If you are earning $24,000 per year, this prime time is now worth approximately $37.50 per hour, and if you are on a 20 percent commission basis, you have to sell $187.50 worth of goods and services each of those hours. Impossible! Not at all —thousands of good professional men and women sales representatives are doing just that each working day in many countries.

The lesson should be very clear: In order to achieve the success you desire, every hour of your working time must count. You should place the proper monetary value on your time and never forget how valuable it is. Richard Prentice Ettinger, a leading American publisher, summed it up as follows:

Time is the most important and valuable asset you have. You and you alone know whether you are using it in the most effective and profitable manner. The self-discipline you exercise in your use of your time determines the success you make of your life and of the company for which you work. It will pay you to make every minute count.

Efficient Territory Analysis

Since sales results are so closely related to efficient use of time, you should concentrate on calls that pay off and eliminate as far as possible nonprofitable calls. This is true even for route calls, in which you have to regularly call back on a set customer list.

A basic step in efficient planning is to analyze your territory carefully in order to identify in advance if possible who your best prospects are and where they are located. This process is often called *territory-screening*. Some sales representatives do this screening by setting up two separate sets of account card files.

Current accounts. Taken from past company records and rated (prime, good, etc.) in order of past business and future potential, current-account cards are grouped into easy-to-work geographical clusters.

Potential accounts. These are new, uncalled-on potential customers. Your research has indicated that if developed properly each could give you a certain amount of business. These cards are rated, grouped, and filed in the same way as are current accounts.

The purpose of such an account file system is to develop an efficient basic working tool; you can systematically list on these cards other information, either initially or as you learn it. For example, you may want to list the name of the key buyer, periods of the month or year when purchasing decisions are made, and bank and credit references. Maintenance of such a list is constant. You gather information on both current and potential accounts from many sources: company records, trade associations or directories, personal observation, and trade journals or newspapers, and from constantly asking questions, and calling on new prospects.

All too few sales representatives take the time to carefully set up and constantly use and improve such an account card file. Yet it can be a very efficient and scientific system for up-to-date *territory analysis*. Through it, you can pinpoint key potential customers and thus be able to plan the amount of time required for their maximum development. Just as importantly, your analysis can pinpoint the unprofitable segments of your customer list. Eliminating them completely or reducing call time spent on them means more time to get to the right places at the right time.

Account Classification for Bigger Sales

Once you have made your basic territory analysis and set up your account card files, you may find it extremely profitable to continually refine your analysis and classification of current and potential accounts. You will have to develop the techniques either by yourself or with the help of your sales supervisors, but basically the idea is to rate your accounts accurately as to current business and, more importantly, as to potential. This rating is important in view of two generally accepted sales principles:

1. Up to 80 percent of profitable business in most sales areas comes from only about 20 percent of the customer list.
2. It is easier to sell more to a current, satisfied customer than to develop new customers.

Once you have accurately classified your accounts in such a manner, you can plan your work to sell more to these better customers first and then to develop the other customers in a systematic way as time permits. Here are some sugges-

ROUTE SCHEDULE

Sales Representative _____

Home Territory _____ For week beginning _____ 19 ____

Date	Time of arrival	City	State/Province and Country	Hotel and address	Time of departure	Planned calls upon

Tentative advance schedule for following week

Key objectives:

Additional comments:

FIGURE 19.1 Example of a Typical Sales Representative's Route Schedule Sheet

tions for obtaining more sales than before from these prime customers you have so carefully analyzed and classified.

1. Plan to call on at least one more good customer or potential customer per day than originally scheduled. Doing this may mean making eleven calls per day instead of ten.
2. Plan to sell each one more of or a wider range of your goods or services. Do not overlook any possibility.
3. Plan to sell higher-priced items; concentrate your planning and presentations on big-ticket items. It is often just as easy to make a big sale as it is to make a small one. Start with the higher-priced items in your line; you can always work down the price scale (please note that this guideline applies to *outside selling*; for instore *retail selling*, as noted on page 338, Chapter 16, the best guideline is to start in the middle price range and trade up).

Covering Your Territory Most Effectively

Your first sales trip around your territory should further clarify your initial planning, analyzing, and forecasting of who influences purchasers and where and when the most purchases are made. The second and future trips give you fresh thoughts on how to concentrate your time and efforts where they are most likely to pay off. By recording all important information on your account cards, you learn through constant evaluation where to spend your time most profitably the next trip.

Sales call patterns usually follow either (1) a fixed routing, where customers are called on repeatedly at regular intervals, or (2) an irregular routing, where frequency of calls is left up to the sales representative. If you follow a fixed route, develop your own route sheet and list on it brief notes that will be useful references for succeeding calls. Such a route sheet may look something like the one in Figure 19.1.

If you follow an irregular-routing schedule or itinerary, you might set up a separate (different-color) index card for each prospect, listing important information that you want to refer to later on. Then file the cards by date in a simplified

FIGURE 19.2

```
                                              UP Aug. 15
                                              _____

      Texon Chemical Company
      112 Broad Street
      Andersonville, Vt.      Tel. 236-4589

      Mr. G. Wood - Purchasing Officer

      No funds on my 3/12 visit; asked me to call back
      around Sept. 1, might consider three Z-range cal-
      culators, model 486, if fourth-quarter funds allow.
```

up-file. It may look something like the one in Figure 19.2 for an office-machines sales representative. Other scheduling permitting, the sales representative can review on August 15 whether to make an appointment for a personal call or at least to follow up by letter, telephone, or telegram.

Some Basic Routing Plans That Save Time

Once you have classified your accounts, determined where the best potential lies, and worked out a basic plan for most efficient coverage, you can devote some planning time to the most efficient *route coverage*. Here are a few ideas that may help you plan such a route most efficiently, depending on the type of selling you are engaged in.

1. *If you cover a large territory or area*, it may help to purchase both an over-all map and detailed sectional maps (road maps are excellent) as well as maps of key cities. You can mark in symbols of your own choice the location of customers and prospects and plan an itinerary and work schedule that will enable you to see the greatest number of customers or potential prospects (based on business potential) most efficiently, at least cost, in a given area. You should keep these considerations in mind regarding trips outside your home area.

   A. Travel costs versus expected sales
   B. Amount of time you can afford to be away at one time from your home or key area
   C. The fact that it may be best to start working the outer areas first, working in toward your home or key area. Thus if you are called back there in an emergency, you will not have so far to travel to pick up the route on a future call.

FIGURE 19.3

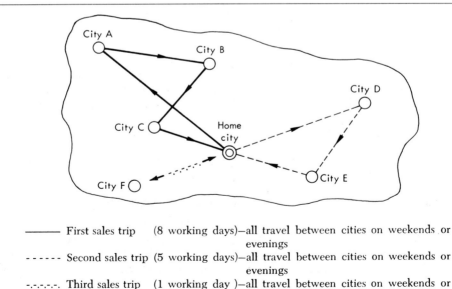

——— First sales trip	(8 working days)—all travel between cities on weekends or evenings
- - - - - - Second sales trip	(5 working days)—all travel between cities on weekends or evenings
-.-.-.-. Third sales trip	(1 working day)—all travel between cities on weekends or evenings
◯ in home city	(6 working days)

Such a simplified map may look something like the one in Figure 19.3 for a four-week itinerary involving three separate trips out of the home city and returns to it in between.

2. *If you cover a city or small territory within a two-hour radius of your home or office,* it may help you to divide it into zones, working a zone at a time, again starting with the outermost customer and working in and covering them as best you can (1) in order of business potential and (2) on the most direct route from one to the next. Such a zone and route plan may look something like the one in Figure 19.4.

FIGURE 19.4

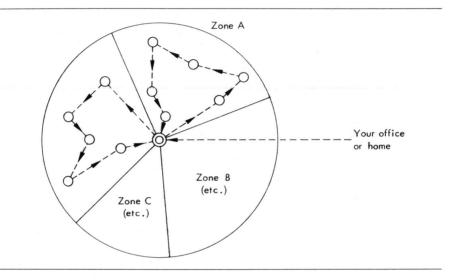

3. *If you are a door-to-door or office-to-office sales representative,* the most efficient system is to work every house or every office in a given area before moving on to the next. The law of averages works for you if you hit every potential prospect in the area. This routing is most effective for cold-call, or one-call, selling.

     Do not in area selling simply wander around looking for a door that appeals to you before knocking. Professional door-to-door sales representatives recommend hitting them all. A systematic door-to-door block routing plan may look something like the one in Figure 19.5.

WORKING THE PLAN—THE FOLLOW-THROUGH OF SELLING

Having carefully planned your work, as we have discussed, your next step is to follow-through on it. *Follow-through,* in management terminology, means systematically working your planned sales program. It involves constant analysis and checks on progress and results, both by yourself and management, of these factors:

Number of calls per day	Size of average order
Sales-call ratio	Daily productivity
Number of sales per day	Profitability of productivity versus expenses

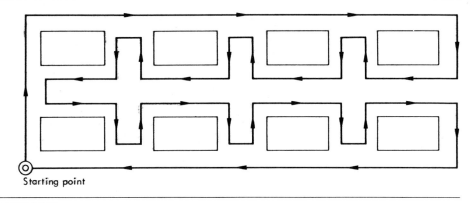

Starting point

FIGURE 19.5

After analysis of such information over a period of time, you can evolve the most effective sales-call pattern, and after a time-analysis review, you can make the pattern operationally efficient.

Establishing *controls* over your activities involves making daily, weekly, monthly, quarterly, or yearly reports or summaries. Information contained in such reports provides feedback from your customers either to you, if you are self-employed, or to your company.

Company controls during the follow-through are usually based on the sales representative's field reports, which cover the above points. Such reports can be either quantitative or qualitative in nature.

Quantitative reports. These include one or all of those listed below. Sales supervisors can compare efforts and results of one sales representative against another and thus set norms against which you can pace yourself, or they can statistically point up weaknesses in specific areas.

Daily Work Plan. This brief report, usually prepared at least a day in advance, lists the prospects you plan to see and the results you expect to accomplish.

Daily Call Report. This brief report outlines daily activity along with the results. This report can be compared with your daily work plan to show how effectively you work your plan.

Weekly Summary Report. For some companies this report takes the place of the daily call reports. Others require it as a brief recap of weekly activities in addition to the more detailed daily call report. In either case, when compared with your itinerary and call objectives, it shows (1) actual results and (2) how effectively you worked your plan.

Monthly Reports. These are usually brief statistical recaps of the more detailed daily call reports. In many companies, the area manager prepares these for submission to the head office. In other companies, you, as a sales representative, prepare them, in a further effort to force you to constantly evaluate your own performance.

Quarterly or Semi-annual Reports. These are over-all progress reports. They may be only one page in length, but their purpose is to ask you to submit in writing (1) a review of your own performance to date versus your sales and expense budget, and (2) what specific plans you have to ensure that goals will be met during the next similar period.

Qualitative reports.   Required by some companies, these reports are more personalized and detailed than quantitative, factual reports in that you are asked to write your personal estimate or opinion of the customer. Such a report may be especially useful to your company credit manager if the customer is overdue in his accounts. Your report may indicate that the owner-manager was and still is sick and that problems will be settled as soon as he gets on his feet again. Your on-the-spot opinion may thus save the credit rating of a good customer who is having temporary difficulties.

How to Manage Paperwork and Reports

Selling, unfortunately, involves many details. You, as a sales representative, are constantly communicating ideas to and between people and are persuading others at distant points to take action for you. The ideas you work with are frequently not your own, and, as a customer-oriented problem solver, you must report problems and facts completely and accurately to your home office. Conversely, when a customer asks something of you in writing, you must be able to communicate intelligently and clearly. Also, in gathering market-research material, you must assemble accurate and specific details of value to you and your home office. All these situations, plus your normal reports, follow-up letters, account card files, etc., involve paperwork. Making the sales call itself is only part of the job; you must see that the necessary follow-up steps are taken, by either yourself or others.

Sales representatives in general are not known for their ability to shuffle papers across a desk. By nature they prefer to be out where the action is rather than writing reports. But, if you want to achieve success in your sales career and most certainly if you aspire to a managerial position, you have to learn to manage your paperwork efficiently. Time means money in selling, and paperwork involves nonproductive selling time. But, you have to get it done, and the secret is to get it done as rapidly, thoroughly, and efficiently as possible within the least amount of time.

You can do many things to make the paperwork side of your sales job less burdensome. All of them require a certain amount of self-discipline until they become habit, but once they become fixed, they can make your work far more pleasant than it was before. Here are a few good habits that, if developed, can help you manage your paperwork efficiently.

1. Do All Routine Paperwork Daily!   The technique of handling paperwork is to get it done as it comes up rather than to let it accumulate. The secret once again: Get today's paperwork done today! This includes the daily work plan for tomorrow and the daily call report for today.

2. Note-Taking.   This should be done during the interview whenever possible and certainly should be completed right after each interview, while the facts are still fresh in your mind. Do not wait until later and run the risk of forgetting; take a few minutes to complete it, according to your own shorthand and system, right after the interview or on any other occasion when you need to jot down facts learned.

3. *Memos.*   Those to the home office or brief thank-you or follow-up notes can often be written during waiting periods in prospects' offices or during lunch. An average, brief, factual memo takes only from two to five minutes to write. There is rarely a day when you do not have ten minutes or so of free or waiting time. It makes sense to get necessary memos out of the way during those free minutes and not to have to do them at night.

4. *Weekly summary reports or weekly expense reports.*   These should be done regularly on Friday evenings, at the end of the day and before returning home. If you get into this habit, you feel relaxed during the weekend. Fail to do it, and little stomach worry-knots over that undone task may actually ruin your weekend!

5. *Order forms.*   These should always be carried. Fill in all details briefly, yet accurately and completely, after the sale is completed, and mail to the home office that day.

Some tips on how to write a good report.   The most important part of your job is selling, but almost as important is reporting activities in the field to the home office. This reporting not only enables management to appraise and evaluate your performance and to proffer advice and help wherever indicated but also is essential for effective coordination of overall company sales activities. A success in your area may be parlayed into successes in many areas providing management receives sufficient facts to make an intelligent appraisal.

Be it a monthly report, an annual report, a special report on a particular situation, or even a plain memo, following certain guidelines will make it effective.

Be specific.   Avoid generalities and stick to facts. Explain facts with reasons. For instance, if your sales are down, the home office knows it before you do. They normally have the figures from monthly computer run-offs. What they do not know right away is why your sales are down; there may be a valid reason, but it has to be supplied from your end. They need to know why they are down and what you plan to do about it.

Avoid clichés.   Statements like "I will do my best" are meaningless. Substitute specifics such as "I plan to increase sales by 20 percent to a total of $1,000." "The exhibition was a great success" does not convey why it was a great success. Because of the number attending or the products sold? Only facts can give the answer. Statements like "I will solve the problem by a positive sales program" are meaningless. The major advantage of specific reporting is that it forces you to supply answers rather than to rely on pulling something out of a hat. So remember the previously discussed fundamentals of good reporting—who, what, when, where, why, and how.

Comparisons help understanding.   Figures themselves are neither good nor bad. Only comparison with other figures can breathe meaning into them. When talking about sales or potential sales, always relate them to comparative figures for the previous year and to budgets for the current year. Where possible, relate them to competitive figures and to the potential of your market.

Be realistic.   Wishful thinking is out of place in business; it is a treacherous bog into which many sales representatives have fallen. Your reports are filed and thus become a matter of record at the home office. If they reflect muddled thinking, management forms a poor opinion of your judgment and your promotion potential. If your report is important, you should perhaps draft it, sleep on it, try reading it objectively from the home-office point of view, and then prepare it for submission in careful, final form.

Be brief. The best reports are concise and are written in telegraphic business style. Winston Churchill refused to read reports stretching beyond one page. Without going to that extreme, you can boil most reports down to essentials by eliminating unnecessary verbiage. The person who thinks clearly expresses himself or herself clearly in writing. And the discipline of forcing yourself to write factually and concisely helps clarify your thinking. Muddled thinking often tries to camouflage itself in a maze of words.

Some Concluding Thoughts
on Effective Planning and Working the Plan

It has been interesting comparing your planning activities to those of your company president, or managing director, but let us reflect once again on those five hungry competitors who, statistically at least, are also after your prime and potential prospects' business. If you do not get to work and get the business, they will! General Nathan Bedford Forrest, a famous yet virtually illiterate Confederate cavalry commander in the American Civil War, summed up his secret for winning battles in these words: "Git there fustest with the mostest." That is not a bad strategy for sales success either, but like General Forrest, you know that a lot of planning, organization, energy, enthusiasm, and plain hard work lie behind the winning of any military or sales campaign.

You and your statistical five sales representative competitors start off with the same basic natural ingredients each day: your head, your feet, and eight average working hours. As in a long-distance foot race, victory is most likely to go to the one who plans his strategy, follows his plan, paces himself, turns on the steam at the proper moment, and is flexible enough to recognize and take advantage of unexpected opportunities.

Management judges you on your productivity, so you have to plan your activities and spend your time in selling where it will pay the greatest dividends. You have to develop habits that make planning, organizing, and implementing your work second nature. You must get in the habit of doing the following:

1. Qualifying your customer and prospect list so you know their potentials and how much time to allocate to each.
2. Planning an efficient travel and work schedule consistent with profitable sales versus expenses.
3. Scheduling appointments whenever possible to avoid excessive waiting time. And keep those appointments! Be there on time!
4. Learning all you can about your customer and planning a presentation tailored to his needs before the interview.
5. Scheduling time for your reports and paperwork. Prepare them carefully since they automatically go on record, and get them in on time. Learn to anticipate questions management will ask and answer them via your reports before they are asked of you.
6. Systematically searching out new prospects.
7. Being flexible and adaptable in mind and schedule to be able to recognize and take advantage of unexpected opportunities.

SUMMARY

We have covered in this chapter several important concepts of how a newly hired outside sales representative can plan coverage of his or her sales territory most efficiently. Many of these principles are equally valid, as adapted, to sales promotion or instore retail selling activities.

Building on the four basic management functions of planning, organizing, executing, and controlling surveyed in Chapter 3, we first considered such topics as forecasting, programming, and scheduling—all essential to good planning. Then, as guides to most effective working of the plan we considered the importance of management of time, efficient territory analysis, account classification for bigger sales, efficient territory coverage, and time-saving basic routing plan suggestions. Many practical illustrative examples were presented.

Yardsticks used to measure performance and evaluate progress were discussed, as were types of reports commonly required of sales representatives. Several practical suggestions on how to manage paperwork and reports were offered, as well as some thoughts on how to develop good planning and work habits that will lead to more rapid personal sales success.

CHAPTER REVIEW

CONCEPTS TO REMEMBER*

_____ potential accounts   _____ qualitative reports   _____ scheduling
_____ forecasting   _____ territory-screening   _____ account
_____ composite inventory   _____ fixed-routing plan   classification
_____ value analysis   _____ territory analysis   _____ programming
_____ quantitative reports

*For memory reinforcement, fill in the page number or numbers where these terms were described.

QUESTIONS FOR ANALYSIS AND DISCUSSION

1. All things being equal between you and a sales competitor, what is your best secret weapon to outperform him over any given period of time?
2. What does programming, as related to salesmanship, mean to you?
3. In managerial and sales terms, what do controls mean to you?
4. Why is it so important for a sales representative to continually refine his analysis and classification of current and potential accounts?
5. Since sales results are so closely related to efficient use of time, what types of sales calls require greatest attention? Why?
6. Concerning account classification, what two generally accepted sales principles might help you rate your accounts most accurately, both as to current and potential business?
7. What two types of routings do sales call patterns usually follow?
8. A sales representative's call reports can be either quantitative or qualitative in nature. What is the difference between the two?

BEST FOODS
STORE-PROCEDURE SELLING FEATURES
SOLID OBJECTIVES AND SYSTEMATIC PLANNING

CPC International, Inc. is a multinational company with operations in 45 countries throughout the world, comprising over 112 plants and research facilities. Its annual sales of almost $2 billion are 80 percent in the food category, with the balance in a wide variety of nonfood fields, including products for such industries as textiles, drugs, and paper. U.S. sales account for about 54 percent of the total. Over 42,000 people produce and market these products; almost two-thirds of them work for the international affiliates, and the majority of them are nationals of the countries in which they work. Operations of the company are divided into five major profit centers: *Best Foods, U.S. Industrial, CPC Europe, CPC Far East,* and *CPC Latin America.*

The success of Best Foods, a Division of CPC International, Inc., is built on a solid base of (1) systematic overall marketing planning and (2) a time-tested and successful approach to retail sale calls.

Best Foods sales representative's training manual terms its modern and highly successful approach to retail calls "store procedure." At the heart of this concept are the solid objectives, thorough planning, basic selling, and merchandising procedures, reporting, and follow-through necessary to make any call by a Best Foods sales representative a worthwhile investment of his time. Company insistence on careful precall planning is of chief interest to us in this case study as well as how they work that plan during the sales call itself and the follow-up preparation of records and reports.

Best Foods sales representatives call basically on (1) grocery stores (i.e., independent stores, chain stores, and convenience stores—all supermarkets) and (2) the important central buying headquarters of chain-store organizations, voluntary groups, co-ops, and other large-volume direct accounts. Planning is more detailed in the second case because of the greater potential of the call, but in both cases, the sales representative carefully plans his work in advance and follows the plan during the call, as outlined below.

I. *Planning* is done the night before the call and is concerned chiefly with these items.
   A. *Account review*
      1. The overall operation and background of the account as gathered from industry sources such as *Progressive Grocer,* "Facts in the Grocery Business," and other trade publications such as the Dillon study and the Colonial Stores study.
      2. Specific information from Best Foods account records that points out previous successful promotions, distribution problems, or other such matters of record.
      3. Special factors, such as personality of dealer, competitive activity, advertising tie-ins, and what items and promotions the headquarters has authorized for the store.
   B. *Specific sales objectives.* This is important since the Best Foods sales representative has over 120 items and sizes to sell, ranging from Mazola oil to Hellmann's Best Foods mayonnaise, dressings, Karo syrup, Mazola and Nucoa margarine and Shinola shoe polish. He has to plan which product or group of products has to be presented to this specific store in the limited *interview time* available, which is often no more than 5 minutes. By studying his account records and the specific items the company is pushing that week, he pinpoints key items which thus become key sales objectives. He

then relates these to advertising tie-ins and other promotional activities in effect at the time of his call.

C. *Final presentation review.* This involves a quick personalizing and dressing up of the suggested order slip and pitch sheet as a final plan and review of the sales presentations for the next day.

II. *Basic selling procedure (or the complete presentation).* Best Foods sales training prepares the sales representative to follow a basic, step-by-step selling procedure on each call. It starts with the preapproach and continues through completion of the daily report. Careful working of the plan—following each step in the order listed below—is expected during every call.

A. *Preapproach.*
   1. Briefly review plans and fix objectives in mind before each call.
   2. Greet the dealer.
   3. Check distribution to make certain all authorized brands and items are on the shelf. Plan presentation on items not stocked or temporarily out of stock.
   4. Get into stockroom and adjust planned assortment according to stock on hand.
   5. Observe competitive store activity.

B. *Approach.*
   1. Get a friendly reception from dealer.
   2. Secure dealer's undivided attention.
   3. Obtain harmony of mind, yes response.

C. *Presentation.*
   1. Present promotions in logical order and in an enthusiastic and convincing manner.
   2. Make complete presentation on authorized brands and sizes not in stock.
   3. Appeal to dealer by effective use of *sales material* (brochures, flyers); pitch sheet and suggested order form; samples and dummy cartons (particularly for initial sales); demonstrations; other aids such as ad layouts (proofs, P.O.P. material).
   4. Avoid negative suggestions, such as "You don't need any—do you?"
   5. Anticipate objections and include positive selling points to counter them.

D. *Close.*
   1. Ask for the order or display and reach agreement on how to handle temporary out-of-stock conditions.
      a. Phrase close to fit dealer.
      b. Use suggested order slip to gain acceptance of suggested assortment.
      c. Keep quiet after presenting suggested order slip.
   2. Thank dealer for order.

E. *Determine method and date of delivery.*

F. *Place order in order guide, order book, or order form.*

III. *Follow-up records and reports* are completed and handled in this way.

A. *Route books.* Enter complete and accurate information immediately after each call. Enter remarks as an aid to planning and selling on next call.

B. *Daily report.* Complete after each call; make sure it is accurate and legible; and mail at the close of business each day. Place other pertinent data on reverse side so daily report acts as a daily letter.

QUESTIONS FOR WRITTEN REPORTS OR CLASS DISCUSSION

1. Are the Best Foods store-procedure planning steps outlined above concerned more with long-range or short-range planning? Explain.

2. What follow-through steps are covered in the Best Foods store-procedure plan? Outline and explain.

3. How does the Best Foods sales representative employ forecasting techniques in his planning?

4. Would the Best Foods after-call daily report noted above be considered a quantitative or a qualitative report? Explain.

PLANNING, SCHEDULING, TIMING, HUSTLING: KEYS TO SALES SUCCESS FOR BROOKLYN INDEPENDENT KOSHER MEAT AND POULTRY WHOLESALER

When Irving Krasner, ex-Navy pilot, returned to civilian life several years ago, he had but one specific career objective in mind: To get into a self-owned and run business where intelligence and hard work would earn him a good living, and where he could be his own boss.

Friendly and outgoing in personality, he decided that a growth-area service business where he could call on prospects and customers in a limited geographical area might suit him. His problem was to find a business where effective personal salesmanship could produce rapid short-term profitable results and lasting long-term growth, yet prove both interesting and challenging.

Centering on his home area in Brooklyn, N.Y., with its large Jewish population, he made a market survey and decided that the fast-moving wholesale Kosher fresh meat and poultry business met his specifications. Although Jewish, he was not himself particularly religious. Kosher meat and poultry, slaughtered in a certain ritualistic way under the supervision of a rabbi, has to be sold by retailers within a week. He felt that this business was particularly suited to a hustling independent wholesaler, since quality and timing of delivery from factory to retailer to ensure maximum freshness is so important.

He selected fifty delicatessens and restaurants as his potential customer targets, with an initial sales goal of selling himself as wholesaler to about twenty, to which he would offer the best possible specialized service and personally selected products. His initial sales approach was, "Will you give me a chance to show you how well I can supply and service your needs?" Within a short time he had his twenty customers, every one of whom still buys in large quantities from him today. Over the years he has delivered what he promised; he spares no effort to keep his customers satisfied.

His is a highly competitive business; not only does he face constant competition from other independents, but also from large, well-advertised national brand companies such as Hebrew National Kosher Sausage, Inc., and Zion Kosher Sausage Products Co., both subsidiaries of large, nationally-known conglomerates. One great selling point he enjoys is his personal servicing, versus their salary-plus-commission hired route sales representatives who often don't feel his deep personal motivation to work for customers.

Since his customers want the best possible product delivered at the time they specify, he buys personally selected items from different provision factories. These include such items as the freshest possible sausage from a factory specializing only in sausage, fresh roasts from specialty butchers, and fresh chickens from poultry houses that can meet his own high standards of quality and freshness. His large competitors have to buy from their own single factory. In order to get the best from each supplier, Krasner has sold himself to them over the years as a good selective customer, so they save the best for him. Thus his follow-through personal selling is to those he buys from, as well as those he sells to.

Planning and organizing his work is done on a weekly basis, starting each Sunday night with phone calls to each customer, since weekends are their busiest period. Some need replacement items early Monday, so he is up at 4:30 A.M. to make his purchases, often visiting two different poultry houses, three butchers, and two factories to select the best—ahead of his competitors. His routing and scheduling are flexible—to service individual customer needs promptly. Route drivers of his large competitors have to wait their turn at their factory and can only deliver as they get supplied; so by working hard and fast, Krasner can normally outsell them in terms of both fresh, selected products, and better delivery timing. He buys, and delivers to each customer, two or three times a week in this fashion. In addition, he telephones each customer daily to keep in closest possible personal touch. Careful working of his weekly plan, plus proper timing, are vital to sales success.

Calculated social involvement with his customers and dealers, except where personal friendship developed, has not been part of his sales philosophy. But he is invited to, and does attend many customer-related affairs such as weddings, bar mitzvahs, and funerals, and visits those who are ill at home or in the hospital. These involvements follow from the very personal relationships developed with customer and dealer alike. Since he sees and telephones them so often, he knows all their problems and is accepted by all almost as a friend of the family, even where a close personal friendship does not exist.

Krasner has found both monetary reward and deep personal satisfaction in his work. He is a successful, independent businessman. His success and enjoyment of his work stems from and is based on his thoroughly professional and warm human salesmanship, and the best possible customer-oriented selling and servicing. He rates his follow-through sales success in these three points of descending importance: (1) best possible products, (2) his personal performance, and (3) price.

QUESTIONS FOR WRITTEN REPORTS OR CLASS DISCUSSION

1. From a theoretical point of view, so described in the chapter material, what does Krasner's planning involve? In theory is such planning for his one-person company any different than that done by his larger competitors? Explain.

2. Krasner's composite inventory and constant value analysis is done in his head; he does not maintain a card-file system as do route-drivers of his large competitors. Do you feel his system or theirs is best? Why?

3. Seven important habits sales representatives in any business should develop to help make planning, organizing and implementing work were presented on page 392 in the chapter. Which two of them does Krasner appear not to be following? Should he be doing them? Explain.

4. Do you feel Krasner's planning his work and working his plan each week are built around all four of the basic management functions discussed in the chapter material? Explain.

HOW CAN SALES REPRESENTATIVES INCREASE THEIR "ACTION TIME" TO GAIN MORE SALES?

"Increase your 'action time' (the minutes you actually spend with your prospect during a sales presentation)—and you'll increase your sales," say some sales authorities.

They are referring to the unproductive time wasted by most sales representatives during any given working day. Since some spend only 20 percent of their actual time selling, where does the other 80 percent go? The answer is, in many cases: 30 percent traveling, 25 percent waiting to see people, 20 percent spent on paperwork, and 5 percent on other things. That leaves only 1/5 of their total time for "action."

QUESTION FOR WRITTEN REPORTS OR CLASS DISCUSSION

Can you list and explain four good ways an average sales representative, through careful planning and efficient management of his time, could cut down on the 80 percent unproductive (but often necessary) part of his daily time and increase his valuable selling or "action" time?

---

programming your career toward higher earnings and management

When you have mastered the content of this chapter, you should be able to:

Describe three basic ways to get to the top through selling.

Summarize the importance of personal goal-setting and self-management as essential to career success in both personal selling and management.

Analyze what is meant by "the secret" of how to reach high sales and earnings.

List several basic personal and professional qualities or characteristics one must possess in order to achieve success in management.

List several aspects of knowledge and performance levels expected of a manager.

Summarize what one should do in order to advance most rapidly within a company or organization.

We have now completed our study of the basic attitudes, planning, organization, strategies, and techniques of and for successful salesmanship. If you understand and have accepted the principles and techniques outlined in the preceding chapters, then you know how to achieve success in selling. From here on, success basically depends on how efficiently you put into practice what you have learned.

If you have only moderate ambitions in life—just want to know enough to get along—then you have largely accomplished your objectives in studying this book. But if you want more than the ordinary in life and in work, if you want to earn a lot of money through selling or if you desire to reach the top in management, then this chapter is worth your special and serious consideration.

But first, a warning! Reaching the top in personal selling or through management within a company or organization requires constant hard work, dedication, creative thinking, and above-average drive and determination.

FEWER THAN ONE IN FIFTY WILL REACH THE TOP

Opportunities to rise to the top through selling have never been greater. The needs and demands of our exploding world population in this exciting age of human and technological change are unparalleled. Industry is expanding at an unprecedented rate to fulfill those needs and is searching avidly now for those individuals capable of leadership in the future.

Yet, from among all those who, along with you, are reading this book, fewer than one in fifty will rise to the top 10 percent in earnings or job positions. Many will fail more from lack of proper attitude, drive, or determination than from lack of intelligence. In the end, all things being somewhat if not altogether equal, success is up to you.

What about it? Do you want to give it a go, to try to reach the top? If you do not try you will never know whether you can. If so, then let us put our mind and will power into high gear and consider how you can most rapidly achieve your goals and ultimate objective.

PERSONAL GOAL-SETTING IS THE BASIC KEY TO SUCCESS

There are basically three ways to get to the top through selling.

1. *Becoming and remaining a full-time professional sales representative either independently or within the framework of a company.* This means forgetting about management as a goal and striving for increased earnings and relative freedom of action through personal management of your activities. Your aim thus becomes that of obtaining more and bigger sales that directly result in higher earnings and personal accomplishment.

Such a professional career potentially offers great freedom of action, independence, satisfaction, and the opportunity to earn a great deal of money as a direct and immediate result of your own efforts. This opportunity to realize high earnings and to remain your own boss exists in many fields: real estate, insurance, and investments to name but a few. You can also find such rewards as a manufacturer's representative or agent or in many of the service or direct-selling areas.

You become, in effect, manager of your own business, one which you can enter without any capital investment, other than that of your own time, efforts, and intelligence. If the market and need is there, success largely depends on how hard you work and on the efficiency of your self-management.

If you have the attributes of a good sales representative, enjoy the excitement of face-to-face selling, and either lack or dislike the analytical and impersonal requirements for top sales or corporate management positions, then this career goal could well be the one toward which you should set your sights.

2. *Personally selling a good, need-filling product or service anywhere in the world and building toward your own small, medium, or large company.* Many young men and women have done this both in the United States and in other parts of the world. Opportunities exist everywhere to start selling even an idea that can quickly develop into a profitable and growing company.

If you have an unusual amount of drive, ambition, and business acumen, what could be more challenging than to start your own company from nothing? The best way to start such an enterprise without much or any capital is to sell successfully something produced by someone else who needs success-minded individuals to sell or market his product.

Potential gains are high in this area; for some individuals the sky is the limit. The risks of such undercapitalized efforts are great, and only a few make it, but who is to stop you from trying? If you have the idea and the product or service and if the need is there, perhaps this is the direction in which you should set your sights. One valuable how-to reference that will help you get started in your own sales business is a book called *How to Make Big Money As an Independent Sales Agent.*[1]

3. *Working up through the sales ranks of an existing company to sales manager, marketing director, and even president or managing director.* If you lack that touch of business acumen or genius necessary for going it alone to form your own company, perhaps you can best reach your goals as a member of a team in an

---

1. Edwin E. Bobrow, *How to Make Big Money As an Independent Sales Agent* (Englewood Cliffs, N.J.: Parker Publishing Co., 1967).

20

existing company. Small or large, such companies are seeking now those individuals who one day will, in top management capacity, guide their organizations.

Since ours is a customer/society-oriented marketing economy, the sales/marketing function is of vital importance to overall company effort. By starting as a sales representative with an enlightened company whose policy is to consider you manager of your territory and a vital member of the management team, you have the opportunity immediately to learn and put into practice the concepts and techniques of top management. This fact alone can put you potentially far ahead of the people in the financial, legal, or computer areas when the time comes for considering you for a top management position. You alone understand what your customers want, how they buy, and how they use company products.

While there will always be room for independent operators and small and specialized companies, the overall trend, in the United States at least, is toward fewer, larger, and more highly diversified companies run by well-trained, professional managers. These managers of the future will have to know not only about such things as computers and scientific decision-making but also how to use them in terms of the human element. Thus sales will continue to be perhaps the fastest road to top management.

SELF-MANAGEMENT IS ESSENTIAL FOR SUCCESS NO MATTER WHAT YOUR GOAL

In order to illustrate the importance of self-management and professionalism, let us focus our attention on two specific goals you might wish to set for yourself: (1) setting your sights for high earnings as a professional sales representative, and (2) programming your career for management. The first, of course, can lead into the second if you elect, or remain a career end in itself. To pursue a sales management or top management goal through selling requires that you first establish a superior record in personal selling.

SETTING YOUR SIGHTS FOR HIGHER SALES AND EARNINGS

Charting your career to reach the top ranks in sales and earnings success requires the same careful planning and follow-through involved in an important military or business operation. Thinking of your sales territory management problems in terms of the managerial concepts we have presented throughout these pages enables you to review and take advantage of all the latest theoretical principles and practical practices and techniques of selling developed over the years. You must now consider them professionally, and decide on your own initiative how to plan, analyze, and take advantage of every possible product and profit opportunity.

Your first step is to study and analyze such opportunities in your specific area of selling for possible application to your own sales activity. In other words, start where others have successfully left off, by putting their hard-won, effective ideas to work for you from the start. Adapt these ideas to your own problems and needs, improve them where possible, and then add your own ideas. This procedure is the quickest and most effective way to move into high-volume selling.

Let us start to put this thinking into practice by considering some of the methods developed by successful professional sales representatives to achieve high sales and earnings. Although we will consider them in the light of managerial concepts and terminology, you should seek those *high-powered, practical tech-*

niques that can most quickly produce profitable volume for you in your own area of selling.

Basic laws for success in selling include the following:

1. The more efficiently you work, the more you achieve.
2. The more carefully selected calls you make, the more interviews you obtain.
3. The more interviews you obtain, the more presentations you make.
4. The more presentations you make, the greater your chances of closing sales.
5. The more sales you close the greater your volume and, if it is profitable volume, the more income for you!
6. Careful planning, efficient work habits, and setting sales goals on big potential customers and big-ticket items lead to increased volume and income.

Progressive development of these laws or principles will lead to increased sales and higher earnings. The degree of success and speed in achievement depends on careful planning, efficient follow-through, careful analysis and controls, and proper management of time and effort. While we have already made many suggestions for practical implementation of forecasting, programming, scheduling, and follow-through in Chapter 19, *let us consider them briefly again in a high-gear, thoroughly professional manner.* Our aim is to present some very practical, maximum-income sales-producing ideas useful to you or any ambitious sales representative, no matter what type of outside selling you are in. If you feel you are merely rereading much of what was presented in part in Chapter 19, then *study* what you have read and are reading *more closely!*

Forecasting.   Increased sales volume alone is not enough to bring high sales and earnings. The secret is to make profitable sales, and to do so you must understand both the profit potential of your product line and the market potential of your territory. One valuable reference that outlines simple methods for evaluating sales procedures and profits is a book called *The Arithmetic of Sales Management.* [2]

Effective forecasting can be based only on facts; yet few sales representatives spend enough time obtaining concrete facts upon which to accurately forecast or base their planning. Here are some suggestions to help make your personal analysis and forecasting effective.

1.   Pay special attention to selecting customers or prospects which your company or industry records indicate not only order but also pay promptly. Such selection helps eliminate bad debts that could affect your end-of-the-year net sales results.

2.   Thoroughly research all the needs of your current good customers and of all their branches. It is nearly always easier to sell more to current customers than to seek out new ones.

3.   Within your territory, carefully analyze who buys what products, why, and how they use them. This analysis not only enables you to intelligently prepare to sell them more but also furnishes ideas for selling to others.

4.   Analyze prospects sold, what they purchased, and the size of their purchases. This information helps you forecast potential business with accuracy.

5.   Prepare from your analysis and forecasts a list of target accounts, keep up-to-date files on them, and use this list in scheduling your calls.

6.   Analyze not only sales of previous years but also new sales figures in order to determine how time can be spent most profitably.

2. Fred M. Truett, *The Arithmetic of Sales Management* (New York: American Management Association, 1968).

7. As you uncover factors that seem to be working against you, try to discover positive angles that can alter the situation in your favor. Then take these new facts into consideration in your forecasting and planning.

8. Analyze and forecast around these goals: (1) selling to a higher percentage of customers and prospects, (2) selling more to each, (3) selling higher-priced items to each, and (4) selling to bigger customers, who have the need and ability to buy more.

9. If your analysis indicates past calls that do not appear to be paying off, investigate further to see whether those accounts are growing businesses that justify further cultivation. You may elect to drop them completely as unprofitable accounts or to handle them by telephone or mail alone.

Programming. Effective programming involves (1) placing the proper value on your time and (2) determining the number and types of calls that enable you to reach your sales or earnings goal. Here are some examples of the value that must be placed on your time if you are to reach selected annual earnings goals. They are based on an average 1,920 working hours in a year of 240 days, noted previously.

Yearly earnings goal	Value of an hour	Value of a minute
$ 5,000	$ 2.60	$ .043
10,000	5.20	.086
20,000	10.40	.174
30,000	15.60	.260
40,000	20.80	.346
50,000	26.00	.433

But, since you are probably only able to spend one-third of your time in profitable, face-to-face sales interviews, the value of your effective selling time is much greater, as these figures show.

Yearly earnings goal	Value per hour of effective selling time	Value per minute of effective selling time
$ 5,000	$ 7.80	$ .13
10,000	15.60	.26
20,000	31.20	.52
30,000	46.80	.78
40,000	62.40	1.04
50,000	78.00	1.30

You will never reach the top in sales or earnings until you place the proper value on your time! Once you do, your problem becomes how to use your valuable time most effectively.

When planning your program, you are basically concerned with (1) making as many calls as possible within the time available, (2) trying to close a sale on every call, (3) trying to sell as much or as many extras as possible on each call. The suggestions that follow for accomplishing these steps are worth your careful consideration.

1. Try to sell something on every call. This simple objective is a powerful psychological incentive to continue trying to close, even if the resulting order is small. Small, foot-in-the-door orders give you a chance to prove your claims of after-sale service and provide reasons for callbacks.

2.   Sell across the board. Try to find some use for any and all of your various product lines if you carry a range.

3.   Try for the biggest possible sale first. It is easier to come down in quantity or price than to trade up. If a customer or prospect asks for a specific item, present the benefits of your top-of-the-line product if you have one. It always pays to ask.

4.   Sell selectively by giving careful attention to low-volume items that, because of higher unit price, can add up to high total sales and profits. Too many sales representatives think of volume alone.

5.   When programming sales calls, concentrate on selling new customers products or services which are currently successful. It is easier to sell something of proven value in most cases than to sell something entirely new. One great secret of profitable selling is to find new markets for current products.

6.   Whenever possible, give up or cut down on selling items that do not produce volume commensurate with the time and effort spent on their promotion.

7.   Carefully review customer-call frequency in terms of actual or potential business. Such analysis may indicate that you are calling on some customers too often and on others not enough.

8.   Do not forget that persistence can pay off. Many sales are often made in some types of selling only after several calls. If the need, the potential, and the ability and authority to buy are there, one more call may do the trick.

9.   Try to sell the biggest potential buyers possible. It takes no more effort to sell a big buyer than to sell a small one, although since the stakes are bigger, your effort may require extra-careful planning.

10.   Program your work to fill in seasonally slack periods (such as around Christmas or during vacation periods) with calls on customers or prospects who will be available and in a position to make buying decisions at that time. To a professional sales representative, there is no slack selling time.

Scheduling.   One great secret of maximizing profitable sales is to spend time and effort only in those areas where maximum results are obtainable. This fact seems almost too obvious to mention, yet here are three of the greatest mistakes commonly made by sales representatives.

Following a milk route through habit and failing to evaluate or change that habit.

Failing to check past or present sales volume against the amount of time and money expended.

Taking it easy and continuing to call mainly on people they know or feel will pleasantly welcome them.

Scheduling is basically concerned with planning your work; it involves scheduling routing and time so that sales result. Successful professional sales representatives around the world have developed many ideas to enable your time spent per call to bring profitable results. Here are but a few ideas that you should take into consideration when scheduling.

1.   Sell where the money is! This involves both analysis of past sales and forecasts of future ones to determine where and how you should spend your time and concentrate your efforts. If 10 percent of past customers have given you 80 percent of past business, then perhaps you should spend more time with these prime customers to try to sell them more.

2.   Keep professional hours—that is, work as early and continue as late as prospects or customers are willing to see you.

3. Because it is often just as easy to sell a complete program or system as to sell the individual parts, consider first overall needs and try for a big sale.

4. As you conclude a sale, try to think of a second sale that will make the first one even more useful. A customer who buys is in a buying mood, and it will pay you to try to take advantage of it by offering something else.

5. Use the telephone effectively to save time. You can use it as a selling instrument to help you qualify customers, handle appointments, keep in touch with small or outlying accounts, clear up misunderstandings, or relay important information rapidly. Proper use of the telephone gives you more time for that most valuable part of selling—face-to-face interviews with the best potential customers.

6. Plan to spend your prime selling time only with those prospects or customers with the money and authority to buy.

7. Swim with the tide; concentrate on selling the products or services that follow current industry developments or interests. And concentrate further on your current, tested, quality items.

8. Make long-term appointments with key customers who require specific visits at specific times and with key new prospects.

9. Group weekly or daily calls to cut down on travel time, and review ahead the specific purpose and results expected from each of these calls.

10. Confirm important appointments ahead of time by mail or phone, and plan your travel or eating time around customers' work or meal habits. This procedure helps cut down waiting time.

Follow-through. As noted previously, we are now using the term *follow-through* in the managerial sense of working your plan rather than in the strictly sales sense of after-sales procedure. Thus we are concerned with the efficiency and profitable productivity of your overall selling efforts within the time allocated for them. This portion of your sales effort is a logical result of planning your work, as we have just covered it. We have discussed many follow-through ideas throughout the entire book. Thus we will add only a few new ones for your consideration.

1. Always try to sell more or extras to your current customers. You may suggest increased quantities, related items, new items, or items on sale.

2. Be creative in your selling and try to find new uses for old products or unthought-of uses for new products.

3. See to it that, when orders are filled by your company, the customers are resold through enclosed sales material that again describes benefits.

4. Find out why your customers buy, and get evidence and endorsement from them in the form of testimonials. Then use that evidence to sell new customers.

5. Aim always to turn small, current, satisfied accounts into large accounts.

Establishing controls. Controls are essential reviews of the effectiveness of your performance not only for you but also for your company. Ideally you should conclude each day with a careful, hour-by-hour review of your activities. Your purpose is to give a step-by-step analysis of your performance. Such analysis should then be entered on a daily performance or evaluation record. Continue this summary or analysis on a weekly, monthly, or quarterly basis as dictated by personal need or company requirements. Here are some suggestions that may help make such control evaluations, summaries, or reports useful and effective.

1. Evaluate results at the end of each day and learn to recognize any sig-

nificant data encountered, such as why sales were lost, competition price or product changes, customers' changing needs, or new trends or developments in the industry that could affect your future sales.

2.   Keep accurate, daily, personal time records so that you will know where your time was spent and how it could be spent most profitably.

3.   Set up a personal, quick-reference, cross-index system to enable you to file and find information easily and rapidly. You should file brief notes jotted down immediately after a sales presentation as a matter of course. Because most people cannot retain facts for long, place every scrap of potentially useful information in your files. This information can provide the basis for specific controls, reports, analyses, forecasts, and plans.

4.   In order to save everyone's time, make any reports or communications for your personal records, to your company, or to your customers simple, clear, complete, concise, and effective. Unless you learn this art, you may never qualify for any top management position.

THE SECRET OF HOW TO REACH HIGH SALES AND EARNINGS

Many entire books explain how to earn high income through personal selling. The relatively few specific ideas just presented within a managerial framework are sound enough yet certainly not comprehensive enough to cover the subject in depth.

However, when coupled with the sound principles and practical techniques of selling contained in preceding sections of this book, they are certainly enough to provide you with a sense of direction.

Is there any secret for success in personal selling as so many sales books and articles seem to claim? If so, what is it? What does one have to learn or do to reach one's sales and earnings goal? We can best answer this question rather simply by observing why most sales representatives will fail to reach their highest objectives and how the one in fifty will succeed.

Failure will be largely due to not putting into practice those lessons which have already been learned through studying this book.

Success will most likely come to those who do put this knowledge into constant, day-by-day, enthusiastic practice.

PROGRAMMING YOUR CAREER FOR MANAGEMENT

According to latest census figures 5.3 million Americans are engaged in some form of sales work. Of these, 2.2 million are in the manufacturing and service industries, and 3.1 million are in retail selling. From among these will come the sales/marketing managers and possibly up to 40 percent of every top U.S. corporate leadership in the late 1970s and the 1980s. If you are an American, man or woman, between the ages of eighteen and forty and aspire to one of these future positions as sales manager, marketing director, or president of a company, you should start planning for and working toward that ultimate objective now.

Most of your millions of potential competitors will spend their careers with private companies. Since the trend in the United States is toward fewer, very large, and highly diversified companies, you should consider how business and marketing changes in the next two decades may affect them and you. No one can predict exactly what may happen economically or politically in the United States or throughout the world over the next two decades. But certainly the needs and wants of the exploding world population will be far greater than they are today, and private companies or nationalized organizations will be fulfilling the marketing function of supplying those needs. Assuming that your career will be closely tied to one or more of these companies or organizations during this period, your advancement via the sales route to a managerial position will be within the marketing framework.

You need to pay careful attention to how you can program or further your own progress toward your desired managerial position. How can you manage that most important business of all—your own career? Here are some questions you may ask; answers will be given in the remainder of this chapter.

1. What will selling and sales management be like in the future?
2. What are the opportunities for reaching management level in the next few years?
3. What are your personal chances of reaching management level?
4. Do you have what it takes to be a manager?
5. How do your superiors judge your managerial potential?
6. What knowledge and performance level does a managerial role require?
7. How can one develop managerial knowledge, skills, and abilities?
8. How does one advance most rapidly within an organization?

WHAT WILL SELLING AND SALES MANAGEMENT BE LIKE IN THE FUTURE?

The successful professional sales representative or sales manager of 1975 may well be the failure of 1985—a victim of progress! The next ten or twenty years will be ones of rapid, even profound change, of problems, of new challenges, and of great opportunities for those companies and individuals who can rise to the occasion.

What will these changes be? Science and technology will produce a host of new and now unthought-of products, and entire new service industries will arise as a result. Customers will be better educated and will be more sophisticated and demanding in their buying. As ever-increasing wealth and affluence spreads to more people, they will have the leisure to enjoy the desire for new and better products and services. Socio-economic pressures and government reaction to them may cause sweeping changes in many aspects of business life.

In this fluid situation, businesses will face increasing competition in searching for new products, in lowering costs, in producing with greater efficiency, and in making higher profits. Automation will bring many changes in the way of doing business—in marketing and selling as in other functional areas. These developments will greatly affect both the professional and the personal lives of sales representatives and sales managers.

Although the need for competent sales/marketing executives will be greater than ever, the situation will require some changes in their role. The scientific approach will become highly important, requiring mathematical and symbolic competence as well as the current creative approach to solving complex sales/marketing problems. In this situation, individual knowledge and competence will be all that count. Like doctors, sales representatives will have to go to school or follow a constant program of self-study in order to stay abreast of the rapid changes in their field.

This study will have to extend to learning about the other functions within the organization. The sales/marketing managers of the future will have to understand the total corporate business picture as well as the interdependent roles of functions such as finance, personnel, production, and advertising.

Global thinking, rather than that along national lines, will be the order of the day, and the new managers will be internationalists at heart. Ideally, they will have a good background in one or more foreign languages; certainly they should have a cultural background that allows them to understand and accept all individuals, nationalities, and races.

These sales/marketing managers will play an important role because they, and they alone of all the functional people in the organization, will be the vital link between company and customer, representing one to the other.

WHAT ARE THE OPPORTUNITIES FOR REACHING MANAGEMENT LEVEL IN THE NEXT FEW YEARS?

Opportunities have never been better! In fact, the United States, Canada, and most European nations are beginning to face a shortage of executive talent. This shortage is especially acute in the middle-management range as a result of low birth rates during the 1930s and, to some extent, of the casualties during World War II.

A high percentage of middle and top management falls in the forty to fifty-five age bracket, the age group that will be in relatively short supply during the next decade especially. As a result, many companies are already seeking bright young men and women capable of moving into key positions in the future.

And while we are on this subject, it is interesting to note one past American Management Association study regarding the best path to take for promotion to top management. Their survey of 200 American company presidents showed that nearly 50 percent now head the companies which gave them their first jobs. An additional 20 percent changed jobs only once in their careers. If this survey is truly representative, it seems to indicate that the best path to the top lies in joining a progressive company in a growth industry and staying with it, rather than job-hopping.

WHAT ARE YOUR PERSONAL CHANCES OF REACHING MANAGEMENT LEVEL?

Since the opportunity for advancement has never been better, the question really becomes, "Can you make the grade?" The answer depends basically on your attitudes toward life and work, knowledge, organization, ability to manage time, and how others judge your capabilities and performance. It also depends on your basic human qualities, character qualities, intelligence, and aptitude for management.

In previous pages we have covered the attitudes, aptitudes, basic human and character qualities, professional skills, and work habits necessary to ensure success in selling. Thus we will assume you do possess these basic ingredients and will relate them only to specific qualities needed by a manager (or leader) as contrasted to a sales representative.

Later we shall consider what your superiors look for in their evaluation of you as a potential manager. For the moment, however, we are concerned only with your evaluation of your ability to fulfill such a role. Many men and women are simply unsuited for management and would not like the role or the responsibilities it places on them even if they were given the opportunity.

Management requires some special personal characteristics. You have to set an example and lead others by demonstration as well as by talk. Thus you lose some personal freedom of action or independence, and you place the team above self. In sales management especially, since it is a line function, you have to work hard, outperform if possible, and often put the welfare of others ahead of yourself if you are to gain their respect and confidence in you as a leader. And, as you move into higher management, a staff function, certain analytical abilities are necessary in addition to those personal leadership characteristics basic to successful line management.

Here are a few of the basic qualities or characteristics you must possess, both from a personal and professional point of view, if you hope to achieve success in management.

Personal characteristics	Professional characteristics
Self-confidence	Good organization
Consideration of others	Good planning abilities
Punctuality	Ability to write accurate reports
Open-mindedness	Ability to devise practical ideas
Consistency	Ability to see the company viewpoint
Creativeness	Orderliness
Initiative	Ability to produce quality work
Ambition	Ability to manage time efficiently
Enthusiasm	Good motivation

Sales management, as contrasted to pure personal selling, is more concerned with managing in the sense of planning, organizing, problem-solving, and goal-setting. We can illustrate this in a practical way by considering some of the key responsibilities outlined by any typical large company.

Figure 20.1 on page 410 may seem like a mere summary of the steps (previously covered in this book) necessary for success in selling. The difference is that a manager has to put them into practice even more devotedly and efficiently than does a sales representative. A sales manager must not only be professionally capable in every respect but also possess the initiative, drive, and stamina to lead and to show others how to do an outstanding job. His enthusiasm and constant attempts to do the job better must rub off on others and are thus vital to success.

If you possess the necessary attitudes, aptitudes, characteristics, knowledge, and skills and are willing to work hard, then your chances of reaching management level are excellent. Thinking you have them or wanting to acquire them is not enough however. Performance is the only thing that counts in selling, and outstanding performance, as judged by superiors in your company or organization, in the end determines your ability to be promoted to management level.

HOW DO YOUR SUPERIORS JUDGE YOUR MANAGERIAL POTENTIAL?

An outstanding sales record is but one of the many factors your superiors have to evaluate when considering you for promotion to a managerial position. The new role requires leadership abilities and certain other aptitudes, abilities, and qualities not essential to success in normal sales activities. Thus your superiors consider all aspects of your performance and also take into consideration your personal qualifications, knowledge, skills, and other overall abilities required for a managerial role. Here are some of the characteristics they evaluate within these areas.

FIGURE 20.1 Territory sales managers' job responsibility chart

To yourself	To the company	To your customers
Increase basic selling skills.	*Be proud* of your association with your company.	*Work* closely with deciders and influencers in each account.
Develop management abilities.	*Maintain* company standing and standards with all customers.	*Point* out the advantages of an association with your company.
Keep pace with changes, trends, and developments in the territory.	*Inform* headquarters and supervisors, through established channels, of changes and developments within your territory.	*Keep* accounts current on all company advertising and promotional activities.
Study to be up to date on products, promotions, policies, and procedures.		*Suggest* ideas, methods, techniques, and tips that can stimulate their sales.
Stay alert for new sales and merchandising ideas.	*Be prompt* in handling records, reports, correspondence, and requests.	*Inform* customers of trends within their areas.
Grow so that you can assume greater responsibilities as opportunities permit.	*Cut* selling costs by economical routing, good use of time, better planning, and greater awareness of opportunities.	*Handle* complaints efficiently and to their complete satisfaction.
Maintain the appearance and deportment expected of a territory sales manager.	*Check* demand and movement of products in the territory.	*Suggest* best techniques for selling your products to their customers.
Analyze your weaknesses and strong points; then do something about them.	*Report* on the activities of competitors.	*Organize* presentation to inform and save time.
	Strive to meet and beat sales goals.	*Alert* customers to changes in company policies or procedures.
	Ask for help when you need it.	*Simulate* and maintain enthusiasm for your products.
	Cooperate with other departments within the company.	*Build* and maintain goodwill.

Personal qualities.   You do not have to look like a movie star to be a manager, but good personal appearance does command respect. Thus good grooming and neatness are important factors. Your manner, as exemplified in your self-confidence, enthusiasm, and sincerity, leads to respect, confidence, pride, and trust in the minds of customers, subordinates, and superiors.

Perhaps the best way to consider the personal attributes or qualities others look for in you is to picture successful businessmen or executives whom you know. What is it about them that commands your attention and respect? Your answers probably tie in fairly closely with the list of personal and professional qualities and characteristics noted on page 409. Generally, as you view and evaluate their personal qualities, so do superiors evaluate yours.

Simple virtues are most likely to impress the boss—punctuality, strict observance of company or organization rules, concentration, trustworthiness, willingness, patience, and self-control. And, the qualities of a team player—one who puts the welfare of the group before selfish personal interests—also are important. You do not have to give up your ambitions or individuality, but you do have to be a cooperative and willing member of the organization team.

Performance record.   A successful sales record, as noted earlier, is but one factor your superiors consider in evaluating your overall performance. They note the soundness of your opinions, your ability to profit from mistakes, your memory, and the way you put plans into action and follow through. They also consider the consistency, reliability, creativity, adaptability, and willingness you displayed in creating that successful sales record. They note your attendance record, how you organize your time, your ability to learn, and the neatness and accuracy of your reports. Other evaluations include these.

How well you handle yourself in different situations.

How well you keep management informed of competitors' activities, customer reactions, and other business and credit information.

How neatly and how effectively you maintain and use sales manuals, visual aids, and records.

Above all, they are interested in the overall soundness of your judgment, your adherence to the organization viewpoint and methods, and the creativity of your ideas and suggestions. Your superiors are not seeking a superperson, but they do realize that a sound balance of these ingredients is essential to success at management level. It is your overall performance record that counts most to them.

Knowledge and skill.   In order to be considered for promotion to a managerial position, you have to exhibit the depth of your knowledge and skills. Some sales representatives can build a good record around superficial knowledge and a few successful techniques. This background is not sufficient for sales management since in that position you must have a depth of knowledge, theory, and practical skills in order to teach others with varied personalities and levels of experience and ability.

We will consider in a moment some of the specific knowledge and skills required in a management role. For now, it is enough to say that your superiors expect you to show comprehensive knowledge about your customer, product, and company and to demonstrate professional skills through performance and results before they consider you for promotion to management.

Special management aptitudes and abilities.   It is normally harder to show others how to sell successfully, to supervise their activities, and to motivate them than it is to do the job yourself. Therefore, in addition to normal sales skills, character qualifications, job knowledge, and a balanced, successful performance record, other special aptitudes and abilities are necessary for success in management.

A manager works at executive level, and the basic function of any executive is to get things done through subordinates who are confident of his abilities and talents and who trust his decisions. How he accomplishes this function is less important than that he possess the gift of leadership—the ability to persuade others to work as a team under his direction to accomplish certain designated objectives. This gift of getting others to perform willingly under one's direction is perhaps the most important aptitude necessary for success. Because it is a difficult quality to pin down, your superiors have to evaluate your personality and performance record carefully to see whether you have it.

Some other special aptitudes and abilities necessary for success in management include analytical gifts, organizational and administrative talents, the ability to plan group efforts, and good communication skills.

WHAT KNOWLEDGE AND PERFORMANCE LEVEL
DOES A MANAGERIAL ROLE REQUIRE?

What does being a manager entail? We have just discussed the fact that a manager has to be a leader, but what else does he have to know and do in order to hold his position? Management is the art, skill, or act of controlling, directing, or administering activities or affairs. Thus, a manager is a director or controller.

In order to plan, organize, direct, and control others toward successful accomplishment, a manager must know the business thoroughly. Having such knowledge requires constant study and application in the face of an ever-changing market situation. Second, he must have leadership qualities in order to get results.

His basic tasks while working with and through others are to make an analysis of what has to be done, to plan the best way to do it, and to put the plan into action. He then has to follow through to see that the plan is accomplished because his performance is judged on results.

Here are some attributes or qualities other than the personal and professional characteristics noted earlier needed by a manager to fulfill his role.

> Be able to speak, write, and listen well.
> Profit from mistakes.
> Take calculated risks.
> Simplify the task.
> Tie up loose ends.
> Set high standards.
> Establish objectives to give a sense of direction.
> Praise in public.
> Criticize in private.
> Be demanding yet considerate of others.

We must further stress some very basic qualities necessary to achieve success. If you aspire to a management role, you must honestly decide whether you possess them. They are key factors to your superiors when they evaluate your past performance and future managerial potential.

Judgment.   A managerial role involves responsibility, and the soundness of your analyses and recommendations becomes more important the higher you rise. Do you have the ability to analyze problems calmly and objectively and are you willing to be held accountable for your decisions?

Ability to plan.   The higher your managerial position, the more time you have to spend planning. At the very top, the effectiveness of your planning determines the profitability of your division or company. The stakes are high—failure can even affect survival. Do you have the analytical abilities of a planner or do you prefer to be out on the firing line, face-to-face with prospects and customers?

Communication skills.   A manager has to be able to communicate his plans effectively and persuasively, verbally or in writing. He has to sell his ideas to begin with in competition with courses of action advocated by others within the organization and to persuade others to accomplish them afterward.

The sincerity, logic, and clarity of his expression in times of crisis can lead to success in spite of seemingly impossible obstacles. The best example of this is the eloquence of Prime Minister Winston Churchill during the Battle of Britain in World War II. His verbal and written words alone at that time lifted his nation from physical and emotional defeat to ultimate victory.

Do you have the ability to think clearly and to communicate your thoughts rationally, forcefully (if not eloquently), and persuasively?

Reliability and moral courage. Consistency and dependability are two very necessary qualities in management. A manager, because of the key role he plays, is considered one who can be depended upon by top management and subordinates alike. And consistent with reliability and dependability is the moral courage to make prompt decisions, to take prompt action, and to bravely accept the consequences of wrong decisions. Are you reliable? Do you have the moral courage to face the possibly adverse consequences of important decisions?

Ambition and persistence. These two qualities are also necessary for success in management. Ambition, if channeled in the right direction, is something to be proud of. It helps feed the inner drive necessary for success. Unless one is ambitious, why put up with the constant strain and risk that come with managerial responsibility? Persistence, or determination, is also essential to managerial follow-through, especially when the going is rough. Are you ambitious enough to face the risks and strains of a responsible managerial role? Are you determined and persistent enough to see every project through to the end whether it be a success or a failure?

HOW CAN ONE DEVELOP MANAGERIAL KNOWLEDGE, SKILLS, AND ABILITIES?

Up to this point, we have observed that while the door to management level is wide open, there is room at the top only for those who can produce results. Knowledge and certain abilities or qualities, along with a natural gift for leadership, have been outlined as prerequisites. While describing these in the light of how superiors evaluate them when considering you for promotion, we also asked you to evaluate them in yourself.

Do you at this point feel that you have the inner characteristics and qualities essential for success in management? Would you like a managerial job, in which you may spend most of your time in brain work at a desk, as contrasted to field sales work? If you are determined to try, then let us see how you may most rapidly develop the knowledge, skills, and abilities that will lead you to success.

Start by programming and managing your own career. Start by thinking like a manager about your own career. Do you recall the four basic functions of a manager which we discussed a few pages back? Let us think of them in terms of your own situation and use them as a basis for programming your career toward whatever managerial goal you elect. Remember that you will be judged all along the way by superiors on your performance and results.

1. Make an analysis of what has to be done to reach your objective.
2. Plan the best way to reach it.
3. Put the plan into action.
4. Follow through to see that you accomplish your plan.

We will not attempt, in this brief section, to outline such a plan for you. That is your responsibility. But we can dwell on three of the most important areas of growth necessary for success: knowledge, managerial and organizational skills, and communication skills.

As an introduction, we can briefly consider two other important factors: development of analytical skills and judgment. If you were not blessed at birth with analytical traits you simply have to work hard, work through others, study constantly, and use your basic intelligence to build through application onto whatever natural abilities you do possess.

As for judgment, we can best cite the philosophy of that famous American World War I flying hero and modern business executive, the late Captain Eddie Rickenbacker. To him, life is a series of experiences, which add up to knowledge, which hopefully gives one judgment.

Knowledge Comes through Study

Basic to success at any level of management is your overall knowledge. Since the best way to learn is to see, hear, and do, the assimilation of knowledge is a never-ending, day-by-day task. Knowledge can be acquired on the job, at home by reading, through professional associations, and through formal course study.

What kind of knowledge do you need? You need to know everything possible about selling, marketing, and business in general, about your customers and their needs, and about company operations and products. You also need a good general background to be able to understand the complexities of our fast-changing world in the areas of history, international relations, politics, economics, psychology, mathematics, sociology, and technology, to name but a few.

As you plan your continuous program of self-study, you should keep in mind the changing skills that will be demanded of the new breed of managers over the next two decades. Here are some suggestions as to how you may go about acquiring and developing the knowledge necessary for success in management.

Selling, marketing, and business knowledge can be gained on the job by studying your customers' operations and needs and by asking why and how questions. Within your company you can get to know key men and learn from them about managerial techniques, controls, accounting, advertising, credit, personnel, production, shipping, and data processing. The more you learn day by day and the sooner you attempt to apply your knowledge, the more interesting your work becomes and the faster you develop professionally.

All types of knowledge can be gained through formal study—through courses offered by correspondence schools, colleges, universities, professional institutes, and business or community organizations. Here is a guide to some of these courses in the United States. There are many other excellent schools or courses in addition to the ones noted, but this listing gives you a start for investigating possibilities.

1. *Correspondence courses* are offered by the National Sales Development Institute, Waterford, Conn., Alexander Hamilton Institute Inc., La Salle Training College, and International Correspondence Schools, among others.
2. *University, college, and community-college courses* are offered in hundreds of cities throughout the country, day and evening.
3. *Three major professional associations* often sponsor management-level courses in business, sales, and marketing.
    A. *Sales and Marketing Executives International, Inc.* Head office: 380 Lexington Avenue, New York, N.Y., 10017. The most active association for sales/marketing in the world, it has a membership of more than 25,000 in over 230 affiliated clubs in 49 countries of the Free World.

    Its Youth Education Center works closely with associated clubs to provide advice and career guidance to young people who desire a sales/

marketing career. This is the best single source to contact for information about such careers.

The organization also offers sales and field-sales management workshop courses in major U.S. cities throughout the year and a well-known summer graduate course in sales management and marketing at Syracuse University, Syracuse, N.Y.

B. *American Management Association*, 135 West 50th Street, New York, N.Y., 10020, sponsors many courses around the country, including specialized ones in sales management.

C. *American Marketing Association*, 222 South Riverside Plaza, Chicago, Ill. 60606, also sponsors courses of interest to sales/marketing people from time to time in different cities.

4. *Other courses* are offered throughout the country by numerous private sales schools, business colleges, and community groups such as the Chamber of Commerce. The latter organization is the best source for finding out about such courses in your area.

Managerial and Organizational Skills

These can be learned through formal study, by observing others and asking questions, and by application. Because the best way to learn is by doing, you should seize every opportunity to accept responsibility, to take on tasks that others may shirk because of the extra work involved, and to do as many jobs, surveys, or reports as you can.

All this responsibility involves heavy extra work, but you will be rewarded with knowledge that is difficult to get in any other way. Opportunities to learn new skills and to apply them come every day in many different ways if you look for them. Once you decide what skills are necessary for success, then you can plan how to acquire them over a period of time.

Communication Skills

These also can be learned through formal study and practice. Many books and courses are available on report writing and effective oral communication. When you make written reports, spend all the time necessary to do them carefully and properly. Then ask your superiors to constructively criticize them so that you can do a better job next time.

Joining a local Toastmaster's Club, where you can practice public speaking before friends, is one of the best ways to improve your oral communication skills. You can also tape a sales presentation and play it back so that you can hear yourself as others hear you. Your wife or husband, friends, or business associates can help point out areas that need improvement.

HOW DOES ONE ADVANCE MOST RAPIDLY WITHIN AN ORGANIZATION?

Sell yourself if you want to be considered for a management position. Let your superiors know that you are capable of performing a bigger job than the one you currently hold. As in all selling situations, you have to determine their needs and wants and present your product (you) in terms of value and benefits to them.

Since requirements for management are different from those for line selling, you have to prove that you fit the needs and requirements of the better position.

The best proof you can offer is to demonstrate constantly by action and results your capabilities and potential in every aspect of your work.

Accept the fact that every task assigned to you represents opportunity. Most men and women consider difficult tasks or assignments problems. What a difference it can make in your life and career if you look upon problems as opportunity in disguise! Seek those tasks or assignments others may try to avoid, and through superior performance prove your willingness and capabilities.

Selling your own capabilities depends in part on how well you program your goals within the organization, how well you perform at each stage, and how effectively you let your superiors know of each new qualification you have. You need not be embarrassed to sell yourself if you are capable and are producing good results. Top executives are busy people and may not notice your efforts unless they are somehow called to their attention.

Find out what your superiors want and need and give it to them.   This involves a total commitment to the organization effort, complete loyalty as a subordinate so that you are trusted, and willingness to take advantage of every opportunity offered. Opportunity to prove your abilities in a new situation may come in the form of a request to relocate anywhere in the United States or the world. Many men and women fail to be promoted because they are unwilling to relocate. Yet top executives as a group are highly mobile, and as in the military or diplomatic service constant relocation is part of the game.

Pattern yourself after successful superiors.   In American companies a newly promoted executive quite often takes two or three trusted subordinates along with him. If you are offered the opportunity to work with an executive on the way up and prove to be highly competent and dependable, you may help make him look good and even become crucial to his upward moves. Such an association does not mean that you have to be a yes-person or lose your individuality. Even if you do not move with him, you can apply his successful methods to your own work.

The ability to adapt rapidly to new situations is important to success.   One of the main functions of executives is to solve new problems or problems subordinates for one reason or another are unable to solve. The ability you display in grasping, adapting to, and handling successfully new assignments or problems gives superiors a good clue to your managerial potential. If you can prove such competence in new assignments, your pathway to the top will be smooth.

The ability to be promoted does not depend on intellectual ability alone.   Being a poor student in school does not necessarily reduce your chances for reaching even top management. Dwight Eisenhower did not graduate in the top part of his West Point class. Yet because of his leadership abilities, he surpassed all his classmates to become commander of the Allies in World War II and later president of the United States.

You may not have to be an intellectual giant or technical expert to reach the top through sales/marketing, but you must have the executive ability to work with those who are. You must know how to meet and talk with highly intelligent experts or technicians, how to select key facts from their knowledge, and how to use these facts in making sound decisions.

The ability to work with others is important to any team effort.   This ability is just as important within the company or organization as outside it. Organization charts look good on paper, but coordination among different functional or department heads is usually achieved informally. If you know personally, get along with, and understand the problems of these individuals in your organization, you can often accomplish goals faster than you could through formal meetings. Thus, the ability to work well informally with others is an important aspect of teamwork.

How not to get ahead in management! We have delved at some length throughout this chapter into what you have to do to succeed in management. But we should note in passing some of the things one should not do if he or she wants to get along with others or to be promoted to management level. Perhaps this brief listing is sufficient warning.

How not to get along or ahead

Harbor resentment	Worry all the time
Be an office politician	Criticize too quickly
Act self-important	Be a slave driver
Complain all the time	Be a crybaby
Be an apple polisher	Undermine colleagues

Strive at all times to think and act like a professional. A successful manager, executive, or leader is a professional. He or she has the ability to analyze problems, develop solutions, and lead others to successful conclusion of a planned action. If you can do these things in a disciplined way and can inspire trust and confidence in others, then you are a professional and certainly deserve to fill the managerial role of your ambitions.

SUMMARY

We directed this chapter to those readers who have the desire, through hard work and dedication, to reach the higher income bracket in personal selling, or to advance to sales management or top management via the sales route. Opportunities for each have never been greater.

Three basic ways to get to the top, in income or promotion, through personal selling were noted: (1) as a full-time professional sales representative, (2) as a developer of one's own business, or (3) as a member of a company team. Personal goal-setting and effective self-management are essential to any of these areas.

Building on previous chapters, we outlined many new high-gear professional ideas concerning forecasting, programming, scheduling, follow-through, and controls, as guides to higher sales and earnings. And we offered the secret of how to reach top dollar sales and earnings: that is, simply to put into efficient, day-by-day, enthusiastic practice the knowledge already obtained through studying this text.

Through a series of eight questions, we then discussed opportunities for promotion to management in the future and outlined the knowledge, characteristics, and qualities needed for such promotion.

We covered the level of knowledge and performance required of a manager and discussed how to develop the managerial knowledge, skills, and abilities necessary for success.

Our conclusion was that a managerial role requires special attributes not necessarily essential to success in selling itself. These include well-rounded knowledge, plus cited special human and character qualities, analytical abilities, reasonable intelligence, and certain basic aptitudes for management. We also noted that a natural gift for leadership is essential for success.

Reaching the top requires a total commitment to your company or organiza-tion, including, if necessary, frequent relocation. You should view such moves or the assignment of difficult tasks as opportunities to further prove your abilities. Since management is a team effort your commitment must be that of a team player, although it need not affect your ambitions or individuality.

CHAPTER REVIEW

CONCEPTS TO REMEMBER*

_____ sell across the board	_____ personal time records	_____ swim with the tide
_____ customer call frequency	_____ global thinking	_____ slack selling time
_____ selective selling	_____ performance record	_____ failure in selling
_____ second sale	_____ communication skills	_____ success in selling

*For memory reinforcement, fill in the page number or numbers where these terms were described.

QUESTIONS FOR ANALYSIS AND DISCUSSION

1. What does it take to get to the top in personal selling or sales management?
2. What does programming mean in terms of managerial planning?
3. Increased sales volume alone is not enough to achieve high sales and earnings. What else is vitally important?
4. What factor, within your control, could keep you from reaching the top in sales or earnings, and what can you do about it?
5. On what two major areas do your superiors judge you throughout your career?
6. What effect will the profound technological and other changes expected over the next quarter century have on professional sales representatives and sales man-agers?
7. What factors other than a successful sales record do superiors consider in evaluating your overall career performance?
8. What three very basic qualities are necessary to achieve managerial success?

Case Study 20–1

TWO KEY WORDS COMPANIES ARE LOOKING FOR IN SALES/MARKETING EXECUTIVES' RESUMES— "PLANNING" AND "STRATEGY"

"Planning for profits is industry's mandate for the new marketing man," reports DUN'S magazine, in noting the rapidly increasing demand in many different indus-tries for imaginative sales/marketing executives.[3] As the marketplace gets tougher in the mid-1970s, companies are looking hard for more sophisticated such executives.

3. Material in this case study extracted from the article, "The Remaking of the Marketing Man," *Dun's* (May 1974), pp. 105–107. Reprinted by special permission from DUN'S, May 1974. Copyright, 1974, Dun & Brad-street Publications Corporation.

Some surveys, for example, show that nearly 15 percent of all jobs searches of recent times are for marketing and sales executives.

"But the marketing managers being sought," the article goes on to note, "are a different breed than their counterparts of a decade ago. More than at any time in the past, the two key words that companies are looking for in marketing executive resumés are 'planning' and 'strategy.' That is because today's marketing man is being given direct profit responsibility. With industry's emphasis on market position and cost controls, he is expected to mastermind everything in a product from pricing, shipping and distribution to market analysis, planning and promotion.

"The modern model of a model marketing executive is the member of the management team who can think through the introduction of a product to determine the prospects of selling it and putting the right price on it. In addition to control over marketing strategy and sales campaigns, he is now expected to interact with design, production, engineering and even finance.

"The discipline's new sophistication is evident in another way. Not only must the marketing executive be a master of many trades, he must arrive at strategy sessions armed with advanced degrees. In consumer goods and retailing, an undergraduate degree in marketing and an MBA are not uncommon. But in heavy industry, until recently few companies demanded advanced credentials of marketers. Now a bachelor's degree in engineering, along with an MBA, is becoming almost mandatory, and increasingly not just MBAs out of school, but those with experience.

"The search for the right marketing man is not all that smooth. First, there are the stiff new qualifications that automatically eliminate many candidates. At the same time, industry is competing so heavily for competent marketing people that there are not that many good marketers to go around. Add to that the gloomy economic forecasts that inhibit seasoned marketing executives from leaving solid jobs for something new. 'It's difficult to find the right people,' says consultant Donald DeVoto of DeVoto, Bass, Brookhouser & Associates. 'Companies have precise requirements and executives are very selective.'

"To make matters worse, marketing is fast becoming a discipline that many companies demand of their general managers. Scarcely a request for a general manager goes out that does not specify that experience in marketing and merchandising is essential.

"The same trend is surfacing even in senior sales executive posts. A vice president of sales, for instance, is now expected to be almost as heavy in marketing know-how as he is in sales. Says Martin Everett, senior editor of *Sales Management:* 'Companies are looking for a different commodity in sales executives these days. Special qualifications, such as strong financial capability, as well as solid marketing experience, are being stipulated.'

"Not surprisingly, the demand for sharp marketers has produced a correspondingly sharp hike in salary levels. A vice president of marketing and distribution to head up a major expansion program for a paper company, say, can start negotiating at a minimum of $60,000 plus incentives. Many directors of marketing are well into the $45,000 range. For that matter, luring a marketer from his present job nowadays takes a total package increase of about 15% to 20%.

"Wanted as they are, though, seasoned marketing executives have a mighty tough row to hoe in today's uncertain economy. As Don DeVoto puts it, 'Companies are looking for experienced, decisive marketing executives who can steer them away from costly mistakes. They want people who can see ahead, around the corner and underneath everything.''

QUESTIONS FOR WRITTEN REPORTS OR CLASS DISCUSSION

1. What are some of the sweeping changes that the world's sales/marketing executives of the late seventies and eighties can expect to face?
2. What special personal characteristics do you think companies are looking for in their eagerly-sought sophisticated sales/marketing executives, as contrasted to technical and academic requirements?
3. What, in the end, determines a sales representative's ability to be promoted to a managerial position?
4. Will the ability to work with others informally be as important a trait of the good sales/marketing executives of the late seventies and eighties, as it was in the sixties and early seventies?

Case Study 20–2

RATING YOURSELF ON MANAGEMENT LEADERSHIP POTENTIAL

How do you determine whether you are presently qualified for sales management or top executive authority—for administrative or emergency leadership? The following statements, extracted from a leading management book, help you analyze your leadership attributes.[4]

1. I have the ability to analyze a complicated problem and to explain it in an orderly, logical manner.
   Yes_____ No_____
2. I respond to the stimulus of a difficult assignment and am fully confident that I can carry it through.
   Yes_____ No_____
3. I lack confidence in my decisions if they affect important operations and prefer to have my superior review my recommendations before I take action.
   Yes_____ No_____
4. I am a bug on details. Once I am given an assignment and am told exactly how it is to be accomplished, I carry it through to the letter.
   Yes_____ No_____
5. I seek the difficult jobs. By accomplishing them I add to my reputation.
   Yes_____ No_____
6. I need my superior's approval. I am upset if he criticizes my performance.
   Yes_____ No_____
7. I want responsibility and diplomatically seek to enlarge my authority by acting on my own initiative when I have the chance. Usually I am successful.
   Yes_____ No_____
8. When there are several alternate approaches to accomplishing an objective, I have no hesitancy in choosing a course of action.
   Yes_____ No_____
9. I like living by a schedule and am comfortable when my responsibilities are clearly laid out for me.
   Yes_____ No_____

4. James Menzies Black, *Assignment Management* (Englewood Cliffs, N.J.: Prentice-Hall, Inc., 1961), pp. 188–89.

10. I like to complete a job once I start it. It annoys me to be asked to handle two or three important assignments simultaneously.

    Yes_____ No_____

11. I do not like to delegate. I always have a feeling of confidence when I am doing the job myself or if it is necessary to delegate, when I am supervising the work of my subordinates.

    Yes_____ No_____

12. I dislike details and prefer to work on broad problems and to delegate the routine to assistants.

    Yes_____ No_____

13. I avoid arguing with my superior even when I disagree with his decisions. After all, he is responsible for the outcome. Besides, he may not like me to oppose him.

    Yes_____ No_____

14. My subordinates respect me but consider me a middle man in the relaying of instructions.

    Yes_____ No_____

15. I am perfectly willing to accept the responsibility for decisions I make that go wrong. After all, I want to be accountable. That way I get credit for success.

    Yes_____ No_____

Yes answers to seven of the above questions (1, 2, 5, 7, 8, 12, and 15) indicate that you have the temperament for successful leadership in any situation. They indicate that you have an analytical mind, are independent in your thinking, have confidence in your decisions, and do not fear criticism.

No answers to these seven and yes answers to the remaining ones indicate that you are probably an able administrator but shy away from ultimate responsibilities.

QUESTIONS FOR WRITTEN REPORTS OR CLASS DISCUSSION

1. Do you accept the judgment that failure to answer yes to these seven questions indicates a lack of leadership potential on your part? Why do you feel this way?
2. Regardless of how you judge your own characteristics in the above index, what is the value in honestly asking yourself such questions?

21
your personal audit: that magic 10 percent plus

We have now come full circle! We commenced by talking about you—your hopes, your fears, and your realistic ambitions in life. We have tried to show how you can overcome any fears and realize your hopes and ambitions through the challenging, interesting, and economically rewarding career of salesmanship. Now we are nearing the end of our study; after these concluding summary thoughts and suggestions you will be on your own.

Early in Chapter 1, it was stated that one of the major aims of this text was to help you evaluate selling as a suitable profession for achieving your personal career goals. The advantages and disadvantages of a sales career were presented early so you could keep them in mind as the concepts, principles, practices, and techniques of modern salesmanship unfolded.

By now you should know whether or not a sales career is for you. If it is, you may be wondering whether or not you have what it takes to be successful in selling. Let us turn our concluding thoughts to some practical and motivational aspects that will help you answer that very personal and important question, and how to get started in this exciting career field.

POSITIVE ATTITUDES AND BROAD GOAL-SETTING
ARE ESSENTIAL FIRST STEPS TO SUCCESS

The basic key to success in selling or any other career field and in life itself is within you. If you have a strong desire to succeed and a positive rather than a negative approach to life and work, then you probably can and will succeed. Once you have decided to succeed, the only question is how to do it.

As a first step in deciding how you can achieve your career ambitions, please fill out this rough outline of the short-term and long-range stages toward your ultimate goal. You may not know exactly what you want to do right now, but you can at least insert in Figure 21.1a what you think you might like to be doing (career position) and the income you would like to be earning. There are approximately 1,920 working hours in an average working year of 240 days.[1] Divide the

---

1. Based on an estimated three weeks annual vacation and a one-week total of national holidays. This leaves 48 working weeks, each made up of five eight-hour working days.

	Next year	+5 years	+10 years	+20 years
What do you want to be doing (position)?				
How much do you want to be earning per year?				

FIGURE 21.1a

How much will your time be worth?				

FIGURE 21.1b

yearly earnings you would like to have by the number of working hours, and fill out in Figure 21.1b what your time will be worth at each stage.

This initial goal-setting gives you a broad outline of a plan for success. As you go along, you fill in details of the plan based on your increasing knowledge, skills, and sense of direction. The essential step is to start a plan or course of action now. After that, will power, persistence, knowledge, adaptability, and hard work will help you overcome most if not all obstacles along the way. Most failures are caused by people not getting past this psychological barrier. They offer excuses for inaction (negative thinking) rather than action itself (positive thinking). Let us discuss some of these topics in connection with the vital subject of proper attitude as follows.

ARE YOU PREPARED TO WORK HARD TO ACCOMPLISH YOUR GOALS?

Most people would like to make enough money to buy all the things that will satisfy their creature comforts, and most people would like to have a position and status of which they, their family, and friends can be proud. But not everyone is willing to put forth the effort to earn these things. First then, you have to decide whether you really want to work hard enough, mentally and physically, to earn them.

You might best decide now that unless you have inherited wealth or position you will have to work hard and competitively to achieve above-ordinary goals. If that challenge appeals to you, then you may find that a sales career offers you unusual opportunity to achieve your goals.

If you really do want to get ahead via a sales career, it can be done —regardless of your age, sex, social, or financial position, national or racial origin. But you must want to put forth the effort, have the will to persevere in spite of all obstacles, and believe in yourself.

Assuming that you agree with these conclusions, you may now ask yourself, "What must I do to achieve my goals?" A good way to start is by evaluating your basic attitudes toward life and work.

ARE YOUR ATTITUDES REALISTIC?

It is true in selling, as in many other careers, that sound philosophies, positive attitudes, enthusiasm, and good work habits are more responsible for success than are any learned techniques. These characteristics result from the character and human qualities listed here.

Basic character qualities	Basic human qualities
Ambition	Personality
Self-discipline	Loyalty
Persistence	Tact
Dependability	Sincerity
Courage	Cheerfulness
Initiative	Willingness to cooperate
Stability	Positive mental outlook
Honesty	Enthusiasm
Thoroughness	Empathy

Psychologists tell us that principles, beliefs, and motives are central factors in individual improvement. The question now is, "Do you believe that the positive principles, beliefs, and motives accepted generally by the world and specifically by the society in which you live provide a structure within which you can work?" It is important to answer this question because success in selling or in most occupations involving work with other people entails a certain amount of conformity to group values. You do not have to lose your individual personality because you work for a large private company or government agency, but if you want to get ahead, you have to work within the established value norms.

In fact, to achieve real success, you have not only to accept these values, but also to believe in them. The many pressures of our modern world, in which onrushing technology often seems to outstrip man's intellectual and spiritual attempts to control it, cause some people to give up, to quit trying to compete. Many of these people believe it is outmoded or square to believe in anything. But mankind's progress through the ages has been made not by quitters, but by doers and believers.

To be successful you must have a positive attitude toward life in general and toward your work in particular. In selling especially, you must believe strongly in the value of the work you do; if you do not, it will show in your attitude—and in your sales volume.

You are the only one who can honestly rate your personal attitude in light of the basic character and human qualities we have just noted. Here are some questions you should ask yourself to determine your real feelings toward your present or future work.

Your Job

Do you think you are now in the right line of work or that the work you plan to do will be right for you? Do you think this work is vital to your national economy and to society? Do you consider it to be as worthy as any other? Would you want your son or daughter to engage in it?

The Company or Organization You Work For

Do you believe that your company or organization or the one you hope to work for has a worthwhile function? Do you believe that its management has worthwhile policies toward its public? Toward its employees? Do you or are you prepared to make a positive contribution toward its collective effort? When a short-term decision toward accomplishment of overall goals differs from your own ideas, do you or will you loyally try to carry it out as well as you can?

The Customers or Public You Serve

Do you really like the people you now serve or plan to serve? Do you think these people like you or will like you? Do you or are you prepared to put forth the necessary time and effort to determine their real needs and to try to satisfy them? Do you sincerely want to offer them what is best for them?

Your Work Habits

Do you now or are you prepared to keep professional hours—to start as early and to finish as late as necessary each working day to serve your customers or public? Do you now or are you prepared to put forth your very best effort each hour of your working day? Do you believe that your determined effort, even if others around you are slackers, will ultimately lead to success; or that, if you fail for any reason, it is still worth the effort?

CAN BASIC ATTITUDES BE CHANGED?

If the answer to most of the above questions is "yes," congratulations—you have the basic positive attitudes essential to success. If your answer to many is "no," take warning and examine the reasons for your negative attitudes; they do not conform to the generally accepted attitudes in American society. You may find it worth your while to change these attitudes.

Can you adjust your own personality, knowledge, and innate aptitudes in such a way as to achieve the personal success you desire? Because few of us are perfect, certain changes may be necessary for you, but you may honestly wonder whether you can change these ingrained habits or attitudes. Leading psychologists and successful men and women in every country, however, say you can change if you really want to. William James, the great psychologist, put it this way: "The greatest discovery of my generation is that human beings can alter their lives by altering their attitudes of mind."

WHAT AREAS DO YOU HAVE TO DEVELOP TO ACHIEVE YOUR GOALS?

Let's assume the psychologists and successful men and women are right, that you can adjust personally and thus achieve your own goals in life and in work. What specific areas do you have to develop to achieve them? We can only generalize here because you are the only one who knows the real you; but if you apply the following concepts to yourself, you may find some positive and helpful concrete suggestions.

Four traditional areas of education are: (1) *knowledge,* (2) *skills,* (3) *attitudes,* and (4) *habits.* We have already noted the belief of many psychologists that principles, beliefs, and motives are central factors in individual improvement. They also believe that if you really want to succeed, you can improve by relating positive principles of success to your goals. This involves developing positive mental attitudes toward life and work. Unless you have the proper attitudes, you cannot succeed in selling.

How Can You Improve Your Self-Image and Attitudes?

Psychologists tell us that each individual has a self-image—a mental picture of the kind of person he is. This private evaluation of abilities—an evaluation you can make by using Figure 21.2—is a motivating force which the individual tends to subconsciously fulfill or live out. Often this self-image is filled with negative as well as positive thoughts. If your negative thoughts can be eliminated and positive ones substituted in their place, it is quite possible, say the psychologists, that your new attitude can change your life and help you achieve your goals.

You may ask yourself, "Can I really change my personality so as to develop positive attitudes that will give me personal and financial success? If so, how do I go about it?" Many excellent books offer scientific, spiritual, and practical suggestions for self-improvement in this area. Many are listed in the bibliography of this book; it will be worth your time to refer to them often.

In general, however, changing your self-image means honestly evaluating your basic attitudes and actually changing them by replacing negative thoughts with positive ones. You fill your mind consciously each day in practical ways by thinking positve, happy, successful thoughts, and eliminating consciously and immediately any negative thoughts that produce inward tension. Since many psychologists feel that our physical life is determined in large part by our emotional condition, and that in turn by our mental attitude, it follows that if you can fill your mind with positive or successful thoughts your personality can change for the better.

Proper Attitude and Personality Can Improve Habits

If you have proper attitudes toward life and work, your personality becomes a key factor in determining the degree of success you will have in achieving your goals. Certain qualities of personality, such as those listed below, make it easier for you to succeed when working with other people, especially in selling. Very few people are blessed at birth with all the qualities of a successful personality, but fortunately many of these qualities can be developed as can the muscles in your body—by intelligent exercises; or, as with the self-image patterns, through daily substitution of negative traits by positive ones. Through practice, these positive attitudes can become habits.

Enthusiasm is certainly one of the greatest personality traits of successful sales representatives, as it is of leaders and successful people in all occupations. Enthusiasm is contagious; it makes people want to buy, enables sports teams to sweep to victory, and can cause an entire nation to follow one leader.

How do you develop enthusiasm? Frank Bettger, a business failure at 40, who changed his life by switching to positive thoughts and went on to business fame and fortune in the American insurance world, puts it this way: "To become enthusiastic, act enthusiastic. Act enthusiastic about every aspect of your life and work." "Start today—now," he says in effect, "force yourself to act enthusiasti-

FIGURE 21.2 Sales Aptitude Self-Evaluation Chart*

	Needs Improving	Average	Strong Asset	Very Strong Asset
Pleasant personality				
Even temperament				
Good appearance				
Analytic ability				
Memory for faces and details				
Vocabulary and word usage				
Harder than average worker				
Self-confidence				
Persuasiveness				
Ability to make friends				
Original and creative ideas				
Competitive attitude				
Persistence				
Accepts criticism and advice				
Problem-solving ability				
Practical-minded				
Poised and self-assured				
Adaptability				
Sincerity				
Sales ability				
Determination to succeed				
Reliability				
Enthusiasm				
Ability to learn quickly				
Good listener				

*This Chapter points out some of the basic personal attitudes and characteristics essential to success in selling. Based on those, does your self-image as pictured in the above chart indicate that you might be successful as a sales representative? It is important that you first ask this question of yourself since you are the only one who knows the real you.

cally, and you'll become enthusiastic. Be alive and your enthusiasm will be catching."[2]

Sincerity is another necessary personality trait. You can develop it by involving yourself thoroughly in your work and by treating other people as you would like them to treat you.

Courtesy on your part stimulates courtesy on the part of the people with whom you work; such cheerfulness helps make life and work and having friends enjoyable.

Initiative and persistence are two more key personality traits essential to success. You can develop initiative each day by the way you tackle each task. You should try to do each one 10 percent better than it has been done before. This 10 percent extra effort in all tasks, every day, builds attitudes and habits that cannot help but lead to success.

We have thus noted some of the important positive attitudes essential to success and have pointed out that by putting them into practice daily you can make them habits. These have been illustrated in many practical ways throughout the text.

Knowledge and Skills Can Be Acquired

Knowledge and skills are the two other traditional areas of education that we need to touch on briefly. Knowledge especially is tied in with the mental qualities and the education obtained at home, in society, at school, and at work. Combined with it are certain traits that, if properly directed, can help you reach your goals faster. These include judgment, business sense, flexibility, observation ability, analytical ability, teachability, foresight, and good memory.

The point in discussing these traits here is that, while you may not have been born with all of them, you can train yourself to develop them. Good memory, for example, can be obtained through the use of many practical techniques; your local library offers many books on this subject. Many world leaders and successful businesspeople have not had university educations, but they have developed their memory, judgment, flexibility, and foresight.

HOW CAN YOU GET STARTED TOWARD YOUR GOALS?

None of these things we have talked about up to this point in this chapter will mean anything to you in selling or in life in general unless you put them into effect. The time to start is now. As with starting the engine of a car, you have to kick over or turn on your will power to get yourself started—to get the wheels turning. If you can force yourself to do that, you will, as James has pointed out, reach within yourself deeper levels of energy that will keep you propelled by some inner want rather than by a coercive "ought to." You will find that you do more work, more efficiently, and with less expenditure of energy.

The first step is to take another look at the "want-to" goals you filled in at the beginning of this chapter. Then, taking into account the proper attitudes, habits, personality changes, and skills we have discussed, outline for yourself, on a piece of paper, the "how-to" steps you feel will be necessary in order to accomplish your goals.

2. Frank Bettger, *How I Raised Myself from a Failure to Success in Selling* (Englewood Cliffs, N.J.: Prentice-Hall, Inc., 1949), p. 11.

Start now. Force yourself to outline a few realistic short-term goals that will enable you to get where you want to be, earning the money you want to earn, a year from now. These realistic short-term goals should be just beyond your present reach, but near enough to seem possible. No matter how insignificant they seem, put them down on paper now. And, even though you may change some of these short-term targets as you improve habits or acquire knowledge and skills, your basic goals or objectives will never change.

The next step is to force yourself each day to try to meet your targets. Do not wait until you feel hot or are in the mood. Simply try to continue improving. Gradually you will find that your inner drives, or wheels, will be warmed up and turning and will keep up the momentum. You will work hard and efficiently because you want to, and you will accomplish more with less effort. As you accomplish your short-term steps, your confidence will increase and with it your will to win. Successful completion of these goals, step by step, will make the big goal seem possible and attainable.

BELIEVE IN YOURSELF AND YOU WILL SUCCEED

Thus, you now have on paper both the one-, five-, ten-, and twenty-year long-range, or big, goals and the intermediate, or little, goals that are stepping stones along the way. Do not be afraid to think big—to think of the distant goal you ultimately intend to achieve. Believe in yourself, have faith in your abilities, and with sound self-confidence and hard work you can and will succeed.

Because you believe in yourself, have the proper mental attitudes, and are developing the proper habits, knowledge, and skills, you put confidence and enthusiasm into everything you do. This confidence and enthusiasm, if honestly felt and projected, can become a powerful, driving force in your life and in your selling. Your attitude makes the difference!

WHAT DOES THIS KNOWLEDGE MEAN TO YOU?

The knowledge you have gained from studying this book will benefit you only to the extent that you accept it, study it, apply it to your own needs, and put it into persistent practice. We said that fewer than one in fifty readers will rise to the top 10 percent in earnings and positions. Success for that one in fifty means putting into efficient, day-by-day, enthusiastic practice the knowledge gained through studying this text.

What is the success secret of sales representatives and executives who pull ahead of the crowd? Ralph Waldo Emerson summed it up: "Take what you want but pay the full price." In most cases, those who have gone farthest are simply those who decided that success is worth the price. They were no brighter than the rest. Their education was not better. They were not luckier. But they made the decision to give themselves over to the overwhelming will to succeed, which may spring from pride, fear, desire for reward, need to command, love of position, or mixed motivations. It is the vital ingredient in every man or woman who has moved ahead.

To achieve real success, you must be prepared to work longer and more efficiently than others and must be willing to do more than is asked or even expected of you. You must exercise self-discipline, be willing to make decisions for which you will be held accountable, and stick with problems until you overcome them.

You must eagerly seek added responsibility and new opportunities and accept the challenges, not just the rewards. If you desire to succeed then start today putting the knowledge presented here into practice; start demonstrating what you can do!

Where Do You Go from Here?

Putting your five-, ten-, and twenty-year objectives down on paper is your first step toward success, based on the very sound psychological principle that if you write your goals on paper they stare you in the face, challenging you to take action. Most people have goals in mind, but that is where the goals usually stay: Most companies require their executives to write out their specific goals and objectives, and since you are chairman of the board of you, the most important enterprise of all, you should require yourself to fulfill this simple request as a basic practical step in managerial thinking and acting.

Now that you have some realistic short-, medium-, and long-range objectives in mind, you can start to plan a course of action toward fulfilling them. Although you may not even have a specific sales job at this point in your sales career, you should never cease striving to improve upon these five specific areas:

1. Your attitudes
2. Your human-relations skills
3. Your knowledge
4. Your sales techniques
5. Your work habits

You should critically evaluate how you currently stand on these points and then decide what steps to take in the future to improve weak areas. Statements and questions raised throughout the book indicate subpoints to these, and you in addition can make up your own from reading, questions, or observation. Consideration of how you can continue to improve in each of these areas is a never-ending task.

What Problems Will You Encounter?

The pathway to success is not always smooth and trouble free. Few mortals are perfect, and most sales representatives are not exceptions when it comes to meeting the constant challenges of their profession. Certain problems seem to give sales representatives in general more trouble than others do. These have been summed up, as shown below, in a book by Percy H. Whiting, for years the managing director of the Dale Carnegie organization. He based his conclusions on returns from questionnaires sent to 3,000 members of the New York Sales Executives Club. These questionnaires asked, "What are the greatest problems of salesmen?"

The five great problems of salesmen[3]

1. Salesmen fail to organize their selling.
2. Salesmen do not think creatively.
3. Many salesmen do not know how to answer objections effectively.
4. Salesmen do not know how to motivate themselves to do their best work.
5. Salesmen rarely communicate effectively.

3. Percy H. Whiting, *The Five Great Problems of Salesmen and How to Solve Them* (New York: McGraw-Hill Book Company, 1964), Preface to Part One.

Whiting, who also wrote the famed Dale Carnegie Sales Course, went on to give his expert thoughts on how to solve these problems. We have throughout this book provided many practical examples of how you can solve both these and other problems you encounter in your own sales career.

Other problems you will face and practical solutions for them are to be found in scores of excellent publications that treat this subject by providing practical solutions for many different problems. Many of the books in this area are listed in the bibliography of this text; others have been listed within chapter pages.

One problem that many of these authors seem to have overlooked is the selling slump you will encounter from time to time. Few if any sales representatives manage to work all the time at peak capacity. Psychologists tell us that most effective work is done in spurts to a certain level. After each spurt comes a relaxation period, or slump, as you gather energy for another burst at a higher level of achievement. Such progression is much like climbing a staircase with many rests at landings.

Thus it is natural to feel a let-down or slump at times. The trick is to overcome this feeling as fast as possible so as to remain on a steady, consistent, progressive course. The best way to overcome these slumps is to follow a few simple rules employed by productive people to squeeze more accomplishment into any given period of work time. These rules include such steps as the following.

1. *When you face a task or problem*, get started at once on it. Writing down the words *who, what, when, where, why,* and *how* is often all that is required to trigger positive mental thoughts which lead to prompt action.

2. *When you do not think you have time*, set a deadline for yourself and establish priorities so that you take care of important things first.

3. *Concentrate your attention, time, and energy on important things first,* and through concentration complete those tasks first. Ruthlessly eliminate less important or nonessential thoughts or tasks.

4. *Organize a natural work flow*, and conserve your energy with breaks for rest and relaxation. Churchill had the ability to drop into complete and utter relaxation and rest for short periods of time, arising to face energetically a constant work load that would have exhausted less organized men.

5. *Strive to complete tasks once you have started them.* It is easy to think up a new idea or start a new task but quite a different thing to finish it. The secret is to define your project, to plan how and when you will complete it, and to work to do just that. Thus when that task is completed you can move on confidently to the next, not beset with worries of having to complete countless unfinished tasks.

TEN PERCENT PLUS SPELLS THE DIFFERENCE

One simple guideline, if followed consistently throughout your sales career, can spell the difference between success and failure. That guideline is to strive to be 10 percent better than your fellow sales representatives in all things, at all times.

What a difference that 10 percent can make! Ten percent plus causes you to stand out from others. Your superiors are not looking for geniuses or supermen; they are looking for the men and women who are consistent producers, who are reliable and dependable—men and women who can be counted on at all times.

Consider for a moment the 10 percent minus person! He always fails by just a small margin to meet even average expectations. Constant little failures lead to great ones, and in time, he becomes a failure in his career and in life. What a pity to fail by so small a margin!

Success in selling, as in most other careers, usually comes to a person not because he is a genius but because he or she is just a fraction better, consistently, in all the things that count. Being 10 percent better can make all the difference: being 10 percent earlier in getting on the job; staying on the job 10 percent longer; being 10 percent better at making decisions, smaller ones first, then larger ones; making 10 percent fewer errors; being 10 percent more industrious, efficient, loyal, and dependable. If your attitude is positive and your enthusiasm genuine, you can achieve that extra 10 percent of excellence that will enable you to win out in fair, hard competition over your competitors.

Which would you rather be—a 10 percent plus or a 10 percent minus sales representative? The choice is yours. Ten percent plus in all things, at all times, day in and day out, year in and year out is all that is required for success. Here are some areas where 10 percent plus counts.

Attitude	Persistence
Knowledge	Imagination
Empathy	Resourcefulness
Human relations	Initiative
Observation	Inquisitiveness
Accuracy	Persuasiveness
Memory	Ambition
Reliability	Sincerity
Sales techniques	Work habits
Industriousness	Efficiency
Loyalty	Sound decisions

How can you start being a 10 percent plus person in all these things? Here are suggestions advanced by one authority.

1. Be healthfully dissatisfied with everything that you now do.
2. Challenge everything you do now.
3. Get facts.
4. Make prompt decisions.
5. Take prompt action.

In conclusion, here is a thought from the late Captain Eddie Rickenbacker: "A winner never quits, and a quitter never wins."

AND NOW IT IS UP TO YOU!

All good things must come to an end, and so it is with this attempt to pass on some useful knowledge. The words and thoughts in the preceding pages represent a sincere desire to communicate and to interact—to fulfill your needs or wants by outlining how you can achieve success in selling. The personalized nature of this approach may seem odd in what is basically a textbook of salesmanship, but you are the sole judge of its success. Whatever your decision, you are to be commended for sticking with it this far. May your author now say to you, "Thank you for your attention and interest; good luck to you in your life's work!"

EBONY:
A STORY OF LITTLE GOALS
GROWING INTO A GREAT MAGAZINE

How publisher Robert Johnson set and accomplished little goals one after another until they grew into his big goal is described by noted author Dr. Norman Vincent Peale[4] as follows:

Recently, I had the pleasure of conferring a Horatio Alger Award of the American Schools and Colleges Association upon Robert Johnson, editor and publisher of the highly successful publication *Ebony* and other periodicals. He had an idea for a great magazine to serve the Negro community but was, as is often the case, short on money. So he was advised to "forget it."

It is some years later, and those so-called friends still cannot forget that they might have owned stock in what is now an immensely profitable enterprise. Mr. Johnson and his wife own all the stock today because he was the only one who had enthusiasm for the project. His enthusiasm bred faith, and faith stimulated action. Robert Johnson is a living example of Charles M. Schwab's declaration that "a man can succeed at almost anything for which he has unlimited enthusiasm."

As Mr. Johnson developed *Ebony* magazine, he decided not to attempt immediately to achieve the large goals to which enthusiasm for his project inspired him. Instead, he wisely chose to set and accomplish what he called "little goals" one after the other. The attainment of one small goal gave him the feeling of success and taught him techniques to use later. Then with added experience he tackled the next little goal, and presently those small goals added up to an immense goal.

QUESTIONS FOR WRITTEN REPORTS OR CLASS DISCUSSION

1. What basic question did Johnson probably first ask himself in contemplating his immense goal?
2. What one thing above all do you feel led to his success?
3. What did Johnson prove by his success that has meaning to you?
4. What is the definition of realistic little goals?

4. *Enthusiasm Makes the Difference* (Englewood Cliffs, N.J.: Prentice-Hall, Inc., 1967), pp. 5–6. Reprinted by permission.

A FEW GUIDELINES TO EFFICIENCY

Some of the many excellent thoughts on guidelines to personal efficiency outlined in a monthly letter published by the Royal Bank of Canada[5] are listed below. They offer serious food for thought to anyone entering a sales or any other career and provide a fitting conclusion to our study of modern applied salesmanship.

In a simpler world the pioneer could follow the lead of his instinct in tackling jobs, but in the complex life of today we need consciously to apply efficiency even in making a plan for doing the chores.

Efficiency gets things done in the smoothest way, with least wear and tear, and with the smallest expenditure of energy. This involves a certain amount of thinking. One must observe, and apply knowledge and experience to the circumstances, and decide what is to be done and how to do it. An efficient person will use facts and skill: he needs also good judgment.

Some ingredients of efficiency are: knowledge, time, energy and material. One of the most important of these is time. Procrastination is the great enemy of efficient time use. Putting off necessary tasks causes additional labor, and reduces the time that is available for the development of new ideas.

FACING DIFFICULTIES

The person who works efficiently is in good position to face difficulties with assurance. He has, in fact, an inclination to look for and to like difficult tasks, because it is in doing them that he shows his worth.

When difficulties thicken upon him, the efficient person has the tendency to persevere. He recognizes the problems and anxieties that may arise in a task, but does not dwell upon them.

To the efficient person a mistake is part of his learning process. He is not always on top of the world: even the great musicians and painters have their comparatively uninspired periods.

Every person who contributes anything significant to life is wrong some of the time: that is why pencils have erasers, but the eraser should not wear out ahead of the lead.

CONCENTRATION AND VERSATILITY

Method, simplicity and concentration are the backbone of efficiency in every profession and job.

Concentration means bringing things to a common center. Once an efficient person has thought through to a conclusion and made plans, he does not go off half-cocked because of something he hears. He refuses to be side-tracked, no matter how pleasing the byway appears.

5. "A Few Guidelines to Efficiency," *The Royal Bank of Canada Monthly Letter*, Vol. 55, No. 1 (January 1974), pp. 1–4.

PERSONAL EFFICIENCY

The success or failure of any human project turns upon the integrity and capability of a man or a woman.

Personal efficiency includes other qualities than those associated with one's job. Just as a person needs to adapt himself to advancement in the state of his art or science, so he needs to fit himself to constantly changing social conditions.

INTELLIGENCE AND PRINCIPLES

The intelligent person bases his actions upon clear understanding of sound rules and principles. He does not waste time arguing about how things ought to behave, but tries to learn how they do behave.

When he cannot change conditions, he analyses them and adjusts himself to them.

In everyday living, efficiency includes making routine doings as habitual and automatic as possible, thus leaving the brain free for consideration of important matters.

BE CONFIDENT

Having worked up your plans with the greatest efficiency you can command, whether they are plans for business expansion or solving a household problem, move with confidence. Knowledge that you have prepared efficiently raises your morale, and your cheerful, confident and zealous manner will inspire others with a sense of purpose, enthusiasm, and a feeling for success.

This may appear to be a large order, and in truth it is, but it is the only known way to move from mediocrity to excellence. Being efficient means the difference between wavering performance and fixed indubitable achievement. A person's efficiency is the secret of his value to the world.

PURPOSE AND ENTERPRISE

The efficient person does not indulge in restless change. He has something specific, concrete and definite to do. He knows that hitting a nail on the head is a praiseworthy action, but only if the nail is needed and is in the right place.

He uses his imagination to put together ideas, to picture what might be done better, and to originate. Ideas of genius status do not spring from a heap of unrelated memories, but from facts that have been mentally sorted and stored in an orderly way.

Success at this point depends upon the enterprise a person used in observing, selecting and filing facts and experiences. There is no place in a person's career where he may stop these processes and continue to do effective work.

Being efficient is far from meaning that you have fixated on a level of competence; your ideal is not having and resting but growing and becoming. You see not only the job on which you are working competently, but what may lie over the horizon, and you prepare for it.

GETTING READY

The accumulation of knowledge is a prerequisite to efficiency. Superiority is neither accidental nor a matter of luck. It rests upon a solid basis of preparation suitable to your hopes and aspirations. To write poetry you must study metre, to build bridges you must be learned in the strength of material under various strains and stresses, to operate a business you must develop a sense of trading.

The efficient person knows what the standard is in everything with which he is concerned. His safe rule is to aim for the standard which is the symbol of excellence. What this is can be learned readily by seeking counsel in the best sources: qualified people, books and personal observation. To talk things over with a person who knows about them is far different from chattering about them with a casual acquaintance. To read a book profitably means selecting one that deals in an authoritative way with the subject in which you are interested. Observation entails more than looking: it means paying attention and asking questions.

It is foolish for a person to think that by giving his work an air of complexity he attains anything worth while. The efficient person finds his satisfaction in his ability to simplify. He does the big job one step at a time.

QUESTIONS FOR WRITTEN REPORTS OR CLASS DISCUSSION

1. In what ways do you feel that thinking out possible short-term and long-term personal goals, and putting them down on paper now, indicates consciously applied efficiency?
2. What is meant by the statement in the above case study, "Personal efficiency includes other qualities than those associated with one's job. A person [also] needs to fit himself to constantly changing social conditions."
3. Explain the statement, "Having worked up your plans with the greatest efficiency, you can command—move with confidence."
4. Under the subheading "Getting Ready" above is a comment that an efficient person knows how to read a book profitably. What does that statement mean to you in terms of your reading *Modern Applied Salesmanship?*

Special Study Project

DEVELOPING A SALES STRATEGY, PLAN, AND MANUAL FOR QUEEN OF SHEBA HIDDEN-BED SOFA

It is one thing to read about how others have solved sales/marketing problems; it is quite another to be confronted with a real-life problem requiring conceptual visualization and development of a strategy and plan of how to solve it, and putting such a plan down on paper in the form of a succinct, concrete, practical, clearly-written proposal.

Modern selling, at all levels, is concerned with problem solving. Part of the excitement of selling lies in the fact that no two situations, or any two sales interviews, are exactly the same; each is different, new, and challenging. Early in Chapter 8, stress was placed on the conceptual, strategic importance of recognizing *what* the problem is and understanding the *why* steps involved in thinking through a possible solution. Some of the basic problems to be faced for each new sales/marketing situation were pinpointed on page 154.

With this orientation in mind, let us now develop a typical sales/marketing problem, presented as an assignment that will require you to tie together this problem-solving concept with all the "how-to" applications studied in this text. Our vehicle will be a term project suited to either individual or small groups within a class application, based on developing a sales strategy, a plan, and a "how-to" sales manual for a consumer product called "Queen of Sheba Hidden-Bed Sofa."

FRAMEWORK OF THE SPECIAL STUDY PROJECT

The problem, factual information, and assignments follow. The exercise is open-ended, with no 100 percent right or wrong answers. Basic answers to all questions lie in the text itself; creative extension or development of the questions asked are yours to seek outside the classroom through library research and practical surveys of businessmen in your local community. This special study project can be undertaken as a running assignment concurrent with your progressive study of the text, or as an end-of-study or term project. Its purpose is to require you to apply what you have been studying in a practical, interesting, and challenging manner. What you get out of it will depend entirely on the energy, enthusiasm, thinking, and creativity you put into it.

THE PROBLEM

You have secured exclusive franchise rights in your local area (a geographic area of 50,000 population) to market and sell a newly developed consumer household furniture item called Queen of Sheba Hidden-Bed Sofa. Your task is to make a rough market survey of possible need for and use of your product, decide who your prospects are and what competition you face, and develop a strategy and specific plan for selling it, which you will put down on paper.

You are to utilize any or all possible methods to sell your product—through retailers and direct to end-consumers; via direct mail, telephone, exhibitions, and house-to-house. Once your sales/marketing strategy and plan is developed, you are to develop a comprehensive "how-to" sales manual containing precise instructions, presentations to the different type prospects selected, and sales-kit materials to be used in such presentations by yourself or other sales representatives. While you are free to incorporate advertising, publicity, and sales promotion ideas as part of your sales plan "mix," emphasis is to be placed largely on personal, face-to-face selling of the product to the various types of prospects selected, with the aim of closing a sale each presentation.

PRODUCT INFORMATION[1]

A sofa is one of the most important pieces of furniture a family ever purchases. A good sofa costs anywhere from $200 to $2,000. Due to its cost, it should offer quality, such as quality construction and durable materials, so it won't sag, buckle, or budge.

Most people simply judge a sofa by its cover and seldom stop to check any other possible features or advantages. This is because most people don't really know what to check for. The following description of Queen of Sheba Hidden-Bed Sofa offers suggestions about what to look for in a sofa:

Queen of Sheba offers four styles to choose from, including a new style designed especially for narrow rooms. It comes in a choice of over thirty fabrics, in a choice of four custom tailoring options like quilting, deep tufting and contrast welting, and in a choice of base and back treatments.

It also offers three choices of cushion filling, ranging from soft to springy, all made of superior materials. The foam filling is a high-density polyurethane foam made exclusively for us. Polyester fibers were selected for their softness and resilience. The new super-soft cushion, a combination of superior polyurethane wrapped in polyester fibers, offers super luxury.

All cushion cores are specially cut to fit the curve of the sofa, so they won't gap apart when someone sits down. Queen of Sheba foam cushions inner cores are 4¾ inches thick, so the foam will hold up and offer firm, comfortable support. Some competitor's foam cushions are only 4 inches or less.

A special feature of Queen of Sheba is its "hidden bed." Since its price is in line with ordinary sofas, it is likely that a buyer may not be getting full value for his money unless the sofa purchased includes a hidden bed.

The quality mattress is a source of special pride, since it offers such sleeping comfort. It is a full-length mattress (75 inches). Most other convertible mattresses are only 72 inches long. And our mattresses are protected from germs and mildew by a special process.

Queen of Sheba's hidden bed is set in so neatly it won't interfere with seating comfort. And the back is comfortably angled to the seat at the ideal sitting angle. Many other sofas don't offer any slant at all, which can make those who sit on them feel like they are sitting in a straight-backed chair.

We are proud of the fact that our beautiful upholstery is made to stay beautiful. Since the outer surface of any sofa needs extra protection to keep the fabric neat and secure, all our thirty especially selected fabrics provide the necessary extra "give." Most other convertibles have nothing like it and their fabric can wrinkle or

1. Product information material was extracted largely from an excellent 1973 national magazine advertisement by Simmons Company for their Hide-A-Bed Sofa.

pucker and filling materials can work loose into the frame. To those who buy a Queen of Sheba Hidden-Bed Sofa, we also make available, at extra cost, extra fabric for drapes. But we also give some extra fabric free—to make arm covers or patch up disasters like cigarette burns. And all of our fabrics are stain-resistant so as to require only minimal care.

Our hidden bed mechanism is easy to open—it requires only twenty pounds of pull-effort, compared to thirty or forty for most other convertibles. Queen of Sheba has a "lock stop" control as an extra safety measure so the bed won't spring out, and recessed moving parts to prevent bumped shins or bruised fingers. This mechanism is so well designed it won't have wear marks on rugs.

Queen of Sheba guarantees the frame, mechanism, mattress, and upholstery filling against defects in workmanship or materials, for the specified time period and within the reasonable limitations contained in our written guarantee. And because ours is a nationally known company with a fine reputation to live up to, our guarantee is good anywhere in the United States or its territories or possessions.

Price of any combination of Queen of Sheba Hidden-Bed Sofa is $499.95 retail (apart from a 25 percent discount to retailers, you are *not* to offer any price reductions or offer premiums as a reason for buying now; all sales are to be made at full retail price).

SPECIAL STUDY PROJECT ASSIGNMENTS

Listed under each of the following numbered topics are several assignment questions which will help guide your thinking and planning. You are expected to develop your own questions, in addition to these. A good way to start is to first review the chapter material in which major concepts or topics were first presented, then carefully study the index to the text in order to make certain you haven't missed anything. This will help acquaint you with using the text as a valuable reference handbook or guide, useful not only for this project, but also for any future sales project in which you might become involved.

I. *FORECASTING (Market Survey)*
   A. Approximately how many family units are there in your 50,000 population local market area? Does each family unit represent a prospect for your product?
   B. Approximately how many new sofas, regular or convertibles, are sold annually in your area by retailers?
   C. Based on your findings from A and B above, what is the maximum number of Queen of Sheba Hidden-Bed Sofas you feel you can sell in your territory (1) the first year, and (2) in two to five years?
   D. Based on C above, what is your sales target or objective for the first year (e.g., how many sofas do you plan to sell): (1) through retailers, and (2) direct to consumers.

II. *STRATEGIC PLANNING*
   A. From a managerial point of view, what is the meaning of the term *planning?*
   B. What channels of distribution will you employ?
   C. What are the four parts of the "promotional mix" you can employ?
      1. List all methods you feel suitable under each of the four.
      2. What proportion of "promotional mix" will you employ?

D. Based on your number of units sales objective, will you do all sales/ marketing yourself, or will you employ sales representatives to assist you?
1. If you plan to employ sales representatives, how many will you employ, and how will you compensate them?
2. Assuming you buy at 60 percent discount, prepare a sales and expense budget for (a) yourself and (b) each sales representative, if any are to be employed (in preparing these, allow 20 percent for all overhead expense, and don't forget that retailers get a 25 percent discount).
3. If you hire sales representatives, how will you train and supervise them?

III. *YOUR PRODUCT VERSUS YOUR COMPETITION*
We will assume you have full information about your well-known company and its standing in the industry, and enough information about your own product, but need to learn more about the industry and competition.
A. Collect all information possible about sofas, both regular and convertible, from the library, trade associations, local retailers, and other sources. This means everything you will need to know about such products and their market, in addition to local area sofa sales estimates asked for under I (B).
B. Relate and compare (in writing) your findings from A above to facts presented about Queen of Sheba Hidden-Bed Sofa under product information. Your aim is to be able to intelligently answer all possible questions prospects might ask about your product.
C. Visit local retail stores and learn about sofa and convertible competition, customer buying habits, and questions customers ask. Your aim is to be able to handle competition's claims and make comparisons in your sales presentations.

IV. *WHAT DO BUYERS LOOK FOR IN A SOFA?*
A. Restudy Chapter 4 and product information material and list all possible factors affecting buying behavior you might anticipate from a sofa prospect and how, from a psychological point of view, you will direct your sales appeals.
B. Visit local retailers and question sofa salespersons regarding your listing from A above; further refine your list prior to planning specific sales presentations.

V. *PROSPECTING*
A. What methods will you employ to find both (1) retail and (2) end-consumer qualified prospects in your sales area?
B. Prepare a direct-mail letter to be sent to households asking for an appointment to discuss your product in their home.
C. Prepare a pre-call telephone outline of a call you will place direct to households inviting the husband and wife to visit (by appointment) a display center where you can demonstrate your product to them.

VI. *PLANNING YOUR PRESENTATION*
  A. Prepare a complete (approach through close) written planned presentation for your product for each of these specific situations:
    1. To a retailer in his store, using your sales-kit materials.
    2. To a husband and wife in their home, using your sales-kit materials.
    3. To a husband and wife at an exhibition where you are able to make a quick demonstration of your product.
    4. To a husband and wife, in a retail store situation where you have both your product to display and competing sofas at hand for comparison, and ample presentation time.
  B. Assemble all possible sales-kit materials for use in the above sales presentation situations.

VII. *PLANNING TO HANDLE OBJECTIONS*
  A. List all possible objections you can think of for not buying your product now, in any of the VI (A1-4) sales situations, and prepare written planned responses.
  B. Explain briefly in writing the meaning of a "trial close" and how and when to employ it in connection with handling objections, for purposes of educating and instructing any sales representative you might employ.

VIII. *TACTICAL PLANNING AND ORGANIZING TO MEET YOUR SALES OBJECTIVES*
  A. Based on all market information data you have gathered and your forecasts and target objectives, prepare a composite inventory (including a value analysis) for prospects in your sales territory.
  B. Outline the programming activities or procedures necessary to accomplish your sales goals (to include both production requirements and production plans) for the first year.
  C. Outline the route planning and scheduling you and your sales representatives (if any) will follow for one typical week (prepare this from actual prospect lists made up from your area). Prepare samples of the forms and records you will use.
  D. Summarize the control procedures you will employ to check both your personal performance results, and that of your sales representatives (if any), against planned objectives.
  E. Prepare samples of daily, weekly, or other report forms you will employ (as in D above).

IX. *PREPARE A SALES MANUAL*
  Part A: to incorporate the above I-VIII materials suitable (1) for your personal reference, or (2) for any sales representatives you hire, as a training and operations manual.
  Part B: to include factual and visual materials suitable for use in any type of face-to-face sales presentation situation with (1) a retail store buyer, or (2) an end-consumer prospect.

glossary
of sales terms

The following selected terms, most of which are used in this text, are commonly used in selling. The definitions are drawn from authoritative sources, are based upon general acceptance, and are related to selling. In some instances the definitions have been extended to include the practices connected with the terms.

Not all the terms or definitions included in the text appear on this list; only the most important or commonly used ones are given.

Account classification The rating of customers according to current business and, more importantly, according to potential.

Advantage In sales, the way a feature of a product or service can help solve problems or meet needs.

Agent middleman (merchant middleman) One who negotiates purchases or sales or both, but does not take title to the goods in which he deals.

Annual report A printed and most often illustrated message to stockholders that is signed by the chairman of the board and president and that incorporates the company income statement and balance sheet for the latest fiscal year, usually with comparisons to previous periods, comments on past performance, and prospects for the future.

Appeal The motive toward which a sales point is directed in the hopes of stirring the prospect to favorable consideration of the product or service being presented.

Approach phase The part of the sales presentation that covers the introduction and quick selling of self, product, and company, in that order, to get and hold attention and interest and thus develop INP (Information, Need, Product).

Authority The power to make decisions and enforce them.

Automation The complete performance of a complex mechanical act without human intervention.

Bad debt An uncollectible receivable.

Balance sheet A financial statement of the condition of an enterprise as of a specified date.

Benefit In sales, a need that has been met.

Bonus An extra compensation because of high productivity, contractual agreement, or a similar reason.

Brand name The spoken trademark or part of a trademark, as contrasted to the pictorial symbol.

Budget A financial plan of proposed expenditures for a stated period, often combined with a forecast of revenues.

Business In the economic sense it relates to the buying and selling of goods and services; in the commercial sense it relates more to a person, partnership, or corporation engaged in manufacturing, commerce, or service. In both senses it relates to profit-seeking activities.

Business ethics The socially accepted rules of conduct that influence businessmen to be honest and fair in their dealings with others.

Buyer (1) in retailing, an executive responsible for purchasing and other duties of departmental management; (2) any person who is open to acquire merchandise for monetary consideration, thus, one who buys.

Buyer's market Where goods and services are plentiful and prices relatively low.

Buying signals Any words, facial expressions, or physical actions on the part of a prospect, at any time during the sales interview, which may indicate that he feels psychologically compelled to buy.

Callback The approach that a sales representative makes on the second or subsequent attempt to sell a prospect.

Canned presentation A prewritten and memorized sales presentation which is verbally presented word for word.

Canvass To call on individuals personally or by telephone to make a survey or to sell goods or services.

Capitalism An economic system based on the freedoms of ownership, production, exchange, acquisition, work, movement, and competition.

Cash discounts Discounts off the list price offered to buyer in return for prompt payment for merchandise bought.

Catalogue Printed matter listing items for sale, usually with descriptions, illustrations, and prices.

Chain stores A group of retail outlets which may or may not have the same ownership, but which operate under the same central management and business policy.

Channel of distribution (see **marketing channel**)

Close or closing In sales, the prospect's verbal or signed agreement to buy the product or service being offered.

Cold call The act of going to see a prospect without an appointment, in the hope of either getting an interview on the spot or of making an appointment for one.

Cold-canvassing Finding leads independently, such as following up a telephone book Yellow Pages listing of specific potential users.

Commission A percentage of a sale price paid to a sales representative, broker, or agent.

Composite inventory A collection of facts about customers or prospects, including everything that can be related to the who, what, where, why, and how of basic reporting or fact-finding.

Consignment Goods on which title is conveyed to the consignee only when he resells and pays, with the consignee retaining the right to return the unsold portion of the goods.

Consumer One who consumes or uses up.

Consumer goods (or **products**)   Those goods, products, or services bought by consumers for their own personal use.

Consumer market (see market)   Consumers who buy for personal or family consumption.

Consumerism   The interaction of consumers, politicians, consumer advocates, business, and industry toward the achievement of consumer rights.

Consumerist movement   Social action to achieve consumerism.

Controls   The checks employed by both the sales representative and his management to compare progress or results against the preplanned sales program.

Convenience goods   Those consumer goods that are normally bought at nearby or convenient outlets without shopping for better prices, styles, or other features.

Cooperative advertising   Advertising placed by retailers and paid for at least in part by the manufacturers or suppliers whose products are advertised.

Cost of sales   (1) To a trading business, the cost of goods purchased less the excess of inventory at the end of the period over inventory at the beginning; (2) to a manufacturing business, the cost of goods manufactured less the excess of the inventory of finished goods at the end of the period over the inventory of finished goods at the beginning.

Current accounts   Those customer names taken from past records and rated (prime, good, etc.) in order of past business and future potential.

Customer-oriented   In sales, the attempt to understand problems, wants, and needs from the customer's point of view and to help him fulfill his desires.

Customer/society-oriented marketing concept (see marketing concept)   A sales/marketing orientation backed by integrated marketing aimed at fulfilling consumer needs with something of value and benefit that will bring lasting satisfaction and provide as well for net improvement in the quality of life for all consumers and to the long-term benefit of society.

Dealer   One who confers quantity utility (breaks lots into smaller quantities for resale) and other utilities on goods or services.

Decision-maker   In sales, the individual or key individual in a group who either has the authority to decide himself or the ability to influence others.

Decision-making   The process of resolving open choices into one opinion or course of action so that, when backed by authority, it becomes policy.

Decision-making group   Individual decision makers, often specialists, who share responsibility for purchase decisions. (The final decision is usually a consensus of the individual decisions.)

Direct, or door-to-door, or house-to-house, selling   The sales representative's taking of a product or service directly from the manufacturer or supplier to the customer in his home or office, thus cutting out all middlemen in the process.

Direct mail   Advertisements sent to prospects or customers (printed pieces, catalogues, circular letters, postcards, and telegrams).

Discount   To offer something for sale at a reduced price below the normal list price.

Distribution In marketing, the separation, breaking down, or spreading out of units or parts to apportion them among different layers and levels of groups.

Drummer An old-fashioned American sales representative who called on retailers of soft goods or greeted them as they went into buying centers.

Emotional buying motives Nonrational motives, such as impulses, habits, and drives.

Empathy In sales, the ability to detect by perception how a prospect feels and what his attitudes and opinions are.

Ethical responsibility The professional standards of a sales representative as related to moral character, motives, and actions.

Exclusive (1) Obtainable only at certain stores or from a limited number of designated distributors or dealers; (2) an agreement to confine sales in an area to a single retailer.

Executive A person whose position calls for the making of decisions and the exercise of power over others in the conduct of the affairs of a company or organization.

Expense account Monies which are advanced by a company to a sales representative meet travel, entertainment, or other specified costs and for which he is held accountable.

Feature In sales, the characteristic of a product or service that produces a benefit.

Feedback In sales, market information from the field obtained from interviews or surveys.

Field survey A sampling of opinion or facts among industry members, dealers, or consumers that is assembled from interviews on the premises of those interviewed.

Firm order A definite order, either verbal or written, that cannot be canceled.

Fixed routing A sales-call pattern whereby customers are called on repeatedly or at regular intervals.

FOB price Most merchandise is sold FOB (Free On Board) shipping point. This means the seller pays transportation costs to that point, and the buyer pays charges from that point.

Follow-up or follow-through (1) In management, the systematic working of a preplanned sales program both up to and following a closing attempt; (2) in sales, actions taken after the closing of the sale to ensure delivery, satisfaction, etc.

Forecasting The collection of facts or data upon which one tries to calculate or estimate what will happen within a specific time.

Forestalling objections The incorporation into the planned sales presentation of some commonly expressed objections and the answering of them in the course of the presentation, before they can be raised as objections.

Free enterprise The freedom of a business or an individual to organize and operate competitively for profit without undue government interference.

Fringe benefits Compensation for labor in a form other than wages, such as health insurance, pensions, paid vacations, etc.

Goal-setting The stages leading to or including the end of one's aims or objectives.

Goods (see **product**).

Goods and services   The output of industry and labor, equaling, in economic terms, the gross national product for any given year.

Group selling   Involves selling to a group of two or more individuals as contrasted to a single person.

Hard sell (high-pressure selling)   A method of selling which is direct, forceful, and insistent (the opposite of soft sell).

House organ   A publication of a business concern that contains articles of interest to its employees and customers.

Impulse buying   The purchasing of goods or services on impulse rather than by plan or according to need.

Inducement   An additional consideration to persuade a person to make an agreement.

Industrial goods (or products)   Those goods, products or services consumed by businesses, and those used in the manufacture of other goods.

Industrial market (see market)   Consumers who buy to further production of other goods and services.

Industry   An industry represents a level in the Standard Industrial Classification (SIC) system developed by the United States Bureau of the Census to cover all commercial activity.

INP   Abbreviation for Information-Need-Product; a "sales handle" often taught to sales trainees to help them remember the simple, logical, step-by-step progressive development of a sales presentation in any common sales situation.

Interaction   In sales, the reciprocal action, influence, or understanding between the sales representative and his prospect or customer and between him and his company.

Irregular routing   A sales-call pattern in which frequency of calls is left up to the sales representative.

Jobber   A marketing middleman or company that buys in quantity from wholesalers and resells in smaller lots to retailers.

Lead (sales lead)   A possible but unqualified prospect or customer.

Lead-in   That part of a discussion that allows a sales representative to move into a sales presentation; or, during a presentation, into a close.

Leadership   The exercise of qualities of guidance and command in a resourceful and responsible manner in a company or organization.

Line and staff   A form of organization characterized by direct-line authority, with staff assistants provided to those in the higher ranks.

List price   Published, basic prices; normally found in sellers' price lists, catalogues, and advertisements. Normally considered the highest price on a product, since it is often subject to discounts.

Management   The process whereby resources are combined into an integrated system in order to accomplish the objectives of the system. Management, at its many levels, plans and sets objectives and strives to ensure that they are met.

Management by objectives (MBO) A way of practicing the four basic management functions of planning, organizing, executing, and controlling—a way of managing.

Management functions Are four generally accepted action processes essential to meeting objectives: planning, organizing, executing, and controlling. They may occur simultaneously in different ways, at different managerial levels, at different times.

Manager A person charged with the control or direction (all or in assigned part) of a business, an organization, or the like.

Managerially oriented One who thinks like a manager in terms of setting and controlling efforts toward a predetermined goal or objective.

Mannerisms Peculiarities of speaking or acting or in one's bearing.

Mark-down A reduction in price commonly employed to encourage buying.

Markup To fix the selling price of an item by adding seller's cost price and selling expenses to reach desired profit level.

Market The total or aggregate demand of the potential buyers for a product or service; *aggregate* is the composite demands of many consumers for a specific item. From a sales/marketing viewpoint, there are two broad market divisions—the consumer market and the industrial market.

Market research Research to gather the facts upon which a marketing decision can be made.

Market segment Groups of potential buyers who demand specific different requirements for the same item.

Marketing The performance of business activities that direct the flow of goods and services from producer to consumer or user.

Marketing channel A path traced in the direct or indirect transfer of ownership to a product, as it moves from a producer to ultimate consumers or industrial users. (This same definition also applies to **channel of distribution**.)

Marketing concept (see **customer/society-oriented marketing concept**) A customer orientation backed by integrated marketing aimed at generating customer satisfaction as the key to satisfying organizational goals.

Marketing mix The combination of four elements to achieve sales/marketing strategic objectives: the product, channels of distribution, pricing policies, and promotional methods.

Marketplace Relates, in the commercial sense, to the activities of business and trade.

Merchandising The planning and promotion of sales by presenting a product to the right market at the proper time, by carrying out organized, skillful advertising and sales promotion. It includes nearly every activity that influences consumers to buy the product except personal selling (but even here a sales representative often sells merchandising plans).

Merchant One who takes title to (that is, buys) and resells merchandise.

Middlemen Those who specialize in performing activities that are directly involved in the purchase and sale of goods in the process of their flow from producer to final buyer. Middlemen can also fall into categories such as agent middlemen, merchant middlemen, retailers, and wholesalers.

Motivational needs   Basic common denominators of desire, such as psychological, biological, social, or self-fulfillment needs.

Net price   When one reduces list price by the discounts applicable, he arrives at the net price.

No sale final   A management policy meaning that no sale is final until a customer is completely satisfied with his purchase.

Objections   To a sales representative, questions or doubts in the prospect's mind which he is happy to answer.

Objective (or **goal**)   Something specific to be achieved.

Order form   A previously prepared or printed form containing information about a product or service being offered for sale which, to save time, the sales representative often fills out in front of the customer, often asking for an approval signature.

Peddler   One who travels and retails or hawks small quantities of goods.

Personal leadership qualities   The ability to persuade others to work under one's direction as a team to accomplish certain designated objectives.

Persuasion   To move a person or persons to a belief, a position, a point of view or a course of action.

Physical inventory   An inventory taken by actual count of merchandise rather than from existing records.

Planned presentation   A preplanned, structured sales message in which only key points are memorized and presented in word-for-word sequence, the parts in between being presented more informally as the situation requires.

Planning   A predetermined course of action that starts with the establishment of goals and objectives.

Point-of-purchase (POP) advertising   Interior store displays and literature distributed at retail counters or for window displays.

Preapproach   Involves (1) finding out as much as possible about the prospect prior to the interview, and (2) determining how to get the specific interview—through prior appointment or without an appointment.

President or managing director   The highest-ranking operating company official, who is responsible to the board of directors for company policy and management.

Price control   When a manufacturer exercises price control, the buyer-for-resale is not permitted to determine his own selling price.

Product (goods)   A product is what a seller has to sell; it can be goods, services, or ideas. *Goods* and *products* mean the same thing in a sales/marketing sense.

Professional standards   In sales, the conduct, aims, and qualities generally agreed on as opposed to amateur or nonprofessional standards.

Profit   The difference between income received from sales and all costs or expenses.

Profitability   The ability of a business to earn a profit and the extent of the profit it can earn.

Programming The specific activities or procedures necessary to accomplish planned goals or objectives.

Promotional mix In attempting to communicate with, inform, persuade, and sell goods, services or ideas to consumers, a firm or organization employs a four-part promotional mix consisting of advertising, publicity, sales promotion, and personal selling.

Proposal A verbal or written recommendation or offer.

Prospect A potential customer.

Prospecting The process of looking up and checking out sales leads.

Purchasing agent An officially appointed buyer for a large company or organization.

Put-off (or **stall**) A pretext, ruse, or trick often expressed by prospects in the form of objections to delay or avoid a buying decision.

Qualified prospect A prospect who has a need or want for any given product or service, is able to afford it, and is able to make the decision to purchase it.

Qualitative reports More personalized and detailed than quantitative reports in that a personal estimate or opinion is included.

Quantitative reports Brief factual reports that help compare efforts expended versus results in the preplanned sales program.

Quantity discounts Discounts off list price offered to buyers in return for buying in large volume.

Question technique The sales technique of directing questions to a prospect in order to find out what he knows, thinks, or feels about what is being offered, and to secure his agreement on various sales points made.

Radiation (selling) methods Involves exploiting a single sale as a center from which to attempt other sales out from it in a widening circle or area based on using it as an example.

Rapport In sales, the affinity, understanding, accord, or harmony between sales representative and prospect.

Rational buying motives All costs affecting the buyer, including cost in money, cost of use, length of usage, degree of labor, and ultimate benefit.

Real salesmen (or **sales representatives**) Those specialty (outside) sales representatives who are vitally concerned with closing sales on most calls.

Referral leads Names of potential prospects given by satisfied users, unsold prospects, or other individuals.

Results-oriented In sales, the understanding by sales representative that he is paid to sell products in the marketplace and that he will be judged on results.

Retail (inside) salesperson One who normally works inside stores and has customers come to him.

Retailer A merchant, or occasionally an agent, whose main business is selling directly to ultimate consumer.

Retailing Consists of the activities involved in selling directly to the ultimate consumer. Retailers, of course, are engaged in retailing, but so is any other institution that sells directly to ultimate consumers.

Rifle technique A sales concept that concentrates on a few items of greatest interest to the prospect in a planned, systematic, effective manner which, through involving him in the buying process, leads directly, rapidly, and persuasively to a buying decision (the opposite of shotgun approach).

Sale The transfer of title to goods or property or the agreement to perform a service in return for payment of cash or for the promise to pay.

Sales anchors Planned statements kept in mind, ready for use at any time, to help sales representatives handle certain standard objections, especially those of a stalling nature.

Sales aptitude The natural potential, capacity, or ability to achieve success as a sales representative according to the qualities, characteristics, and demands of the sales profession.

Sales manual (sales kit) A handbook or manual offering details about a product or service; can be employed for instructional uses only, or as a visual sales tool, or a combination thereof.

Sales/marketing A term often used to describe the modern interrelationship of marketing and personal selling, perhaps the most important of the four marketing functions.

Sales pitch A line of reasoning or persuasive argument intended to persuade someone to buy, accept, or do something.

Sales presentation The complete sales process of telling a prospect or a group about a product or service, from personal introduction to asking for the order.

Sales promotion Those elements of marketing that embrace display, selling schemes, publicity-winning ploys, and advertising other than in regularly paid, space-and-time media.

Sales representative (see **salesman**).

Sales trainee A newly hired sales representative engaged in basic sales training.

Salesman (sales representative or **salesperson)** One who sells goods, services, or ideas. The term *salesperson* is most often used to describe those who sell goods in a retail store; *sales representative* is the modern term (replacing the older term *salesman*) most often used to describe those men and women engaged in outside selling, where they call on prospects in their homes, offices or places of business.

Salesmanship The art/skill/science of persuading someone to accept or follow ideas and thus to take the action desired (buying).

Sample or sampling The distribution of small lots of a product to permit prospective buyers to become familiar with it, thus promoting its sale, or, simply, a model used for sales demonstrations and booking orders.

Scheduling In sales, the arrangement and management of the time necessary to carry out a sales program.

Second sale When a customer has just made a purchase, he is in a buying mood. This offers opportunity to suggest something else to him which he might purchase readily as a second item.

Self-image One's private evaluation of his abilities or what he would like to be seen as, thus, his inner, personal, mental picture of the kind of person he is.

Self-management The personal organization of planning, time, and work.

Seller's market Where goods and services are scarce and prices relatively high.

Selling The personal or impersonal process of assisting and/or persuading a prospective customer to buy a commodity or service and to act favorably upon an idea that has commercial significance to the seller.

Shopping center An area that is planned and engineered as a place for retail trade, free from manufacturing and residential dilution, with stores, shops, and parking in one specialized location away from the heart of an urban area but readily reached by automobile.

Shopping goods The products a consumer buys infrequently after shopping around to compare price, style, and other features.

Shotgun approach A sales approach that covers a wide area in an irregular, ineffective, haphazard way based on the hope that by sheer luck something might be said or done that will interest or persuade a prospective buyer.

Soft sell A method of selling which is quietly persuasive, subtle and indirect (the opposite of hard sell).

Specialty (outside) sales representative One who goes outside to call on prospects in their homes, offices, or places of business.

Telephone sales itinerary A plan outlining in advance exactly which prospects or accounts will be called, and in what frequency.

Territory-screening An analysis of a customer or prospect list to identify in advance the best customers in terms of potential and of location.

Testimonial A statement in praise of a product or service made by a satisfied user and publicized by a company through advertising or sales promotion.

Tickler file A follow-up folder in which correspondence, memoranda, etc., are filed by future dates and reviewed on the respective dates.

Trade discount A deduction from the list price of an item granted by manufacturer or supplier to a retailer.

Trade reference An individual or company in business to which a seller is referred for information concerning an applicant's credit standing.

Trade show A public exhibition or showing of products offered by sellers to prospective buyers.

Trade up To show or move up to items of higher quality or price.

Traveling salesman (or sales representative) or commercial traveler A firm's traveling representative who solicits orders.

Trial close An attempt, based on listening or observation, to induce action (to buy) at any stage of the sales presentation prior to the final, planned closing attempt.

Turnover The number of times a stock of merchandise is replaced in one year.

User calls The callbacks a sales representative makes on a customer who has made a purchase through him or through his company.

Value The worth of any property, good, service, right, or thing: (1) at market; (2) as agreed; (3) as determined by legislation; (4) at the owner's minimum selling price; (5) as determined in a dispute or by judicial decree; (6) intrinsically; (7) in the long run; (8) at par or face; or (9) at maturity.

Value analysis   The sorting out and classifying of customers or prospects into a simplified grouping to establish an order of priority for calls and for time to be allocated.

Warranty or guarantee   A seller's declaration, enforceable in a suit for damages, that merchandise is as represented.

Wholesale   The level of marketing between manufacturing and retailing.

Wholesaler   One who buys and resells merchandise to retailers and other merchants and to industrial, institutional, and commercial users, but does not sell in significant amounts to ultimate consumers.

Wholesaling   Involves selling to buyers other than to ultimate customers.

bibliography

This brief, selective bibliography represents only a partial listing of the many excellent classic and newer North American-published books in the areas noted. However, these books will provide rich source materials for further study by interested readers. Constantly updated comprehensive book and periodical bibliographies in dozens of sub-areas of selling, personal salesmanship, marketing, business, and management can be found in most large libraries.

PRINCIPLES AND PRACTICES OF SALESMANSHIP

Baer, E. E. *Salesmanship*. New York: McGraw-Hill Book Company, 1972.

Ernest, J. W., and Ashman, R. *Salesmanship Fundamentals*, 4th ed. New York: Gregg Division, McGraw-Hill Book Company, 1973.

Grief, E. *Personal Salesmanship: New Concepts and Directions*. Reston, Va.: Reston Publishing Co., 1973.

Haas, K. B., and Ernest, J. W. *Creative Salesmanship: Understanding Essentials*. Beverly Hills, Calif.: Glencoe Press, 1974.

Jones, M. et al. *Miracle Sales Guide: Student Edition*. Englewood Cliffs, N.J.: Prentice-Hall, Inc., 1973.

Kirkpatrick, C. A. *Salesmanship*, 5th ed. Cincinnati, Ohio: South-Western Publishing Co., 1971.

Pederson, C. P., and Wright, M. D. *Salesmanship: Principles and Methods*. 5th ed. Homewood, Ill.: Richard D. Irwin, Inc., 1971.

Russell, F., Beach, F., and Buskirk, R. H. *Textbook of Salesmanship*, 9th ed. New York: McGraw-Hill Book Company, 1974.

Thompson, J. W. *Selling: A Managerial and Behavioral Science Analysis*, 2nd ed. New York: McGraw-Hill Book Company, 1973.

SALES/MARKETING AND MARKET RESEARCH

Beckman, T. N., Davidson, W. R., and Talarzyk, W. W. *Marketing*, 9th ed. New York: The Ronald Press Company, 1973.

Bolt, G. J. *Market and Sales Forecasting—A Total Approach*. New York: Halsted Press, 1972.

Buzzell, R. D., Nourse, R. E. M., Matthews, J. B., and Levitt, T. *Marketing: A Contemporary Analysis*, 2nd ed. New York: McGraw-Hill Book Company, 1972.

Carman, J. M. et al. *Marketing Principles and Methods*, 7th ed. Homewood, Ill.: Richard D. Irwin, Inc., 1973.

Crane E. *Marketing Communications*, 2nd ed. New York: John Wiley & Sons, Inc., 1972.

Davis, K. R. *Marketing Management*, 3rd ed. New York: The Ronald Press Company, 1972.

Enis, B. *Marketing Principles: The Management Process*. Pacific Palisades, Calif.: Goodyear Publishing Co., 1974.

Green, P., and Tull, D. *Research for Marketing Divisions*, 3rd ed. Englewood Cliffs, N.J.: Prentice-Hall, Inc., 1974.

Kollat, D. T. et al. *Strategic Marketing.* New York: Holt, Reinhart & Winston, Inc., 1972.

Kotler, P. *Marketing Management: Analysis, Planning and Control,* 2nd ed. Englewood Cliffs, N.J.: Prentice-Hall, Inc., 1972.

Lazer, W. and Kelley, E. J., eds. *Social Marketing: Prospective and Viewpoints.* Homewood, Ill.: Richard D. Irwin, Inc., 1973.

Luck, E., and Wales, H. *Marketing Research,* 4th ed. Englewood Cliffs, N.J.: Prentice-Hall, Inc., 1974.

Mallen, B. et al, *Marketing in the Canadian Environment.* Toronto, Canada: Prentice-Hall of Canada, Inc., 1973.

Rachman, D. *Marketing Strategy and Structure.* Englewood Cliffs, N.J.: Prentice-Hall, Inc., 1974.

Still, R., and Cundiff, E. *Essentials of Marketing,* 2nd ed. Englewood Cliffs, N.J.: Prentice-Hall, Inc., 1972.

Stuteville, J. R. *Marketing in an Affluent Society.* Belmont, Calif.: Wadsworth Publishing Company, Inc., 1973.

SALES PROMOTION, ADVERTISING, AND PUBLIC RELATIONS

Brann, C. *Direct Mail and Direct Response Promotion.* New York: John Wiley & Sons, Inc., 1972.

Burke, J. D. *Advertising in the Marketplace.* New York: McGraw-Hill Book Company, 1973.

Burton, P. W. *Advertising Copywriting,* 3rd ed. New York: International Textbook, 1974.

Canfield, B. R., and Moore, H. F. *Public Relations: Principles, Cases and Problems,* 6th ed. Homewood, Ill.: Richard D. Irwin, Inc., 1973.

Cohen, D. *Introduction to Advertising.* New York: John Wiley & Sons, Inc., 1972.

Cutlip, S., and Center, A. *Effective Public Relations,* 4th ed. Englewood Cliffs, N.J.: Prentice-Hall, Inc., 1971.

Dunn, S. W., and Barbon, A. M. *Advertising: Its Role in Modern Marketing,* 3rd ed. Hinsdale, Ill.: Dryden Press, 1974.

Grosse, W. H. *How Industrial Advertising and Promotion Can Increase Marketing Power.* New York: AMACOM, 1973.

Kernan, J. B. et al. *Promotion: An Introductory Analysis.* New York: McGraw-Hill Book Company, 1970.

Kleppner, O. *Advertising Procedure,* 6th ed. Englewood Cliffs, N.J.: Prentice-Hall, Inc., 1973.

Lewis, H. G. *The Businessman's Guide to Advertising and Sales Promotion.* New York: Gregg Division, McGraw-Hill Book Company, 1974.

Mandell, N. *Advertising,* 2nd ed. Englewood Cliffs, N.J.: Prentice-Hall, Inc., 1974.

Mills, K. et al. *Creative Distinctive Displays.* Englewood Cliffs, N.J.: Prentice-Hall, Inc., 1974.

Nicosia, F. M. *Advertising, Management and Society: A Business Point of View.* New York: McGraw-Hill Book Company, 1974.

Tillman, R., and Kirkpatrick, C. A. *Promotion: Persuasive Communication in Marketing,* Rev. ed. Homewood, Ill.: Richard D. Irwin, Inc., 1972.

RETAIL SELLING AND RETAILING

Boale, Y. G. and Corey, J. A. *Retail Selling.* New York: Gregg Division, McGraw-Hill Book Company, 1972.

Butcher, B. C., and McAnelly, J. R. *Fundamentals of Retailing.* New York: The Macmillan Company, 1973.

Duncan, D. J. et al. *Modern Retailing Management: Basic Concepts and Practices,* 8th ed. Homewood, Ill.: Richard D. Irwin, Inc., 1972.

Moseley, L. W. *Customer Service: The Road to Greater Profits.* New York: Chain Store Age Books, 1972.

Rachman, D. *Retail Strategy and Structure,* 2nd ed. Englewood Cliffs, N.J.: Prentice-Hall, Inc., 1974.

Robson, P. et al. *Successful Retail Salesmanship,* 3rd ed. Englewood Cliffs, N.J.: Prentice-Hall, Inc., 1961.

Wingate, I. et al. *Problems in Retail Merchandising,* 6th ed. Englewood Cliffs, N.J.: Prentice-Hall, Inc., 1973.

CONSUMERISM AND CONSUMER BEHAVIOR

Aaker, D. A., and Day, G. S. *Consumerism: Search for the Consumer Interest,* 2nd ed. New York: The Free Press, 1974.

Bennett, P., and Kassargian, H. *Consumer Behavior.* Englewood Cliffs, N.J.: Prentice-Hall, Inc., 1972.

Britt, S. H. *Consumer Behavior and the Behavioral Sciences.* New York: John Wiley & Sons, Inc., 1966.

Engel, J. F. et al. *Consumer Behavior,* 2nd ed. New York: Holt, Reinhart & Winston, Inc., 1973.

Farley, J. V. et al. *Consumer Behavioral Theory and Application.* Boston, Mass.: Allyn & Bacon, 1974.

McNeal, J. V. *An Introduction to Consumer Behavior.* New York: John Wiley & Sons, Inc., 1973.

Ward, S. et al. *Consumer Behavior: Theoretical Sources.* Englewood Cliffs, N.J.: Prentice-Hall, Inc., 1973.

Webster, F., Jr., and Wind, Y. *Organizational Buying Behavior.* Englewood Cliffs, N.J.: Prentice-Hall, Inc., 1972.

SELF-MOTIVATION IN SELLING

Bettger, F. *How I Raised Myself from Failure to Success in Selling.* Englewood Cliffs, N.J.: Prentice-Hall, Inc., 1958.

Bristol, C., and Sherman, H. *TNT–The Power Within You.* Englewood Cliffs, N.J.: Prentice-Hall, Inc., 1954.

Hill, N. *Think and Grow Rich.* Greenwich, Conn.: Fawcett Publications; Inc., 1960.

Hill, N. *The Master Key to Riches.* Greenwich, Conn.: Fawcett Publications, Inc., 1965.

Mandino, O. *The Greatest Salesman in the World.* New York: Frederick Fell Publishers, Inc., 1968.

Peale, N. V. *The Power of Positive Thinking.* Englewood Cliffs, N.J.: Prentice-Hall, Inc., 1952.

Peale, N. V. *Enthusiasm Makes the Difference.* Englewood Cliffs, N.J.: Prentice-Hall, Inc., 1967.

Stone, W. C. *Success Through a Positive Mental Attitude.* Englewood Cliffs, N.J.: Prentice-Hall, Inc., 1965.

ADVANCED OR PROFESSIONAL SALES PRINCIPLES AND TECHNIQUES

Bark, R. *How to Avoid Talking Yourself Out of a Sale*. Englewood Cliffs, N.J.: Prentice-Hall, Inc., 1974.

Barr, A. *Master Guide to High-Income Real Estate Selling*. Englewood Cliffs, N.J.: Prentice-Hall, Inc., 1974.

Black, G. *Sales Engineering: An Emerging Profession*. Houston, Texas: Gulf Publishing Co., 1973.

Blake, R. R. *The Grid for Sales Excellence*. New York: McGraw-Hill Book Company, 1970.

Dane, L. *Big League Sales Closing Techniques*. Englewood Cliffs, N.J.: Prentice-Hall, Inc., 1971.

Dane, L. *Amateurs Don't Make a Dime Selling Hardgoods: 14 Steps to Big Money Success*. Englewood Cliffs, N.J.: Parker Publishing Co., 1974.

Dunlap, J. *Personal and Professional Success for Women*. Englewood Cliffs, N.J.: Prentice-Hall, Inc., 1972.

Edlund, S. *There Is a Better Way to Sell*. New York: AMACOM, 1973.

Feldman, B. *Creative Selling for the Seventies*. Rockville Center, N.Y.: Farnworth Publishing Co., 1974.

Hanan, M. et al. *Consultative Selling*. New York: AMACOM, 1973.

Harrison, J. *Profitable Self-Management for Salesmen*. Englewood Cliffs, N.J.: Prentice-Hall, Inc., 1972.

Kenian, P. R. *You Can Become a Super Salesman*. New York: Drake Publishing, Inc., 1972.

Kissel, I. R., and Grun, A. K. *How to Handle Claims and Returns: A Manual for Manufacturers and Retailers*. New York: McGraw-Hill Book Company, 1973.

Ling, M. *How to Increase Sales and Put Yourself Across by Telephone*. Englewood Cliffs, N.J.: Prentice-Hall, Inc., 1963.

Lund, P. R. *Compelling Selling: A Framework for Persuasion*. New York: AMACOM, 1975.

McCall, C. H., Sr. *How to Use Showmanship to Multiply Success at Every Step in Selling*. Englewood Cliffs, N.J.: Executive Report Corporation, 1974.

Romes, H. *Dynamics of Motivating Prospects to Buy*. Englewood Cliffs, N.J.: Prentice-Hall, Inc., 1973.

Shook, R. L., and Shook, H. M. *How to Be the Complete Professional Salesman*. New York: Frederick Fell Publishers, Inc., 1974.

Smith, A. *Complete Guide to Selling Intangibles*. Englewood Cliffs, N.J.: Prentice-Hall, Inc., 1971.

Susser, S. S. *The Truth About Selling*. New York: Paul S. Ericksson, Inc., 1973.

SALES MANAGEMENT

Buzzotta, L., and Buzzotta, S. *Effective Selling through Psychology: Dimensional Sales and Sales Management Strategies*. New York: John Wiley & Sons, Inc., 1972.

Carney, G. J. *Managing a Sales Territory*. New York: American Management Association, 1971.

Carney, G. J. *The Complete Field Sales Program*. New York: AMACOM, 1973.

Cyr, J. *Training and Supervising Real Estate Salesmen*. Englewood Cliffs, N.J.: Prentice-Hall, Inc., 1973.

Edgett, J. *How to Manage Your Way to the Top*. Englewood Cliffs, N.J.: Prentice-Hall, Inc., 1974.

Goodman, C. S. *Management of the Personal Selling Function*. New York: Holt, Rinehart & Winston, Inc., 1971.

Humble, J. W. *How to Manage by Objectives*. New York: AMACOM, 1973.

Malinick, S. *The Making of the Manager*. New York: Anchor Press, 1974.

Miller, M. R. *Climbing the Corporate Pyramid*. New York: AMACOM, 1973.

Raia, A. P. *Managing by Objectives*. Glenview, Ill.: Scott, Foreman and Co., 1974.

Stroh, T. H. *Training and Developing the Professional Salesman*. New York: AMACOM, 1973.

Tonning, W. *How to Measure and Evaluate Salesmen's Performance*. Englewood Cliffs, N.J.: Prentice-Hall, Inc., 1973.

Wotruba, T. R. *Sales Management: Planning, Accomplishment and Evaluation*. New York: Holt, Rinehart & Winston, Inc., 1971.

BUSINESS:
PRINCIPLES, ORGANIZATION, MANAGEMENT

Baumback, C. M. et al. *How to Organize and Operate a Small Business*, 2nd ed. Englewood Cliffs, N.J.: Prentice-Hall, Inc., 1974.

Brown, L. *Effective Business Report Writing*, 3rd ed. Englewood Cliffs, N.J.: Prentice-Hall, Inc., 1973.

Cohn, T., and Lindberg, R. A. *Survival and Growth: Management Strategies for the Small Firm*. New York: AMACOM, 1973.

Drucker, P. F. *Management: Tasks, Responsibilities, Practices*. New York: Harper & Row, 1973.

Lesikar, R. V. *Report Writing for Business*, 4th ed. Homewood, Ill.: Richard D. Irwin, Inc., 1973.

Mahoney, T., and Sloane, C. *The Great Merchants*, Updated and enlarged ed. New York: Harper & Row, 1974.

Massic, J., and Douglas, J. *Managing: A Contemporary Introduction*. Englewood Cliffs, N.J.: Prentice-Hall, Inc., 1973.

Musselman, V., and Hughes, E. *Introduction to Modern Business: Analysis and Interpretation*, 6th ed. Englewood Cliffs, N.J.: Prentice-Hall, Inc., 1973.

Pickle, H., et al. *Introduction to Business*, 2nd ed. Pacific Palisades, Calif.: Goodyear Publishing Co., 1974.

Poe, J. B. *An Introduction to the American Business Enterprise*, Rev. ed. Homewood, Ill.: Richard D. Irwin, Inc., 1972.

Robock, S. H., and Simmonds, K. *International Business and Multinational Enterprises*. Homewood, Ill.: Richard D. Irwin, Inc., 1973.

Terry, G. R. *Principles of Management*, 6th ed. Homewood, Ill.: Richard D. Irwin, Inc., 1972.

Weimer, A. M. et al. *Introduction to Business*, 5th ed. Homewood, Ill.: Richard D. Irwin, Inc., 1974.

index

459